DANTE'S "OTHER WORKS"

The William and Katherine Devers Series in Dante and Medieval Italian Literature

Zygmunt G. Barański, Theodore J. Cachey, Jr., and Christian Moevs, editors

---

VOLUME 20   *Dante's "Other Works": Assessments and Interpretations* • Edited by Zygmunt G. Barański and Theodore J. Cachey, Jr.

VOLUME 19   *Liturgical Song and Practice in Dante's* Commedia • Helena Phillips-Robins

VOLUME 18   *Dante and Violence: Domestic, Civic, and Cosmic* • Brenda Deen Schildgen

VOLUME 17   *A Boccaccian Renaissance: Essays on the Early Modern Impact of Giovanni Boccaccio and His Works* • edited by Martin Eisner and David Lummus

VOLUME 16   *The Portrait of Beatrice: Dante, D. G. Rossetti, and the Imaginary Lady* • Fabio A. Camilletti

VOLUME 15   *Boccaccio's Corpus: Allegory, Ethics, and Vernacularity* • James C. Kriesel

VOLUME 14   *Meditations on the Life of Christ: The Short Italian Text* • Sarah McNamer

VOLUME 13   *Interpreting Dante: Essays on the Traditions of Dante Commentary* • edited by Paola Nasti and Claudia Rossignoli

VOLUME 12   *Freedom Readers: The African American Reception of Dante Alighieri and the* Divine Comedy • Dennis Looney

VOLUME 11   *Dante's* Commedia: *Theology as Poetry* • edited by Vittorio Montemaggi and Matthew Treherne

VOLUME 10   *Petrarch and Dante: Anti-Dantism, Metaphysics, Tradition* • edited by Zygmunt G. Barański and Theodore J. Cachey, Jr.

VOLUME 9   *The Ancient Flame: Dante and the Poets* • Winthrop Wetherbee

VOLUME 8   *Accounting for Dante: Urban Readers and Writers in Late Medieval Italy* • Justin Steinberg

DANTE'S "OTHER WORKS"

Assessments and Interpretations

Edited by

ZYGMUNT G. BARAŃSKI

and

THEODORE J. CACHEY, JR.

University of Notre Dame Press
Notre Dame, Indiana

Copyright © 2022 by the University of Notre Dame
Notre Dame, Indiana 46556
undpress.nd.edu

All Rights Reserved

Published in the United States of America

Library of Congress Control Number: 2021921331

ISBN: 978-0-268-20238-5 (Hardback)
ISBN: 978-0-268-20239-2 (Paperback)
ISBN: 978-0-268-20240-8 (WebPDF)
ISBN: 978-0-268-20237-8 (Epub)

ABOUT THE WILLIAM AND KATHERINE DEVERS SERIES
IN DANTE AND MEDIEVAL ITALIAN LITERATURE

The William and Katherine Devers Program in Dante Studies at the University of Notre Dame supports rare book acquisitions in the university's John A. Zahm Dante collections, funds a visiting professorship in Dante studies, and supports electronic and print publication of scholarly research in the field. In collaboration with the Medieval Institute at the university, the Devers program initiated a series dedicated to the publication of the most significant current scholarship in the field of Dante studies. In 2011 the scope of the series was expanded to encompass thirteenth- and fourteenth-century Italian literature.

In keeping with the spirit that inspired the creation of the Devers program, the series takes Dante and medieval Italian literature as focal points that draw together the many disciplines and lines of inquiry that constitute a cultural tradition without fixed boundaries. Accordingly, the series hopes to illuminate this cultural tradition within contemporary critical debates in the humanities by reflecting both the highest quality of scholarly achievement and the greatest diversity of critical perspectives.

The series publishes works from a wide variety of disciplinary viewpoints and in diverse scholarly genres, including critical studies, commentaries, editions, reception studies, translations, and conference proceedings of exceptional importance. The series enjoys the support of an international advisory board composed of distinguished scholars and is published regularly by the University of Notre Dame Press. The Dolphin and Anchor device that appears on publications of the Devers series was used by the great humanist, grammarian, editor, and typographer Aldus Manutius (1449–1515), in whose 1502 edition of Dante (second issue) and all subsequent editions it appeared. The device illustrates the ancient proverb Festina lente, "Hurry up slowly."

Zygmunt G. Barański, Theodore J. Cachey, Jr.,
and Christian Moevs, editors

ADVISORY BOARD

Albert Russell Ascoli, Berkeley
Teodolinda Barolini, Columbia
Piero Boitani, Rome
Patrick Boyde, Cambridge
Alison Cornish, New York University
Christopher Kleinhenz, Wisconsin
Giuseppe Ledda, Bologna
Simone Marchesi, Princeton
Kristina M. Olson, George Mason
Lino Pertile, Harvard
John A. Scott, Western Australia
Heather Webb, Cambridge

In memory of our dear friend Steven Botterill

CONTENTS

	List of Illustrations	xi
	Preface	xiii
	Abbreviations and Editions	xvii
1.	The Lyric Poetry MANUELE GRAGNOLATI	1
2.	*Fiore* and *Detto d'Amore* CHRISTOPHER KLEINHENZ	35
3.	*Vita nova* ZYGMUNT G. BARAŃSKI	71
4.	*Epistles* CLAIRE E. HONESS	125
5.	*Convivio* SIMON GILSON	154
6.	*De vulgari eloquentia* MIRKO TAVONI	186
7.	*Monarchia* PAOLA NASTI	221
8.	*Questio de aqua et terra* THEODORE J. CACHEY, JR.	270
9.	*Egloge* DAVID G. LUMMUS	306

10.	Philosophy and the "Other Works"	333
	LUCA BIANCHI	
11.	Theology and the "Other Works"	363
	VITTORIO MONTEMAGGI	
	Bibliography	388
	List of Contributors	445
	Index of Names	449

ILLUSTRATIONS

FIGURE 6.1. "T and O" *mappa mundi*. London, Lambeth Palace Library, ms. 371, fol. 9v, ca. 1300. Courtesy of Lambeth Palace Library, London.   *192*

FIGURE 6.2. Dante's biblical and postbiblical linguistics superimposed onto a "T and O" *mappa mundi*.   *193*

PREFACE

Zygmunt G. Barański and Theodore J. Cachey Jr.

Thirty years ago, the late Steven Botterill, to whose memory this volume is dedicated, wrote an essay in his memorably gracious style on the modern history of Dante studies in America as viewed through the lens of *Dante Studies*. He reported that between 1966 and 1990 almost 80 percent of the nearly two hundred scholarly essays that had appeared in the journal were primarily concerned with the *Commedia*, and that the neglect of Dante's so-called minor works was particularly striking: "nine articles on the *Vita nuova*, five on the *Convivio*, three on the *Rime*, one each on *De vulgari eloquentia*, *Monarchia* and *Quaestio de aqua et terra*."[1] Today, these statistics strike us as astonishing. Botterill attributed the cause for the lack of interest in Dante's "minor works" to the contemporary character of American Dante studies and the defining role played in it by the scholarship of Charles S. Singleton, who, despite having written an early pioneering book on the *Vita nova*, was overwhelmingly concerned with the *Commedia*.[2]

How times have changed. In the first place, it seems quaint to recall a time when one spoke of Dante studies in the United States as an autochthonous tradition, under the sway of a single scholar. Indeed, the sweeping internationalization and fragmentation of the field have constituted, arguably, the most important shift in scholarly perspectives of the last thirty years. Another macroscopic change that has taken place since Botterill wrote his essay is the amount of attention now dedicated to Dante's "minor works." Even a cursory consultation of the *Bibliografia internazionale dantesca / International Dante Bibliography*—significantly, a collaboration between the Dante Society of America (DSA) and the Società dantesca italiana (SDI)—reveals the great burgeoning of titles and of collective scholarly focus on the poet's "other" writings over the last thirty or so years.[3] With the publication of new editions and commentaries of all the texts during this same period, it would be fair to say that our appreciation of the so-called minor works, both in America and internationally, has been transformed.

The present volume grows out of a series of lectures given at the University of Notre Dame during the spring and fall of 2015, titled "Dante's 'Other Works': A Celebration of the 750th Anniversary of Dante's Birth."[4] We are pleased to present our book in time for the celebrations in 2021 of the seven-hundredth anniversary of the poet's death. Rather than speak of Dante's "minor works," according to an age-old tradition of Dante scholarship going back at least to the eighteenth century, we have preferred the designation "other works," both in light of their enhanced status and as part of a general effort to reaffirm their value as autonomous works. Indeed, had Dante never written the *Commedia*, he would still be considered the most important writer of the late Middle Ages for the originality and inventiveness of the "other works" he wrote besides his monumental poem. For us, the "other works" embrace the *Rime*, the *Fiore*, the *Detto d'Amore*, the *Vita nova*, the *Epistles*, the *Convivio*, the *De vulgari eloquentia*, the *Monarchia*, the *Questio de aqua et terra*, and the *Egloge*.

Cosponsored by the Devers Family Program in Dante Studies and the Center for Italian Studies at Notre Dame, the original lecture series brought together prominent scholars from the United States, Italy, and the United Kingdom, who delivered lectures at Notre Dame in the Hesburgh Library's Department of Special Collections. The majority of those lectures have become chapters in this volume. Each chapter addresses one of the "other works" by presenting the principal interpretative trends and questions relating to the text and by focusing on aspects of particular interest. Two special contributions on the relationship between the "other works" and the issues of "philosophy" and of "theology" were also part of the original lecture series, and these too have been included in the volume. The excitement and energy around the study of Dante's "other works" of recent years, including the most up-to-date scholarship, inspire and inform the chapters, which have been written by leading authorities, whom we should warmly like to thank for their commitment and patience. Our aim in collecting these essays has been quite straightforward: to make available the first "companion" to Dante's "other works" in English.

As we write these brief prefatory remarks, we find ourselves in June of 2020 in the midst of a worldwide health crisis, a predicament that has caused many of us soberly to reflect on and to reassess our priorities and commitments, both private and public. This time of travel restrictions, spatial distancing, and face masks has also brought a new appreciation of the many boons that we have enjoyed over a very long time as a scholarly community but that we can now no longer take for granted, including the freedom to travel and to gather together in person in the same place so that we can enjoy spending time together and discussing matters sundry and not just Dantesque. We can only hope that some of this collegiality, so fundamental to scholarship, can be recovered during the 2021 Dante anniversary. For now, colleagues have already begun to adapt, as we have also here at Notre Dame, to what is being termed the "new normal" of virtual scholarly communication and of webinars.

This volume, as we have noted, is dedicated to the memory of our dear friend Steven, who graced a different time with his scholarship and his warm and witty conversation, a time that, tragically, like Steven, cannot return. Steven in fact was one of the original contributors to this project, offering a droll and trenchant assessment of the *De vulgari eloquentia* in the Hesburgh Library's Special Collections.[5] Sadly, he was unable to turn his lecture into a chapter for our volume. And yet it is vital that that time and especially Steven should continue to inspire our work and help us deal with the demands of the present.

A Personal Postscript

Steven and his husband Craig were part of our family. We had the privilege and joy of being at their civil partnership in Brighton in 2007, among the first to take place in the United Kingdom and famously recorded by the BBC. However, it was Steven and Craig's regular visits to Reading that tightened our bonds of affection. Among my fondest memories of Anna and Edward's early years is their running into Steven and Craig's bedroom and leaping onto their bed, accompanied by shrieks and laughter. Few children could have asked for more attentive and caring "uncles." With Steven's cruel and untimely passing, Maggie, Anna, Ed, and I have lost an irreplaceable part of our lives. (zgb)

Notes

1. Botterill, "*Dante Studies*," 97.
2. Singleton, *Essay*.
3. http://dantesca.ntc.it/dnt-fo-catalog/pages/material-search.jsf.
4. The seminar series was organized by the coeditors of the volume, together with the excellent Anne Leone, assistant director of the Italian Studies Program at Notre Dame (2011–18), who has since joined the faculty of Syracuse University, where she is assistant professor of Italian. We should also like to record our gratitude to Eli Bortz, our series editor at the University of Notre Dame Press, for his support, advice, and efficiency as regards not just the present volume but also the many book projects on which we have worked and continue to work together.
5. We are extremely grateful to Mirko Tavoni for agreeing to write at relatively short notice the chapter on the *De vulgari eloquentia*. We are fortunate to have one of the foremost authorities on the treatise among our contributors.

ABBREVIATIONS AND EDITIONS

The following editions are used throughout, unless otherwise stated.

Albert the Great's works are cited from *Alberti Magni Opera omnia*, ad fidem codicum manuscriptorum edenda curavit Institutum Alberti Magni Coloniense. 41 vols. Cologne: Aschendorff, 1951–.

Bonaventure's works are cited from *Opera Omnia*. 10 vols. Quaracchi: Ex typographia Collegii S. Bonaventurae, 1882–1902.

Thomas Aquinas's works are cited from *Opera omnia*. 25 vols. Parma: Fiaccadori, 1852–73; we have used the reprint: New York: Musurgia, 1948–50.

Classical Latin authors, unless stated otherwise, are cited from the Loeb Classical Library.

Reference to annotated editions of Dante's works is made by using the editor's name followed by "ed.": for instance, Gorni ed. In the Bibliography the editions are listed under "Alighieri, Dante."

Bible	*Biblia Sacra iuxta vulgatam versionem*, edited by Robert Weber and Roger Gryson. 5th ed. Stuttgart: Deutsche Bibelgesellschaft, 2007.
Commedia	*La Commedia secondo l'antica vulgata*, edited by Giorgio Petrocchi. 2nd ed. 4 vols. Florence: Le Lettere, 1994.
Conv.	*Convivio*, edited by Franca Brambilla Ageno. 3 vols. Florence: Le Lettere, 1995.
Detto	*Il Fiore e il Detto d'Amore attribuibili a Dante Alighieri*, edited by Gianfranco Contini, 483–512. Edizione Nazionale a cura della Società Dantesca Italiana, vol. 1. Milan: Mondadori, 1984.
DDP	Dartmouth Dante Project: https://dante.dartmouth.edu/.

Dve	*De vulgari eloquentia*, edited and translated with commentary by Pier Vincenzo Mengaldo. In Dante Alighieri, *Opere minori*, 2:1–237. Milan: Ricciardi, 1979–88.
Ecl.	*Egloge*, edited by Marco Petoletti. In Dante Alighieri, *Epistole. Egloge. Questio de aqua et terra*, edited by Marco Baglio, Luca Azzetta, Marco Petoletti, and Michele Rinaldi, 489–650. Rome: Salerno, 2016.
Ep.	*Epistole*, edited by Arsenio Frugoni and Giorgio Brugnoli. In *Opere minori*, 2:505–643. Milan: Ricciardi, 1979–88.
Fiore	*Il Fiore e il Detto d'Amore attribuibili a Dante Alighieri*, edited by Gianfranco Contini, 1–467. Edizione Nazionale a cura della Società Dantesca Italiana, vol. 1. Milan: Mondadori, 1984.
GDLI	Accademia della Crusca, *Grande dizionario della lingua italiana*: http://www.gdli.it/.
Inf.	*Inferno*.
Mon.	*Monarchia*, edited by Prue Shaw. Florence: Le Lettere, 2009.
Par.	*Paradiso*.
Purg.	*Purgatorio*.
Questio	*Questio de aqua et terra*, edited by Michele Rinaldi. In Dante Alighieri, *Epistole. Egloge. Questio de aqua et terra*, edited by Marco Baglio, Luca Azzetta, Marco Petoletti, and Michele Rinaldi, 651–751. Rome: Salerno, 2016.
Rime	*Rime*, edited and commented by Domenico De Robertis. Florence: SISMEL and Edizioni del Galluzzo, 2005.
TLIO	*Tesoro della lingua italiana delle orgini*, founded by Pietro Beltrami. Florence: http://tlio.ovi.cnr.it/TLIO/.
Vn	*La vita nuova*, rev. ed., edited by Michele Barbi. Florence: Bemporad, 1932.

CHAPTER 1

The Lyric Poetry

MANUELE GRAGNOLATI

Dante's lyric poems, usually referred to in Italian as *Rime*, have been a very debated topic in the last two decades, arguably the most debated within a field like Dante studies that, as is well known, elicits a lot of discussion among scholars. In this chapter, which engages with some of the most important questions that have been raised about Dante's lyrics, I will refer to some work that I have done in the past, both within a comparative project on performance and performativity in the Middle Ages and as author of the line notes for Teodolinda Barolini's 2009 Italian edition of the first volume of Dante's *Rime*.[1] As will become clear, Barolini's scholarship has deeply shaped my understanding of Dante's lyric poetry and, although my emphasis is sometimes different, I am greatly indebted to it.

This chapter is divided in three parts: first, it offers an overview of Dante's lyrics; then it explores Dante's *Vita nova* as an early and particularly telling example of what I call the "performative power" of collecting lyrics; and third, it discusses the most important editions of Dante's *Rime* in the twentieth and twenty-first centuries, which cannot avoid taking a position on what kind of performative power they (want to) exert.

DANTE'S LYRICS

I shall begin by reiterating the way in which the Italian philologist Gianfranco Contini opened the introduction to his 1939 commented edition of

Dante's *Rime*: Dante's lyric poems are freestanding, independent lyric poems that Dante wrote occasionally without collecting—and the term *rime* is precisely meant to indicate a difference from the term *canzoniere*, which after Petrarch is associated with the sense of a "unitary work" and an "organic adventure of the soul."[2] In this sense, Contini continues, and on this point too he is right, Dante's *Rime* differs not only from Petrarch's collection of lyrics but also from Dante's own *Vita nova* and, to a lesser extent, the *Convivio*, which collect some of the lyric poems written by Dante in the past and, with the help of a prose framework and with a different degree of cohesion, insert them into a unitary work of which they are an integral component and from which part of their meaning derives.[3]

Dante's lyrics were written between circa 1283 and circa 1307–8. Their circulation began immediately, and their first extant transcriptions are found in notarial registers from Bologna, the so-called Memoriali bolognesi, already in 1287, when the notary Enrichetto delle Quercie transcribed in Memoriale 69 the sonnet "No me poriano za mai far emenda" [Never can [my eyes] make amends to me], and in 1293, when Pietro Allegranza copied in Memoriale 82 some verses of the canzone "Donne ch'avete intelletto d'amore" [Ladies who have understanding of love], which is also copied in the late thirteenth-century *canzoniere* Vaticano Latino 3793.[4] In addition to the separate circulation of the poems eventually included in the *Vita nova* and the *Convivio*, the manuscript tradition of the *Rime* includes more than five hundred documents. Its oldest and most authoritative strands come from the Veneto (as in the case of mss. Escurialense e.III.23 and Barberiniano Latino 3593) and Tuscany (as in the case of ms. Chigiano L VIII 305) or are connected to Boccaccio's editorial work, to which I will return later and which was also a source for the now-lost Raccolta Aragonese (an anthology of Italian lyrics assembled by Angelo Poliziano between 1476 and 1477 as a gift from Lorenzo de' Medici to Federico d'Aragona) and the so-called *Giuntina di Rime antiche* (Florence, 1527), the first printed edition of Dante's lyrics.[5]

The *Rime*'s exact number of poems depends on several factors, the most important one being the question of whether the lyrics eventually included in the *Vita nova* and the *Convivio* belong to an edition of Dante's *Rime* or not. For reasons that will become clear later on, I agree with some important editors, like Michele Barbi, Kenelm Foster and Patrick Boyde, and Teodolinda Barolini, that an edition of Dante's lyrics should include all of them and that their number is therefore approximately ninety poems. Although it is difficult to date most of them with any certainty and although critics debate not only their date of composition but also the criterion for ordering them, one possible way to group Dante's lyric poems is the following, which combines the reconstruction of a plausible chronology with thematic and formal criteria:[6]

1. Early poems written in the Sicilian and Tuscan manner dating from the early to the late 1280s, including:

1A. Exchanges with contemporary poets, like those on the nature of love with Dante da Maiano, which deploy the dense and convoluted style and rhetoric inspired by Guittone d'Arezzo; the sonnet "A ciascun alma presa e gentil core" [To every captive soul and gentle heart] (which, as we shall see later, will become the first sonnet of the *Vita nova*); the envoi to Guido Cavalcanti "Guido i' vorrei che tu Lapo ed io" [Guido, I wish that you and Lapo and I], which is a "wish-poem" (Foster and Boyde) fantasizing about union and companionship among fellow poets. (To this sonnet one can link the sonnet "Amore e monna Lagia e Guido e io" [Love and Lady Lagia and Guido and I], which was long placed among the lyrics of dubious attribution but which Domenico De Robertis has recently convincingly attributed to Dante.)

1B. "Double sonnets" (or *sonetti reinterzati* in Italian), that is, metrical variations on the traditional fourteen-line structure of the sonnet—a variation that also shows the influence exerted by Guittone d'Arezzo on the young Dante: "Se Lippo amico sé tu che mi leggi" [If you who read me are friend Lippo], which accompanies the *stanza di canzone* "Lo meo servente core" [My loyal heart]; "O voi che per la via d'Amor passate" [O you who walk along the path of love], which is a traditional *lamentanza* for a love that has been taken away; and "Morte villana, di pietà nemica" [Savage death, compassion's enemy], which bemoans the death of a young lady.

1C. The so-called floral *ballate*, written in a light, fresh manner inspired by some poems by Cavalcanti: "Per una ghirlandetta" [For a little garland] and "Deh, Violetta, che 'n ombra d'amore" [Ah, Violetta, you who in love's form].

1D. Diverse sonnets, ranging from "Sonar bracchetti e cacciatori aizzare" [The beagles belling and the hunters' cries] written in a "comic-realist" manner à la Folgore da San Gimignano, to the playful "No me poriano za mai far emenda" [No, never could they hope to make amends] and "Com più vi fere amor co' suo' vincastri" [The more love strikes you with a shepherd's stick], the latter of which suggests that one should surrender to love and also uses, for the first time, a harsh language and style.

2. Poems belonging to the phase that in *Purgatorio* 24 Dante will retroactively call *dolce stil novo* (sweet new style), from roughly the late 1280s to the mid-1290s.[7] Some of these poems were eventually collected and commented upon in the *Vita nova*, where, as we shall see, they often changed and acquired a different meaning. Like the poems belonging to the previous group, these are also quite varied, but what unites them is precisely a process of simplification and contraction of style[8]—a purified style that is *dolce* in the sense of elegant and apparently simple and that reacts against the convoluted and overtly complicated manner of the previous Tuscan poets, in particular Guittone d'Arezzo.

2A. Poems of *amore doloroso*, painful love, also inspired by Cavalcanti, but not the positive, airy Cavalcanti of the floral ballads mentioned in group 1C—rather the Cavalcanti who, often drawing from contemporary medicine, describes love as a sensual and incontrollable passion attacking the body and impairing the subject's physiological and psychological faculties.[9] They include the sonnets that will be placed in the *gabbo*—mocking—episode in the *Vita nova*; the two canzoni "Lo doloroso amor" [The grievous love] and "E' m'increscie di me sì duramente" [I feel such deep compassion for myself]; and the two sonnets "Degli occhi della mia donna si move" [A light emerges from my lady's eyes] and

"Ne le man vostre, gentil donna mia" [My gentle noble lady, in your hands], which combine the Cavalcantian influence with other sources, such as the Bible or the poet Guido Guinizzelli and, like the two canzoni, are excluded from the *Vita nova*.

2B (or 5E?). The canzone "Aï faus ris, pour quoi traï aves" [Alas, false smile, why have you betrayed], a trilingual *descort* that Barbi had placed among the lyrics of dubious attribution and that De Robertis has now reattributed to Dante. It is a virtuoso piece written in Latin, Florentine, and French (featuring some forms admissible only outside of France [Contini]), and while thematically it is a conventional lament over the lady's indifference, technically its linguistic and metric features represent a novelty in the Italian tradition and attest to Dante's incessant experimentalism. Indeed, differently from other medieval poems (such as Raimbaut de Vaiquerais's, where the plurilingualism was meant to express the confusion of a wounded heart), "Aï faus ris"'s plurilingualism has been mainly read as not having any stylistic or content-related justification but as mere virtuosity, motivated only by the poet's desire that its "chanson" travel throughout the world (Contini and Giunta). The composition date is uncertain, and while De Robertis seems to believe it is an early poem and writes that "non si dovrebbe essere lontani da un testo come . . . *Lo doloroso amor*" (2005 ed., 223) [with which it indeed shares the theme and some metrical features], it is also plausible that the poem belongs to the postexilic phase and dates around 1306–8, when Dante was sojourning in Lunigiana at the court of the Malaspina family. And in this case, Massimiliano Chiamenti has argued that, despite the banality of its occasional character, "Aï faus ris" is more than an empty exercise and attains a certain degree of formal and rhetorical intensity.[10]

2C. "Praise" poems, which shift the focus from the condition of the lyric "I" to the praise of the lady's worth, beauty, and angelic, salvific features. Some will be placed in the *Vita nova* to exemplify precisely a new manner of writing (*stilo della loda*) and are among the most famous poems by Dante, such as the sonnets

"Amor e 'l cor gentil sono una cosa" [Love and the noble heart are one sole thing], "Negli occhi porta la mia donna Amore" [My lady carries love within her eyes], "Tanto gentile e tanto onesta pare" [My lady shows such grace and dignity], "Vede perfettamente ogne salute" [Whoever sees my lady with her friends], and the canzone "Donne ch'avete intelletto d'amore" [Ladies who have intellect of love], which Dante will always consider a pivotal text and which he will also mention both in the *De vulgari eloquentia* and, as the poem inaugurating the *dolce stil novo*, in *Purgatorio* 24.[11]

2D. Poems written after the lady's death and other poems that will be mainly placed in the *Vita nova*, such as the canzone "Li occhi dolenti per pietà del core" and the sonnets "Era venuta nella mente mia" and "Lasso per forza di molti sospiri," as well as the sonnets that will become part of the episode of the "donna gentile," the noble lady, and the sonnets "Deh pellegrini che pensosi andate" and "Oltre la spera che più larga gira."

3. The poems of the so-called cycle of the "donna gentile," which revolve around the emergence of a new love that replaces the poet's love for Beatrice after her death: the two canzoni "Voi che intendendo il terzo ciel movete" and "Amor che ne la mente mi ragiona" (which will be both included and commented upon as allegorical in books 2 and 3 of the *Convivio* and then cited in the *Commedia*), the *ballata* "Voi che savete ragionar d'Amore," and the two sonnets "Parole mie che per lo mondo siete" and "O dolci rime che parlando andate." These poems, which are written in the same style as the *dolce stil novo* poems mentioned above and develop the motif of the volubility of desire (in this case specifically after the death of the beloved), have been the object of a long and intense debate, in particular the two canzoni eventually included in the *Convivio*. The major questions they raise concern the date of their composition (whether at the time of the other *dolce stil novo* poems or later), whether they all share the allegorical meaning that the two canzoni have in the *Convivio* (where the "donna gentile" is interpreted as a symbol of Philosophy, to which Dante would have dedicated himself as a form of

consolation after Beatrice's death), and especially whether the allegorical meaning that the two canzoni have in the *Convivio* was already present in the original lyrics.

4. The poems composed from around 1295, the time of Dante's entrance in Florentine politics, to Dante's exile in 1302. This phase comprises several types of poems, which are often very different from one another but which are all somewhat "denser" than before and which often abandon the *dolce stil* in favor of linguistic and stylistic, sometimes "radical," experimentalism and intensity.

> 4A. The two "doctrinal" canzoni "Le dolci rime d'amor ch'io solia" [The sweet love poetry] and "Poscia ch'Amor del tutto m'ha lasciato" [Since love has completely abandoned me]. Albeit not a love poem and therefore not liable to an allegorical interpretation like the two canzoni that preceded it in the *Convivio* ("Amor che ne la mente mi ragiona" [Love, speaking fervently in my mind] and "Voi ch'intendendo il terzo ciel movete" [O you who move the third heaven]), the former was written in about 1294–96 and was subsequently placed by Dante in the fourth book of the *Convivio* dedicated to the discussion of nobility. The canzone proclaims the abandonment of love poetry and turns into a small treatise that challenges the traditional understanding of *gentilezza* as long-standing possession of wealth accompanied by pleasing manners and conceives of it as a moral virtue independent from lineage. The canzone mixes Aristotle's *Nicomachean Ethics* with the ethical tradition in the vernacular and represents a "form of early humanism."[12] As emphasized by Foster and Boyde, it represents a turning point in Dante's career insofar as for the first time the didactic aim predominates. Moreover, not only does the style change from *dolce* (sweet) to *aspr' e sottile* (harsh and subtle), but this new mode of argumentative poetry also implies that the readership has widened from the restricted circle of the *Fedeli d'Amore* to the same addressees as the *Convivio*, namely, all those possessing intelligence but lacking a higher education.[13]

Tightly connected chronologically, thematically, and stylistically with "Le dolci rime" is the other doctrinal canzone, "Poscia ch'Amor del tutto m'ha lasciato," which describes the courtly virtue of *leggiadria* (a term that can be loosely translated as "liberality") and takes a moralizing tone against the corruption of contemporary society.

4B. The so-called lyrics of the "pargoletta" [the young lady]: the two *ballate* "I' mi son pargoletta bella e nova" [I am a young girl, lovely and marvelous] and "Perchè ti vedi giovinetta e bella" [Because you see you are so young and fair] and the sonnet "Chi guarderà giammai sanza paura" [Who will ever look without fear]. They portray the beautiful young lady as angelic and graceful like Beatrice in the *Vita nova* but express a different notion of love from the positive and salvific view formulated in the *libello*, one that continues to partake, instead, of Cavalcanti's dysphoric sense of love as a lethal, sensual passion.

4C. The canzoni "Amor, che movi tua vertù da cielo" [Love, who sends down your power] and "Io sento sì d'Amor la gran possanza" [So much do I feel love's mighty power]. Some critics, like Barbi-Pernicone, connect these two canzoni with the "pargoletta" cycle, and it is also debated whether they are allegorical or not (and indeed some other critics, like Foster and Boyde, link these canzoni with those written for the "donna gentile"/*Filosofia* and referred to above as Group 3). What is most interesting about these lyrics is that they seem to represent another phase in contrast to that represented by "Le dolci rime" and "Poscia ch'Amor," which have left love behind. In "Amor, che movi" and "Io sento sì d'Amor," love comes back powerfully, but whereas in the previous lyrics it remained in a mainly Aristotelian context, it is here a cosmic force that combines a Platonic sense of emanation with a Christian creationism and has also been identified with the Holy Spirit.[14]

4D. The "Tenzone con Forese Donati": a six-sonnet exchange between Dante and Forese Donati, of which all that is known is that the sonnets were written before Forese's death in 1296, although it cannot be excluded that they were written before the composition of the *Vita nova*.[15] This *tenzone* belongs to the strand of the so-called *poesia giocosa* whose most famous practitioners are poets like the Florentine Rustico Filippi and the Sienese Cecco Angiolieri, although this style was also practiced by other poets, including not only Dante but also Guinizzelli and Cavalcanti. It is a genre belonging to the "comic" register, which uses a very concrete, material, often scurrilous style and jargon and deals with everyday and frequently offensive themes that do not pertain to the higher, lofty, and more idealized modes of courtly poetry. The insults that the two poets address to each other in the *tenzone* range from Dante's accusing Forese of sexual impotence, gluttony, thieving, and illegitimacy to Forese's accusing Dante of poverty, cowardice, and not avenging his father. In the past the authenticity of the exchange was questioned because it was deemed implausible that the lofty poet of Beatrice could lower himself to such a level of vulgarity and aggression, while today their attribution seems to pose no more problems.[16]

4E. The four canzoni that form the so-called *Rime petrose*: "Io son venuto al punto de la rota" [I have come to that point on the wheel], "Al poco giorno ed al gran cerchio d'ombra" [To the short day and the great circle of shadow], "Amor, tu vedi ne che questa donna" [Love, you see well that this lady], and "Così nel mio parlar vogli'esser aspro" [I want to be as harsh in my speech]. They are called *petrose* because they concern the poet's love for a young, cruel lady who is as hard as stone and whose *senhal* is precisely "petra." The poems' main features are the expression of a negative and dark concept of love as an obsession of the senses that paralyzes the lyric "I" and leads the poet to death, and the deployment of a technical and metrical virtuosity that reveals a direct knowledge and engagement with Occitan poets, in particular Arnaut Daniel's *trobar clus*, a "difficult" style relishing metrical and rhetorical complexity as well as deliberate obscurity. In this respect, one has to mention at least the use of the sestina form in "Al poco giorno ed al gran cerchio d'ombra," which

Dante takes from Arnaut and which will be taken up by Petrarch. The poems do not always circulate together in the manuscript tradition, but it is quite certain that they form a group, and even Claudio Giunta, who seems reluctant to acknowledge any connection between Dante's lyrics, claims that, if not necessarily connected with one another, they are nonetheless the outcome of the same *Kunstwollen*.[17]

5. Postexile poems, that is, poems written after 1302.

5A. The "canzone of exile" "Tre donne intorno al cor mi son venute" [Three women have come round my heart], which has the technical peculiarity of two *congedi* (and there has been much discussion as to whether they were written at the same time or whether the second *congedo*, which is not present in all the manuscripts and utters a request for peace to Florence, has been added at a second stage).[18] This canzone imagines a dialogue taking place around the poet's heart between Love and three women allegorizing three different forms of Justice: *ius naturale, ius gentium*, and *ius civile* [natural law, the law of nations, and civil law] (Pietro di Dante).[19] The canzone addresses the theme of contemporary evil and degeneracy and takes Dante's exile as the ultimate symbol of that degeneracy. Connected with this canzone is the sonnet "Se vedi gli occhi miei di pianger vaghi" [Lord, if you see my eyes desiring to weep], which is a prayer to God that he may restore justice on earth.

5B. The canzone "Doglia mi reca ne lo core ardire" [Grief brings boldness to my heart], which gives the courtly version of the degeneracy described in "Tre donne." It is an ethical canzone that proposes the connection, otherwise unthinkable in the courtly world, between lust and avarice. Dante cites it in the *De vulgari eloquentia* (2.2.9) to stage himself as the Italian *cantor rectitudinis*, that is, as the moral poet of Italy.[20]

5C. The sonnet exchanges with Cino da Pistoia. Several exchanges with Cino are extant that Dante wrote after his exile and that address, in different and often contradictory ways, the issue of the heart's fickleness and of the poet's falling in love with a new woman. For instance, while the sonnet "Io sono stato con Amore insieme" [I have been together with love] maintains that one must yield to the new love because it is absurd to try to resist its power, the sonnet "Io mi credea del tutto esser partito" [I thought, messer Cino, that I had] maintains that Cino should control the volatility of his heart through his virtue.[21]

5D. "Amor, da che convien pur ch'io mi doglia" [Love, since after all I am forced to grieve] or the *canzone montanina* (as it is defined in line 75 with reference to its composition in the mountains of the Casentino). It is usually considered Dante's last poem and describes, in terms similar to those of Cavalcanti's negative physiology of love, the poet's overwhelming and lethal passion for a cruel lady. It is accompanied by an epistle in Latin to the marquis Moroello Malaspina, which was probably written in 1307, and which explains that, ever since the poet fell in love with a woman in the Casentino, his free will has been conquered by Love and cannot but obey Love's commands.

This is a very general overview of Dante's lyric poems, but it allows us to make two points: on the one hand, as Foster and especially Boyde have shown, it is possible to detect a general development in the style of Dante's lyric poetry, first toward the simplification of the *dolce stil novo* phase, and then toward a greater intensification and density. It is also possible to detect a few cases of connections among poems, as, for instance, in some sonnets that accompany another poem (as in "Se Lippo amico" [If you who read me are friend Lippo], "Messer Brunetto, questa pulzeletta" [Messer Brunetto, this young girl], and "Sonetto, se Meuccio" [Sonnet, when Meuccio has been pointed out]) or, less traditionally and more interestingly, as in the post–*Vita nova* "cycles" of the "donna gentile," the "pargoletta," or the *Rime petrose*.[22] But, on the other hand, it also seems that, when considered in their entirety, Dante's lyrics show great range and variety, and indeed most critics agree that their main characteristic is their incessant experimentation.

A significant aspect of Dante's lyrics is indeed their ability to touch upon very different, often contradictory modes, genres, and styles both synchronically and diachronically. I will give only a few examples of what Teodolinda Barolini has called "fascinating examples of discontinuities."[23] For an example of synchronic discontinuity one can take the rarefied celebration of the lady as an angelic creature who elevates and improves the poet-lover in some of the *dolce stil novo* poems *versus* the scurrilous and vulgar accusations of sexual impotence leveled at Forese Donati in the sonnet exchange with him (where Forese's wife is also misogynistically portrayed as "suffering" from her husband's lack of sexual interest). For a diachronic example, I will refer once more to Barolini and recall that in Dante's sonnet to Cino da Pistoia "Io sono stato con Amore insieme," written more than a decade after the spiritualized love for Beatrice in the *Vita nova*, the poet "characterizes love as an overriding force that dominates reason and free will, and admits to having first experienced such love in his ninth year, that is, vis-à-vis Beatrice."[24] Furthermore, in Dante's "tragic" last canzone, "Amor, da che convien pur ch'io mi doglia," not only is Love a sensual, deadly passion of the Cavalcantian kind, but also the style is surprisingly "untimely."[25]

My point is that a certain open-endedness and fluidity inherent in the genre of lyric poetry in the Middle Ages seem also present in Dante's *Rime*, namely, a certain possibility for the poet to change position without any sense, even implied, of breaking the consistency of the lyric "I." And, indeed, one need only think of the lyric corpus of poets like Guido Guinizzelli and Guido Cavalcanti to appreciate their variety and "freedom" to wander among very different styles and themes. For us (post) modern subjects it is difficult to think of a lyric "I" that is different from a modern sense of well-defined and fixed identity, but this is precisely what is interesting about the medieval position. Here I would like to propose that the fluidity of this nonlinear sequence of poems that doesn't seem to correspond to a (subject's) development could be considered as a trace of the medieval lyric's less defined sense of selfhood. This is a debated issue, and several critics now insist on the individuality characterizing the lyrics of the *dolce stil novo* poets.[26] But, as I will shortly argue, while working on the difference between the *Rime* and the *Vita nova*, I was often reminded of Contini's emphasis on the collective and choral character of the lyrics by the *dolce stil novo* poets, who are not always interested in stressing the distinctiveness of their own individuality—a distinctiveness that, on the contrary, is emphatically asserted in the *Vita nova*. With Contini, therefore, I would like to propose that the sense of "interchangeability" that characterizes some of the *dolce stil novo* poets (including the pre–*Vita nova* Dante) is the expression of the nonessential character of possession and individuality.[27]

In other words, what is particularly noteworthy and interesting about the *Rime*, especially in the poems up to those eventually included in the *Vita nova*, is their fluidity, not only in the sense of thematic nonlinearity and discontinuity, but also in the sense of not always expressing an "I" that is fixed or fully individualized. On the one hand, this is not surprising in itself given that a certain porosity and openness were the traditional mode of medieval lyrics, which were originally not meant to be listened to or read together and whose transmission itself was often instable and could even produce very different selves. With respect to this possibility I have found very inspiring Simon Gaunt's balanced take on the controversial phenomenon of *mouvance*, that is, the mobility of stanza order in transmission that was common in the troubadour and *trouvère* love lyric and that Gaunt analyzes in the case of Bernart de Ventadorn's "Can vei la lauzeta mover."[28] In particular, Gaunt comments upon the fact that the manuscripts transmit different stanza orders and shows how Bernart's poem produces different selves according to the order of the stanzas that the modern editor decides to follow. On the other hand, vestiges of this less fixed "I," which could be considered the trace of a medieval mode of composing, performing, and transmitting lyrics, are striking in an author like Dante, whose *Divine Comedy* has been celebrated by Erich Auerbach as the beginning of the modern individual and whose other works stage a strong sense of personality and individuality.[29]

In order to appreciate the fluidity and openness of medieval lyric poetry that is to an extent also present in Dante's *Rime*, I shall now consider what I call the *Vita nova*'s "performative power," focusing in particular on what happens when some of the lyrics are inserted within the unitary narrative of the *libello*. I hope that in this way two points will become clear: that Dante's lyrics function differently according to whether they are read as the freestanding poems that they were originally meant to be or within the *Vita nova*, and that the operations of selection, order, and commentary exert a great power on the lyrics' meaning and the kind of authorship they create.

The *Vita nova* and the Performative Power of Selection, Order, and Commentary

As is well known, the *Vita nova*'s textual operation represents Dante's first act of self-exegesis and consists of assembling thirty-one lyrics, most of which were certainly composed in the past, and inserting them within a prose narrative that is meant to explain their origin and meaning.[30] As I have shown elsewhere, the operations of selection, ordering, and commentary can be understood as a "performance of the author" in two senses:[31] first, in the sense that the protagonist-narrator's memorial account stages an ideal development from uncertain beginnings to a correct way of loving and writing that grants him exemplary, ethical, and authoritative significance; and, second, in a stronger sense that involves the creation of an author through language and draws on John Austin's original distinction between constative and performative utterances—that is, between utterances that simply describe something and can therefore be judged as true or false and utterances that, like oath swearing or promises, ship naming or marrying, "do" something and respond primarily to the criteria of the success or failure of the actions that they seek to accomplish. (In this case, the criterion according to which we assess these utterances is not their truth but their success, or "felicity.")[32]

Returning now to the *Vita nova* and its operation of collecting preexistent, stand-alone lyrics and of glossing them with a prose commentary, I have shown that, unlike what it claims, Dante's *libello* neither reveals nor describes the true meaning of the poems it contains, but rather creates new lyrics that, notwithstanding the fact that they almost always appear textually identical to their pre–*Vita nova* state, function differently than before. Scholars had already noticed that the poems change depending on whether they are read by themselves as freestanding poems or through the prose frame of the *Vita nova*, but, before Barolini reopened the issue in her edition of Dante's *Rime giovanili e della "Vita Nuova,"* they had rarely focused on the double meaning of the poems, exploring mainly their "true meaning" (*sententia*, *VN* (I.1 [1.1]), which the *Vita nova* claims to reveal.[33] For example, in an article on Dante's poems, Michelangelo Picone points out how the poetic texts have a different meaning according to whether they are read on their own or in the contexts of the *Vita nova* or the *Con-*

vivio,³⁴ but he maintains that once an individual lyric has been incorporated into one of those two works, it has lost the characteristics of an impromptu effort, since it is now part of a literary totality from which each poem receives its meaning.³⁵ This last assumption leads him to draw the conclusion that the lyrics included in the *Vita nova* (or the *Convivio*) lose their original status as freestanding poems and therefore should not be published in an edition of Dante's *Rime*—and, indeed, we shall see that various twentieth-century editions of Dante's poems, including Gianfranco Contini's magisterial and influential enterprise, omit the lyrics included in the *Vita nova* and those found in the *Convivio*.

Barolini offers a different perspective, discussing Picone's argument and noting that his conclusions are conditioned not only by the drive to reveal the magisterial and influential enterprise, namely the *Vita nova* (thus believing what Dante says he is doing), but also by Petrarch's *Rerum vulgarium fragmenta*, or *Canzoniere*.³⁶ Barolini's edition therefore includes every lyric poem written by Dante, and, as we shall see, her commentary traces Dante's intellectual development as well as the connections between his lyric poems and the *Commedia*.

From my standpoint, that is, looking at the *Vita nova* from a performative perspective, the importance of the question of the "true" meaning of the lyrics is diminished compared to the question of how the *libello* manages to rewrite those poems, creating new meanings in such a convincing manner that they have managed to erase and replace their original ones, as if a different meaning had never existed. While, at certain points in the *Vita nova*, Dante introduces variants at the moment of the inclusion of the lyrics in his new text, it is more commonly the new prose frame that effectively rewrites them and succeeds in bestowing on them a new meaning.

Here I will consider the first sonnet of the *Vita nova*, which represents a good example of how, without necessarily changing them textually, the *Vita nova* rewrites previously written lyrics and turns them into new poems:

> A ciascun'alma presa e gentil core
> nel cui cospetto vèn lo dir presente,
> in ciò che mi riscrivan suo parvente,
> salute in lor segnor, cioè Amore.

Già eran quasi che aterzate l'ore
del tempo che omne stella n'è lucente,
quando m'apparve Amor subitamente,
cui essenza membrar mi dà orrore.
   Allegro mi sembrava Amor tenendo
meo core in mano, e nelle braccia avea
madonna involta in un drappo dormendo.
Poi la svegliava, e d'esto core ardendo
lei paventosa umilmente pascea.
Apresso gir lo ne vedea piangendo.
               (III.10–12 [1.21–23])[37]

[To every captive soul and noble heart / before whose eyes my present words appear, / beseeching them the favor of reply, / accept my greeting in the name of love. / A third of night had almost run its course, / a time that every star is shining bright, / when Love appeared before me suddenly, / the memory of whose manner frightens me. / Jubilant, Love seemed to hold my heart / within his hand, and in his arms he held / my Lady wrapped within a cloth, asleep. / He woke her then, and she, beset by fear, / began to humbly eat my burning heart. / And then I saw him go away in tears.]

Originally, "A ciascun'alma presa e gentil core" is a poetic riddle presenting quite an erotically charged, if obscure, description of a dream, circulated among contemporary poets so that they would oblige by deciphering its opaque and therefore interpretable, "porous" meaning. Through this envoi, the young Dante wanted to establish a dialogue and a relationship with other fellow poets, and we know that this aim was achieved by the three replies that have survived, which, in their diversity of tone and content, give an indication of the openness to interpretation of Dante's sonnet: Dante da Maiano replies in a comic register with the sonnet "Di ciò che stato sei dimandatore" [The matter you asked me about], maintaining that the fellow poet is talking nonsense and recommending that he cure his love-sickness by washing his testicles: "che lavi la tua coglia largamente / a ciò che stinga e passi lo vapore / lo qual ti fa favoleggiar loquendo" (7–9) [give your testicles a good wash, so that the vapors that make you talk nonsense be extinguished and dispersed];[38] according to Terino da Castelfiorentino (or, less likely, Cino da Pistoia), the dream indicates that the poet's lady reciprocates his feelings; and also Guido Cavalcanti gives a positive reading of the dream as a sign of achieved happiness. Of these reply-sonnets, only Cavalcanti's, "Vedeste, al mio parere, onne valore" [What you saw, I think, was all nobility], is mentioned in the *Vita nova*, to demonstrate how this poetic exchange led to the start of a friendship between the two poets.

The *Vita nova* changes the meaning of Dante's sonnet, which from an "open" riddle becomes the definitive account of a vision prophesying Beatrice's ascent to heaven. As Foster and Boyde have argued, nothing in the sonnet itself indicates that the lady held by Love in the vision is Beatrice,[39] and it is only in the *libello*, which is centered on Beatrice's death and opens and closes with the image of her glory in heaven, that the dream described in the sonnet can represent a premonition of the lady's death. The creation of this new meaning is achieved by some details added in the *Vita nova*: for instance, while the sonnet ends with the image of Love's departure, the prose adds that Love goes to heaven ("verso lo cielo")—a detail that would otherwise be absent in the sonnet.

Usually commentators indicate that the dream's true meaning is revealed by Beatrice's death, but I would rather say that this meaning is created by the way in which this sonnet is placed and commented upon in the *Vita nova*. In other words, if it is unlikely that this sonnet referred originally to Beatrice, it is not Beatrice's death that allows the author and everybody to understand what it really meant. On the contrary, the sonnet's new meaning is a textual *performance* of the *Vita nova*, which refers the lyric to Beatrice for the first time, inserts it in a context centered on her glorious destiny, and adds some significant details. This performance is so successful that after it has taken place, it is difficult to go back and see the open meaning that the poem had as a stand-alone lyric, a meaning that does not refer to the lady's death or even to Beatrice.

Moreover, while "A ciascun'alma presa" was originally composed as a "porous" poem that was open to interpretation and circulated among fellow poets to create a space of exchange and dialogue with them, in the *Vita nova* it has a different aim and acquires a fixed, providential meaning that distinguishes its author from his fellow poets, in particular Guido Cavalcanti.[40] In other words, not only does "A ciascun'alma presa" change its meaning in the *Vita nova*, where it is effectively rewritten into another poem, but a greater individuation of the speaker's voice also takes place with respect to the more choral and collective stance from which the poem was originally written.

In the case of "Ciascun'alma presa e gentil core" it is its context in the *Vita nova* and the prose commentary that change its meaning and contributes to the emergence of a new author, but the operations of selecting which lyrics to include and which to leave out and of placing them in a particular order also exert a great degree of power over the kind of performance realized in Dante's text and the sort of author emerging from it. In the case of the poems left out of the *Vita nova*, for example, it is interesting to consider that, as Barolini has argued, some canzoni, like "Lo doloroso amore" and "E m'increse di me sì duramente," are left out of the *Vita nova* because they bear witness to a poetic output in which Beatrice is explicitly the bringer of death rather than life, so that they cannot enter into the *libello*'s world.[41] And, in the case of the ordering of the lyrics, suffice it to think of those that bear the hallmarks of Cavalcantian inspiration in the so-called episode of the *gabbo* and that, precisely because they are placed in a specific position within a teleological order, assume the value of a negative poetic experience to which they do not otherwise attest if read as independent, unconnected poems.

While I can only hint at the performative power of selection and order, I want to briefly mention one final case of resignification that takes place in the *Vita nova*, that is, the well-known sonnet "Io mi sentii svegliar dentro a lo core" (XXIV [15]):

> Io mi sentii svegliar dentro a lo core
> un spirito amoroso che dormia:
> e poi vidi venir da lungi Amore
> allegro sì, che appena il conoscia,
> dicendo: "Or pensa pur di farmi onore";
> e 'n ciascuna parola sua ridia.
> E poco stando meco il mio segnore,
> guardando in quella parte onde venia,
> io vidi monna Vanna e monna Bice
> venir inver lo loco là 'v'io era,
> l'una appresso de l'altra maraviglia;
> e sì come la mente mi ridice,
> Amor mi disse: "Quell'è Primavera,
> e quell'ha nome Amor, sì mi somiglia."

[I felt a spirit of love begin to stir / within my heart, where it was fast asleep; / then I saw Love approaching from afar / (I barely recognized him for his cheer), / who said, while smiling after every word: / "Now only think how you might honor me." / And while my Lord remained with me a while, / I turned my eyes to see from where he'd come / and saw the ladies Joan and Beatrice / draw near the place where I was standing then, / one marvel followed by a second one. / And as my memory now recollects, / Love said: "This one is Spring, the other's name / is Love, because she so resembles me."]

As a freestanding poem, this sonnet is a description of the poet feeling the power of love at the arrival of his lady ("monna Bice") accompanied by Guido Cavalcanti's lady ("monna Vanna") and it celebrates the friendship between the two poets. The prose commentary of the *Vita nova* adds an additional meaning, and by creating an analogy between Giovanna and John the Baptist and between Beatrice and Christ it not only contributes to Beatrice's divinization but also distinguishes Dante from Cavalcanti and indicates that, no matter how significant, Guido Cavalcanti is a precursor of Dante and is to be surpassed by him.[42]

Furthermore, while in the *Vita nova* the sonnet belongs explicitly to Dante and serves to mark a difference between him and Cavalcanti, it is interesting to note that in some of the manuscripts transmitting it outside the *Vita nova* the sonnet can be attributed to Cavalcanti—and this could represent another indication of the greater fluidity or "interchangeability" of the pre–*Vita nova* lyric "I" and of the distinction between poets that the *libello* seeks, if not to create from nowhere, at least to bolster.

If through selection, ordering, and commentary the *Vita nova* rewrites Dante's lyrics and gives them a new meaning, it also creates a new, individualized, and well-defined author. As Albert Ascoli has shown, it is precisely by creating an individual and personalized character and by inserting it into the largely impersonal and ahistorical category of the medieval *auctor* that the *Vita nova* represents one of the first instances in which a new kind of author begins to emerge who is similar to that of modern texts[43]—and this author, as I have shown, does not preexist the text but is performed by it.

Rather than allowing ourselves to be convinced by the authority of its author, we can reopen the closure that Dante's *libello* wishes to impose on its lyrics, recovering their archaeological complexity and appreciating their double temporality and existence. Seen from this perspective, the *Vita nova* neither reveals nor explains the true meaning of the poems within it but, often without changing them textually, writes new poems that continue to exist alongside the originals. Recently I have proposed that, in this sense, the poems that Dante includes in the *Vita nova* can be considered as multistable figures, or *Kippbilder* in the original German, like the "duck-rabbit" discussed by Ludwig Wittgenstein in the *Philosophische Untersuchungen*, which, without changing materially, can appear either as a duck or as a rabbit, depending on how one looks at it.[44]

Therefore, it is to my mind necessary that an edition of Dante's *Rime* contain all the lyrics, including those later included in the *libello* and the *Convivio*. The question remains of how one should order the *Rime* in such an edition. If the authorial intervention and the prose make the performative power of the *Vita nova* very clear, once this idea of an author has come into being, it also applies to any collection—and, indeed, any edition of Dante's *Rime* contributes in different ways to the production of an author. Seen from this perspective, the very act of collecting the *Rime* in an edition (which includes selection, order, and often also commentary) cannot but exert some power on lyrics that were written as freestanding. Thus I would propose that it is possible to draw an analogy between the performative power exerted by the *Vita nova* on the lyrics included and that exerted on them by an edition that arranges them into a collection. Keeping in mind some of the questions and issues raised so far by the *Rime*, I shall now consider what the most important editors and commentators of the twentieth and twenty-first centuries have done with them in their editions.[45]

Dante Performed: Twentieth- and Twenty-First-Century Editions of the *Rime*

Michele Barbi, with Francesco Maggini and Vincenzo Pernicone

Michele Barbi's critical edition was published with the patronage of the Società Dantesca Italiana in 1921 and was followed by an edition with commentary, on which two pupils of Barbi worked after his death: Francesco Maggini and Vincenzo Pernicone. Barbi's edition includes the poems of both the *Vita nova* and the *Convivio* for a total of eighty-eight poems. It also contains twenty-nine poems by various authors who seem more or less closely connected with Dante and is followed by an appendix with twenty-six poems of dubious attribution (*rime dubbie*). The eighty-eight "authentic" poems and those by other authors connected with them are distributed among seven books (as they are called in the 1921 edition) or parts (as they are called in the 1956 and 1969 editions) that combine biographical-chronological logic with formal and thematic principles: (i) *Rime della "Vita Nuova"* [Poems of the *Vita Nuova*], placed in the same order as they appear in the *libello*; (ii) *Rime del tempo della "Vita Nuova"* [Poems from the time of the *Vita Nuova*] ordered according to a chronological criterion; (iii) *Tenzone con Forese Donati* [Tenzone with Forese Donati]; (iv) *Rime allegoriche e dottrinali* [Allegorical and doctrinal poems], namely, the poems from the *Convivio* and those related to them; (v) *Altre rime d'amore e di corrispondenza* [Other love poems and poetic exchanges], which include nonallegorical poems supposedly written after those grouped in the previous book: here one finds both the two canzoni "Amor che movi" and "Io sento sì d'amor" and the cycle of the "pargoletta" that could be related to them—and all these poems are considered nonallegorical. This book also contains some exchange sonnets, like the first exchanges with Cino; (vi) *Rime petrose* [Stony poems]; and (vii) *Rime varie del tempo dell'esilio* [Various poems from the time of exile], which more or less correspond to the last group (v) of the overview sketched above and include the canzoni "Doglia me reca," "Tre donne intorno al cor mi son venute," the *canzone montanina*, and the late sonnet exchanges with Cino.

Gianfranco Contini

Between Barbi's 1921 critical edition and the Barbi-Maggini and Barbi-Pernicone commented editions (1956 and 1969), in 1939 Gianfranco Contini published his commented edition of Dante's *Rime* (which was republished in 1946 and 1965).[46] Contini's collection includes fifty-four poems (plus twenty-six *rime dubbie*) rather than Barbi's eighty-eight because Contini thinks that Dante's *Rime* are only the *estravaganti* (those that wander outside, that is, the poems that have not been collected by Dante in either *Vita nova* or *Convivio*), and he therefore leaves out the poems included in these two works. In terms of order, Contini eliminates Barbi's division into books but follows (with some minor alterations) his reconstruction of an ideal chronology. The result is "la più superba collezione di 'estravaganti'" [the most superb collection of *estravaganti* poems].[47] It may be "superb," but Contini's collection is deprived of thirty-one lyrics and therefore partial, and indeed the term *estravaganti* has a certain flavor of "residues" or "leftovers" (with respect to something for which they were in fact never intended).[48] With respect to Barbi, Contini also reduces the choral atmosphere around some poems and, for instance, does not always include the replies or the envois by other poets—a surprising choice, given that, as we have seen, in his introduction Contini insists on the choral character of the *dolce stil novo*.

Kenelm Foster and Patrick Boyde

Kenelm Foster and Patrick Boyde's 1967 commented edition of *Dante's Lyric Poetry* takes a different track from both Barbi's and Contini's editions: like Barbi's, it includes the poems of the *Vita nova* and the *Convivio* but, like Contini's, it eliminates Barbi's division into books/parts and arranges the poems in a plausible chronological order, interspersing the *Vita nova*'s poems with the others written by the young Dante. Foster and Boyde base the reconstruction of their plausible chronology "on considerations of style, theme, and tone, where external evidence is lacking, as it often is."[49] They follow Barbi's chronology but with some alterations (and one different attribution in the "Tenzon del duol d'amore," the exchange on the pain of love with Dante da Maiano, so that the number of Dante's poems increases to eighty-nine). They eliminate Barbi's appendix of twenty-six poems of doubtful attribution and reduce the number of poems by other poets, which now become eighteen (rather than the twenty-nine of Barbi's edition).[50] Foster and Boyde's plausible chronology is mainly interested in showing the different stages of Dante's poetic development, and the reconstruction of a chronological sequence creates a sense of stylistic evolution that marks Dante's innovations with respect to his earlier procedures.

Domenico De Robertis

Domenico De Robertis's 2002 critical edition for the Società Dantesca Italiana is the result of almost fifty years of intense philological work and was followed by his 2005 annotated edition. In terms of the selection, De Robertis reassigns eight poems to Dante that according to Barbi were of doubtful attribution, and from the *Vita nova* includes only those thirteen poems that exist materially in a redaction prior to the *libello*,[51] to which he adds the *Vita nova*'s first sonnet, "A ciascun'alma presa," although it does not have a different redaction preceding the *Vita nova*. The most striking feature of De Robertis's edition is the attempt, in the absence of an order decided by Dante, to avoid the editor's imposition of his subjective views on the *Rime* by resisting the temptation to suggest a chronological development of Dante's lyric poetry, opting instead to order the lyrics according to the way in which they were transmitted in the most ancient and authoritative codices. The result is an edition that contains seventy-nine poems by Dante, thirty-one by other poets, and nineteen of dubious attribution. It can be divided in two parts.

The first part begins with fifteen canzoni, including the three of the *Convivio*, which Boccaccio called *distese* (that is, pluristrophic) and copied in the same order in three different codices (Toledano 104.6, Chigiano L.V.176, and Riccardiano 1035):

1. "Così nel mio parlar vogli'esser aspro"
2. "Voi che 'ntendendo il terzo ciel movete"
3. "Amor che nella mente mi ragiona"
4. "Le dolci rime d'amor ch'io solea"
5. "Amor che movi tua vertù dal cielo"
6. "Io sento sì d'Amor la gran possanza"
7. "Al poco giorno ed al gran cerchio d'ombra"
8. "Amor, tu vedi ben che questa donna"
9. "Io son venuto al punto della rota"
10. "E' m'incresce di me sì duramente"
11. "Poscia ch'Amor del tutto m'ha lasciato"
12. "La dispietata mente che pur mira"
13. "Tre donne intorno al cor mi son venute"
14. "Doglia mi reca nello core ardire"
15. "Amor, da che convien pur ch'io mi doglia"

The *canzoni distese* are found in the majority of the manuscript tradition, which follows the medieval custom of dividing poems in manuscripts according to their metrical genre (usually canzoni first, followed by *ballate* and sonnets, and then the *Rime di corrispondenza*). In De Robertis's editions, they are followed first by the other canzoni not included in the series ("Lo doloroso amor" [The sorrowful love], "Traggemi de la mente Amor la stiva" [Love draws the load of my mind], of which only the incipit is extant, and the trilingual "Aï faus ris, pour quoi traï aves" [Alas false smile, why have you betrayed], which De Robertis considers authentic) and then by the "satellite" poems, that is, those poems that are somewhat connected with the *canzoni distese*: "Voi che savete ragionar d'amore" [O you who know how to reason about love], "Parole mie che per lo mondo siete" [Words of mine that have gone about], "O dolci rime che parlando andate" [O you sweet poems that go about], "I' mi son pargoletta bella e nova," "Perché tti vedi giovinetta e bella," "Chi guarderà giammai sanza paura," and "Se vedi gli occhi miei di pianger vaghi." If the first part of De Robertis's edition is occupied by the *canzoni distese* and their satellite poems, the second part contains the remainder of the *Rime* and the lyrics by other poets that De Robertis intersperses between Dante's poems.

De Robertis's attempt to break the chronological order of Dante's *Rime* aims at conveying their nonplanned and occasional character, and indeed it produces a different experience of Dante to the reader: less an individualized "author" who can be followed in his development than a scattered juxtaposition of texts that are often not easily distinguishable from those of other poets. While this is a very interesting choice, De Robertis's edition also has some blind spots: first of all, as Barolini has made clear, while De Robertis claims that choosing the ordering of the manuscript tradition is a "neutral" choice in the absence of an order by Dante, that choice is not only as subjective as any other choice but also influenced by Boccaccio;[52] and second, De Robertis makes a "philological" choice and follows the manuscript tradition only in placing the fifteen *canzoni distese* at the beginning of his edition, but the rest of the collection is, for the most part, "historiographical" and ordered according to the traditional chronological reconstruction (which would of course be fine if De Robertis did not claim otherwise).[53] Moreover, De Robertis's edition, which includes only fourteen of the thirty-one poems of the *Vita nova*, is incomplete, and his choice of including only poems that exist materially in a redaction preceding the *libello* is particularly striking in the case of poems that, as with canzone "Donne ch'avete intelletto d'amore," we know for certain were circulating before the *Vita nova*.

Teodolinda Barolini

Only the first part of the edition by Teodolinda Barolini has come out so far: first in Italian in 2009 as *Rime giovanili e della Vita Nuova* (and it is for this edition that I wrote the line notes to the poems) and then, without my line notes, in English in 2014. Barolini is now completing the second volume, which will contain the rest of Dante's poems. When possible, Barolini follows the text reconstructed by De Robertis, but, for the first time in an Italian edition, she endorses Foster and Boyde's choice to arrange the lyrics in a chronological sequence. Barolini knows well and reiterates the fact that Dante never intended to collect his poems and that any choice with respect to the chronological ordering of the poems cannot but be editorial; she also takes the corpus of Dante's *Rime* as a helpful reminder of some of the paths that Dante at a certain point tried out but decided not to take. The choice she consciously takes as editor of the *Rime* is that of showing how "Dante became Dante": "My aim is to illuminate the conceptual itinerary that led a young courtly poet of the final decades of the thirteenth century to become the writer of the vast and visionary *Commedia*. . . . Throughout the commentary I look more forward than back, in terms of Dante's own trajectory. . . . These poems on the one hand testify to the paths not taken, and on the other allow us to identify with greater clarity when, how, and by what incremental and gradual steps Dante ventured along the path that would ultimately become his."[54] Indeed, even more than with Foster and Boyde, what results is more of a unitary author whose poetic development is reconstructed teleologically as finally arriving to write the *Divine Comedy* (and the stress on Dante's individual character is also highlighted by the fact that, with respect to previous editions, Barolini eliminates many of the poems by other poets). So, for instance, Barolini writes in the introduction to the English edition: "I want to show how that development, beginning in Dante's youthful lyrics, leads to the *Commedia* and is epistemologically essential to our understanding. My commentary essays on the fifty-eight poems move in a teleological direction and form a narrative in which I endeavor to tell a coherent story, one that I hope will reward a reading that moves from beginning to end."[55]

Claudio Giunta

The 2011 edition by Claudio Giunta provides some clear explanations and interesting commentaries on the poems that, rather than focusing on the intertextual connections between the poems, which for Giunta are a less important feature of medieval poetry than usually argued, situate them within both the historical and cultural context and the literary genres and rhetoric of medieval Romance, Latin, and even German literary culture.[56] But Giunta's edition also raises some unresolved tensions. The first concerns the number of poems to include. In an article that preceded the publication of his edition, Giunta first agreed that an edition of Dante's *Rime* should "ideally" contain all of Dante's lyric poems: "Le *Rime* di Dante sarebbero, a rigore, tutte le poesie composte da Dante" [Strictly speaking, Dante's *Rime* would be all the poems written by Dante]. But then he claimed that "in practice" scholars consider as *Rime* only those poems not included in the *Vita nova* and the *Convivio*: "Di fatto, gli studiosi chiamano *Rime* solo una parte di questo *corpus*, e cioè tutte le poesie volgari di Dante che non sono comprese nella *Vita nova* e nel *Convivio*."[57] In this way not only does Giunta not seem to acknowledge as scholars all those for whom this is not true (like Barbi, Foster and Boyde, and Barolini), but he also explicitly privileges the supposedly scholarly habit ("fatto") over what is correct ("rigore"). Giunta's actual edition indicates only that the *rime* consist of Dante's lyrics not included in the *Vita nova* and the *Convivio*, explicitly presenting them as a residue rather than a choice ("Non si tratta dunque di una scelta, ma di un residuo"),[58] and thereby making it clear that this is what is really meant by the term *estravaganti* first coined by Contini and then used by several other critics. Another tension that characterizes Giunta's edition concerns the lyrics' order. Giunta acknowledges that there are some connections among them but maintains that "il grosso del corpus dantesco non mostra al suo interno traiettorie di sviluppo riconoscibili" [the greatest part of the Dantean *corpus* does not show internally any recognizable trajectories of development].[59] He claims that the most appropriate solution would be that of ordering the lyrics according to their metrical genre or, even better, alphabetically, insofar as these would be "scelte avalutative" [neutral choices], which do not give to the reader "false impressioni di coerenza o consequenzialità" [false impressions of coherence or consequentiality].[60]

However, while even ordering by genre or alphabet would not be a neutral choice, quite unexpectedly, Giunta decides to follow Barbi's sequence (although without the lyrics of *Vita nova* and *Convivio*, and without the division into books, and with some alterations). This ultimately means that his selection is the same as Contini's, albeit updated after De Robertis's reassessment of the attribution of Dante's poems ("la stessa selezione di Contini salvo le ovvie rettifiche, dopo il lavoro di De Robertis, circa le inclusioni e le esclusioni dal canone" [the same selection as Contini's with the obvious corrections, after De Robertis's work, on the inclusions and exclusions from the canon]),[61] that is, a total of fifty-nine poems, which also in this case represent only a partial selection of Dante's lyrics.

Marco Grimaldi and Donato Pirovano

The new annotated edition of Dante's works coordinated by Enrico Malato has published the first part of *Vita Nuova; Rime*, edited by Donato Pirovano (*Vita Nuova*) and Marco Grimaldi (*Rime*), while the second part with the rest of the *rime* recently appeared in 2019. This two-part volume follows Barbi's criteria and therefore publishes all of Dante's lyrics, including those of the *Vita nova* and the *Convivio*, and organizes them according to Barbi's division in separate sections.[62] The unusual and interesting choice, which, at the risk of being redundant, acknowledges the fact that, as I have indicated above, Dante's lyrics included in the *Vita nova* and the *Convivio* have a double existence, is that of publishing the *Rime della "Vita Nuova" e altre rime del tempo della "Vita Nuova"* in the same volume with the *Vita nova* itself.

Having reviewed the most important editions of Dante's *Rime* of the twentieth and twenty-first centuries, I want to conclude this overview by mentioning one more question that has arisen recently, namely, the hypothesis of the so-called *Libro delle canzoni*. It is a hypothesis that originates from De Robertis's edition, which suggests that the sequence of the fifteen *canzoni distese* that crystallized in the most ancient and authoritative manuscript tradition is not an invention by Boccaccio (as was believed for a long time) but actually predates him. That is, it would not have been Boccaccio who created the sequence of the *canzoni distese*, but rather he would have found it already formed, and its creation would date back to Dante's time. (And indeed De Robertis could consult some important manuscripts that were not available to Barbi, like the Riccardian 1050 or the British Library, Additional 26772 or the *Raccolta aragonese primogenita*.) Some critics argue that it is actually not at all certain that the sequence of the fifteen *canzoni distese* predates Boccaccio, and that the tradition indicated by De Robertis to defend his hypothesis is actually influenced by Boccaccio,[63] but some scholars connected to De Robertis, in particular Giuliano Tanturli, Natascia Tonelli, and Lino Leonardi, have pushed his claims further and argued that the sequence of the *canzoni distese* not only predates Boccaccio but is to be attributed to Dante himself.[64] In other words, according to this hypothesis, Dante himself would at a certain point have decided to collect the fifteen *canzoni*, and this sequence would therefore represent an authorial choice. In addition to the idea that the sequence predates Boccaccio, a proof for this would be that the sequel of the fifteen *canzoni distese* would more or less correspond to the same order of the fourteen *canzoni* that Dante was planning to comment on in the *Convivio* plus an introductory one. These critics also argue that it is possible to find formal connections among the fifteen canzoni, which would also reveal an authorial intention behind them.

As Tonelli argues, the consequence of this hypothesis is that the poems contained in De Robertis's edition would form two anthologies of Dante's lyric poems, each with a very different status: an organic series of canzoni that could be called the *Libro delle canzoni*; and the rest of the poems, mainly not canzoni, which, using Contini's formula, would now form a "raccolta di estravaganti": no longer "superb" like Contini's, but just a collection of modest leftovers.[65] And this is precisely the concept informing the recent volume *Libro de las canciones y otro poemas*, edited in 2014 by Juan Varela Portas.[66] This volume, which is closely connected to the sustained work done on the *rime* by the Spanish Grupo Tenzone and its yearly Madrid journal *Tenzone* since 2000, includes the fifteen *canzoni distese*, followed by some of their satellite poems and a few other canzoni, as well as by the "Tenzone with Forese Donati" and the exchanges with Cino.[67]

The hypothesis of the *Libro delle canzoni*, which would include poems expressing a sensual, irrational, and "anti-Beatrician" concept of love, raises interesting questions,[68] but I do not find it convincing for the reasons lucidly indicated by Barolini:[69] it seems far from certain that the sequence predates Boccaccio and that it corresponds to the one hypothetically planned for the *Convivio*. Even if that were the case, there is no reason why the planned order of the *canzoni* in the *Convivio* should correspond to how Dante would have collected them in another context; and, especially, differently from what we know about Petrarch's way of working and assembling the *Rerum vulgarium fragmenta*, there is no material evidence whatsoever that can justify the claim of the supporters of the hypothesis of the *Libro delle canzoni*. Moreover, there does not seem to be any formal connection between the fifteen *canzoni distese*, and it seems to me that the analyses provided in support of the book's unity not only fail but actually prove the opposite.

In any case, what matters to my argument here is that, even on a hypothetical level (and I stress hypothetical because I don't believe that the theory is plausible), if the *Libro delle canzoni* represented an authorial choice, then it would certainly make sense to read these poems in that order (and it certainly does make a lot of sense if one is interested in Boccaccio's reading of Dante), but, as in the case of *Vita nova* and *Convivio*, they would have become something else without ceasing to be part of the poetic production that Dante wrote in the form of (mainly) occasional and stand-alone lyrics. Therefore, as in the case of the *Vita nova* and the *Convivio*, an edition of Dante's *Rime* should contain them all, in all their variety, experimentation, and even multiple existence.

Indeed, unlike most other works by Dante that aim at staging a unitary and ultimately consistent self (as is the case of the *Vita nova*, the *Convivio*, *De vulgari eloquentia*, and the *Commedia*), the *Rime* convey less a sense of consistency or coherence guaranteed by the identity of an individual. If this is especially true for the poems of youth (while it may be possible to detect the signs of an emerging individuality in some of the post–*Vita nova* poems), one of the most interesting features of Dante's *Rime* is their openness and fluidity. My proposition is that one could consider them as an example of "erranza senza errore," a sort of "errorless errance," a multifarious wandering and straying without a sense of norm that contrasts not only with the *Vita nova*'s performance of unity but also with the twists and turns of Petrarch's *Rerum vulgarium fragmenta*, which are fascinating in their resistance to linearity and conversion but which, unlike the *Rime*, presuppose a consistent authorial "I."

I hope to have shown how it is both fascinating and complex to think of an edition that collects Dante's *Rime* and that it cannot but alter their fluidity and openness. My final suggestion is that the very debated concept of *mouvance*, to which I have alluded before while mentioning Gaunt's reading of Bernart de Vertadorn's *Can vei la lauzeta*, could be usefully, if metaphorically, transposed from the order of the stanzas within one poem to the ensemble of the editions of Dante's *Rime*, insofar as they give different organizations of the poems that are legitimate from a manuscript point of view but that also produce different selves and authors. Would it be possible to think of Dante's *Rime* as a fluid and simultaneous combination of all their different editions? Given that collecting Dante's *Rime* in an edition necessarily curtails their errant nature, the concept of *mouvance* could help to preserve, at least ideally, the fluidity of poems that for the most part were composed not in connection with other poems but rather in a state of disconnected singularity. And might such a flexible edition, in which the individual reader has to take control and responsibility, not be achieved quite well online rather than in print?

Notes

1. Gragnolati, "Authorship and Performance"; Gragnolati, "Trasformazioni e assenze"; and Dante Alighieri, *Rime giovanili*; more recently, Gragnolati, "Without Hierarchy," and Gragnolati, "Performance senza gerarchia."

2. "Meglio che di *Canzoniere*, . . . è prudente discorrere di *Rime* di Dante: poiché alla cinquecentesca accezione di 'canzoniere' involontariamente si associa, dopo l'esperienza petrarchesca, l'idea di un'opera unitaria, dell'avventura organica di un'anima, e si tende così a riportare al duecento l'esigenza d'una cosciente costruzione psicologica almeno tanto quanto stilistica, chiusa nell'armatura d'una storia perspicua, e nella quale lo stile è, appunto, anzitutto quello sforzo perenne d'eliminazione e semplificazione" [Better than *Canzoniere*, . . . it is more prudent to speak of the *Rime* of Dante: for the reason that the sixteenth-century understanding of "canzoniere," after Petrarch, is inevitably associated with the idea of a unified work, of the organic adventure of a soul; and tends to in this way project back to the thirteenth century the need for a self-conscious construction, as much psychological as stylistic, enclosed within the framework of a coherent story, whose style is, precisely, before anything else, defined by an unending process of elimination and simplification] (Contini, "Introduzione" [to *Rime*], liii). Contini's introduction was written in 1938 and published in 1939, and although Contini introduced some changes to his edition in 1946 and 1956, it remained largely unchanged; on this and the impact of Contini's introduction, see Barański, "Dante 'poeta' e 'lector.'"

3. As we shall see, from these correct premises, Contini draws the less correct conclusion that only those poems that he terms *estravaganti*, that is, that have never been collected by Dante in either the *Vita nova* or the *Convivio*, should belong to an edition of Dante's *Rime* ("Introduzione" [to *Rime*], liii); on this point, see Barolini, "Editing Dante's *Rime*."

4. Steinberg, *Accounting for Dante*, 17–60.

5. On the manuscript tradition of the *Rime*, see De Robertis's critical edition of 2002 and, for a more succinct account, Contini, "Nota al testo."

6. See the discussion in Varela-Portas de Orduña, "*Libro de la canciones*," 24–27, and Barolini, "Dante and the Lyric Past," esp. 37–45.

7. The concept of *dolce stil novo*, which was coined by Dante in *Purg.* 24.57 and imposed itself in Italian literary history after Francesco De Sanctis's 1870–71 *Storia della letteratura italiana*, is controversial, and it has been intensely debated to what extent it corresponds to a legitimate historiographical category. See the clear discussion in Pirovano, *Dolce stil novo*, 15–38.

8. Boyde, *Dante's Style*, 317.

9. Tonelli, *Fisiologia della passione*, 3–70 (on Cavalcanti's connections with contemporary medical treatises on love sickness) and 71–124 (on the persistence in Dante's *Rime* of a physiological understanding of love as an irrational passion in harming the body).

10. Chiamenti, "Aï faus ris," 9–22.

11. Barolini, *Dante's Poets*, 40–57.

12. Barolini, "Aristotle's *Mezzo*."

13. On Dante's "lay" and political attitude toward knowledge that increases after the exile, see Imbach, *Dante*.

14. Giunta, "Amore come destino."

15. Forese was a member of the powerful Donati family and the brother of Corso Donati, the leader of the Black Guelfs and one of those responsible for Dante's exile in 1302. Those familiar with the *Divine Comedy* will remember the encounter between Dante and Forese in the terrace of gluttony in *Purgatorio*—as well as the pilgrim's encounter with Forese's sister Piccarda Donati in the Heaven of the Moon in canto 3 of *Paradiso*.

16. For a recent, comprehensive study of the Tenzone and its literary afterlife in Dante himself and Boccaccio, see Alfie, *Dante's "Tenzone."*

17. Giunta, "Nuovo commento." On the *Rime petrose*, see the now-classic Durling and Martinez, *Time and the Crystal*.

18. Carrai, "Doppio congedo."

19. Pietro di Dante, "*Commentarium*," 132–33.

20. Barolini, "Guittone's *Ora parrà*." On Dante's canzone, see also Bausi, "Doglia mi reca"; on the canon of the *De vulgari eloquentia*, see Ascoli, *Dante*, 157–69.

21. See Ferrara, "'Io mio credea.'"

22. For these and other connections among Dante's poems, see Camboni, "Philologie et langue," esp. 5–6.

23. Barolini, "Dante and the Lyric Past," 39.

24. Ibid., 40.

25. As Contini put it, it is impossible to explain the inconsistency of this late canzone, which, also on the stylistic level, finds itself "su una linea involutiva, quasi d'errore" [along a backward, almost erroneous trajectory] ("Introduzione" [to *Rime*], lxx). It has also been proposed that the canzone was actually composed during Dante's youth and that its *congedo* (the shorter, final stanza that is placed in conclusion of a canzone that in this case contains a reference to Dante's exile) was added later. See Allegretti ed., Dante, *Canzone montanina*, and Fenzi, "Ancora sulla *Epistola*." On the presence of Cavalcanti in "Amor, da che convien pur ch'io mi doglia," see Barolini, "Dante and the Lyric Past," 41.

26. See, for instance, Giunta, *Versi a un destinatario*.

27. Contini, "Introduzione" [to *Rime*], lix. See also Gragnolati, "Performance senza gerarchia." On the communal character of medieval subjectivity and its difference from a post-Romantic sense of individuality, see Bynum, "Did the Twelfth Century."

28. Gaunt, "Discourse Desired." The concept of *mouvance*, introduced by Paul Zumthor in his *Essai de poétique médiévale* and subsequently developed in several other publications, was fiercely debated; see Rosenstein, "Mouvance."

29. Auerbach, *Dante*. See also Ascoli, *Dante*, and Gragnolati, *Amor che move*.

30. On Dante's self-exegesis, see Barański, "Dante Alighieri."

31. Gragnolati, "Authorship and Performance" and "Trasformazioni e assenze."

32. Austin, *How to Do Things*. Later Austin would distinguish between locutionary, illocutionary, and perlocutionary acts. For a discussion of Austin's theory and its significance for literary and cultural criticism, see Culler, "Philosophy and Literature." For a discussion of Austin's role in contemporary performance theory, see Wirth, "Performazbegriff im Spannungsfeld," and Fischer-Lichte, *Ästhetik des Performativen*, 31–57.

33. Barolini, "Editing Dante's *Rime*." The indication of the text of the *Vita nova* is first given according to its traditional subdivision into forty-two chapters and then followed by its indication according to the subdivision into thirty-one paragraphs proposed by Gugliemo Gorni in Gorni ed., *Vita nova*.

34. "Ha . . . ragione Barbi nel ritenere essenzialmente diversa una lirica letta nel contesto della *Vita Nuova* o del *Convivio* dalla stessa lirica letta invece singolarmente. Una rima accompagnata o meno dal commento dell'autore non viene insomma recepita allo stesso modo dal lettore" (Picone, "Dante rimatore," 174) [Barbi is right in believing that a lyric that is read in the context of the *Vita Nuova* or the *Convivio* is essentially different from the same lyric when it is read

individually. In short, a *rima* is interpreted differently by the reader whether it is accompanied or not by the author's commentary].

35. "Ha perduto il suo carattere di prova estemporanea, per entrare a far parte di una totalità letteraria e di un ingranaggio compositivo dai quali soltanto riceve il suo significato" (ibid.) [It has lost its character of an extemporaneous exercise, becoming instead part of a literary whole and a compositional mechanism from which it entirely receives its meaning].

36. Barolini, "Editing Dante's *Rime*," 267–69.

37. The text of Dante's lyrics is quoted from Dante, *Rime giovanili*.

38. Dante da Maiano, *Rime*, 151.

39. Foster and Boyde ed., *Dante's Lyric Poetry*, 2:23. See also Barbi and Maggini ed., *Rime della "Vita Nuova*," 8–9.

40. Dante's attitude toward Guido Cavalcanti in the *Vita nova* is ambivalent, and if, on the one hand, Dante's *libello* acknowledges his significance and celebrates the companionship between him and its younger protagonist, on the other, it stages a progressive distinction between the two poets, which corresponds to Dante's explicit rejection of Cavalcanti's love theory, presented as too negative and irrational. The bibliography on the matter is very extensive and can be found in Gragnolati, "Authorship and Performance," but see also Rea, "*Vita Nuova*," which maintains that at the moment of Dante's composition of the *Vita nova*, Cavalcanti would have ceased writing poetry and committed only to the study of philosophy. The relationship between the two poets staged in the *libello* would therefore express not rivalry but succession.

41. See Barolini's introductions to the poems in her edition of Dante's *Rime giovanili*.

42. For further discussion of Cavalcanti's relationship to Dante, see Barański, chapter 3 of this book, the section "In Lieu of a Conclusion."

43. Ascoli, *Dante*, 178–201. See also the recent discussion in Steinberg, "Author."

44. See Gragnolati, "Without Hierarchy" and "Performance senza gerarchia."

45. The following overview of editions relies on Barolini's "Editing Dante's *Rime*," and "Dante's Lyric Poetry," esp. 13–17 (except for Giunta's edition, which came out after these articles were written); in both publications by Barolini one can also find a discussion of the editorial history of Dante's *Rime* until the sixteenth century, which focuses in particular on the role played by Dante himself, Boccaccio, and the Giuntina; see also Varela-Portas de Orduña, "*Libro de la canciones*," 21–31.

46. I refer to Barbi and Maggini ed., *Rime della "Vita nuova*," Barbi and Pernicone, *Rime della maturità*, and the 1995 reprint of Contini ed., *Rime*.

47. Contini ed., *Rime*, LIII.

48. Barolini, "Editing Dante's *Rime*," 268.

49. Foster, "Introduction," 1:xxxix.

50. They include "either 'letter-poems' addressed to Dante, to which his own reply is extant, or replies to similar 'letters' by him'" plus Cecco Angiolieri's sonnet on the last sonnet of the *Vita nova*, "which seemed too interesting to be omitted" (ibid., xxxvii).

51. On them, see De Robertis, "Sulla tradizione estravagante."

52. Barolini, "Editing Dante's *Rime*," 271.

53. Camboni, "Philologie et langue," esp. 8–9, and Grimaldi, "Nota ai testi," 319.

54. Barolini, "Dante's Lyric Poetry," 3–4.

55. Ibid., 27.

56. On Giunta's controversial take on medieval intertextuality, see the balanced remarks by Zinelli, "Dante TQ," 27.

57. Giunta, "Che differenza c'è," 17.

58. Giunta, "Nota al testo," 61.

59. Ibid.

60. Ibid., 69.

61. Ibid., 68.

62. For the minor differences with respect to Barbi's edition, see Grimaldi, "Nota ai testi," 320–21.

63. See, for instance, Eisner, *Boccaccio and the Invention*, 68–73, and Grimaldi, "Boccaccio editore." See also the recent discussion by Berisso, "Dante di De Robertis."

64. Tanturli, "Edizione critica"; Leonardi, "Nota sull'edizione critica"; Tonelli, "Rileggendo le *Rime*."

65. Tonelli, "*Rime*," 207. See Varela-Portas de Orduña, "*Libro de las canciones*," 28–29.

66. Dante, *Libro de las canciones*.

67. All the issues of *Tenzone* can be consulted online at http://pendiente demigracion.ucm.es/info/italiano/acd/tenzone.

68. See Pinto, *"Rime" di Dante*.

69. Barolini, "Critical Philology."

CHAPTER 2

Fiore and *Detto d'Amore*

CHRISTOPHER KLEINHENZ

For more than a century the *Fiore* and *Detto d'Amore* have posed many and diverse interpretive problems, and the Italian phrase *male gatte da pelare* (nasty cats to skin) seems an apt way to characterize them, as does the related English expression, "There's more than one way to skin a cat." Indeed, for many years and without clear consensus scholars have proposed tentative answers for the primary question raised by these two works: Who is the author? As will be evident in the following pages, the debate over authorship, while continuing apace, has in recent years been sharing the critical spotlight with a variety of other issues, and the appearance of several new editions has served to generate new interest in these poems. This essay divides into the following five sections: (1) the history of the unique manuscript; (2) the two poems in light of their source text, the *Roman de la Rose* (*Romance of the Rose*); (3) the editorial history of these works; (4) the question of authorship; and (5) interpretive trends.

The Manuscript

The story of these two poems properly begins with manuscript H438, in what was once the Library of the Faculty of Medicine in the French university city of Montpellier.[1] The date of the codex, written in a Tuscan hand and containing the two untitled works, ranges from the late thirteenth to the mid-fourteenth century.[2] Codicological evidence indicates that the *Fiore* preceded the *Detto* in the manuscript, but this does not imply that it was composed first or even by the same author. At some point, probably in France in the mid-fifteenth century, this codex and another containing a version of the *Romance of the Rose* were bound together, with the Old French text placed first.

For some five centuries following its initial composition, the codex was relatively unknown, passing through several private owners and libraries before it was eventually acquired by the library in Montpellier in 1804. And there its modern history would begin, thanks to the actions of Count Guglielmo Libri, the appropriately named bibliophile and mathematician turned book thief. As it happens, Libri was part of a commission "to investigate the manuscript collections of the provincial libraries and create catalogs of their holdings,"[3] and in his listings for the Montpellier library he refers to the manuscript as being divided into two parts—"Le Roman de la Rose" and "Sonetti italiani"[4]—but he fails to mention the *Detto*, although the poem was clearly indicated on the fly leaf of the codex when it was in the library of Jean Bouhier in Dijon: *Romant / de la Rose / par M. Iean Mehun / Sonnets, et / Chansons en Italien / Du dict Romant*, where the indication "Chansons en Italien" clearly refers to the *Detto*, which was part of the manuscript until Libri removed it and wrote his catalog description.[5] Having removed the final four folios containing the *Detto*, Libri combined them with three other manuscripts to form a new codex that would eventually come to the Laurentian Library in Florence in 1884 as part of the collection of Lord Ashburnham.[6]

In the small format of the original manuscript (20 x 14 cm) the text of the *Fiore* is arranged in two columns, four sonnets per page,[7] and the *Detto* is written in double columns of thirty lines per folio. This format follows the general *mise-en-page* of most *Rose* manuscripts.[8]

The *Romance of the Rose*, the *Fiore*, and the *Detto d'Amore*

The *Romance of the Rose*

The *Rose* is an allegorical work, a dream vision, written in the thirteenth century by two Old French poets, Guillaume de Lorris and Jean de

Meun.⁹ It enjoyed great popularity, as the more than three hundred extant manuscripts attest.¹⁰ However, as Sylvia Huot has noted, there is not a single *Rose* but many medieval *Roses*.¹¹ The *Rose* is not an easy text to read or understand, for the poem is not a unified whole; indeed, its two sections are radically different in tone and purpose. The author of the first part, Guillaume de Lorris, wrote his four thousand–plus verses in the second quarter of the thirteenth century (1237) and left the work incomplete. Some forty years later (ca. 1280), Jean de Meun completed Guillaume's unfinished allegorical dream vision, employing a much different style and tone. In the second part of the *Rose*, consisting of an additional seventeen thousand–plus verses, Jean counters Guillaume's courtly idealism with his own extensive philosophical digressions and social commentary. Guillaume sets his poem in springtime and frames it within the context of "courtly" love, drawing his material from Ovid (*Ars amatoria*), from the earlier lyric traditions of the troubadours and *trouvères*, and from the treatise by Andreas Capellanus (*De amore*). On a May morning Guillaume's narrator/protagonist enters the walled Garden of Pleasure (*Deduit*), planted by Courtesy (*Courtoisie*), and sees a beautiful rosebud. Wounded by the God of Love's arrows, he falls in love with the Rose and swears his fealty to Love, who then locks his heart with a key. The Lover's difficult quest to win the Rose is portrayed through the interaction of allegorical figures, who represent different aspects of the complex psychological and social drama. Some of these present obstacles to love, for example, *Dangier* (Resistance), *Jalousie* (Jealousy), and *Male Bouche* (Slander), while other characters assist the Lover in his quest, such as *Bel Accueil* (Fair Welcoming), *Ami* (Friend), *Pitié* (Pity), and *Esperance* (Hope). To help the lover overcome these obstacles, the God of Love reappears and provides him with a set of rules, Love's Commandments, as well as the code of courtship behavior outlined in Ovid's *Ars amatoria*. Love encourages the lover to cultivate the virtues of a courtly knight as a means to conquer the *Rose*, and this the lover does. With the intercession of Pity and Openness (*Franchise*), the obstacle to the rose posed by Resistance is overcome, and with Venus's persuasion of Bel Accueil the Lover kisses the rose. As a consequence of this rash act, the guardians of the Rose—Jealousy, Fear, and so on—enclose the Rose and Fair Welcoming behind even stronger fortifications, and the Lover laments his situation. At this point Guillaume's poem breaks off.

While the first part of the *Romance* invokes the fusion of Love and Courtesy (*Amour* and *Courtoisie*), the courtly behavior presented in many medieval French romances, Jean de Meun, in his continuation of the work, adopts a moralizing tone and encyclopedic scope. He, too, employs personified characters, such as Reason, Nature, and Genius, to make extensive commentaries on a variety of topics—free will versus determinism, optics, Fortune, planetary influence on human behavior, the mendicant orders, and so on—topics only incidental to the main action of the poem.[12] In contrast to Guillaume's lyrical and psychological overtones, Jean's style is polemical. He often satirizes women, parodies religious orders, and raises questions about the relationship between the sexes and about social and class differences. Jean concludes the poem with a vivid account of the plucking of the rose, achieved through deception and violence, which is very unlike Guillaume's idealized conception of the love quest.

The *Fiore*

On the face of it, the *Fiore*—so named by its first editor (Ferdinand Castets)—is a rather faithful and lively redaction and reduction of the *Rose* in 232 sonnets, whose protagonist and probable author is named Durante.[13] Adding to the large and growing corpus of "translated," "Italianized" works from the Latin and French traditions, the *Fiore* offers insights on literary transmission and tastes in medieval Florence.[14] However, the *Fiore* is not what one usually considers to be a "translation," for in length it is only about one-seventh the size of the *Rose*: 3,248 verses in the Italian sonnets,[15] compared to the 21,750 verses of the Old French text. In its reconstructed and recomposed form and despite its numerous Gallicisms, the *Fiore* is very different from the rather pedestrian, sentence-by-sentence *volgarizzamenti*, generally in prose, that characterize Latin and Old French works in the same period.[16] Huot has termed the *Fiore* "a creative reworking of the *Rose*,"[17] and other scholars have commented on its reduced and more focused state: for example, John Took notes that the major theme is "the submission of reason to sensitive appetite," while Peter Armour calls it "una guida, scritta nello stile 'comico', all'*ars amandi*" [a guide to the "art of loving" in the comic style] and Fabian Alfie "a type of parodic *ars amandi*."[18] Zygmunt Barański has correctly noted the metaliterary dimension of Falsembiante's words in sonnet 103—"Così vo io mutando e suono e verso / e dicendo parole umili e piane" [And thus I go changing both tone and verse / and saying humble and simple words]—which "describe and synthesize perfectly the means the author of the *Fiore* uses to translate his source text": he "transforms the sounds of the *Rose* not only by rendering them in Italian but also by reordering a large part of the poem"; he also alters the metrical structure and describes the style as uniformly "comic" ("parole umili e piane") and thus capable of a syncretism that anticipates in certain ways Dante's *Commedia*.[19] As previously noted, the *Fiore*'s *mise-en-page*—four sonnets per page arranged in two columns—is similar to that of many double-columned *Rose* manuscripts; moreover, almost every sonnet has a rubric, which follows the practice in most *Rose* codices of "using narrative and thematic rubrics both to create subsections" and to identify speakers.[20] We do not know which *Rose* manuscript or manuscripts may have served as the model for the *Fiore*;[21] of the some three hundred manuscripts, only a few may date from the end of the thirteenth century, and the handful in Italy are "not among the earliest."[22]

The *Fiore* has a number of similarities with and differences from the *Rose*.[23] The Italian poem begins *in medias res* when Lover (*Amante*), gazing in rapture at a flower in the Garden of Pleasure, is wounded by the God of Love:[24]

Lo Dio d'Amor con su' arco mi trasse
Perch'i' guardava un fior che m'abellia,
Lo quale avea piantato Cortesia
Nel giardin di Piacer; e que' vi trasse
Sì tosto c[h]'a me parve ch'e' volasse,
E disse: "I' sì ti tengo in mia balìa."
Alló·gli pia[c]que, non per voglia mia,
Che di cinque saette mi piagasse.
La prima à non' Bieltà: per li oc[c]hi il core
Mi passò; la seconda, Angelicanza:
Quella mi mise sopra gran fredore;
La terza Cortesia fu, san' dottanza;
La quarta, Compagnia, che fe' dolore;
La quinta apella l'uon Buona Speranza.[25]

[With his bow the God of Love pierced me / while I was gazing at a Flower that pleased me, / the Flower that Lady Courtesy had planted / in the garden of Pleasure. Love came / so quickly that it seemed to me he flew, / and said: "I have you in my power." / Then as was his pleasure, and no desire of mine, / he wounded me with five arrows. / The first, named Beauty, passed my eyes / and transfixed my heart; the second, Angel-Like, / gave me a bitter chill; / the third without doubt was Courtesy; / the fourth, Social Grace, caused pain; / the fifth is called Good Hope.]

Two important differences are clear from the beginning: (1) this is not a dream vision, and (2) instead of a rose we have simply a lovely, generic flower.[26] The *Fiore* presents a series of events and conversations told in a linear, narrative style.[27] While the entire action of the *Rose* takes place in one day, the plot of the *Fiore* unfolds over the course of some two years. As we learn in the third sonnet, the action of the poem begins in the month of January, and not in May, as did the *Rose*, and perhaps the harsh setting is intended to suggest the difficulties the Lover will have in achieving his amorous goal. In his insightful reading of the first thirty sonnets of the *Fiore*, Barański rightly focuses on the manner in which the first sonnet begins, reflecting the prescriptions of the medieval poetry manuals[28]— which anticipate the five journalistic W's: Who? What? When? Where? Why? We are introduced to the principal players, the place, the dominant theme, and so on. Barański also notes the importance of the spoken words in the text and how they enhance the dramatic quality of the whole.[29]

After Lover pledges fealty to the God of Love, we see, in the fifth sonnet, another major innovation of the *Fiore*, the idolatry of love effected through ironic use of biblical phraseology:[30]

L'Amante e Amore
Con grande umilitate e pacïenza
Promisi a Amor a sofferir sua pena,
E c[h]'ogne membro, ch'i' avea, e vena
Disposat' era a farli sua voglienza;
E solo a lui servir la mia credenza
È ferma, né di ciò mai nonn-alena:
"Insin ched i' avrò spirito o lena,

I' non farò da·cciò giamà' partenza."
E quelli allor mi disse: "Amico meo,
I' ò da·tte miglior pegno che carte:
Fa che m'adori, ched i' son tu' deo;
Ed ogn' altra credenza metti a parte,
Né non creder né Luca né Matteo
Né Marco né Giovanni." Allor si parte.

[*Lover and Love* // With much humility and patience / I promised Love that I would suffer his pain / and that my every limb and vein / were prepared to do his will. / And my mind is set to serve him and him alone / and will never cease to do so. / "As long as I live and breathe, / I will never depart from this promise." / And Love then said to me: "My friend, / your pledge is better than any written promise: / be sure to worship me, for I am your god; / and set aside every other belief: / do not believe Luke or Matthew, / Mark or John." And then he departs.]

The next twenty-seven sonnets feature the allegorical figures of Resistance (*Schifo*), Reason (*Ragione*), Mercy (*Pietà*), Sincerity (*Franchezza*), and so on, and their actions are virtually identical to those presented in Guillaume de Lorris's portion of the *Rose*, but with the significant change in gender of the figure known in the *Rose* as the masculine *Bel Acueil* (Fair Welcoming), who becomes the feminine *Bellacoglienza* in the *Fiore*. In part due to the gender of the noun passing from French to Italian, this change does "make Bellacoglienza more directly the representative of the lady whose love Amante seeks. . . . The feminine gender of Bellacoglienza allows her to merge more directly with the figure of the beloved and certainly creates a stronger feminine presence in the poem."[31]

The transition from the first to the second part of the *Rose* occurs in sonnets 33–34 of the *Fiore*.[32] Here a new metaphor is introduced, "the voyage by boat for the protagonist's erotic quest,"[33] in which the author makes it clear that in his rewriting of the *Rose* he is independent, able to pick and choose from his source text, following and changing it as he wants. This assertion is part of an overall strategy to make the *Fiore* a vibrant and "original" Italian poem, one that consciously downplays or ignores its French model and indeed French cultural hegemony in general.³⁴ These two sonnets also focus on the psychological description: the extreme anxiety of Lover, who finds himself in difficult straits because of love. The presence of several precise phrases—"una piaggia," "terra . . . salvaggia," "salvaggio loco," "pena de·ninferno"—which call to mind the anxious mood and desolate landscape of the early cantos of *Inferno*, has indicated, for some critics, the hand of Dante in the composition of the *Fiore*.³⁵

Of the remaining 198 sonnets in the *Fiore*, 125—more than half the poem—are given over to long monologues by Friend (*Amico*), False Seeming (*Falsembiante*), and the Old Woman (*La Vecchia*),³⁶ and Jean de Meun's extensive digressions have been omitted.³⁷ After Reason tries in vain to dissuade Lover from pursuing his amorous quest, Friend, in the course of twenty-six sonnets (47–72), advises Lover on the trickery of love. The temporal element reenters the narrative when the God of Love, wishing to reward Lover for his one-year resistance to all of his obstacles, summons his Barons to plan their strategy for conquering the castle. In his monologue of forty sonnets (88–127), False Seeming, who appears dressed as a Dominican friar, embodies—indeed, embraces—ecclesiastical hypocrisy and assures his faithfulness to the God of Love. Once inside the castle, Lover strikes a deal with the Old Woman to convince Fair Welcome to yield, and then, over fifty-nine sonnets (141–99), the Old Woman gives Bellacoglienza advice on seduction, recounting her youthful errors and urging women to use deceit to betray and profit from men as well as to have several lovers simultaneously. The army of the God of Love attacks the castle, and large-scale slaughter ensues, until a truce is called (206–14). Venus intervenes by setting fire to the castle and routing the enemy (215–25). Lady Courtesy persuades Fair Welcome to receive Lover (226–27), who then, in a mock religious ceremony celebrating the successful conclusion of his pilgrimage, deflowers the Flower, all this being described in highly eroticized metaphorical language (228–30). In the final two sonnets Lover thanks his benefactors and rejoices at the successful accomplishment of his mission in the face of many obstacles.

By eliminating Jean's digressions, the author of the *Fiore* concentrates on the art of love as presented in the first part of the *Rose* and redirects his poem's narrative to this end.³⁸ We might say that, in doing this, he follows Guillaume de Lorris, who states that his poem is called "the *Romance of the Rose*, in which the whole art of love is contained" [ce est li *Romanz de la Rose*, / ou l'art d'Amors est tote enclose], (37–38), as well as accomplishing Jean de Meun's principal objective as well, that of making the *Romance of the Rose* a "Mirror" or encyclopedia for lovers ("*Le Mirouer aus Amoureus,*" 10,651).[39]

The *Fiore* does not distinguish between the two parts of the *Rose*. Indeed, the author removes the story from its original courtly and didactic frames[40]—Guillaume's lyrical style and Jean's encyclopedic and digressive formulations—and casts it in the style of the so-called Italian comic poets (the *poeti giocosi*). The "mixed idealism and realism of the *Rose* are reduced to 'pure realism' in the *Fiore*,"[41] and this can be seen in the obscene metaphors found in some poems.[42] As it has been argued, the choice of the sonnet form would indicate the author's intent both to dissociate his work from the French text and to place it within a distinctively Italian poetic tradition, as well as to enhance the "sense of order and harmony."[43] While often used for courtly texts in the high style, the sonnet was the preferred form of more popular poets, such as Cecco Angiolieri, Rustico Filippi, and others.[44] The use in the *Fiore* of sonnets as narrative units is unusual,[45] but it is not completely unprecedented, for there are *corone* or sonnet cycles by Guittone d'Arezzo and the so-called Amico di Dante.[46] Therefore, the use of the sonnet form as the meter of the *Fiore* may be viewed as a conscious literary choice that enabled its author to represent the pivotal points of the *Rose* in discrete units that can be linked poetically, as necessary, to foster continuities and syntheses.[47]

The *Detto d'Amore*

Despite their common origin in the *Rose*, the *Fiore* and the *Detto d'Amore* are two very different works, both structurally and thematically.[48] While not possessing the narrative structure of the *Fiore* or sharing with it many source passages from the *Rose*, the *Detto* can be called a *summa* of courtly love—the love that ennobles the lover as he searches for perfect and loyal service to the God of Love:[49]

> E questo fin asemr' è
> A ciascun amoroso,
> Sì c[h]'Amor amoroso
> No·gli sia nella fine.
>   (10–14)

> [And this will be a perfect example / for every lover, / so that Love will not be bitter to him in the end.]

With this statement of intent the *Detto* aligns itself with Guillaume de Lorris's portion of the *Rose*—"in which the whole art of love is contained" [ou l'art d'Amors est tote enclose], (38).[50]

The *Detto* is incomplete, lacking at least one folio (and thus, at a minimum, some 120 verses) and an indeterminate number of lines at the end.[51] Its 480 extant verses are in rhymed heptasyllabic couplets with many equivocal and composite rhymes. The *Detto* is divided into two parts: the first, consisting of 270 verses, presents the psychology of love; the second, verses 271–480, delineates the social ethics upon which courtly society and love affairs are based with recourse to some personifications such as *Ricchezza* (Riches), *Gelosia* (Jealousy), *Folle-Larghezza* (Foolish Generosity), *Povertà* (Poverty), and so on. The *Detto* reflects the poet's familiarity not only with the first part of the *Rose* but also with the preceding Italian lyric tradition from the Sicilian School to Guittone d'Arezzo and his followers,[52] as well as to the early poetry of Guido Guinizzelli and the *poemetti* of Brunetto Latini (*Il Tesoretto* and *Il Favolello*). In the prologue to the first part, the author declares the objectives of the poem and gives it, as it were, its "title"—the *Detto d'Amore*:

> Amor sì vuole, e par-li,
> Ch'i'n ogni guisa parli
> E ched i' faccia un detto,
> Che sia per tutto detto,
> Ch'i' l'ag[g]ia ben servito.
> (1–5)

> [Love so decrees, and deems it proper, / that I should speak in this particular way / and compose a *detto*, / so that it may be proclaimed everywhere / how well I served him.]

In verses 6–74, the poet declares his allegiance to the God of Love, but Reason urges him to seek higher goals:

> Perdio, or te ne getta
> Di quel falso diletto,

> E fa che si'a diletto
> Del mi', ched egli è fine,
> Che dà gioia sanza fine.
> (106–10)

[For God's sake, get away / from that false pleasure, / and let my pleasure be yours / for it is perfect / and gives unending joy.]

Responding to Reason, the poet declares his happiness with the way things are:[53]

> Tu mi vuo' trar d'amare
> E di' c[h]' Amor amar' è:
> I' 'l truovà' dolce e fine
> E su' comincio e fine
> Mi pia[c]que e piacerà,
> Ché 'n sé gran piacer' à.
> (141–46)

[You want to keep me from loving / and you say that Love is bitter, / but I have found him sweet and perfect, / and I liked and will like / his beginning and end, / because in him there is great pleasure.]

Bidding farewell to Reason, the poet then announces the next part of his poem:

> "Adio, ched i' mi torno,
> E fine amante torno
> Per devisar partita
> Com' ell' è ben partita
> E di cors e di membra,
> Sì come a me mi membra."
> (161–66)

["Goodbye, for I am leaving, / and I will return to being a perfect lover / in order to compose another part / to describe how well-proportioned she is, / both in her body and in her members, / just as I remember them."]

In verses 167–270, he praises the beauty and fine qualities of his lady, and the physical description begins with the lady's head, as is customary in love poetry of the time:[54]

> Cape' d'oro battuto
> Paion, che m'àn battuto,
> Quelli che porta in capo,
> Per ch'i' a·llor fo capo.
> (167–71)

[Her fine head of hair / seems fashioned of gold, / golden strands that conquered me, / and with these I'll begin.]

The lady is transformed into an object of the poet's own invention to be contemplated:

> Il su' nobile stato
> Sì mette in buono stato
> Chiunque la rimira.
> Per che 'l me' cor si mira
> In lei e notte e giorno,
> E sempre a·llei ag[g]iorno,
> Ch'Amor sì·ll'à inchesto,
> Néd e' non à inchesto
> Se potesse aver termine,
> C[h]'amar vorria san' termine.
> (223–32)

[Her noble condition / puts everyone who gazes at her / in a blissful state. / For this reason my heart gazes / on her day and night, / and with thoughts of her I always greet the dawn, / because Love has willed it so, / nor has my heart asked / if this could come to an end, / for it would want to love endlessly.]

In opening a space between desire and its fulfillment, the poet implicitly rejects base eroticism by idealizing the feminine in terms of medieval *fin'amors* and using this *topos* to elevate corporeal reality into a disembodied ideal—an ideal that adheres to the feudal precepts of courtly society.[55]

The second part of the *Detto* describes the perfect lover who must behave according to the rules of courtly society. Following a lacuna beginning after verse 360, the remainder of the text (361–480) contains the advice Love gives to the lover regarding proper modes of behavior, personal hygiene, and social interaction, and the following two passages follow closely similar commandments in the *Rose*:[56]

> Cortese e franco e pro'
> Convien che sie, e pro'
> Salute e doni e rendi:
> Se·ttu a·cciò ti rendi,
> D'Amor sarai in grazia,
> E sì ti farà grazia.
> E se se' forte e visto,
> A caval sie avisto
> Di punger gentemente
> Sì che la gente mente
> Ti pongan per diletto.
>   (403–13)

[You must be courteous / and loyal and valiant, / and you must give and return his greeting graciously. / If you do all of these things, / you'll be in Love's favor, / and he will compensate you well. / And if you're strong and skillful / be advised when on horseback / to use your spurs elegantly, / so that the people / may look at you with delight.]

> Della persona conto
> Ti tieni; e nul mal conto
> Di tua boc[c]a non l'oda,
> Ma ciascun pregia e loda.
> Servi donne ed onora,
> Ché via troppo d'onor' à
> Chi vi mette sua 'ntenta,
> S'alcuno il diavol tenta

Di lor parlare a taccia,
Sì li dì che·ssi taccia.
        (439–48)

[Keep your appearance elegant, / and let no evil things / be heard from your mouth, / but esteem and give praise to everyone. / Serve and honor women, / for whoever sets his mind to do it / will receive much honor. / And if the devil tempts someone / to speak badly about women, / tell him to be quiet.]

The poem ends abruptly at verse 480.

In addition to recalling the courtly mythology of Guillaume's section of the *Rose*, the *Detto* appears, as Luigi Vanossi has noted, to signal the "transition between traditional Italian courtly love poetry and the new poetics of the *Dolce Stil Novo*."[57] In the *Detto* the tension that dwells in the space between desire and the fulfillment of that very desire provides the inspiration for the poet to explore the phenomenology of love and the nature of the lover's adherence to the precepts of courtly love. The metaphor of the perfect lover describes a love that transcends the real and transports the poet into an ecstasy focused on the ideal.

Dating the *Fiore* and the *Detto* and Their Editorial History

Dating

Determining the date of the composition of the *Fiore* is not without problems.[58] Internal references to historical events would place the writing within the period 1284–95:[59] the murder of the philosopher Siger of Brabant around 1282–84 in Orvieto (sonnet 92); the renewed persecution of the Paterines in Tuscany between 1283 and 1287 (sonnet 126); and the revolt of the bourgeoisie against the nobility between 1282 and 1293 (sonnet 118). These events, together with the date of completion of the *Rose*, would establish the *terminus a quo* in the early 1280s. We have no comparable ways of dating the *Detto*, given the absence of historical references.

Editions and Translations

The critical history of the *Fiore* began in 1878 with Ernesto Monaci's announcement of Alessandro D'Ancona's discovery of the manuscript in Libri's catalog.[60] Monaci and D'Ancona abandoned their proposed edition of the work when Castets announced his intention to edit the entire poem, which was published in 1881.[61] Less than a decade later, in 1888, Giuseppe Mazzatinti's edition appeared, accompanied by Egidio Gorra's extensive introduction.[62] A few decades later, in 1922, Ernesto Giacomo Parodi produced the first truly critical edition in 1922 for the Società Dantesca Italiana, and this served as the base text for many subsequent editions for more than half a century.[63] One year later, Guido Mazzoni's facsimile edition of the Montpellier manuscript appeared. In 1984 Gianfranco Contini published his magisterial edition, which rapidly became the standard text for both the *Fiore* and the *Detto*.[64] Subsequent editions of the *Fiore*, of which there have been six, reflect various critical attitudes: Luca Carlo Rossi (1996) adopts Contini's text with some minor modifications; Took (2004) presents both a diplomatic text of the *Fiore* alongside Contini's edition with an English translation; Menotti Stanghellini (2009) follows Contini's text with some emendations, but believes that Cecco Angiolieri is the author; Paola Allegretti (2011) follows the general model of Parodi's text with a number of variations from Contini's edition; and Luciano Formisano (2012) follows Contini but with emendations intended to be more faithful to the manuscript. Santa Casciani and Kleinhenz's translation of both poems (2000) follows Contini's edition with reference to Rossi's text.

The first complete edition of the *Detto* was published in 1888, by Salomone Morpurgo, who discovered the text.[65] He determined (1) that the same scribe copied both the *Detto* and the *Fiore* and (2) that similarities in language and style between the two poems, as well as their common source in the *Rose*, would suggest that a single author wrote both works.[66] In 1922 Parodi was the first editor to join the *Fiore* and the *Detto* in the same volume.[67] L. C. Rossi follows Contini's 1984 text, as does Formisano,[68] while Allegretti uses Parodi's edition as her base text.

The Question of Authorship

The *Fiore*

Over the years the most controversial issue for both works has been the attempts to identify the author.[69] We can imagine the excitement experienced by late nineteenth-century scholars when, out of the blue, the seemingly closed canon of Dante's works was potentially reopened by the discovery of these unknown poems. Two questions immediately arose: Was the protagonist/author named Durante really Dante Alighieri?[70] And were both works written by the same author? With regard to the latter question, in his 1922 edition Parodi noted that "one poem cannot be separated from the other, and . . . if the *Fiore* is attributed to Dante, or Durante, Alighieri, then it is necessary to attribute the *Detto d'Amore* to him as well."[71] However, even though both poems derive from the *Rose*, they present obvious differences in form, style, and register.[72]

Contini's research on the question of authorship would lead him to the conclusion evident in the title of his magisterial 1984 edition:[73] "*Il Fiore*" *e* "*Il Detto d'Amore*" *attribuibili a Dante Alighieri*.[74] In the last two decades no fewer than three scholars, L. C. Rossi, Took, and Allegretti, have signaled their acceptance of the Florentine poet as author by omitting Contini's carefully chosen words, *attribuibili a Dante* ("that may be attributed to Dante"), from the title page of their editions. Even though they discuss, to a greater or lesser degree, the *vexata quaestio*, their choice of title and author leaves little room for doubt as to their views on the matter. Of the recent editors only Formisano continues to classify the two poems among the "Opere di Dubbia Attribuzione" ("Works of Dubious Attribution").

The following presentation outlines some of the arguments advanced in favor of Dante's authorship;[75]—Contini characterizes these as "external" and "internal."[76] First and foremost among the "external" arguments is the so-called signature of the author in the text.[77] Given that the name Durante appears twice in the text, Dante, being the shortened, familiar form of this name, became a prime candidate even in the first edition of the poem.[78] The God of Love says to his Barons as they prepare to wage war on the castle:

> "Ch'e' pur convien ch'i' soccorra Durante,[79]
> Chéd i' gli vo' tener sua promessione,
> Ché trop[p]o l'ò trovato fin amante.
> Molto penò di tòr[r]elmi Ragione:
> Que' come sag[g]io fu sì fermo e stante
> Che no·lle valse nulla su' sermone."
> (82.9–14)

["For I [the God of Love] must help Durante, / since I want to keep my promise to him, / for I have found him to be a very refined lover. / Reason tried very hard to take him away from me; / but that one was so wise and tenacious and constant / that Reason's speech had no effect at all."]

After assurances from Fair Welcome, Lover is about to touch the flower:

> Delle sue cose i' non fu' rifusante;
> Ma spesso falla ciò che 'l folle crede:
> Così avenne al buon di ser Durante.
> (202.12–14)

[I did not refuse her things; / but often what fools believe does not come to pass: / thus it happened to the good ser Durante.][80]

This "naming" of the protagonist—and possibly also of the author—is found in places similar to that in the *Rose* (10526–30, 10658–660, and 10565–69), where the God of Love refers to and names the two authors, Guillaume and Jean. However, we may ask if it is legitimate to conflate the protagonist of the poem with the author. Be that as it may, with the possibility that Dante was the author, the critical floodgates opened, and various arguments were made either to bolster his case or to deny it by proposing other candidates.

To be sure, as Guglielmo Gorni has noted, the name Durante is fairly common in Tuscany in this period, but only twice does it refer to Dante Alighieri:[81] once in a notarial document of 1343 drawn up on behalf of Dante's son Jacopo, where we read "Durante, called Dante, Alagherii" ("Durante, ol. vocatus Dante, cd. Alagherii") and another time in the

Florentine history of Filippo Villani.[82] Some scholars have considered the name Durante to be a sort of "nome parlante," that is, the present participle of *durare*, which indicates the quality of an individual who "endures," who is "constant," "patient," "suffering," or "tenacious."[83] Another interpretation, along the lines of *interpretatio nominis*, was offered by Lino Pertile, who argued that the language of sonnet 82 would suggest that the name *Durante* is used as an epithet, not to name the author, but to synthesize in one word the sexual role of the Lover throughout the entire text,[84] for, after all, Durante rhymes with *fin amante* and *fermo e stante*, and, in sonnet 60 verse 3, Lover is advised to show himself to be "forte e duro" (i.e., strong and resolute, or "hard") when he is in his lady's arms.[85]

Among the several external arguments is the reference to the murder of the philosopher Siger of Brabant in sonnet 92.9–11—"Master Siger did not meet a happy end: / with a sword I made him die with great pain / in the court of Rome, at Orvieto" ("Mastro Sighier non andò guari lieto: / A ghiado il fe' morire a gran dolore / Nella corte di Roma, ad Orbivieto"). Siger is not present in the *Rose*,[86] but the mention in the *Fiore* would anticipate his unexpected presence in the heaven of the Sun in Dante's *Paradiso* 10.133–38. These two—the only two—references to Siger would attest to Dante's uncommon interest in him and his demise.[87]

The "internal" arguments are based largely on Contini's research on the intricate concatenation of language and ideas beginning with the *Rose*, proceeding through the *Fiore*, and culminating in the *Comedy*,[88] as well as his minute textual analyses detailed in his 1984 edition. Patrick Boyde describes the typology of Contini's analysis as the discovery of "the verbal resemblance between the language and style of the 3,248 hendecasyllables in *Fiore* and the heterogeneous corpus of Dante's acknowledged works in vernacular verse (c. 17,000 lines). These likenesses . . . [range] from rare individual words or individual words used in rare senses, to increasingly complex phrases that are prominent and similar by position or by metaphorical usage, to passages where the phonetic, rhythmical, lexical, and stylistic resemblances are so intertwined that they can be explained only on the assumption that they proceed from the same mind or from an author's memory of his own work."[89] Contini's "regina delle prove"—the "queen of proofs"—involves those passages where "the repetition of semantic elements are accompanied by repetition of phonic evidence in analogous rhythmical and syntactical circumstances."[90] More recently

Lino Leonardi has examined Contini's correspondences within the larger context of the entire Italian poetic production of the thirteenth century and found that 30 percent of the likenesses may be attributed to the general poetic language of the period, that another 30 percent are uncertain, but that 35–40 percent of the resemblances are applicable only to the *Fiore* and the Dantean poetic corpus.[91] While these results are not and cannot be considered definitive, they would certainly appear to provide strong support for Dante's authorship of the *Fiore*.[92] However, we should note here Michelangelo Picone's still-relevant reservations on Contini's method, which does not consider the importance of "context" and "deep structure."[93] In addition to some studies of a linguistic nature, scholars have used "resemblances" to argue both sides of the issue—either for Dante or for another poet—as well as computer analyses "of vocabulary, of rhymes, and of accentual structure" or word frequency, syntax, and meter for similar ends.[94]

The 1994 Cambridge Conference, which resulted in the volume *The "Fiore" in Context*, was devoted primarily to the question of authorship of the poem and its relationship to the *Rose* and to its larger literary context, without, however, resolving the question.[95] The volume of "readings"— *Lettura del "Fiore"*—is also a major contribution toward a better understanding of the poem.[96]

As noted earlier, the *Fiore* and the *Detto* could not have been written earlier than the 1280s, and a later date, say sometime after 1300, could raise questions about the currency of the historical references. If Dante is the author, then questions arise concerning when in his early years he would have been able to compose these two works. Recently Luciano Rossi has shown that Jean de Meun was at the university in Bologna from 1265 to 1269 and that he could have come into contact with Guido Guinizzelli, Guittone d'Arezzo, and Monte Andrea, relationships that could be extended to Brunetto Latini and Dante.[97]

As part of his examination of Dante and the *Rose*, Vanossi has studied the many Gallicisms in the *Fiore*—the numbers range from 350 to 500[98]— and this research has continued more recently with studies by Riccardo Viel and Pasquale Stoppelli.[99] Parodi's description of "an orgy of brazen Gallicisms" poses a problem for Dante's authorship,[100] in that their use would reflect the knowledge that only someone who had lived for a long time in France would have. If Dante did indeed travel to Paris (perhaps after his sojourn in Bologna), this objection would fall.[101]

Scholars have proposed numerous candidates as the author of the *Fiore*; however, given the limitations of space, the following list will suffice:[102] Durante di Giovanni;[103] Dante da Maiano;[104] Brunetto Latini;[105] Rustico Filippi;[106] Lippo Pasci dei Bardi[107] (or "Amico di Dante"[108]); Dante degli Abati;[109] Folgore da San Gimignano;[110] Antonio Pucci;[111] Guido Cavalcanti;[112] Francesco da Barberino;[113] Immanuel Romano;[114] Cecco Angiolieri;[115] and Guillaume Durand.[116]

Perhaps one of the most cogent arguments against Dante's authorship of the *Fiore* is his silence about it in his canonical works,[117] as well as that of his contemporaries.[118] It could also be that Dante wanted to dissociate himself from the *Fiore* because of its scabrous content.[119] However that may be, the truth of the matter is that we do not and may never know the true identity of the author, unless other documents come to light to resolve the question.

The Authorship of the *Detto*

Given the absence of external evidence relating to the question of the authorship, the *Detto d'Amore* poses fewer problems than the *Fiore*.[120] Scholars have noted that internal evidence in the form of stylistic similarities would argue for Dante as its author.[121] However, critics have often cited the equivocal language of the *Detto*—language recalling that of Guittone[122]—or the metrical resemblance to Brunetto Latini's *Tesoretto* to justify their opposition to Dante as author, while nonetheless relating these to Dante's early poetic apprenticeship.

Interpretive Trends—Past, Present, and Future

The search for the identity of the author of the *Fiore* and the *Detto* has driven and continues to drive much of the criticism,[123] but this quest has also encouraged research on a number of related textual cruxes and literary topics;[124] these include, but are not limited to, considerations of the poems' relationship to the *Roman de la Rose*, their intrinsic literary value and cultural merits, the influence of political-philosophical culture in late Duecento Italy, and their place in and contribution to the developing Italian literary tradition.[125] Other areas that have been partially mined and hold promise as sources for future research are the history of the sonnet, the relationship to the oral tradition of the *cantari* and to the comic-realistic poets, the importance of intertextual relations with classical and biblical literature and commentary, the reflection of contemporary social customs and attitudes, the intersection of (for lack of a better phrase) French and Italian attitudes and mores, and the general practice of "translation," "rewriting," and *volgarizzamenti* in this period.[126] Critics have commented on the remarkable ability of the author to present a dramatic narrative, and related to this point are Barański's comments on what he terms Durante's great discovery ("trovata"): the recognition and exploitation of the "sonnet's narrative possibilities."[127] Vanossi's volume (*Teologia poetica*) remains the only extended study of the *Detto*.[128]

Some critics have looked at the earlier literary traditions in France and Italy in the attempt to situate the author of the *Fiore* and the *Detto*, thematically and rhetorically, within this larger frame. For example, Leonardi has investigated the potential influence of Guittone d'Arezzo's sonnet cycle, and Domenico De Robertis has done the same with Cavalcanti.[129] Along these lines Lucia Lazzerini has demonstrated that further research on the literary traditions of the *langue d'oc* and *d'oïl* will prove profitable;[130] Huot has done similarly for the manuscript tradition of the *Rose* and Kevin Brownlee for the rewriting of the *Rose* in the *Fiore*, as well as the cultural meanings that attach to *translation* and the nature of cultural authority and/or dominance.[131]

Given the three recent, richly annotated editions of the *Fiore* (and, in two cases, the *Detto*), we now have a mine of materials that will enable scholars to pursue actively many different lines of inquiry.[132] In her edition of the two poems Allegretti presents several ways of assessing the intricate verbal fabric (the "tessuto verbale") and the consummate metrical structure of the *Fiore* through the examination of meaningful "distant" parallel verbal structures, the use of rhymes (including internal rhymes), and other verbal linkages within individual and contiguous sonnets.[133] These considerations may be useful for investigating the more general history of the development of the sonnet form. With reference to the *Rose* and to the rubrics in the Italian redaction, Allegretti also presents arguments for the significance of the overall narrative structure of the *Fiore*, both numerical and geometric,[134] and she adduces symmetries in language, phraseology, and themes to demonstrate the poet's attention to detail and the overarching structure.[135] In addition to the very informative introduction to his edition and the interpretive notes and contextualizing remarks that accompany each sonnet, Formisano provides a list of the Gallicisms and a table of correspondences between the *Rose* and the *Fiore*, as well as a *rimario* of the *Fiore* and *Detto*.[136] With its diplomatic edition of the unique manuscript, rich introduction, and extensive commentary, Took's edition-translation of the *Fiore* opens up a number of new critical avenues for future research. In short, these three recent editions offer a wealth of resources that present many interesting research possibilities, and Montefusco ("Novità") suggests new and promising avenues for approaching the two poems.

The exceedingly valuable critical studies that have appeared over the past several decades stand as monuments to the interest stirred by these in many ways enigmatic texts.[137] The meticulous readings of the *Fiore* contained in *Lettura del "Fiore"* are models of their genre, as are Vanossi's insightful interpretive volumes on the two poems (*Dante e il "Roman de la Rose"* and *La teologia poetica*) and Sebastio's more recent study (*Strutture narrative*), which argues for greater literary, historical, and philosophical contextualization of the poetic themes of the *Roman de la Rose* and the *Fiore*. Even those critics who propose authors "other than Dante" for the *Fiore* and *Detto* are valuable, for their considerations—literary, historical, cultural—of these lesser-known poets offer different perspectives on these works as well as bringing them and the talents of their presumptive authors to the attention of interested readers. In the end, however, barring the discovery of a new manuscript or archival document, the question of authorship appears destined to remain open.

Therefore, since these *male gatte*—*Fiore* and *Detto*—have not yet been completely *pelate* and may never be with regard to the author's identity, scholars have appropriately directed their attention to a host of other, related topics with probing and insightful analyses, thus confirming that the proverbial nine lives of these particular felines have provided and will continue to provide much impetus for continuing research in the areas of literature, prosody, linguistics, comparative cultural studies, and social, intellectual, and institutional history.

Notes

1. Now called the Bibliothèque Inter-Universitaire, Section Médicine. The most detailed account of the vicissitudes of the manuscript and its editorial tra-

dition is in *Fiore*, Formisano ed. The manuscript is found on fols. 111r–139v, which may be viewed in the *Roman de la Rose* Digital Library, http://roman delarose.org/#read;MontpellierH438.111r.tif.

2. According to the paleographer Emanuele Casamassima (whose opinion Contini requested), the hand is *bastarda fiorentina*, a cross between the more formal *littera textualis* and the more casual *corsiva cancelleresca* (Dante, *Fiore*, Contini ed. (Ed. Nazionale), lv; De Robertis Boniforti, "Nota sul codice," 57–60). In the discussion that follows her study ("Nota sul codice," 82–86), De Robertis Boniforti clarifies that, in paleographical terms, a Tuscan hand at that time would also include parts of Umbria and even Bologna. The titles of the two works do not appear in the manuscript and are modern designations. The date of the manuscript may be as late as 1320 or even after 1350. De Robertis Boniforti ("Nota sul codice," 63) argued for its composition during the first two decades of the fourteenth century but later changed her view to a date after 1350, according to Tonelli ("Ragione," 232 and 246n1). However that may be, except for holographs, the date of a manuscript is not necessarily the date of original composition.

3. See the Special Collections Processing at Penn website, https://penn rare.wordpress.com/, and specifically Abby Lang's post, "'I can do only two things in this world: love and read.'—book thief Guglielmo Libri to François Guizot, 1845," October 22, 2012, https://pennrare.wordpress.com/author/ abbyrare/.

4. Libri notes that "these sonnets are nearly all in dialogue" [ces sonnets sont presque tous en dialogue] and then provides some of their rubrics ("Lamante et amore"; "Lamante e lo Schifo"; "Lamante e la ragione"; etc.).

5. See *Fiore*, Formisano ed., xxii–xxiii.

6. First known by shelf number Ashburnham 1234, the codex is now cataloged as 1234 *bis*, after the folios containing the *Detto* were removed to form a separate codex.

7. This small format is similar to that of two early Italian lyric manuscripts (Laurentian Rediano 9 and the Biblioteca Nazionale Centrale Banco Rari 217) and is virtually identical to Riccardiano 2908 (Brunetto Latini's *Tesoretto*) in size and format, a very intriguing similarity.

8. For an account of the *mise-en-page*, see, among others, De Robertis Boniforti, "Nota sul codice" and the following editions of the *Fiore*: Contini ed. (Ed. Nazionale), xlix–lvii; Took ed., xiii–xiv; Allegretti ed., 131–37; and Formisano ed., lxxvii–lxxix. On this and related matters for the *Detto*, see Gorni, "Gemello del *Fiore*."

9. This section reproduces much of the section "Background: The *Romance of the Rose*" (3–4), as found in Kleinhenz and Casciani, "Introduction to the *Fiore*." Passages from the *Roman de la Rose* follow Guillaume de Lorris and Jean de Meun, *Roman de la Rose*, Lecoy ed., and *Romance of the Rose*, Dahlberg's English translation.

10. For a study of the *Rose*'s reception and manuscript tradition, see Huot, *Romance of the Rose*.

11. Huot, "*Fiore*," 155.

12. Jean includes a comprehensive disquisition on love and courtship, introducing moral and scientific themes stemming not only from European texts but also from classical authors. See F. D. Kelly (*Internal Difference*, 52–91) for the scientific and philosophical modes of treatment and Fleming ("Jean de Meun") for the subject of classical *auctores*.

13. This section reproduces some portions of the sections "The *Rose* in Italy and the Appearance of the *Fiore*" and "The Content of the *Fiore*," as found in Kleinhenz and Casciani, "Introduction to the *Fiore*," (5–6, 9–10).

14. See, among others, Barański, "Ethics of Literature," and "*Fiore* e la tradizione"; and Brownlee, "Conflicted Genealogy" and "Practice of Cultural Authority."

15. Three sonnets (121, 132, 144) are each missing one verse, and part of a verse is missing in 228.

16. Parodi, "Prefazione," xi, referred to the "orgia di sfacciati francesismi" [orgy of brazen Gallicisms], while Contini ed. (Ed. Nazionale), xcvii, noted that the *Fiore* exhibits "un 'creolo' meramente letterario" [a merely literary "creole"]. See also Moroldo, "Emprunts," and Viel, "Impronta." For *volgarizzamenti* in general, see Cornish, *Vernacular Translation*.

17. Huot, "*Fiore*," 153.

18. Took, "Towards an Interpretation," 526; Armour, "Lettura dei sonetti LXI–XC," 58; Alfie, "Durante's *Ars Amandi*," 5. In terms of the subject matter, Armour ("*Roman de la Rose*," 69) notes that the Italian author "is apparently anti-rational and anti-intellectual, skeptical in religious and moral matters, uninterested in erudition, almost single-mindedly preoccupied with the quest for the pleasure of the flower."

19. Barański notes that the phrase "descrive e sintetizza perfettamente i mezzi con cui l'autore del *Fiore* traduce la sua fonte . . . trasforma i *suoni* del *Roman de la Rose* non solo rendendoli in italiano ma anche rimaneggiando gran parte dell'originale" ("*Fiore* e la tradizione," 32–33).

20. See Huot, "*Fiore*," 154.

21. Huot provides much valuable information on the manuscript tradition, noting that although the source text for the *Fiore* may have been an abridged version, this is unlikely, since "sections of the *Rose* eliminated from the poem do seem nevertheless to have left their mark" ("*Fiore*," 158).

22. Grayson, "Dante," 195.

23. The readings of the 232 sonnets contained in Barański, Boyde, and Pertile, *Lettura del "Fiore*," are excellent examples of a variety of critical perspectives on and a deep understanding of the Old French and Italian works. See also, among others, Vanossi, *Dante*.

24. The *Fiore* essentially begins around verse 1681 of Guillaume's part of the *Rose*, thus omitting the apparatus of the dream vision, the description of vices and virtues on the enclosing garden wall. See, among many others, Harrison, "Bare Essential," 293, and Caballot, "Exemple de 'naturalisation,'" 19. Harrison ("Bare Essential," 293–94) notes the "essentialism of the Italian work" and the "boldness" of the author of the *Fiore* "to drop the entire first half of Guillaume's narrative and then to condense over two hundred verses of the French text into a single sonnet" (i.e., the first). Citations from the *Fiore* and the *Detto d'Amore* are from Contini's edition (Ed. Nazionale) and from Casciani's and my translation.

25. The *Rose* has "Biaus Semblance." Various reasons have been advanced for the departure, from a scribal error to a conscious alteration by the author. See, among others, Gorni, "Sul *Fiore*," 92–93), and *Fiore*, Formisano ed., 7.

26. In this regard Porcelli ("Nominazione," 222–23) notes that the "generico fiore compatibile col gennaio . . . è nella tradizione letteraria italiana l'equivalente della femminilità. Il fiore, privato non solo del nome originario ma anche dei roseti e del verziere, cessa di essere la bivalente figura della *Rose* per acquistare quasi esclusivamente consistenza carnea," and that it thus assumes a "posizione antifrastica rispetto ai nobili fiori 'di vertù,' 'di filosafi,' di 'belle cortesie' che i letterati contemporanei o di poco posteriori coglievano nei verzieri della cultura."

27. *Fiore*, Formisano ed., xlv: "Eliminata la cornice del sogno, ser Durante mira al sodo, a un racconto lineare e coerente."

28. Barański, "Lettura dei sonetti I–XXX," 14–22.

29. Ibid., 15. For the theatricality of the *Fiore*, see also Vanossi, *Dante*, 110–13, 124, 140, 149, etc.

30. Rossi ("Dante, la *Rose*," 23) notes the possible allusion in the fifth sonnet to Gerardo da Borgo San Donnino and his (lost) *Liber Introductorius ad Evangelium aeternum* (1254), an allusion also made in the *Rose* (11760–866). This and other allusions to the *Evangelium aeternum* in the *Fiore* would suggest a common interest in Joachimite ideas on the part both of Durante and of Dante. The poet of the *Fiore* "retained the notion of erotic love and its 'code' as a form of idolatry, one that parodies Christian rites and dogma. Numerous biblical echoes in the first five sonnets of the *Fiore* clearly set up erotic love as a parody of Christian faith and charity: Amante vows to serve no other god but Cupid, to love him with all his heart. Cupid himself insists that his rule must take the place of the Gospel. . . . Amante's substitution of Cupid for the Christian god is emphasized by the explicit reference to Christ in the discourse of Ragione, whose advice he spurns" (Huot, "*Fiore*," 159–60). See also Took's ironic perspective on the nature of love in the *Fiore* ("Towards an Interpretation," 508–10).

31. Huot, "*Fiore*," 154.

32. Allegretti ed., 133, notes that in the manuscript of the *Fiore* there is an extra blank line separating sonnets 33 and 34, a unique occurrence in the text and one that indicates the passage from the first to the second part of the *Rose*.

33. Brownlee, "Jason's Voyage," 176.

34. See, among others, Brownlee, "Practice of Cultural Authority," and Barański, "*Fiore* e la tradizione." See also the sections "The *Fiore* and the *Rose*: Questions of Influence and *Translatio*," "Rewriting the *Rose*: Omission and *Textus Interruptus*," and "The Relationship to Alan of Lille" in Kleinhenz and Casciani, "Introduction to the *Fiore*," 10–18, 18–23, 23–31.

35. The following are the parts of the two sonnets in question with the pertinent words and phrases in bold:

L'Amante
Quand' i' vidi i marosi sì 'nforzare
Per lo vento a Provenza che ventava,
C[h]' **alberi e vele e ancole fiac[c]ava**,
E nulla mi valea il ben governare,
Fra me medesmo comincià' a pensare
Ch'era **follïa** se più navicava,
Se quel maltempo prima non passava
Che dal buon porto mi facé' alu[n]giare:
Sì ch'i' allor m'ancolai a **una piag[g]ia**,
Veg[g]endo ch'i' non potea entrar in porto:
La terra mi parea molto **salvaggia**.
I' vi vernai co·molto disconforto.
Non sa che mal si sia chi non asaggia
Di quel d'Amor, **ond'i' fu' quasi morto**.

[Lover / When I saw the waves rise ever higher, / because of the wind that blew from Provence, / such that masts and sails and anchors broke, / and my good steering was to no avail, / I began to think in my heart of hearts / that it was madness to pursue my course, / until that bad weather passed, / which was keeping me far from the good harbor. / Thus, I anchored myself upon a beach, / seeing that I could not enter the harbor; / the land seemed very inhospitable to me. / There I passed the winter in much discomfort. / He does not know what pain is who has not experienced / the pain of Love, because of which I almost died.]

L'Amante
Pianto, sospiri, pensieri e afrizione
Eb[b]i vernando **in quel salvag[g]io loco**,
Ché **pena de·ninferno** è riso e gioco

Ver' quella ch'i' soffersi a la stagione
C[h]'Amor mi mise a tal distruzïone.

[*Lover* / With weeping, sighs, thoughts and affliction / I passed the winter in that harsh place, / for the pain of Hell is laughter and play / compared to that which I suffered that season / when Love put me in such distress]

See, among others, Took, "Towards an Interpretation," "Lettura dei sonetti XXXI–LX," and several sections in "Introduction," xl–xlii, xlvi–xlviii, lxvi–lxviii; Harrison, "Bare Essential," 297–98; and Brownlee, "Conflicted Genealogy," 274–75. For a slightly differing perspective, see Sebastio, *Strutture narrative*, 127–30. See also the fine analysis of these two sonnets by Maffia Scariati, "Spigolature," 37–43.

36. Rossi has suggested that the statements of Amico reflect ideas held by Guido Cavalcanti ("Dante, la *Rose*," 26).

37. The author of the *Fiore* more than likely considered these digressions as examples of *amplification* and unnecessary to the poem. For example, Reason's discourse in the *Rose* takes up some three thousand verses, which include "a long exposition of the various forms of love with recourse to various authorities and including the identification of the role of pleasure in sexual desire as the means to the end of procreation and the continued existence of the human race" (*Fiore*, Formisano ed., xlv). The only traces that remain of this long digression in the *Fiore* are found in sonnet 39 and 40. Similarly missing in the *Fiore* are, among others, the digressions on the fickleness of Fortune, Nature's extended commentary on cosmological and philosophical matters (another three thousand verses!), and Genius's sermon.

38. For major studies on the relationship between France and Italy and the fortune of the *Romance of the Rose* in Italy, see, among others, Contini, "Nodo della cultura medievale"; Dionisotti, *Geografia*; Segre, *Lingua, stile e società*; and Took, "Dante and the *Roman de la Rose*."

39. Barański, "Lettura dei sonetti I–XXX," 26–27.

40. On this point, see, among others, Sebastio, *Strutture narrative*, and Took, "Towards an Interpretation."

41. *Fiore*, Formisano ed., xlvi.

42. For example: 60.1–4 (see *Rose* 7690–691) and 66.12–14 (see *Rose* 9816–817).

43. Barański notes that the sonnet "è un mezzo eccellente con cui rafforzare tale senso di ordine e di armonia" ("Lettura dei sonetti I–XXX," 30; see also 27–32).

44. In *De vulgari eloquentia*, 2.3.5–6, Dante relegates the sonnet (and the *ballata*) to the inferior ranks of poetry. Poems written in this stylistic register coexisted with the more conventional courtly lyrics, a literary situation already

present in the Sicilian School and in many of the sonnets by Guido Cavalcanti and Dante.

45. It has been suggested that the consistent rhyme scheme for the octet—ABBAABBA—may be an attempt to reproduce the rhymed couplets of the *Rose* (*Fiore*, Formisano ed., xlvii).

46. See Leonardi, "*Fiore*."

47. Some of the techniques include *coblas capfinidas* and internal rhymes. It may also be that it was intended, at the same time, to launch a counterattack against thirteenth- and fourteenth-century French cultural hegemony in Italy. See Barański, "Lettura dei sonetti I–XXX," 27–28.

48. This section reproduces some portions of "The Content of the *Detto d'Amore*" and "The *Detto d'Amore*: Questions of Influence and Translation" as found in Kleinhenz and Casciani, "Introduction to the *Detto d'Amore*," 503–4, 504–7).

49. For the text of and translations from the *Detto*, see note 24 above.

50. The *Fiore*, on the other hand, follows the Jean's satirical/parodic stance in the *Rose*. Furthermore, the *Detto*, like the *Fiore*, reflects a new art of translation of the *Rose*, or as Harrison states of the *Fiore*, "The poem becomes provocative primarily in those features that set it off from the *Rose*," thus becoming an emblematic adaptation of the *Rose* ("Bare Essential," 293).

51. On the basis of codicological evidence, Vela ("Per la misura") suggests that the *Detto* originally had 720 verses.

52. Because of its rhymed couplets and equivocal rhymes, Guittone's canzone "Tutto, s'eo veglio o dormo" is often cited as a model for the *Detto*.

53. The presence of the large blue initial would indicate a break in the text, and this corresponds to two similar moments in both parts of the *Rose* (3073 and 4359). See *Detto d'Amore*, Formisano ed., 360.

54. This accords, in particular, with the description of *Oiseuse* ("Idleness") in the *Rose* (527–74). See *Detto d'Amore*, Formisano ed., 363.

55. For a study of the genres of courtly literature, see Hult, *Self-Fulfilling Prophecies*, 186–262.

56. See *Detto d'Amore*, Formisano ed., 376–79.

57. See Vanossi: "trapasso dai modi lirici tradizionali alla nuova poetica stilnovistica" ("*Detto d'Amore*," 394), as well as his more extensive treatment in *Teologia poetica*.

58. As noted earlier (see note 1), any attempt to square the date of the physical production of the two poems with Dante's possible authorship is difficult, if not impossible.

59. G. Mazzoni ("Se possa," 681) argues for its composition in the period around 1295, while Contini dates it to the years 1285–90 (Ed. Nazionale, cix–cx), which are closer to Petrocchi's proposed dates of 1286–87 ("Biografia," 9, 20–21, 35). The dates proposed by Contini and Petrocchi are much more appro-

priate, because they agree with internal references in the *Fiore* to historical events relating to the period 1282–93. However, on the basis of strong historical evidence, Montefusco ("Novità per il *Fiore*?," 414–16) has recently made a good argument for the later mid-1290s date. Discussions of these historical events are also found in many studies, including all the recent editions of the poem (Contini ed. [Ed. Nazionale], cix–cxiii; Rossi ed., vii–xiii; Took ed., xliii; Allegretti ed., 183–205; Formisano ed., xl–lxii), as well as other studies (e.g., Armour, "*Roman de la Rose*," 71–72).

60. For an extensive overview of the editions, see *Fiore*, Formisano ed., lxxx–xcvi. In his short essay, Monaci ("Redazione") provides an edition of the first three sonnets, as well as the last, with the pertinent portions of the Old French text and the rubrics for the entire *Fiore*.

61. *Fiore, poème italien*, Castets ed. Formisano (ed., xxii–xxvi), provides the most extensive and illuminating account of the interactions of Castets, Monaci, and D'Ancona, as well as Gaston Paris and Adolfo Mussafia, leading up to the eventual publication of the 1881 edition.

62. Mazzatinti's edition of the *Fiore* was incorporated, three decades later, by Della Torre in his unannotated, posthumous volume of all of Dante's works.

63. See the *Fiore* editions of Di Benedetto (1941), Petronio (1951), Blasucci (1965), and Marchiori (1983); Parodi's edition was also reprinted in the "Opere di Dante" section of the *Enciclopedia dantesca* (1984). See Formisano, "Postille," for a study of the annotations made by Parodi in the course of editing the two poems.

64. Contini published two editions in 1984, one for specialists (the Edizione Nazionale of the Società Dantesca Italiana, published by Mondadori)—and the other for more general readers (the annotated volume in the Ricciardi series). Some reviewers provide valuable commentary on the philologically oriented edition; see, for example, Lazzerini ("*Fiore, il Roman*") and Vanossi (*Dante*), as well as Cassata ("Sul testo del *Fiore*"), who proposes a number of emendations and parallel texts, and Milani ("*Fiore*"), who examines the metrical aspects of the manuscript and Contini's regularization of individual verses. For an assessment of the importance, both to Romance philology and to Italian literature in general, of Contini's essay ("Nodo della cultura medievale") on the *Fiore* as the point of connection between the *Roman de la Rose* and the *Commedia*, see Montefusco, "Contini e il nodo." For the value and pertinence of Contini's general philological methodology with a few references to the *Fiore*, see Leonardi, "Attualità di Contini filologo."

65. Earlier in 1888 Monaci published the first 222 verses in the separately distributed second fascicule of his *Crestomazia* and gave the poem its name. See Morpurgo, "Detto d'Amore."

66. Stoppelli, *Dante e la paternità*, 91, provides a substantial list of textual similarities between the *Detto* and the *Fiore*.

67. Portions of Parodi's text appeared in various anthologies, and it was the basis for Vanossi's 1974 slightly revised edition of the *Detto*.

68. *Fiore*, Formisano ed., xcv. Rossi and Formisano follow this text with some emendations and alterations

69. A number of studies present an overview of this issue, chief among them Barański and Boyde, *Fiore in Context*. See also Coglievina, "Attribuzione"; *Fiore*, Formisano ed., xxix–lxi; and the recent monograph by Stoppelli, *Dante e la paternità*. For some eloquent essays disputing Dante's authorship, see, among others, Lanza, "*Fiore*." From a historical perspective, the first editor, Castets, was favorable toward Dante as the author, but the poem's second editor, Mazzatinti, was opposed to this attribution. Included among early supporters of Dante as its author are Rajna, "Questione del *Fiore*," and G. Mazzoni, "Se possa," but among the opponents to the attribution we find Renier, "Di una imitazione"; D'Ancona, "*Romanzo della Rosa*"; Gorra, "Codice H 438"; Zingarelli, "Falsa attribuzione"; Borgognoni, "*Fiore*"; and Parodi, "Prefazione." In addition to Contini, firm believers in the possibility of Dante's authorship include Vanossi, *Dante*, and Vallone, "*Fiore* come opera." More recent critics who dispute his authorship are Wunderli, "*Mortuus redivivus*"; Armour, "Lettura dei sonetti LXI–XC"; Fasani, "Attribuzione del *Fiore*" and all his other works; Pertile, "Lettura dei sonetti CLXXXI–CCX"; and Cursietti, "Ancora per il *Fiore*." For an overview of the question, see *Fiori*, Contini ed. (Ed. Nazionale), xxvii–xliv, and Lanza, "*Fiore*."

70. For an overview of the question, see Gorni, "Ser Durante."

71. See Parodi: "Un poemetto non può scompagnarsi dall'altro, e . . . se si attribuisce il *Fiore* a Dante, o Durante, Alighieri, conviene anche attribuirgli il *Detto d'Amore*" (Parodi, "Prefazione," xix). However, Parodi does not believe that Dante is the author. See also, among others, Tonelli, "Ragione," 231, 233.

72. Novati, *Attraverso il Medio Evo*, 260, believed that different authors were responsible for the two works, as does Benedetto, "*Roman de la Rose*," 121, and "Di alcuni rapporti," who also suggests that the *Detto* was composed before the *Fiore*. See *Fiore*, Formisano ed., xxviii.

73. Contini, "Fiore, Il," "Nodo della cultura medievale," and "Questione del *Fiore*." See Coglievina, "Attribuzione," for a thorough review of the scholarship focusing on Contini's contributions.

74. As *Fiore*, Contini ed. (Ed. Nazionale), xx, and others have noted, the key word, *attribuibili*, reflects Latin *tribuendi*, which would suggest a strongly favorable opinion regarding Dante's authorship.

75. Vanossi, *Dante*, 349, calls the *Rose* "la fonte volgare di gran lunga più importante per la *Commedia*" [by far the most important vernacular source of the *Commedia*]. For the relationship among the *Rose*, the *Fiore*, and the *Commedia*, see, among others, Contini, "Nodo della cultura medievale," Davie, "*Fiore* Revisited," and Maffia Scariati, "*Fiore Inferno in fiere*."

76. *Fiore*, Contini ed. (Ed. Nazionale), lxxi–xcv. Excellent overviews of these arguments are found in Boyde, "*Summus minimusve poeta?*" and Barnes, "Uno, nessuno e tanti," as well as in Leonardi, "'Langue' poetica," and *Fiore*, Allegretti ed., 183–236, and Formisano ed., xxix–xxxvi.

77. Some of these external arguments are essentially the same as those noted early on in *Fiore*, Castets ed., xiv–xvi, Gorra, "Codice H 438," 421–32, and numerous others over the years.

78. See *Fiore*, Castets ed., xv.

79. See "Vez ci Guillaume de Lorriz / . . . / se je ne pens dou secourir" (10526, 10530).

80. The use of *ser*, an honorific that normally indicates a notary, would appear to be humorous along the lines of "ser Baratto" (129.10) and "ser Mala-Bocca" (136.1).

81. See Gorni, "Dante, Durante," 253–63.

82. F. Villani, *De origine civitatis Florentie*, 75–76. See, among others, Gorni, "Dante, Durante," and Porcelli, "Nominazione." There is, of course, at least one other poet with that name: Dante da Maiano.

83. *Fiore*, Formisano ed., 131n.

84. Pertile, "Lettura dei sonetti CLXXXI–CCX," 149–53, disagrees with Vanossi's suggestion that the name "Durante" should be interpreted seriously according to the principle of *nomina sunt consequentia rerum* following Dante's practice in the *Vita nova* 24.4 and in *Paradiso* 12.79–81 (*Dante*, 39). See also Rossi, "Tradizione allegorica," 153–54.

85. The practice of *interpretatio nominis* should be viewed in the more general context of Duecento and Trecento literature, where it serves both serious and comic ends. In this regard Pertile notes the juxtaposition of Beatrice to Becchina ("Lettura dei sonetti CLXXXI–CCX," 152). For a rebuttal of Pertile's suggestion, see Maffia Scariati, "Spigolature," 47–51, and Porcelli, "Nominazione," 224.

86. Unlike the mention in the following tercet of William of St. Amour, who is explicitly mentioned in the *Rose*, 11505–508.

87. Other singular historical references in the *Fiore* accord with Dante's political views, such as the persecution of the Patarine heretics in Tuscany and the power struggle between the old aristocracy and the new bourgeoisie that would culminate in the Ordinances of Justice in 1293 (but on these points, see Indizio, "Supplemento a *Fiore*"). Other external arguments include the sonnet, "Messer Brunetto, questa pulzelletta," which would have as its addressee Brunetto Latini (and not Betto Brunelleschi). The "pulzelletta" would be the *Fiore*, the "frati Alberti" = the Dominicans, and "Giano" = Jean de Meun. See, among others, Gorni, "*Pulzelletta* per messer Brunetto," and Rossi, "Dante," 26–29, and "Tradizione allegorica," 172–77. Another argument concerns the seemingly independent circulation of sonnet 97, "Chi della pelle del monton fasciasse," in the

Trecento, for which see, among others, *Fiore*, Contini ed. (Ed. Nazionale), lxxiv–lxxvii and the "Appendice," 475–81; Quaglio, "Per l'antica fortuna"; Coglievina, "Frammento estravagante"; *Fiore*, Allegretti ed., 177–82; *Fiore*, Formisano ed., xxxi–xxxii; and especially Alfie ("Wolves in Sheep's Clothing"), who examines thoroughly the extant versions of the sonnet attributed to Bindo Bonichi in light of the *Fiore* and medieval translation practices.

88. Contini, "Nodo della cultura medievale" and "Questione del *Fiore*." Casciani views the rose in the *Paradiso* as the proper revision of the *Roman de la Rose* ("Consider the Rose"). Following Contini's lead, Paolazzi ("'Comico' tra *Donna pietosa*") adduces lexical correspondences among Dante's canzone "Donna pietosa," the *Inferno*, and the *Fiore*, and Orelli ("Sonetto del *Fiore*") focuses on the connections between the fourth sonnet of the *Fiore* and the *Rime*, *Vita nova*, and *Commedia*, a practice followed also by Vanossi, *Dante*.

89. Boyde, "*Summus minimusve poeta?*," 27.

90. "Ma la regina delle prove si tocca quando alla ripetizione di elementi semantici si accompagna quella di dati fonici in analoghe congiunture ritmiche e sintattiche" (*Fiore*, Contini ed. [Ed. Nazionale], lxxxviii, and "Fiore, Il," 899).

91. Leonardi, "'Langue' poetica," 288–89.

92. For a study of words and phraseology in Dante and other poets of his time in relation to Contini's and Parodi's editions, see Cassata, "Sul testo del *Fiore*."

93. Picone, "*Fiore*," 150: "Il grande elemento assente nell'analisi continiana mi sembra che sia proprio questo: il contesto" [The large element absent in Contini's analysis seems to me to be precisely this: context]. Other reservations to Contini's approach have been voiced, for example, by Fasani, in *Lezione del "Fiore*."

94. For linguistic studies, see Ramacciotti, *Syntax of "Il Fiore*," Langheinrich, "Sprachliche Untersuchung," and Peirone, *Tra Dante e "Il Fiore*." For a statistical analysis of the *Fiore* and the view that it is not by Dante, see the studies by Barber, "Prospettive," and "Statistical Analysis." For another dissenting voice, see Moroldo, "Emprunts." For computer analyses "of vocabulary, of rhymes, and of accentual structure," see Robey, "*Fiore* and the Comedy," 109.

95. See Boyde, "Results of the Poll," for an overview of the findings of the Cambridge conference and his own "propositions" (376) for future research on the question. See also Rossi's review of the volume.

96. In addition to those *letture* mentioned specifically in the notes, the volume also contains excellent essays by John Barnes ("Lettura dei sonetti CXXI–CL"), Patrick Boyde ("Lettura dei sonetti CCXI–CCXXXII"), Mark Davie ("Lettura dei sonetti CLI–CLXXX"), and Peter Hainsworth ("Lettura dei sonetti XCI–CXX").

97. See Rossi, "De Jean Chopinel," "Du nouveau," "Jean de Meun," and "Tradizione allegorica," as well as Cornish, *Vernacular Translation*, 88–89.

Indeed, Dante might have become aware of the *Rose* precisely during his presumed residence in Bologna in 1286–87 and again in 1291–93.

98. Vanossi identifies some 350 Gallicisms in the *Fiore* (*Dante*, 236), while Formisano, in his edition of the *Fiore*, puts the total at 500 (xlix).

99. See Viel, "Impronta," and Stoppelli, *Dante e la paternità*, 75–93. Grayson ("Dante," 194–95) notes that many of these are unattested in Italy before the fourteenth century, including fifty that occur only in the *Fiore*.

100. See note 16 above.

101. On this topic, see, among others, Boyde, "*Summus minimusve poeta?*," 29–30.

102. The late Remo Fasani proposed no fewer than five candidates—Folgore da San Gimignano, Antonio Pucci, Amico di Dante, Brunetto Latini, and Immanuel Romano. For excellent overviews of the question of attribution, see Barnes, "Uno, nessuno e tanti," and *Fiore*, Formisano ed., li–lxi.

103. Borgognoni, "*Fiore.*"

104. His candidacy raised some initial interest with Castets, "Introduction," xviii, and D'Ancona, "*Romanzo della Rosa*," and recently received strong support from Stoppelli, *Dante e la paternità*, 107–35.

105. Recently Canettieri ("*Fiore* e il *Detto d'Amore*"), using an algorithm constructed to analyze texts based on a number of criteria, has concluded that the *Fiore* and the *Detto* are by the same author, probably Brunetto. Others who support Brunetto's candidacy are Muner, "Perché il *Fiore*" and "Paternità brunettiana"; Richards, *Dante*; Armour, "*Roman de la Rose*" and "Lettura dei sonetti LXI–XC"; and Fasani, "*Fiore* e Brunetto Latini."

106. Pèrcopo, "*Fiore.*" Buzzetti Gallarati ("Memoria") examines the numerous correspondences between the poetry of Rustico and the *Fiore*, noting that they—and Dante—share a "common cultural *milieu* that bears the mark of Brunetto Latini" [un commune *milieu* culturale di impronta brunettiana] (68).

107. *Fiore*, Di Benedetto ed.

108. Fasani, "Attribuzione del *Fiore.*"

109. Filippini, "Possibile autore del *Fiore*" and "Dante degli Abati."

110. Fasani, *Lezione del "Fiore.*"

111. Fasani, *Poeta del "Fiore,"* "Ancora per l'attribuzione," "*Fiore* e la poesia," and *Metrica*.

112. Cursietti, "Ancora per il *Fiore.*"

113. Fratta, "Lingua del *Fiore.*"

114. Fasani, *"Fiore" e il "Detto d'Amore.*"

115. See the commentary in Angiolieri, *Fiore*, Stanghellini ed.

116. His candidacy was suggested by Palma di Cesnola in two studies: "Battaglia del *Fiore*" and "Durante francese?" However, Formisano, in his edition of the *Fiore* (1), has called this suggestion an "ipotesi bizzarra"; see also Gorni, "Dante, Durante," 256–57.

117. Dante's general practice is to cite earlier works in later ones (e.g., the reference to the *Vita nova* in *Convivio* and the citations of his three *canzoni* in the *Commedia*).

118. However, an interesting suggestion has been made that in his sonnet ("Dante Allaghier, Cecco, 'l tu' servo e amico") written in response to Dante's last sonnet in the *Vita nova* ("Oltre la spera che più larga gira"), Cecco Angiolieri refers to "lo dio d'Amore / il qual è stat' un tu' signor antico" (3–4), a phrase that, appearing in the first verse of the *Fiore* but nowhere else in Dante's works, would suggest Cecco knew the poem and associated it with Dante. See Mazzucchi, "A proposito," as well as Gorni, "Sul *Fiore*," 92, and *Fiore*, Formisano ed., xxxvi.

119. Perhaps the most personal argument against Dante's authorship was expressed by Torraca ("*Fiore*," 245), whose opinion may be shared subconsciously by others: "I never believed that a semi-obscene poem—the *Fiore*—had come from the same mind that produced the *Divine Comedy*" [Io non ho mai creduto che un poemetto semi-osceno fosse uscito dalla stessa mente, onde uscì la *Divina Commedia*].

120. For a study that contested Dante's authorship of the *Detto*, see Parodi, "Prefazione."

121. Commenting on the language of the *Detto*, Vanossi (*Teologia poetica*, 2) argues that its versification resembles the technical language found both in Dante's early rhymes and in the *rime petrose*. Specifically, he sees the sonnet "Non canoscendo, amico, vostro nomo" (*Rime*, 3a [XLIV]) as incorporating a style very close to that of the *Detto*, for in this particular poem Dante constructs a discourse based on equivocal rhymes. Peirone ("*Detto d'Amore*") also believes in Dante's authorship of the *Detto*.

122. See Leonardi, "*Fiore*."

123. For some concise, synthetic presentations of the two poems, see Contini, "Fiore, Il," Vanossi, "*Detto d'Amore*," and Bellomo, "'Fiore' and 'Detto.'"

124. See, for example, Contini, "Santorre Debenedetti" and "Sul testo del *Fiore*"; Castellani, "*Cruces* del *Fiore*"; and Breschi, "Ancora su *Fiore* CCXI 13."

125. On the influence of the "civiltà di tipo 'podestarile-consiliare,'" see Montefusco, "*Mostrando*." For some recent studies on the *Fiore* in relation to the Italian literary tradition, see, among others, Orelli, "Sonetto del *Fiore*"; Bernardo, "Sex and Salvation"; Dragonetti, "Specchi d'amore"; Senior, "Authority and Autonomy" and "Love, Sex, and Gender"; Alfie, "Durante's *Ars amandi*"; Sebastio, "'Ragion la Bella'" and "Tra *Roman de la Rose*"; and López Cortezo, "Presencia." Two essays by Allegretti ("*Decretale* dello scandalo" and "Rapporto") have been expanded and included in the introduction to her edition.

126. Given that he once identified the author of the *Fiore* as Antonio Pucci, Fasani has been particularly interested in its relation to the oral tradi-

tion of the *cantari* (*Metrica* and *Poeta del "Fiore"*). Along these lines, Formisano ("Postille") notes that in the annotations preparatory to his edition of the *Fiore* Parodi also supports the view regarding the influence of the tradition of the *cantari*. In connection to the comic-realistic poets, see, for example, Buzzetti Gallarati, "Memoria." Abrame-Battesti ("Trivilisation"), who focuses on the *Fiore*'s more "mercantile" or "realistic" treatments of subjects than was the case in the *Rose*: Amico's parody of courtly discourse, generally more obscene language, women's venality, and so on. In connection to classical and biblical literature, see, among others, Chiamenti, "Modulo della negazione." In connection to "translation," "rewriting," and *volgarizzamenti*, see Cornish, *Vernacular Translation*; Richards, *Dante* and *"Fiore"*; and Barański, *"Fiore"* and "Ethics of Literature."

127. "La grande trovata di Durante, maggiore persino della sua invenzione linguistica, è di riconoscere le possibilità narrative del sonetto" (Barański, "Lettura dei sonetti I–XXX," 31). Perrus ("Avant-propos," 13) notes the unusual union of narrative (the "poemetto") and lyric poetry (the sonnet) in the *Fiore*.

128. In addition to comments on particular verses of the *Detto*, Picone ("Osservazioni") has studied the influence of Guittone and the "Mare amoroso" on the poem ("Glosse al *Detto d'Amore*").

129. See Leonardi, *"Fiore"*; De Robertis, "Traccia del *Fiore*"; and Cursietti, "Ancora per il *Fiore*." Stoppelli (*Dante e la paternità*) has extended Leonardi's research, indicating the many commonalities joining the *Fiore* to the lyric tradition.

130. See, among others, Lazzerini, *"Fiore,"* and Buzzetti Gallarati, "Postilla oitanica al *Fiore*."

131. Huot, *Romance of the Rose*, "Authors, Scribes," and *"Fiore* and the Early Reception"; Brownlee, "Conflicted Genealogy" and "Practice of Cultural Authority."

132. See the detailed reviews of Allegretti's and Formisano's editions by Montefusco and Leonardi and by Rinoldi ("In margine") only for the latter volume. In a separate review article, Montefusco ("Novità") examines the innovations of these two new editions and argues cogently for a number of new research directions vis-à-vis the *Fiore*, focusing on a greater contextualization of the historical elements in the text and providing extremely apt examples (e.g., the dating of the poem and the identity of Falsembiante as a Franciscan).

133. Vanossi, *Dante*, and Maffia Scariati, "Spigolature," 35, have also investigated these points.

134. This concerns a pattern suggesting the division 34 (Guillaume de Lorris's part)–163 (the speeches of the principal characters, Ragione, Amico, Falsembiante, and La Vecchia)–34 (the battle, burning of the castle, and the conquest of the flower), based on the Old French poem, and another division

77–77–77–1, based on the rubrics for the individual sonnets. For other numerological considerations, see Gorni, "Ser Durante," 60–63, and *Lettera nome numero*, 88–98.

135. Allegretti also provides long lists that may prove valuable to future investigations of the relationship of the *Fiore* and the *Detto* to the *Rose*, such as the direct translations from the Old French text and the incipits of the sonnets vis-à-vis the capital letter section indicators in the *Rose*.

136. In his essay ("Commentare il *Fiore*") Formisano provided a sampling of what would subsequently become the extensive annotations of his edition.

137. Two recent edited collections contain presentations from specific conferences/workshops sponsored by the Società Dantesca Italiana and devoted wholly or in part to the *Fiore*: (1) Tonelli, *Sulle tracce del "Fiore,"* features essays by Alessio Milani, Luciano Rossi, Enrico Fenzi, Riccardo Viel, Paolo Canettieri, Antonio Montefusco, Raffaele Pinto, Elena Stefanelli, and Maria Rita Traina; and (2) Gragnolati et al., *Atti degli incontri*, contains essays by Paola Allegretti, Luciano Formisano, Luca Carlo Rossi, and Pasquale Stoppelli. In addition to the section ("Dante and the *Rose*") in John Took's recent book (*Dante*), other recent contributions include Allegretti, "È il *Fiore* adespoto?"; Giuseppe Alvino, "Ancora sulla serie" and "Memoria del *Fiore*"; Marco Berisso, "Cosa chiedere al *Fiore*"; Formisano, "Qualche riflessione sul *Fiore*"; Inglese, "*Fiore* XLIX 3"; and Laura Nieddu, "Processo all'immagine."

CHAPTER 3

Vita nova

ZYGMUNT G. BARAŃSKI

Well, I once knew love—I knew how love felt
Yeah I knew love—love knew me
And when I walked—love walked with me
—John Prine, "All the Best"

DEFINITION AND PROBLEMS OF DEFINITION

The *Vita nova*, which was composed in Florence in the early to mid-1290s, is a *prosimetrum*, a text that integrates prose and poetry, specifically thirty-one of Dante's preexisting love lyrics, which are encased within a multilayered prose framework that integrates narrative, doctrinal, exegetical, scientific, and devotional prose.[1] The poems are distinguished into twenty-three standard sonnets, two *sonetti rinterzati*, three canzoni, one canzone interrupted at the end of the first stanza, two stanzas of a canzone, and a *ballata*.[2] Taken together, prose and verse constitute an alluring compendium of vernacular writtern forms. Beyond the importance of the work in itself, it is the prose, as we shall see, that is especially significant both as regards Dante's career as a writer and apropos the development of vernacular literature in Italian. In straightforward narrative terms, the *Vita nova* recounts in the first person the story of the lover's relationship with his beloved, Beatrice, both before and after her death on

June 8, 1290 (*Vn* XXIX.1 [19.4]). The story, spanning a period of nearly twenty years, emerges and gains significance as a consequence of the poet-lover pondering on the poetry that he previously wrote over a period of circa nine years.[3]

The *Vita nova* incorporates both an anthology of this poetry and a record, written in prose, of, again, a selection of the most meaningful recollections, ideas, associations, and interpretations that, reflecting on the verses, the poet-lover extrapolated: "non tutte [le parole], almeno la loro sentenzia" [not all the words, but at least their vital meaning].[4] The "libello" [little book], which Dante claims is a faithful if redacted copy of the "libro de la mia memoria" (I.1 [1.1]) [book of my memory], thus alternates between sections in prose specifically penned to be included in its pages and retranscribed texts of poems that were originally conceived as discrete self-standing compositions, but that are now resemanticized by being collected together and placed in a new overarching and unifying structure.[5] Dantists have tended to privilege the poetry over the prose, deeming the latter to be subordinate to the former. The prose is judged to have auxiliary functions: to interpret the poems and to contextualize them by illuminating the circumstances of their genesis. As a result, the *Vita nova*, namely the work in its entirety, which Domenico De Robertis famously termed, calquing Dante, "il libro della *Vita Nuova*" [the book of the *Vita Nuova*], or what modern scholarship would term the *Vita nova* as macrotext, has been interpreted primarily within a lyric, subjective, and erotic framework:[6] the text is a ritualized symbolic representation of different facets of love and other emotions, and a sublimation of psychological experiences.[7] Yet the prose is strikingly more varied, both in style and in genre, and hence in subject matter, than the exclusively love lyric tenor of the poems. It weaves together a narrative register that recounts private and public events alongside the lover's thoughts and dramatically shifting psychological states; a standard scholastic hermeneutic register, the *divisio textus*—the partitioning and paraphrasing of a text—that either precedes or follows the poems; and a rich doctrinal and explicatory register (perhaps "registers" in the plural might in fact be more appropriate) that includes topics as varied as medical lore, astronomy, personification allegory, literary history, and etymology and semantics.[8] It is thus the prose rather than the poetry that provides a sense of the *Vita nova*'s remit, even if I must immediately stress, and as this chapter hopes to demonstrate, that it is the interplay between poetry and prose that fundamentally establishes the *libello*'s textual identity, its interests, and its groundbreaking qualities. Thus, in broad literary terms, the *Vita nova* is characterized and determined by its formal and structural identity as a prosimetrical compilation, which both stylistically and in its *materia* transcends any single set of writerly and intellectual concerns, although it is important to stress that such a definition only in part fixes its genre. The difficulty of establishing the *libello*'s genre stems, in the first instance, from the fact that no work similar to the *Vita nova* had previously been composed, in Italian or in any of the Romance vernaculars. Indeed, as I shall discuss, no comparable work had been written in the Latin tradition[9]—a remarkable achievement for an author who, at most, had just celebrated his thirtieth birthday.

In ideological terms, however, what lies at the *Vita nova*'s core is the realization, fruit of the poet-lover's ruminations, that his interactions with Beatrice, who is dubbed a "miracle" (XXIX.3 [19.6]) and an emanation of God, were not contingent but divinely willed.[10] Their relationship transcended conventional, earthbound ties between a woman and a man. Instead, their rapport was meant to help the poet-lover appreciate how to live a good Christian life, and so endeavor to achieve salvation. In an original maneuver, the *Vita nova* integrates secular and religious views about love, which are presented not as necessarily antithetical but as potentially harmonizing. At the same time, the impact of Beatrice on his life encouraged the poet-lover to reflect on his literary activities and to write the *Vita nova*, so that others too might benefit from his experiences, which, because of their providential character, are thereby deemed to be exemplary. As such, the *Vita nova* oscillates between the subjective and the universal; and it is the work's universalism, its privileged position within the intricacies of a theocentric reality, that serves to legitimate and to begin to account for the breadth of its concerns.

Problems of Interpretation

It is curious, to say the least, that a work of the complexity and originality of the *Vita nova*—the first major literary self-commentary of the Western canon, a facet that further underlines its generic intricacy and fluidity—

should have been assessed and interpreted within relatively narrow cultural, historical, and critical parameters. In fact, Dante scholarship has only recently begun to take cognizance of the revolutionary fact of its pioneering status as self-commentary and as a literary *unicum*. Instead, and now for over a century, the primary focus has been on the *Vita nova*'s relationship to the Romance vernacular lyric.[11] More recently, by building on the historic, albeit sporadic and unfairly criticized, contributions of Aristide Marigo, Charles Singleton, and Vittore Branca, increased attention has been paid to its ties to the scriptural tradition.[12] The *libello*'s distinctive dual literary heritage controls one of the two dominant and interrelated ways in which Dantists now interpret it. According to this reading, the *Vita nova* is an innovative attempt both to discriminate between and to integrate secular and Christian ideas about love. Concurrently, Dante also relates the story of his own poetic progress in light of developments in the Romance lyric in general and in the Italian branch of this in particular. This metaliterary reading, which has developed substantially, if somewhat unsystematically and reductively, over the last fifty or so years, constitutes the second main critical viewpoint on the *Vita nova*;[13] the *libello* is interpreted as a major meditation on the achievements and potential of vernacular literature, the most sophisticated expression of which ends up being Dante's own *libello*.[14] At the same time, by largely limiting the discussion to Romance vernacular poetry, scholars have minimized the significance of the prose, as well as of the relationship between prose and poetry. In some extreme instances, the metaliterary has "overwhelmed" the erotic, once more trivializing the *libello*'s range: "The *Vita Nuova* is a treatise by a poet, written for poets, on the art of poetry."[15]

Even when brought together, the two dominant critical strands end up by marginalizing, arguably "concealing," other significant features that characterize the *Vita nova*—elements, in fact, that point to Dante's intent to engage with a more comprehensive set of issues that goes beyond the Bible and the Romance lyric. Indeed, the ambitious range of the subjects treated and of the formal experiments attempted anticipates, even if in minor key, the *Commedia*'s totalizing formal and thematic "encyclopedism." Scholars have, of course, noted the presence in the *Vita nova* of characteristics that fall outside the immediate purview of scripture and of the love lyric. It is enough to remember its occasional references to classical culture, to matters of doctrine, and to hagiography; its likely dependence on the works of Augustine and of Boethius; and its engagement with Brunetto Latini, the leading Florentine intellectual of the late thirteenth century. Nevertheless, despite the contemporary cultural weight of such elements, Dantists have normally subsumed these into the dominant erotic-salvific and metaliterary readings of the *Vita nova* rather than evaluating them as potentially "self-sufficient," albeit integrated, parts of a complex and wide-ranging textual and intellectual mechanism.

The main limitation of most of the secondary literature on the *Vita nova*, as we have begun to see, is the guiding conviction—now affirmed as a critical truism—that, for all its elegance and sophistication, its remit is narrow (as befits its status as a "youthful" work). In this regard, on account of its privileging of the canzone "Donne ch'avete intelletto d'amore" (*Dve* 2.8.8 and 12.3) [Ladies who have understanding of love], which in the *Vita nova* marks the major shift in its ideological perspective (see below), the *De vulgari eloquentia* has been read as, *inter alia*, legitimating the *libello*'s poetics, of which "Donne ch'avete" is deemed to serve as an emblem. As a result, the *Vita nova* is transformed into the quintessential stilnovist text.[16] Thus its register, it is maintained, is monolingual, its subject matter is love and the literature on love, and its ideological interests are circumscribed by the stilnovists' refined intellectualism and by theologically determined Christian views on Providence, love, and salvation.[17] It is an elitist work written for an elite audience, hence its tendency toward an idealized, atemporal, and exemplary abstraction. The setting is "la cittade," the city, and never Florence. If it is largely valid to judge the poems in such terms, the same is far from the case as regards the prose (see "Plurilingualism, Language, Literature" below) and, by extension, the *Vita nova* as a whole. By having recourse to the *De vulgari*, scholars have interpreted the *prosimetrum* from the anachronistic and distorting perspective of a later, postexilic work, whose concerns were no longer those of the *libello*.[18] Thus the treatise's determining and ultimately abstract notion of the "illustrious vernacular," a supraregional form of Italian modeled on the status of Latin as *gramatica* and in clear opposition to the peninsula's local vernaculars, has no place in the *Vita nova*, where the "problem of the language" pivots around the concrete question of the relationship between Latin and the vernacular as literary languages—a supremely practical question in light of linguistic developments in late medieval culture (see below for a fuller discussion of this point). Furthermore, as some scholars have recently recognized, the *Vita nova* in fact addresses other concrete, historically inflected issues, from matters relating to gender and to social relations between women and men to funerary customs, and from pilgrimage to the obligations of friendship and social rank to the urban environment.[19] Indeed, a symbolic Christian trope such as exile, which was used to describe our life on earth and which helps underpin the *libello*'s religious structure, is manipulated by Dante so that it subtly establishes important connections with contemporary political banishment, a form of punishment regularly used in Florence.[20]

There is little doubt, at least as far as I am concerned, that the *Vita nova*, culturally and connotatively, is a thickly stratified and complex text. Nonetheless, the dominant critical approach, tightly focused on the *Vita nova*'s engagement with love and lyric, continues to downplay its multifacetedness and hence its interpretive challenges, despite the fact that the *Vita nova* persistently and openly underscores its engagement with difficulty and complication: demanding poems that require clarification and a protagonist who has to resolve existential, artistic, and intellectual problems (see, for example, XII.5 [5.12]). In truth, the most difficult text of all is the *Vita nova* itself. The personal status of the "book of memory" underscores the need for appropriate guidance in what, at first sight, looks like a "private" realm. The same need for guidance holds good for its insistent and wide-ranging literary *novitas*. The poet is acutely aware that his writing is a source of "doubts" and thus needs clarification (XII.17 [5.24]; and compare XXV.1 [16.1]).

The *Vita nova* is a perplexing text. It is a work of *subtilitas*—"ma più sottilmente pensando, e secondo la infallibile veritate. . . . Forse ancora per più sottile persona si vederebbe in ciò più sottile ragione" (XXIX.3–4 [19.6–7]; and compare XXXIII.2 [22.2]; XLI.9 [30.9]) [but more subtly thinking, and according to the infallible truth. . . . Perhaps by a yet more subtle person a more subtle reason would be seen in this]—which, paradoxically, is nevertheless accessible to "tutte le persone" (XXVI.15) [all persons] and to "li più semplici" (III.15 [2.2]) [the most simple].[21] And this is just one among many such large-scale conundrums that go to the very core of the *Vita nova*'s textual status and ideological and formal integrity. It is a text that appears to stand at a bewildering and innovative cultural crossroad. One merely needs to think about the striking tensions that arise from the coexistence in the *libello* of Latin and the vernacular, of prose and poetry, of Christian and pagan imperatives, and of sacred and secular elements; and all this before we are faced with having to decide what the "book of memory" might actually include or what its precise relationship to the *Vita nova* might be; and then there is the matter of the status of the book's author-protagonist . . .[22] Dante is keenly aware of his responsibilities in coming to his readers' aid and in "rimuov*ere* alcuna dubitazione" (XXXVII.4 [26.4]). However, the manner in which he does this, the ways in which he interprets and guides our interpretation, despite the *prosimetrum*'s seeming close reliance on the established norms of medieval literary exegesis, is itself a source of disquiet. Rather than offer clear-cut, comfortable, and conventional explanations using standard procedures, Dante involves us in a complex, potentially destabilizing, and hugely original exegetical exercise.[23] The more problems he poses, the more the need to interpret is highlighted. Even more significantly, the fundamental standing of the *Vita nova* as a text that both is a work of interpretation and is itself interpretable is affirmed. In fact, Dante goes a step further and appears to suggest that the *libello*, at least as far as the poems are concerned, provides the "correct," namely the rationally sanctioned, elucidation of their meaning (VII.2 [2.13] and VIII.3 [3.3]). In this regard, it is difficult not to agree with Justin Steinberg that one of the reasons for the *Vita nova*'s composition is to be sought in Dante's dissatisfaction with his reception in the late 1280s and early 1290s and, especially, in his anxiety regarding the "misreading" of his verses.[24]

THE *VITA NOVA* BETWEEN THE *COMMEDIA* AND THE *CONVIVIO*

The critical appreciation of the "little book" has also been adversely affected by its being too closely associated with some of Dante's later works and, as a consequence, by its being evaluated in respect of these, especially as such rapprochements invariably reaffirm its status as a text on love. Given the hope expressed at the close of the *Vita nova*—"Io spero di dicer di lei quello che mai non fue detto d'alcuna" [I hope to say of her what has never been said of any woman] (XLII.2 [31.2])—readers have been tempted to consider the *prosimetrum* as, in essence, a sort of youthful preamble to the *Commedia* and have interpreted it accordingly. In line with this view, by restoring Beatrice to a position of prominence in the

Commedia after the perceived philosophical seductions of the "gentle lady" of the *Convivio*, the poem marks an orthodox and unproblematic return to the religious and erotic purview of the *Vita nova*, as well as to its core salvific concerns.[25] The *Commedia* and the "little book" thus resemble two paired panels of an artistic and ideological diptych that narratively explores the ties between God and humanity, as well as those linking human beings, by concentrating on the interactions between this world and the next, the universalizing setting common to both works. That the two major texts involving Beatrice can be considered together and that they are to a degree complementary is self-evident. At the same time, however, we need to be clear about the implications and limits of such an approach. Thus, as regards each text's possible original functions, remit, and meanings, it is incumbent to recognize that, given the order of their composition, the *Vita nova* can bear directly on the *Commedia* but the reverse is not possible. In truth, there is no evidence to suggest that, when Dante announced his aspiration to celebrate Beatrice at some point in the future, he was thinking, however vaguely, of the poem. To put it differently, when assessing the *Vita nova*, we ought not judge it through the lens of the *Commedia*, not least because the poem exploits the *libello* for its own purposes, subordinating and restricting the work to its own needs. Instead the *Vita nova* ought to be assessed on its own terms, as a vernacular text composed in 1290s Florence,[26] a time and place untouched by the magnificent yet oppressive shadow of the *Commedia*. Indeed, the *prosimetrum*'s concerns should not be circumscribed by its apparent ties to the *Commedia*, especially as these would appear to bind it exclusively to questions of love, self, Providence, and salvation.

Furthermore, in the *Commedia*, Dante seems intent on criticizing the *Vita nova*'s formal solutions, and hence its effectiveness and standing as a work of literature. In particular, first in *Inferno* 1 and 2 and then in *Purgatorio* 30 and 31, while evoking its language, he presents the *libello* as a text whose artistic solutions he has left behind. In the same way as occurs with the many other works that Dante evaluates in the poem, the *prosimetrum* is deemed to be constrained by its adherence to a restrictive traditional poetics that the *Commedia* challenges and supersedes.[27] Such an assessment, which is entirely at the service of the poet's vindication of the *Commedia*'s experimentation, deliberately conceals the *Vita nova*'s equally noteworthy experimental literary character (on which a significant part of this chapter concentrates) and the breadth of its *materia*. In other words, the poem sidesteps the *prosimetrum*'s actual and foregrounded "newness."

Beginning in the nineteenth century, much scholarship too has underplayed its originality. Since the *Vita nova* deals with the poet-lover's youth, it is judged to be—as I have intimated—a "youthful" work, and consequently one that cannot but lack the artistic sophistication and boldness of Dante's later "mature" works, with, of course, the *Commedia* at their head. Such a reading seems to find support in the *Convivio*: "E se nella presente opera, la quale è Convivio nominata e vo' che sia, più virilmente si trattasse che nella Vita Nova, non intendo però a quella in parte alcuna derogare, ma maggiormente giovare per questa quella; veggendo sì come ragionevolmente quella fervida e passionata, questa temperata e virile essere conviene" (1.1.16) [And if in the present work, which is called *Convivio* and I wish it to be (a banquet), matters are treated in a more virile manner than in the *Vita nova*, I do not intend however to detract from that in any part, but more to benefit that work, thanks to this one: seeing how it is reasonably appropriate for that to be fervid and passionate, this temperate and virile] and "Per lo quale ingegno molte cose, quasi come sognando, già vedea, sì come nella Vita Nova si può vedere" (2.12.4) [Thanks to this intelligence, many things, as if dreaming, I already saw, as can be seen in the *Vita nova*]. Both descriptions fix the *Vita nova* as a worthy albeit immature and intellectually deficient text that needs to be bolstered by a "virile" work. However, as is obvious, such a definition functions, as with the *Commedia*'s treatment of the *libello*, not to the latter's benefit but to that of the "present work," which Dante was keen to portray as a new and enhanced departure in his personal and artistic *iter*. Accordingly, the poet introduced the *Convivio* as his first attempt at writing an intellectually rigorous text with "encyclopedic" ambitions, though the *Vita nova* too has not dissimilar ends.[28] In addition, by terming the *Vita nova* "fervid and passionate," attributes conventionally associated with ardent "adolescent" behavior, Dante defined it as work whose subject matter was emotive rather than rational.[29] Consequently, given the *Vita nova*'s focus on the lover's relationship to Beatrice, such a definition meant that its *materia* could not but be overwhelmingly if not exclusively amorous.

Structure, Ideology, Diegesis

It is time to provide an inkling of the range, variety, and artistic, intellectual, and cultural verve and originality of Dante's extraordinary "little book."

The structure of the *Vita nova* is elaborate and subtle, and hence serves as a further mark of its ambition and novelty. At the same time, while some patterns are self-evident, others remain the source of controversy. It is very likely that the work's original version, like the "book of memory," was organized into "major paragraphs," what we might term "chapters" or, perhaps better, "sections," since the latter term implies a less rigorous and clear-cut type of ordering than the idea of a text divided into chapters:[30] "verrò a quelle parole le quali sono scritte ne la mia memoria sotto maggiori paragrafi" (II.10 [1.11]).[31] However, since no manuscript in Dante's hand, whether of the *Vita nova* or of any of his other works, has survived, we can only conjecture about the arrangement of the *prosimetrum*'s holograph, given that the evidence offered by the oldest manuscripts of the *libello* is inconclusive (see the subsection "Appearance" below). These contain signs that appear to point to breaks in the text; however, such signs are inconsistently introduced across different manuscripts and have been interpreted differently by textual editors. Two versions of the *Vita nova* are currently used by most scholars: one is divided into forty-two chapters and associated with Michele Barbi's fundamental critical edition of the *libello*; the other, proposed by Guglielmo Gorni, is partitioned into thirty-one chapters, the same number as the poems, thereby granting the *Vita nova* an apparently alluring harmony.[32] While Barbi recognized the artificiality and shortcomings, as well as the practical imperative, of his set of divisions, Gorni insisted—if truth be told, without the necessary philological support—that his text conformed to Dante's organizational intentions. If pushed, my sense is that Gorni's configuration of the *Vita nova* may indeed be closer, even if not identical, to the original.[33]

The *libello* is thus divided into prose and poetry and into an indeterminate number of discrete textual units, each of which always incorporates parts in prose and, normally, at least one poem (Gorni was unable to introduce a poem into each of his chapters; his edition includes three chapters exclusively written in prose). However, there are other, less contentious, elements in the *Vita nova* that highlight the care with which Dante structured his work. In narrative terms, it can most obviously be divided into two: before and after Beatrice's death, namely into chapters I to XXVII [1–18] and XXVIII to XLII [19–31].[34] However, the extent to which Dante may have deemed such a division as significant is moot. The suspicion persists that attention has been drawn to it by the anachronistic influence of Petrarch's division of the *Canzoniere* into a section *in vita* and another *in morte* rather than by the *prosimetrum*'s actual organizational logic.

Scholars have convincingly argued that the *Vita nova* is more likely divided into three parts.[35] Different tripartite divisions have been proposed. What follows is the most cogent such partition in terms of markers present in the *libello* itself. Chapters I–XVI [1–9] present the lover struggling to find a proper balance in his relationship with Beatrice. His mistake is to treat and react to the "benedetta" as if she were an ordinary woman, and hence according to established secular erotic conventions. This section draws extensively on the commonplaces of the Romance literature on love, from screen ladies to a Cavalcantian pessimism that judged love to be a destructive and irrational force,[36] and from personifications of Love to the Occitan *gab* (Italian *gabbo*), the mocking of the lover by the woman and her friends, with which this part closes.

Chapters XVII–XXVII [10–18] are prefaced by the declaration "A me convenne ripigliare matera nuova e più nobile che la passata" (XVII.1 [10.1]) [It seemed fitting to me to take up again a new and more noble subject matter than the past one], thereby stressing a marked shift in the *Vita nova*'s unfolding, a sort of new beginning. This change is predicated on the "stilo de la sua loda" (XXVI.4 [17.4], but see in particular XVIII.6–9 [10.8–11]) [style of her praise], the new morally and spiritually appropriate way of interacting with the beloved, namely, altruistically celebrating her in a manner akin to the praise that a Christian ought to direct toward God. The lover thus begins to recognize and acclaim Beatrice's divine nature and hence begins to consider love in religious and ethical terms as a charitable and ennobling experience that can lead to salvation. Although the emphasis is unquestionably Christian—a significant departure in the history of secular writing about love—Dante also recognizes that Guido Guinizzelli's idea of love is valid and not incompatible with his new sense of the emotion: "Amore e 'l cor gentil sono una cosa, | sì come il saggio [Guinizzelli] in suo dittare pone" (XX.3 [11.3]) [Love and the gentle heart are one thing, | as the wise man places in his writing].[37] At the same time, the tones of celebration are menacingly countered by an increasingly doomladen sense of the inevitability of Beatrice's death, indicating that the lover has still not fully grasped the woman's miraculous nature and providential function.

Chapters XXVIII–XLII [19–31] open with the proclamation that "lo segnore de la giustizia chiamoe questa gentilissima a gloriare sotto la insegna di quella regina benedetta virgo Maria" (XXVIII.1 [19.1]) [the lord of justice called this most gentle woman to glory under the emblem of that blessed queen the virgin Mary]. Immediately prior to making this announcement, Dante declares that Beatrice died as he was composing a canzone praising the effects on him of seeing her (XXVII.2 [18.2])—a canzone of which he had written the opening stanza (which is reproduced in the preceding chapter), and which he now cannot but leave unfinished. Once again, Dante underlines that the *Vita nova*'s subject matter has altered and that a new section has begun: "quasi come entrata"—the reference is to the Latin epistle to the "rulers of the land" informing them of Florence's piteous state after Beatrice's death—"de la nuova materia che appresso vene" (XXX.1 [19.9]) [almost like the introduction to the new subject matter that comes next]. The dominant register of this last section is overtly Christian. It includes a scripturally inflected temptation: the lover espies "una gentile donna giovane e bella molto, la quale da una finestra mi riguardava" (XXXV.2 [24.2]) [a gentle young woman and very beautiful, who was looking at me from a window] and reacts to her as if she were a conventional "gentle" lady (3 [3]), a regressive step and a mark of his grief-stricken confusion, since the woman is in fact a temptress, the Florentine manifestation of the archetypical woman at the window, Jezabel: "Hiezabel . . . depinxit oculos suos stibio et ornavit caput suum et respexit per fenestram" (2 Kings 9:30) [Jezabel painted her eyes with stibic stone and adorned her head and looked out of a window]. Beatrice miraculously appears to him and helps him to "discacci*are* questo . . . malvagio desiderio" (XXXIX.2 [28.2]) [drive away this evil desire]. There are also references to the Veil of Veronica and to pilgrimage, before the lover's sigh rises up to the Empyrean to contemplate Beatrice among the "benedette anime" (XLI.6 [30.6]) [blessed souls]. The *libello* begins to come to a close with a final "mirabile visione" (XLII.1 [31.1]) [marvelous/miraculous/wondrous vision] that makes the poet realize he must cease writing until such time as he is capable "degnamente trattare di lei" (1 [1]) [worthily to treat of her]. The *Vita nova* then concludes, appropriately given its key salvific intent, with allusions to the lover-poet's not unlikely future salvation, to God's omnipotence, and to Beatrice's key role as mediatrix between her lover and God: "E poi piaccia a colui che è sire de la cortesia, che la mia anima se ne possa gire a vedere la gloria de la sua donna, cioè di quella benedetta Beatrice, la quale gloriosamente mira ne la faccia di colui *qui est per omnia secula benedictus*" (XLII.3 [31.3]) [And then may it please him who is the lord of courtesy, that my soul may go and see the glory of his lady, namely of that blessed Beatrice, who gloriously gazes on the face of him who is blessed forever and ever]. The final sentence succinctly captures the book's overarching view of reality and its fundamental religious priorities. It also affirms the divinely sanctioned "truth" of the preceding narrative. At the same time, Dante underscores his personal responsibility as a writer in disseminating this truth and its future ramifications: "Io studio quanto posso. . . . Sì che . . . io spero di dicer di lei quello che mai non fue detto d'alcuna" (XLII.2 [31.2]) [I study as much as I can. . . . So that . . . I hope to say/write about her that which has never been said/written about any woman]. Literature and life, the man and the author—and hence his writing, with the *Vita nova* in prime position as bearer of a divine revelation—become one and are legitimated "forever and ever."

The *libello*'s tripartite division complements and is sustained by the providential roles that the numbers nine and three play in the lover-poet's growing appreciation of the divine significance of his love: "Dunque se lo tre è fattore per se medesimo del nove, e lo fattore per se medesimo de li miracoli è tre, cioè Padre e Figlio e Spirito Santo, li quali sono tre e uno, questa donna fue accompagnata da questo numero del nove a dare ad intendere ch'ella era uno nove, cioè uno miracolo, la cui radice, cioè del miracolo, è solamente la mirabile Trinitade" (XXIX.3 [19.6]) [Thus if three is the factor by itself of nine, and the factor by itself of miracles is three, namely the Father and the Son and the Holy Spirit, who are three and one, this woman was accompanied by this number of nine to make it understood that she was a nine, namely a miracle, whose root, namely of the miracle, is solely the marvelous/miraculous/wondrous Trinity]. The *Vita nova*'s structure, as with the *Commedia*'s interplay of threes and tens, upholds that its primary model is the numerically harmonious order of creation—a detail that, by extension, highlights its divine credentials. Notions of coherence and orderly development thus characterize both the narrative and the text.[38] As I hope I was able to make clear in my discussion of the three parts of the *libello*, the different stages, despite the crises that accompany each of them—crises that recall the ups and downs of human life as recorded most significantly for Dante in Augustine's *Confessions*—are soundly progressive. An emblematic example of this fundamental evolutionary structure is provided by the first and final sonnets: "A ciascun'alma presa e gentil core" (III.10 [1.21]) [To every captive soul and gentle heart] and "Oltre la spera che più larga gira" (XLI.10 [30.10]) [Beyond the sphere that turns widest]. The former, with its emphasis on the draped sleeping figure of Beatrice who is forced to eat the lover's heart, is vividly physical, even sexual in tenor. Indeed the sexual element is heightened in the prose that precedes it: "una persona dormire nuda, salvo che involta mi parea in uno drappo sanguigno leggeramente" (III.4 [1.15]) [a person sleeping naked, except that she seemed to me to be lightly wrapped in a blood-red cloth] and "E tanto si sforzava per suo ingegno, che le facea mangiare questa cosa che in mano li ardea" (III.6 [1.17]) [And [the lord] was trying so hard with his ingenuity, that he made her eat this thing that burned in his hand]. Conversely, in the closing sonnet, the lover's disembodied "sigh" rises up to gaze on Beatrice enjoying beatitude. The contrast between the two accounts and experiences could not be greater or more significant: a journey from transient sexual desire to eternal spiritual contemplation. Some scholars have seen in this movement an allusion to the development of the Romance love lyric,[39] from the adulterous, carnal longings of the first Occitan poets to the Christian spirituality of the *Vita nova*. Given the *prosimetrum*'s emphatic metaliterary designs and the care with which Dante organized it, this is not an unreasonable suggestion. More likely, however, is that, by means of the ordering of his poems, Dante was pointing not simply to the development of his own poetic history but also to that of the Italian love lyric. The latter elucidation is anachronistic, or, perhaps better, idealized and personalized, since, in chronological terms, it begins appropriately with poems written in the manner of the Occitan-leaning followers of Guittone d'Arezzo, the so-called *siculo-toscani*, before introducing texts in the manner of Guido Cavalcanti. However, it then moves on, but also "backwards," to compositions that draw on the "sage" Guido Guinizzelli, who, in actuality, belonged to the literary generation predating that of the "first friend"; he was in fact a contemporary of Guittone d'Arezzo and many of his epigones. Finally, the *Vita nova*'s oblique history of Italian poetry reaches its inevitable apogee in the Christian poetics of Dante's "praise style."[40]

The *libello*'s interwoven ideological and structural allusiveness is a hallmark of its intellectual and artistic ambition. To disentangle the different strands and patterns, in line with the *Vita nova*'s general hermeneutic emphases, demands an interpretive effort, which, as with any act of interpretation, is open to question and revision. Yet there is one design that is not open to discussion, as it is laid out with mathematical precision, thereby serving, I believe, and we are thus back in the realm of interpretation, as an emblem of the *prosimetrum*'s organizational sophistication, as well as of its dependence on the *Deus artifex*, who "omnia mensura et numero et pondere disposuit" (Wisd. 11:21). The thirty-one poems are "disposed" into a chiastic configuration based on the distinction between the *Vita nova*'s major metrical forms, the three canzoni, and its remaining minor forms, the sonnets, the partial canzoni, and the ballad. The poems fan out symmetrically as follows: 10 + canzone I + 4 + canzone II + 4 + canzone III + 10. The system pivots around "Donna pietosa e di novella etate" [A compassionate woman of a young age], the canzone that describes the prophetic vision of the story's pivotal event, Beatrice's death and her assumption into heaven. The other two canzoni also appear in structurally and ideologically marked positions: the first, "Donne ch'avete intelletto d'amore" [Ladies who have understanding of love], heralds the arrival of the "praise style"; while the third, "Li occhi dolenti per pietà del core" [Grieving eyes through compassion for the soul], serves to preface the verses written after Beatrice's death.[41]

The text's multifaceted orderliness is backed by the rigid linearity of its story. Yet, although in chronological terms this linearity is unquestionable, if one considers the *Vita nova* narratologically a much more complex and fragmented structuring becomes apparent.[42] Thus it is normal for the same event to be presented from two slightly differing perspectives: on the one hand, the poetic account and, on the other, the prose narrative, as we saw earlier with respect to the sexual dynamics of the first "maravigliosa visione" (III.3 [1.14]) [marvelous/miraculous/wondrous vision]. In addition, not infrequently, an incident is further complicated by the *divisio textus*'s prose paraphrase, which provides a third take on it. A good example of this graduated storytelling may be found in Dante's treatment of the lover's encounter with Amore "come peregrino leggeramente vestito e di vili drappi" (IX.3 [4.3]) [like a pilgrim lightly/skimpily dressed in shabby clothes], who explains the need to change his screen lady:

A me parve che Amore mi chiamasse, e dicessemi queste parole: "Io vegno da quella donna la quale è stata tua lunga difesa, e so che lo suo rivenire non sarà a gran tempi; e però quello cuore che io ti facea avere a lei, io l'ho meco, e portolo a donna la quale sarà tua difensione, come questa era." (IX.5 [4.5])

[It seemed to me that Love was calling me, and was saying these words to me: "I come from that woman who has long been your defense, and I know that her return will not be for a long time; and therefore that heart which I had you give to her, I have it with me, and I carry it to a woman who will be your defense, as this one was."]

Quando mi vide, mi chiamò per nome,
e disse: "Io vegno di lontana parte,
ov'era lo tuo cor per mio volere;
e recolo a servir novo piacere."
(IX.11–12 [4.11–12])

[When he saw me, he called me by name, | and said: "I come from a distant part, | where your heart was by my will; | and I bear it to serve a new pleasure."]

Ne la seconda [part of the sonnet, namely, the lines cited above] dico quello ch'elli mi disse, avvegna che non compiutamente per tema ch'avea di discovrire lo mio secreto. (IX.13 [4.13])

[In the second part I say/write that which he said to me, albeit not fully for fear that I had of revealing my secret.]

Each version introduces new details. The cumulative effect is to present an experience of some complexity—a complexity that can be achieved only by the coming together of the *libello*'s three primary forms through which the story is told: narrative prose, poetry, and critical prose, thereby highlighting the fundamental and unassailable unity of the "book of the *Vita nova*." It is the interplay of its different registers that defines the *libello*, is the source of its *novitas*, and bears its salvific message. By portraying an event from a variety of angles, Dante stresses the intricacy of things, especially if divinely willed. In temporal terms, he reminds us that the *Vita nova* brings together texts composed at different times and records intuitions belonging to different moments, thereby underscoring the complexity of providential time in which past, present, and future congruently coalesce.[43] In psychological terms, he appears to be hinting at the fragmentariness of memory—the patchwork ways in which we reconstruct the past. At the same time, he also draws attention to the act of writing: the rhetorical *variatio* of composition and his own mastery of such "variation," as well as the control that he is able to exercise over his *materia* and its representation. Nevertheless, I suspect that the main reason for this approach is made clear in the *Vita nova*'s opening: "sotto la quale rubrica io trovo scritte le parole le quali è mio intendimento d'assemplare in questo libello; e se non tutte, almeno la loro sentenzia" (I.1 [1.1]) [under which rubric I find written the words that it is my intention to copy in this little book; and if not all, at least their vital meaning]. Words in themselves are never enough, even if backed up by other words, especially as it is impossible to "copy" "every word." Ultimately, our responsibility is to go beyond "words," namely beyond the text's literal level and its style, by interpreting their divinely sanctioned "sentenzia." And yet, it is only thanks to the poet's "parole" that the *prosimetrum*'s "essential meaning" can be appreciated.

The *Vita nova*'s narrative flow is further disrupted by its recurring digressions that veer between topics as diverse as the effects of Beatrice's "mirabile saluto" (XI.1 [5.1]) [marvelous/miraculous/wondrous greeting], the theory of personification, connections between literary languages, numerology, different calendrical types, various forms of pilgrimage, physiology and psychology, and even a foray into lexicography. In any case, as I noted earlier, the *libello* actually tells two stories, that of the lover and that of the poet—stories that, like the prose and the poetry (see the subsection "Appearance" below), increasingly merge. The *Vita nova*'s didactic ambitions involve not only salvation but also other aspects of life. The aim seems to be to acknowledge the intricate weave of reality. Complexity, the central medieval tenet of plurality in oneness, namely, the intimate relationship between macrocosm and microcosm, structures the *libello*. Two such microcosms, the female and male protagonists, are, appropriately, both emblems of involvedness. Beatrice integrates conventional love lyric elements with behaviors and social connections proper to a well-born Florentine woman, to which Dante adds Marian and hagiographic elements, tesserae taken from the love story told in the Song of Songs and its exegetical tradition, and, most boldly, Christological details. Indeed, as the story's third protagonist declares, the *donna* even subsumes him into herself: "E chi volesse sottilmente considerare, quella Beatrice chiamerebbe Amore, per molta simiglianza che ha meco" (XXIV.5 [15.5]) [And who would like to consider subtly, would call that Beatrice Love, for the similarity that she has with me]. The man, in his turn, is a lover, a citizen, a member of the city's elite, an intellectual, and, of course, a writer[44]—a writer in fact, as the *prooemium* categorically asserts, who, unusually, is a master of all aspects of his trade. He is a *scriptor*, a *compilator*, a *commentator*, and an *auctor* (see below), who, when he composes the *Vita nova*, is in almost perfect control of his *materia* and *ars*.

PLURILINGUALISM, LANGUAGE, LITERATURE

Despite conventional critical claims regarding the *Vita nova*'s formal and thematic monolingualism, the *libello*, in fact, is a rigorously organized—I suspect that this feature too has encouraged ideas regarding its supposed standardization—"hybrid" and heterogeneous text. The range of its interests is reflected in the variety of its style and, in particular, in the range of its sources and vocabulary. I thus believe that it is appropriate to define the *Vita nova* as Dante's first attempt at composing a "plurilingual" work. In Dante scholarship, the term *plurilinguismo* is normally restricted to the *Commedia* and is used to describe the poem's experimental, theoretically self-reflective, and stylistically, structurally, and linguistically eclectic character,[45] in which the highest forms of classical oratory merge with the incomprehensible splutterings of demons without each discrete formal element losing its own singularity. Yet, while no other of Dante's works comes close to the *Commedia*'s revolutionary heterogeneity, this does not preclude the *Vita nova*, the *Convivio*, and even some of Dante's poems from having their own plurilingual ambitions. The "absolute" *plurilinguismo* of the *Commedia* constitutes the end point of a complex stylistic and intellectual undertaking, while that of the *Vita nova* reveals Dante at the beginning of this process, as he attempted to find ways to bring together different genres, textual forms, and discourses, and, specifically, their different registers and vocabularies.

Let's consider three concrete examples of the diverse ways in which, in the *Vita nova*, Dante worked with, adapted, and integrated the languages and literary traditions with which he had come into contact. I deliberately begin with the least ostentatious case, building up to the most bold expression, since I wish to make clear both the distinctiveness and variety of the *libello*'s plurilingual procedures and their dissimilarities from the *Commedia*'s *plurilinguismo*. The poem's experimental eclecticism had a long gestation, and, with the *Vita nova*, we ought not forget, we are at its birth.

Dante meticulously clarifies the reasons for the intensity of Beatrice's grief at her father's death:

> Onde con ciò sia cosa che cotale partire sia doloroso a coloro che rimangono e sono stati amici di colui che se ne va; e nulla sia sì intima amistade come da buon padre a buon figliuolo e da buon figliuolo a buon padre; e questa donna fosse in altissimo grado di bontade, e lo suo padre, sì come da molti si crede e vero è, fosse bono in alto grado; manifesto è che questa donna fue amarissimamente piena di dolore. (XXII.2 [13.2])

> [Hence given that such a departure is painful for those who remain and had been friends of the one who goes; and there is no friendship so intimate as that of a good father toward a good child and that of a good child toward a good father; and given that this woman was in the highest grade of goodness, and her father, as many believe and is true, was good in a high grade; it is manifest that this woman was most bitterly full of grief.]

The explanation for Beatrice's pain is structured as a syllogism, with the start of the opening premise—"con ciò sia cosa che"—and the beginning of the proposition—"manifesto è"—calquing and translating Latin scholastic argumentative formulas. At the same time, the remainder of the long phrase draws on the language of the literature on friendship, with its origins in Cicero; on scripture—"Nemo novit Filium nisi Pater, neque Patrem quis novit nisi Filius" (Matt. 11:27) [Nobody knows the Son if not the Father, nor does anyone know the Father if not the Son]—; and on the Marian tradition of the acute suffering of the *Mater dolorosa*. What is striking is not so much the range of sources making up the syllogism, though its diversity is suggestive, but the fact that Dante should have efficiently synthesized the discrete elements into a new single whole. Despite the diversity of its makeup, Dante ensured that, thanks to a syntax centered on repetition, balance, and alliteration, the sentence achieves something akin to cohesion of register that, thereby, controls and harmonizes the sundry constituent parts. In formal, if not in ideological terms, the phrase is marked by what might be termed a "flattening out" of difference. At the same time, it is important to stress that "flattening out" is not identical to negating or avoiding "difference": scholastic formulas and scriptural intertexts are each still distinguishable and hence distinct.[46] This procedure is, of course, unlike Dante's approach in the *Commedia*, where the stylistic synthesis is firmly predicated on bringing out the unique characteristics of the assorted elements.

The above sentence offers an example of what we might term the moderate end of the *Vita nova*'s plurilingualism. In other passages Dante is more obviously intent on bringing out distinctions between different sets of vocabulary, as in the following sentence:

> E poi che alquanto mi fue sollenato questo lagrimare, misimi ne la mia camera, là ov'io potea lamentarmi sanza essere udito; e quivi, chiamando misericordia a la donna de la cortesia, e dicendo "Amore, aiuta lo tuo fedele," m'addormentai come un pargoletto battuto lagrimando. (XII.2 [5.9])

> [And then that this weeping had somewhat eased, I went to my room, there where I could lament without being heard; and here, calling out for mercy to the lady of courtesy, and saying "Love, help your faithful one," I fell asleep like a beaten small child weeping.]

Weeping lovers who implore their ladies for mercy and avoid the company of others while addressing Love and declaring their fealty are erotic and lyric commonplaces; and some of the vocabulary evidently comes from this tradition: *lamentare, donna, cortesia, Amore, fedele*. Other terms, most notably *sollenare* and *lagrimare*, are also present, albeit (very) rarely, in early Italian vernacular amatory lyric poetry. Most interesting, naturally, are those words that have no precedent in writing about love: *camera, misericordia, addormentare, pargoletto*, and *battere*. Thus *camera* is present in a range of early Florentine prose texts and in Brunetto's *Rettorica* and vernacularization of Cicero's *Pro rege Deiotaro*, before its flourishing in the *Vita nova*;[47] *misericordia* may be found in religious and moral prose, including Brunetto Latini and Bono Giamboni, and in the *Novellino*; *addormentare* is rare, a few instances in early Florentine prose;[48] *pargoletto*'s earliest attestation seems to be in the *Vita nova*;[49] finaly, *battere* has a fairly wide dissemination occurring several times in the *Novellino*, in Bono's *volgarizzamento* of Orosius, in some early Florentine prose texts, and even in verse 8 of Brunetto's *Tesoretto*.[50] The situation that Dante is describing in XII.2 [5.9] is conventional; however, the formal means he employs to evoke the lover's piteous state, and its emblematic capture in the domestic and lifelike simile of the "pargoletto battuto," are anything but standard. Indeed, Dante's aim appears to be to broaden the vocabulary (and imagery) of writing about love by drawing on other traditions and possibly even on external reality, while highlighting the artificiality of generic restrictive lexica. Significantly, given the *Vita nova*'s prosimetrical character, he enriches the lyric treatment of love by introducing words overwhelmingly tied to writing in prose.

The most radical and sustained instance of the *Vita nova*'s plurilingualism is found in one of the *libello*'s strategically most important zones. As was common in the Middle Ages, the book's opening serves to introduce the work as a whole by establishing its main concerns, its principal formal and structural characteristics, and its major sources.[51] Although Dante himself refers to the "proemio che precede questo libello" (XXVIII.2 [19.2]) [the proem that precedes this little book], we cannot be certain of its remit. According to Gorni, the "proem" stretches at least as far as paragraph 13 of the third chapter of Barbi's text; and, in keeping with its traditional proemial functions, it offers considerable insight into the *prosimetrum*, and especially into its plurilingual goals.[52] Thus the lexical and connotative range of the chapter in Gorni's edition is quite remarkable. It embraces the language and structures of exegesis, of scripture, of science (especially astronomy, physiology, and psychology), of linguistic theory (the reflections on Beatrice's name), of symbolism, of scholastic logic, of different types of religious writing, of the classical epic (the reference to "quella parola del poeta Omero" (II.8 [1.9]) [that word of the poet Homer]), of vision and dream literature, and of the Romance lyric. It further enriches its Italian with Latinisms, Gallicisms, and phrases in Latin.[53] This is a heady stylistic mix, almost as radical for the mid-1290s, not least given the conditions of Italian prose at the time, as the *Commedia* would be for the early years of the new century.[54] And not to recognize the links between the experimentation of the two is, I believe, to ignore how profound and sustained were Dante's deliberations on the languages of his world, or better, on the possibilities they offered to a writer bold enough to try to integrate them. The *Vita nova*'s prologue stands as an unambiguous statement of stylistic intent, ambition, and "uniqueness"; and it is an essential function of its declarative aims that, in it, Dante's plurilingualism should be so persistent and extensive. Indeed, as far as I have been able to ascertain, no other section of the *prosimetrum* is as formally and intellectually eclectic as the "proemio." As convention dictated, from the outset, Dante wanted to leave no doubt as regards the *forma tractandi* of his *libello*.

Definition of the *forma tractandi*, the "form of treatment," was a basic feature of the medieval *accessus*, the scholastic introductions to a text and its author.[55] Confirming both the *prooemium*'s introductory functions and the *Vita nova*'s close ties to contemporary literary criticism, other elements belonging to the *accessus* tradition are discernible in its opening. Thus the book's *titulus* is clearly stated, as is its *materia*, "subject matter." The key phrase "*Incipit vita nova*" signifies both "The/my new life begins" and "The title is *Vita nova*" (I.1 [1.1]). Indeed, one way of considering the *libello* is as an extended commentary on its title, so that it can be read as a kind of "super-*accessus*"—more generic hybridity—a characteristic that is strengthened by the fact that it can also be seen as a comprehensive presentation of its *causa efficiens*, "efficient cause," namely its *auctor*, and the *vita auctoris* was also a regular *accessus* feature. Finally, Dante alludes to the *intentio auctoris*, another *accessus* subheading: "sotto la quale rubrica io trovo le parole le quali è mio intendimento d'assemplare in questo libello; e se non tutte, almeno la loro sententia" (I.1 [1.1]) [under which rubric I find written the words that it is my intention to copy in this little book; and if not all, at least their vital meaning].[56]

In the *proemio*, Dante illuminates the *Vita nova*'s plurilingual "form of treatment"—arguably its most original trait—not just thanks to the impressive range of the prologue's vocabulary and interests, but also thanks to its evoking the main obstacle to linguistic and "stylistic" assimilation, the *genera dicendi*. According to the classificatory category of the "types of speaking," every literary work belonged to one of three "styles" (the "high," the "middle," and the "low"), with each *stilus* deemed a quasi-self-sufficient system defined by its own particular class of text, exemplary authoritative works, topics, and vocabulary. Of the various medieval classifications of literature it was not just the most influential but also, because of its emphasis on the need for authors to ensure that, in general though not necessarily absolutely, the three *stili* were to be kept separate, the one that most affected and determined the formal character of medieval writing.[57] Thus, when Dante recorded verbatim the outburst in Latin of each of the three psycho-physiological *spiriti* deeply perturbed on seeing Beatrice, he was also intent on making a metaliterary point (II.4–6 [1.5–7]). "Heu miser, quia frequenter impeditus ero deinceps!" [Oh unhappy me, because from now on I will be frequently impeded] is a pithy example of the "low" style, one of whose distinguishing features was *soloecismus*.[58] In the same vein, the mix of scriptural and "tragic" classical intertexts that characterizes the first phrase qualifies it as "high" in register: "Ecce deus fortior me, qui veniens dominabitur michi" [Here is a god stronger than me, who coming will have dominion over me].[59] Finally, the exclusively scriptural character of the words of the "spirito animale" [animal spirit] marks them out as *sermo humilis*—"Apparuit iam beatitudo vestra" [Your beatitude has already appeared][60] which, by the late thirteenth century, had become increasingly associated with "comedy" and hence the "middle" *stilus*.[61] In light of the prologue's rich plurilingualism and of the strategic placement of the three spirits, when Dante alluded to the *tria genera dicendi*, he was making a defiant statement of poetics and self-definition: his *libello* was a "hybrid" text that could boldly and unusually incorporate the three discrete *stili*.

To speak of the *Vita nova* as a plurilingual text is not usual. Yet, as evidenced by the spirits' speech, the *libello* is a work in which different languages do coexist. To date, these intriguing snippets of Latin embedded in the *prosimetrum*'s prose and, in one instance, in its verse, have been seen as the sole element conventionally connecting the *Vita nova* to the tradition of medieval plurilingual writing.[62] In this respect, scholars tend to treat them as largely unexceptional instances of the far-from-uncommon practice in the Middle Ages of enriching, usually for contrastive purposes, the predominant language of a text with fragments in a different tongue. Although there is little doubt that, at a quite basic level, the *Vita nova*'s Latin expressions can be subsumed under this stylistic procedure, their significance increases in import and originality if they are also, and principally, considered as part of a sustained and wide-ranging plurilingual experiment that deliberately strives to go beyond established writerly norms.

As a consequence, the *Vita nova*'s assessment of the relationship between Latin and the *volgare*—always at the center of Dante's thinking and art—cannot but also increase in complexity.

It is striking that rather than draw traditional distinctions between Latin and the vernacular, with the former language always in a position of privilege, Dante redimensioned established perceptions of the relationship between Latin and the *volgare*. Instead of presenting this in clichéd hierarchical terms, he stressed the connections, similarities even, between the two languages.[63] Thus Dante openly highlighted the ease with which Latin could be transformed into the vernacular. Glossing the incipit of "O voi che per la via d'Amor passate" [Oh you who pass along the way of Love], he explained that, in the sonnet's opening, he had employed Jeremiah's actual words: "Intendo chiamare li fedeli d'Amore per quelle parole di Geremia profeta che dicono: 'O vos omnes qui transitis per viam, attendite et videte si est dolor sicut dolor meus'" (VII.7 [2.18]) [I intend to call Love's devotees by means of those words of the prophet Jeremiah that say: "Oh all of you who pass along the way, consider and see if there is a grief like my grief"]. The fact that the prophet's words were in Latin, as the poet himself underlined by quoting them, is not considered an issue. The impression created is of a fluid, "unproblematic" interchangeability between the two languages—an exchange between equals.[64] Long before Dante asserted that "se alcuna figura o colore rettorico è conceduto a li poete, conceduto è a li rimatori" (XXV.7 [16.7]) [if any figure or rhetorical color is conceded to the poets, it is conceded to the those who write rhymes], since "dire per rima in volgare tanto è quanto dire per versi in latino" (XXV.4 [16.4]) [to write in rhyme in the vernacular is the same as to write in verse in Latin], he had begun to dismantle the barriers that traditionally divided the "natural" from the "artificial" language, and hence their users. Thus nowhere in the *Vita nova* does the poet assert the linguistic supremacy of Latin. In chapter XXV [16], language is not an issue. Dante exclusively focuses on the role of the *auctores* as literary and not as linguistic models for "vernacular poets" (XXV.4 [16.4])—a status they had acquired largely as a result of the fact that they had begun to write "anticamente" (XXV.3 [16.3]) [in ancient times], rather than as a consequence of some inherent superiority.[65]

Dante makes it evident that, in his writing, matters of esteem, whether linguistic or of subject matter, have no bearing on his choice of language. Indeed, what *materia* could be more prestigious than Beatrice's assumption into heaven (XXVIII.1 [19.1])? Instead, Dante reveals that the determination as to which language he should employ is conditioned either by personal preference ("lo intendimento mio," namely, "my intention") or by practical factors: writing to "li principi de la terra" (XXX.1 [19.8]) [princes of the earth/land] he needs to utilize a language, Latin, that his addressees will understand.[66] Questions of value and hierarchy have no bearing on his linguistic decision-making. As far as he is concerned, the two languages constitute equal alternatives and are in essence interchangeable, as he indicates in the title of his *libello*, given that it is impossible to establish whether *Vita nova* is to be read as a Latin or as a vernacular phrase.[67] Dante's claims for the *volgare* in the *libello* were indisputably radical and new. Yet by investigating the potential of the vernacular as a broad language of culture, and by offering concrete confirmation of its expressive and intellectual, namely plurilingual, capacities, the poet left little doubt that his claims were anything but unfounded. Ultimately, if the *volgare*, like Latin, had not been a language of considerable sophistication, range, and flexibility, he could never have written the *Vita nova*. As far as Dante was concerned, the vernacular, as the plurilingual character of the *Vita nova* eloquently indicated, was potentially as rich and as significant a language as Latin.

The *libello*'s linguistic and stylistic plurilingualism and its wide-ranging engagement with an extensive array of texts and traditions (see the following subsection)—the building blocks of its composite character—are effectively controlled by a narrative development that, for all its fragmentariness and shifts in perspective, attests to providence's inexorability. More significantly, the *Vita nova* is regulated by the coherence of its ideological and cultural interests. Thus the lesson on spiritual salvation is complemented by the declaration of literary *renovatio*. Both concerns announce the need for and the possibility of renewal; and, just as salvation entails a radical transformation, so the shift from Latin to the vernacular requires an equally sweeping process of change—a process, in fact, that, as with the coming into being of the *homo novus*, affects every area of life. Consequently, the *Vita nova*'s plurilingualism and rich intertextuality are also signs of its effort to engage with the complexities of the contemporary world. At the end of the Duecento, love in its Christian and secular ramifications was a vital and multifaceted concept that touched on many areas of experience. It was therefore the ideal hook on to which to hang the *libello*'s overarching religious and cultural reassessment. For Dante, love was a point of departure rather than of arrival. The *Vita nova* plots and reveals the vernacular's capacity to deal with the spiritual and intellectual richness of reality, of which love, for all its significance, is just one aspect. In fact, the "little book" does rather more than this. It innovatively confirms the vernacular's ability to accommodate and integrate the density of the real in a new, flexible, stratified, and overarching textual form—"il libro della *Vita Nuova*." As the only authentic deity of love—the "sire de la cortesia" (XLII.3 [31.3]) [lord of courtesy], the good and merciful Lord—the Christian God is the *Amore* from whom emanates the complexity of being, "colui a cui tutte le cose vivono" (XLII.2 [31.2]) [he for whom all things live]. In light of the *Vita nova*'s functions as a *vestigium* of the divine and of the divinity's presence in our lives, it is God who fundamentally inspires and legitimates the breadth of its interests. To write about love is necessarily to write about "everything"; and deeply conscious of this, the poet brings the *libello* to a close by recognizing his present limitations and the need to "study as much as he can" (XLII.2 [31.2]). Only thanks to this effort will he acquire the intellectual and artistic proficiency that, in the future, will allow him to "speak of" his beloved Beatrice in a manner that suitably recognizes the universal realities of which she is a *signum*.

Models, Sources, Unity

The way in which Dante drew on the diverse registers and languages of his world in order to create a new plurilingual synthesis that revealed the potential of the vernacular, or more precisely of the *lingua di sì*, and established his own standing as the supreme *auctor* and *auctoritas* of this new literary tradition is a hallmark of his writerly ambition and of the seriousness of the *Vita nova*'s engagement with contemporary literature and intellectual culture. Accordingly, the *libello*'s linguistic and stylistic eclecticism is complemented by the range of its sources, the variety of traditions that it evokes, and its generic fluidity.

I do not believe that it is an exaggeration to assert that the *Vita nova* constitutes a new literary genre. As we have begun to see, it shares characteristics with a number of long-established and broad arch-genres, such as the *prosimetrum* and the *comentum*, as well as with a variety of other clearly recognizable textual forms. At the same time, it cannot conveniently and tidily be subsumed under any of these. Thus its metaliterary vigor and its tight integration of prose and verse have no precedent in canonical prosimetrical works such as Boethius's *Consolation of Philosophy*, Martianus Capella's *De nuptiis Philologiae et Mercurii*, or Alan of Lille's *De planctu Naturae*.[68] Equally, conventional commentaries lack the narrative and critical coherence of the *Vita nova* and were never, as we have seen, the result of an act of self-commentary. Bob Hollander is correct to note that the *libello* "has no precise or certain model in Western literature.... The *Vita nuova* is, as one can rarely say with such certainty, unique. Nothing in the tradition of Dante's Romance predecessors, or indeed of any precursors, serves as a sufficient model."[69] Yet scholars persist in trying to squeeze Dante's pre-exilic masterpiece into inappropriately restrictive textual cages, claiming that its primary, and therefore controlling, influence is to be sought in elegy, in glossed manuscripts of Ovid, in the Occitan *razos* and *vidas*, in Cicero's *De amicitia*, in Romance narrative and lyric works (in particular authorially organized lyric collections), in Augustine's *Confessions* and *Retractationes*, in hagiography, in Brunetto Latini's *Rettorica,* and in the various other texts and traditions that have suggestively been put forward as antecedents of Dante's "little book." Most of these proposed models and sources, to a lesser or greater extent, do indeed lie behind the *libello*. However, not one of them is able on its own to account either for the *Vita nova*'s ambitious ideological aims or for its formal range and quality. The texts that come close to achieving this are the glossed manuscripts of some of the poetic scriptural books, specifically the Lamentations of Jeremiah, the Psalter, and the Song of Songs.[70] The annotated *Canticum* in particular, thanks to its blend of verse and narrative and exegetical prose, as well as its emphasis on love, salvation, and large-scale metaliterary reflection, offered Dante an alluringly rich and complex model to follow as he endeavored to create a new and totalizing text that could establish the potential of the vernacular as a language of culture.

The only contemporary text that can unquestionably and completely account for the *Vita nova*'s "hybrid" and plurilingual aims and identity is the Bible, which, according to standard medieval belief, drew on every language and every *genus* in order to portray its providential account of salvation through a harmonious mix of prose and verse. The supreme prosimetrical work of the Middle Ages, it should not be forgotten, was God's book; and it is thus more than fitting that, in addition to the *Vita nova*'s register and ideology, the Bible—no other text is as visibly and extensively present in the "little book"—should legitimate too its most obvious formal feature, as well as its capacity to fuse the plurality of its antecedents into a logically unified and evolving narrative and ideological whole—a whole, in fact, that is confidently greater than the sum of its parts, as befits a work modeled on the *exemplum* of the *Deus artifex*.

As medieval proemial convention dictated, Dante affirmed the *libello*'s consistency—and also its uniqueness—from the very start of the *Vita nova*. The source of both these fundamental attributes, the poet made clear, is to be sought in two closely related elements: first, in the proem's distinctly biblical register, which resounds with scriptural echoes,[71] and, second, and just as significantly, in the "libro de la mia memoria" [book of my memory] and specifically in "quella parte" [that part] where "si trova una rubrica la quale dice: *Incipit vita nova*" (I.1 [1.1]) [is found a rubric that says: *Incipit vita nova*]. Dante claimed that he was not inventing anything but simply copying from ("assemplare") and glossing ("la loro [of the "words"] sentenzia," namely, "their vital meaning") a preexisting scripturally inflected text,[72] whose unity is guaranteed by its being a "book"—and not just any book but one worthy of dissemination and commentary—the distinctiveness of which is assured by the possessive *mia*. Furthermore, as the *Vita nova* progresses, and as the providential character of the story it tells increasingly emerges, it becomes ever more apparent that its ultimate author—its primary *causa efficiens*, as the Aristotelian *accessus* would have put it—is God.[73] The "book of memory" and "la divina scrittura" (*Par.* 29.90) have a supreme and unimpeachable common origin, which, in the last instance, unproblematically accounts for the former's close dependence on the latter. What we are reading is a divine *signum*, the work of an "inspired" *scriba Dei*, which has at its core an account of God's symbolic presence in the world. No doubts can thus reasonably be entertained about the *Vita nova*'s logic and exceptionality.

A problem, nevertheless, arises in connection with my scriptural-cum-plurilingual reading of the *libello*. Given the prominence granted to classical writers in chapter XXV—according to Gorni, the book's central, because sixteenth, chapter—why did Dante cite the *auctores*, and what might their relevance be for the *Vita nova*?

Their functions, whether individually or collectively, are in fact quite complex. Thus it is likely that the allusion to Virgil and the *Aeneid* is meant to highlight the *Vita nova*'s ties to the "tragic" "high" style, while that to Lucan—for the Middle Ages both a poet and a historian—indicates the truthfulness of the *prosimetrum*'s account. In addition, the epic poetry of Homer, Virgil, and Lucan points to and authorizes the *Vita nova*'s narrative ambitions, while its lyric dimension is presented as having its precedent in Horace, the archetypal *liricus*, and in the love poetry of Ovid, the *magister Amoris*. More than anything, what the "bella scola" (*Inf.* 4.94) of *auctores* highlights is that the *libello* cannot conventionally be subsumed under the "authority" of any one of them. To put it another way, the *Vita nova* is more than just another book about love with its roots in Ovid. Instead, their co-presence confirms that it is a markedly original composite work that fuses different traditions and *stili*, as Dante had intimated in the *proemio*, while at the same time transforming and adapting these to its new needs as a vernacular and Christian text dealing with that most demanding and essential of subjects, the relationship between God and humanity.

For both Dante and the *libello*, however, the most interesting reverberations are those arising from the reference to Horace.[74] As is well known, it is in the *Vita nova*, while explicating his own poems, that Dante for the first time presented himself in the guise of both vernacular *auctor* and *commentator*, the very same profile that, since antiquity, only Horace, among the canonical writers, was considered to have.[75] Although Dante highlighted his status as an *auctor* by pointing to his affinities to the major classical literary *auctoritates*, only Horace the *praeceptor* and the *Ars poetica*, his magisterial work of literary reflection, could properly authorize Dante's credentials as a theorist and critic of poetry, as is immediately obvious from the manner in which the ancient poet and his work are introduced: "Per Orazio, parla l'uomo a la scienzia medesima sì come ad altra persona; e non solamente sono parole d'Orazio, ma dicele quasi recitando lo modo del buono Omero, quivi ne la sua Poetria: *Dic michi, Musa, virum*" (XXV.9 [16.9]) [For Horace, the man speaks to the science itself, but says, reciting the mode of good Homer, here in his *Ars poetica*: Tell me, Muse, about the man]. Even more significantly, as far as the *Vita nova*'s textual remit is concerned, Horace signals and validates another of its key traits—its standing as literary criticism.[76]

And there is more in the chapter. As far as I am aware, when scholars examine the implications of its classical allusions, they fail to notice that the chapter includes a sixth and preliminary reference: "Dico che lo vidi venire; onde, con ciò sia cosa che venire dica moto locale, e localmente mobile per sé, secondo lo Filosofo, sia solamente corpo, appare che io ponga Amore essere corpo" (XXV.2 [16.2]) [I say that I saw him coming; hence, since to come indicates local motion, and to be locally mobile by itself, according to the Philosopher, is something that belongs to the body only, it appears that I posit Love to be a body]. In addition to its various other discourses, the *Vita nova* also speaks the language of philosophy and doctrine. In Dante's *libello*, or rather, in its treatment of prosopopeia, Aristotle merges with the *poetae*,[77] just as the *auctores* merge with each other; and the effects of these syntheses can be felt across the *Vita nova* as a whole, not least because, as De Robertis has argued, the issues raised by prosopopeia can be extended to the work in its entirety.[78]

By evoking classical culture, Dante succeeds in establishing the ambition, range, and variety of his work, as well as the integration within it of its different strands. There is little doubt that the references to the ancients authorize both the vernacular poet and his text, as well as elevate the pair to a level close to the pedestal on which the Middle Ages placed the classical world.[79] Furthermore, the allusions help foreground the tremendous potential and flexibility of the vernacular *auctor* and his language and literature, given that the *Vita nova* is able to accommodate key elements epitomizing each of the classical *auctores*. And all this is expertly and effectively done by making recourse to the most respected and appropriate *auctoritates*. At the same time, the *Vita nova*'s relationship to classical culture is largely generic. It bears principally upon the work's broad ambitions and its intellectual and artistic macrostructures. Indeed, before the chapter on prosopopeia, apart from the reference to Homer, there are no other markers to suggest any kind of real affinity, never mind a close one, between the *Vita nova* and classical literature. Unlike the other two authors, Guido Cavalcanti and Jeremiah, representatives of the Romance and scriptural traditions—traditions that, throughout the *libello*, have a major and constant bearing both on the details and on the overarching structures of its form and content—until chapter XXV, classical poetry's sway over Dante's text is, at best, marginal. Indeed, classical literature, with its championing of the discrete *genera dicendi*, stands in direct opposition to Dante's *modus tractandi*, unable to legitimate and account for the *prosimetrum*'s plurilingualism and calculated defiance of the doctrine of the *genera*. There is thus a sizable gap between the *Vita nova*'s striking formal and ideological syncretism, not to mention the minutiae of its style and language, and the literary solutions of the *auctores*. As will be one of his hallmarks throughout his career, Dante bends the great authors of antiquity to his needs, subordinating them to the demands of the new Christian and vernacular realities of his world and to his own writerly ambitions, as well as utilizing them as tools to aid in the interpretation of his "little book." Furthermore, as we will soon see, there were also local, Florentine reasons for citing the *auctores* (see the concluding subsection).

EXEGESIS: RESOLVING PROBLEMS OF INTERPRETATION

There is, nonetheless, a glaring yet vital paradox at the heart of the *Vita nova*'s metaliterary structure. At first sight, in the *libello*, Dante seems anything but the kind of author who encourages and expects his readers to exercise their critical skills. Thus the *prosimetrum* seems effectively constrained and determined by the forms of the *comentum* tradition: the opening sentences recall an *accessus*, while large swaths of the prose are given over to the scholastic expository technique of the *divisio textus*. It would appear, therefore, that Dante was actually intent on delimiting, denying even, independent interpretation by rigorously controlling textual meaning. However, the immediate impression created by the poet's large-scale recourse to the typical conventions of medieval hermeneutics is almost certainly partial, if not actually misleading. It is significant that these critical structures are overwhelmingly applied just to the poems and are employed to analyze and define individual poems as self-sufficient textual entities. The *Vita nova*, with the possible exception of its first two *accessus*-like sentences, does not benefit from a similarly traditional commentary.

That, in its second sentence, the *Vita nova* should be introduced as a *compilatio* made up of copied "words" and exegesis was not in itself unusual. This was, in fact, the basic defining characteristic of many medieval manuscripts in which selected texts were accompanied by critical glosses. The *libello* takes a decidedly strange turn, however, with the entry of "A ciascun'alma presa" toward the proem's close. It now becomes clear that the copyist, who is equally the *compilator* and the *commentator*, is also the *auctor* of the "parole." The *Vita nova* is unique, a text without precedent, since it is the product of and integrates writerly activities that were normally, not to say, invariably, considered as distinct.[80] Moreover, ahead of the *libello*, sustained self-commentary that expressly made recourse to the forms of scholastic criticism was unknown in Western literary culture. To complicate matters further, the idea that vernacular texts were worthy of commentary was, at the very least, highly challenging. The *Vita nova* thus quickly defines both itself and its author as exceptional. At the same time, and as will become common in Dante's oeuvre, it also recognizes its roots in and debts to the tradition. The *libello* openly highlights its profound interest in exegesis by repeatedly returning to established interpretive structures, such as those of the *divisio textus*. However, as I adumbrated, this conservative analysis is restricted to the poems, whose formal and metrical character is already fixed in the tradition. Even "Donne ch'avete"'s *novitas* is to be sought in its content and not in its form: "E però propuosi di prendere per matera de lo mio parlare sempre mai quello che fosse loda di questa gentilissima" (XVIII.9 [10.11]) [And therefore I proposed always to take as subject matter of my speech that which would be praise of this most gentle woman]. To put it simply, when it came to his poems, Dante conventionally applied the methods of traditional commentary to traditional texts.[81] Conversely, since there is little that is obviously traditional about "the book of the *Vita Nuova*," he found it necessary and appropriate to develop a new type of exegesis for the new type of literature he was forging. It was a type of exegesis, in fact, that did not find its raison d'être outside the text, in established critical procedure, but that, as I have been attempting to document, emerged from within the new text itself;[82] it therefore assumed a new type of *lector* who, subtly steered by the *auctor*, would become directly involved in fashioning the new criticism. Most strikingly, the readers of the *Vita nova* no longer needed to be versed in the practices of scholastic criticism. They simply needed to allow their sensibilities and wit to be guided by the text, so that even "li più semplici" (III.15 [2.2]) [the most simple] could profit from it, as befitted a work of salvation. At the same time, the "subtle," by exercizing their learning and intelligence, would appreciate the *libello* as a work of revolutionary cultural and intellectual complexity, as well as of deliverance.[83]

It is thus clear that the *Vita nova*'s originality as a metaliterary text transcends both its status as one of the first Italian vernacular translations of Latin critical language and its standing as the first self-commentary of the Western literary canon. In the *libello*, Dante was also intent on developing a new sort of criticism apt to clarify and accompany his new Christian vernacular literature. The *Vita nova* may not be commentary as this had been understood since the times of the ancients, but it is unquestionably profoundly interested in exegesis and in the potential of this to fuse with other textual forms while at the same time illuminating them. Indeed, the complexity, ambition, and coherence of Dante's critical enterprise can properly be appreciated only if considered in the round. As with the *Vita nova* in general, the "little book"'s metaliterary operation too is a composite. It is thus through the productive tension between the forms of the old and the new criticism that the full extent of *Dante critico*'s achievement, and hence of the *prosimetrum*'s metaliterary inventiveness, can be gauged. Just as the lyric poems are granted "new life" by being included in the *libello*, so established exegetical structures are revived by being incorporated into the *Vita nova* and "vernacularized." At the same time, the traditional character of both the verses and their critical prose accompaniment is underscored by the *novitas* of the *Vita nova*'s overarching literary and hermeneutic forms. The old prepares for and is subordinated to the new; and the *libello* announces and describes the birth not just of the *homo novus* but also of the *canticum novum* and the *commentarium novum*.

Appearance

Yet, on account of its difficulties and formal innovations, for all the poet's efforts at exercising control over his text and at providing its readers with a tailor-made exegetical framework, the *libello*—as we noted earlier—is a work very much prey to misreading. Its manuscript transmission offers telling evidence of this. The *Vita nova* creates doubts in the minds not just of its readers but also of its copyists. Thus, if one compares the oldest extant fourteenth-century manuscripts of the "little book," the differences in the ways in which they present Dante's *prosimetrum* are striking.[84] It soon becomes apparent that there is limited consistency in their paragraphing, in their use of initial capitalization, and in their textual layout.

Indeed, on occasion, the divergences are substantial. It is enough to think of Boccaccio's notorious decision to separate off and "marginalize" the *divisiones* in the two autograph manuscripts now preserved in the Capitular of Toledo and in the Vatican Library—a decision that marks a startling failure to appreciate the fundamental coherence of the "libro della *Vita Nuova*" and that can be deemed the most obvious example of the contemporary unease regarding the *Vita nova*'s textual identity.[85] Another area of scribal doubt concerns the treatment of the poetry, and hence its relationship to the prose. Thus the Strozzi codex sets the sonnets apart from the prose by means of paragraphing, spacing, and initial capitals, and, more specifically, by employing the established scribal format—two verses per line—to copy them. Conversely, the Chigiano L. VIII. 305, the oldest extant manuscript of the *Vita nova*, treats the verse as if it were prose. However, even if not always consistently, it does introduce line markers, something that, when copying the canzoni, the renowned early codex Martelli, produced between 1330 and 1350, omits to do. At the same time, the Martelli manuscript transcribes the sonnets by copying each verse on a new line and further emphasizes the poems' autonomy by using capitals at the start of quatrains and tercets. Boccaccio's autograph Chigiano L. V. 176, on the other hand, treats "le rime a mo' di prosa" [the poems as if they were prose], as also occurs in the Toledano.[86]

Even if, as is well known, the layout of prose and of poetry in medieval manuscripts could be the same, it is also very much the case that, logically, given the mutual exclusivity of the scribal solutions, not all (or perhaps any?) of the fourteenth-century manuscripts of the *Vita nova* can be said to reflect Dante's original layout for his *prosimetrum*. To try to establish how the poet might have wanted his exceptional *libello* to look is a matter of some import. This is not just for reasons of philological precision. In the *Vita nova*, Dante strove to fashion a new relationship between prose and poetry,[87] one that raised fundamental questions about the distinctiveness and functions of the two forms. In this respect, it is suggestive that, despite their individual solutions and eccentricities, if taken together, the fourteenth-century manuscripts of the *libello* do, in fact, reveal something about Dante's intentions as regards its appearance. With one exception, all the codices in their design and arrangement diminish the differences between prose and verse[88]—a solution that was anything but usual in the scribal treatment of texts that, in one way or another, brought together the two forms. This is, of course, self-apparent in those manuscripts that present the poetry as if it were prose. However, even the Martelli, by being written in two columns, whose width tidily matches the span of a hendecasyllable, and by using capitalizations at the beginning both of poems and of distinct sections of the prose, standardizes the appearance of the text. It thus seems reasonable to hypothesize that those manuscripts that transcribe the poetry as if it were prose, especially in light of the Martelli's harmonizing tendencies, were not simply following scribal convention but attempting to replicate a feature originally sanctioned by the poet himself. That this is not unlikely is supported by another trait that Dante introduced into the *Vita nova*, and that Wayne Storey has valuably highlighted: "Before each poem Dante always notes in the prose the poetic genre of the composition that will follow and either its partial or complete first verse. In the prose which immediately follows the poem, Dante reiterates the genre. . . . This essentially scribal system of reiteration establishes both linkage and framing devices for the physical act of copying the poems."[89] It is hard to imagine that, unless the poet aimed to present the prose and verse in a very similar, possibly identical, manner, such careful marking of the boundaries between the two forms would have been necessary. That Dante should have wanted to diminish, possibly elide, the difference between verse and prose fits in well both with his reevaluation of the role and standing of the two forms and with his aim to make of the *Vita nova* a new composite syncretic "book," in which poetry and prose come together to fashion a new type of fused literary language.

The manuscripts also disclose another key aspect of the visual form that Dante probably chose for the *Vita nova*. The evidence of their quirks and discrepancies strongly points to the fact that the "look" of the *Vita nova* on the page was peculiar. The *prosimetrum*'s atypical characteristics engendered what Storey has correctly termed scribal "uncertainty,"[90] which, in its turn, inevitably led to different solutions when the *scriptores* began the practical task of transcription. The problem, I suspect, was that copyists found it difficult to establish their scribal bearings when faced with Dante's *prosimetrum*, since, as we have seen, it was a work that lacked an obvious precedent. Thus, given the predominance of prose in the *libello*, vernacular lyric collections offered little guidance on how the *Vita nova* might best be reproduced. Equally, when judged against its most obvious

Latin textual models, the *libello* was neither a prosimetrical work in the manner of the *Consolation of Philosophy* nor a standard commentary to a corpus of lyrical texts, both of which had developed well-established and recognizable traits as regards their format on the page—traits to which, in both cases, the *Vita nova* did not evidently conform. In particular, it is normal for medieval manuscripts of Boethius's *Consolatio* visibly to distinguish between the prose and the poetry by means of decorated initials and paragraphing that separates the two forms. As a result, the metrical characteristics of the poems are carefully respected and each line of verse is plainly distinguished; in addition, the *metra* are at times written in two columns. Finally, marginal, interlinear, and other modes of commentary are clearly distinguished from Boethius's text by their collocation and by the size of their script, as occurs too in glossed lyric collections.[91] The problem with the *Vita nova* as far as its scribes were concerned was that Dante had not respected such traditional types of textual organization and difference.

Instead, the poet was intent on challenging and reconfiguring conventional distinctions between prose and verse, artistic text and commentary, narrative and lyric, in order to develop not just a new sort of macrotext but also a new idea of textuality. Consequently, I think that it is not unreasonable to assume that among Dante's aims when he composed the *Vita nova* was that of fashioning a new type of textual appearance—one that might grant his *libello* a distinct identity, not to say canonicity, that straight away would distinguish it from the established forms, not just of Latin textuality, but also of vernacular writing. In addition, the *Vita nova*'s original look would "prefigure" some of its primary concerns, most notably its committed engagement with *novitas*, which finds its principal literary expression, as with the *libello*'s outward form, through its dialectical relationship to the tradition. Dante's homogenizing synthesis of prose and verse alters not just the conventional manuscript layout in which the two forms were presented together but also the ways in which such hybrid texts were read. The poet's identical treatment of the prose and the poetry eliminated any sort of hierarchical relationship between the two, thereby countermanding the standard ranked rapport between canonical poetic text and subordinate prose commentary. Dante thus developed the traditional graded interdependence between verse and prose, which worked entirely in favor of the authoritative poetic text, since the status, though not the integrity, of the former was guaranteed by the presence of the latter, into a new system of mutual reliance, whereby the integrity of each form was absolutely predicated on the presence of the other within the macrotext, to whose overarching integrity both made a vital contribution. Differently from a conventional glossed poetic manuscript of an *auctor*, in which "the page was organized to present text and commentary simultaneously," the *Vita nova*'s poems and their accompanying prose could not be read "simultaneously" but had to be read consecutively, namely sequentially, as part of a logically developing, chronologically determined, narrative and argument, which assured the coherence of the "libro della *Vita Nuova*."[92] Thus, when Dante first arranged the manuscript of the *Vita nova*, in all likelihood he attempted to structure his page in a manner that would guarantee that his "little book" would be read "correctly." Indeed, I cannot but wonder whether one reason for the various exordial references to the "libro," its layout, and its copying was to draw attention to the novelty of its appearance. To tamper with Dante's design, as Boccaccio chose to do when he removed the *divisiones*, meant destroying the *Vita nova*'s rigorous coherence and negating its newness.

The far-reaching yet perplexing *novitas* of Dante's operation is emblematically captured in the failure of the *Vita nova*'s scribes adequately to appreciate the poet's structural experimentation and resystematization. Indeed, Dante introduced elements into the *Vita nova* that were meant to help guide its copyists.[93] To resolve the doubts of his readers was a responsibility that the poet accepted unflinchingly. Indeed, as I have already suggested, Dante was bent on illuminating and regulating every aspect of the interpretation and dissemination of the *libello*. An intense preoccupation with form, tradition, and exegesis, inseparable from an equally profound sense of his work's novelty and of its moral and salvific purpose, lies at the heart of the *libello*.

In Lieu of a Conclusion: A Quintessentially Florentine Work

Dante's aims in the *Vita nova* are thus quite concrete, one might even say "practical," as is confirmed by the fact that its audience—"li più semplici" (III.15 [2.2]) [the most simple]—is broad, as befits a work of salvation. The *libello* is not a text written exclusively for an elite, as for too long has been maintained, but, like the Bible, and later the *Commedia*, one aimed at everyone; and it is "subtle" precisely because it deals with matters divine and is itself a *vestigium Dei*—matters that, despite their "subtlety" as befits their divine origin, are necessarily addressed to every believer.[94] Yet, on account of its perceived abstraction, aestheticization, and literariness, these are not attributes commonly associated with the *libello*. In particular, the *Vita nova* has normally been detached from its immediate Florentine context, as if the "grubbiness" of city life, like Beatrice and the "misery" of the damned, cannot "touch" it (*Inf.* 2.92). Nevertheless, it is a quintessentially Florentine work: composed in the city, for a Florentine audience, with many of its determining traits having specifically Florentine roots, connotations, and solutions. This is an area of study that has remained almost entirely unexplored.[95] In what follows, I discuss, in a highly preliminary and, frequently, a highly conjectural manner, a few issues regarding the *Vita nova*'s Florentineness that, I believe, might be worth further investigation.

One important feature of the *libello* is unmistakably Florentine: the role played in it by Guido Cavalcanti, Dante's so-called "first friend" (III.14 [2.1]).[96] Although Guido is never named, the references to him are easily recognizable and would have been much more so in late thirteenth-century Florence. In the early 1290s, not simply because of his intellectual and poetic abilities but also because of the prominence of his family, Guido was the leading figure among those younger poets who, like Dante, were trying to differentiate themselves from often older poets in the city, such as Chiaro Davanzati and Monte Andrea, who wrote in the manner of Guittone. Dante presents both Cavalcanti and himself rejecting and criticizing the *siculo-toscani* and their mentor: "E questo mio primo amico e io ne sapemo bene di quelli che così rimano stoltamente" (XXV.10 [16.10]) [And this my first friend and I know well about those who thus compose rhymes stupidly]. At the same time, while apparently acknowledging his ties to Guido, Dante also calculatedly refuted his intellectual and, just as significantly, his artistic lessons. As scholars have long recognized, concentrating almost exclusively on their substantial ideological differences concerning the nature of love, the *Vita nova* is an anti-Cavalcantian work, which makes its dedication to Guido pointedly polemical: "questo mio primo amico a cui io ciò scrivo" (XXX.3 [19.10]) [this my first friend for whom I write this]. What colleagues have failed to note, however, is the boldness of Dante's maneuver in terms of the Florentine literary, social, and possibly even political milieu, especially given his concomitant dismissal of the city's other principal lyric grouping. As I have already discussed, Dante was keen to stress the uniqueness of his *prosimetrum* and the singularity of his own experiences and achievements.[97] Indeed, this strategy comes even more sharply into focus on recognizing the formal differences between Guido's exclusively poetic endeavors with their roots down deep in the soil of the Romance lyric and Dante's increasingly religiously (scripturally) inflected verses, his shift to a plurilingual prose, and his integration of the two forms (*prosimetra* were in fact almost unknown to vernacular writing,[98] although Brunetto Latini—on whom below— claimed in the *Tesoretto* that he intended to add passages in prose to his *poemetto* [411–26, 909–14, 1116–24]). As chapter XXIV [15] makes evident, Cavalcanti is presented as preparing the way for Dante, who, it is strongly implied, is going to far surpass his precursor. To snub a scion of the powerful Cavalcanti family so unceremoniously was no trifling matter. Even when it may seem that Guido has offered Dante a useful guideline, a polemical edge emerges. Dante explains that "lo intendimento mio non fue dal principio di scrivere altro che per volgare. . . . E simile intenzione so ch'ebbe questo mio primo amico a cui io ciò scrivo, cioè ch'io li scrivessi solamente volgare" (XXX.2–3 [19.9–10]) [my intention was from the start to write not other than in the vernacular. . . . And I know that this my first friend for whom I write this had a similar intention, namely that I should write to him solely in the vernacular]. Yet, by this stage in the *libello*, we are well aware that this is not actually true, as there are in it "parole . . . tutte latine" (XXX.2 [19.9]) [words . . . all in Latin]. In addition, in contrast to Cavalcanti's exclusive literary vernacularism—it was a commonplace in the Trecento to present him as someone who disdained Virgil and the other *auctores*[99]—in chapter XXV [16], immediately after having relegated Guido to a supporting role, Dante ostentatiously engages with classical poetry by quoting its preeminent poets. In doing so, he was not just taking a swipe at his supposed "friend" but also passing comment on the Florentine cultural environment more generally.

It has long been recognized, and indeed recently confirmed on the basis of substantial new evidence, that in late Duecento Florence the poetic classics played a relatively minor role in both the educational and literary culture of the city,[100] even though their *auctoritas* remained untainted. This crucial fact has largely been ignored or downplayed by most scholars of medieval Italian literature, and especially so by Dantists. Rather than a mark of Dante's and Florence's ease with the classics, chapter XXV [16] offers a glimpse of how fraught was the relationship between the "moderns" and the "ancients," especially given the marginality of Latin literature in the Romance lyric.[101] The six *sententiae* are normally treated as having exclusively illustrative purposes—random instances of prosopopoeia excerpted from the writings of the four Latin poets.[102] Yet for Dante to treat quotations from other writers in such a superficial manner would be quite unparalleled. Indeed, he employs the extracts in a way that had no precedent in the tradition: his choice of citations is individual and bent to distinctive ends. What is most striking about the six passages is the fact that only one, the first, Juno's address to Aeolus, regularly circulated autonomously. The others, as far as I have been able to establish, either had a minimal independent transmission or were not normally excerpted.[103] This, I believe, is significant. Dante appears to have selected the quotations because of their lack of familiarity. In a context, such as that of late Duecento Florence, where awareness of the *auctores* and their texts would have been mostly mediated, partial, and secondhand, the poet was trying to create the impression that his appreciation of, and hence recourse to, the classics was based on a direct reading of their works. Dante employed the Latin excerpts to establish his own cultural "authority" and to confirm that the links he was forging between himself and the *auctores* and their writings were the result of serious reflection. In an environment in which rhetorically based education and a burgeoning literature in the *volgare* had increasingly pushed the study of the *auctores* into the background, Dante was making a case for a new type of literary classicism that could cooperate effectively with both vernacular and Christian culture—a position that, in essence, he would continue to uphold throughout his career.[104]

Again, Dante was announcing the distinctiveness of his voice inside the walls of Florence, boldly distinguishing himself from his immediate lyric peers and, as I discussed earlier, despite his recourse to them, also from the great poets of antiquity. However, in chapter XXV [16], he was also making a general point, as I have intimated, about the status and influence of classical culture in the city that transcended the strictly literary. If the poetic *auctores* were neglected, the same was not true of Cicero and Aristotle and, to a lesser extent, of "moral Seneca" (*Inf.* 4.141). Brunetto Latini, the leading Florentine intellectual of the generation before Dante's, and very much the city's ethical, political, and rhetorical mentor until his death in late 1293, drew substantially on classical prose writers as he bent them to the needs of the present. Although, as recent studies have shown, Brunetto utilized Cicero to enhance his own standing (an approach that predates Dante's tactics of self-authorization), both the manner in which he aligned himself to the Roman author and his *forma tractandi* point to his subordinate position and to a deficiency in artistic ambition.[105] Thus, in his vernacular *Rettorica*, Brunetto translates and glosses at some length the opening parts of Cicero's *De inventione* (up to 1.17.24). The work is more than just a straightforward *volgarizzamento* and commentary, even though it is written in "uno stile piuttosto semplice e discorsivo,"[106] since, basing itself on Cicero, it aims "not only [to] provide rhetorical instruction to its readers, but also [to] make the case for Brunetto's own authoritative reincarnation of the Ciceronian *magnus vir et sapiens*, namely, the great wise man, whose eloquence inculcates civic values within the political community."[107] In addition, as Dante would do in chapter XXV [16], Latini saw himself as mediating classical culture to his fellow citizens. The question thus arises of the implications—beyond the obvious one of drawing a distinction between himself and yet another Florentine worthy—of the tensions that Dante created between his own poetic classicism and Brunetto's prosaic one.

Dante's relationship to Latini is complex, and, I believe, requires considerable further study. First and foremost, it is useful to acknowledge that it falls into different phases. Thus, until Dante began to compose the *Vita nova*, one way of thinking about his career is as in deliberate opposition—possibly polemically so—to Brunetto's literary and intellectual profile. Dante wrote for an elite, Brunetto for a broad audience; Dante concentrated on love, Brunetto on a wide range of doctrinal and practical questions; Dante primarily had recourse to lyric poetry, Brunetto to prose and to narrative verse; Dante indulged in a rarefied and escapist poetic activity, Brunetto involved himself in the life of his city. The contrasts are striking. Things change with Latini's death, which created a significant cultural and political void in Florence. If initially Dante was careful to forge an authorial identity that was clearly distinct from Brunetto's, once the older man had died, he felt able to begin to attempt to take over the latter's public mantle.[108] The *Vita nova* may be considered as contributing to this process of communal self-legitimation, which would necessarily imply that the *libello* was likely begun circa 1293/4. At first blush, it may seem that by bringing together text and gloss as in the *Rettorica* and by deciding to use prose, Dante was dutifully following in Brunetto's artistic footsteps,[109] and hence also in his cultural and social ones. Yet the nod to his predecessor, as so often in Dante's oeuvre, is in fact the basis on which to establish their differences. Thus Dante wrote self-commentary, Brunetto glossed and vernacularized the work of another. Differently from his predecessor, Dante succeeded in composing a *prosimetrum*. Furthermore, unlike Brunetto, who largely kept separate his narrative and broadly didactic aspirations, Dante integrated these in the *Vita nova*, implying that his poetic classical models offered him a literary self-confidence that the prose *auctores* could not: "Con ciò sia cosa che a li poete sia conceduta maggiore licenza di parlare che a li prosaici dittatori, e questi dicitori per rima non siano altro che poete volgari, degno e ragionevole è che a loro sia maggiore licenzia largita di parlare che a li altri parlatori volgari" (XXV.7 [16.7]) [Since to poets is conceded greater license to speak than to prose writers, and since these writers in rhyme are none other than vernacular poets, it is worthy and reasonable that greater license be granted to them to speak than to other vernacular speakers]. At the same time, differently from Brunetto, Dante was making a strong pitch for vernacular culture's respectful independence from the ancient world, while also appealing to his fellow citizens to appreciate a much richer swathe of classical culture than was customary in Florence. Equally, the quality of their prose was strikingly different: Dante's richly plurilingual, Brunetto's functionally pedestrian while mechanistically and predictably switching its registers.[110] Most significantly, Brunetto's approach and concerns are overwhelmingly local and secular—classical rhetorical teaching, moral thought, and examples dominate his writings—while Dante's key point of reference is scripture and hence God, so that his remit is first universalizing and only secondarily local. They share a commitment to others, but Brunetto's focus is narrowly earthbound, while Dante's is eternal: "Oltre la spera che più larga gira" (XLI.10 [30.10]) [Beyond the sphere that turns widest].[111]

As with other vernacular prose texts circulating in Florence—from *volgarizzamenti* of Latin and Old French works to doctrinal *compilationes* on a wide range of subjects, and from moral treatises to historical and legendary narratives, as well as applied texts of instruction and cautionary collections of tales and anecdotes, such as the *Novellino*—Brunetto's *Rettorica* and Dante's *Vita nova* have a clear practical bent. What distinguishes the *libello* from any other contemporary prose work, beyond its metaphysical priorities, is its literary ambition and sophistication.[112] Prose was in fact the overwhelmingly dominant mode of vernacular writing in Florence. Such texts were valuable, instructive, and worthy—a medieval would have termed them "useful";[113] they served the growing intellectual curiosity of an expanding class of *laici* in the city.[114] Yet, from a literary perspective, such texts were formally humdrum.[115] Dante, I suspect, when he composed the *Vita nova*, was intent on demonstrating that doctrinal and practical matters could be presented with literary and narrative verve and inventiveness. Prose could aspire to the same artistic status as (lyric) poetry. Indeed, the two could usefully collaborate, as could Aristotle and the poetic *auctores*, scripture and the Romance tradition, love and reason.[116] Different intellectual and cultural activities could be brought together. The local and the universal could integrate. Dante was ever a syncretist; and the plurilingual *Vita nova* marks his first serious effort at achieving synthesis—a synthesis that had its points of reference in contemporary Florence and in the various poetic and prose vernacular forms circulating in the city, and that was meant to establish its author's literary and intellectual uniqueness and *auctoritas*.[117] Dante was thereby affirming that he was a more than worthy successor to Brunetto when it came to offering moral and cultural leadership to his city. The *Vita nova* confirms to the poet's contemporaries that his intellectual interests were no longer narrowly erotic but, more so than Brunetto's, were broadly based, spiritually invigorating, communally useful, reliant on an up-to-date body of knowledge, and presented with an unusual literary complexity. The *libello* offered the account not just of how an exemplary individual transformed himself into Paul's *homo novus* (Eph. 4:24) but also of how a whole community might renew itself.[118] The *Vita nova* confidently announces, and embodies in its *forma tractandi*, that the possibility of spiritual, artistic, social, intellectual, and cultural *renovatio* is available to each of us, as well as to the societies of which we are part.[119]

Notes

I should like to thank warmly Ted Cachey, Lorenzo Dell'Oso, Filippo Gianferrari, Simon Gilson, David Lummus, Matteo Favaretto, Paola Nasti, and Lino Pertile for their comments on an earlier version of this chapter. As I explain below, I prefer the form *nova* rather than *nuova* as the adjective in the work's title; see esp. note 67.

1. Scholars have proposed two plausible dates of composition: 1292/3–1294/5 and 1293–96.

2. For an authoritative treatment of Italian metrical forms, see Beltrami, *Metrica*. In "the *sonetto rinterzato* (literally 'layered sonnet') or *sonetto doppio*," the "layering" is "achieved by inserting *settenario* verses (seven-syllable verses) between a sonnet's fourteen canonical hendecasyllables (eleven-syllable verses)" (Barolini ed., *Dante's Lyric Poetry*, 63). Dante introduces six *settenari* into each sonnet, thereby expanding them to twenty lines.

3. The lover first saw Beatrice in spring, possibly May 1274, when she was nine years old (II.1 [1.2]), and the story ends around Holy Week 1292 (XL.1 [29.1]). Of the previously written poems, "A ciascun' alma presa" was composed in May 1283 (III.1 [1.12]), while "Oltre la spera" was composed in early spring 1292.

4. Unless indicated otherwise, all translations are my own. In translating my aim is literal accuracy rather than idiomatic elegance.

5. On the resemanticization of the lyric poems, see Manuele Gragnolati's important contributions: in particular "Authorship and Performance" and "*Performance* senza gerarchia."

6. See De Robertis, *Libro della "Vita Nuova.*" Henceforth, whenever I use the designation *Vita nova*, I refer to the *libro* in its entirety.

7. See the classic formulations in Croce, *Poesia di Dante*, 35, and Eliot, *Dante*, 61.

8. With regard to the narrative register, Dante's treatment of the poet-lover clearly anticipates Petrarch's presentation of the same figure in the *Canzoniere*. On astronomy in the work's explicatory register, see the excellent Chisena, "Astronomia di Dante."

9. Filippo Gianferrari, in "Dante," has recently suggested that, despite their overwhelmingly evident differences, there are some interesting points of contact between the *Vita nova* and a popular schoolroom text, Prosper of Aquitaine's *Liber epigrammatum*, which accompanies prose excerpts from Augustine's oeuvre with original poetic maxims that serve as glosses to the *sententiae*.

10. On Beatrice's miraculous nature, see Santagata, "Donna del miracolo," and Vecce, "'Ella era uno nove.'"

11. See, for example, Cappello, "*Vita Nuova*"; Picone, "*Vita Nuova*" e tradizione romanza and Percorsi della lirica duecentesca, 249–65.

12. For rather too long, indeed since the latter years of the nineteenth century, (Italian) Dante scholarship, on account of its secularizing bias, has tended to underplay the religious character of the poet's oeuvre. Recently, things have changed significantly. See Marigo, *Mistica e scienza*; Singleton, *Essay*; Branca, "Poetica del rinnovamento" and "Tradizione francescana." On ties to the scriptural tradition, see in particular Cristaldi, "*Vita Nuova*"; Nasti, *Favole d'amore*; Martinez, "Mourning Beatrice" and "Poetics of Advent Liturgies"; Paolazzi, "*Vita Nuova*."

13. Despite some notable contributions, scholars have not infrequently failed to examine the *Vita nova*'s reflections on literature in a systematic manner. Thus, until very recently, no study existed of the extent to which Dante's references to literature and his deployment of the language and procedures of medieval literary theory and criticism were to be read as constituting a coherent, organic, and evolving structure that might cast light not just on the poet's thinking about literature in the 1290s but also on the interpretation and status of the *Vita nova* itself. Thus it is likely that Dantists have often underestimated the novelty and experimental character of the *libello* precisely because they have failed to appreciate the complexity and unity of its metaliterary discourse, which Dante largely developed to legitimate and illuminate his work's innovations. Finally, and at a more general level, limited attention has been paid to the possible relationships between the poet's literary, linguistic, cultural, and ideological concerns in the *Vita nova*. This chapter endeavors to address some of these issues; see also Barański, "Dante 'poeta,'" "'Lascio cotale trattato,'" "Roots of Dante's Plurilingualism," and "'Valentissimo poeta'"; Todorović, *Dante*.

14. The best scholarship normally moves between the erotic and the metaliterary examining the ways in which they bear on and illuminate each other.

15. B. Reynolds, "Introduction," xiii.

16. See for instance, Scott, *Perché Dante?*, 38–39 and 118; Pirovano ed., 27–28.

17. On the use of *dolce stil novo* as a literary historiographical concept, see Pirovano, *Dolce stil novo*, esp. the first chapter. On the *Vita nova* as the supreme stilnovist work, see De Robertis ed., 11.

18. I return in greater detail to the matter of the *Vita nova* as a "youthful" text and the question of its relationship to Dante's other works in the next subsection.

19. Dante, *Dante's Lyric Poetry*, Barolini ed.; Borsa, "Identità sociale"; Turco, "Restaging Sin."

20. Hooper, "Exile and Rhetorical Order."

21. Dante's reference to "the most simple" is obviously scriptural in character: for instance, Matt. 11:25; Luke 10:21; 1 Cor. 1:26–27. I shall have something to say about the seeming contradiction between "subtlety" and "simplicity" in due course.

22. I discuss the remit of the "book of memory" and especially the status of the author-protagonist below.

23. However much, in constructing the *Vita nova*, Dante may have relied on easily identifiable independent critical structures, such as the *divisio textus*, his aim, as with the poems, was not to maintain their autonomy but to integrate these into a new, unified, and coherent form (see the subsection "Exegesis").

24. Steinberg, *Accounting for Dante*, 2, 62–66, 81.

25. Recent scholarship has begun significantly to redimension the *Convivio*'s standing as a rigorously (Aristotelian) philosophical text by emphasizing its generally scriptural and specifically sapiential characteristics, thereby calling

into question the extent to which Beatrice and the "donna gentile" ought to be perceived in antithetical terms; see Gilson, chapter 5 of this book, the section "Structure, Organization, Subject Matter, and Language." This new reading of the *Convivio* obviously complicates the traditional view of the relationship between it, the *Vita nova*, and the *Commedia*.

26. For a reading in this key, see in particular the closing subsection.

27. See Barański, "Genesis," 210–16, and "'New Life' of 'Comedy.'"

28. In light of my analysis in this chapter of the remarkable richness and originality of the *Vita nova*'s prose, it would appear that the prose of the *Convivio* owes substantially more to the *libello* than has normally been recognized.

29. "Della prima [età = adolescenza] nullo dubita, ma ciascuno savio s'acorda ch'ella dura in fino al venticinquesimo anno; e però che infino a quel tempo l'anima nostra intende allo crescere e allo abellire del corpo, onde molte e grandi transmutazioni sono nella persona, non puote perfettamente la razionale parte discernere" (*Conv.* 4.24.2) [Regarding the first [age = adolescence] nobody has doubts, but each wise person agrees that it lasts until the twenty-fifth year; and therefore until that time our soul is concerned with the growth and beautifying of the body, whereby many and great transformations are in the person, the rational part cannot discriminate perfectly]; "A questa etade è necessario d'essere rifrenato, sì che non transvada" (4.25.4) [At this age it is necessary to be restrained, in order to avoid transgressing]. On medieval ideas on youth as "a time of immaturity and passion," see Minnis, *"Magister amoris,"* 55–61 (the quotation is on p. 57). The assessment of the *Vita nova* in the *Convivio* suggestively recalls standard criticism of Ovid's *Ars amatoria* as a youthful and problematic work about love: "The *Ars amatoria* is put firmly in its place, as the expression of a young man, with all that implied in medieval culture" (56). In reality, as ought to become clear during the course of this chapter, the *Vita nova* is deeply concerned with and defines itself in relation to reason and standards of rationality. This is especially apparent in Dante's original association between love and reason: "Ne la prima [parte] dico quello che Amore, consigliato da la ragione, mi dice" (XV.8 [8.8]) [In the first part I say what Love, counseled by reason, says to me].

30. In the Middle Ages, *paragraphus* is "generally used for text divisions smaller than chapters. . . . The term was commonly used for the sign marking the beginning of a section (a subdivision of a chapter), and, metonymically, also for the section itself": Teeuwen, *Vocabulary*, 229. The *Vita nova*'s structure ought to be studied in light of the increased interest in textual division and organization in the late medieval period, something that Dante scholarship has so far failed to do; see Parkes, "Influence"; Weijers, *Dictionnaires et répertoires*.

31. Dante also refers to the *Vita nova*'s "proemio" (XXVIII.2 [19.2]) [proem] as a separate textual entity.

32. There is a rarely utilized third version—Cervigni and Vasta ed.—that, in keeping with the *Vita nova*'s manuscript tradition, does not introduce num-

bering into its text. Instead, mimicking highlighted initial capitalization in medieval manuscripts, including some of those of the *Vita nova*, the editors emphasize typographically what they deem to be the start of a new section. To partition their version of the *libello*, Cervigni and Vasta rely on the "criterion" of "temporality," since "temporal expressions provide the clearest internal pattern of textual junctures, and the only consistent pattern sufficiently extensive to provide the number of divisions necessary for understanding and interpreting the text" ("Introduction," 27, and see also 19–28, 37–41), namely, a *Vita nova* divided into thirty segments. There is merit to some of Cervigni and Vasta's suggestions, so that their edition deserves to be better known.

33. When citing, I first provide Barbi's numbering but then give Gorni's in square brackets. I should like to note that, in agreement with most Dantists, I firmly prefer Barbi's text of the *Vita nova*, and hence, both in the present chapter and throughout this collection, all quotations are taken from his edition. See below for further discussion of the section divisions, including an explanation of why, cautiously and only up to a point, I am willing to accept Gorni's proposal.

34. See, in particular, Gorni, *Lettera nome numero*, 98–102; Harrison, *Body of Beatrice*.

35. See Pirovano, "Nota introduttiva," 9–15; see also Hirsh, "Prose Structure."

36. On Guido Cavalcanti's important role in the *Vita nova*, as both a poetic and an intellectual foil, see below.

37. On the Christian emphasis as a departure in the history of secular writing about love, see Malato, "Amor cortese."

38. Gorni, *Lettera nome numero*, 102–7, argues that the prose is formally characterized by its "programmatic" (102) dependence on tripartite stylistic structures. See also Sbacchi, "Andamanto ternario," who associates this feature of Dante's style with a similar procedure in Matthew's Gospel.

39. See most recently Brugnolo, "Conservare per trasformare."

40. See in particular Picone, *"Vita Nuova" e tradizione romanza* and *Scritti danteschi*, 23–46.

41. McKenzie, "Symmetrical Structure."

42. Barolini, "'Cominciandomi dal principio infino,'" discusses at some length the "programmatic *contaminatio*" (140) that characterizes the *Vita nova*'s narrative makeup. On the *Vita nova*'s narrative structure, see also Carrai, *Dante elegiaco*, 43–75; Cristaldi, *"Vita Nuova"*; Moleta, *"Vita Nuova."*

43. On the importance of time in the *Vita nova*, see, for instance, Cervigni and Vasta, "Introduction," 28–44; Harrison, *Body of Beatrice*, 93–157; Pirovano, "Nota introduttiva," 16; Sbacchi, "Indicazioni orarie"; Singleton, *Essay*, 52–54; Tonelli, "Tempi della poesia."

44. On the different Dante figures of the *Vita nova*, see Sparrow, "Dante's Self-Characterization." It is a critical commonplace to consider the *libello* an "autobiography": "The book illustrates an autobiography that is to be

understood neither in a realistic sense (the recording of actual events dealing with the narrator's love life) nor in a strictly historical-cultural sense (the narrator's love life as a metaphor for his artistic and intellectual formation), but in a poetic context (the narrator's love life as the typological realization of the preceding poetic tradition)" (Picone, "*Vita Nuova*," 874); on the *Vita nova* and "autobiography," see especially Guglielminetti, *Memoria e scrittura*, 42–72, who convincingly calls into question the *prosimetrum*'s ties to an "autobiographical" reality, as do Carrai, *Dante elegiaco*, 58; Corti, *Percorsi dell'invenzione*, 41–42; Cristaldi, "*Vita Nuova*," 60; Moleta, "*Vita Nuova*." I am reluctant to use the designation *autobiography* since it is anachronistic. It introduces modern notions of writing about oneself into a cultural context whose ideas about subjectivity, individuality, and their representation were different from those that developed during subsequent centuries; see, for instance, S. Kay, *Subjectivity in Troubadour Poetry*; C. Lee, *Soggettività nel Medioevo*, 5–44; Zink, *Subjectivité littéraire*. At the same time, there is no doubt that Dante constructs a complex life story centered on the *io*-figure, who himself is psychologically, intellectually, and socially complex. What the relationship might be between the I-figure of the *Vita nova* and the historical Dante Alighieri is, to say the least, contentious and, I suspect, unresolvable. I should like, however, to make an observation on this matter. If it is the case, as I argue in the final subsection, that the *Vita nova* is a work that addresses specifically Florentine issues, the interesting problem arises of how a contemporary Florentine readership would have reacted to a treatment of its first-person protagonist that strayed too far and too frequently from local knowledge about its author.

45. Contini, "Preliminari," 171–72. See also Barański, "Roots of Dante's Plurilingualism."

46. On this sentence, see Paolazzi, "*Vita Nuova*," 136.

47. *Vn* II.4 and 5 [1.5 and 6], III. 2 and 3 [1.13 and 14], XII.2, 3, and 9 [5.9, 10, and 16], XIV.9 [7.9], and XXIII.10 and 12 [14.10 and 12]). See *Testi fiorentini*, Schiaffini ed., 76, 122, 130, 137, 142, 161, 243, 253, 287, 311, and 333.

48. *Testi fiorentini*, Schiaffini ed., 162 and 190.

49. *Pargolo* is rare: some instances in moral and rhetorical prose, and in *volgarizzamenti*.

50. On *battere* in early Florentine prose texts, see *Testi fiorentini*, Schiaffini ed., 157, 175, 205, 212, 322, and 326. I base my analysis in this paragraph primarily on *GDLI* and *TLIO*. See the final subsection for an assessment of Duecento Florentine prose and its relationship to the *Vita nova*.

51. On medieval prologues, see Gallo, "Matthew of Vendôme," 59–60; Lausberg, *Handbuch der literarischen Rhetorik*, 2:150–63.

52. I wonder whether the *proemio* ought, in fact, stretch as far as VII.7 [2.18] in Barbi's edition. Given the centrality of the Romance lyric and of scripture in the *Vita nova*, one would expect to find clear reference to these in the prologue. Thus, rather than find them relegated to a second chapter, as in

Gorni's edition, it would make more sense for Cavalcanti (III.14 [2.1]) and for Jeremiah (VII.7 [2.18]), the emblematic representatives of their respective traditions, to be present in the *libello*'s proem.

53. My assessment of the prologue's connotative and lexical range is largely based on the notes in De Robertis ed., Gorni ed., and Pirovano ed. On the *Vita nova*'s prose, see Baldelli, "Lingua e stile," 82–88; Baldelli too stresses the range of the *Vita nova*'s prose, highlighting its use of technical vocabulary, of Latinisms, and of terms with concrete associations (82–83, 86–87). See also Bertoni, "Prosa"; Tartaro, "Prosa narrativa antica," 641–46; Terracini, "Prosa poetica."

54. On early Italian prose, see at least Baldelli, "Lingua e stile," 61–62; Casapullo, *Storia della lingua italiana*, 49–182; D'Agostino, "Itinerari e forme"; Frosini, "Volgarizzamenti"; Segre, *Lingua, stile e società*, 13–270; Tartaro, "Prosa narrative antica"; Tesi, *Storia dell'italiano*, 15–183. See also the concluding subsection below.

55. On the medieval *accessus*, see Hunt, "Introductions to the *artes*"; Minnis and Scott, *Medieval Literary Theory*, 12–36; Minnis, *Medieval Theory of Authorship*, 9–72. On the relationship of chapter I per Barbi's numbering to the *accessus* tradition, see Picone, "*Vita Nuova*," 61–63.

56. On the Dante's recourse to and departures from standard critical conventions in the *Vita nova*, see the subsection "Exegesis."

57. See Quadlbauer, *Antike Theorie*. See also Barański, *Dante, Petrarch, Bocaccio*, 209–56, especially 224–26.

58. Spitzer discusses the phrase's grammatical infelicities: "Osservazioni," 108–9; see also Gorni ed., 10. On the rhetorical status of solecism, see Lausberg, *Handbuch der literarischen Rhetorik*, 1:268–74.

59. The phrase combines Isa. 40:10, Matt. 3:11, and Luke 3:16 with *Aen.* 1.283 and 285, and 6.46.

60. The phrase recalls Luke 1:11, Titus 2:11, and 3:4.

61. See Auerbach, *Literary Language*, especially 25–81. On the relationship between the *sermo humilis* and "comedy," see Bene Florentinus, *Candelabrum* 1.6; see also Barański, *Dante, Petrarch, Boccaccio*, 282–83; Pertile, "*Cantica*."

62. These are conveniently collected at the end of Gorni ed. in the section "Frasi in lingua latina," 390.

63. The implications of this claim for Dante's treatment of Latin and the vernacular in the *Convivio* and in the *De vulgari eloquentia* lies beyond the remit of this chapter. On Dante's lingusitic reflections in the *Vita nova*, see the illuminating Lombardi, "Pensiero linguistico."

64. Contini, *Idea di Dante*, 63. For further examples of Dante's synthesis of Latin and Italian in the *Vita nova*, see Barański, "Roots of Dante's Plurilingualism," 112–15.

65. See Barański, "Dante 'poeta,'" 95–99. For further discussion of chapter XXV [16] as well as of Dante's treatment of the classical *auctores*, see the following and the concluding subsection.

66. My association of Latin with the "princes of the earth" privileges the traditional universalizing interpretation of the phrase in contrast to recent proposals that see in the rulers Florence's governing elite. In any case, the two readings are far from mutually exclusive.

67. See Gorni, *Dante prima della "Commedia,"* 111–32. The form *nuova*, of course, is exclusively vernacular. As well as giving the title as *Vita nova* at the start of the *libello*, Dante repeated it in *Conv.* 1.1.16, 2.2.1, and 12.4. Arguments in favor of *nuova* are in fact philologically weak; see Pirovano ed., 50.

68. Recent research has confirmed the important status enjoyed by Boethius's *Consolatio philosophiae* in late medieval Italy in general and Florence in particular, and hence in Dante; see Lombardo, "'Alcibiades quedam meretrix,'" *Boezio in Dante*, and "Primi appunti," 25–29; Nasti, "Storia materiale" and "'Vocabuli.'" See also Carrai, *Dante elegiaco*, but this overstates the *Vita nova*'s elegiac characteristics.

69. Hollander, *Dante*, 13–14.

70. See Martinez, "Mourning Beatrice"; Nasti, *Favole d'amore*; Stillinger, *Song of Troilus*.

71. See most recently Candido, "Per una rilettura."

72. Since Dante is "copying," the obvious implication is that the *libello*'s scriptural tenor is already a feature of the "book of memory," thereby offering a further early clue of the extraordinary character of the events that the protagonist experienced in his "new life."

73. Divinely motivated literature had two authors: God provided the inspiration, while the human *scriba* was responsible for the textual execution. See Minnis, *Medieval Theory of Authorship*, 90–102.

74. On Dante and Horace, see Barański, *"Magister satiricus,"* which includes an extensive bibliography on Horace's influence on Dante and on his medieval reception. See in addition Barański, "Inferno I"; Tavoni, *Qualche idea su Dante*, 335–69.

75. On Horace in the Middle Ages, see at least Bernardi, *Orazio*; Friis-Jensen, *Medieval Horace*; Gillespie, "Study of Classical Authors," 160–78; S. Reynolds, *Medieval Reading*; Villa, "Per una tipologia."

76. Barański, "'Valentissimo poeta.'" See also Paolazzi, *"Vita Nuova,"* 56–57, 89–91.

77. On the relationship between philosophy and poetics in chapter XXV [16], see Pinto, *Dante*, 109–19.

78. De Robertis, *Libro della "Vita Nuova*," 231–38.

79. For an in-depth discussion of Dante's self-authorizing tactics in the *Vita nova* that has interesting points of contact with my presentation, see Ascoli, *Dante*, 178–201.

80. See Ascoli, *Dante*, 6.

81. Indeed, as I suggested earlier, Dante claims to be offering the definitive explanation of the poems. In this way, readers are invited not to expend their

critical energy on the poems, as there is really nothing more to say about them, but to focus their exegetical attention on the new text that the poet has fashioned for them.

82. For further examples, see Barański, "'Lascio cotale trattato,'" 12–23, and the next subsection.

83. The fact that the *Vita nova* can be appreciated by different categories of readers is another mark of its dependence on the Bible, since, in line with Gregory the Great's influential dictum, this is a fundamental feature of scripture: "Habet in publico unde paruulos nutret, seruat in secreto unde mentes sublimium in admiratione suspendat. Quasi quidam quippe est fluuius, ut ita dixerim, planus et altus, in quo et agnus ambulet et elephas natet" (*Moralia in Iob, Epistola reverendissimo et sanctissimo fratri Leandro* 4) [It has out in the open nourishment for children but keeps hidden away the things that fill the minds of the subtle with awe. Scripture is like a river, as I have said, shallow and deep, in which the lamb can walk and the elephant can swim].

84. I base my discussion on Chigi L. VIII. 305; Martelli 12; Magliabechiano Cl. VI. 143 (normally termed the Strozziano on the basis of its earlier provenance); Toledo, Archivo y Biblioteca capitulares, ms. Zelada 104.6; and Chigi L. V. 176. I also make the occasional reference to the three Trecento manuscripts that include fragments of the *libello*: Laurenziano Acquisti e Doni 224; the Trespiano preserved in S. Maria degli Angeli in Florence; and BNCF Tordi 339. I have not consulted the manuscripts directly but have relied on the reproductions in Barbi ed. and in Storey, "Following Instructions," 127–30. For descriptions of the manuscripts, see Barbi, "Introduzione," xix–lxxxviii, as well as the excellent updated and detailed descriptions found at http://vitanova.unipv.it. See also P. Trovato, *Testo della "Vita Nuova."*

85. On Boccaccio's *Vita nova*, see Banella, *"Vita Nuova" del Boccaccio.*

86. Quote from Barbi, "Introduzione," xxiv. On the Toledano, see *Mostra di manoscritti*, 1:103.

87. See especially Barański, "'Lascio cotale trattato,'" 12–16 and 23–26.

88. The exception is the Strozzi manuscript. The fragments too copy the verse as if it were prose.

89. Storey, "Following Instructions," 122. See also Pacioni, "*Auctoritas poetica,*" 60.

90. Storey, "Following Instructions," 125; see also 117.

91. One effect of the allusion to the "altro chiosatore"—"e però lascio cotale trattato [discussing Beatrice's death] ad altro chiosatore" (XXVIII.2 [19.2]) [and therefore I leave such a treatment to another glossator]—is to stress that the exegetical passages in the macrotext have a different status from that of a conventional literary commentary, which, unlike Dante's *divisiones*, was always presented as distinct from the work it was glossing.

92. Irvine, *Making of Textual Culture*, 389.

93. See Storey, "Following Instructions," 122–25; Pacioni, "*Auctoritas poetica,*" 59–61.

94. Pacioni, too, refers to the *Vita nova*'s "ambizione a un pubblico più vasto" [ambition to address a broader audience], as confirmed by Dante's reference to "tutte le persone" (XXVI.15 [17.15]) [all persons] ("*Auctoritas* poetica," 58–59).

95. Beyond the *Vita nova*'s deceptive allusiveness, the main reason for this neglect is almost certainly linked to the fact that "l'ambiente fiorentino risulta assai . . . sfuggente" (De Robertis and Milani, "Contesto fiorentino," 67) [the Florentine environment turns out be rather elusive]. For studies of the *libello* that do pay some attention to its ties to Florence, see the works cited at notes 19 and 20.

96. The extensive scholarship on Dante and Guido rarely discusses their relationship in terms of its Florentineness. On the two poets' complicated relationship, see also Gragnolati, chapter 1 of this book, the section "The *Vita nova* and the Performative Power of Selection, Order, and Commentary."

97. In the diegesis, the poet's uniqueness is confirmed by the exceptional, because divinely ordered, nature of his experiences, whose import is universal and not local, even though the setting is largely restricted to the "sopradetta cittade" (VII.1 [2.12]) [abovementioned city], which, as I am suggesting, nevertheless makes its presence felt in the *Vita nova*.

98. *Novellino* 64 closes with a "canzonetta"; a letter by Guittone (26) and one by Meo Abbracciavacca to Guittone (31) include sonnets; while a further letter by Guittone incorporates a stanza of a canzone (36). See also Delle Donne, "Tra retorica e poetica."

99. See Barański, *Dante, Petrarch, Boccaccio*, 455–57 and 459.

100. See Black, *Humanism and Education*. See also Davis, "Education in Dante's Florence"; Faini, "Prima di Brunetto." On Florentine education, see in particular Gianferrari, "Dante," which includes an insightful discussion of methodological issues related to the study of Dante's education, as well as a very good bibliography, and "*Pro patria mori*."

101. But see Marcozzi, "Stilnovisti ed elegia latina"; Van Peteghem, "Vernacular Roots."

102. Dante cites (i) Virgil, *Aen.* 1.65; (ii) 1.76–77; (iii) 3.94; (iv) Lucan, *Phars.* 1.44; (v) Horace citing Homer, *Ars poetica* 141; (vi) Ovid, *Remedia amoris* 2.

103. Barański, "Roots of Dante's Plurilingualism," 108–10.

104. Vitale, "Pagan Gods," is a highly suggestive reading of the quotations from the *Aeneid* in chapter XXV [16] through the filter of Servius's commentary. This is an important proposal that needs to be examined further in light both of Dante's relationship to and knowledge of the *auctores* in the 1290s and of the documented presence of the text in Santa Croce.

105. For a study on Brunetto's use of Cicero, see in particular Keen, "Florentine *Tullio*."

106. Segre, *Lingua, stile e società*, 178.

107. Keen, "Florentine *Tullio*," 1.

108. In the wake of Fenzi's pioneering suggestions (*"Sollazzo e leggiadria,"* 215), a few scholars have begun to consider Dante's Florentine activities from 1294 onward as conditioned by the reverberations of Brunetto's passing. See Barański, *Dante, Petrarch, Boccaccio*, 31–33; Diacciati, "Dante," 263.

109. This is the standard critical view; see De Robertis, *Libro della "Vita Nuova,"* 209–14; Sarteschi, "Dalla *Rettorica*." Lombardo helpfully alludes to Dante's approach to the writings of Brunetto and Bono Giamboni, the other major established Florentine intellectual who had likely died a year or so before Latini, as having "un senso emulativo, che di superamento" ("Primi appunti," 23) [an emulative sense, as well as of overcoming].

110. Lombardo, "Primi appunti," 33; Segre, "Introduzione," xxix. In line with the opposition that Dante established between poets and prose writers, the limitations of Brunetto's style were also an implied critique of his prose models. Given Latini's fundamental reliance on Cicero, such criticism could not but involve the Roman author, whose standing, in Florence, as a rhetorical and moral *auctoritas* was paramount. Once more, Dante was differentiating himself from his fellow citizens.

111. For further differences between the two, see Lombardo, "Primi appunti," 30–31.

112. That, in composing the *Vita nova*, Dante should have drawn on these local traditions, and on their leading exponents, Brunetto and Bono, is, in itself, unsurprising. It is enough to recall the range of issues treated in the *libello*'s prose sections. The key question, I believe, is how to evaluate their points of contact: an organic and largely pacific development, as is conventionally assumed, or, as I am suggesting, a more radical agonistic, contrastive, and self-authorizing attitude, closely akin to the poet's treatment of his sources in the remainder of his oeuvre. On connections between Florentine prose and the *libello*, see Dell'Oso, "Tra Bibbia"; Lombardo, "Primi appunti." See also Lombardo, "'Talento m'è preso.'"

113. See Librandi, "Ristoro."

114. *Laicus* refers to those medievals who, like Dante, had a limited formal education and were not directly connected to higher educational institutions: see Imbach, *Dante*. See also Diacciati and Faini, "Ricerche."

115. Segre, "Introduzione," xxxv–xxxix.

116. See most recently Rea, "Amore e ragione."

117. The question of the *Vita nova*'s possible relationship to other intellectual centers with which the young Dante may have come into contact is one that Dantists have not yet posed.

118. There are other areas that ought to be examined as regards the *Vita nova*'s ties to Florence. (i) The nature and ramifications of Dante's relationship to Bono Giamboni are only now beginning to be studied. Bono was a leading

legal and rhetorical authority and, as the *volgarizzatore* of Orosius and Vegetius, an important mediator of classical culture. What distinguished him from Brunetto was the expressly Christian character of some of his writings. His *Libro de' vizî e delle virtudi* adapts and rewrites the traditional Latin psychomachia, the timeless allegorical battle between personified vices and virtues, a genre with an ostentatious moral and even salvific purpose. The *Vita nova* too has these same goals, and, particularly with the figure of Amore, has recourse to personification. On the other hand, the *libello* is strikingly different from the *Libro*: it is a first-person prosimetrical account set in a contemporary and familiar (Sbacchi, "Due luoghi") environment and at a particular time with recognizably human rather than symbolic actors. Indeed, Dante first carefully delimits personification allegory, and then, with the disappearance of Love, eliminates it. In metaliterary terms and as a mark of the *Vita nova*'s newness, this maneuver speaks volumes. Modern scholarship, unlike that of the past, prefers to avoid interpreting the *libello* in narrow allegorizing terms. (ii) Given its religious ambitions, especially as regards the treatment of Beatrice, the question arises of its connections to forms of popular, and hence largely vernacular, religious practice: see Pegoretti, "*Civitas diaboli*"; see also Biasin, "Indagine," Hawkins, "Religious Culture," and, even if primarily concerned with the *Commedia*, Nasti, "Religious Culture." Xiaoyi Zhang, a doctoral student at the University of Notre Dame, is completing a dissertation on the impact on the *libello* of contemporary thinking and practice relating to the emotions. (iii) In light of the *Vita nova*'s doctrinal interests and its overt recourse to Aristotle in its latter stages (XXV.2 [16.2] and XLI.6 [30.6]), the matter of its relationship to the advanced educational institutions in the city, the mendicant *studia*, is a question of some import. Dell'Oso, "How Dante Became Dante," has established suggestive and highly plausible connections between topics discussed at the Franciscan convent of Santa Croce and the *Vita nova*. Even more intriguingly, but entirely in keeping with Dante's strategy in the *libello*, Dante developed solutions to these issues that were different from and critical of those propounded by the friars. The poet's attempt to "far parte per se stesso" (*Par.* 17.69) thus took in an impressively broad swathe of Florentine cultural and intellectual life.

119. I completed this chapter in "lockdown." As we attempt to come to terms with the tragic and perplexing reverberations of COVID-19, I found Dante's and the *Vita nova*'s message of hope and rebirth reassuring. Indeed, as a nonbeliever, I found it especially apt, since it does not narrowly touch on just matters of faith. Nonetheless, it is almost certain that, given his theocentric view of the universe, Dante would not have been in sympathy with my drawing of distinctions. God was one, his creation harmoniously reflected this loving oneness, and the *Vita nova* affirmed these truths.

This chapter is dedicated to the memory of John Prine, a truly great singer-songwriter, who died after contracting coronavirus. As I write, I imagine John and Dante talking about how "love walked with *them*."

CHAPTER 4

Epistles

CLAIRE E. HONESS

Thirteen extant Latin letters are traditionally attributed to Dante, although the authenticity of one of these—to which I shall return shortly—is still hotly debated, while recent claims about the Dantean authorship of a fourteenth remain to be proved.[1] We are dealing, then, with a relatively modest body of texts, although it seems probable that this may be only a small sample of the work of a much more prolific letter writer, many of whose writings in this form—by their very nature, occasional and scattered—have simply not been preserved for posterity. Certainly Dante presents himself as a letter writer from as early as the time of the *Vita nova*, when he claims that he wrote a letter to the "principi de la terra" (XXX.1 [19.8]) (probably meaning Florence's civic leaders, rather than literally the "princes of the earth") describing the bereft state of his hometown after the death of Beatrice. And Boccaccio, in his *Trattatello in laude di Dante*, asserts that Dante wrote "molte *Pistole* prosaiche in latino, delle quali ancora apparisco no assai" [many prose letters in Latin, of which a great number survive];[2] while Leonardo Bruni, in his 1436 *Vita di Dante*, numbers among his works "molte *Epistole* in prosa" [many prose letters] and claims to have seen some of these, written in Dante's own "perfect" handwriting, for himself.[3]

It does not fall within the remit of this chapter to indulge in conjecture about those letters that have not survived.[4] These form part of the "myth" of Dante: the "Dante" constructed by his readers, at different points in history, to be a commentator on *their* times rather than his own.[5] However, it is interesting to note that those letters referred to by contemporary and near-contemporary commentators, such as Boccaccio, Bruni, and the Florentine chronicler Giovanni Villani, suggest a broader output, which may have been more prolific than that which has survived, but which was not very different in kind. Villani, for example, states that, alongside two letters that can be confidently identified with those known today (numbered 7 and 11 in modern editions of the epistles), Dante wrote "al reggimento di Firenze dogliendosi del suo esilio sanza colpa" [to the government of Florence, complaining about his unjust exile]: a letter that does not seem to have survived but may be the same letter mentioned by Bruni, who states that, in his desire to return from exile, Dante wrote a number of letters both to individual Florentines and to the city's government, including a long letter that opens, "Popule mi, quid feci tibi?" [Oh my people, what have I done to you?].[6] Bruni also mentions a number of other letters that have not survived, including one describing the Battle of Campaldino and two discussing Dante's role in Florentine politics before his exile, including his period as prior; and in the fifteenth and sixteenth centuries various other letters were attributed to Dante, often highly implausibly, including letters to the king of Hungary, to Pope Boniface VIII, and to Guido da Polenta.[7] A significant common thread characterizes all of these, the plausible and the spurious alike: without exception, they identify Dante as a writer of what we might term public-facing (rather than strictly private or personal) letters—letters that are broadly political in subject matter and that return time and again to the subject of his exile. The letter sent in 1312 in the name of Cangrande della Scala, Lord of Verona, to the Emperor Henry VII, which Paolo Pellegrini has recently attributed to Dante, would, if shown to be genuine, also fit into this category of "public" or "political" letters, written on behalf of a patron.[8] However, the evidence adduced by Pellegrini is scant and his reasoning decidedly circular, and this chapter will not therefore treat this text as part of Dante's epistolary corpus.[9] Nonetheless, the general picture of Dante the letter writer evoked by accounts is, as we shall see, entirely in keeping with that which emerges also from those texts that can be reliably identified as his.

Four of the letters that can be attributed with relative certainty to Dante were written on behalf of a third party or group.[10] As such, there may be little here that is distinctively Dantean, although it is clear that, even in these cases, Dante writes only in support of causes in which he believes. This is clearly true in the case of the letters written on behalf of the Countess of Battifolle to Margaret of Brabant, the wife of the Emperor Henry VII. For all their conventionality, these brief texts express an enthusiasm for the Italian expedition of the emperor that is entirely in keeping with the strong support for Henry's campaign expressed in *Epistles* 5, 6, and 7, written in Dante's own voice.[11] *Epistle* 11, which deals with that other great medieval institution, the church, follows naturally from this series of six "imperial" letters and expresses a political pessimism that will be familiar to any reader of the *Commedia*. Meanwhile, the turbulent political situation of Florence, which is the subject of *Epistle* 1, is also prominent in *Epistles* 6 and 7—where it is interwoven with imperial concerns, as mentioned above—and comes to the fore again in *Epistle* 12, in relation to the conditions of Dante's exile. Indeed, it is significant that, of the letters written in Dante's own voice, there is only one—the letter to the cardinals—that *does not* mention his exile. Finally, three letters—*Epistles* 3, 4, and 13—are linked to Dante as poet and seem to have been intended to accompany, and perhaps to elucidate, a specific piece of poetry.[12]

Epistles 1, 2, 4, 5, 6, 7, 8, 9, and 10 are found in a 1394 manuscript, now in the Biblioteca Apostolica Vaticana, MS Palatino Latino 1729, produced for, and in part transcribed by, Francesco Piendibeni. The manuscript also contains Dante's *Monarchia* and Petrarch's *Bucolicum carmen*. *Epistles* 5 and 7 are also found in another manuscript from the second half of the fourteenth century (S. Pantaleo 8) in the Biblioteca Nazionale Centrale in Rome, and a further, late fifteenth-century, copy of *Epistle* 7 is found in the Biblioteca Nazionale Marciana in Venice (MS Lat. XIV 115 (4710)). *Epistles* 3, 11, and 12 can be found, transcribed in Boccaccio's own hand, in the so-called *Zibaldone boccaccesco*, produced around 1350 and held in the Biblioteca Medicea Laurenziana in Florence (Plut. XXIX 8).[13]

The history of *Epistle* 13, addressed to Cangrande della Scala, Lord of Verona, is hugely complex and fiercely contested: a "political football in Dante studies," as Barolini has accurately asserted.[14] The primary aim of the present chapter is to reconsider and to highlight the importance of those letters that are certainly Dantean, and consequently discussion of the authenticity of *Epistle* 13 falls beyond its scope. The history of the

Cangrande debate shows how easy it is for scholarly discussions of the *Epistles* to be sidetracked by this particular question of attribution, to the exclusion of all else. This chapter will resist that temptation, not because it seeks to minimize the importance of *Epistle* 13, but out of a desire to consider the importance of *Epistles* 1–12, in terms both of their importance as works in their own right and of the light they cast on Dante's broader career as a writer and as a political thinker. While it is undoubtedly true that, unlike Petrarch's *Familiares* and *Seniles*, the *Epistles* were never intended to form a single coherent literary text, this does not, I believe, mean that they cannot be considered "literary"; nor does it mean that they cannot illuminate the Dante whom we read in his other works, including the *Commedia*.[15]

For the sake of completeness, however, it is impossible to proceed without paying some attention to the thorny issue of the letter to Cangrande. That much more could be written is a given, and I refer the interested reader to my bibliography for indications of scholarly works that engage more fully with this text, from all sides of the debate.[16]

The letter to Cangrande was first formally attributed to Dante at the beginning of the fifteenth century by Filippo Villani.[17] However, it seems to have been known, minus the Dantean attribution, well before this date, by many of the Trecento commentators, including Guido da Pisa, Jacopo della Lana, Pietro Alighieri, Boccaccio, Francesco da Buti, and Benvenuto da Imola, all of whom repeat material from the letter verbatim,[18] although this material is often of a commonplace character. This letter is not included in either of the two manuscripts that contain Dante's other letters, and the question of attribution is complicated by the fact that the oldest manuscript copies that have come down to us (dating from the fifteenth century, so already further from Dante's own time than the manuscripts containing the other letters) contain only the first four paragraphs of the text, which is to say the part that clearly presents itself *as a letter*, in contrast to the commentary section that follows in paragraphs 5–33.[19] This is, in fact, not at all atypical: both *Epistle* 3 and *Epistle* 4 of Dante's accepted corpus also refer to a work "appended below," which is not, however, appended at all in the manuscript copies that have come down to us.[20] Nonetheless, this late and fragmented manuscript tradition, along with the fact that there is a marked difference in style between the opening "epistolary" paragraphs of the letter and the rest, with the first part being much more typically Dantean, has contributed to further complicating the controversy surrounding the letter. Thus while some commentators claim that the whole letter is by Dante, and some deny its Dantean authorship entirely, others accept only the first four paragraphs as genuine.[21]

Debates around the authenticity of the letter focus principally, though not exclusively, on three issues. The first of these is the question of allegory (discussed in §7), and specifically the appropriateness—or otherwise—of the application of the fourfold way of reading associated with the interpretation of scripture to the "poema sacro" (*Par.* 25.1).[22] The second is the issue of the title of the poem (discussed in §10) and the extent to which the definition of *comedy* given here fits—or does not fit—with the scope and ambition of the poem that Dante refers to in the *Inferno* as "la mia comedìa" (21.2).[23] And, third, commentators have pointed to the differences in the use of the distinctive rhythmic phrase endings, or *cursus*, typical of medieval Latin prose, between the "commentary" part of the letter and Dante's canonical Latin works.[24] With arguments around each of these issues (and others) being mustered both for and against attribution of the letter to Dante, and with definitive proof of authorship based on new hard-and-fast evidence unlikely to be forthcoming, the debate around *Epistle* 13 looks set to continue to generate scholarly disagreement well into the twenty-first century.

As I have already indicated, it is my aim in this chapter to ensure that the heat and light generated by the contentious thirteenth *Epistle* do not serve to relegate its twelve fascinating cousins to the cold, dark forgotten corner of Dante studies. Rather, I hope to show how Dante, the great experimental poet, experiments also with the epistolary form, and in ways that both reflect and illuminate his other works, and, in particular, the *Commedia*. To do so, it will be necessary to draw attention briefly to the rules of the medieval *ars dictaminis* or art of letter writing—an art to which, ironically enough, the author of the letter to Cangrande (whether Dante or another) makes explicit reference. In the sentence that draws the initial epistolary section of the letter to a close and opens the commentary that follows, the author refers explicitly to the "formula epistole," the formula prescribed for letter writing.[25] What is this formula? And to what extent does Dante, in his letters, adhere to it?

The *ars dictaminis*, as Dante would probably have known it, began to be formalized toward the beginning of the twelfth century, at least in part in response to the changing bureaucratic and administrative needs of the newly emerging communes with their literate, but often not classically educated, bourgeois or mercantile classes.[26] The writing of letters appears to have been seen as an intensely practical undertaking, closely associated with speechmaking—and indeed official letters may well have been designed to be read aloud, blurring this distinction still further.[27] Twelfth-century *artes dictandi* or letter-writing manuals clearly set out the sort of formulaic approach alluded to by the author of the Cangrande letter and described by Witt as exercising a "tyranny of stylistic prescriptions."[28] The letter was typically divided into five main parts, which, with minor differences, remained the same for all types of communication, and which were reinforced through the provision of multiple examples taken from sample letters, both real and invented (or adapted) for the purpose.

Dante's letters do not, on the whole, adopt this formulaic approach. The influence of the *ars dictaminis* tradition was, in any case, waning by the end of the thirteenth century, but beyond this and as we shall see, Dante's letters are intended to bridge literary and practical traditions in a way that reaches far beyond the bureaucratic remit of the *artes dictandi*. Nonetheless, on those occasions when Dante writes as a bureaucrat or perhaps as a diplomat—when he writes on behalf of, and at the behest of, others—the standard patterns and structures recommended by the textbooks do tend to emerge, as is amply illustrated by the example of *Epistle* 10, one of the letters written on behalf of the Countess of Battifolle to Margaret of Brabant. A brief analysis of this letter therefore provides an illustration of the letter-writing "formula" that Dante will bend and stretch to suit his literary and political needs in his more personal and heartfelt letters.

The first key element of a letter is the *salutatio* or greeting. This often received the most detailed treatment in the *artes dictandi*, for it was vital that the precise form of greeting used should be appropriate to the social status of both sender and recipient. Indeed, in many cases, the *artes dictandi* conflated social categories with the conventional stylistic categories of the *genera dicendi*—high, middle, and low—ensuring that style was appropriately mapped onto status.[29] Ordinarily, the *artes dictandi* recommended the "humble" style as being the most appropriate for the practical purposes of letter writing. In the case of Dante's letter, however, we see our author ventriloquizing a woman of some considerable status, the

Countess of Battifolle, who is herself addressing a woman of an even higher status, an empress, and who therefore, in an opulent register, declares herself, with all due humility, to be her faithful, compliant, and devoted servant.[30]

The next section of the letter was the *exordium*, sometimes also referred to as *captatio benevolentiae*:[31] a term that clearly identifies the purpose of this section: to charm the reader or listener and, hopefully, ensure her or his sympathetic ear. In the letter to Margaret of Brabant, then, we see further expressions of humility and of shared joy at positive news previously received—both clearly designed to convey unanimity between writer and recipient. It was also often recommended that the *exordium* contain proverbs,[32] and Dante's comment about the way in which the hearts of devoted servants are gladdened by the good fortune of their lords certainly has something of the set phrase about it.[33]

The letter writer then progressed to the *narratio*, the least formulaic part of the letter, since the set of circumstances giving rise to each individual letter would be different. Relatively little space was given to the *narratio* in the *artes dictandi*, except to stipulate that it should be brief, setting out the facts to be conveyed as sparely and as clearly as possible. *Brevitas* and *claritas* were the dual keywords of the *narratio*, and, indeed, Dante's letter is short and to the point here: Henry is making good progress toward his goal.[34]

The standard letter finally comes to its point in the next section, the *petitio* or request. In Dante's letter it is clear that this request is purely rhetorical. In prose whose tortuous complexity belies the simplicity of its message, he requests permission from the empress to respond (on behalf of the Countess) to the question posed in the former's previous letter, a question that, when stripped of its rhetorical flourishes, can be reduced to a simple inquiry after the health of the Countess.[35] The point here, it seems, is not the question asked, nor its equally banal answer,[36] but the fact that it is framed specifically as a *petitio*: "Petentis audeo iam inire officium" (*Ep.* 10.2) [I now dare to assume the voice of the petitioner].

The letter closes with a formal *conclusio*: in this case simply a statement of the date and place of writing, the castle of Poppi on May 18, 1311 (*Ep.* 10.6).

This letter is paradigmatic in its formulaic conformity to the rules of the *ars dictaminis* tradition that had developed in Italy in the twelfth century. Its banality is precisely the point, reflecting Dante's familiarity with this tradition and its rules and structures, which serves only as a starting point and springboard for a much more interesting epistolary output, drawing not only on the *ars dictaminis* but also on subsequent developments to the genre. Through the thirteenth century a new approach to letter writing had developed, especially in Italy, influenced by the professional correspondence produced by the papal and imperial courts. This more sophisticated and stylistically complex approach, known as the *stilus rhetoricus*, was characterized by the frequent use of interjections and interrogatives, by a heavy reliance on both biblical and classical quotations, and by the use of the *cursus*.[37]

The earliest letter of Dante's that has come down to us can perhaps be seen as a product of this tradition. The addressee of this letter is Cardinal Niccolò da Prato, who had been sent to Tuscany by Pope Benedict XI to act as "peacemaker," and who, at the time of the letter, was negotiating with the Ghibellines and White Guelfs in exile.[38] Still written in an "impersonal" voice, on behalf of the Florentine Whites in exile in Arezzo, the letter follows the basic formula just outlined: after its greeting is a fairly blatant *captatio benevolentiae* in which Dante apologizes, on behalf of his companions, for any perceived tardiness in responding to the cardinal's previous communication,[39] and there follows an exposition of the concerns and priorities of the *parte bianca*, which culminates in the request that the cardinal continue to work to bring peace to the exiles' troubled city and to guarantee their safe return. All the parts of the conventional, formulaic letter are in place, therefore; but so too are some of the typical features of the *stilus rhetoricus*. We see an insistent use of rhetorical questions: "Et ad quid aliud in civile bellum corruimus, quid aliud candida nostra signa petebant, et ad quid aliud enses et tela nostra rubebant, nisi ut qui civilia iura temeraria voluptate truncaverunt, et iugo pie legis colla submitterent, et ad pacem patrie cogerentur?" (*Ep.* 1.5) [For what other reason did we plunge into civil war? What else did our white standards seek? For what other reason were our swords and our spears stained red, if not in order that they who have destroyed civil rights through their own mad desires should submit their necks to the yoke of the rightful laws and be forced to contribute to the peace of the city?]; and these are combined with a number of classical quotations and allusions, particularly from Virgil, such as the phrase "dignas grates persolvere" (1.7) [to render due thanks], which occurs twice, in almost identical forms, in the first two books of the *Aeneid*.[40]

Hints at the way in which Dante's mature letter writing would develop are, perhaps, already present here, but they are very much constrained and kept beneath the surface by the fact that he is here writing not in his own voice but as the mouthpiece of a broader group: a group whose views he shares, and is able to articulate, only for a very short time, as any reader of the Cacciaguida cantos of the *Paradiso* knows, for it will not be long before this "compagnia malvagia e scempia" [wicked and senseless company] turns against Dante, making his only honorable course of action to become a "parte per [se] stesso," a party of one, a lone voice (*Par.* 17.62 and 69).[41] These cantos, at the very center of the *Paradiso*, are central also to our understanding not only of the *Commedia* but of Dante's poetic and political development—indeed, of his human trajectory in its entirety—and it is worth keeping in mind, therefore, as we read Dante's letters, Cacciaguida's encouragement of this lone voice to speak out and tell the truth, no matter whom it may offend, for the sake of the message that it carries for all who hear it, whether they care to listen or not:

> Ma nondimen, rimossa ogne menzogna,
> tutta tua visïon fa manifesta;
> e lascia pur grattar dov' è la rogna.
>   Ché se la voce tua sarà molesta
> nel primo gusto, vital nodrimento
> lascerà poi, quando sarà digesta.
>   (*Par.* 17.127–32)

[Nonetheless, setting falsehoods aside, reveal everything that you have seen, and let those you make squirm scratch that itch. For if your voice tastes bitter at first, it will provide vital nourishment once it has been digested.]

Cacciaguida is speaking here of the message to be conveyed by the *Commedia*, but he could well also have been referring to that of many of the letters Dante would write following his break with the Whites, shortly after writing his letter to Niccolò da Prato.

The impact of this imperative to tell the truth no matter what emerges particularly clearly in *Epistles* 5, 6, and 7, the letters that Dante would write in 1310 and 1311 at the time of Henry VII's descent into Italy. While they share the basic subject matter of the three Battifolle letters, and were written at roughly the same time, they could not be more different in style and tone. The change in emphasis is hinted at, in fact, right from the start, in the apparently innocuous opening sections devoted to *salutationes*. In line with the rules of the *ars dictaminis*, the author (or, rather, the implied author) of the letters written on behalf of others, such as *Epistle* 1 and *Epistle* 10, already discussed, remains anonymous: "Reverendissimo in Christo patri dominorum suorum carissimo domino Nicholao . . . devotissimi filii A. capitaneus, Consilium et Universitas partis Alborum de Florentia semetipsos devotissime atque promptissime recommendant" (*Ep.* 1) [To the most reverend Father in Christ, their most beloved lord, Niccolò . . . his most devoted sons, A. the Captain, the Council, and all the members of the White party of Florence commend themselves with devotion and zeal]; "Illustrissime atque piissime domine domine Margarite . . . fidelissima sua G. de Batifolle . . . se ipsam et voluntarium ad obsequia famulatum" (*Ep.* 10) [To the most illustrious and most gracious lady, Lady Margaret, . . . her most faithful servant, G. di Battifolle, . . . offers herself and her willing and compliant service]. When writing in his own voice, however, Dante does not hesitate to name himself, using the now-famous formulation "Florentinus et exul inmeritus" [a Florentine undeservedly in exile]. Even more strikingly, in the letter to the Florentines he reverses the usual order whereby the more humble writer is indicated only after the more illustrious addressee of the letter, as seen in the examples above. Here, in this most status-conscious part of the letter, he elevates his own position—morally more than socially—in comparison with the "wicked" Florentines, already anticipating in the *salutatio* the highly critical and derogatory tone that the letter will go on to take: "Dantes Alagherii florentinus et exul inmeritus scelestissimis Florentinis intrinsecis" (*Ep.* 6) [From Dante Alighieri, a Florentine undeservedly in exile, to the most wicked Florentines within the city]. The logical conclusion of Dante's claiming for himself of the moral high ground is visible in the *salutatio* of *Epistle* 7. Here, as in the letter to Niccolò da Prato, where peace and the greater good of Florence are stated as the exiles' principal concerns, Dante claims to speak for those Tuscans who desire peace:[42]

"Sanctissimo gloriosissimo atque felicissimo triumphatori et domino singulari domino Henrico divina providentia Romanorum Regi et semper Augusto, devotissimi sui Dantes Alagherii Florentinus et exul inmeritus ac universaliter omnes Tusci qui pacem desiderant, terre osculum ante pedes" (*Ep.* 7) [To the most holy, most glorious, and most fortunate conqueror and sole lord, the lord Henry, by divine providence king of the Romans and forever Augustus, from his most devoted Dante Alighieri, a Florentine undeservedly in exile, and from all Tuscans who desire peace, who kiss the ground beneath his feet]. In the later letter, this stance does not contradict Cacciaguida's definition of Dante after 1304 as a "lone voice" but rather confirms it. Dante does not—and cannot—now write as the spokesman for a group, but only as himself, the Florentine undeservedly in exile, and for any others who believe, like him, in an ideal of peace that may already be starting to appear unrealizable. Whether this phrase is intended to be read as a true "esortazione alla guerra" [call to arms] or, rather, as a shifting of the hope for peace onto a future, eschatological plane is unclear; what is clear, however, is that the "Tuscans who desire peace" here evoked do not represent any specific political faction.[43]

Peace is, in fact, a constant theme in these letters, emerging right from the start of *Epistle* 5, in which Dante announces the arrival of Henry VII in Italy with the words: "'Ecce nunc tempus acceptabile,' quo signa surgunt consolationis et pacis" (*Ep.* 5.1) ["Now is the favorable time," when signs of solace and of peace are emerging]. Henry of Luxembourg had been chosen as king of the Romans and emperor-elect in November 1308, and crowned by the archbishop of Cologne in Aachen in January 1309. Almost immediately, he began to plan what he hoped would be a triumphal journey to Italy, in order to be crowned as emperor in Rome. After encouraging preliminary negotiations with the cities of Lombardy and Tuscany and with the papacy, Henry set out for Italy and crossed the Alps in October 1310.[44] *Epistle* 5 is set directly against this backdrop, and against the context of Dante's conviction—set out most clearly in the *Monarchia* and in book 4 of the *Convivio*—that only a universal emperor, freed by his very universality from the sin of *cupiditas* [greed or self-interest], could bring an end to the wars and conflicts that plagued Italy and the world, and that had led directly to the poet's own traumatic exile.[45] This letter is unlike any of the letters that Dante had written previously and is very far from the formulaic and practically oriented stock letters of the *artes dictandi*: more a piece of political propaganda—a "manifesto," as Toynbee defines it—than a letter as such,[46] as the breadth of the addressee list in its *salutatio* already begins to suggest: "Universis et singulis Ytalie Regibus et Senatoribus alme Urbis nec non Ducibus Marchionibus Comitibus atque Populis" (*Ep.* 5) [To each and every one of the kings of Italy, and to the senators of the Holy City, and also to Italy's dukes, marquises, and counts, and to her people].

The tone for Dante's fervent—almost fanatical—support for the emperor-elect is set in the letter's opening words. Dante's quotation of St. Paul's "Ecce nunc tempus acceptabile" (2 Cor. 6:2) is more than just a form of words implying some unspecified hope for the future. Rather, in Paul's letter, this "favorable time" is linked precisely, through biblical citation, with the mission of Christ and of his first followers. Paul quotes Isaiah to suggest that the church at Corinth should take comfort in the fact that the "favorable time" prophesied by Isaiah has now definitively arrived.[47] Paul claims, in other words, that Christ fulfills the words of the prophets, bringing those who are in darkness into the light and those who are slaves to freedom; and Henry, Dante argues, has a very similar function for contemporary Italy: Isaiah's prophecy points forward to the figure of Christ, but they both—at least in that particular time and place—point forward to the figure of Henry. Already, then, in this letter's first sentence we are brought face to face with a wealth of biblical references and allusions that is very different from what we have seen hitherto. Indeed, the letter to Niccolò da Prato, though addressed to a cardinal, does not contain a single biblical reference.

If the letter's first sentence suggests that Henry may be, in some sense, a second Christ, his messianic status is confirmed and intensified as the letter goes on, through a further series of biblical parallels that are striking both for sheer quantity and for the audacity of the comparisons. Henry is the "Leo fortis de tribu Iuda" (*Ep.* 5.1) [great lion of the tribe of Judah];[48] he is a new Moses, who will transform the Egyptian wasteland of contemporary Italy into a land flowing with milk and honey—"Moysen alium . . ., qui de gravaminibus Egiptiorum populum suum eripiet, ad terram lacte ac melle manantem perducens" (*Ep.* 5.1)—;[49] in an echo of the *Nunc dimittis*, he is described as "gloria plebis tue" (*Ep.* 5.2) [the glory of [Italy's] people],[50] and, as in the Song of Songs (traditionally interpreted as an account of the mystic marriage of Christ and his church), he is the bridegroom, hastening to be joined with his beloved.[51] Claiming that Henry's authority will come not from his human electors and supporters, and not even from papal endorsement, but from God himself, Dante bolsters his arguments with a further series of biblical quotations. In the letter's fourth paragraph he urges the Lombards to accept Henry as their legitimate ruler, on the basis that "potestati resistens Dei ordinationi resistit" [anyone who resists authority is rebelling against God's decision]. This injunction is a direct quotation from St. Paul's letter to the Romans,[52] and it is followed immediately, and supported by, a further reference to Paul in the phrase "Durum est contra stimulum calcitrare" (*Ep.* 5.4) [It is hard for you, kicking like this against the goad], which indicates the futility of any resistance to Henry and is taken from the account of the conversion of St. Paul on the road to Damascus.[53] The parallels here are clear. Those who resist the emperor are like Saul, who persecutes not only the early Christians but also, by extension, Christ himself,[54] a parallel that equates Henry, once again, with Christ.

Space in the present context does not allow me to enumerate all the biblical references to be found in *Epistle* 5.[55] Although such references are typical of letters written in the *stilus rhetoricus*, here they far outnumber the classical references with which they are traditionally intermingled. Indeed, the sheer quantity of biblical references, combined with the emphatic way in which Dante deploys them, suggests that his presentation of Henry as a Christ-like figure who has come to cleanse Italy of her (political) sins and restore her to peace needs to be read as more than just an enthusiastic rhetorical flourish. Unlike those passages of the *Commedia* (and, in particular, of the *Purgatorio*) where Dante's imperial ideal is alluded to with regret and lament, the tone here is, rather, one of confident hope.[56] This instinct is confirmed by a reading of *Epistle* 7, the letter Dante writes in April 1311 to Henry himself, expressing both his continued hope for the establishment of a divinely willed imperial peace and the increasing worry that Henry might not, after all, be able to deliver on his promise. Having been crowned in Milan in January 1311, Henry had immediately met with difficulties: Florence had refused to send representatives to the coronation and had instead sought in every way possible to ally itself ever more closely with the papal court, and Henry had met with resistance too among the cities of Lombardy, so that the coronation in Rome that would confirm his imperial authority was starting to look ever more distant and uncertain.

In the letter to Henry, Dante does not hide the frustration that he feels at these various delays and setbacks; and yet his frustration does not dim his conviction that Henry and Henry alone can restore the empire and bring peace to the world and happiness to the individuals within it. Rather, the slow and difficult progress made by Henry only goes to confirm, in Dante's eyes, the emperor-elect's identification with Christ, as Dante maintains that the doubts of Henry's followers inspire them to cry out "in vocem Precursoris . . .: 'Tu es qui venturus es, an alium expectamus?'" (*Ep.* 7.2) [with the words of Christ's precursor . . . : "Are you the one who is to come, or have we got to wait for someone else?"].[57] The Gospel reply given by Christ to the followers of John the Baptist when they ask him this same question confirms his messianic status in no uncertain terms, while exhorting them not to lose faith: "Caeci vident claudi ambulant leprosi mundantur surdi audiunt mortui resurgunt pauperes evangelizantur et beatus est qui non fuerit scandalizatus in me" (Matt. 11:5–6) [The blind see again, and the lame walk, lepers are cleansed, and the deaf hear, and the dead are raised to life and the Good News is proclaimed to the poor; and happy is the man who does not lose faith in me]. Likewise here, the biblical quotation enables Dante to reiterate the Christological status of Henry VII, while providing encouragement for his doubting supporters. And this renewed statement of confidence in Henry is given an even stronger expression just a few sentences further on, when Dante explains that he has, himself, seen and paid homage to the emperor-elect: "Cum pedes tuos manus mee tractarunt et labia mea debitum persolverunt . . . exultavit in te spiritus meus, cum tacitus dixi mecum: 'Ecce Agnus Dei, ecce qui tollis peccata mundi'" (*Ep.* 7.2) [When my hands touched your feet, and my lips paid homage to you . . . my spirit exulted in you, and I silently said to myself: Behold the lamb of God that takes away the sins of the world]. This sentence contains two further confirmations of Henry's Christ-like status, which, taken together, could scarcely be more emphatic. The first is an echo of the *Magnificat*— "Exultavit spiritus meus in Deo salutari meo" (Luke 1:47) [My spirit has rejoiced in God my savior]—while the second is a reflection of the *Agnus Dei* (John 1:29); in both cases the passages are not only biblical but also liturgical, meaning that their repercussions would have been unmistakable for Dante's readers. Dante presents Henry as God's representative on earth, working to free human beings, not from their sins *tout court*, like

Christ himself, but specifically from the sins of the political sphere, which prevent political stability and impede peace in earthly community and happiness in the individuals who make them up.[58]

Perhaps even more interestingly, though, the parallel that Dante sets up here between Henry and Christ has implications also for the letter writer himself. For the *exul inmeritus*, the lone voice crying in the political wilderness of contemporary Italy, is clearly presented here as standing in an anticipatory and prophetic relationship to the quasi-messianic emperor, like that of John the Baptist to Christ. Far from being the formulaic work of a mere anonymous spokesman, the letter, in this period of Dante's epistolary production, is transformed into a sort of "oracle" (a term to which I shall return shortly), the work not of a scribe or bureaucrat but of a prophet and visionary.[59]

The fact that John the Baptist was the patron saint of Florence—the city that was Henry's most tenacious opponent—makes the parallel that Dante sets up in the letter to the emperor all the more ironic. Dante's claiming of his isolation—his becoming a "parte per se stesso"—as a badge of honor may recall John's voluntary retreat into the wilderness; but at the same time the relationship with Florence that these letters convey is strongly reminiscent of the relationship of the Old Testament prophets with the city of Jerusalem. For Isaiah and Jeremiah, Jerusalem remains God's chosen city, even as they rebuke its wicked citizens in the harshest of terms;[60] and in the same way Dante is never just an *exul inmeritus*, he is also, always, *Florentinus*, and as such he claims for himself the right to address the city as one of its own, even while acknowledging his estrangement from it.[61] In the *Convivio* he had claimed that "chiamare solemo la cittade quelli che la tengono, e non coloro che la combattono, avvegna che l'uno e l'altro sia cittadino" (*Conv.* 2.6.8) [when we refer to a city we mean those who hold it, not those who are attacking it, even though both groups are citizens], and this assertion resonates strongly, for example, in the *salutatio* of *Epistle* 6, in which Dante, a Florentine outsider, boldly addresses the "scelestissimis Florentinis intrinsecis" [the most wicked Florentines *within* the city], claiming, as we have seen, against all social, political, and epistolary conventions, the superiority of the former over the latter.[62] And the overturning of convention continues here into the *exordium*, where we find no *captatio benevolentiae* but rather the threatening voice of a hellfire and damnation preacher: "In hanc Dei manifestissimam voluntatem quicunque temere presumendo tumescent . . . ex nunc severi iudicis adventante iudicio pallore notentur" (*Ep.* 6.1) [Let all those who, in their blind arrogance, resist these clear signs of God's will now turn pale at the thought of the impending judgment of such a severe judge].

This powerful and unconventional opening, then, points the reader toward the way in which, in this letter, Dante will explicitly appropriate the voice of the prophet, when, having foretold, in three paragraphs of pure vitriol, the complete and utter destruction of Florence, he adds the only apparently concessive "si presaga mens mea non fallitur" [if my prophetic gift does not deceive me]—only apparently concessive because he then goes on to assert that Florence's terrible fate is revealed by "sic signis veridicis sicut inexpugnabilibus argumentis" (*Ep.* 6.4) [unequivocal signs and unquestionable arguments], leaving very little room for doubt. These three paragraphs take the *stilus rhetoricus* to a new level. Biblical quotations sit cheek by jowl with classical ones, as in the passage immediately preceding Dante's reference to his prophetic gift, where Lucan gives way to Jeremiah;[63] rhetorical questions become so insistent as to create almost the feeling of a cross-examination: "Quid . . . pium deserentes imperium nova regna temptatis . . . ? Cur apostolice monarchie similiter invidere non libet, ut si Delia geminatur in celo, geminetur et Delius? . . . An septi vallo ridiculo cuiquam defensioni confiditis? (*Ep.* 6.2–3) [Why . . . do you insist on forsaking the holy empire and on trying to build new kingdoms . . . ? Why do you not regard the church with similar envy? If you would like to see two moons in the sky, why not also two suns? . . . Do you believe that your pathetic fortifications will protect you?] (§§2–3), and so on. And this is all skillfully interwoven with the sort of "legalese" typical of the letter-writing genre, as when Dante distinguishes carefully between public and prescriptive rights.[64]

We might set alongside these examples of the rhetorical tools employed in the letter to the Florentines a truly striking passage of invective against his hometown in which Dante indulges in the letter to Henry. With what may be a passing nod to the questions of social *convenientia* with which the *artes dictandi* were so preoccupied, it is almost as if Dante feels liberated by the fact that, in *Epistle* 7, he is speaking about Florence (and to a social and political superior at that) rather than to her (or her representatives) directly, and the full strength of his frustration with the city here emerges in a torrent of abuse, in which he piles metaphor upon metaphor of animalistic violence, sickness, corruption, and self-destructive rage:

> An ignoras, excellentissime principum, nec de specula summa celsitudinis deprehendis ubi vulpecula fetoris istius, venantium secura, recumbat? Quippe nec Pado precipiti, nec Tiberi tuo criminosa potatur, verum Sarni fluenta torrentis adhuc rictus eius inficiunt, et Florentia, forte nescis?, dira hec pernicies nuncupatur. Hec est vipera versa in viscera genetricis; hec est languida pecus gregem domini sui sua contagion commaculans. . . . Vere matrem viperea feritate dilaniare contendit. . . . Vere fumos, evaporante sanie, vitiantes exhalat, et inde vicine pecudes et inscie contabescunt. (*Ep.* 7.7)

> [Do you not realize, most excellent prince, have you risen so high, your Highness, that you cannot see where it is that this stinking vixen has gone to earth, safe from the hunters? It is not, to be sure, from the swift waters of the Po, nor from your own Tiber that this troublemaker drinks. Rather, her snarling jaws continue to pollute the rushing course of the Arno, and—did you really not know it?—Florence is the name of this ill-omened beast. She is the viper who turns against the vitals of her own mother; she is the sick sheep, which infects her master's flock with her disease. . . . With all the ferocity of a viper, she strives to tear her mother to pieces. . . . She gives off fetid fumes, dripping with gore, which cause any nearby flocks still unaware of her ways to waste away.]

Epistles 6 and 7 thus stand as examples of Dantean texts that draw on the traditional norms of medieval letter writing but also go beyond and, where necessary, invert these in order to convey a powerful message intended (in the spirit of Cacciaguida's injunction in *Paradiso* 17) to provide nutritious, if hard-to-swallow fare for his readers, in which the complexity of the metaphorical language strongly reinforces, rather than obscuring, the message to be conveyed.[65] In the passages highlighted above (and in many more that space does not allow me to discuss in detail), it is possible to identify an approach to tradition long seen as typical of the mature Dante's poetic practice. He makes use of the genre, even while pushing back against its rules and conventions, making of it something unexpected, recognizably of the genre and yet not constrained by it, in a way that clearly recalls the way he approaches questions of style and genre in the writing of the *Commedia*.

This characteristically Dantean approach should be borne in mind also when considering Dante's other great political letter: that addressed to the Italian cardinals following the death of Pope Clement V (*Epistle* 11).[66] In some ways this is a more "practical" letter than the three letters written during Henry VII's Italian campaign, which for all their rhetorical sophistication and vehemence are really no more than strongly worded but ultimately fairly generic statements of support for the imperial cause. *Epistle* 11 has, at least, a clear *petitio*: the request that the Italian cardinals at the conclave band together against the "Gascons," who, in 1305, elected Clement V and initiated what Dante would see as the papacy's "Babylonian exile" in Avignon, to ensure the election of an Italian pope and, more importantly, the return of the institution to its "rightful" place in Rome. And although it lacks a *salutatio*—indeed, the second person is not introduced until the fourth paragraph—it nonetheless returns, somewhat obsessively even, to questions of *convenientia*. The whole of the fifth paragraph, for instance, is devoted to Dante's defense of himself against the charge of speaking out of turn to those in ecclesiastical authority, and he returns to this theme—"Pudeat ergo tam ab infra . . . argui vel moneri" (*Ep*. 11.9) [You should be ashamed, therefore, at being condemned and rebuked by such a humble person]—at the point of transition to the *petitio*, turning the apparent inappropriateness around so that it reflects badly, not on the letter's humble author, but on its high-ranking recipients, who are so tainted by cupidity that they are unable to recognize (or to repent of) their misdeeds for themselves.

If the three imperial letters had been characterized above all by a prophetic tone and by the fervent hope for the realization of peace on earth, this letter, while having lost none of the anger of its predecessors, is instead characterized above all by this tone of disappointment. Henry had died of malaria in 1313 without ever having united Italy (let alone the world) under the universal empire of which Dante dreamed; the papacy had been removed to Avignon; Rome was deprived of both her suns; and Dante saw little hope for the future. Even the biblical quotation with which the letter opens, despite its having been taken from a prophetic text, appears to look only to the past: "Quomodo sola sedet civitas plena populo! Facta est quasi vidua domina gentium" [Oh how lonely she sits, the city once thronged with people. She who was great among the nations has become like a widow].⁶⁷ The quotation from Lamentations confirms from the outset that the peace and renewal that Dante dreamed of in 1311 have not come about, for he notes that while he too, like Jeremiah, finds himself compelled to weep for a widowed, lonely city, unlike the prophet, who tells of the future destruction of Jerusalem, Dante expresses his grief only after the event: "Cum Ieremia, non lugenda prevenientes se post ipsa dolentes, viduam et desertam lugere compellimur" (*Ep.* 11.2) [We too, like Jeremiah, find ourselves compelled to weep for our own widowed, lonely city; not in anticipation of things to come, but rather in suffering after the event]. I have argued elsewhere that the failure of Henry's campaign, in particular, brings about a dramatic shift in the way in which Dante conceives of the notion of peace and of the possibility of the attainment of political peace and harmony on earth, and specifically, I have suggested that, in those of his works written after the failure of Henry's campaign, he shifts his hopes for peace, stability, and perfect citizenship between individuals from the earthly to the heavenly plane.⁶⁸

This is a complex question, the repercussions of which go far beyond the remit of the present chapter. Nonetheless, I would contend that a close reading of *Epistle* 11 supports such a view and points to an abrupt change in Dante's mind-set between the period of the "imperial" letters in 1310–11 and that of the letter to the cardinals, written in 1314. Here, in keeping with the way in which he appropriates the quotation from Lamentations in the letter's opening, Dante speaks no longer as a prophet, as he did when writing about Henry, but as a resigned realist, one who is compelled to speak truth to power, even when he knows that his voice is unlikely to be heard. The letter closes, in fact, with a very small opening toward hope—the church, the Bride of Christ, may be saved if only the cardinals are able to work together to bring her back to Rome;⁶⁹ but the foregoing paragraphs serve only to reinforce in the mind of the reader how unlikely a prospect this collaboration really is. And, meanwhile, the letter's only prophetic pronouncement—uttered as an aside, but a significant one, suggests that if this does not happen the church will necessarily remain corrupt "usque ad ignem, cui celi qui nunc sunt et terra sunt reservati" (*Ep.* 11.11) [until the fire for which the present heaven and earth are destined], that is, until the Day of Judgment.

If the letter to the cardinals were Dante's final surviving letter, it would be tempting to draw this chapter to a close with that reference to the Day of Judgment, which would, at least, give it a nice finality. However, the occasional nature of the epistolary genre means that, as long as the author remains alive, there is always the chance of a further word, some new statement, an excursion into a new theme with a new correspondent. I shall end, then, not with the Last Judgment but with a return (in writing, if not in person) to Florence, for the last extant letter that can be definitively attributed to Dante returns to the subject that runs right across his epistolary output: his exile. *Epistle* 12 can be dated with some certainty to after an amnesty announced by the government of Florence on May 19, 1315. In it, Dante scornfully rejects the offer of a return to his hometown on what he deems to be humiliating conditions: the payment of a fine and a ceremony of penitence in the Baptistery, which Dante will not entertain. The rhetorical questions with which he earlier scorned Florence's stance against Henry VII are now used to deride the city's risible offer to its political exiles. The writer who so forcefully appropriated for himself the prophetic voice of Florence's patron will not be led to the Baptistery like a conquered slave:[70] "Estne ista revocatio gratiosa qua Dantes Alagherii revocatur ad patriam, per trilustrium fere perpessus exilium? Hocne meruit innocentia manifesta quibuslibet? hoc sudor et labor in studio? Absit a viro phylosophie domestico temeraria tantum cordis humilitas... quasi vinctus ipse se offerri!" (*Ep.* 12.3) [Is this, then, the gracious recall of Dante Alighieri to his native city, after the miseries of nearly fifteen years of exile? Is this the reward for innocence that is evident for all to see, and for the sweat and toil of relentless study? Heaven forfend that a philosopher should submit to such a senseless act of humiliation, presenting himself for the ceremony... like a common criminal in chains!]. Some ten years earlier, in the letter that he had written to the Conti Guidi on the occasion of the death of their uncle (*Epistle* 2), Dante had alluded to the state of quasi-servitude to which his exile had reduced him. Poverty, he claimed, had confined him to a prison cell, without horses or arms.[71] Then, his only aim had been to free himself and return to Florence; but much has happened in the meantime—not least the imperial adventure of the years 1310–13—and Dante's relationship with his hometown, perhaps conditioned by its reaction to Henry and by the way in which he had come to think, and to write letters, about it during that period had been irrevocably damaged.

A sort of midway point between these two positions can be found in the letter that Dante writes to Moroello Malaspina (*Epistle* 4), traditionally dated to somewhere around 1308. This letter presents the writer's political allegiances in a much more ambivalent way, which expresses neither the immediate desire to return to Florence at any cost (as seen in *Epistles* 1 and 2) nor the later, more cautious, approach, characterized by the taking on of that lone voice of truth recommended by Cacciaguida and influenced, no doubt, by the behavior of Florence toward Henry VII. In this letter, as Catherine Keen has argued very persuasively, Dante walks a fine line:[72] on the one hand, he declares his allegiance to Moroello (a statement that, significantly, appears in the letter's *exordium*, the paragraph traditionally associated with the *captatio benevolentiae* that this statement clearly represents),[73] and, on the other, he asserts his freedom to take that allegiance as he wills and give it to some other lord (in the letter the lord of love who controls him utterly, in a way that Moroello never could).[74] In the letter, these bonds are described in the language of the feudal courts, of serfs and lords, rather than through the language of citizenship most often associated with Dante's Florence.[75] But these two worlds come together in the *congedo* of the *canzone* that is usually associated with this letter, the so-called *canzone montanina* ("Amor, da che convien pur ch'io mi doglia" [Love, since it behooves me to grieve]), where Dante sends his poem to Florence, but only to reject the city in his powerlessness to stray from the new love that holds him:

> O montanina mia canzon, tu vai:
> forse vedrai Fiorenza, la mia terra,
> che fuor di sé mi serra,
> vota d'amore e nuda di pietate;
> se dentro v'entri, va dicendo: "Omai
> non vi può far lo mio fattor più guerra:
> là ond'io vegno una catena il serra
> tal, che se piega vostra crudeltate,
> non ha di ritornar qui libertate."
>   (*Rime* 15.76–84)

[Off you go, my mountain song, and perhaps you'll see Florence, my city that has banished me, empty of love and denuded of pity. If you go inside, say, "Now you can no longer harm my maker. In the place where I've come from a chain holds him, so that even if your cruelty were to end he would no longer be free to return."]

In her recent Meridiani edition of the letters (2014), Claudia Villa has suggested a later dating for this letter, and—taking up a suggestion of Boccaccio's—an association of the text not, as has been almost universally supposed for nearly two centuries, with the *montanina* but with the *Purgatorio*, and specifically with the cantos of the Earthly Paradise (*Purg.* 28–33).[76] Constraints of space do not allow me to explore this suggestion in detail in the present context, but, on the basis of the evidence presented in this chapter, the letter's political ambivalence in relation to Florence, exile, and the relationship between the civic and courtly worlds seems much more typical of the pre-Henry period of Dante's political thought (and of his epistolary production) than of the single-mindedness (one might even say "obsessiveness") of Dante's support for the imperial cause and of his determination (one might even say "stubbornness") with regard to his own exile that we have identified in the letters written from late 1310 onward.

The letter to the Florentine friend (*Epistle* 12), on the other hand, seems to me to be perfectly in keeping both with Cacciaguida's injunction that Dante should value truth above all else in his writing and with the purely imaginary return to Florence that Dante stages in *Paradiso* 25,[77] where he imagines a return to the city, not in chains in the guise of a petty criminal, but as its honored poet:

> Se mai continga che 'l poema sacro
> al quale ha posto mano e cielo e terra,
> sì che m'ha fatto per molti anni macro,
>   vinca la crudeltà che fuor mi serra
> del bello ovile ov'io dormi' agnello,
> nimico ai lupi che li danno guerra;
>   con altra voce omai, con altro vello
> ritornerò poeta, e in sul fonte
> del mio battesmo prenderò 'l cappello.
>   (*Par.* 25.1–9)

[If it ever comes to pass that this sacred poem, to which both heaven and earth have set their hand so that it has made me waste away for many years, should overcome the cruelty that banishes me from the beautiful sheepfold where I slept as a lamb, an enemy of the wolves that attack it, then, with another voice and another fleece, I shall return as a poet, and, at the font where I received my baptism, I shall receive the laurel crown.]

Only this kind of return to Florence would be acceptable to Dante. But the Dante who wrote *Epistles* 6 and 7 must have known that it was highly unlikely ever to happen. It is not a coincidence that this daydream of return is situated precisely in the canto devoted to hope. Dante's hopes now, are not, in reality, of a return to Florence (as *Epistle* 12 makes abundantly clear) but only of heaven. If Dante had written himself out of hope in the letters to and about Henry, he had also, by the time he was drafting the final cantos of the *Paradiso*, written himself out of the despair of the letter to the cardinals. The letter to the Florentine friend does not speak of resignation and certainly not of defeat; in it Dante writes with a clear conception of his own worth and of that of his work, the fruit of his "sudor et labor in studio" (*Ep.* 12.3) [sweat and toil in study]. He writes, not with the voice of a letter writer and an exile hopeful of return, but with the confident voice of a poet and a citizen not of any earthly city but of "quella Roma onde Cristo è romano" (*Purg.* 32.102) [that Rome of which Christ is a Roman].

Notes

    1. All translations in this chapter are my own; translations from *Epistles* 5, 6, 7, and 11 are taken from Honess ed. and trans., *Four Political Letters*.

    2. Boccaccio, *Trattatello*, ed. Maier, 79.

    3. Bruni, *Vite di Dante*, 43.

    4. On these "missing" letters, see Montefusco, "Lettere di Dante," 22–27.

    5. See, for example, Giorgio Inglese's recent biography of Dante, which seeks to draw distinctions between "'certezza' . . . , probabilità ragionata e . . . semplice plausibilità" [the certain . . . , the logically probable, and . . . the merely plausible] (Inglese, *Vita di Dante*, 12).

    6. G. Villani, *Nuova cronica* 10.136; Bruni, *Vite*, 43. The opening words cited by Bruni here echo the Good Friday *Improperia* [Reproaches] in a way that may recall Dante's quotation of the book of Lamentations in the openings of *Epistle* 11 and the letter on the death of Beatrice mentioned in *Vn* 30.

7. See Toynbee, "Introduction," xxviii–xxxvi.

8. See Pellegrini, "Quattordicesima epistola." The text of this letter can be found in Zaccagnini, *Vita dei maestri*, 212–13.

9. For a compelling rebuttal of Pellegrini's arguments, see Casadei, "Nuova epistola di Dante?"

10. These are *Epistle* 1, written on behalf of the exiled White Guelfs of Florence, and *Epistles* 8, 9, and 10, written on behalf of the Countess of Battifolle, the wife of Count Guido, who hosted the poet at the castle of Poppi in the Casentino, to the east of Florence, in the spring of 1311. On the authenticity of these letters, which was considered dubious until the twentieth century, see Moore, "'Battifolle' Letters."

11. *Epistles* 6 and 7 were also written at Poppi, as the texts themselves attest. See *Ep.* 6.6 and 7.8.

12. *Epistle* 3 is linked with the sonnet "Io sono stato con Amore insieme" (*Rime* 104); *Epistle* 4 is conventionally associated with the canzone "Amor, da che convien pur ch'io mi doglia" (*Rime* 15). The controversial epistle to Cangrande is connected with the *Paradiso*.

13. On the manuscript tradition of the *Epistles*, see Pastore Stocchi, "Epistole," 705–6, and Montefusco, "Lettere di Dante," 7–22.

14. Barolini, "For the Record," 140; and for an illustration of the occasionally heated nature of this debate, see H. Kelly, "*Cangrande* and the Ortho-Dantists" (with Hollander's "Response," and H. Kelly's further "Reply to Robert Hollander").

15. My approach is therefore a more inclusive one, in terms of Dante's literary canon, than that of Ahern, who contends that the letters "were never intended to be read together (*or separately*) as literary texts. Nor were they meant to shed light on the *Commedia*, with the possible exception of the letter to Cangrande, or on any of his other literary works" (Ahern, "*Epistles*," 353; my italics).

16. I make no attempt, in this context, to give an exhaustive bibliography but refer the reader to the further reading and in-depth discussions contained in Azzetta ed., 273–324, Brugnoli, "Introduzione," and Villa ed., 1565–83, and in the more recent contributions to the debate by (among others, including those referred to above) Ascoli ("*Epistle to Cangrande*"), Azzetta ("Chiose"), Barański ("*Comedìa*"), Bellomo ("Epistola a Cangrande"), Casadei ("Sull'autenticità"), Hall and Sowell ("*Cursus*"), Hollander (*Dante's Epistle to Cangrande*), Jennaro-MacLennan (*Trecento Commentaries*), H. Kelly (*Tragedy and Comedy*), and Pertile ("*Canto-cantica-Comedìa*").

17. F. Villani, *Expositio*, 32.

18. See Hollander, *Dante's Epistle to Cangrande*, 4.

19. On the manuscript tradition of *Epistle* 13, see Brugnoli, "Introduzione," 512–13.

20. "Redditur, ecce, sermo Calliopeus inferius" [Please find attached below a poetic composition] (*Ep.* 3.2); "Regnat itaque Amor in me, nulla refragante

virtute; qualiterque me regat, inferius extra sinum presentium requiratis" (*Ep.* 4.5) [Love, therefore, reigns within me, unchecked by virtue; and just how Love reigns you will discover below, beyond the present letter].

21. See for example, Mancini, "Nuovi dubbi"; Nardi, *Punto*. Authorship of the latter part of the letter is often attributed to one of the Trecento commentators who cite it, and in particular Guido da Pisa (see, for example, H. Kelly, *Tragedy and Comedy*) and Boccaccio (see, for example, Ginzburg, "Dante's Epistle to Cangrande").

22. See, for example, Barolini, "For the Record"; Nardi, *Punto*.

23. See, for example, Barański, "*Comedìa*."

24. See, for example, Hall and Sowell, "*Cursus*"; H. Kelly, *Tragedy and Comedy*.

25. "Itaque, formula consumata epistole" (*Ep.* 13.4) [Therefore, having completed the formula prescribed for letter writing].

26. See, for example, Davis, "Education in Dante's Florence."

27. See Witt, "Arts of Letter-Writing," 70–71.

28. Ibid., 71.

29. Camargo, *Ars dictaminis, ars dictandi*, 22.

30. "Illustrissime atque piissime domine domine Margarite divina providentia Romanorum regine et semper Auguste, fidelissima sua G. de Batifolle Dei et imperialis indulgentie gratia comitissa in Tuscia palatina, cum promptissima recommendatione se ipsam et voluntarium ad obsequia famulatum" (*Ep.* 10.1) [To the most illustrious and most gracious lady, Lady Margaret, by divine providence Queen of the Romans and always Augusta, her most faithful servant, G. di Battifolle, by the grace of God and by imperial indulgence Countess Palatine in Tuscany, offers with eager devotion herself and her willing and compliant service]. For an analysis of the specific subgenre of "letters written on behalf of female rulers," see Bartoli Langeli, "Scrivere all'imperatrice," 434–45.

31. Camargo, *Ars dictaminis, ars dictandi*, 22; Witt, "Arts of Letter-Writing," 71.

32. Witt, "Arts of Letter-Writing," 73.

33. "Cum pagina vestre Serenitatis apparuit ante scribentis et gratulantis aspectum, experta est mea pura fidelitas quam in dominorum successibus corda subditorum fidelium colletentur" (*Ep.* 10.2) [When Your Serenity's letter reached the one who writes this letter and sends this greeting, my sincere devotion showed the extent to which the hearts of devoted servants are made glad by the good fortune of their lords].

34. Camargo, *Ars dictaminis, ars dictandi*, 24; "Nam per ea que continebantur in ipsa, cum tota cordis hilaritate concepi qualiter dextera summi Regis vota Cesaris et Auguste feliciter adimplebat" (*Ep.* 10.2) [For from the contents of your letter I gathered, with great rejoicing in my heart, how the right hand of the great king was successfully realizing the wishes of Caesar and Augusta].

35. "Verum quia nonnulla regalium clausularum videbatur hortari ut, si quando nuntiorum facultas adesset, Celsitudini regie aliquid peroptando de status mei condizione referrem, quamvis quedam presumptionis facies interdicat, obedientie tamen suadente virtute obediam" (*Ep.* 10.4) [Since a sentence in the royal letter seemed to urge that, should the opportunity to send a message arise, I should provide your Royal Highness, in accordance with my own desires, some details of my own circumstances and condition, although I am constrained by the fear of appearing presumptuous, yet, won over by the virtue of obedience, I will obey].

36. The response can be reduced to a simple "We are well, thank you": "Audiat, ex quo iubet, Romanorum pia et serena Maiestas, quoniam tempore missionis presentium coniunx predilectus et ego, Dei dono, vigebamus incolumes, liberorum sospitate gaudentes, tanto solito letiores quanto signa resurgentis Imperii meliora iam secula promittebant" (*Ep.* 10.4) [May it please the gracious and serene majesty of the Romans to learn, since she so commands, that at the time of writing my beloved husband and myself, by the gift of God, were prospering and in good health, rejoicing in the welfare of our children, and more joyful than usual since signs of the improving imperial fortunes were promising happier times to come].

37. Witt, "Arts of Letter-Writing," 76–78.

38. See Reggio, "Niccolò da Prato." This letter is dated to March/April 1304.

39. "Et si negligentie sontes aut ignavie censeremur ob iniuriam tarditatis, citra iudicium discretion sancta vestra preponderet" (*Ep.* 1.1) [And should we be judged guilty of negligence or sloth by fault of our tardiness, may your holy discretion fall short of condemnation].

40. Quis vobis dignas grates persolvere attentabit? [Who can attempt to render due thanks to you?] (*Ep.* 1.7; and compare *Aen.* 1.600–601 and 2.537).

41. For a reading of this crucial turning point in Dante's political engagement with his hometown and, by extension in his career as a writer, see Tavoni, "*Epistole* I e II."

42. See the passage from *Ep.* 1.5 quoted above.

43. See Brilli, "Enrico VII," 421. I agree entirely with Brilli that Dante cannot here be referring to any formal political group, but my own interpretation (see, for example, Honess, "'Ritornerò poeta . . .'") points more toward eschatological hope than immediate war.

44. For a detailed analysis of Henry VII's Italian campaign, see Bowsky, *Henry VII in Italy*.

45. See *Conv.* 4.4; *Mon.* 1.5. On the link between Dante's conception of peace in *Epistle* 5 and his arguments in favor of a universal emperor in *Convivio* and *Monarchia*, see Honess, "Ecce nunc tempus acceptabile,'" 485–91.

46. Toynbee, "Introduction," xiii. Ferrante describes this group of letters as works of "undisguised political propaganda" (*Political Vision*, 108).

47. "Haec dicit Dominus in tempore placito exaudivi te et in die salutis auxiliatus sum tui . . . ut diceres his qui vincti sunt exite et his qui in tenebris revelamini" (Isa. 49:8–9) [Thus says Yahweh: At the favorable time I will answer you, on the day of salvation I will help you. . . . I will say to the prisoners, "Come out," to those who are in darkness, "Show yourselves"]; "Ait enim tempore accepto exaudivi te et in die salutis adiuvavi te ecce nunc tempus acceptabile ecce nunc dies salutis" (2 Cor. 6:2) [For he says: *At the favorable time I have listened to you; on the day of salvation I came to your help.* Well, now is the favorable time; this is the day of salvation].

48. This is a common biblical term with Messianic overtones. Compare Gen. 49:9–10; Rev. 5:5.

49. Compare Deut. 6:3.

50. Compare "gloriam plebis tuae Israhel" (Luke 2:32) [the glory of your people Israel].

51. "Sponsus tuus . . . ad nuptias properat" (*Ep.* 5.2) [your bridegroom . . . is hurrying to his wedding]. On this comparison, see Pertile, "Dante Looks Forward," 7–8; Nasti, *Favole d'amore*, 143–45.

52. Compare Rom. 13:2.

53. Compare Acts 26:14.

54. "Ego sum Iesus quem tu persequeris" (Acts 26:15) [I am Jesus and you are persecuting me].

55. For a more complete enumeration, see the footnotes in Honess ed. and trans., *Four Political Letters*, 47–56.

56. Compare *Purg.* 6, 16, and 32, in particular. This fundamental difference makes me skeptical about Somaini's suggestion that *Purgatorio* 6 and *Epistle* 5 were intended as a sort of "dittico poetico-letterario e retorico-politico" [poetic/literary and rhetorical/political diptych] to be presented to Henry himself ("Epistola V," 288).

57. Compare Matt. 11:3; Luke 7:19.

58. Happiness, according to the *Convivio*, is the goal of human and communal life: "La umana civilitade . . . a uno fine è ordinate, cioè a vita felice" (4.4.1) [Human civilization . . . is ordered toward one end; that is, a happy life].

59. On Dante's letters as prophetic utterances, see Montefusco, "Competenze."

60. On the importance—and ambivalence—of the city of Jerusalem in medieval culture and for Dante, see Honess, *From Florence*, 107–50.

61. Dante's lone voice of truth "acts upon the world by being outside of it" (Mazzotta, *Dante*, 138).

62. On this letter, see Marcozzi, "Epistola di Dante."

63. "Videbitis plebem circumquaque furentem nunc in contraria, pro et contra, deinde in idem adversus vos horrenda clamantem, quoniam simul et ieiuna et timida nescit esse. Templa quoque spoliata, cotidie matronarum frequentata concursu, parvulosque admirantes et inscios peccata patrum luere

destinatos videre pigebit" (*Ep.* 6.4) [Now the population, divided against itself, rages indiscriminately, some for you and some against you, but then you will see it united in raising its voice terribly in opposition to you, since a starving mob is incapable of fear. Likewise you will be ashamed to see your holy places, where groups of women congregate each day, defiled, and your children, bewildered and ignorant, destined to pay for the sins of their fathers]. Compare Lucan, *Phars.* 3.58: "Nescit plebes ieiuna timere" [a starving people is incapable of fear]; Lam. 5:7: "Patres nostri peccaverunt . . . et nos iniquitates eorum portavimus" [Our fathers have sinned . . . and we ourselves bear the weight of their crimes].

64. "An ignoratis, amentes et discoli, publica iura cum sola temporis terminatione finiri, et nullius prescriptionis calculo fore obnoxia?" (*Ep.* 6.2) [Are you unaware, in your absurd perversity, that public rights cannot be restricted by arguments based on prescription and can be brought to an end only with the end of time itself?]. On the legal implications of this letter, see Steinberg, "Messianic and Legal Time."

65. See also Tomazzoli, who notes that, no matter how dense the figurative language of these letters may become, comprehensibility is always Dante's priority ("Funzioni delle metafore," 159).

66. For a discussion of the historical context of this letter, see Honess ed. and trans., *Four Political Letters*, 83–84.

67. *Epistle* 11.1. The reference is to Lam. 1:1, a verse also quoted by Dante in the *Vita nova*, where he claims to have used it as the *incipit* of his letter to the rulers of Florence on the death of Beatrice (*Vn* XXVIII.1 [19.1]; XXX.1 [19.8]), and paraphrased in the invective against Italy of *Purg.* 6 (78 and 112–13).

68. See Honess, "Ecce nunc tempus acceptabile" and "Ritornerò poeta."

69. "Emendabitur quidem . . . si unanimes omnes qui huiusmodi exorbitationis fuistis auctores, pro Sponsa Christi, pro sede Sponse de Roma est, pro Ytalia nostra, et ut plenius dicam, pro tota civitate peregrinante in terries, viriliter propugnetis" (*Ep.* 11.11) [Amends certainly will be . . . if all those of you who were the authors of this transgression will now go forth together to fight bravely for the Bride of Christ, for the Seat of the Bride which is Rome, for our Italy and, in more general terms, for the whole of the City of God on pilgrimage in this life]. See also Lokaj, "Fonti biblico-patristiche."

70. On this letter and questions of reputation and infamy, see Steinberg, *Dante and the Limits*, 16–20.

71. "Inopina paupertas quam fecit exilium . . . , equis armisque vacantem iam sue captivitatis me detrusit in antrum . . . , et nitentem cunctis exsurgere viribus, hucusque prevalens, impia retinere molitur" (*Ep.* 2.3) [The unlooked-for poverty brought about by exile . . . has thrust me, deprived of horses and arms, into her prison cell [. . .], and though I struggle with all my strength to get free, so far this wicked one has prevailed against me].

72. Keen, "Florence and Faction."

73. "Ne lateant dominum vincula servi sui . . . ad conspectum Magnificentie vestre presentis oraculi seriem placuit destinare" (*Ep.* 4.1) [Lest my lord be ignorant of the bonds of his servant . . . it has seemed good to me to address this letter to the eyes of your Magnificence].

74. "Ne contra se amplius anima rebellaret, liberum meum ligavit arbitrium, ut non quo ego, sed quo ille vult, me verti oporteat" (*Ep.* 4.4) [In order to prevent my spirit rebelling against him, he bound my free will, so that I had to go not where I wish but where he wishes].

75. On citizenship in Dante, see Honess, *From Florence*, especially 37–70; Keen, *Dante and the City*, especially 50–91.

76. See Villa ed., 1529–40, and Villa, "Tempi dell'epistolario dantesco."

77. On the relationship between *Par.* 25 and the *Egloge*, see Lummus, chapter 9 of this book, the section "Dante's Laurel Crown."

CHAPTER 5

Convivio

SIMON GILSON

All of Dante's "other" works are—as is becoming increasingly well known—richly complex and multifaceted; they all have their own histories (histories that include to varying degrees the history of their relations with the *Commedia*); and they all have their own cultural programs, as well as their own rhetorical ends and argumentative imperatives. This chapter deals with the *Convivio*, exploring some of the interpretative trends and issues raised by a work whose overall meaning and value have been highly contested, especially in the last hundred years. The *Convivio* has indeed been almost a crucible for polemics at various points in the last century. At the same time, and certainly in the last twenty-five years, there has been a remarkable resurgence of critical interest, with new Italian and German editions and commentaries, alongside major monographic studies, important volumes of collected essays, several dedicated study days, and a new English translation. This work looks set to continue with a major new Italian edition planned for publication after the 2021 anniversary year.[1]

Given such critical ferment, the heated disputes, and the now quite daunting bibliography, on the one hand, as well as the remarkable philosophical and exegetical complexity of the work, on the other hand, one inevitably sets out with some trepidation in any attempt to make sense of Dante's "quasi comento" (1.3.2) [almost commentary]. In what follows, we have four main aims divided into four sections. We will first provide a general overview of the work's structure, organization, content, main themes, and language. Second, we will outline some background regarding its textual state, transmission, and early reception, since such matters have significant bearing on later interpretative questions. The third aim is to attempt to provide a critical overview of the varied approaches to categorizing and interpreting Dante's treatise in the twentieth- and early twenty-first century. The sections dealing with the second and third aims will also broach the question of the relations between the *Convivio* and Dante's poem. However, a fourth and final section will offer, by way of a coda, some more detailed reflections on the ways in which the work has been utilized in relation to the *Commedia*.

Structure, Organization, Subject Matter, and Language

The *Convivio*, as it is titled—even if it takes some time for this designation to settle down, and early terms used include *chiosa* or *Amoroso Convivio* (recalling 3.12.12) or *Convito*—is of course a *prosimetrum*, that is, a work combining both verse and prose commentary on that verse. Crucially, however, it is also a work of self-commentary, since the verse is Dante's own in the form of three major doctrinal canzoni. In this narrow sense at least, the work can be related to Dante's earlier prosimetrical self-commentary, the *Vita nova*. The *Convivio* is unfinished and has come down to us in four books, even though fifteen seem to have been projected, since in the first book Dante tells us of his intention to provide commentary on fourteen of his canzoni (1.1.14; see also 3.15; 4.26 and 4.27).[2] Given Dante's acute attunement to the importance of intricate correspondences, symmetries, and proportion (1.5.13; 2.13.17–18), the number fifteen (the opening book plus the book-length expositions on the fourteen earlier poems) takes on a structural role in the overall design of the work. Fifteen acts as the basic unit for books 2 and 3, which have fifteen chapters each, and for book 4, which has thirty; and other numerical correspondences may also help to inform parts of the work's organization.[3]

Of the four books or *trattati* that have come down to us, the opening one has twelve chapters and is often designated as a prologue in manuscripts and early printed copies. This book does indeed offer a complex and fascinating set of prefatory discussions, drawing in large part upon the tradition of the *accessus ad auctores*, that is, the preparatory discussions found in works of biblical, philosophical, and literary commentary. This academic prologue tradition explained such headings as the purpose, utility, and title of the work, its formal and structural features (such as the number of books and their division), the kind of knowledge conveyed, and information about the author, including his life. Dante broaches nearly all these matters in book 1, although, as we will see, he innovates extensively on the tradition.

He begins the book with Aristotle, the "Philosopher," and the celebrated opening of book 1 of the *Metaphysics* (1.1.980a 21), which states that all humans naturally desire to know. With other Aristotelian passages (*Nicomachean Ethics* 10.7.117a 12–17) and contemporary discussions in mind, Dante states that humans are providentially driven by nature toward knowledge and that through such knowledge they reach their ultimate perfection and attain ultimate felicity (1.1.1). The pursuit of learning is not straightforward, however. Many impediments or defects, both intrinsic and extrinsic to humankind, can slow down or even cancel out this inbuilt desire. The defects "dentro dall'uomo" (1.1.3) [within humans], bodily and mental, are not blameworthy, but most reprehensible are the extrinsic ones, those "fuori dall'uomo" (1.1.4) [outside of humans], that are caused by family and civic concerns ("la cura familiare e civile," 1.1.4) and by a lack of a seat of learning or nearby scholars in the place where a person is born. As a result, few people attain knowledge and the vast majority "sono li 'mpediti che di questo cibo sempre vivono affamati" (1.1.6) [are hindered and live forever hungry for this food]. Continuing the food metaphor and enriching it with biblical echoes, Dante exclaims that few and blessed are those who sit "a quella mensa dove lo pane delli angeli si manuca!" (1.1.6) [at that meal where the bread of angels is eaten!]. Dante does not sit at the "beata mensa" (1.1.10) [blessed meal], but he has nonetheless escaped the common herd and has been able to gather up bit by bit the scraps that have fallen at his feet from those who do sit at the table (once more biblical echoes are strong here: Luke 16:21; Matt. 15:26–27). Understanding the sweetness residing in such scraps and moved by compassion for the ignorant, he now prepares a table for "un generale convivio" (1.1.11) [a general banquet]. Elaborating further the rich interlocking metaphorical fields of eating, hunger, and banqueting, Dante goes on to explain that the food of the banquet is set out in fourteen courses (1.1.13), that is, fourteen early canzoni on themes of love and virtue. The bread for the banquet will be provided in the form of Dante's own exposition, his self-commentary.[4] At the end of the first chapter, Dante explains—in a passage that has generated much discussion and controversy—how his new *Convivio* is related to the *Vita nova*. The earlier work is not superseded but can in fact be read with greater utility through the current one. If the *Vita nova* as a work of Dante's youth was "fervida e passionate" (1.1.16) [fervid and passionate], the *Convivio* is one that is "temperata e virile" [temperate and virile], for it is fitting to write in different ways at different stages of life. This relationship with the *Vita nova* is one to which Dante will return in books 2 and 3, as he re-presents and resemanticizes the "donna gentile" [gracious lady], the central figure of an entire episode in the *Vita nova* (XXXV–XXXIX [24–28]) in which this lady is presented as a malignant distraction from the worship of the dead Beatrice. The chapter closes with Dante stating that he will use "allegorica esposizione" (1.1.18) [allegorical exposition] to unveil the true intention of his verse. The opening book of the *Convivio*, then, already offers its readers a rich yet representative indication of how sophisticated and original the work is to be. While balancing Aristotle and contemporary discussions on the nature of knowledge, perfection, and happiness alongside prominent biblical echoes, Dante presents himself as a collector of scraps of knowlege, the expositor and allegorizing interpreter of his own earlier verse, and the author of the *Vita nova*. At the same time, he innovatively covers ground set out in some of the principal headings from the *accessus* tradition, such as work's title, intention, number of books, and utility.

No earlier Dantean verse is expounded in book 1. Instead, Dante must first clear up a range of issues concerning his own role in what he calls the "quasi comento" (1.3.2) [almost a commentary]: the phrase seems an aside but is most significant, and we will return to it in the third section. In chapters 2–4, and staying in metaphor, Dante removes any perceived stains or "macule" from the bread of his self-commentary. The flaws are of two kinds: first that "parlare alcuno di se medesimo pare non licito" (1.2.3) [it is not admissible to speak about oneself] without a compelling reason; and second that it is unreasonable to "parlare in espondendo troppo a fondo" (1.2.3) [to be overly abstruse in an exposition]. Dante establishes two eventualities in which contemporary ordinances against self-speaking can be contravened, and he uses two major Latin *auctores*—Boethius and Augustine (1.2.13–14)—as antecedents, or one might say models, for his own behavior. The first circumstance for rule breaking is if there is a need to speak about oneself in order to avoid infamy (as Boethius did in his *Consolation of Philosophy*). The second arises when there is an imperious need for divulgation of knowledge, and this is what Dante, perhaps rather disingenuously, says Augustine does in his *Confessions*. The infamy that Dante helps to avert is that the canzoni apparently reveal extremes of his earlier sensual passion (1.2.16), but their true meaning and motivating cause is virtue, a meaning that is hidden "sotto figura d'allegoria" (1.2.17) [beneath the figure of allegory].

As regards the difficult, abstruse quality of the exposition, the defense of this point leads to an arresting "autobiographical" outburst (1.3.3–4; see *Dve* 1.6.3), beginning with an impassioned, regret-laden exhortation that God might have allowed things to be otherwise. Ejected from the sweet breast of his home city, Florence, he has wandered, tired and destitute, throughout the Italian peninsula, a land notably designated periphrastically as having one language: "le parti . . . alle quali questa lingua si stende" (1.3.4) [the regions . . . where this language reaches]. In his peregrinations, buffeted like a rudderless boat to various ports, he has become ever more aware of the damaging effects of hearsay and explains its causes at some length. Since Dante may be more "vile" (1.4.13) [base] in appearance than in reality, the *Convivio* allows him the opportunity to raise up his besmirched reputation and give him authority. This is "life writing" that, in its sophistication and subtlety, is at a distant remove from the tradition of biography in the *accessus* tradition.

The remainder of book 1 (1.5–1.13) deals with a further possible "macula," not an accidental but a substantial one (the terminology is philosophical), and this is Dante's use of the vernacular rather than Latin, or as he puts it in a further extension of the bread metaphor, "biado" [coarse grain] rather than "frumento" (1.5.1) [grain]. The use of such a lesser language, one not previously employed to treat the most serious topics, is justified on three main grounds. First, since the poems to be commented upon are composed in the vernacular, it would have been inappropriate to use the superior language, Latin, to expound them. Second, since the aim of the work is to diffuse knowledge and love for it, it was more fitting to do this in a language that could be understood and useful to the many. Third, since everyone naturally loves their own mother tongue, it is only right to use the vernacular. The account has received much discussion, notably for the views on the vernacular as a servile, lesser language to Latin, the reference to the plan to write a little book on language, "di volgare Eloquenza" (1.6.10) [about eloquence in the vernacular], and the celebrated affirmation of the untranslatability of poetry (1.7.14–15).[5] At one point, which has been seized upon understandably enough by some critics and commentators, Dante writes how, in contrast to the elite readership in Latin, the vernacular "servirà a molti" (1.9.4) [will serve many]. He writes in particular for those who have left learning to be abused and prostituted, that is, "Questi nobili sono principi, baroni, cavalieri e molt'altra nobile gente, non solamente maschi e femmine, che sono molti e molte in questa lingua, volgari, e non literati" (1.9.5) [These nobles are princes, barons, knights, and many other noble people, not only male but female, among whom there are many in this language who use the vernacular and are not learned]. The imprint of exile and a noncivic, non-Florentine context can be felt keenly here, and the attention to women readers is noteworthy, though we should perhaps be wary about regarding this statement as identifying the only readership intended for the work (see section 3). Equally important is the emphasis on the perils of earthly motivations debasing learning, an issue Dante returns to elsewhere (3.11.10).

A further motivation becomes clear in the tightly argued defenses and motivations set out against those who write in other languages. This concerns the desire to demonstrate "la gran bontade del volgare di sì" (1.10.12) [the great goodness of the vernacular of *sì*"] and its ability to handle aptly, fully, and elegantly "altissimi e novissimi concetti" [sublime and novel concepts]. Dante turns his fire on those "sects" who belittle their own vernacular but praise others (1.11.2). His implicit target here is undoubtedly Brunetto Latini, his fellow citizen and the major figure in Florence before his death in 1293 in providing Latin-informed civic education for the Florentine laity via vernacular translations and encyclopedic works. Latini offered the most important precedent as "cominciator e maestro in disgrossare i Fiorentini" [initiator and teacher in making Florentines less uncouth],[6] but one whose principal work of compilation, the *Trésor*, had been written in French and had defended that linguistic choice. The final chapter of the first book presents strongly personal notes on how the vernacular both made Dante exist (it brought his parents together to conceive him) and made him "good" by introducing him to learning, explaining how his very early Latin schooling was assisted by use of the vernacular (1.13.4–9). The chapter concludes with a salvo of biblically charged language (Isa. 9:2; Matt. 4:16), as Dante states that his work, in both its content and its use of the vernacular, will be like a "luce nuova, sole nuovo, lo quale surgerà là dove l'usato tramonterà, e darà lume a coloro che sono in tenebre ed in oscuritade, per lo usato sole che a loro non luce" (1.13.12) [a new light, a new sun, which will rise where the customary sun will be setting, and it will give its light to those who are in darkness and obscurity, because the customary sun does not shine for them]. As Ruedi Imbach rightly recognized, this is a dramatic moment in which knowledge in the vernacular is programmatically presented to a non-Latin literate laity, and learning breaks out of its traditional institutional settings in the universities and the *studia* of the religious orders.[7]

With book 2 we have our first canzone, "Voi ch'intendendo il terzo ciel movete," a composition that most likely dates back to the period of the *Vita nova* and tells of the battle in the poet's mind for a new love who eventually triumphs over the former one, Beatrice. Dante begins the book with an account of how the bread presented in the previous book should be "eaten" by discussing the multiple senses conveyed by texts in general (2.1.2–15). He suggests that writing in general can be interpreted according to four senses: the literal; the allegorical, exemplified by Ovid's account of Orpheus taming the beasts, trees, and rocks (standing for the imparting of humility and the education of the ignorant); the moral (the need to have only a few intimates present at major revelations), with the example of Christ's transfiguration; and the anagogical, as demonstrated in Psalm 113 regarding the Israelites' flight from Egypt (betokening the soul liberated from sin; 2.1.2–7).

The passage has received detailed attention, and the interpretative problems it raises are far from being settled, in part because of the corruption of the text (especially at 2.1.2), but also because of the richly layered complexity of the discussion itself with the self-referential quality of the allusion to Orpheus, the slippage between examples from the Bible and from ancient literature, and the fact that Dante is commenting on his own text.[8] What is clear is the strong emphasis that Dante places on the primacy of literal sense and its foundational role (2.1.8), a point he reiterates as at the close of the chapter when he confirms that "sopra ciascuna canzone ragionerò prima la litterale sentenza, e appresso di quella ragionerò la sua allegoria" (2.1.15) [I will first discuss the literal meaning of each canzone, and after that I will discuss its allegory]. In the following chapter, Dante then connects the canzone with the *Vita nova* and the "donna gentile" and sets out a division of the canzone following the contemporary exegetical practice of textual division (*divisio textus*) (1.2.6–10). Dante uses this technique throughout the *Convivio* (e.g. 2.2.7; 3.2.1; 3.5.1–2; 4.3.3). He also deploys related techniques such as *ordinatio*—the hierarchical arrangement of disparate material within a work. However, the exegetical practice he utilizes most frequently and most extensively is a related one, *compilatio*, that is, the rearrangement of texts and *auctoritates* (authority-conferring extracts of texts) into a new textual unity. Rather than referring solely to specific genres, compilation can be understood as a set of mental habits and related textual practices that Dante uses with exceptional freedom and sophistication to organize and rearrange knowledge in his "quasi comento," often (but not always) drawing upon works that are themselves *compilationes* or have compilatory elements such as commentaries, collections of *auctoritates*, and encyclopedias.[9] *Compilatio* is employed throughout books 2, 3, and 4, and already in the opening chapter of book 1 this preoccupation is marked out in the image of Dante's gathering of food that has fallen at his feet: "Ricolgo di quello che da loro cade" (1.1.10) [I gather up from what falls from them].

Chapter 3 offers much material on the universe, astronomy, and cosmology. The chapter sets out the number, arrangement, movements, and sites of the ten heavens, discussing different opinions, beginning with Aristotle on the eight planetary heavens and adding information on the ninth heaven or First Mover from Ptolemy (2.3.8–12). The approach here is doxographical in that the "scientific" information is arranged on the basis of reportage following the views of major schools or thinkers. It is also compilatory in that Dante has reworked material based on the teachings of these authorities that he has accessed through works containing their own compilatory doxographies (and much else), such as the Aristotelian commentaries of Albert the Great and Thomas Aquinas. Dante adds a tenth theological heaven, the Empyrean, to the other nine physical ones, and, in so doing, he reconciles its existence and inclusion with Aristotle's teachings. The desire for synthesis and syncretism are notable here. The following chapter continues the cosmological interests and the syncretic spirit displayed in the previous one by providing an account of the number of the movers or intelligences responsible for the movement of the heavens and identifying these with the angelic hierarchies. Dante again presents us with a doxographical account that moves from Aristotle to Plato and on to Christian views. Once more Aristotle's doctrine is reconciled with Christian teaching, with an especially strong syncretic urge displayed in the way the Christian angels are associated with pagan deities (2.4.6–7). The account continues in chapter 5, where Dante gives a more pronounced set of biblical examples and enumerates the order of the nine angelic hierarchies (2.5.6–8).

After these three chapters, Dante returns to literal exposition of the canzone (2.6–11). The techniques he uses here include further divisions of the text; lexical explanations of certain terms such as the adjective *soave* (2.7.5) [mild] and the noun *cortesia* (2.10.7–8) [courtesy]; rhetorical comments (2.7.12), and more expansive discussion of themes raised—above all the issue of the immortality of the soul (2.8.7–16). Here again Dante marshals the views of the ancients and Christian teachings, even going so far as to discuss how dream divination demonstrates the soul's immortality. Other scientific material brought into the discussion includes elements of optical and visual theory (2.9.4–5; see 3.10). With the final four chapters of the book, Dante undertakes his own allegoresis of his earlier canzone (2.12–15). Chapter 12 brings us back to the "donna gentile" episode of the *Vita nova*, offering a remarkable, radical resemanticization of that earlier figure in order to provide scaffolding for his allegorized reading of the canzone. Dante now explains how in the period after Beatrice's death he was consoled not by a real woman but by Philosophy, whom he reimagines as the "donna gentile." The first two Latin books he read in his quest for conslation—Boethius's *Consolation of Philosophy* and Cicero's *On Friendship*—led to many others, as the pursuit of learning provided succor for his grief but also prompted the quest for "vocabuli d'autori e di scienze e di libri" (2.12.5) [the words of authors, of fields of knowledge, and of books]. In considering these authorities, Dante is led to the following conclusion: "Giudicava bene che la filosofia, che era donna di questi autori, di queste scienze e di questi libri, fosse somma cosa. E imaginava lei fatta come una donna gentile" (2.12.5–6) [I determined there and then that philosophy, who was the lady of these authors, these sciences and these books, was a supreme thing. And I imagined her to be like a gentle woman]. The autobiographical insertion continues as he goes on to explain how his intellectual ardor was so piqued that he searched out this lady where she truly existed in his home city of Florence, that is, in the *studia* of the religious orders and the public lectures or quodlibetal disputations held there, namely "nelle scuole delli religiosi e alle disputazioni delli filosofanti" (2.12.7) [in the schools of the religious orders and at the disputations of the philosophers]. In the remaining three chapters, Dante uses the conceit that each heaven corresponds to a particular art or science (2.13.2) to provide a map of the entire cosmos. He aligns the features shared by the seven lower heavens with the arts of the trivium (grammar, dialetic, rhetoric) and those of the quadrivium (arithmetic, astronomy, music, geometry); and, most unusually, he makes the final three "cieli" correspond to physics/metaphysics, ethics, and theology (2.13.2–30; 2.14.1–21). At the same time, he discusses more aspects of cosmological lore and compiles information on each of the disciplines mentioned. The account of how Mars may be compared to music, for example, leads Dante to bring together comments on harmony, the number five, the fiery properties of the heaven that result from burning vapors, observations of the heaven recorded by Albumasar and Seneca, and the effect of music on human spirits and the soul (2.13.20–24). The final chapter returns us to close textual exposition in line with the allegorized vision Dante has set out of the "donna gentile."

The third tractate continues with the exposition of the canzone "Amor che nella mente mi ragiona," another poem from the 1290s but one whose philosophical freight is more readily apparent in its depiction of Love's effects on the poet's intellect, of a celestial influx into the noble lady, and of the descent of divine light through her to those on earth, as well the effects of her smile and eyes as conveying the delights of Paradise. The tractate develops a hymn of praise to the "donna gentile" and the power of philosophy to bestow happiness on those who love her. Book 3 is remarkable for the ways it celebrates philosophy, the nature of love, and the complexity of the human in their relationships to the universe and to God.[10] Chapter 1 opens with a carefully articulated justification for praising the beloved, and it closes with a division of the canzone into three main parts (3.1.14). Beginning the discussion of the first part of the canzone, Dante establishes the grounds for interpreting the words *Love* and *mind* in its first line. He presents Love as the spiritual union of the soul (3.2.3) with the beloved thing, a formulation that recalls notions of love as a unitive force that we find in the so-called Pseudo-Dionysius, the sixth-century Christian Platonist, though here again Dante is probably dependent on intermediary sources such as the commentaries of Albert and Aquinas and other independent works.[11] With another Platonizing authority in mind, the *Book of Causes*, Dante goes on to explain how, since every effect retains something of the nature of its cause, it follows that noble forms, such as the human soul, receive more of divine nature than any others (3.2.4–8). As regards "mente" (3.2.10–19) [mind], on the basis of Aristotelian authority, he details the powers of different kinds of creatures, including plants, animals, and humans, noting how the human soul "è perfettissima di tutte l'altre . . . la quale colla nobilitade della potenza ultima, cioè ragione, participa della divina natura a guisa di sempiterna Intelligenza" (3.2.14) [is most perfect of all the others . . . which with the nobility of its most elevated power, reason, participates in the divine nature in the manner of a sempiternal Intelligence].

Chapter 3 continues to bolster this remarkable philosophical vision of the place of humans and the human soul within the hierarchy of being and uses it to interpret the canzone. All things in the universe have a specific love drawing them toward a place. The human being is, Dante explains, an especially complex composite of other natures: "E però che l'uomo . . . per la sua nobilitade, ha in sé e la natura d'ognuna di queste cose, tutti questi amori puote avere e tutti li ha" (3.3.5) [And since humans . . . have divine nature within themselves, they can and do have all these loves]. Humans, then, have five natures, from their simple body, which tends downwards, to the fifth and highest power, which is truly human, "o meglio dicendo angelica, cioè razionale" (3.3.12) [or to put it better the angelic, that is the rational one]. Chapter 4 contains further crucial elements in the anthropology elaborated as it explains the ineffability of the experience described in the canzone as related to the fact that the intellect is unable to draw on a mental faculty of the body, phantasy, and so cannot rise up to certain things such as the understanding of substances separate from matter (3.4.9). Chapter 5 examines the second stanza and its reference to the sun, providing an extensive account of helocentrism and the views of Pythagoras, Plato, and Aristotle. Notable here is the way Dante calls on his readers' imagination and provides them with domesticated examples—the poles of the Earth are named after Mary and Lucia. Notable too is his explicit reference to Albert the Great's treatises on cosmology and geography (3.5.12), as well as his impassioned call to humanity to raise its gaze to the heavens (3.5.21–22). Soul theory informs again chapter 7 as Dante once more turns to Albert in developing ideas about humanity's distinctive ontological place in the universe: humans are up to their necks in matter, but their heads, their rational parts, emerge from it (3.7.5). Humans are here at the boundary between the divine and natural realms, an emphasis that continues in the following chapter with its preoccupation with how the union of three natures in one form makes humakind "mirabilissimo" (3.8.1) [most marvelous].

Having outlined the first two parts of the canzone, chapter 9 turns to the third part with a notable "digressione" (3.10.1) [digression] on visual and optical theory that is intended to exonerate the canzone from reproach when it is compared with an earlier *ballata* by Dante, "Voi che savete ragionar d'amore." After concluding the literal exposition (3.10), the tractate continues to provide scientific and philosophical material. Thus, in discussing the allegorical reading of the sun (3.14.3–5), Dante states how no better sensory image is offered than the sun to represent God, and extends the analogy of heating and illuminating to the divine diffusion of intelligibility and goodness. Later in the same chapter he quotes Avicenna (once more he is compiling from other sources) in articulating the different sense of words for light (3.14.15). The allegorical sections of the book make dramatic assertions regarding how the "donna gentile" manifests the presence of the Creator God and make strong claims for compatibility between rational truths of philosophy and revealed truths of religion. At the same time, these chapters are steeped in complexities concerning the relations between divine wisdom and earthly philosophy, and the limits and jurisidiction of human knowledge in this life.

The final tractate, book 4, comprises, as noted, thirty chapters and has no allegorical commentary (4.1.8). The canzone expounded is "Le dolci rime d'amor ch'io solìa," the longest and most scholastically wrought of the three canzoni in the "quasi comento." This book has often been viewed as separate, conceptually and stylistically, even as a later work with different finalities, though the matter remains conjectural. It certainly has less prominent autobiographical insertions than the earlier two tractates and deals more prominently with ethical and civic themes. Its argumentative structure, even more than the canzone, adheres to that of the scholastic *questio*.[12] Book 4 also seems to reveal how Dante has acquired a deeper understanding of classical literature, above all Virgil's *Aeneid* but also Statius's *Thebaid*. However, we should not forget the strong scholastic patina to be found in the earlier books nor neglect the stylistic and philosophical hybridity that we continue to find in book 4. Dante is careful to connect book 4 to the metaphysical questions (4.1.8) regarding the relationship between God and prime matter broached at the end of book 3 (3.15.6). His inability to deal with the relation between God and prime matter has led him to deal with an error regarding human goodness, its origin and basis, and to "gridare alla gente che per mal cammino andavano" (4.1.9) [call out to people who were on a bad path]. Dante continues to display a capacity for reconciling passionately vehement outbursts within a tightly woven tissue of arguments, distinctions, objections, and clarifications.

In book 4, Dante spends fifteen chapters refuting the thesis that nobility, in the view of Frederick II, consists in "antica richezza e belli costumi" (4.3.6) [old wealth and courteous ways] and then devotes a further fifteen to elaborating his own viewpoint. In chapters 4–6, Dante prepares the terrain for this view by explaining why he disagrees with the imperial authority of Frederick and the philosophical authority of Aristotle in his statement that what is apparent to the majority cannot be wholly false. He does this first by disclosing the roots of imperial authority, setting out the essential lineaments of his own political thought on the empire as being foundational in order to satisfy the needs of human society and the way it is ordained to happiness (4.4.1). He proclaims the divine origin of the Roman Empire: "Non da forza fu principalmente preso per la romana gente, ma da divina provedenza, che è sopra ogni ragione" (4.4.11; see 4.5.2) [Not through force was it originally taken by the Roman people but through divine providence, which is above every particular reason or law]. Notably Dante now uses Virgil as the "spokesperson" for this view, translating a passage from the *Aeneid* to support his thesis. In chapter 5, he explains the entire process by which God's will brought about the Roman Empire and placed it and Rome at the center of universal history as the "ottima disposizione" (4.5.4) [optimal disposition] for Christ's entry into the world. The biblical account is coordinated with Aeneas's own peregrinations and founding of Rome (4.5.6). Chapter 6 then establishes the philosophical authority for his discussion. The chapter provides a general account of authority and its definition and addresses a paean to Aristotle's supremacy in teaching us the end of human life. Aristotle is the "maestro e duca della ragione umana in quanto intende alla sua finale operazione"

(4.6.8) [master and guide of human reason insofar as it is occupied by its final end]. Dante emphasizes such authority after a further doxographical survey of ancient views and approaches. Chapters 7–8 return us to the exposition of the canzone and resolve the falsity of popular opinion and the view that he, Dante, is irreverent to the authority either of the emperor or of Aristotle. In chapter 9 he explains, again through carefully ordered argument, the essential baseness of wealth. The discussion continues in the following two chapters, making distinctions, dealing with doubts, and quoting a range of classical and biblical *auctoritates*. In chapter 12, he adduces a wealth of authorities (Boethius, Cicero, Solomon, Seneca, Horace, and Juvenal) in order to stress the deficiencies of wealth and its hidden defects (4.12.4–11). Having established how the pursuit of wealth is imperfect because it always generates desire, Dante now addresses a possible objection regarding the desire for knowledge by setting out a vision of human desire, its shifting from one object to another throughout life, and humans' supreme desire to return to God as the ultimate object of desire (4.12.17). The following chapter concludes that in the desire for knowledge, unlike the desire for wealth, "successivamente finiscono li desiderii e vienesi a perfezione" (4.13.5) [desires come to an end one after the other, in a progression, and reach perfection]. The final two chapters, returning to the canzone, refute the idea that "antica ricchezza" (4.14.1) [old wealth] is the cause of nobility, highlighting multiple inconsistencies in the arguments of his opponents and counteracting the view that nobility is related to the long-standing duration of wealth and cannot be generated anew (4.15.3).

The *pars construens*, or constructive part, of Dante's argument begins in chapter 16. The chapter's opening words are Dante's translation of a resonant quotation from Psalm 62:12 regarding the closed mouths "di coloro che parlano le inique cose" (4.16.1) [of those who speak things contrary to justice]. Dante now proceeds to his own exposition "della veritade" (4.16.2) [of truth], concentrating on the intrinsic, essential properties of nobility. In humans, then, he states that nobility is the seed of the virtues, and he discusses the eleven Aristotelian moral virtues as each being a mean between vices (4.17.4–7). Virtue, in this Aristotelian context, stems from one principle, that is, the habit of our good choices, and consists in an "abito elettivo consistente nel mezzo" (4.17.7) [an elective habit existing in the mean]. With chapter 20 we come to a definition of nobility: Dante notes that true nobility comes from God (4.20.3), who confers it on the well-disposed soul regardless of family or lineage, so that human nobility is nothing else than the "seme di felicitade" (4.20.9) [seed of happiness] placed into the soul whose body is perfectly disposed. Chapter 21 clarifies how goodness descends into humans, explaining this in both naturalistic and theological terms (4.21.1). Drawing on a range of philosophical works, but above all Albert the Great, Dante creates his own personal account of how the soul is generated (4.21.2–14). Dante goes on to discuss how nobility can be cultivated by directing of the will, and the outward signs by which the noble person may be recognized (4.22–23). Chapters 23–24 digress on the ages of human life, enumerating the four ages (4.24.1), "adolescenza" [youth], "gioventute" [early adulthood], "senettude" [middle age], and "senio" [old age], and compiling material from astrology, medicine, and law. Significant too is Dante's use of the *Aeneid* to illustrate the arc of human life in stages (4.24.9). Each age receives a separate chapter and is illustrated by the works of the poet assigned to it, Statius (4.25.6 and 8), Virgil (4.26.8–13), Ovid (4.27.17–21), and Lucan (4.28.13–16). Having cleared up two further problems or "questioni," the final chapter comments on the envoy of the canzone, noting how "Contra-li-erranti mia" is related to Thomas Aquinas's *Summa contra Gentiles* (4.30.3).

As regards the language of *Convivio*, the work has rightly been singled out for the way it marks a new phase in Dante's development as a prose writer. Beginning with a seminal essay by Cesare Segre and important work by Ignazio Baldelli, critics have become increasingly aware of the importance and sophistication of the prose, and more recent work, by Andrea Mazzucchi and others, has stressed its formal qualities and the way in which the work might be seen as a stylistic training ground for the writing of the *Commedia*.[13] Of course, the *Vita nova*, for all its fervently passionate tonality, had begun to incorporate scientific, scholastic, and philosophical language in its prose. However, the *Convivio* marks a significant intensification and enrichment of these interests. Linguistically and stylistically, the work speaks to Dante's embrace of new horizons, intellectually, socially, and politically, as a result of his exile and the opportunities for new sites of study and new programs of reading. The prose of the *Convivio* is rationally and symmetrically organized, just as each book is, and indeed the entire projected work would have been. Dante develops a richly articulated, often syllogistic, syntax in which tightly reasoned argumentation extends out in complex but organized sentences, often beginning with a conjunction and proceeding through a chain of multiple hypotactic clauses before returning to the main clause. The desire to emulate Latin so as to express ideas aptly, fully, and attractively (1.10.12) is a major concern throughout. The *Convivio*'s lexicon is rich in scientific and technical terms drawn from a wide range of disciplines from astronomy to geometry, from medicine to the theory of the soul. Thus we find terms from astronomy and cosmology such as *epiciclo* and *cerchio equatore* (2.3.16) [epicycle, equatorial circle], from geometry such as *triangulo, quadrangulo, pentangulo*, and *quadrare* (4.7.14; 2.13.27) [triangle, quadrangle, pentangle, circumference, square], and from medicine such as *complessione, omori, spirito visivo*, and *umido radicale* (3.3.4, 4.20.8; 3.9.8; 4.20.8) [complexion, humors, visual spirit, radical humor]. Notable too are the ways that Dante's prose calques the argumentative or introductory modes of scholastic Latin, not only with its use of verbs such as *argomentare, disputare*, and *riprovare* (4.2.13; 4.9.1) [to argue, to dispute, to refute], but also and especially with an extensive range of formulations reminiscent of scholastic expressions such as "redeuntes autem ad principale intentum/intentio"; "unde manifestum est quod"; "et ratio huius est"; "hic sciendum est"; "et per hoc solvitur quaestio"; and "quare notandum est."[14] The *Convivio*, then, shows us a Dante who has mastered the art of expressing the most complex ideas through the technical terminology and argumentative framework of late medieval Latin scholasticism. However, at the same time we should not forget that the prose is open to a range of other models, including of course the Bible and the writers of Latin antiquity, but also contemplative writings: one thinks of *ineffabile* (2.15.4; 3.2.1) [ineffable]; *inebrarsi* (3.8.14) [to get drunk].[15] The final chapters of book 4 are, moreover, especially notable for the use of similes (4.27.4; 4.28.1–7), and, as we have noted above, Dante gives prominent attention throughout the entire work to metaphors, excalamations, rhetorical questions, and figures of speech.

Textual Tradition and Early Reception

As with all of Dante's works, we lack any autograph or even partial autograph copy. Scholars have used the extant manuscripts to reconstruct an archetype that was quite demonstrably in a parlous textual state. The modern critical edition prepared by Franca Brambilla Ageno has some twenty lacunae and over one thousand errors in the archetype. With characteristic verve and borrowing analogies from the natural sciences, Guglielmo Gorni once speculated about the original manuscript being in a gaseous state as opposed to a solid one, as representing no more than sets of scattered notes.[16] From what we know about the manuscript tradition, now forty-six manuscripts in total, the *Convivio* is a work that we nearly did not have at all. Until recently, it was believed that there were only two extant copies from the fourteenth century, but renewed investigations have shown that there are in fact four.[17] The earliest of these copies (MS. BAV, Barb. Lat. 4086) dates from the late 1320s to the early 1330s. Dante's eldest son, Pietro, who visited Florence in the 1320s, may well have brought a copy of the treatise with him to the city. Pietro appears to have had his own private copy, since he uses the work extensively (though never actually mentioning it) in redactions of his Latin commentaries from the 1340s onward. All our other evidence relating to the work in the first half of the fourteenth century comes from a Florentine context. The evidence is relatively sporadic and begins in the third and fourth decades of the Trecento, most notably in two early Dante commentators, the so-called Ottimo commento and Andrea Lancia, who both seem to have known Dante personally (or at least they tell us they did). Lancia, an important Florentine notary, uses the work conspicuously and intelligently in his glosses on Dante's poem circa 1343–45. He openly refers to the title of the *Convivio* and employs it for variety of purposes, discussing Dante's imperial allegiances, his use of imagery, and his views on matters such as avarice, cosmology, and angelology. He always does so in complete and absolute harmony with proposed parallel passages in the *Commedia*.[18] The other most important early witness is found in Giovanni Villani. In redactions of Villani's life of Dante, inserted into book 10 of his *Cronica* (ca. before 1348), a passage refers at some length to the *Convivio*, linking it to the *De vulgari eoloquentia* and referring to its incomplete state, its remarkable artistry, and its philosophical and scientific qualities. Significantly, Villani treats the work as a late one, almost an unfinished swan song that is interrupted by Dante's death.[19] In his life of Dante, dating from the early 1350s, Boccaccio mentions the *Convivio*; he also understands it to be a late work, interrupted by death, and he too pairs it with the *De vulgari eloquentia*. Boccaccio seems not to have known the treatise directly and is most probably dependent on Villani here. All the other major Dante commentators before the end of the century—Francesco da Buti, Benvenuto da Imola, the Anonimo Fiorentino—do not know the work.

One should stress how important for the early reception and interpretation of the work the late dating has been. What may seem like a minor (and erroneous) detail of biography actually helps to govern the way the *Commedia* is read, at least until the early nineteenth century. Before then, for almost all early readers and commentators, the fact that the work was believed to be composed very late in life and left incomplete at Dante's death means it was understood to offer particularly privileged access to the *Commedia*. The idea that it might contradict the poem was almost never entertained, except for a few very exceptional cases.

When we reach late Trecento and early Quattrocento Florence there is some evidence of knowledge of the work in the first generations of humanists, above all Coluccio Salutati (in one of his Latin letters) and his circle.[20] But the *Convivio* still has a relatively thin presence, and the work seems not to have been copied, or at least not to have been copied widely, until the 1440s, when we enter a new period of intense scribal activity, still in the Tuscan environment. The *Convivio* is now studied for its scientific and cosmological information, and we get a flourishing interest in copying the text. Over forty of the forty-six extant manuscripts date to the next three to four decades. We know that merchant copyists, such as Antonio Tuccio Manetti, took a very strong interest in the work, which they copied, read against the *Commedia*, and used for their own cosmographical theories. Marsilio Ficino was also thoroughly familiar with the treatise and echoed its language in his own vernacular works in the late 1450s and 1460s. By the 1460s, the text was being read and reused by the city's best-known poets, humanists, and artists. We know, for example, that Lorenzo de' Medici, Angelo Poliziano, Leonardo da Vinci, and Girolamo Benivieni knew the work directly, even if there still remains space to understand better the extant codices, their layout and textual variants, and the diverse uses made of these texts in art, architecture, cosmography, and other forms of self-commentary.[21]

In close connection with the manuscript tradition and the burgeoning Florentine interest, the first print edition, an unadorned *octavo*, was published in the city in 1490. What is most important for us is that printing allowed the text to become both a pan-Italian phenomenon and even an extra-Italian one. Three more Venetian prints followed in the 1520s and early 1530s (Milton was to own a copy of the 1529 print), with an address to the reader, portraits of Dante, and a lengthy table of contents that increased its usability and the ease with which cross-reference to the *Commedia* could be made. In spite of some sporadic and occasional criticism, throughout the sixteenth century the treatise tended to be considered positively and used very widely as an authority, for linguistic matters (the *Convivio* is cited repeatedly in the first major Italian dictionary of 1612, the *Vocabolario della Crusca*) but also and especially for its doctrinal teachings. It is quoted not only in commentaries on literary works (including ones on Boccaccio, Petrarch, and Cavalcanti) but also in dialogues, *lezioni*, and treatises of all kinds. Pietro Bembo and Torquato Tasso both owned and annotated print copies: Bembo's annotations on his own copy of a 1490 edition were made with a real eye to parallels in the *Commedia*. Bembo places, for example, a large, elegant manicula next to the "selva erronea" discussed at *Convivio* 4 and provides a parallel quotation from *Inferno* 1.[22] From the 1520s, the *Convivio* was soon swept up into language dispute, the so-called *questione della lingua*. Passages, such as the celebrated closing lines of book 1, were extracted from context to offer chauvinistic support of pro-Florentine linguistic positions on the vernacular. At the same time, the treatise was widely used in grammars and other kinds of lexicographical and linguistic aids. In debates over the authenticity of the *De vulgari eloquentia*, discussion centered on the extent to which the views on language expressed in the *Convivio* were consistent with the Latin treatise. Most interesting and relevant for us today is the way the *Convivio* was again utilized for the parallels it offered with the *Commedia*. All the major Dante commentators and readers used it, and often quite extensively, in order to discuss the cosmography of hell, explain Dante's language, reconstruct and clarify his philosophical and scientific interests, especially ethics, astronomy and cosmology, offer details of his exile, pinpoint characters, situations, and ideas shared between the two works, and even highlight word choices and stylistic features. The *Convivio* was a useful interpretative tool for understanding the *Commedia* and was read almost always in a strongly harmonizing key. Amid hundreds of parallels posited by commentators, only Lodovico Castelvetro emerges as an exception in seeing contradictions between the treatise and the *Commedia*, but this kind of reading was, in his case, in line with his critical method of searching for coherence or its absence in Dante's text.[23]

Trends and Issues in Twentieth- and Twenty-First-Century Criticism

Even though there continued to be interest in the *Convivio* in the eighteenth century (Antonio Maria Biscioni prepares a 1723 print edition), it was principally in the early nineteenth century that the treatise was studied with renewed vigor,[24] and sophisticated textual work was undertaken for the editions prepared by Vincenzo Monti, Karl Witte, Giambattista Giuliani, and Edward Moore. The revitalized interest in the textual tradition grew alongside its use within a new and growing tradition of Dante commentary on the *Commedia* that began to mine the *Convivio* even more deeply than its sixteenth-century readers and exegetes had. In Niccolò Tommaseo's edition and commentary of 1826, for example, we find nearly four hundred references, in Giovanni Scartazzini's 1874–82 Italian edition nearly five hundred, and by the early twentieth-century commentary of Francesco Torraca we reach almost seven hundred. Significantly, too, as early as the 1820s, scholars such as Monti and Foscolo began to draw strong attention to some of the discrepancies between the *Convivio* and the *Commedia*.[25] This concern becomes increasingly apparent in the tradition of Dante commentary by the middle of the century. In his 1856 commentary, Raffaello Andreoli, for example, emphasizes divergences with respect to the treatment of Guido da Montefeltro in *Inferno* 27 and the account of the Moon spots in *Paradiso* 2. In the 1860s, Luigi Bennasutti argues that *Purgatorio* 16 corrects Dante's earlier and excessive enthusiasm for astrological doctrines. Scartazzini himself uses the idea (and the language) of retraction when discussing Dante's treatment of fortune in *Inf.* 7.69–70, the Moon spots in *Paradiso* 2, and the order of angelic hierarchies in *Par.* 28.97–129. Significant, too, in the first half of the nineteenth century (as again both Foscolo and later Scartazzini show) are also new estimates of the likely dating of the *Convivio* as a much earlier work than previously thought.[26]

Let us now look more closely at the last century and some current interpretative trends, issues, and themes in relation to the work itself. One might signal at least seven major critical questions that have animated discussion on the work: (i) how one might categorize the work in terms of genre; (ii) who are its addressees, its intended public; (iii) what are its primary models and sources; (iv) what are its likely dating and possible place(s) of composition; (v) how does one interpret Dante's celebration of philosophy; (vi) how is the *Convivio* to be understood and used in relation to the *Commedia*; and, underpinning many of these questions, (vii) what does the *Convivio* mean in terms of Dante's development as an intellectual and writer? Of course these are not the only questions that have been posed or the only topics investigated. For example, some excellent recent work has been done on Dante's use of specific authorities, most notably Boethius, Cicero, Livy, and Albert the Great, as well as on the meaning and significance of specific passages and doctrinal elements and the relations between the *De vulgari eloquentia* and the *Convivio*.[27]

All the same, much of the work undertaken on the *Convivio* in the past has tended to be inflected in relation to the work's content and ideas, often bringing with it a concomitant sense of the work's status as a philosophical or enyclopedic work.[28] For understandable reasons, the *Convivio* has been a favorite quarry for historians of ideas—one need only think of the editions by Cesare Vasoli and Gianfranco Fioravanti, or that by Ruedi Imbach with the assistance of Ricklin and Cheneval. It is, in fact, only recently that important renewed attention been paid to work's formal, generic, and metaliterary issues, and such matters as the interest in raising the potential of poetry and ennobling it.[29]

Even a preliminary survey of some of my suggested questions illustrates how varied critical discussions have been and continue to be and how remarkably innovative and complex the work is. Time and again, the *Convivio* resists easy categorization when we take into account the complexity of its structure, its incorporation of multiple genres, and its syncretic hybridity, both formal and conceptual. In all these ways, we might begin to think of the *Commedia* itself. On the question of genre, it has been traditional to associate the work with the vernacular encyclopedia. However, we are becoming increasingly aware that, the *Convivio* is not a traditional enyclopedia at all: one thinks of its emphasis on beauty, on metaphor, on similes, of its prominent autobiographical strands, and its status as self-commentary: "quasi comento." This is not to say that the idea of the encyclopedia should be disgarded but rather that it might be more helpful to think of encyclopedism in terms of its techniques rather than its content, and to connect it with the practice and mentalities associated with compilation, as we noted in the first section. Of course, Dante's handling of the material, and indeed the ways he structures it, remain highly personal, even peculiar, at times. One good example is provided by the carefully crafted analogies between the heavens and the sciences in book 2.13, in particular its treatment of ethics and theology. Analogues have been presented in numerous earlier writings from Alan of Lille's *Anticlaudianus* to Alexander Neckham's *De naturis rerum*, from Boncompagno da Signa's *Rhetorica Novissima* to Michael Scot's *Liber introductorius*.[30] But the analogies never quite fit or satisfy. The *Convivio* bears the traces of many other genres, including the commentary. We have already noted how elements of the *accessus ad auctores* or prologue tradition in medieval commentary are notably built into the first book;[31] and throughout the use of digressions, division of text, argumentative structures, and even precise technical terms of expressions often recall the tradition of *commentaria*, which is itself a fluid and hybrid genre and one allowing for elements of authorial intervention. We need to attend also to different kinds of commentary, not only philosophical commentaries but also literary and biblical ones. As Paola Nasti has demonstrated in particular, biblical commentary (notably that on the Song of Songs) leaves a deep imprint upon the treatise;[32] and some suggestive work has been done and might be developed further to investigate possible similarities with so-called Chartian commentaries, above all William of Conches's glosses on Plato's *Timaeus* and those on Boethius's *Consolation of Philosophy*.[33]

When reflecting on the generic hybridity of the work, then, one needs bring into discussion many different types of text, from the Bible and theological works (the *Summa contra Gentiles* is one of the works we noted in the previous section), to scientific and philosophical texts (including primary base texts such as Sacrobosco, Albumasar, Alfraganus), rhetorical treatises, works of spiritual autobiography, classical literature, and even humble *volgarizzamenti*. Even more important and destabilizing is the need to place Dante into the work—he is, as so often, self-consciously at the center of it all. The emphasis on self is a major feature (there are over 150 occurrences of the pronoun *io*), and, as part of this privileging of his own subject position, there comes a construction of himself as a passionate, if amateur, lover of knowledge, a lay intellectual, an undeserving exile, alongside a strongly personal vision about how he approaches knowledge that is more than simply compiling lore. As with the *Commedia*, we need to recognize that ultimately what Dante is already concerned with in the *Convivio* is to fashion his own original structure, one that allows him to address his own concerns and himself with fuller and greater fluidity. Related to these observations, and again with bearing for the *Commedia*, one might add the *Convivio*'s pronounced tendency toward syncretism that we touched upon in the earlier overview, that is, its complex structuring of various tiers of knowledge in pursuit of an overall vision of truth, the cosmos, and humanity's place in it (and notably too of Dante's own role and personal history in that cosmological system). Such features are evident from the very opening lines of book 1, where Dante combines a celebrated Aristotelian quotation (though one notably mediated) with Christian notions of providence and a biblical calque of "pan de li angeli" (Psalms 77:25). In the subsequent presentation of the banquet itself, Dante mobilizes a series of biblical elements, as well as further Aristotelian and neo-Platonic components.[34]

As regards the public and addressees, important recent interventions have been made on the subject by a number of scholars.[35] It is perhaps easier to see who Dante is not addressing: he is most certainly not writing for those *literati* who hark after knowledge purely for monetary gain, and those who use other vernaculars are treated with similar disdain. The addressees are not really seated at the banquet of learning at all but are viewed as gathering crumbs that fall from the table of learning because various impediments—civic and family concerns and a lack of time—have not allowed them to pursue intellectual inquiry fully. Ruedi Imbach, as we have noted, stressed how the *Convivio* represents a profound laicization of culture and displays a deep-rooted zeal in spreading knowledge: "dare a molti e giovare a molti" (1.8.3) [to give to and help many people]. At the same time, if this appears to be an antielitist conception of knowledge diffusion, it is not a straightforward democratization of knowledge but a complex cultural operation, and at points, especially in book 1, Dante appears to be addressing a specific, and noble, section of this vernacular public, made up of princes, barons, and knights and including women, as we quoted in our account of book 1.[36]

Regarding Dante's sources, models, and "library," as we have noted, some fine work has been done here, but again further research remains to be done to appreciate better the precise ways in which Dante read his authorities. In several areas, the *Convivio* speaks to Dante's encounter with a world of books and a depth and range of learning that do not seem to have been present to the same degree in the Florentine environment. We are beginning to recover the mediated nature of some of this contact, but further work is required in these areas in relation to major authorities such as Augustine, Cicero, and Boethius, and by book 4 to understand more thickly references to the *auctores* of classical literature—Virgil, Ovid, Lucan, and Statius. The presence of Aristotle is especially notable: the Stagirite is named and quoted around one hundred times and is the single most important philosophical authority, with the *Nicomachean Ethics* being particularly important. However, the *Convivio* demonstrates Dante's assimiliation of a hybrid and complex Aristotelianism, and a highly mediated one, even in its opening quotation, and especially through the works of Albert the Great, who lies behind many of the Aristotelian references and is quoted directly with regard to several specific short treatises.[37] At the same time, we should not neglect Neoplatonic works, including quotations from the *Book of Causes*, or the work of "moderns" including Aquinas's *Contra Gentiles*, which we have already mentioned, and Giles of Rome's *De regimine principum* (4.24.9).[38] We also need to study more closely works that are not cited but that we know or strongly suspect Dante had accessed—William of Conches's *Glosae super Boetium*, Hugh of St. Victor's *Didascalicon*, and Brunetto Latini's *Trésor* are just some of the cases in point.

On the fourth point, that is, questions of the dating (1303–4 to 1307–8 are the most common spans now proposed) and especially of the conjectured place(s) of composition, both of these issues involve intensely complex questions regarding Dante's postexilic movements and intellectual formation. A recent focus has been placed again on Bologna, given its wealth of books, the circulation of ideas there, and the likelihood of Dante's residence in the city from summer 1304 to autumn 1306.[39] This welcome concern to insert Dante into a particular time, moment, and cultural project inevitably brings difficulties given the conjectural nature of our knowledge of Dante's movements and indeed of the materials, libraries, and intellectual circles present in Bologna and elsewhere, in particular Padua. Of course, Dante himself tells us nothing about such a stay, and *Convivio* 2.13 is emphatic in the way it underscores the Florentine character of Dante's engagement with philosophy. There may be here a degree of retrospective projection onto Florence of the learning in Bologna or at least a position that obscures the ways in which books, individuals, and ideas circulated within and between the lay and clerical cultures of both cities. Further work is needed on such pathways of exchange, on libraries, including private libraries, on techniques of teaching, and on the relationships between cities and their lay cultures, as well as on the classicizing and intellectual dispositions of the religious orders.[40] At the same time we may well also need to look outside of the Florence-Bologna axis to Arezzo, Padua, and Lucca as places of learning with which Dante had some contact in the years when he worked on the *Convivio*, asking similar questions in relation to likely book holdings and educational programs in *studia* and any such related learned environments.

The fifth point, the *Convivio*'s overall approach to philosophy and its autonomy, is one that has seen most attention and has created the most distortions and problems. The presentation of the "donna gentile" as a "figlia di Dio" (2.12.9) [daughter of God] and the celebration of reason have been seen as remarkably unorthodox (3.7.16; 4.1.8). Heated polemics surfaced at various points in the last century, first with the disputes between Luigi Pietrobono and Michele Barbi. Pietrobono regarded the *Convivio* as a phase of excessive rationalization that was then recanted in the *Commedia*.[41] The rigidity of Pietrobono's arguments was shown up by Barbi's pointing to the presence of nonrationalist elements in *Convivio* and of rationalizing ones in *Commedia*.[42] And its artificiality can be felt in the forced quality of Pietrobono's arguments for a double redaction of the *Vita nova*. Later disputes have demonstrated the difficulties of defining too rigidly or narrowly the work's philosophical and religious outlook. Emblematic of such tendencies is Giovanni Busnelli's 1934 commentary, which remains valuable in many parts but forced Dante and the *Convivio* into neo-Thomist straitjackets and for this reason was effectively dismantled by Bruno Nardi, who was instead concerned to stress quite rightly a more eclectic vision of Dante's philosophical allegiances.[43] More recently, Maria Corti's celebrated book *La felicità mentale* argued for phases of rationalism and Averroism in book 3 before a return to Thomist religious orthodoxy in book 4. Once again, such assertions have been rightly disputed and rigorously recontextualized by both Falzone and Fioravanti.[44]

Convivio and *Commedia*

The question of philosophy brings us back to some concluding remarks on the relations between the *Convivo* and the *Commedia*, and here we touch on the sixth and seventh questions raised above. One major interpretative approach has been the concern to read the *Convivio* in terms of the palinode, relying on ideas of recantation and a vision of the treatise as often revealing an excessive, even sinful, pursuit of rationality, of secular-based learning, or even of heterodox thought. Palinodic approaches to the *Convivio* represent a critical position that has been notably developed in North America, though as the previous section showed, it has also attracted supporters in Italy, including some recent ones.[45] In such presentations, though variously understood and inflected, the *Commedia* often represents a "narrow escape" from the "dead-end" represented by the *Convivio*.[46] Certainly, a good number of passages can be seen as opposing views earlier expressed in the *Convivio*. The best-known ones are the treatment of Guido da Montefeltro (*Inf.* 27; *Conv.* 4.28.8) and that of Bertran de Born (*Inf.* 28; *Conv.* 4.11.14). But there are also doctrinal divergences such as the explanation of the Moon spots in *Paradiso* 2.61–148 (*Conv.* 2.12.9) or the arrangement of the celestial hierarchies in *Paradiso* 8 and 28 (*Conv.* 2.5.6). And these are only the most celebrated points of discrepancy: critics have also noted a range of other areas (*Inf.* 10.14–15 and *Conv.* 4.6.11–12; *Inf.* 26.118–20; *Purg.* 19.1–8; *Purg.* 20.1–3 and *Conv.* 1.1.9; *Purg.* 31.133–38 and 3.15.23; *Purg.* 33.85–90 and *Conv.* 2.12.7; *Par.* 2.10–12 and *Conv.* 1.1.7).

We need, however, to assess each proposed reference carefully and to discriminate appropriately. As Lino Pertile reminded us in a lively open letter he exchanged with Robert Hollander, the noncirculation of *Convivio* needs to take into account in such discussions, since we should not assume that Dante intended his reading public to recognize any reference to the earlier work. For "Amore che nella mente" and *Purgatorio* 2 (where Casella gives voice to the composition and prompts the severe reprimands of Cato) we also need to be aware of the circulation of earlier redactions of the canzone before the allegorization undertaken in the *Convivio*.[47] Scholars have also argued strongly against the theory of the palinode on other grounds. One of the best accounts of the suggestive correspondences between the two works is provided by John Scott. Scott draws attention to how Dante's thinking on imperialism and the myth of Rome is developed in the earlier work, and emphasizes how the scientific and philosophical interests on hierarchy, causality, and cosmology help to provide building blocks for the *Commedia*.[48] As the previous section suggested, this not only is a matter of shared ideas but also concerns hybridity in both language and thought, as well as the complex articulation of Dante's individual agency within the cosmic system. Others who have argued against the palinode include Mario Trovato when demonstrating the Neoplatonic elements in books 2 and 3, and Teodolina Barolini in her attention to passages in *Convivio* that act almost as a "blueprint" of the *Commedia*.[49] Several passages in book 4 are also of potential relevance here. Indeed a careful reading of criticism on the *Convivio* shows how even on what appear to be different sides of the debate finer discriminations are often made. Hollander, for example, while discussing the divergences often in a strongly recantative vein in his own commentary (see, e.g., his commentary to *Purg.* 33.85–90; *Par.* 2.10–12; 4.139–42; 8.3), also draws attention to how useful the *Convivio* can be in understanding the poem.[50] For his part, too, Scott is keenly aware of what is absent from the *Convivio*, such as the realm of grace, any privileged revelatory vision, the guides, and of course poetry.[51]

The *Convivio*, as we have seen, has often been haunted by varied and competing visions of Dante's development and by associated conjectures regarding its relations to the *Commedia*. In the last fifteen years or so, however, the very way in which this question has been framed has begun to be questioned, and we might end with two further examples of important recent tendencies here. First, one notes the more probing and historically precise assessments provided by Falzone's 2010 monograph and how these have begun to present a less organic reading of Dante's development, in which the discussion focuses on nonlinearity and the importance of bearing in mind the coexistence of philosophy and theology.[52] A final example is found in what is, to my mind, the most important single contribution, even though it is not exclusively concerned with the *Convivio*, namely, Ascoli's alert critique of the palinode. Rather than seeing the palinode as expressing Dante's lived experience, Ascoli stresses its instability and fragility, its representational status, and its power as a rhetorical device, and he reminds us how the ideal telos of the *Commedia* has had a major impact on discussions.[53] As we move beyond the anniversary year, it will be fascinating to see not only how the questions proposed above are tackled (or indeed if they are picked up at all or if other ones will emerge) but also how the critical tools provided by scholars such as Ascoli will inform the treatment of the work.

NOTES

1. See the Bibliography for the critical editions by Ageno (1995) and the major editions and commentaries by Cesare Vasoli (1988), Gianfranco Fioravanti (2014), and Ruedi Imbach with Thomas Ricklin and François Cheneval (*Gastmahl IV*, 2004). For the major book-length studies, see Dronke, *Dante's Second Love*; Falzone, *Desiderio della scienza*; and Ardizzone, *Reading as Angels Read*. For major volumes of essays/conference proceedings, see Bartuschat and Robiglio, *Convivio di Dante*, and Meier, *Dante's "Convivio."* The most recent English translation (2018) with helpful commentary is Dante, *Convivio: A Dual-Language Edition*, Frisardi ed. and trans. For helpful earlier discussion in English, see Scott, *Understanding Dante*, 107–42; Took, *Dante: Lyric Poet*, 81–122; and Took, *Dante*, 235–86, who calls the *Convivio* "the great work of his middle period" (235). For a proposed new Italian edition, see Mazzucchi, "Proposte."

2. It has been suggested, largely unpersuasively as no supporting evidence exists for the claim, that, in his choice of poems to include in the *Convivio*, Dante would have depended heavily on the so-called *canzoni distese* (on which see Gragnolati, chapter 1 of this book, the end of the section "Dante Performed").

3. See the discussion in Sarolli, "Numero."

4. On the metaphor of the banquet and the role of bread and other imagery, see Barański, "'Oh come è grande,'" 17–20; Callegari, "Dante's Nutritional Vernacular," 59–75; Hooper, "Dante's *Convivio*, Book 1"; Maldina, "Raccogliendo briciole."

5. See at least Grayson, "Nobilior est vulgaris"; Tavoni, "Volgare et latino" (with earlier bibliography).

6. G. Villani, *Nuova cronica* 8.10. On the role of Latini here and in general in Dante's formation at the time of the *Convivio*, see Barański, "On Dante's Trail," 8; Pegoretti, "On Grammar and Justice." See also Barański, "Dante fra 'sperimentalismo'"; Vasoli, "*Convivio* di Dante."

7. Imbach, *Dante*, 137.

8. On some of these points and their complexities, see Ascoli, "Tradurre l'allegoria."

9. On *compilatio* and *ordinatio*, see at least Guenée, "Storico e la compilazione"; Minnis, *Medieval Theory of Authorship*, 190–210, and "'Nolens auctor sed compilari reputari'"; Parkes, "Influence." For its relevance to the *Convivio*, see Barański, "'Oh come è grande,'" 17–20; Camozzi Pistoja, "Testo come eucarestia"; Maldina, "Raccogliendo briciole." A different view is presented in Fioravanti, "Introduzione." On encyclopedism in the *Convivio*, see Vasoli, "*Convivio* di Dante"; Barański, "Dante fra 'sperimentalismo'"; and S. Gilson, "Qualche considerazione su Dante."

10. Took, *Dante*, 253, speaks of the concern in book 3 with the "assimilation of the created to the uncreated mind."

11. See, for instance, Aquinas, *Summa contra Gentiles* 1.91: "Dicitur a Dionysio quod amor est unitiva virtus" [Dionysius says that love is a unifying power]. See also Aquinas, *Sent.* 3.27.1.1; Albert, *Ethica* 7.1.1: "Sicut dicit Ierotheus, quod 'amor virtus unitiva est, superiora movens ad inferiorum providentiam, et in inferiora ad superiorum subjectionem.'"

12. Most recently on book 4 as scholastic *questio* (but also as a polemic against the monetization of learning), see Fioravanti, "Prima trattazione." A different reading of book 4 in light of medieval theories of satire is proposed in Camozzi Pistoja, "Quarto trattato del *Convivio*."

13. Segre, *Lingua, stile e società*, 227–70. See also Baldelli, "Prosa del *Convivio*"; Mazzucchi, *Tra "Convivio" e "Commedia."*

14. For these examples (only a selection), see "al principale intendimento tornando" (1.2.12) [to return to the main discussion]; "Onde è manifesto che" (1.6.8) [Hence it is manifest that]; "La ragione è che" (1.2.4) [The reason is that]; "Ed è da sapere" (2.3.13) [And it should be known]; "E per questo è la dubitazione soluta" (3.15.10) [And so the doubt is resolved]; "Per che è da notare" (4.7.3) [Here it should be noted].

15. On the Bible, see Fioravanti, "Presenze bibliche"; Nasti, *Favole d'amore*, 93–130; Vasoli, "Bibbia."

16. Gorni, "Appunti," 6–7, and much earlier Biscioni, who, in his 1723 edition, had noted pithily that "in sì deplorata condizione non si trova forse alcuno libro d'antico scrittore" [perhaps no book by any ancient writer in Italian is found in such a deplorable state] (*Prose di Dante Alighieri*, vii).

17. See now Ceccherini, "Il *Convivio*." For a new manuscript discovery, see Dusio, "Nuovo manoscritto."

18. See Lancia, *Chiose alla "Commedia,"* ad indicem, and further commentary in Azzetta, "Tradizione del *Convivio*." For the Ottimo's "acquaintance" with Dante, see *Ottimo commento*, ed. Torri, 1:183, 225. For the early reading and transmission of the *Convivio*, see most recently Azzetta, "'Di questo parla l'autore'" with further bibliography.

19. G. Villani, *Nuova cronica* 10.136.48: "E comincia [sc. Dante] uno comento sopra XIIII delle sopradette sue canzoni morali volgarmente, il quale per la sopravenuta morte non perfetto si truova se non sopra le tre; la quale, per quello che·ssi vede, alta, bella, sottile e grandissima opera riusciva, però che ornata appare d'alto dittato e di belle ragioni filosofiche e astrologiche. Altresì fece uno libretto che·ll'intitola *De vulgari eloquentia*, ove promette fare IIII libri, ma non se ne truova se non due, forse per lo affrettato suo fine, ove con forte et adorno latino e belle ragioni riprova tutti i vulgari d'Italia" [Dante starts a commentary in the vernacular on fourteen moral canzoni, but only three are finished because of his death. From what one can see, this work is a very great one, lofty, elegant, and subtle, since it is endowed with a high style of expression and won-

derful philosophical and astronomical explanations. Dante also composed a small book that he called *De vulgari eloquentia*; here he promises to write four books even though only two are found, perhaps on account of its rushed end. In this work with powerful and polished Latin and elegant reasoning he reproves all the other Italian vernaculars].

20. See most recently Azzetta, "Nota sulla tradizione."

21. On Manetti, see De Robertis, "*Convivio* copiato." On the circulation of the *Convivio* in this period, see Arduini, "Episodio" and "Ruolo di Boccaccio"; S. Gilson, "Reading the *Convivio*."

22. See Curti, "Bembo."

23. On the *Convivio* in sixteenth-century Italy, see S. Gilson, "Reading the *Convivio*" and *Reading Dante*, 66–69 and *ad indicem*. For Castelvetro's concern to highlight contradictions, see his "Sposizione," 414 and 417 (*Inf.* 27.79–81 and 28.134); Castelvetro nonetheless reads several passages (*Inf.* 1.1–3; 20.118–19; 21.112–14) in harmony with the treatise. See most recently Tavoni, *Qualche idea su Dante*, 251–92.

24. See Biscioni ed. and note 16 above.

25. Scartazzini ed., Dante, *"Divina Commedia,"* 1:62: "ritratta una opinione da lui emessa nel *Convito*" [retracts a view that he had advanced in the *Convito*]; 3:37: "Qui e' confuta in versi quanto nel *Conv*. aveva detto in prosa" [Here he confutes in verse what he had said in prose in the *Convivio*]; see also 354, 764.

26. Dante, *Convito*, Monti ed., xvii and xviii (on Moon spots); Foscolo, *Poeti italiani maggiori*, 202, 213, 227, for a dating after 1313; and on the "dissomglianze" [dissimilarities] with the *Commedia*, see especially 243–45. See also Colombo, "Karl Witte." The other examples and data in this paragraph are drawn from searches undertaken using the DDP.

27. On Boethius, see for instance Lombardo, *"Quasi come sognando"*; Nasti, "Storia materiale." On Cicero, see Di Fonzo, "Dal *Convivio* alla *Monarchia*"; Marchesi, "Rilettura del *De officiis*." On Livy, see Livraghi, "Dal *Convivio* alla *Monarchia*." On Albert, see Falzone, "'Sì come dice Alberto'"; Vasoli, "Fonti albertiane." On connections between the *Convivio* and *De vulgari eloquentia*, see at least Fenzi, "Dal *Convivio*"; and Tavoni, "*Convivio*." On the doctrine of the Empyrean, see Cristaldi, "Empireo e cosmo"; Italia, "L'Empireo"; Pegoretti, "Empireo." See also Fioravanti, "Dossografie filosofiche." Topics such as law and nobility have also received renewed attention. The examples are only indicative; see also the essays collected in Meier, *Dante's "Convivio,"* and Bartuschat and Robiglio, *Convivio di Dante*.

28. See recently Falzone, "*Convivio* di Dante."

29. See above all Barański, "*Convivio* e la poesia" and "'Oh come è grande,'" and Hooper, "Dante's *Convivio*, Book 1."

30. Still valuable is the discussion in Wieruszowski, "Early Anticipation."

31. See M. Trovato, "Primo trattato."

32. See Nasti, *Favole d'amore*, 93–130.

33. See De Bonfils Templer, "*Donna gentile* del *Convivio*," "Due *ineffabilitadi* del *Convivio*," and "'Prima materia degli elementi.'" On Conches's Boethian commentary, see now Lombardo, *Boezio in Dante*, 8 and *ad indicem*.

34. For discussion of these components and of the opening, see Bianchi, "'Noli comedere'" and "'Ultima perfezione'"; De Bonfils Templer, "Dantesco amoroso uso"; Barański, "'Oh come è grande'"; Gentili, *Uomo aristotelico*, 127–65; Fioravanti, "Presenze bibliche," 250.

35. On the public, see Fioravanti, "*Convivio*"; Tavoni, "*Convivio*" and *Qualche idea su Dante*, 77–103. See also Lansing, "Dante's Intended Audience"; Picchio Simonelli, "Pubblico e società." See also the judicious comments in Ascoli, "'Ponete mente,'" 121n11. See now on the entire question Pertile, "Sulla cronologia."

36. On the issues raised here, see especially Pertile, "Sulla cronologia."

37. See most recently Bianchi, "'Ultima perfezione,'" who shows traces of Averroistic readings of Aristotle in the very opening quotation as mediated by the tradition of philosophical compendia linked to the *Auctoritates Aristotelis*. On Albert and Dante, see Vasoli, "Introduzione," lxviii, and his notes to *Conv.* 2.13.5; 3.5.12 (*De causis et proprietatibus elementorum* and *De natura loci*); 3.7.3 (*De intellectu et intelligibili*); and 4.24.6 in Vasoli ed. Of particular note are the writings associated with the *Parva naturalia*, as well as the *De natura et origine animae* and the *De intellectu et intelligibili*; all these short treatises tended to circulate together.

38. On the *De causis*, see Falzone, *Desiderio della scienza*, 69–80. On Giles, see Papi, "Aristotle's Emotions," 100–104.

39. See especially Fioravanti, "Introduzione," and Tavoni's articles and books listed in Bibliography.

40. On these issues, see at least Barański, "On Dante's Trail"; Dell'Oso, "Per la formazione intellettuale."

41. Pietrobono, *Poema sacro*.

42. Barbi, "Razionalismo e misticismo."

43. Dante, *Convivio*, Busnelli and Vandelli ed. On Busnelli and the context of his neo-Thomism, see now Stabile, "Dante oggi." Nardi recognized that the "donna gentile" represented a remarkably rich construct—bringing together diverse notions, figures, and traditions. But he too was concerned to stress patterns of development in Dante and between his works, often with his own hypthoses on dating, redactional phases, and questions of authenticity that were normally related to his vision of Dante's development; see Nardi, *Dal "Convivio" alla "Commedia."*

44. See Corti, *Felicità mentale*, and the critiques in Fioravanti ed. (for example, on *Conv.* 4.1.8) and especially Falzone, "*Convivio* di Dante."

45. See Gagliardi, *Tragedia intellettuale di Dante*, and traces of such views in Nicola Fosca's recent commentary on the DDP, for instance *Purg.* 2.120–23 and *Par.* 4.139–42 *ad loc*.

46. Quotations in Jacoff, "Post-Palinodic Simile," 116. For other relevant references, see Hollander, "Dante's Deployment."

47. Pertile, "Lettera aperta."

48. Scott, "Unfinished *Convivio*" and *Understanding Dante*, 107–42. On cosmology in the *Convivio*, see Cachey, "'. . . Alcuna cosa.'"

49. M. Trovato, "Against Aristotle"; Barolini, *Undivine Comedy*, 99–101 (on *Conv.* 4.12).

50. Dante, *Inferno; Purgatorio; Paradiso*, Hollander ed.

51. Scott, "Unfinished Convivio."

52. Falzone, *Desiderio della scienza.*

53. See Ascoli, *Dante*, especially 274–78, 284, 297–98; for an earlier version, see Ascoli, "Palinode and History."

CHAPTER 6

De vulgari eloquentia

MIRKO TAVONI

THE STRUCTURE OF THE *DE VULGARI ELOQUENTIA*

Dante wrote the *De vulgari eloquentia* in exile, probably between mid-1304 and early 1306. At the time, he was also working on the first books of the *Convivio*, in which he announced the linguistic treatise and its title: "Di questo si parlerà altrove più compiutamente in uno libello ch'io intendo di fare, Dio concedente, di Volgare Eloquenza" (1.5.10) [This topic will be pursued more fully elsewhere, in a little work I intend to write, God willing, on *Eloquence in the Vernacular*].[1] The *De vulgari* was meant to consist of four or five books, but, abruptly, Dante left it incomplete after the thirteenth chapter of book 2 and never published it. In fact, it remained practically unknown until the beginning of the sixteenth century.

The treatise proposes to teach vernacular eloquence, "Cum neminem ante nos de vulgaris eloquentie doctrina quicquam inveniamus tractasse, atque talem scilicet eloquentiam penitus omnibus necessariam videamus, cum ad eam non tantum viri, sed etiam mulieres et parvuli nitantur, in quantum natura permictit" (1.1.1) [Since I find that no one, before myself, has dealt in any way with the theory of eloquence in the vernacular, and since we can plainly see that such eloquence is necessary to everyone—for not only men, but also women and children strive to acquire it, as far as nature allows].² To achieve this, however, Dante approaches the topic in a roundabout way. He begins by defining human language by comparing it to the modes of communication of angels and of animals. He then moves on to the linguistic history of humanity, beginning with Adam and Eve, before "narrowing" his focus to the ethno-geo-linguistic context of Europe, after which he concentrates on the Romance linguistic and literary sphere. With respect to this, Dante reviews all the municipal vernaculars of Italy, and, against this backdrop, he highlights the brilliant lineage of illustrious vernacular poets who have "deviated" from their own local vernacular. Moving on from these *poete*, Dante constructs a philosophically founded theory of vernacular poetry and literature that is intended to serve as the nucleus of the Italian language—the so-called illustrious vernacular—which would develop, with all its civic functions, around a future imperial Italian court. Book 2 addresses the literary uses of the illustrious vernacular, both in poetry and in prose. Dante then concentrates on poetry, specifying the poets and topics for which the illustrious vernacular ought to be reserved, as well as the style, metrical form, verses, words, and syntactic structures that it should utilize. Finally, Dante considers in detail how the stanza, namely the strophe, of the canzone, the metrical genre most appropriate for the illustrious vernacular, should be constructed.

Given the significant difference in the subject matter of books 1 and 2, should the *De vulgari eloquentia* be considered a treatise on linguistics or on poetics? What were Dante's aims? What kind of message did he want to communicate, and what was his audience? And why did he abandon it so abruptly? We will attempt to answer these questions in the penultimate subsection, after having examined the most salient theoretical points of the treatise.

The Vernacular and Latin

From the very first chapter Dante sets up the dichotomy between the *locutio vulgaris*, or the vulgar tongue based on usage, which is simply the human faculty of language, and the artificial *locutio secundaria*, also termed *gramatica*, which is based on art and is rationally codified. All human beings possess the *locutio vulgaris*, while only some peoples have developed a *gramatica*, which may be acquired only through prolonged study. In practice, the grammatical languages that embody the *locutio secundaria* are Latin (which Dante knew well) and Greek (which Dante did not know, although he was aware of its existence).

Having established the diglossia between the language of everyday use and the exclusive language of intellectuals, Dante comes up with a revolutionary assertion: "Harum quoque duarum nobilior est vulgaris" (1.1.4) [Of these two kinds of language, the more noble is the vernacular]. Dante thus subverts the traditional hierarchy between Latin and the vernacular, which is all the more astonishing since, in book 1 of the *Convivio*, presumably written only a few months prior, Dante had affirmed that Latin is "più bello, più virtuoso e più nobile" [more beautiful, more virtuous, and more noble] because "lo volgare seguita uso, e lo latino arte" (*Conv.* 1.5.14) [the vernacular is shaped by usage, and Latin by art]. In concluding, I will assess the implications of this contradiction, over which much scholarly ink has been spilled.

It is important to point out, however, that, for Dante, Latin is an artificial language only up to a point. It is not a form of "Esperanto," that is to say a completely artificial language deliberately constructed by taking and combining elements from different languages that belong to discrete linguistic families.[3] This would be so only if we were to understand that the "inventores gramatice facultatis" [inventors of the art of grammar], who designed Latin "de comuni consensu multarum gentium" [with the common consent of many peoples], as Dante states in 1.9.11, designed it with the consent of *everyone* in the Christian West who employs Latin as the language of culture, of the church, and of the universities but who speak vernacular languages belonging to different families: Romance, Germanic, and Western Slavonic. But this was not Dante's view, otherwise he would not have been able to nurture the extremely high and sympathetic admiration that he had for the language of Virgil and of the other great Latin poets. Equally, he would not have been able to represent the Italian troubadour Sordello throwing himself at Virgil's feet and exclaiming that the *Aeneid* "mostrò ciò che potea *la lingua nostra*" (*Purg.* 7.17; my emphasis) [revealed what *our language* was capable of].[4] Below we will examine further, in the subsection "Language Change, the Invention of Latin, and the 'Italianness' of Latin," what, according to Dante, was the process whereby Latin was constructed.

A Political Idea of Language

Why does Dante dedicate two entire chapters (1.2–3) to demonstrate that *locutio*, or the faculty of language that is the supreme manifestation of the rational soul, was given exclusively to mankind and not to angels or to inferior animals? The phrase with which the following affirmation concludes reveals the answer: "Non angelis, non inferioribus animalibus necessarium fuit loqui: sed nequicquam datum fuisset eis; *quod nempe facere natura abhorret*" (1.2.2; my emphasis) [It was not necessary that either angels or the lower animals should be able to speak; rather, this power would have been wasted on them, *and nature, of course, hates to do anything superfluous*]. Dante borrows these words from the opening page of Thomas Aquinas's commentary on Aristotle's *Politics* (*Sententia libri Politicorum* 1.1.28–29), where Thomas comments on the famous Aristotelian definition of man as a political animal and identifies in language, a distinctively human faculty, the proof that man is indeed a political animal. From this Dante deduces that clarifying human discourse is of primary importance when endeavoring to reveal the principles of civic coexistence. Additionally, the aim of "locutioni vulgarium gentium prodesse" (1.1.1) [improving the language of people who speak the vulgar tongue], announced in the opening of the *De vulgari eloquentia*, is crucial for his agenda of educating a new Italian ruling class both ethically and politically, an agenda that he was putting into motion by writing the *Convivio*. It is here that we can recognize the development of the linguistic treatise as it grows, gaining its own autonomy, from the political and civic concerns of the *Convivio*.[5]

The Linguistic History of the World: From Adam to the Tower of Babel

If the first three chapters, dedicated to defining what language is, are philosophically marked, drawing on Aristotle and scholastic culture, chapter 4 marks the beginning of what might be termed Dante's recourse to "biblical linguistics," which inaugurates the reconstruction of the linguistic history of the world. First of all, Dante clarifies the circumstances surrounding the *primiloquium* (1.4.1), humanity's primal utterance. The first to speak was Adam, not Eve (1.4.2–3), and his first word was *El*, or "God" (1.4.4–6), which he spoke immediately after God had infused the rational soul into him (1.5.1–2), although Dante was unaware whether this happened inside or outside the Earthly Paradise (1.5.3), in the language that would later be called Hebrew (1.6.7), when, as a consequence of Babel, it survived only among the descendants of Eber, who had not participated in the sinful act of defiance.[6]

In chapters 4–6, Dante devotes himself to "rewriting Genesis," as has been said, using a formula that expresses almost unease for the nonchalance with which Dante aligns himself to the sacred text.[7] Any astonishment diminishes, however, if we turn to Augustine's *De Genesi ad litteram*, which does more or less the same thing. Intending to defend the sacred text from potential detractors, and assuming that the Bible is not, nor is it held to be, perfectly complete and ordered in its presentation of facts, the bishop of Hippo attempts to give to the *lictera* of the text the most rational explanation possible. Thus the family of terms relating to *ratio*, reason, is as present in the *De Genesi ad litteram* as it is in the *De vulgari eloquentia*.

Dante states that God created a "certam formam locutionis" (1.6.4) [certain form of language] in Adam's rational soul. What does this mean? Does it mean that God gave him a specific language already fully formed, an *ydioma*, namely Hebrew? Or does it mean that God endowed his rational soul with mental structures capable of elaborating language, structures that Adam would draw on to "produce" his language, namely, Hebrew? Today there is nearly unanimous agreement in favor of the first interpretation, if for no other reason than that Dante asks "sub quo ydiomate primiloquium emanavit" (1.4.1) [in what language that primal utterance was made], and it would not make sense for him to respond to this question by claiming that God gave Adam linguistic universals.[8]

Banished from the Earthly Paradise, Adam, Eve, and their descendants moved together until they reached the Plain of Shinar. There, incited by the giant Nimrod, the travelers began constructing the Tower of Babel (1.7). To punish them for their wickedness, God caused them suddenly to forget their shared language, which was still the language of grace created inside Adam. Consequently each group of workers fashioned its own language (1.7.6–7). Only Eber's family had not participated in the transgressive act and so was spared from the confusion of languages. From this family "ortus est populus Israel, qui antiquissima locutione sunt usi usque ad suam dispersionem" (1.7.8) [descended the people of Israel, who used this most ancient language until the time of their dispersal], that is until the destruction of the Temple of Jerusalem in 70 CE, "ut Redemptor noster, qui ex illis oriturus erat secundum humanitatem, non lingua confusionis, sed gratie, frueretur" (1.6.6) [so that our Redeemer, who was to descend from them (insofar as he was human), should speak, not the language of confusion, but that of grace].

By representing Babelic punishment as the failure to communicate between different groups of artisans, Dante was also alluding to the *Arti*, or guilds, which governed Florence and other city-states, all of which were wracked by constant unrest. In any case, beginning with this traumatic event:

> Cum igitur omnis nostra loquela, preter illam homini primo concreatam a Deo, sit a nostro beneplacito reparata post confusionem illam que nil fuit aliud quam prioris oblivio, et homo sit instabilissimum atque variabilissimum animal, nec durabilis nec continua esse potest; sed sicut alia que nostra sunt, puta mores et habitus, per locorum temporumque distantias variari oportet. (1.9.6)

> [Since, therefore, all our language (except that created by God along with the first man) has been assembled, at our pleasure, in the aftermath of the great confusion that brought nothing else than oblivion to the original language, and since human beings are highly unstable and variable animals, our language can be neither durable nor consistent with itself; but, like everything else that belongs to us (such as manners and customs), it must vary according to distances of space and time.]

Babel thus marks the clear point of separation between two phases of mankind's linguistic history: monolingual before Babel, plurilingual after Babel. In representing this linguistic history, Dante had in the front of his mind a "T and O" *mappa mundi*, like the one reproduced in figure 6.1. The map is oriented to the East, not to the North, and the Earthly Paradise (*paradisus*) coincides with the cardinal point of the East (*oriens*) at the top of the map. The O is the circumference of the landmass encircled by the ocean, and the T refers to the Cross: the horizontal beam represents the Don (northward) and Nile (southward) rivers, while the vertical beam represents the Mediterranean.

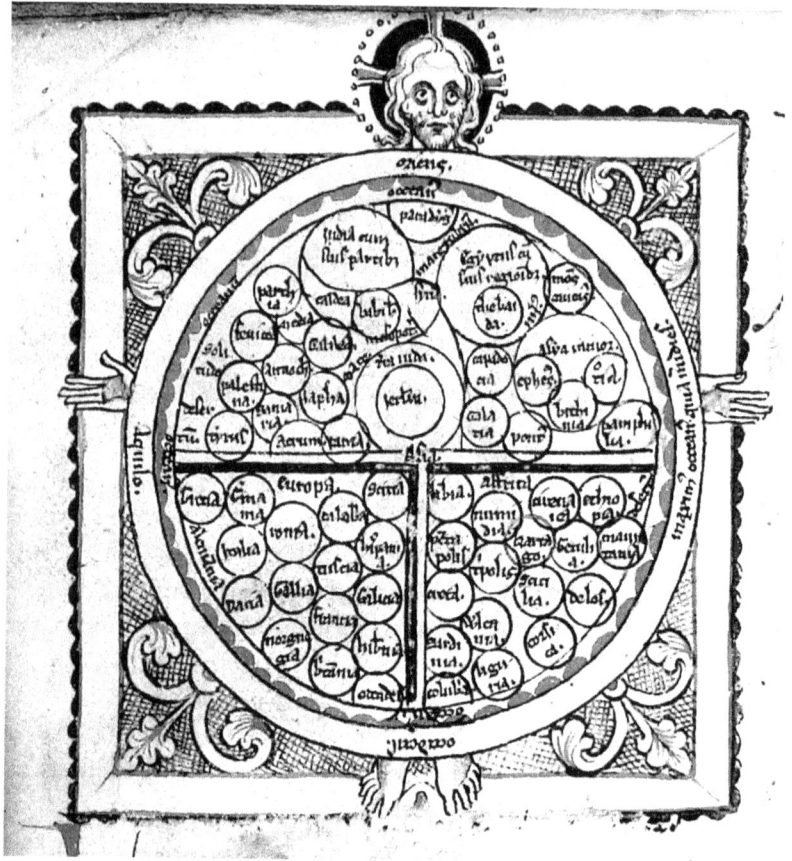

Figure 6.1. "T and O" *mappa mundi.* London, Lambeth Palace Library, ms. 371, fol. 9v, ca. 1300. Courtesy of Lambeth Palace Library, London.

Figure 6.2 projects onto this "T and O" map the migrations of peoples and languages that Dante describes in the *De vulgari eloquentia*. The two phases, pre- and post-Babelic, are represented (1.8.1) through the metaphor of *propaginatio*: a viticulture technique whereby the first vine branch, which is buried, sprouts into many branches. The first vine branch, representing mankind still united in movement, stretches from the Earthly Paradise to the Tower of Babel, in the middle of Asia. From there, following on from the confusion of tongues, many new offshoots of the vine head out in every direction, representing the many human groups on the move, each with its own respective language.[9]

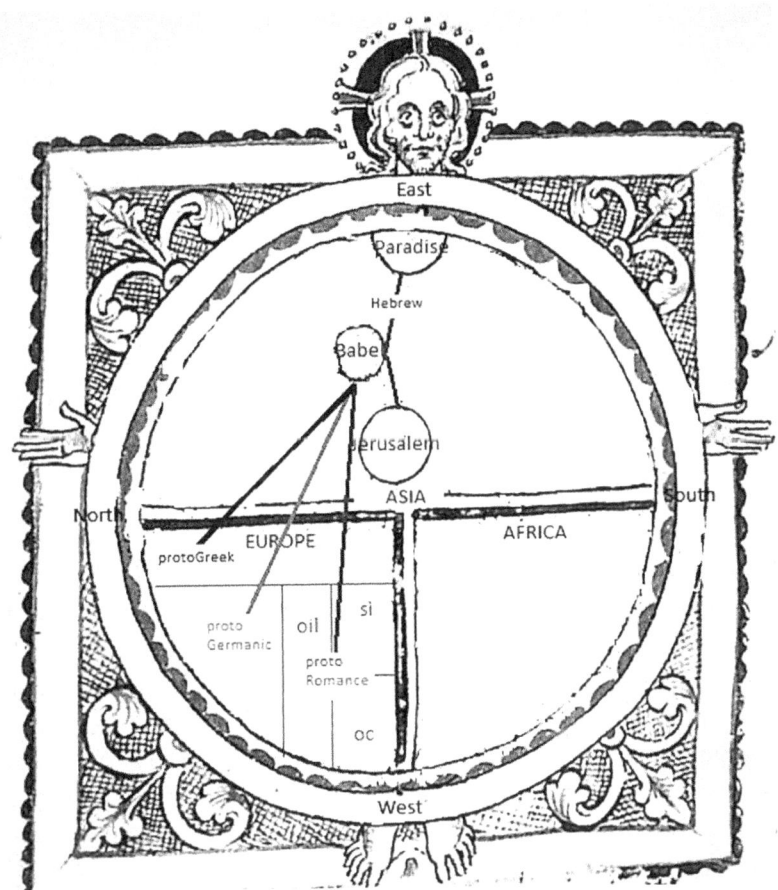

Figure 6.2. Dante's biblical and postbiblical linguistics superimposed onto a "T and O" *mappa mundi*.

The key role of the Tower of Babel is rejected in *Paradiso* 26, where Adam says to Dante:

> La lingua ch'io parlai fu tutta spenta
> innanzi che a l'ovra inconsummabile
> fosse la gente di Nembròt attenta.
>   (124–26)

[The language that I spoke was all extinguished before Nimrod's people turned their attention to the unattainable task.]

Our first parent then deduces from this the general principle that

> Opera naturale è ch'uom favella;
> ma così o così, natura lascia
> poi fare a voi secondo che v'abbella.
> (130–32)

[It is a natural activity for man to speak; but this way or that, nature then leaves it up to you to choose at your pleasure.]

In the *Paradiso*, Dante thus maintains that an original language of grace never existed. This palinode has been explained as the definitive abandonment of the "pregiudizio teologico" [theological prejudice] that would have residually continued to hold sway in the *De vulgari eloquentia* despite the fact that, as the treatise makes clear, Dante had also discovered the rational principle of the intrinsic mutability of all languages. Nevertheless, the Babelic confusion was not an article of faith, so it would be strange for Dante to espouse more rationalist positions in the *Paradiso* than in the *De vulgari*. It seems more likely that Adam's declaration can be explained in light of Dante's supreme appreciation of the vernacular as "una sorta di blasone interno alla *Commedia*, ad autogiustificare il paradosso del poema sacro in una lingua peritura" [a sort of emblem internal to the *Commedia*, to justify the paradox of the sacred poem composed in a language that would pass], whereby "alla definitiva sanzione teologale che garantisce la liceità dell'alta missione alla quale il pellegrino è chiamato si collega la sanzione linguistica dell'opera che di quella missione è veicolo e forma" [to the definitive theological sanctioning that guarantees the legitimacy of the lofty mission to which the pilgrim has been called is linked the linguistic sanctioning of the work that is that mission's medium and form].[10]

The Linguistic History of the World: From the Tower of Babel to the Linguistic Families of Europe

From Babel, three among the various migratory currents headed toward Europe, bringing with them three Babelic languages (1.8.1–2). As we can see in figure 6.2, the bearers of the first language (*ydioma*), which we may call "proto-Germanic-Slavonic," settled in the northwestern part of Europe (1.8.3). The bearers of the second language (*ydioma*), which we may call "proto-Greek," settled in the East astride Europe and Asia (1.8.4). The bearers of the third language (*ydioma*), which we may call "proto-Romance," settled in the southwestern part of Europe (1.8.5-6). Subsequently, each of these Babelic languages further differentiated itself into diverse vernaculars (*vulgaria*), obeying the law of inevitable and constant change of every natural language that Dante had discovered: "Ab uno postea eodemque ydiomate in vindice confusione recepto, diversa vulgaria traxerunt originem" (1.8.3) [Later, from each one of these languages received in that vengeful confusion different vernaculars developed]. In figure 6.2 we can see these three languages having their origin in the confusion of languages at Babel and then differentiating themselves into many vernaculars.

It is at this juncture that Dante's third metalinguistic term comes into play with rigorously semantic specificity. After *locutio*, which signifies the faculty of language, and after *ydioma-ydiomata*, which refers to the particular languages found in scriptural human history (Adam's language and then those of Babel), Dante begins to speak of *vulgare-vulgaria*, which signifies the vernacular languages of modern Europe.

It was long believed that Dante had conceived of a single European Babelic language—an unfounded idea that anachronistically made Dante a precursor of Indo-European linguistics.[11] By establishing his linguistic tri-partition of Europe, Dante is perhaps influenced by the division of the ecumene into three continents—Asia, Europe, and Africa—that was depicted in the "T and O" *mappae mundi*, a division that in turn corresponded to the three sons of Noah: Shem, Ham, and Japheth. As may be seen in figure 6.1, Asia takes up the eastern half of the ecumene, Europe the bottom left quadrant (northwest), and Africa the bottom right quadrant (southwest). In symmetry with the division of the ecumene into three continents, Dante may have also decided to divide the European languages into three, thereby following the same geometrical logic, as we can see in figure 6.2: one language ("proto-Greek") occupying the eastern half, one language ("proto-Germanic-Slavonic") occupying the northwest quadrant, and one language ("proto-Romance") occupying the southwest quadrant. Dante was perhaps also influenced by the analogous tri-partition of the proto-Romance Babelic language into the three vernaculars of *sì* (Italian), *oc* (Occitan), and *oïl* (Old French). It does not seem by chance that, in 1.8.5, he should designate all three with the expression *ydioma tripharium*, the same expression that, in 1.8.2, he uses to indicate the three European proto-languages.

Dante's skill in integrating elements about which he had varying degrees of information into a unique and original overview is noteworthy. Dante knew much about the "proto-Romance" Babelic language, divided into the vernaculars of *sì*, *oc*, and *oïl*, because he knew the three languages well. Conversely, he did not know anything about the "proto-Germanic-Slavonic" language, except that he must have learned somewhere, likely from transalpine students at the University of Bologna, that it used the affirmative particle *iò* (1.8.3). Dante did not know anything about the "proto-Greek" language either, except that Greek existed as a grammatical language and very likely, since this was widely known, that it had five dialects. Yet, from such limited, heterogeneous, and uneven sources of information, Dante succeeded in brilliantly envisioning a unitary linguistic synthesis and overview of Europe: three language families going back to three Babelic languages, with each family differentiated into many vernacular languages and endowed, in two out of three cases, with a grammatical language: Latin and Greek.

Language Change, the Invention of Latin, and the "Italianness" of Latin

How did Dante manage to discover the principle of the inevitable change of all natural languages that he presents in 1.9.6? It was no small feat to recognize that all languages change, given that, on the one hand, Latin had not changed in centuries, while on the other, on account of a lack of written evidence, it was impossible to determine whether vernaculars had altered. If Dante was able to establish that vernacular languages change, it was because he recognized the similarities between the vernaculars of *oc*, *oïl*, and *sì*, from which he deduced that, in the past, they must have constituted a single language that then became differentiated in time and space (1.8.5 and 9.2).

Consequently, the Tower of Babel is not a "theological leftover" in Dante's thought but a perfectly rational point of reference that explains why the vernaculars of *oc*, *oïl*, and *sì* are so similar. At the same time, Babel demonstrates that languages change: if the three vernaculars are so similar, it is because at one point—at the moment of linguistic confusion—they were a single language, and if they are no longer so, it is because languages change. This is enough to exclude the possibility that Adam's palinode in *Paradiso* 26 is the result of Dante's having abandoned an irrational "prejudice." On the contrary, the changed perspective was because, as he composed the *Paradiso*, Dante was no longer interested in the overview of the European linguistic families. He was interested instead in receiving from Adam a full legitimation of the vernacular in which his sacred poem was written.

Another matter that stands out is that words shared by the vernaculars of *oc*, *oïl*, and *sì* are also shared by Latin. Dante could not have imagined that Latin was actually the mother language of the three vernaculars, but he saw clearly that its lexical base was the same as theirs. And this is so because Latin, which was constructed "with the common consent of many peoples," was constructed with the sole consent of southern European peoples that spoke the vernaculars of *oc*, *oïl*, and *sì*, and no one else. Thus Latin is not an "inter-Babelic" language. In figure 6.2 we can see the "proto-Romance" language that is divided into the vernaculars of *oc*, *oïl*, and *sì*. At that point, the *inventores gramatice facultatis*, on the basis of these three sister languages, invent Latin as a *gramatica*. In the same way, the other European *locutio secundaria*, Greek, is also not an "inter-Babelic" language. Equally, the Greek *gramatica* was created upon the exclusive foundation of the Babelic "proto-Greek" language, and only after that language had been differentiated in line with the principle of the inevitability of language change post Babel. Dante had no direct knowledge of these vernaculars, which he posited derived from the Greek Babelic language. However, the widespread notion of the existence of five Greek dialects must have assured him that this process of change had actually occurred.

The relative chronology of these processes is very different from the idea that we have today. Latin literature, which presupposes Latin *gramatica*, is posterior to the existence of the vernaculars of *oc*, *oïl*, and *sì*. Therefore, ancient Latin writers lived immersed in the same diglossia that existed in Dante's day. They wrote in Latin but spoke in the vernacular. In fact, in hell, Virgil quips, using his native Lombard: "Istra ten va, più non t'adizzo" (*Inf.* 27.21) [Now get lost, I won't urge you any more]. And in the *Vita nova* (25.3 [16.3]) Dante writes that "anticamente non erano dicitori d'amore in lingua volgare, anzi erano dicitori d'amore certi poete in lingua latina" [in antiquity no one wrote about love in the vernacular; rather, those who wrote about love were certain poets who used Latin],[12] not because the "vernacular language" did not exist at that time, but because poets were free to choose in which language to write. "E lo primo che cominciò a dire sì come poeta volgare"—that is, the first troubadour, 150 years earlier—"si mosse però che volle fare intendere le sue parole a donna, a la quale era malagevole d'intendere li versi latini" (25.6) [And the first who began to write as a vernacular poet did this because he wanted his words to be understood by women, who found it difficult to understand Latin verses]. It is for this reason that Romance literatures developed later than Latin literature.

The idea that Latin was created only starting from the vernaculars of *oc*, *oïl*, and *sì* is confirmed by the fact that the *positores* of Latin *gramatica*, when choosing their affirmative particle—a word that has strong identificatory value throughout Dante's treatise—chose *sic*, "quod quandam anterioritatem erogare videtur Ytalis, qui *sì* dicunt" (1.10.1) [and this fact would seem to confer a certain preeminence on the Italians, who say *sì*]. And the language of *sì*, in relation to its two sister languages, enjoys this privilege, that "magis videtur inniti gramatice, que comunis est, quod rationabiliter inspicientibus videtur gravissimum argumentum" (1.10.2) [it seems to be closer to the *gramatica* that is shared by all—and this, to those who consider the matter rationally, will appear a very weighty argument]. Therefore, it is clear why Latin is fully "lingua nostra" [our language], as Sordello says to Virgil in *Purgatorio* 9.[13]

Which Is the Best Vernacular in Italy?

At this point (1.10.3–6), Dante launches his geographically based investigation into the vernaculars of Italy, divided between those to the right of the Apennines (corresponding to the Tyrrhenian Sea, since medieval maps placed East at the top, and not North), and vernaculars to the left of the Apennines (those on the Adriatic side). There are fourteen main vernaculars: seven to the right and seven to the left of the Apennines

(1.10.7).[14] Dante's goal is "decentiorem atque illustrem Ytalie ven*ari* loquelam" [to hunt for the most respectable and illustrious vernacular that exists in Italy]. However, before doing that, he declares: "Perplexos frutices atque sentes prius eiciamus de silva" (1.11.1) [Let us begin by clearing the tangled bushes and brambles out of the wood], namely the worst vernaculars: those of Rome (1.11.2), Ancona (1.11.3), Milan and Bergamo (1.11.5), and Aquileia and Istria (1.11.6).

Having eradicated the worst, Dante moves on to the best: first and foremost Sicilian (1.12), exemplified by Guido delle Colonne's canzoni "Ancor che l'aigua per lo foco lassi" [Although water flees from fire] and "Amor, che lungiamente m'hai menato" [Love, who long have led me] (1.12.2). The primacy of Sicilian is due to "illustres heroes Fredericus Cesar et benegenitus eius Manfredus" [those illustrious heroes, the Emperor Frederick and his worthy son Manfred], who gathered around their court "excellentes Latinorum" [the most gifted individuals in Italy], who, in their turn, created the first illustrious poetry in the vernacular of *sì* (1.12.4). In order to do so, those poets distanced themselves ("diverterunt") from their native Sicilian vernacular, which, according to Dante, sounded like a drawl, as in the verse "Tragemi d'este focora se t'este a bolontate" [Get me out of this fire, if you would be so kind]. The Apulian poets at the Frederician court did the same thing, moving away from their native vernacular, which sounded low, as in the verse "Bòlzera che chiangesse lo quatraro" (1.12.6–7) [I would like the boy to cry], in order to produce illustrious poems such as "Madonna, dir vi voglio" [Lady, I wish to tell you] and "Per fino amore vo sì letamente" [I go so happily for true love's sake] (1.12.8).

From the excellent Sicilians Dante moves on to the deplorable Tuscans, "qui, propter amentiam suam infroniti, titulum sibi vulgaris illustris arrogare videntur" (1.13.1) [who, greedy in their foolishness, seem to lay claim to the honor of possessing the illustrious vernacular]. Dante vents his disdain for all the municipal vernaculars of Tuscany, each with its plebeian "stigma," a dialectal expression that characterizes each of them: his list includes Florence, Pisa, Lucca, Siena, and Arezzo. In contrast, the stilnovist poets from Florence and Pistoia—Guido Cavalcanti, Lapo Gianni, Dante himself, and Cino da Pistoia—"vulgaris excellentiam cognovisse" (1.13.4) [have known the excellence of the vernacular] by "deviating" [diverterunt] from their natural way of speaking.

The juxtaposition of excellent Sicilians and deplorable Tuscans points to the political moment that Dante was experiencing in the early years of his exile. Offended by the banishment that his fellow citizens had inflicted upon him, in the midst of a civil war that he saw as the climax of the communal violence that was bloodying Italy, Dante derided the Tuscan vernaculars as emblems of local linguistic self-interest. Accordingly, he exalted the Sicilians, who blazed the trail for a supraregional Italian poetry under an imperial aegis that Dante identified as the remedy to the permanent state of conflict plaguing the city-states.

Having completed his assessment of the right side of Italy—that is, the Tyrrhenian side—Dante crosses the Apennines of Tuscany and Romagna and arrives at the left side of Italy, on the Adriatic (1.14.1). In other words, he leaves Tuscany and reaches the Po Valley. He now seems to find himself at a crossroads between two opposing macro-areas: that of the Romagnol vernacular, judged to be too effeminate (1.14.3), and that of the "Lombard" vernaculars, namely, Emilian, Lombard, Venetian, and Piedmontese, deemed to be too harsh (1.14.5). This impressionistic dichotomy does not have any actual basis in the Gallo-Italic dialects; and yet Dante forcefully asserts it. He likely does this because, in so doing, he can award the prize of the most beautiful municipal vernacular to Bolognese, which tempers the defects of both macro-areas thanks to its strategic position between the two. Indeed, the citizens of Bologna "accipiunt etenim . . . ab Ymolensibus lenitatem atque mollitiem, a Ferrariensibus vero et Mutinensibus aliqualem garrulitatem, que proprie Lombardorum est" (1.15.3) [take . . . a soft, yielding quality from those of Imola, and from the people of Ferrara and Modena, on the other hand, a certain abruptness that is more typical of the Lombards], so that "eorum locutio per commixtionem oppositorum ad laudabilem suavitatem remaneat temperata" (1.15.5) [their language, tempered by the combination of opposites mentioned above, should achieve a praiseworthy degree of elegance].

I believe that Dante granted preferential treatment to Bolognese because Bologna was where he resided while writing the treatise, as well as the place where he saw political and cultural conditions that promised to guarantee him a future as an intellectual (see the concluding subsection). But not even the Bolognese vernacular could be identified as the linguistic ideal that Dante was seeking: "Non etenim est quod aulicum et illustre vocamus; quoniam, si fuisset, maximus Guido Guinizelli, Guido

Ghisilerius, Fabrutius et Honestus et alii poetantes Bononie, nunquam a proprio divertissent" (1.15.6) [For it is not what we could call "aulic" or "illustrious" language; if it were, Bolognese poets like the great Guido Guinizzelli, or Guido Ghislieri, or Fabruzzo or Onesto or many others, would never have left off using it], which, of course, they did, as demonstrated by their various canzoni that Dante cites.

THE PANTHER AND THE ILLUSTRIOUS VERNACULAR

Therefore, the best vernacular in Italy that Dante has so far been hunting is like the "panther" of the bestiaries, "redolentem ubique" [whose scent is left everywhere], and yet "necubi apparentem" (1.16.1) [which is nowhere to be seen]. It can be found, however, in the illustrious canzoni of those vernacular poets who "have deviated" [diverterunt] from their local vernacular, as is the case with the poets of the Sicilian School (1.12), the Bolognese with Guido Guinizzelli at their head (1.15), and the stilnovists of Florence and Pistoia (1.13). To catch the *panthera*, Dante undertakes "a more closely reasoned investigation" [rationabilius investigemus] (1.16.1), no longer empirical-inductive (as we would say today) but hypothetical-deductive: a method based on the Aristotelian principle of *reductio ad unum*, whereby all things belonging to the same genus can be referred to a single entity that is the measure for all the others, as the numeral 1 functions for numbers and white for colors. In the same way, among the vernaculars there must be one—the simplest—that serves as the unit of measurement for all the others. This vernacular will be one of the "simplicissima signa, et morum et habituum et locutionis, quibus latine actiones ponderantur et mensurantur: que quidem nobilissima sunt earum que Latinorum sunt actiones" (1.16.3) [most simple signs, of customs and habits and speech, by which the actions of the people of Italy can be weighed and measured: and these signs are the most noble among the actions performed by Italians].

Around the same time as Dante was composing the *De vulgari eloquentia*, theorists of the subordination of the emperor's authority to that of the pope also made recourse to the principle of the *reductio ad unum*, which Aristotle discussed in book 10 of the *Metaphysics*. Among such thinkers were Giles of Rome, who propounded his views in the *De ecclesiastica potestate* [On ecclesiastical power], and Pope Boniface VIII, who expressed similar ideas in the bull *Unam sanctam* [One holy]. Subsequently, in *Monarchia* 3.11.1, Dante would energetically and originally challenge the hierocrats' recourse to this principle.[15] However, already in the treatise, Dante made use of the notion to maneuver out of the impasse into which his empirical search for the best Italian vernacular had fallen.

Following this a priori line of reasoning, Dante declares that, "adepti quod querebamus" [having found what we were seeking], he is thus able to define as the "illustre, cardinale, aulicum et curiale vulgare in Latio, quod omnis latie civitatis est et nullius esse videtur, et quo municipalia vulgaria omnia Latinorum mensurantur, ponderantur, et comparantur" (1.16.6) [illustrious, cardinal, aulic, and curial vernacular in Italy that which belongs to every Italian city yet seems to belong to none, and against which the vernaculars of all the cities of the Italians can be measured, weighed, and compared]. In practice, Dante confers a metaphysical status on the common language found in the illustrious poetry of the Sicilians, the Bolognese, and the Tuscan stilnovists. In this way, as has been noted, he brings about a process that goes "from the many to the one." This newly identified unitary language—the illustrious vernacular—is not artificial like *gramatica*; rather, it is natural. It is not a nostalgic or regressive recovery of the linguistic unity that was lost at Babel. It is instead a rational instrument constructed *ad placitum* that operates within the linguistic reality of Italy.[16]

This "most simple" vernacular deserves the title "illustrious" because "illuminans et illuminatum prefulgens . . . et suos honore sublimat et gloria" (1.17.2) [it gives off light or reflects the light that it receives from elsewhere . . . and is capable of exalting those who use it in honor and glory]. Indeed, it confers so much honor as to lift those who use it to unbelievable social heights: "Nonne domestici sui reges, marchiones, comites, et magnates quoslibet fama vincunt?" (1.17.5) [Does not the fame of its devotees exceed that of any king, marquis, count, or warlord?]. And Dante ends on a poignant, personal note: "Quantum vero suos familiares gloriosos efficiat, nos ipsi novimus, qui huius dulcedine glorie nostrum exilium postergamus" (1.17.6) [And I myself have known how greatly it increases the glory of those who serve it, I who, for the sake of that glory's sweetness, have the experience of exile behind me].

The illustrious vernacular is also "cardinal" because, just as a door follows the hinge, "sic et universus municipalium grex vulgarium vertitur et revertitur, movetur et pausat, secundum quod istud, quod quidem vere paterfamilias esse videtur" (1.18.1) [so the whole flock of languages spoken in the cities of Italy turns this way or that, moves or stands still, at the behest of this vernacular, which thus shows itself to be the true head of their family]. Thus Dante does not consider the illustrious vernacular as statically counterpoised to local vernaculars. Rather, he presents it as endowed with a regulatory prestige capable of advancing the entire system of inferior vernaculars, each of which has its own legitimate communicative function in its respective social context.

Finally, the illustrious vernacular is "aulic" and "curial," two epithets typically related to politics: "aulic" in the sense of an *aula*, or imperial courtroom (1.18.2–3); and "curial" in the sense that this vernacular is destined to be the instrument of communication of the curia, namely, the sum of governmental functions that surround the emperor (1.18.4–5). With these two final epithets, Dante clarifies the imperial origins of his idea of the common Italian illustrious vernacular. Just as the language of Italian poetry was born in the Sicilian curia of Emperor Fredrick II, so the future imperial curia in Italy, once restored, would fully realize this language as the political language of government in an Italy saved from municipal fragmentation. In the meantime, those poets who received this language from the Sicilians and who have kept it alive function as the virtual limbs of this future Italy, "gratioso lumine rationis unita" [brought together by the gracious light of reason], one day also united under a single monarch (1.18.5).[17]

Dante concludes, "Hoc autem vulgare quod illustre, cardinale, aulicum et curiale ostensum est, dicimus esse illud quod vulgare latium appellatur" (1.19.1) [So now we can say that this vernacular, which has been shown to be illustrious, cardinal, aulic, and curial, is the vernacular that is called Italian]. Indeed, as every city (for instance, Cremona), every region (say, Lombardy), and each side of Italy (left and right) have their own vernacular, "sic istud quod totius Ytalie est, latium vulgare vocatur. Hoc enim usi sunt doctores illustres qui lingua vulgari poetati sunt in Ytalia, ut Siculi, Apuli, Tusci, Romandioli, Lombardi et utriusque Marchie viri" (1.19.2) [so this last, which belongs to all Italy, is called the Italian vernacular. This is the language used by the illustrious authors who have written vernacular poetry in Italy, whether they came from Sicily, Apulia, Tuscany, Romagna, Lombardy, or either of the Marches]. This progressive rising up from the particular to the universal has a strong aprioristic character, and the same may be said of the metaphysical Aristotelian argument regarding the local vernaculars' *reductio ad unum*. Nevertheless, Dante likely recognized some sort of empirical substance in these, as well as in the distinction between the "vulgare semilatium" (1.19.1) [half-Italian] of the right and left sides. There are two possible explanations for this: first, the part of the Apennine ridge of which Dante had personal experience was that of Tuscany, Emilia, and Romagna, which in reality does separate the northern vernaculars from those of the center and south; second, Dante may well have connected these two halves of Italy to the "Tyrrhenian and Adriatic corridors" through which had passed "i principali flussi di poesia lirica volgare che dal Sud giungevano in Toscana e nell'Italia settentrionale" [the principal currents of vernacular lyric poetry that from the south had reached Tuscany and northern Italy].[18]

The Poets and the Language of *Sì*

The succession of vernacular poets who in different regions elevated their language to that of the illustrious vernacular sketches a general political design.[19] At its origin is found the Sicilian School, an imperial creation that establishes the Italian illustrious tradition. Dante does not cite by name the Sicilian and Apulian "perplures doctores" (1.12.2) [many masters of eloquence], likely because he viewed them not as individuals but as a group, whom Fredrick II and his son Manfred had meritoriously gathered together at their curia. The second group to stand out is that of the Florentine poets Guido Cavalcanti, Lapo Gianni, and Dante himself, along with Cino da Pistoia—in other words, those poets that have come to be known as stilnovists, and who, by distinguishing themselves from the municipal Tuscan poets, "vulgaris excellentiam cognovisse" (1.13.4) [have known the excellence of the vernacular]. The third and final group is that of the Bolognese: the "maximus," namely the "great" Guido Guinizzelli, Onesto, Guido Ghisilieri, and Fabruzzo dei Lambertazzi (1.15.6). Tommaso da Faenza and Ugolino Buzzola Manfredi, two little-known poets from Faenza, are no more than a coda to the Bolognese group

(1.14.3). It is almost certain that Dante did not include the pair among this rarefied elite for their poetic merits, which are nonexistent, but out of respect for the Ghibelline *signorie* of Romagna who were allied to Bologna against the despised Marquis Azzo VIII of Este. Moreover, as we have already seen, the Bolognese draw their vernacular "utrinque" (1.15.5) [from both sides], from both Romagna and Lombardy. However, the complementary defects of these languages—the former as too effeminate, the latter as too harsh—do not appear to be of equal weight given that little Faenza has been able to produce two poets, while "Ferrariensium, Mutinensium, vel Regianorum—which is the same as saying the Marquisate of Este—nullum invenimus poetasse" (1.15.4) [we find that no one from Ferrara, Modena, or Reggio has written poetry], since their *garrulitas*, namely, their stridency, of Longobard origin absolutely prevents poetic composition.

The role of Cino is essential to the poetic equilibrium of the *De vulgari eloquentia*, for he and Dante represent those Florentine and Pistoiese poets who wrote in the best vernacular. And Cino, rather more than Dante, is the ideal *trait d'union* between this group and the Bolognese poetic community. In fact, as a jurist, Cino was a regular at the Bolognese *studium*, and it is well known that vernacular poetic activity in the city was implicated with legal and notarial circles. It is enough to think of Guido Guinizzelli, both a judge and a poet. This is why Dante continuously places Cino before himself by means of the repeated formula "Cynus Pistoriensis et amicus eius" (1.10.2) [Cino da Pistoia and his friend]. I believe that Dante did this so that Cino's name might strengthen his own ties to the university and poetic environments of Bologna.[20]

The leading poets in Italy—Cino, poet of *venus*, and Dante, poet of *virtus*, love and virtue respectively (see the next subsection)—were both exiles: Cino was exiled from Pistoia for being a Black Guelf, and Dante was exiled from Florence for being a White Guelf. The symbolic value of this fact is significant for two reasons. First, it denotes that injustice dominates in Italy (see 1.12.5). Second, it demonstrates that the victims of this rampant injustice fall on both sides of the political divide. Throughout the treatise Dante is careful to avoid associating the concept of empire to which he was so drawn with either of the two warring factions. Rather, the idea that Dante wants to communicate is that "Cynus Pistoriensis et amicus eius" are victims, from opposing sides, of an all-enveloping injustice.

In any case, while waiting for a future Italian curia to reunite Cino and Dante and to honor them, just as the *Magna Curia* of Fredrick II had reunited the "excellentes Latinorum" (1.12.4) [most gifted individuals in Italy], the White Guelf city of Bologna of the years 1304–5 is the place where the pairing of Dante and Cino makes more sense than anywhere else in Italy.

The Subjects and "Style" Befitting the Illustrious Vernacular, and the Nature of Poetry

In book 2, Dante addresses the literary uses of the illustrious vernacular. He first declares that "latium vulgare illustre tam prosayce quam metrice decere proferri" (2.1.1) [the illustrious Italian vernacular may as fittingly be used for writing prose as for writing poetry]. This is exactly what he does in the contemporaneous *Convivio*, where he comments in prose on a selection of his own canzoni. Then, concentrating first on poetry, "quia quod inventum est prosaycantibus permanere videtur exemplar, et non e converso" (2.1.1) [because what is set out in poetry serves as a model for those who write prose, and not the other way about], he mandates that "non omnes versificantes sed tantum excellentissimos illustre uti vulgare debere" (2.2.1) [not all poets, but only the very best of them, should use the illustrious vernacular] and that "sola optima digna sint ipso tractari" (2.2.5) [only the best subjects are worthy to be discussed in it].

To establish these subjects, Dante daringly builds on the Aristotelian concept of the tripartite human soul: the vegetative, the animal, and the rational. "Nam secundum quod vegetabile quid est, utile querit, in quo cum plantis comunicat; secundum quod animale, delectabile, in quo cum brutis; secundum quod rationale, honestum querit, in quo solus est, vel angelice sociatur nature" (2.2.6) [For insofar as they are vegetable beings, they seek the useful, and they have this in common with plants; insofar as they are animal, they seek pleasure, and this they share with beasts; and insofar as they are rational, they seek the good, and in this they stand alone, or may be related to the nature of angels]. And only the loftiest things in each of these categories, "salus videlicet, venus et virtus, apparent esse illa magnalia que sint maxime pertractanda, hoc est ea que maxime sunt ad ista, ut armorum probitas, amoris accensio, et directio voluntatis"

(2.2.7) [safety, love, and virtue, appear to be those most important subjects that are to be treated in the loftiest style; or at least this is true of the themes most closely associated with them, prowess in arms, ardor in love, and control of one's own will]. These are the three "magnalia" worthy of being sung in the illustrious vernacular. In the Occitan tradition, an exemplary poet had composed on each topic: Bertran de Born on arms, Arnaut Daniel on love, and Guiraut de Bornelh on the proper exercise of the will. In the Italian tradition, however, no one had written of arms, and so there are only two exemplary poets: Cino da Pistoia for love and "his friend," as Dante with showy modesty puts it, for rectitude (2.2.8).

Such a philosophical basis and classification of poetic genres is quite new, and it represents a crucial step for bringing vernacular poetry into the realm of philosophical discourse. By privileging *virtus*, Dante closes the circle that he opened at the start of the treatise when he linked the *De vulgari* to Aristotle's *Politics* with Aquinas's commentary. It is poets—all poets—but markedly those who compose on *virtus*, and hence Dante Alighieri, as exemplified by the doctrinal canzoni that are cited in the treatise, almost a preview of the operation undertaken in the *Convivio*, who shape the vernacular in order to communicate "in utili et nocivo, iusto et iniusto, et aliis huiusmodi" (Thomas Aquinas, *Sententia libri Politicorum* 1.1.28–29) [what is useful and damaging, just and unjust, and similar matters], thereby rendering language capable of fulfilling the goal for which Nature granted it to humanity, namely, the creation of societies.

Among the various metrical forms, which include sonnets, ballads, and canzoni, only the canzone is excellent, and thereby is the only form worthy of being associated with the lofty themes and the illustrious vernacular (2.3.3). Dante thus focuses on the form of the canzone (2.4); and it is as part of this discussion that he famously affirms that those who write verses in the vernacular "prorsus poete sunt, si poesim recte consideremus, que nichil aliud est quam fictio rethorica musicaque poita" (2.4.2) [are most certainly poets, if we understand poetry aright: that is, as nothing other than a verbal invention composed according to the rules of rhetoric and music]. It is a crucial statement because it extends the title of *poeta*, previously reserved for poets using a grammatical language, to those writing poetry in the vernacular. The affirmation is fundamental also because it defines the "essence" of poetry in purely technical terms: as an artificial creation achieved (*poìta*, past participle of the Greek verb *poièin*, which corresponds to the Latin *ficta*, from *fingere*, to fashion) through rhetoric, the art of speech, and music, which here indicates meter, the prosodic-rhythmic structure of verses and strophes.

In the *Commedia*, instead, Dante reserves the term *poeta* only for the greatest "tragic" Latin poets, and among the moderns only for himself, and only as regards his sacred poem. This is a mark of the profound change that has occurred in his poetics, from secular and "workman-like" in the *De vulgari eloquentia* to sapiential and prophetic in the *Commedia*. In any case, it is because of this momentous extension of the semantic sphere of the word *poeta*, and thanks to the fact that the *Commedia*'s author would immediately be called *poeta* by all, beginning with the poem's first commenters writing both in Latin and in the vernacular, that today Shakespeare, Góngora, Rilke, Baudelaire, and Pessoa are for us poets.[21]

Dante then distinguishes between three "styles"—the tragic, comic, and elegiac (2.4.5)—where the elegiac is defined according to its content as the "stilum . . . miserorum" [style . . . of the unhappy], while the other two are defined in formal terms as the "high" and "low" style, respectively. As may be expected, the illustrious vernacular is appropriate only for the lofty "tragic style," and vice versa (2.4.6).[22] As regards verse forms, Dante grants primacy to the hendecasyllable, which "videtur esse superbius, tam temporis occupatione, quam capacitate sententie, constructionis, et vocabulorum" (2.5.3) [is clearly the most splendid, both for its duration in time and for its capacity to contain meanings, constructions, and words], which is then followed by the septenary, the quinary, and finally trisyllables (2.5.6), thereby totally rejecting parisyllables (2.5.7).

The Troubadours

Among the troubadours to whom Dante refers, the trio representing the three *magnalia* stand out: Bertran de Born and *salus*, Arnaut Daniel and *venus*, and Guiraut de Bornelh and *virtus* (2.2.8).

Of the three, the one furthest from Dante is undoubtedly Bertran de Born, since martial themes are relatively marginal in Dante's poetic output. In fact, in the *Convivio*, Bertran de Born is cited as an example of liberality (4.11.4) and not of arms-themed poetry. Indeed, in the *De vulgari*, Dante quotes his "sirventese-canzone," "Non puosc mudar" [I cannot refrain], an atypical poem for Bertran, which deals with liberality instead of war. Conversely, the bloody Bertran, besides being decapitated as a sower of discord in *Inferno* 28, also provides one of the subtexts for the representation of the ninth *bolgia* as an infernal parody of a battlefield.

Dante's relationship to Arnaut Daniel and to Guiraut de Bornelh is quite different in the transition from the *De vulgari* to the *Commedia*. In the *Convivio–De vulgari* phase, while Dante presents himself as a poet of *virtus*, it is Guiraut, his Occitan counterpart, who enjoys primacy. Indeed, Dante's doctrinal canzoni belonging to this phase—"Tre donne" [Three women], "Doglia mi reca" [Grief brings], "Poscia ch'amor" [Since love], and "Le dolci rime" [The sweet rhymes]—all echo with elements originating in Guiraut. Although briefly upstaged, Arnaut in reality exerted a more powerful and consistent allure for Dante, beginning with his youthful compositions, "Lo doloroso amor" [Painful love] and "Com' più vi fere Amor" [The more Love wounds you], and then, pivotally, in the *rime petrose*, the "stony rhymes," which would prove essential to the development of the "aspro e choccio" (*Inf.* 32.1) [harsh and rasping] language of the *Commedia*. If, in the *De vulgari*, the "high style" needs to draw on words that are both "combed" [pexa] and "shaggy" [yrsuta] (2.7), thereby rejecting the rhetorical convention that excluded the latter, this was because Dante had absorbed Arnaut's lesson. A major and technically extreme experiment among the *petrose* is the *sestina* "Al poco giorno" (2.10.2 and 13.2) [To the short day], which Dante wrote as an attempt to emulate Arnaut. He did this by adopting the stanza that he deemed most characteristic of Arnaut, the "stantia sine rithimo" (2.13.2) [unrhymed stanza], corresponding to an "oda continua" (2.10.2) [uninterrupted melody], and he follows this with the "double *sestina*" "Amor tu vedi ben" [Love you see well]. These experiments are highly valued in the *De vulgari*. Consequently, the claim that Dante was intent on distancing himself from the *sestine* in 2.13.13 is incorrect. In truth, he compares them to "novum aliquid atque intentatum artis" [something new and previously unattempted in the art], an attempt that should earn him a poetic investiture similar to that of a knight.

In the *Commedia*, the hierarchy of values is inverted, and Guinizzelli declares Arnaut to be the "miglior fabbro del volgar materno" [the better smith of the maternal language], while adding: "e lascia dir li stolti / che quel di Lemosì [Guiraut] credon ch'avanzi" (*Purg.* 26.117–20) [and let the ignorant speak / who believe that the Lemosin surpasses him]. This new hierarchy culminates in the elevation of the bishop Folquet de Marseille, previously a love poet, to the heaven of Venus in *Paradiso* 9.

The overall effect of the reassessment of troubadour poets in the *Commedia* is to redimension moral poetry, which in the "secular" *De vulgari* constitutes the highest of the *magnalia*, and to reevaluate love poetry, both Arnaut's and Folquet's, which provides poetic illumination that can be sublimated in theological terms.[23]

THE ART OF THE *CANZONE*

Which construction is the best, *supprema constructio* (2.6.6)?[24] Answering this question was particularly challenging for Dante, for in his day no theory of sentence syntax had been developed. Thus the notions of main, coordinate, or subordinate clause did not exist. Nevertheless, Dante had his own intuitive idea about what the excellent construction in vernacular poetry ought to be; and, in order to explain his idea, following the *artes dictandi*, the manuals that provided instruction on how to write in Latin prose, he composed a series of Latin phrases of ever-loftier register (2.6.4). He then advised his readers to become familiar with the great classical poets and prose writers (2.6.7), before proposing numerous poetic examples taken from both the Occitan and Italian traditions (2.6.6). As ever, Guittone d'Arezzo serves as the negative counterexample (2.6.8). The careful balancing of the sentence has been identified as the key criterion for assessing the syntactic and rhetorical quality most appropriate for the illustrious vernacular.[25]

The three Latin phrases Dante utilizes to exemplify ever more elevated syntactic and rhetorical registers, from "sapidus" [flavored] to "venustus" [graceful] and "excelsus" [excellent] (2.6.4), are sarcastic phrases used against Charles of Valois and the Marquis Azzo VIII of Este, mortal enemies of both Dante and Bologna.[26] These phrases are also imbued with poignant empathy for the Florentine exiles, including Dante himself, all of whom were the victims of Charles of Valois. The political content of these phrases strongly suggests that Dante was in Bologna while he wrote them and that he embedded them in the text as a precise message to his Bolognese audience.

"Grandiosa modo vocabula sub prelato stilo digna consistere" [the great words worthy to contribute to the style defined above] are the subject of chapter 7. By discarding terms that are "infantile" (*puerilia*, such as *mamma, babbo, mate, pate*), "womanish" (*muliebria*, such as *dolciada, placevole*), "rustic" (*silvestria*, such as *greggia, creta*), "urbane and glossy" (*urbana lubrica*, such as *femina*), and "urbane and unkempt" (*urbana reburra*, such as *corpo*), "sola . . . pexa irsutaque urbana tibi restare videbis, que nobilissima sunt et membra vulgaris illustris" (2.7.4) [you will see that all you have left are urbane words that are combed or shaggy; these are the most noble, and belong to the illustrious vernacular]. Dante gives definitions of "combed" and "shaggy" words, but these cannot be translated into objective phonetic and prosodic features. The metaphor he employs describes the "combed" words that "slide" through the comb, namely when they are pronounced, and the "shaggy" words that offer resistance (but not excessively so, as is the case with "unkempt" words). Thus "combed" and "shaggy" words need to be harmonized in poetry (2.7.7).

"Preparatis fustibus torquibusque ad fascem, nunc fasciandi tempus incumbit" (2.8.1) [Now that we have gathered the sticks and cords for our bundle, the time has come to put the bundle together]. The image stresses that a canzone must be composed with all the elements described up to this point. *Canzone* refers, not to a melody, which can either accompany a poem or not, but rather to "fabricatio verborum armonizatorum" [a composition made up of words arranged with due regard to harmony], which is called *canzone* even though "talia verba in cartulis absque prolatore iacent" (2.8.5) [such words are written down on the page, in the absence of any performer]. Dante thus decisively locates himself after the "separation" that occurred between poetry and music. For him, poetry is a notion full of philosophical dignity, and its potential melodic "covering" is only an accidental quality of the text's performance, even though on the shores of Purgatory his musician friend Casella intones "Amor che ne la mente mi ragiona" [Love that speaks in my mind] "sì dolcemente, / che la dolcezza ancor dentro mi suona" (*Purg.* 2.113–14) [so sweetly, that the sweetness still resounds inside me]. Poetry, in its essence, "nichil aliud est quam fictio rethorica musicaque poita" (2.4.2) [is nothing other than a verbal invention composed according to the rules of rhetoric and music]. However, this "music" that is intrinsic to poetry is nothing more than its metrical structure, both rhythmic and prosodic, which makes it poetry and not prose, insofar as it can be set to music.[27]

Broadly speaking, all poetic compositions are "canzoni"; however, the canzone par excellence "est equalium stantiarum sine responsorio ad unam sententiam tragica coniugatio" (2.8.8) [is a connected series of equal stanzas in the tragic style, without a refrain, and focused on a single theme], and Dante cites as the representative example his own "Donne che avete intelletto d'amore" [Women who have an understanding of love], the famous canzone of the *Vita nova* that inaugurates the "praise style."[28]

The treatise then focuses on the canzone's stanza (*stantia*), which is so called because it is "mansio capax, sive receptaculum totius artis" (2.9.2) [a capacious storehouse or receptacle for the art in its entirety], given that a canzone is made up of a series of stanzas of equal length. The general definition of a stanza is "sub certo cantu et habitudine limitata carminum et sillabarum compagem" (2.9.6) [a coherent arrangement of lines and syllables governed by a particular melody and a clearly defined organization]. The stanza is undivided when it is accompanied by "una oda continua usque ad ultimum progressive, hoc est sine iteratione modulationis cuiusquam et sine diesi; et diesim dicimus deductionem vergentem de una oda in aliam" (2.10.2) [an uninterrupted melody, in an ordered progression from beginning to end—that is, without any repetition of musical phrases or any diesis (and by *diesis* I mean a movement from one melody to another)]. Conversely, the stanza is divided when the part of the stanza that precedes the diesis, or the part that follows it, or both, harbor a repetition of the melody. If the part that precedes the diesis is undivided, it is called "forehead" [frons]; if it is divided, it is separated into "feet" [pedes]. If instead the part after the diesis is undivided, it is called a "tail" [sirma]; if it is divided, it is separated into "turns" [versus]. As regards their arrangement, chapter 11 then explores the different possible combinations of these parts of a stanza, based on the number of verses and syllables that may appear in each.

Chapter 12 establishes the three types of verse—the hendecasyllable, the septenary, and the quinary—which should primarily be used in the stanza of a canzone. Of the three, as already affirmed in chapter 5, "Endecasillabum propter quandam excellentiam in contextu vincendi privilegium promeretur" [The hendecasyllable earns the highest ranking when we try to write poems in the tragic style], such that "quedam stantia est que solis endecasillabis gaudet esse contexta" (2.12.3) [there is a kind of stanza that seems to rejoice in being composed entirely of hendecasyllables]. To illustrate this last point, Dante cites the two most ideologically committed, albeit in contrasting terms, canzoni, namely, Guido Cavalcanti's "Donna me prega"—a manifesto of neo-Averroistic and materialistic love—and his own "Donne ch'avete intelletto d'amore," which records the key stage in the *Vita nova*'s account of spiritually ennobling love.

Chapter 13 deals with rhyme. Dante cautions against three potential flaws: excessive repetition of the same rhyme, useless equivocation, and harsh rhymes (2.13.13). By outlining these defects, Dante may seem to be distancing himself from his *rime petrose*, which were characterized by systematic harshness, as the incipit of the canzone "Così nel mio parlar voglio esser aspro" [I want to be as harsh in my speech] affirms. In addition, the *rime petrose* were also marked by the obsessive repetition of the same rhyme words and the sustained play upon their equivocal meanings, as in the sestina "Al poco giorno e al gran cerchio d'ombra" [To the short day and the great circle of shadow], a virtuoso imitation of Arnaut Daniel, and in the "double sestina" "Amor, tu vedi ben che questa donna" [Love, you see well that this lady]. Yet Dante is not actually moving away from his earlier poetry, given that the harshness of the rhymes can be redeemed if it is "lenitati permixta" [mixed with gentle-sounding rhymes]. Even more significantly, a single rhyme's excessive repetition in a poem should be condemned, unless this excess "novum aliquid atque intentatum artis hoc sibi preroget; ut nascentis militie dies, qui cum nulla prerogativa suam indignatur preterire dietam. Hoc etenim nos facere nisi sumus ibi, *Amor, tu vedi ben che questa donna*" (2.13.13) [claims for itself something new and previously unattempted in the art; then the poet is like a knight on the day of his dubbing, who scorns to let it pass without some special exploit. This is what I tried to do here: "Love, you see well that this lady"]. Thus Dante in fact vindicates the extreme technical difficulty of "Amor, tu vedi ben" and thereby implicitly also that of "Al poco giorno." Indeed, the poems confirm that he deserves to be elevated to the rank of poet, an advancement similar to the investiture of a knight that might be deemed the glorious inauguration of his poetic "militancy."

At this juncture, the treatise is left unfinished.

THE MEANING OF THE *DE VULGARI ELOQUENTIA* AND ITS RELATIONSHIP TO THE *CONVIVIO*

In the second half of the twentieth century, the prevailing idea was that, in the *De vulgari eloquentia*, Dante had wanted to give an interpretation of his own poetry. Given that a key feature of Dante's career was the "perpetuo sopraggiungere della riflessione tecnica accanto alla poesia, quest'associazione di concreto poetare e d'intelligenza stilistica" [constant arrival of technical reflection next to poetry, this association of concrete poetic practice with stylistic intelligence], in other words "il gusto radicato per l'autoesegesi a distanza" [the deeply rooted taste for reflective self-exegesis], the *De vulgari* was seen as the main theoretical moment of the poet's literary self-reflection. In particular, the *De vulgari* was thought to be focused on the "tecnicità della riflessione linguistica e retorica" [technical qualities of linguistic and rhetorical reflection], with the specific aim of theorizing "una ben precisa 'fase,' e si può dire la più recente, dell'attività del lirico, cioè la poesia delle grandi canzoni morali e dottrinarie" [a precise "phase," the most recent one, of Dante's activities as a lyric poet, namely, the poetry of the great moral and doctrinal canzoni].[29] This is Pier Vincenzo Mengaldo's central idea in his fundamental critical edition (1968) and in his annotated edition (1979) of the treatise. In its turn, this position chimed well with the "idea of Dante" that Gianfranco Contini had developed during the preceding thirty years, to use the title of his seminal collection of essays on the poet composed between 1935 and 1968.[30] According to this standpoint, the primary driving force behind each of Dante's cultural projects was poetry: more specifically, the experimental progression of his poetry's various stylistic phases, each of which was accompanied by concurrent or subsequent metapoetic explanations.

As regards the *De vulgari*, this idea is valid but limited, given that book 1's content is irrelevant to Dante's poetics, since it addresses other interests and cultural experiences. Consequently, its aims go well beyond poetry and reveal Dante's interests in addressing a wider and more stratified audience. His objectives, I believe, have more to do with establishing his authorial identity as a "lay philosopher"—an operation in which Dante was engaged when he composed the *Convivio*, which is not a philosophical accessory to the *De vulgari*'s poetics. On the contrary, the *Convivio* constitutes the poet's fundamental and monumental endeavor to disseminate an ethical philosophy at the service of a profound political reform, thanks to which the exiled Dante intended to ascribe to himself a new role as an intellectual. In this regard, his commentary on the canzoni does not have the goal of explaining or valorizing them in the eyes of connoisseurs of poetry. Rather, the canzoni themselves, which have already granted their author the reputation as a doctrinal poet, along with the prose commentary, are meant to validate him especially in the eyes of the governing nobles of the Po Valley, where Dante lived at the time. It is to this particular group that Dante wishes to "spiegare in cosa consista la vera nobiltà" [explain in what true nobility consists].[31] Thus the *De vulgari* was originally intended as an appendix of the *Convivio*, not the other way around. Its function was theoretically to strengthen the justification of writing the commentary to the canzoni in the vernacular—a justification that occupies almost the entirety of the *Convivio*'s first book.

We have already noted the underlying political concerns of the treatise at several points in this chapter. The subsection "A Political Idea of Language" emphasizes the fact that only mankind received the gift of language from Nature for the purpose of realizing its purpose as a political species. Dante's teachings in vernacular eloquence are thus meant to play a civic role that runs parallel to, and is just as important on a formal level, as the role played by the *Convivio*'s instruction in ethics and philosophy. The subsection "The Panther and the Illustrious Vernacular" examines the political implications of the key principle of the *reductio ad unum* of all things belonging to the same genus, a principle that Dante derived from the contemporary controversy on whether or not the emperor's authority should be subjected to that of the pope. Finally, the subsection "The Poets and the Language of *Sì*" highlights the imperial foundation of the illustrious Italian literary tradition. On the basis of this lofty precedent, Dante imagines himself and his friend Cino seated in the curia of a future emperor, just as the first *doctores eloquentes*—Guido delle Colonne and Giacomo da Lentini—were seated in the *Magna Curia* of Fredrick II.

The *De vulgari eloquentia* in Dante's Biography

Along with the suggestion that the *De vulgari* has a vital political inspiration, it has been proposed that the treatise was written in Bologna and that this had a profound effect on its conception and subject matter. In fact, in terms of the renewed critical interest in Dante's biography, the *De vulgari eloquentia* stands as a privileged case study, since it provides powerful evidence in favor of the concrete importance of biographical details if we are properly to understand important aspects of Dante's works.[32]

I have already put forward various elements indicating that the *De vulgari* was written with Bologna in mind. Thus, in the subsection "Which Is the Best Vernacular in Italy," I highlight the distinction between the "Lombard" and "Romagnol" vernaculars, which has no actual basis in linguistic geography, but which seems aimed at placing Bologna at the center between these two "macro-areas," thereby awarding its vernacular aesthetic primacy on account of its "middleness." In the subsection "The Poets and the Language of *Sì*," I discuss the exaltation of Bolognese vernacular poets and their humble Romagnol affiliates, as well as the scornful declaration that there are no poets from Ferrara, Modena, or Reggio Emilia—a judgment that is not based on poetic criteria but traces the borders of the political alliance centered on Bologna against the Estense, Angevin, and Florentine regimes. In the same subsection, I clarify that the poetic celebration of Cino da Pistoia is quite disproportionate to his effective poetic value and to the esteem that Dante actually had for him. In fact, his assessment in the treatise can be accounted in light of the prestige that Cino enjoyed in Bologna as a jurist and vernacular poet. Furthermore, in the subsection "The Art of the Canzone," I demonstrate that the sarcastic political dimension of the examples of syntactic "supprema constructio" (2.6.4) can best be explained as the address of an exiled Florentine White Guelf to his host city of Bologna. Finally, a reason why Dante suddenly interrupted and abandoned his treatise with its deep links to Bologna may be connected to the fall of the city's White Guelf regime in January-February 1306 and its substitution by a regime that was extremely hostile to the poet.

Two explanations—one "external," the other "internal"—have recently been proposed with regard to the contradiction between the greater nobility afforded Latin in the *Convivio* and the greater nobility afforded the vernacular in the *De vulgari eloquentia*, as highlighted in the subsection "The Vernacular and Latin."

The "external" explanation is based on Dante's differing attitudes toward the audiences of the two treatises. In the *Convivio*, Dante presents himself as a "lay philosopher" who disseminates philosophical knowledge to noblemen who do not know Latin (*Conv.* 1.9.4–5), probably those belonging to the Veronese entourage of Bartolomeo della Scala. In this regard, it is logical that he should reaffirm Latin's traditional superiority over the vernacular. Indeed, such a move is coherent with his intent to gather the precious food that has fallen from the "beata mensa" (*Conv.* 1.1.10) [blessed table] of professional philosophers and to give it to those without Latin who are excluded from the feast.[33] In the *De vulgari eloquentia*, however, Dante addresses the professors of philosophy and theology and masters of *artes dictandi* at the Bolognese *studium*, as well as the city's notaries and judges, who knew Latin and passionately cultivated vernacular poetry. Again, it is logical that Dante, in addressing this highly specialized audience, would go so far as to assert, audaciously yet coherently, that the vernacular is actually nobler than Latin.[34] Dante's claim, in its turn, is coherent with the equally audacious affirmation that vernacular poets deserve the title of "poet," which until then was reserved exclusively for Greek and Latin poets (2.4.2).

The "internal" explanation emphasizes that the vernacular described in the *Convivio* is a single entity and less noble than Latin "perché lo latino è perpetuo e non corruttibile, e lo volgare è non stabile e corruttibile" (1.5.7) [because Latin has a permanent form and is not subject to change, whereas the vernacular is unstable and is subject to change]. The vernacular described in the *De vulgari eloquentia*, however, is divided in two: on one hand, there are the local vernaculars, lacking in value, and on the other hand, there is the Italian vernacular (*latium*), simultaneously illustrious, cardinal, aulic, and curial. This illustrious vernacular is a totally new entity and is the "noblest" among the vernaculars (1.16.4; 2.3, 6.1, and 7). Indeed, it can be defined as nobler than Latin because it is much less unstable and corruptible than the local vernaculars and, unlike Latin, is natural.[35]

There is thus no contradiction between the two explanations. They are both valid. Dante would not have been the extraordinary intellectual that he was if he had been unable to transform the stimuli and opportunities offered by the various environments in which he found himself into differing, yet original and coherent ideas and proposals. I firmly believe that being able to discover the stimuli and opportunities to which Dante responded in his writings cannot but increase our understanding of the facts, and consequently our admiration for a way of thinking that was able to fuse so effectively contingent planning with permanent theorizing.

NOTES

Translated from the Italian by Davis Richardson.

1. All translations from the *Convivio* are taken from Dante, *Banquet*, Ryan trans.

2. All quotations from the *De vulgari eloquentia* are taken from Tavoni ed. Here and elsewhere I base my translation on Botterill's translation, although in several instances I adapt it to reflect better the original Latin.

3. See Mengaldo, "Introduzione," l–lxiv; Vinay, "Ricerche," 236–58; Viscardi, "Favella di Cacciaguida."

4. Tavoni, "Volgare e latino" and "Che cosa erano il volgare e il latino," 13–21. Translations from the *Commedia* are my own.

5. Irène Rosier-Catach has the merit of having developed a political reading of the *De vulgari eloquentia*; see "'Solo all'uomo'" and "Man." See also Zanni, "*De vulgari eloquentia*," 299–322.

6. Gambale, *Lingua di fuoco*, underlines right from Adam's *primiloquium* the linguistic urgency, the expressive impulse, that underpins both Dante's reflections on language and his poetry.

7. Barański, "Dante's Biblical Linguistics," 112–14.

8. The interpretation of "cert*a* form*a* locutionis" as "il principio generale strutturante della lingua" [language's general structuring principle], which was put forward by Corti, *Dante*, 47, alongside the proposal that Dante had been influenced by the modistic grammarians, has been widely rejected (see most recently Rosier-Catach, "Dante et le langage"), although it has in part been reproposed by Tesi, *Lingua della grazia*, 35–39.

9. Tavoni, "Dante e la scoperta," 2–5.

10. The first quotation is from Contini, *Idea di Dante*, 42; the second is from Mengaldo, *Linguistica e retorica*, 246. Barolini, "Difference as Punishment," underlines in Adam's palinode Dante's full acceptance of linguistic variety without any taint of sin. See also Corrado, *Dante e la questione*, 65–82. According to Tesi, *Lingua della grazia*, 40–67, there is no palinode in *Paradiso* because Hebrew was not the "language of grace."

11. The expression *ydioma tripharium* (1.8.2) simply signifies "three languages" (a triple murder means three murders). Nonetheless Marigo translated the phrase as "un idioma triforme" [three-formed language], namely, "un *ydioma* già differenziato in tre maniere diverse (*tripharium*) senza perdere tuttavia l'impronta dell'unità originaria" (Marigo ed., 46–47) [an *ydioma* already differentiated in three different ways (*tripharium*) but without losing the imprint of a single origin]. The error has been corrected for some time (Tavoni, "*Ydioma Tripharium*"), but it continues to return: Benucci, "De la tour," 50–52; Sasso, *Lingua, la Bibbia*, 29, 106, 130.

12. Translations from the *Vita nova* are my own.

13. The issues discussed in this subsection are developed more fully in Tavoni, "Volgare e latino."

14. On the possible numerological implications of this doubling of the number seven, see Tavoni "Perché i volgari italiani." On the geography of the regional languages of Italy, see Iwakura, *Pensiero linguistico*, 71–81, and F. Bruni, "Geografia di Dante," which includes geographical maps. On the "rewriting" of this regionalized linguistic map in *Inferno*, see Cachey, "Cartographic Dante."

15. See the discussion in Nasti, chapter 7 of this book, the section "Structure and Argument."

16. Imbach and Rosier-Catach, "De l'un au multiple"; Rosier-Catach, *Présentation*, 50–58. See also Zanni, "*De vulgari eloquentia*," 333–40.

17. On *curialitas* as the mark identifying a new "imperial" intellectual elite, see Zanni, "Tra *curialitas* e *cortesia*." I prefer to define Dante's position as "imperial" (Tavoni, "Idea imperiale") rather than "Ghibelline" (Fenzi, "Introduzione," xxiii, xxxiii, and xxxv; Pinto, "Introducción," 54 and 73) because, in exile, Dante always wanted to exhibit a superior bipartisan attitude toward both the Guelfs and the Ghibellines. One may wonder whether, in the future "excellentissima Ytalorum curia" [most excellent curia in Italy], Dante saw the curia of a kingdom of Italy, equivalent to the "curia regis Alamannie" (1.18.5) [the curia of the king of Germany], as Pinto, "Introducción," 76–78, maintains, or the imperial curia with its seat in Italy, as the precedent of Frederick II's *Magna Curia* would suggest.

18. Tesi, *Lingua della grazia*, 219.

19. On the poets of the *De vulgari eloquentia*, see Iwakura, *Pensiero linguistico*, 41–70, and Montuori, "Rime." Dante's knowledge of these poets comes from a manuscript similar to the two Florentine lyric collections, ms. Vaticano Latino 3793, belonging to a mercantile environment, and ms. Palatino 418 of the Biblioteca Nazionale of Florence, which comes from a courtly environment; see Steinberg, *Accounting for Dante*, 95–144; Manzi, "Dante."

20. That the prominence given to Cino bears little relationship to his poetic merits and to Dante's actual regard for him has been rightly noted by Fenzi, "Introduzione," xlii–xliii and liv–lvi; see also Tavoni, "Esilio dantesco," 25–29. On Dante's relationship to Cino as a jurist, see Nasti, chapter 7 of this book, the section "History, Virgil, Augustine, and the Law."

21. See Tavoni, "Che cosa è la poesia?"

22. On the three "styles" in Dante and in medieval culture, see Barański, "'Tres enim sunt manerie dicendi.'"

23. On the troubadours of *De vulgari eloquentia*, see Formisano, "Rime," who is uncertain as to when and from which manuscripts Dante may have learned about the troubadours and the *trouvières* (267–69).

24. "Est enim sciendum quod constructionem vocamus regulatam compaginem dictionum" (2.6.2) [You need to know that we call "construction" a group of words put together in regulated order].

25. Tavoni and Chersoni, "Ipotesi d'interpretazione."

26. "Piget me, cunctis pietate maiorem, quicunque in exilio tabescentes patriam tantum sompniando revisunt" [I am stricken with sorrow more than most, for whoever drags out his life in exile, revisiting his native land only in dreams]; "Laudabilis discretio marchionis Estensis, et sua magnificentia preparata, cunctis illum facit esse dilectum" [The laudable discretion of the Marquis of Este, and his widely displayed generosity, make him beloved of all]; "Eiecta maxima parte florum de sinu tuo, Florentia, nequicquam Trinacriam Totila

secundus [Charles of Valois] adivit" [The greater part of your flowers, o Florence, having been snatched from your breast, the second Totila advanced in vain toward Trinacria]. In this last phrase there is a concentration of political allusions; see Tavoni ed.

27. See Roncaglia, "Sul 'divorzio tra musica e poesia'"; Lannutti, "'Ars' e 'scientia'"; Lannutti and Locanto, *Tracce*; Persico, *Parole e la musica*; Camboni, *Fine musica*. On the abandonment of music as a sign of the process of philosophical intellectualization of the poetic text, see Pinto, "Introducción," 86–88.

28. See Gragnolati, chapter 1 of this book, and Barański, chapter 3 of this book.

29. The first quotation comes from Contini, *Idea di Dante*, 4, and the remainder come from Mengaldo, "Introduzione," viii, xi–xiii.

30. In line with this tradition, Iwakura entitles the first part of his book (*Pensiero linguistico*) "Il *De vulgari eloquentia* come autointerpretazione dell'opera di Dante" [The *De vulgari eloquentia* as self-interpretation of Dante's oeuvre].

31. Fioravanti, "Nobiltà spiegata ai nobili," 162. Various and divergent interpretations of the *Convivio* and its audience have been proposed, as is clear from the chapters in this volume by Simon Gilson and by Luca Carlo Bianchi. The interpretation that I follow here is, in my opinion, the one that best explains the composition of the treatise in parallel to that of the *De vulgari eloquentia*.

32. Tavoni, "Introduzione," 1113–16, *Qualche idea su Dante*, 77–103, "Esilio dantesco," and "Dante e il 'paradigma'"; Brilli, "Forum Dante and Biography."

33. Tavoni, "Pane degli angeli."

34. Steinberg, *Accounting for Dante*, 17–60; Tavoni, "*De vulgari eloquentia*," 92–93.

35. See Rosier-Catach, "Uomo nobile," 174; see also her "Du vulgaire illustre" and Zanni, "Tra *curialitas* e *cortesia*." See also Pinto, "Grammatica in Dante," 20.

CHAPTER 7

Monarchia

PAOLA NASTI

The *Monarchia* is the only one of his theoretical works that Dante completed. Its dates of composition are uncertain. However, internal and external clues confirm that the work was written during the last decade of the poet's life (1311–18),[1] in response both to developments affecting the late medieval conflict between church and state and to the intellectual debate that ensued between supporters of the two opposing institutions. Written in Latin and divided into three books, the text unveils in a systematic way the author's political philosophy and provides arguments for his advocacy of the Holy Roman Empire as the best possible form of government. To this end, Dante examines the ontological nature of monarchy, the rule of one sovereign,[2] seeking its foundations in scripture, in history, and in metaphysical and philosophical arguments. Through logical arguments and evidence from authoritative texts, Dante attempts to demonstrate that the empire is a providential guide (a *directivum*) established by God to lead humanity toward its earthly ends: understanding truth, achieving intellectual fulfillment, and living happily, justly, and in peace. With a good dose of what Quaglioni terms practical "realism," the poet also intended to prove that this form of government, whose origins are to be found in Roman history, was not a utopian aspiration but a living institution fatally wounded by the arrogant interference of popes and kings who hindered its proper functioning and limited its authority.[3] The *Monarchia*'s aim was thus twofold: it sought actively to defend a contemporary but weak political institution in the context of a continuing and blood-stained controversy, and it tried to do so by demonstrating the empire's worth and status not in the public arena but in theoretical and absolute terms. The most immediate effect of this powerful combination of militancy and intellectual inquiry is the presence in the *Monarchia* of a rich panoply of rhetorical, textual, and logical strategies: Dante is at times polemical against his adversaries, most often analytical, and always prophetic and authoritative in his stance. He also employs different existing genres and registers to address different audiences. In this sense, like all his works, the *Monarchia* is an *unicum* as well as a landmark in the history of political writing and thought.

Structure and Argument

Each of the *Monarchia*'s three books aims to resolve a doubt or a problem concerning the need, the history, and the authority of the monarchy, and Dante formalizes his inquiry in three questions:

> Maxime autem de hac tria dubitata queruntur. Primo nanque dubitatur et queritur an ad bene esse mundi necessaria sit; secundo an Romanus populus de iure monarche offitium sibi asciverit; et tertio an auctoritas Monarche dependeat a Deo inmediate vel ab alio Dei ministro seu vicario. (1.2.3)

> [Now there are three main points of inquiry which have given rise to perplexity on this subject: first, is it is necessary to the well-being of the world? second, did the Roman people take on the office of the monarch by right? and third, does the monarch's authority derive directly from God or from someone else (his minister or vicar)?][4]

By arranging his "inquisitio" (1.2.4) [inquiry] around three questions, Dante immediately makes it clear that he will proceed according to scholastic modes of writing and discussing philosophy, science, or theology.

In the first book, through logical and philosophical arguments as well as evidence drawn from authoritative writers, such as Virgil (1.11.11), Galen, and King David (1.14.13), Dante attempts to demonstrate the ontological necessity of a temporal monarchy ("temporalis monarchia"), which he defines as the rule of one sovereign: "Est ergo temporalis monarchia, quam dicunt imperium, unicus principatus et super omnes in tempore vel in hiis et super hiis que tempore mensurantur" (1.2.2) [Temporal monarchy, then, which men call "Empire," is a single sovereign authority set over all others in time, that is to say over all authorities which operate in those things and over those things which are measured by time]. In his innovative and original attempt to give a metaphysical foundation to his political subject matter, Dante sets off to establish in the opening paragraphs of book 1 (1.2.6–8) the principle upon which his reasoning will be based.[5] Since the "materia" [subject matter] of his work is politics, and since everything that is "politicum nostre potestati subiaceat" (1.2.2) [in the political sphere comes under human control], Dante's primary concern is not theoretical understanding but action. Politics belongs to the realm of praxis, but since praxis is directed by the "ultimus finis" (1.2.2) [the final objective] which causes everything, a scientific investigation needs to ascertain "quid sit finis totius humane civilitatis" (1.3.1) [whatever constitutes the purpose of the whole of human society]. After considering that "Deus et natura nil otiosum facit, sed quicquid prodit in esse est ad aliquam operationem" (1.3.3) [God and nature do nothing in vain; on the contrary whatever they bring into being is designed for a purpose], Dante bases his argument on the Aristotelian principle of finality. He thus concludes that the activity or the ultimate goal that God has providentially decreed for the whole of human society is to be able to learn, by means of the possible intellect, the potentiality of an individual human being to have intellective cognition of all things, as defined by Aristotle in book 3 of his *De anima*. However, Dante observes, the perfection of this intellectual potentiality can be achieved only as a common endeavor by humanity in its entirety ("totaliter"; 1.4.1). To actualize its power first to speculate and then to act according to the findings of the intellect, humanity needs to live in peace. Universal peace is therefore set as a condition that is indispensable if human beings are to achieve their earthly perfection (itself a prerequisite for eternal beatitude). It is also a prerequisite if one is to understand the arguments that the author will present:

> Ex hiis ergo que declarata sunt patet per quod melius, ymo per quod optime genus humanum pertingit ad opus proprium. Et per

consequens visum est propinquissimum medium per quod itur in illud ad quod, velut in ultimum finem, omnia nostra opera ordinantur: quod est pax universalis, que pro principio rationum subsequentium supponatur. (1.4.5)

> [From the arguments developed so far, it is clear what is the better, indeed the best, way of enabling mankind to engage in the activity proper to humanity; and consequently we see the most direct means of achieving the goal to which all our human actions are directed as to their final end. That means is universal peace, which is to be taken as the first principle for the arguments which follow.]

The remaining chapters of book 1 develop eleven arguments through syllogistic reasoning to demonstrate that, in this view of the proper purpose of earthly existence, the monarch guarantees order and peace in the world. Probably the key argument in support of this thesis is found in chapter 11, where Dante, deeming the emperor to be all-powerful and, consequently, not affected by personal ambitions that can distract him, considers him the only ruler able to reign over his subjects inspired by an equitable sense of justice. Dante bases his conclusion on the belief that justice, founded on *caritas*, is the opposite of *cupiditas*, the root of all inordinate passions:

> Ad evidentiam primi notandum quod iustitie maxime contrariatur cupiditas, ut innuit Aristotiles in quinto *ad Nicomacum*: remota cupiditate omnino, nichil iustitie restat adversum. (Unde sententia Phylosophi est ut, que lege determinari possunt, nullo modo iudici relinquantur; et hoc metu cupiditatis fieri oportet, de facili mentes hominum detorquentis). Ubi ergo non est quod possit optari, inpossibile est ibi cupiditatem esse: destructis enim obiectis, passiones esse non possunt. Sed monarcha non habet quod possit optare: sua nanque iurisdictio terminatur Occeano solum, quod non contingit principibus aliis, quorum principatus ad alios terminantur, ut puta regis Castelle ad illum qui regis Aragonum. Ex quo sequitur quod monarcha sincerissimum inter mortales iustitie possit esse subiectum. Preterea, quemadmodum cupiditas habitualem iustitiam quodammodo, quantumcunque pauca, obnubilat, sic karitas seu recta dilectio illam acuit

atque dilucidat. Cui ergo maxime recta dilectio inesse potest, potissimum locum in illo potest habere iustitia; huiusmodi est monarcha; ergo, eo existente, iustitia potissima est vel esse potest. Quod autem recta dilectio faciat quod dictum est, hinc haberi potest: cupiditas nanque, perseitate hominum spreta, querit alia; karitas vero, spretis aliis omnibus, querit Deum et hominem, et per consequens bonum hominis. Cumque inter alia bona hominis potissimum sit in pace vivere—ut supra dicebatur—, et hoc operetur maxime atque potissime iustitia, karitas maxime iustitiam vigorabit et potior potius. (1.11.11–14)

[To clarify the first of these it must be noted that the thing most contrary to justice is greed, as Aristotle states in the fifth book of the *Ethics*. When greed is entirely eliminated, nothing remains which is opposed to justice; hence Aristotle's opinion that those things which can be resolved by law should in no way be left to the judge's discretion. And it is fear of greed which makes this necessary, for greed easily leads men's minds astray. But where there is nothing which can be coveted, it is impossible for greed to exist, for emotions cannot exist where their objects have been destroyed. But there is nothing the monarch could covet, for his jurisdiction is bounded only by the ocean; whereas this is not the case with other rulers, whose sovereignty extends only as far as the neighbouring kingdom, as is the case, for instance, with the kings of Castille and of Aragon. From this it follows that of all men the monarch can be the purest embodiment of justice. Moreover, just as greed, however slight, dulls the habit of justice in some way, so charity or rightly ordered love makes it sharper and brighter. So the man in whom rightly ordered love can be strongest is the one in whom justice can have its principal abode; the monarch is such a man; therefore justice is or can be at its strongest when he exists. That rightly ordered love does what has been stated can be deduced from this: greed, scorning the intrinsic nature of man, seeks other things; whereas love, scorning all other things, seeks God and man, and hence the true good of man. Since among the other goods available to man living in peace is supremely important (as we saw earlier), and justice principally and most effectively brings this about, love most of all will strengthen justice, and the stronger love is the more it will do so.]

The first three arguments focus instead on order and organization. In a universe that, in line with medieval Christian views of creation, is perfectly ordered in all its components, whether natural or social, the empire is seen as the principle that organizes and orders all the single units into which human beings arrange themselves (families, districts, cities, kingdoms) to help them achieve their common goal of happiness. The fourth and fifth arguments, which have a more obvious metaphysical and theological character, maintain that the empire is perfect because it strives to guide humanity to unity so that it can become more like the Creator and the heavens: unified under a single ruler, humanity resembles God, who, being wholly one, directs the heavens. From chapter 12, Dante focuses on the ability of the emperor to establish peace between conflicting rulers or parties and to guarantee freedom. Here Dante discusses freedom from the same perspective as that presented in *Purgatorio* 1: political freedom is necessary to allow humans to exercise their free will, that is, judgment that is not to be undermined by their appetites:

> Et humanum genus potissime liberum optime se habet. Hoc erit manifestum, si principium pateat libertatis. Propter quod sciendum quod principium primum nostre libertatis est libertas arbitrii, quam multi habent in ore, in intellectu vero pauci. Veniunt nanque usque ad hoc: ut dicant liberum arbitrium esse liberum de voluntate iudicium; et verum dicunt, sed importatum per verba longe est ab eis, quemadmodum tota die logici nostri faciunt de quibusdam propositionibus, que ad exemplum logicalibus interseruntur (puta de hac: "triangulus habet tres duobus rectis equals").... Si ergo iudicium moveat omnino appetitum et nullo modo preveniatur ab eo, liberum est; si vero ab appetitu quocunque modo preveniente iudicium moveatur, liberum esse non potest, quia non a se, sed ab alio captivum trahitur. (1.12.1–4)

> [Now the human race is in its ideal state when it is completely free. This will be clear if we clarify the principle of freedom. Therefore it must be borne in mind that the first principle of our freedom is free will, which many people talk about but few understand. For they go so far as to say that free will is free judgment in matters of volition. And what they say is true, but they are very far from understanding what the words mean, just like our logicians who daily enunciate cer-

tain propositions by way of example in their discussions on logic, such as "a triangle has three angles equal to two right angles." . . . Now if judgment controls desire completely and is in no way preempted by it, it is free; but if judgment is in any way at all pre-empted and thus controlled by desire, it cannot be free, because it does not act under its own power, but is dragged along in the power of something else.]

By preventing those in power from guiding people to live in the service of others rather than in the service of the development of their own selves, Dante says, with the support of Aristotle's authority, the empire guarantees the freedom that is necessary to live virtuously: "Unde Phylosophus in suis *Politicis* ait quod in politia obliqua bonus homo est malus civis, in recta vero bonus homo et civis bonus convertuntur. Et huiusmodi politie recte libertatem intendunt, scilicet ut homines propter se sint" (1.12.10) [Hence Aristotle in the *Politics* says that in bad government the good man is a bad citizen, whereas in good government the good man and the good citizen are one and the same thing. And these just forms of government aim at freedom, i.e., that men should exist for their own sake]. If such a unifying power is not present, the poet maintains, the world is condemned to a state of perennial discord that affects individuals' ability to live correctly and thereby to achieve their potential. Since "omnis concordia dependet ab unitate que est in voluntatibus" (1.15.8) [all concord depends on the unity which is in wills], humanity cannot hope for unity unless one will controls and directs all other wills toward one goal, given that the wills of mortals require guidance on account of the seductive pleasures of youth, as Aristotle teaches at the end of the *Ethics*. The argument is not different from the one presented by Charles Martel in *Purgatorio* 16; yet while in *Purgatorio* Dante appeals to the power of affective rhetoric to show the causes of what he considered a deep political crisis, in the *Monarchia* he mostly follows strict logical argumentation to prove his point. Yet even here, the poet's moral preoccupations emerge: plurality is not just disorder, it is sin; unity is not simply concord, it is a divine attribute that humanity should strive to imitate: "Hinc videri potest quod peccare nichil est aliud quam progredi ab uno spreto ad multa; quod quidem Psalmista videbat dicens: 'A fructu frumenti, vini et olei multiplicati sunt'" (1.15.3) [Hence it can be seen that to sin is nothing other than to spurn unity and move toward plurality; the Psalmist saw this when he said: "From the fruit of the corn, the wine, and the oil they have been multiplied"].

Having presented logical and philosophical arguments in favor of the need for a universal monarch, Dante closes the first book in an unexpected way by observing that, in historical terms, the empire confirmed its beneficial effects during the time of the Roman emperor Augustus, who ensured that peace reigned over the whole of the Roman world. It is clear that, in formal terms, Dante uses this last chapter as a bridge to the next *questio*, which investigates whether the Roman people ruled by right. However, there are also other, intrinsic reasons for this sudden turn to history. As Dante claimed at the start of book 1, politics is the realm of action. Consequently, no intellectual assessment of the nature of the empire is able to exclude experience and praxis. Historical evidence, Dante suggests, proves that his theoretical argument can be translated into action and that the contemporary world can be restored to its proper order. Having recourse to Roman history, furthermore, supports a fundamental principle of Dante's philosophical thought: the belief that humankind has been created to look for two kinds of happiness that are achieved through two different means, reason and revelation:

> Duos igitur fines providentia illa inenarrabilis homini proposuit intendendos: beatitudinem scilicet huius vite, que in operatione proprie virtutis consistit et per terrestrem paradisum figuratur; et beatitudinem vite ecterne, que consistit in fruitione divini aspectus ad quam propria virtus ascendere non potest, nisi lumine divino adiuta, que per paradisum celestem intelligi datur. Ad has quidem beatitudines, velut ad diversas conclusiones, per diversa media venire oportet. Nam ad primam per phylosophica documenta venimus, dummodo illa sequamur secundum virtutes morales et intellectuales operando; ad secundam vero per documenta spiritualia que humanam rationem transcendunt, dummodo illa sequamur secundum virtutes theologicas operando, fidem spem scilicet et karitatem. Has igitur conclusiones et media, licet ostensa sint nobis hec ab humana ratione que per phylosophos tota nobis innotuit, hec a Spiritu Sancto qui per prophetas et agiographos, qui per coecternum sibi Dei filium Iesum Cristum et per eius discipulos supernaturalem veritatem ac nobis necessariam

revelavit, humana cupiditas postergaret nisi homines, tanquam equi, sua bestialitate vagantes "in camo et freno" compescerentur in via. (3.16.7–9)

[Ineffable providence has thus set before us two goals to aim at: i.e. happiness in this life, which consists in the exercise of our own powers and is figured in the earthly paradise; and happiness in the eternal life, which consists in the enjoyment of the vision of God (to which our own powers cannot raise us except with the help of Gods light) and which is signified by the heavenly paradise. Now these two kinds of happiness must be reached by different means, as representing different ends. For we attain the first through the teachings of philosophy, provided that we follow them putting into practice the moral and intellectual virtues; whereas we attain the second through spiritual teachings which transcend human reason, provided that we follow them putting into practice the theological virtues, i.e. faith, hope and charity. These ends and the means to attain them have been shown to us on the one hand by human reason, which has been entirely revealed to us by the philosophers, and on the other by the Holy Spirit, who through the prophets and sacred writers, through Jesus Christ the son of God, coeternal with him, and through his disciples, has revealed to us the transcendent truth we cannot do without; yet human greed would cast these ends and means aside if men, like horses, prompted to wander by their animal natures, were not held in check "with bit and bridle" on their journey.]

Once Dante has established that natural reason is the means to achieving earthly happiness, in the conclusion of book 1 he quickly moves from the philosophical examination of the necessity of the empire to a discussion of the role of the Roman Empire. He deems it essential to demonstrate that, since the monarchy as an institution predates the revelation of the Gospels, it can exist independently from any spiritual revelation, teaching, and interpretation. This point is vital in establishing the importance of the separation of the two powers, the secular and the spiritual—a separation that is fundamental if humanity is to achieve the twofold happiness that Dante saw as its divinely instituted end.

Book 2 begins with a palinode: Dante admits that there was a time when he identified the reason for the Romans' supremacy over the world as their military power. However, when he penetrated "medullitus oculos mentis... per efficacissima signa divinam providentiam hoc effecisse" (2.1.3) [with [his] mind's eye to the heart of the matter... and understood through unmistakable signs that this was the work of divine providence], his amazement faded. The personal tone of this observation justifies Dante's present engagement with the topic and his fervent attack, amplified by biblical quotations, against those who oppose "Domino suo et Uncto suo, romano principi" (2.1.3) [their Lord and his Anointed, the Roman prince]. Since he has invoked divine providence to explain human history, Dante now clarifies that his arguments will be supported not just by rational evidence but also by divine authority: "non solum lumine rationis humane, sed etiam radio divine auctoritatis" (2.1.7) [not only by the light of human reason but also by the radiance of divine authority; when these two are in agreement]. From chapter 2 onward, Dante endeavors to establish whether or not the Roman Empire can claim its universal authority by right. As in the preceding book, the poet investigates the premises on which he will base his discussion. The issue at stake in this instance is the nature of right. As we shall see, the definition Dante provides of this concept in the *Monarchia* is both original and ambitious. The poet considers right as existing in the mind of God at its highest degree where it suffers no defects (2.2.4). To reach this conclusion Dante presents his metaphysical view of nature as a more or less perfect divine creation of God:

> Sciendum est igitur quod, quemadmodum ars in triplici gradu invenitur, in mente scilicet artificis, in organo et in materia formata per artem, sic et naturam in triplici gradu possumus intueri. Est enim natura in mente primi motoris, qui Deus est; deinde in celo, tanquam in organo quo mediante similitudo bonitatis ecterne in fluitantem materiam explicatur. Et quemadmodum, perfecto existente artifice atque optime organo se habente, si contingat peccatum in forma artis, materie tantum imputandum est, sic, cum Deus ultimum perfectionis actingat et instrumentum eius, quod celum est, nullum debite perfectionis patiatur defectum (ut ex hiis patet que de celo phylosophamur), restat quod quicquid in rebus inferioribus est peccatum, ex parte ma-

terie subiacentis peccatum sit et preter intentionem Dei naturantis et celi, et quod quicquid est in rebus inferioribus bonum, cum ab ipsa materia esse non possit, sola potentia existente, per prius ab artifice Deo sit et secundario a celo, quod organum est artis divine, quam naturam comuniter appellant. (2.2.2–3)

> [We must bear in mind then that, just as art is found at three levels, in the mind of the craftsman, in his instrument, and in the material shaped by his craft, so too we can consider nature at three levels. For nature is in the mind of the first mover, who is God; then in the heavens, as in the instrument by means of which the image of eternal goodness is set forth in fluctuating matter. And just as, when the craftsman is perfect and his instrument is in excellent order, if a flaw occurs in the work of art it is to be imputed exclusively to the material, in the same way, since God attains the highest perfection and his instrument (i.e., the heavens) cannot fall short of the perfection appropriate to it (as is clear from those things philosophy teaches us about the heavens), our conclusion is this: whatever flaws there are in earthly things are flaws due to the material of which they are constituted and are no part of the intention of God the creator and the heavens; and whatever good there is in earthly things, since it cannot come from the material (which exists only as a potentiality), comes primarily from God the maker and secondarily from the heavens, which are the instrument of God's handiwork, which is commonly called nature.]

Once the theological and philosophical premises of his argument are established, the poet argues in chapter 3 that the Romans did not usurp the role of monarch in the world because the imperial authority belongs to the noblest of people, which is what the Romans were. To prove the nobility of the Romans, as well as their being predestined to rule the world, Dante quotes several examples of Roman virtue (above all Aeneas's) found in Virgil's *Aeneid*, which, like others in the Middle Ages, he treats as a historical source. In chapter 4, the poet searches for supernatural evidence for the nobility of the Romans and lists several miracles performed by God that, in his view, affirmed the supremacy of the Romans and demonstrated the providential character of Rome. The evidence Dante provides includes quotations from a variety of ancient texts that range from Lucan to the Bible. It is in this chapter that the poet makes his only direct reference to Livy's *First Decade*, a text that was not widely available in the early decades of the fourteenth century:

> Quod autem pro Romano imperio perficiendo miracula Deus portenderit, illustrium autorum testimoniis comprobatur. Nam sub Numa Pompilio, secundo Romanorum rege, ritu Gentilium sacrificante, ancile de celo in urbem Deo electam delapsum fuisse Livius in prima parte testatur. (2.4.5)

> [That God performed miracles so that the Roman empire might be supreme is confirmed by the testimony of illustrious authors. For Livy tells in the first part of his work that in the time of Numa Pompilius, the second king of the Romans, a shield fell from heaven into God's chosen city as he was sacrificing according to the pagan rite.]

In chapters 5 and 6, Dante focuses on the law, a key concept in his understanding of justice and government, seen as the foundation of any successful and peaceful society. Here, the poet returns to develop further his interpretation of right as the correct relationship between social parts that guarantees the common good, before asserting with Cicero that the law is necessary to preserve the common good:

> Ius est realis et personalis hominis ad hominem proportio, que servata hominum servat sotietatem, et corrupta corrumpit (nam illa *Digestorum* descriptio non dicit quod quid est iuris, sed describit illud per notitiam utendi illo). Si ergo definitio ista bene "quid est" et "quare" comprehendit, et cuiuslibet sotietatis finis est comune sotiorum bonum, necesse est finem cuiusque iuris bonum comune esse; et inpossibile est ius esse, bonum comune non intendens. Propter quod bene Tullius in *Prima rethorica*: "Semper—inquit—ad utilitatem rei publice leges interpretande sunt." (2.5.1–2)

> [Right is a relationship between one individual and another in respect of things and people; when it is respected it preserves human society, and when it is violated it destroys it. For the description of it

given in the *Digests* does not say what right is but describes it in terms of its practical application. If therefore our definition correctly embraces both the essence and the purpose of right, and if the goal of any society is the common good of its members, it necessarily follows that the purpose of every right is the common good; and it is impossible that there can be a right which does not aim at the common good. Hence Cicero is correct when he says in the *De inventione* that laws are always to be interpreted for the benefit of the community.]

The Romans, in particular, are identified as the champions of the law, and this is confirmed by their noble enterprises that neglected profit and greed for the love of peace. "Signs" of the Romans' love of the common good are reported by illustrious writers, including Cicero, but to strengthen their authoritative views, Dante adds the cases of individual heroes who, thanks to their personal excellence and sacrifice, established the glory of Rome: Cincinnatus, Gaius Fabricius Luscinus, Marcus Furius Camillus, Lucius Iunius Brutus, Gaius Mucius Scaevola, and Cato of Utica. Such displays of heroism are for Dante proof of the fact that the Romans always looked for the common good and therefore at the perfection of the law (2.5.8–17).

Having reiterated his belief in the legitimacy of the Roman Empire, the poet concludes the second book with a series of chapters (7–9) that aim to demonstrate God's positive judgment in favor of the Romans. Given the difficulty for the human mind rationally to understand God's judgments, Dante considers other ways to ascertain the providential will. In light of the fact that putting to the test is one of God's ways of establishing human worth, that the Romans won, even through military might, their exceptional role in the world is seen by the poet, in chapter 9, as confirmation of their legitimacy. Book 2 closes with Dante's strongest claim in support of the empire, one that he also upheld in his other works: the Roman Empire is lawful and divinely willed because the Incarnation took place *imperante Augusto* [under the rule of the Emperor Augustus]:

Sed Cristus, ut scriba eius Lucas testatur, sub edicto romane auctoritatis nasci voluit de Virgine Matre, ut in illa singulari generis humani descriptione filius Dei, homo factus, homo conscriberetur: quod fuit illud prosequi. Et forte sanctius est arbitrari divinitus illud exivisse per Cesarem, ut qui tanta tempora fuerat expectatus in sotietate mortalium, cum mortalibus ipse se consignaret. Ergo Cristus Augusti, Romanorum auctoritate fungentis, edictum fore iustum opere persuasit. Et cum ad iuste edicere iurisdictio sequatur, necesse est ut qui iustum edictum persuasit iurisdictionem etiam persuaserit: que si de iure non erat, iniusta erat. (2.10.6–8)

[But as his chronicler Luke relates, Christ chose to be born of his Virgin Mother under an edict emanating from Roman authority, so that the Son of God made man might be enrolled as a man in that unique census of the human race; this means that he acknowledged the validity of that edict. And perhaps it is more holy to believe that the edict came by divine inspiration through Caesar, so that he who had been so long awaited in the society of men might himself be enrolled among mortals. Therefore Christ acknowledged by his action that the edict of Augustus, who embodied the authority of the Romans, was legitimate. And since someone who issues an edict legitimately must logically have the jurisdiction to do so, it necessarily follows that someone who acknowledges that an edict is legitimate is also acknowledging that the jurisdiction of the authority which promulgated it is legitimate; because if it were not based on right, it would not be legitimate.]

The third and final question to be addressed is, as anticipated, the relationship between the pontiff and the emperor, which constitutes the matter of book 3. Dante warns his reader that the solution to this last *questio* will perhaps be a cause of scandal. At the same time, he presents himself as someone who will embrace his cross for the love of truth, certain of the divine approval: "Quid timeam, cum Spiritus Patri et Filio coecternus aiat per os David: 'In memoria ecterna erit iustus, ab auditione mala non timebit'?" (3.1.4) [What should I fear, when the Spirit who is coeternal with the Father and the Son says through the mouth of David: "The righteous shall be in everlasting remembrance and shall not be afraid of ill report"?]. The problem that Dante bravely addresses is the following one: Does the emperor's authority depend on God or on his vicar on earth, the pope? The question is of course poignantly urgent in the context of the long-lasting conflict between the Holy Roman emperors and the medieval church.⁶ The secular and ecclesiastical powers clashed openly in an controversy over the investiture of bishops in the mid-eleventh century. The Investiture Controversy, resolved in 1122 through the Concordat of Worms, gave the church absolute power over investitures and administered a blow to the emperor's authority. While the conflict caused decades of civil war in Germany, in Italy the Investiture Controversy weakened the emperor and strengthened local rulers and institutions. The political ambitions of both Emperor Frederick I (1159–77) and Emperor Frederick II (1227–50) to increase their authority in Germany and in Italy led to conflicts with the papacy and the Italian city-states. The conflicts reached their climax in the late thirteenth and early fourteenth centuries with the involvement of the French monarchy and the theocratic policies of popes like Boniface VIII. Boniface VIII (1294–1303) was condemned by Dante for his attempt to create a theocratic government to which all other powers would be subordinated. The *Monarchia* was most probably written as a response to the new developments that the recently crowned emperor Henry VII's campaign to restore imperial authority in the Italian territories brought to this conflict. In 1310–11 Henry descended into Italy with the aim of reestablishing peace among the warring factions and city-states. His attempt, however, was thwarted by the alliance between the Guelf and Ghibelline factions, the papacy, and the French monarchy. His premature death in 1313 put an end to his attempt to strengthen the authority of the empire. The church too lost its secular influence and suffered a major setback when Pope Clement V, under pressure from the French crown, moved the curia to Avignon in 1309.

As the second chapter of book 3 makes clear, Dante's aim is to resolve the conflict between the church and the empire by tackling ignorance. According to the poet, ignorance regarding the fundamental need to separate the secular from the spiritual exists because humanity, overwhelmed by passions, abandons the path of reason, especially if the guides appointed to lead it "ipsi nichil intelliguntur" (3.3.5) [fail to make themselves understood]. Three groups of people are opposed to the divinely willed solution to this problem: the pope and his followers, those governed by greed, and the "decretalists," those who believe that the decretals, papal decrees concerning points of canon law, have more authority than the Bible itself. These defenders of the traditions of the church abuse scripture in order to prove the absolute authority of the church and, in so doing, corrupt the truth of revelation. From chapter 4 onward, Dante considers a series of hierocratic statements in favor of the pontiff's absolute authority that are mainly based on biblical passages. One of these false arguments considers the sons of Jacob, Levi and Judas, as allegories of the relationship between religious and secular power (chapter 5). The poet refutes this argument on the basis of an interpretation of the syllogism:

> Et cum arguendo inferunt "Sicut Levi precedit in nativitate sic Ecclesia in auctoritate," dico similiter quod aliud est predicatum conclusionis et aliud maior extremitas: nam aliud est "auctoritas" et aliud "nativitas," subiecto et ratione; propter quod peccatur in forma. Et est similis processus huic: A precedit B in C; D et E se habent ut A et B: ergo D precedit E in F; F vero et C diversa sunt. (3.5.3)
>
> [And when by their reasoning they reach the conclusion "As Levi preceded in birth so the church precedes in authority," I say again that the predicate of the conclusion is a different thing from the predicate of the major premise; for "authority" is one thing and "birth" another, both in respect of their subject and their meaning; and thus there is a logical flaw in the argument. And the reasoning goes like this: A precedes B in C; D is to E as A is to B; therefore D precedes E in F; but F and C are different things.]

In chapters 6 and 7, Dante counters the hierocrats' interpretations of King Saul's investiture and of the gifts of the Magi by means of a similar application of syllogistic reasoning. Instead, in chapters 8 and 9, the poet corrects the interpretation of two Gospel passages (Matt. 16:19 and Luke 22:38) thanks to a careful literal reading.

However, the most controversial rectification of hierocratic positions is found in chapter 10. Here, famously, the poet confutes the validity of the so-called Donation of Constantine to Pope Sylvester of the *Patrimonium Petri*, a Roman imperial decree, proved to be a forgery by the humanist Lorenzo Valla in 1439–40, that the church used to support its claims of political authority over Rome and the western Roman Empire. As in the *Comedy* (especially *Inf.* 19.115–17), Dante courageously dismisses the validity of the Donation even though it was included in a ninth-century collection of Decretals. Dante argues that Constantine did not have the right to transfer temporal authority over Rome to the pope, that is, to deprive himself of a part of the empire in order to donate it to others, because such an action was against the law. Every institution exists before its ministers: the empire is a jurisdiction, so it precedes its judge, the emperor, who cannot transfer the jurisdiction to others:

> Preterea, omnis iurisdictio prior est suo iudice: iudex enim ad iurisdictionem ordinatur, et non e converso. Sed imperium est iurisdictio omnem temporalem iurisdictionem ambitu suo comprehendens: ergo ipsa est prior suo iudice, qui est imperator; qua re ad ipsam imperator est ordinatus, et non e converso. Ex quo patet quod imperator ipsam permutare non potest in quantum imperator, cum ab ea recipiat esse quod est. (3.10.10)

> [Moreover, all jurisdiction is prior to the judge who exercises it, for the judge is appointed for the sake of the jurisdiction, and not vice versa; but the empire is a jurisdiction which embraces within its scope every other temporal jurisdiction: therefore it is prior to its judge, who is the emperor, for the emperor is appointed for its sake, and not vice versa. From this it is clear that the emperor, precisely as emperor, cannot change it, because he derives from it the fact that he is what he is.]

Equally, the ministers of the church, which Christ had established in poverty, did not have the right to accept Constantine's gift. The poet was stoutly affirming that both the church and the empire have their own distinct foundations (3.1.7–8): the foundation of the church is Christ, while that of the empire is human right. Both institutions, therefore, must be kept distinct and independent, but they must both refer back to a single entity, God (chapters 11 and 12). If imperial authority, having been established before the church, is not subject to ecclesial authority, the pontiff must necessarily be willing to accept the emperor, following Christ's example:

> Maior propositio huius demonstrationis declarata est in terminis; minorem Cristus et Ecclesia confirmat. Cristus nascendo et moriendo,

ut superius dictum est; Ecclesia, cum Paulus in Actibus Apostolorum dicat ad Festum: "Ad tribunal Cesaris sto, ubi me oportet iudicari"; cum etiam angelus Dei Paulo dixerit parum post: "Ne timeas, Paule, Cesari te oportet assistere"; et infra iterum Paulus ad Iudeos existentes in Ytalia: "Contradicentibus autem Iudeis, coactus sum appellare Cesarem, non quasi gentem meam habens aliquid accusare, sed ut eruerem animam meam de morte." (3.13.5)

[The major premise of this proof is clear from the terms in which it is formulated; the minor premise is confirmed by Christ and by the church. Christ confirms it by his birth and his death, as was said earlier; the church when Paul in the Acts of the Apostles says to Festus: "I stand at Caesar's judgment seat, where I ought to be judged"; and again when the angel of God said to Paul a little later: "Fear not, Paul; thou must be brought before Caesar"; and again, later, Paul said to the Jews who were in Italy: "But when the Jews spake against it, I was constrained to appeal unto Caesar, not that I had aught to accuse my nation of, but to deliver my soul from death."]

At this point Dante deploys his final arguments against the papalists. He claims not only that he cannot find in scripture any evidence of God's intention to devolve temporal authority to priests but also that both testaments demonstrate that the religious always avoided involving themselves in earthly matters (chapter 14). In sum, the Bible shows that the exercise of temporal power is against the nature or form of the church and so is not one of its faculties. The very form of the bride of God, the *ecclesia*, is Christ (and his teachings). The poet closes the series of biblical episodes analyzed to support his position with a sentence taken from the Gospel of John, the most spiritual of all the Gospels, to pass a final judgment on those who ignore the example of Christ, who unambiguously left this decree to his disciples: "My kingdom is not of this world" (John 18:36).

The *Monarchia*'s closing chapter clarifies how the authority of the empire descends directly from God. Dante presents a grand and precise representation of the order and measure of creation at the center of which humankind stands as one of the primary objects of God. Everything in the universe has a function and a place; everything is geared toward a clear end. Because we are both divine and human, encompassing both natures (body and soul), we need two different guides to achieve our different ends, one corruptible, the other incorruptible: happiness in this life and happiness in eternity. At its end, the *Monarchia* proclaims the principle of the independence of the two main institutions and authorities of the medieval world, a position that has strong Ghibelline aspects. Yet the poet is keen to remind his readers, in his own defense, that the solution that he has proposed to the question should not be misunderstood: the emperor must be somewhat subordinate to the pope, just as earthly happiness is subordinated to the afterlife. The emperor, in other words, should address the pope with that respect that a son owes a father. Scholars have long discussed the meaning of this unexpected closing assertion. To what extent does the "somewhat" clause mitigate the argument in favor of the emperor's independence? Throughout his life, Dante always showed the utmost respect for the seat of Peter, even when he attacked the simonist popes of his times and placed them in hell. Throughout his oeuvre, he never failed to stress the priority of faith over those things that reason cannot grasp. It is difficult, therefore, to consider this final statement as a softening of his views or as a concession to the papalists, given the positions that Dante so energetically and consistently espoused in the *Monarchia*.

What Kind of Text Is the *Monarchia*?

The work is generally defined by scholars as a treatise on political theory that covers "three main points of inquiry" concerning its "materia" [subject matter], the empire: "Maxime autem de hac tria dubitata queruntur: primo nanque dubitatur et queritur an ad bene esse mundi necessaria sit; secundo an romanus populus de iure Monarche offitium sibi asciverit; et tertio an auctoritas Monarche dependeat a Deo inmediate vel ab alio, Dei ministro seu vicario" (1.2.3) [Now there are three main points of inquiry which have given rise to perplexity on this subject: first, is it necessary to the well-being of the world? second, did the Roman people take on the office of the monarch by right? and third, does the monarch's authority derive directly from God or from someone else (his minister or vicar)?].

Scholars' definition of the *Monarchia* as a political treatise follows Dante's own instructions on the *causa formalis* of his work.[7] The poet in fact refers to it as a "tractatus" in the opening of the first book: "Presens tractatus est inquisitio" (1.2.4) [This present treatise is a kind of inquiry]. Yet, as readers of the *Comedy* have learned to expect, bracketing Dante's texts into a single genre is neither easy nor advisable. The poet might describe this work in what appear to be clear terms, yet his prose is littered with technical details that complicate our understanding of the nature of his enterprise. As well as *tractatus*, the poet in fact uses at least three other terms to describe his work. He refers to all three books as *quaestiones*: "Itaque prima questio sit: utrum ad bene esse mundi Monarchia temporalis necessaria sit" (1.5.2) [So the first question is this: is temporal monarchy necessary for the well-being of the world?]; "Igitur fiducie prenotate innixus et testimonio rationis et auctoritatis prefretus, ad secundam questionem dirimendam ingredior" (2.1.8) [Relying therefore on the faith of which I spoke earlier and trusting in the testimony of reason and authority, I proceed to resolve the second question]; and "Questio igitur presens, de qua inquisitio futura est, inter duo luminaria magna versatur: romanum scilicet Pontificem et romanum Principem" (3.1.5) [The present question, therefore, which we are now to investigate, concerns the two great lights, that is the Roman Pope and the Roman Prince]. In book 2 the discussion is, in fact, introduced by a formula that is typical of medieval scholastic *quaestiones*: "Utrum Romanus populus de iure sibi asciverit imperii dignitatem" (2.2.1) [That is, did the Roman people take on the dignity of empire by right?]. Book 3, however, is further classified as a *disputatio*: "Isti vero ad quos erit tota disputatio sequens" (3.4.1) [the whole of the argument which follows]. The *quaestio* and *disputatio* are fundamental genres of medieval philosophical and theological literature, as well as techniques and practices of scholastic teaching. Based on Aristotelian logical and syllogistic reasoning, both had become the favored method of packaging inquiry in any intellectual field, such as medicine, theology, philosophy, and law.[8] Thus, if Dante's decision to present the *Monarchia* as a mini *summa* of *quaestiones* and *disputationes* was not in itself unusual, his mastery of the argumentative procedures has so impressed his readers as to persuade a great admirer of his, Giovanni Boccaccio, to consider the poet to have been formally trained in philosophy.[9]

Though largely skeptical about Boccaccio's claim, modern commentators nevertheless analyze the *Monarchia* as a striking display of Dante as a *loicus*, logician, and philosopher. Not only does the poet offer clear evidence of his knowledge of Aristotelian classics such as the *Ethics*, the

Metaphysics, and the *Politics*, but he also shows himself able to master the analytical method of scholastic inquiry. To discuss his *quaestiones* and to guarantee the rigorous scientific nature of his investigation, following Aristotle, Dante proceeds inductively to seek the principles (or causes) upon which the issues at stake must be founded; from these, through the use of syllogisms, he establishes the points he privileges as logical truths.[10] The resulting text is imbued with technical terms that reveal the clear influence on Dante's argumentative techniques of the lesson of Aristotle's *logica nova* and the *logica modernorum* that had become standard in arts.[11] Alongside generic terms such as *intentio* (1.2.1) [intention], *definitio* (2.5.2) [definition], and *describere* (2.5.1) [to describe], the poet deployed specialist words such as *instantia*,[12] a technical expression used by scholastics to introduce the refutation of the "rationale" (*ratio*) underlying the arguments raised against (*contra*) the problem posed by a *quaestio*. Significantly, in his *disputatio* against the hierocrats in book 3, Dante frequently attempts to dismantle logical fallacies by appealing directly to the *Sophistic Refutations* of Aristotle, a text that led to the recognition in late medieval logic and semantics regarding the need to a focus on the properties of terms. The incorrect use of logic is a frequent target in the *Monarchia*, as much as bad poetry and bad rhetoric are in the *Comedy* and in the *De vulgari eloquentia*. Indeed, to defend an interpretation, Dante flaunts his competence and direct knowledge of the relevant *auctoritates*, as occurs, for example, when he criticizes false syllogisms by quoting the *Ethics* verbatim (6.9 1142b.22–24): "Dicit enim Phylosophus: 'Sed et hoc falso sillogismo sortiri: quod quidem oportet sortiri; per quod autem non, sed falsum medium terminum esse'" (2.5.23) [For Aristotle says: "Yet it is possible to attain even good by a false syllogism: to attain what one ought, but not by the right means, the middle term being false"].

Whether or not Dante had learned such techniques in the classroom, he appears keen to affirm his authority and intellectual standing by demonstrating, as in the following passage that alludes to Aristotle's *De caelo*, his familiarity with the methods of contemporary academic philosophers and his knowledge of their key textbooks: "Deus ultimum perfectionis actingat et instrumentum eius, quod celum est, nullum debite perfectionis patiatur defectum, ut ex hiis patet que de celo phylosophamur" (2.2.3) [Likewise since God achieves highest perfection, and his tool (that is, the heavens) cannot suffer any defect in its condign perfection, as is clear from our philosophical studies on the heavens].[13] However, politics was not included in the academic curriculum.[14] At the same time, university-educated intellectuals, such as Thomas Aquinas and Peter of Auvergne, wrote commentaries on Aristotle's *Politics*, while, toward the end of the thirteenth century, others begun to hold academic "disputed questions," as well as questions *de quodlibet*, related to topics of political philosophy. They wrote in response to political events, especially in the context of the power struggle between the church and secular institutions, or to define political virtues such as prudence and poverty, or simply to discuss matters of policy and constitution within the church itself.[15] At times, such *quaestiones* were turned into treatises that preserved the original scholastic format. In this sense, even though he never formally discussed the *Monarchia*'s topics in an academic forum, Dante's definition of his work as a treatise composed of *quaestiones* fully adheres to the academic practices of his time. It must be noted, however, that, as far as political science is concerned, such a "tradition" was a novelty that did not belong to the scholastic classroom: the first treatises on politics were written during the poet's lifetime, and, as Dante notes clearly at the start of his work, the debate was still in its infancy, since matters both of methodology and of basic principles regarding the discussion of political questions were only slowly being developed.

Not surprisingly, therefore, alongside the main definitions of the text as a *tractatus* and a *quaestio*, in the prologue of book 1, Dante also presents his work as a *notitia utilissima* on hidden truths that need to be brought to light: "Cumque, inter alias veritates occultas et utiles, temporalis Monarchie notitia utilissima sit et maxime latens" (1.1.5) [Now since among other truths which are hidden and useful, a knowledge of temporal monarchy is both extremely useful and most inaccessible]. Just a few lines earlier, marking the incipit of the *Monarchia*, Dante had stated that writing such a *notitia* was an act of our innate love for the truth, as well as one of respect for his own abilities:

> Omnium hominum quos ad amorem veritatis natura superior impressit hoc maxime interesse videtur, ut, quemadmodum de labore antiquorum ditati sunt, ita et ipsi posteris prolaborent, quatenus ab eis posteritas habeat quo ditetur. Longe nanque ab offitio se esse non dubitet qui, publicis documentis imbutus, ad rem publicam aliquid afferre non curat. (1.1.1–2)

[For all men whom the Higher Nature has endowed with a love of truth, this above all seems to be a matter of concern, that just as they have been enriched by the efforts of their forebears, so they too may work for future generations, in order that posterity may be enriched by their efforts. For the man who is steeped in the teachings which form our common heritage, yet has no interest in contributing something to the community, is failing in his duty.]

The solemn opening is of course a reworking of the Aristotelian dictum (*Metaph.* 1.1 980a21) as reelaborated by Thomas Aquinas—"Naturaliter homo desiderat scientiam" [All men naturally desire to know][16]—and as already cited in *Convivio* 1.1.1. Significantly, the poet adapted the *sententia* by exchanging the term *scientia* for *veritas*. The variation on the Aristotelian topos acquires a specific value when *veritas* is seen in combination with the technical term *notitia*. While the latter was used in late medieval scholasticism as a synonym for knowledge, the claim that theologians needed to be allowed to seek *notitia veritatis* against the restrictions imposed by Bishop Tempier's 1277 condemnations has its source in *Quodlibet* 12 by Godfrey of Fontaines, who was regent master in theology at the University of Paris between 1285 and 1303/4.[17] Godfrey strongly advocated for the need for intellectual freedom on matters that were still open to discussion. The subject and the rhetoric, as well as the terminology, employed by Godfrey were soon appropriated by those who first started writing about politics not as a matter of current affairs but as theological *quaestiones* that needed to be clarified to avoid further confusion about the truth, as well as further acrimony between opposing factions: namely, James of Viterbo (*De regimine christiano*, 1301–2) and John of Paris (*Tractatus de potestate regia et papali*, 1302). Regardless of their ideological position, all these theologians appealed to the need to search for the truth (*notitia veritatis*) by means of scientific investigation applied to matters of politics. Dante's deliberate utilization of the same rhetoric as the theologians once again highlights that the *Monarchia* belongs to a specific cultural and intellectual environment, scholasticism. In addition, it points to Dante's awareness of the emergence of a new genre dealing with a new *materia* within the broader context of scholastic treatises and *quaestiones*.

The novelty of politics as a topic for discussion allowed for some flexible uses of the genre. Given how serious he considered the failings of contemporary political life, Dante gave a strong prophetic and apostolic emphasis to the scholastic format of his discussion, transforming his *notitia utilissima* into a sort of divine mandate.[18] By identifying truth with Old Testament wisdom, Dante equates himself to the prophet Daniel and to St. Paul and presents himself as a *scriba Dei*, a divinely inspired author:

> Sed quia de trono inmutabili suo Veritas deprecatur, Salomon etiam silvam Proverbiorum ingrediens meditandam veritatem, impium detestandum in se facturo nos docet, ac preceptor morum Phylosophus familiaria destruenda pro veritate suadet; assumpta fiducia de verbis Danielis premissis, in quibus divina potentia clipeus defensorum veritatis astruitur, iuxta monitionem Pauli fidei loricam induens, in calore carbonis illius quem unus de Seraphin accepit de altari celesti et tetigit labia Ysaie, gignasium presens ingrediar, et in brachio Illius qui nos de potestate tenebrarum liberavit in sanguine suo impium atque mendacem de palestra, spectante mundo, eiciam. (3.1.3)

> [But since truth from its unchangeable throne implores us, and Solomon too, entering the forest of Proverbs, teaches us by his own example to meditate on truth and loathe wickedness; and since our authority on morals, Aristotle, urges us to destroy what touches us closely for the sake of maintaining truth; then having taken heart from the words of Daniel cited above, in which divine power is said to be a shield of the defenders of truth, and putting on "the breastplate of faith" as Paul exhorts us, afire with that burning coal which one of the seraphim took from the heavenly altar to touch Isaiah's lips, I shall enter the present arena, and, by his arm who freed us from the power of darkness with his blood, before the eyes of the world I shall cast out the wicked and the lying from the ring.]

The sacred reverberations of Dante's register tie knowledge to theology, namely, to the interpretation of the Bible as the source of all understanding.[19] From this perspective, the truth that Dante wants to defend appears as one with his awareness of God's will, while his use of the term *notitia* echoes, alongside its scholastic meanings, St. Paul's "Deum habere in notitia" (Rom. 1:28) [to retain the knowledge of God]. Indeed, Dante's description of his task seems very close to St. Francis's Christo-mimetic approach to learning, which, as recorded by Bonaventure in his chapter of the life of the saint dedicated to the interpretation of the Bible and to the spirit of prophecy, coincided with "in notitia veritatis proficere," that is, with "an excellent knowledge of the word of God."[20]

The framing of the poet's mission in religious and providential terms explains why, on the one hand, the *Monarchia* is a collection of *quaestiones* and *disputationes*, generally analytical and scientific in mode and structure, while, on the other, it is also marked by a strong prophetic sense of apostolic engagement, which bursts out especially in the prologues and conclusions to its three books. As in the *Convivio*, the *Comedy*, and the *Epistles*, Dante fashions his prophetic voice on biblical models, appropriating the words of *scribae Dei* such as David, Solomon, Paul, and Isaiah, to present his work as divinely inspired. Furthermore, as in the *Comedy*, the biblical quotations are not an act of simple "ventriloquism"; instead, Dante bends the sacred text to demonstrate that, if the Bible is concerned with the present, as medieval readers most certainly thought was the case, the views that he expresses on the present are in fact inscribed in God's book. Thus, for example, when at the start of book 2 the poet utters the first lines of the messianic Psalm 2, he recasts them, against any possible interpretation of the literal biblical sense, to attack those who do not acknowledge the supremacy of the Roman Empire: "Propter quod derisive, non sine dolore quodam, cum illo clamare possum pro populo glorioso, pro Cesare, qui pro Principe celi clamabat: 'Quare fremuerunt gentes, et populi meditati sunt inania? Astiterunt reges terre, et principes convenerunt in unum, adversus Dominum et adversus Cristum eius'" (2.1.4) [For this reason I can cry out in defence of that glorious people and of Caesar—mockingly, yet not without some feeling of grief—along with him who cried out for the prince of Heaven: "Why did the nations rage, and the peoples meditate vain things? The kings of the earth have arisen, and the princes have gathered together, against their Lord and against his Christ"].

Such attacks against the ignorance and malice of those who deny what the poet considers to be the divine truth go hand in hand with the representation of himself not just as a voice crying out in the desert but also as a prophet who, by calling the powerful to perform their divinely ordained duties, risks being thrown to the lions like Daniel: "Conclusit ora leonum, et non nocuerunt michi: quia coram eo iustitia inventa est in me" (3.1.1) [He shut the lions' mouths, and they did not harm me, for in his sight righteousness was found in me]. By fashioning himself as a prophet of the truth and his work as an announcement (*notitia*) of the will of God, Dante broadens the remit of the genre of the *Monarchia* and shifts the *quaestiones* and *disputationes* examined into the scriptural realm of divine revelation. As Chiesa and Tabarroni have noted, prophetic posturing was certainly congenial to Dante; yet the extent of his self-awareness in the *Monarchia* seems heightened: prophecy and science, philosophy and the sacred page are presented as the poet's two *modi scribendi* and *operandi*. Like all of Dante's masterpieces, the *Monarchia* is a hybrid, and hybridity characterizes every element of this text, from its style to its audience, and from its genre(s) to its hermeneutic aims. This should not be seen as a mark of compositional weakness or expositional failure. On the contrary, the multifaceted manner in which Dante develops his political argument is proof of the complexity of his approach to understanding *humana res* (human things) as a mix of the corruptible and the uncorruptible. If, as the poet had claimed since the *Convivio*, humanity is both divine and human, both natural and supranatural, politics cannot be comprehended solely as the realm of law, right, and philosophical arguments. It needs rather to be set within the context of providential history and requires a correct reading of both the book of nature and the book of God, the Bible.

This is why contamination is more pervasive and reaches further than just a blend of biblical rhetoric and scientific literature. As Boccaccio had already noted in his *Trattatello*, the *Monarchia*'s *quaestiones* employ a variety of methodologies, modes, and sources to explore as fully as possible its main topic:

> Nel primo loicalmente disputando, pruova che a ben essere del mondo sia di necessità essere imperio: la quale è la prima quistione. Nel secondo, per argomenti istoriografi procedendo, mostra Roma di ragione ottenere il titolo dello imperio: ch'è la seconda quistione. Nel terzo, per argomenti teologi pruova l'autorità dello 'mperio immediatamente procedere da Dio, e non mediante alcuno suo vicario, come li chierici pare che vogliano; ch'è la terza quistione.

> [In the first book he proves by argument of logic that the Empire is necessary for the well-being of the world. This is his first point. In the second book, proceeding by arguments drawn from history, he shows that Rome rightly holds the title of the Empire. This is his second point. In the third book by theological arguments he proves

that the authority of the Empire proceeds directly from God, and not through the mediation of any vicar, as the clergy appear to maintain. This is his third point.][21]

The observations are of great importance: Boccaccio perceptively noted the flexibility of Dante's approach to the genre of the *quaestio*. Of particular relevance is Boccaccio's acute characterization of book 2 as "istoriografico." This *quaestio*, as mentioned, aims to demonstrate that the Roman Empire was created and ruled *de iure*, by right. To support his argument, Dante states that he will offer evidence that comes "lumine rationis humane, sed etiam radio divine auctoritatis: que duo cum simul ad unum concurrunt, celum et terram simul assentire necesse est" (2.1.7) [by the light of human reason but also by the radiance of divine authority; when these two are in agreement, heaven and earth must of necessity both give their assent]. As we will see, especially in the first section of the *quaestio*, in order to substantiate his presentation, the poet often relies on what some scholars consider an impressive knowledge of canon and civil law. More frequently, however, particularly from chapter 7 on, Dante supports his case with what he believed to be historical evidence drawn from classical *auctoritates*. In so doing, Dante brings together a chronologically haphazard list of important and memorable events and heroes from ancient Rome. His aim is not to write a *chronica* or a *fiorita* of Roman events; instead, he presents an interpretation of the history of the Roman Empire: in Rome he recognizes the signs of God's will and providential plan. However alien his vision of sacred history might be to us, Dante, like any historian today, develops a thesis that finds a particular logic in the evolution of events. His original focus shifts from one discipline to another: he moves from the treatment of political philosophy in the first book to that of historiography and even to philosophy of history in the second book, further complicating our efforts to interpret the *Monarchia*.[22]

History, Virgil, Augustine, and the Law

Uncovering the sources of Dante's historical knowledge displayed in book 2 of the *Monarchia* reveals the poet's familiarity with the major classics of ancient and medieval historiography. Dante owes his awareness of Roman history mainly to the *Historiae adversum paganos libri VII* by Augustine's disciple Orosius, though access to other sources, whether medieval or ancient, such as Livy's *Ab urbe condita*, appears likely. Yet, in the majority of cases, book 2 of the treatise is more like a poetic digest of the great Roman poets: Virgil, Lucan, and Ovid. Unsurprisingly, among these, Virgil is at the fore. Dante's recourse to literature as part of his historiographical methodology has often been characterized as essentially an homage paid to the great *auctores* by a poet who intended to exalt the art of poetry above all other textual forms. Yet Dante's historiographical method is neither a rhetorical flourish nor a straightforward aesthetic choice: Virgil had long been deployed as a "historian" by Christian authors. The Virgilian cento, *De laudibus Christi*, written by Proba around 362 CE, for example, recounted the biblical story of the world from the Creation to the coming of the Holy Spirit by using 694 lines taken from Virgil's *Aeneid*. This cento was still used in late medieval schools and was well known to Boccaccio, who included its learned author in his list of famous women in the *De mulieribus claris*. However, if we want to remain closer to Dante's concerns, we do not need to look much further than Augustine's *De civitate Dei* as a precedent for using the *Aeneid* as a historiographical source. Here, as is well known, the bishop of Hippo develops an extremely negative interpretation of Roman civilization, which is deemed an aberration of the Christian principles found in scripture. In book 3, the main historical sources for his bleak account of Roman power are Sallust and Terence. In addition, Augustine also frequently quotes Varro to discuss Roman religion, Livy to give examples of Roman virtue, and Apuleius with respect to philosophical matters. Yet, for Augustine, as for Dante, Rome meant, first and foremost, Virgil. The Mantuan poet is repeatedly quoted as the emblematic representative of the earthly city's sinful culture and history that Augustine sought to discredit and dismantle in order to demonstrate the righteousness of the city of God. Throughout the *De civitate Dei*, Augustine turns to Virgil as the key authoritative source on Rome; yet he does so acerbically, to deconstruct the very myth of Rome that the *Aeneid* had fostered.

Dante openly declares that he initially accepted Augustine's negative view of Roman rule: "Admirabar equidem aliquando romanum populum in orbe terrarum sine ulla resistentia fuisse prefectum, cum, tantum superficialiter intuens, illum nullo iure sed armorum tantummodo violentia obtinuisse arbitrabar" (2.1.2) [For my own part, I used to once be amazed that the Roman people had set themselves as rulers over the whole world without encountering any resistance, for I looked at the matter only in a superficial way and I thought that they had attained their supremacy not by right but only by force of arms]. Whether or not he had read the entire *De civitate Dei*, it is obvious that Augustine's recourse to Virgil left a durable impression on him. By polemically engaging with the Christian father's influential text, the *Monarchia* wished to set the record straight not just on the empire but also on Virgil. More precisely, Dante rewrites his anti-Augustinian version of Roman history by drawing on Virgil and the other classical poets in order to reappropriate their words and their authority against the use to which the bishop of Hippo had bent their verses. Thus Dante often reprises the same poetic citations as Augustine employed in the *De civitate Dei* in order to polemically overturn the emphases that the bishop gave them. Indeed, the same strategy is apparent even where references to the *De civitate Dei* are veiled. This is the case regarding Dante's digression on Aeneas's killing of Turnus. The poet notes that the hero would have shown *clementia* to his enemy if Turnus had not previously killed Pallas:

> Nam de primo cum de sede patris Enee, qui primus pater huius populi fuit, verteretur litigium, Turno Rutulorum rege contra stante ... in quo quidem agone tanta victoris Enee clementia fuit, ut nisi balteus, quem Turnus Pallanti a se occiso detraxerat, patuisset, victo victor simul vitam condonasset et pacem, ut ultima carmina nostri Poete testantur. (2.9.13–14)

> [For at the very beginning, when a dispute arose about the abode of father Aeneas, who was the first father of the Roman people, and Turnus king of the Rutuli opposed him ... in this combat the clemency of the victor Aeneas was so great that, had he not caught sight of the belt which Turnus had taken from Pallas when he killed him, the victor would have granted life as well as peace to the vanquished, as our poet's closing lines testify.]

The pertinence of this digression within the context of Dante's wider argument on trial by combat has appeared questionable to scholars;

however, the poet's motivations were in fact extratextual. In the *De civitate Dei* 3.4.1, the section dedicated to the brutality of Roman history, Augustine refers to the *Aeneid* to ridicule the false remorse shown by Aeneas after killing Lausus (*Aen.* 10.821–26):

> Vnde enim aput Vergilium pius Aeneas laudabiliter dolet hostem etiam sua peremptum manu? . . . Quaeso ab humano impetremus affectu, ut femina sponsum suum a fratre suo peremptum sine crimine fleuerit, si uiri hostes a se uictos etiam cum laude fleuerunt. Ergo sponso a fratre inlatam mortem quando femina illa flebat, tunc se contra matrem ciuitatem tanta strage bellasse et tanta hinc et inde cognati cruoris effusione uicisse Roma gaudebat.
>
> [For why do we praise the grief of Aeneas (in Virgil) over the enemy cut down even by his own hand? . . . I demand, in the name of humanity, that if men are praised for tears shed over enemies conquered by themselves, a weak girl should not be counted criminal for bewailing her lover slaughtered by the hand of her brother. While, then, that maiden was weeping for the death of her betrothed inflicted by her brother's hand, Rome was rejoicing that such devastation had been wrought on her mother state, and that she had purchased a victory with such an expenditure of the common blood of herself and the Albans.][23]

Like the majority of citations from the *Aeneid* in the *Monarchia*, so Dante's apparently arbitrary observations on Aeneas's clemency in book 2 function as a deliberate response to the attacks that Augustine persistently launched against Virgil and his great hero.[24] In fact, the *Monarchia*'s anti-Augustinian interpretation of Roman history can, in itself, justify Dante's Virgilian historiographical perspective.[25] From an ideological point of view, however, Dante also challenges the traditional Christian condemnation of the Roman Empire by basing himself on sound principles in law that confirm his knowledge of developments in contemporary legal debates. Encouraged by the study of texts of Roman law, such as the *Corpus juris civilis*, and conscious of the need to arrest the waning of universal and local institutions beset by factionalism and other conflicts, thirteenth-century practitioners of *scientia iuris* had dedicated themselves to pursuing principles that would guarantee order, justice, and the "common good." In this regard, drawing on French examples, Dante's friend the jurist and teacher Cino da Pistoia had introduced a new way of thinking about public law into Italian legal circles:[26] attention was shifted from the study of private law to an understanding of public right (*ius*) and its rationale (*ratio* or *causa*), namely, to the "inner logic" of the law as this found expression in the *Corpus juris civilis*, the compilation of Roman law that was enacted under Emperor Justinian I (ca. 482–565).[27] The *Monarchia* reveals that Dante's thought on jurisdiction, order, and government evolved in light of these new developments and can be deemed to constitute a reflection on the ontology of the law and its philosophical principles. Against the narrowly focused activities of legal annotators, and despite the fact that he lacked formal training in the discipline, Dante seeks to establish "the essence of right" (*ius*). To accomplish this task, the poet is not afraid to comment on the limitations of the *Digest*, the most important part of the Justinian *Corpus*, and to dismiss its classifications as simply descriptive tools prepared for practical purposes. In contrast and as a counter, he offers his own definition of right as "realis et personalis hominis ad hominem proportio" [a relationship between one individual and another in respect of things and people] that has the common good as its end:

> (Nam illa *Digestorum* descriptio non dicit quod quid est iuris, sed describit illud per notitiam utendi illo). Si ergo definitio ista bene "quid est" et "quare" comprehendit, et cuiuslibet sotietatis finis est comune sotiorum bonum, necesse est finem cuiusque iuris bonum comune esse; et inpossibile est ius esse, bonum comune non intendens. Propter quod bene Tullius in *Prima rethorica*: "semper—inquit—ad utilitatem rei publice leges interpretande sunt." (2.5.1–2)

> [For the description of it given in the *Digest* does not say what right is, but describes it in terms of its practical application. If therefore our definition correctly embraces both the essence and the purpose of right, and if the goal of any society is the common good of its members, it necessarily follows that the purpose of every right is the common good; and it is impossible that there can be a right which does not aim at the common good. Hence Cicero is correct when he

says in the *De inventione* that laws are always to be interpreted for the benefit of the community.]

This definition, which explains the nature of right in terms of harmony and measure, is now considered by scholars to be an original and innovative classification based on a synthesis of sources ranging from the Bolognese jurist Irnerius (1050–1125), founder of the tradition of medieval Roman law, to Brunetto Latini. It is not difficult to see how Dante may have arrived at such a position as a logical development of his belief, supported by the *Digest*, that right is one with the will of God, who created the world according to measure and *caritas*. On the other hand, the poet's focus on the common good as the end of the law is very similar to late medieval thought on politics and government, from John of Salisbury's *Policraticus* to Remigio de' Girolami's *De bono comuni*. Dante shared with these political thinkers a belief in the well-being of the *res publica* as the essential condition for achieving earthly happiness. Like Ptolemy of Lucca, he concluded, on the basis of what he considered to be historical evidence, that the Roman Empire had been the highest expression of right as this existed in the mind of God. If, as the actions of Rome's great heroes appeared to confirm, the Romans had put the state, the public good (the *res publica*), above all other goods, then their successes had to be considered victories achieved by right (*de iure*): "Patet igitur quod quicunque bonum rei publice intendit finem iuris intendit. Si ergo Romani bonum rei publice intenderunt, verum erit dicere finem iuris intendisse" (2.5.4) [Therefore if the Romans had the good of the community as their goal, it will be true to say that the achievement of right was their goal].

The Augustinian view that the Romans had ruled by force, invoked by those who in the thirteenth and fourteenth centuries opposed imperial rule in order to attack its legitimacy in favor of the pope and his allies, is thus overturned in *Monarchia* 2 on the basis of a careful "commentary" on history, historiography, and the philosophy of right. The shadow of Augustine, however, stretches also over book 3 of the treatise. Here, a reprise of Augustinian epistemological methods leads Dante further to criticize those that condemn the empire on the basis of Augustine's teachings on Rome and its imperial power. It is unsurprising that many of those who wrote against the empire in this manner at the start of the fourteenth century were, in fact, Augustinian Hermits. Giles of Rome,

James of Viterbo, and Augustinus Triumphus discussed key questions regarding the relationship between church and state, war, justice, ethics, virtue, and civic life interpreted through the lens provided by Augustine. It was these friars, who, focusing on the work of their spiritual leader, developed a full-fledged political theory according to which the pope, representing the *civitas caelestis* on earth, had absolute supremacy (*plenitudo potestatis*) over both secular and sacred affairs.[28]

AUGUSTINE, THE HIEROCRATS, AND THE BIBLE

Although book 3 is devoted to further proving that the emperor has a divine mandate, large parts of the last *quaestio* of the *Monarchia* focus on the definition of the nature of the authority of the church. The question of ecclesial authority is central to the definition of the theology of the church, but, as already mentioned, in the late Middle Ages, following the radicalization of papal claims with respect to the secular sphere, authority and jurisdiction had become major topics of political and scholastic debate. From the ninth century onward, the papacy had extended its temporal power and had developed arguments for the imposition of its authority by limiting the sovereignty of secular rulers. To do so, echoing Innocent III's bull *Per venerabilem* (1202), most supporters of papal supremacy maintained that the pope had inherited absolute authority directly from God, receiving ultimate power over both the temporal and the spiritual realms (what is commonly termed Petrine supremacy). In book 3, Dante holds a *disputatio* against those who believe that temporal power belongs to the pope. Decretalists aside, those who most concerned Dante were the papalists who based their belief in the absolute authority of the church on sources that Dante deemed authoritative and appropriate, namely, arguments "que quidem de Sacra Scriptura eliciunt et de quibusdam gestis tam summi pontificis quam ipsius imperatoris, nonnullum vero rationis indicium habere nituntur" (3.4.1) [which they draw from the holy Scriptures and from certain actions both of the supreme Pontiff and the Emperor himself; but they seek to have some support from reason on their side as well].

As *Monarchia* 3.3 makes clear, these "sons of the church" (3.3.8) employed the hermeneutic strategies of theologians and exegetes and developed a coherent ecclesiology based on reputable biblical, philosophical, and historical sources. Dante, nevertheless, challenges his opponents for their failure to interpret both authorial intention and the literal sense of the Bible correctly. In the poet's eyes, the papalists' ecclesiologies needed to be challenged given that their bad interpretive practices stretched the mystical sense of the Bible beyond what was plausible. To support his condemnation of their hermeneutic practices, Dante presents the types of exegetical errors that can affect the validity of an interpretation: "Advertendum quod circa sensum misticum dupliciter errare contingit: aut querendo ipsum ubi non est, aut accipiendo aliter quam accipi debeat" (3.4.6) [It must be borne in mind that one can make two kinds of error when dealing with the mystical sense: either looking for it where it does not exist, or taking it in some inadmissible way]. To back his understanding of proper hermeneutic procedures, Dante quotes Augustine:

> Propter primum dicit Augustinus in *Civitate Dei*: "Non omnia que gesta narrantur etiam significare aliquid putanda sunt, sed propter illa que aliquid significant etiam ea que nichil significant actexuntur. Solo vomere terra proscinditur; sed ut hoc fieri possit, etiam cetera aratri membra sunt necessaria." Propter secundum idem ait in *Doctrina Cristiana*, loquens de illo aliud in Scripturis sentire quam ille qui scripsit eas dicit, quod "ita fallitur ac si quisquam deserens viam eo tamen per girum pergeret quo via illa perducit." (3.4.7–8)

> [Augustine says in his *City of God*: "Of course one must not assume that all events narrated are symbolic; but those that lack such significance are interwoven in the interest of such as do possess it." As far as the second is concerned in *On Christian Doctrine*, he says, speaking of someone understanding something in Scripture differently from what the writer means, that "he is deceived in the same way as a man who wanders off the path by mistake and rambles in a circle."][29]

Dante's recourse to Augustine's views regarding the risks of bad reading and overinterpretation is of considerable significance for several reasons. First, even though the poet entertained a lifelong dialogue with the great theologian, he very rarely quoted his work directly. Direct quotations from the *Confessions* appear in *Convivio* (1.2.14 and 4.9),[30] whereas the *De civitate Dei* and the *De doctrina christiana* are mentioned only in the passage I am currently discussing. While in *Monarchia* 2 Dante engages with Augustine indirectly, through a subtle yet oblique citational strategy with respect to classical writings, in book 3 the great father of the church features prominently and for combative and polemical ends. As one might expect, the hierocrats, and especially the Augustinians, made extensive use of Augustine's *auctoritas* to support their theological views in their papalist treatises.[31] The highly apposite references to Augustine in the *Monarchia* intend to show that Dante, unlike Augustinian political thinkers, has not ignored the teachings of their spiritual father on biblical hermeneutics. Not only did Augustine often underline that evidence for the authority of the church must be found first and foremost in scripture,[32] but he also clearly set out the exegete's *vademecum* for the interpretation of scripture in the *De doctrina christiana* (in books 1–3). The guiding principle of Augustine's approach to exegesis is that, as long as they do not oppose the tenets of faith, all interpretations are acceptable (*De doctrina christiana* 3.27). At the same time, coherence and virtue are essential to understand scripture properly. Augustine also emphasizes correct motives in interpretation, which coincide with the rule of charity.[33] On the other hand, by explicitly addressing Augustine's epistemology, Dante acknowledges the authority of Augustine in the field of biblical exegesis after he has attacked his historiographical viewpoint. Not by chance, Augustine is the only name mentioned by the poet as an *auctoritas* in the field of theology.[34] More specifically, however, by appealing to Augustine, Dante probably wished to prove his expertise as a *biblicus*, an expert interpreter of scripture, in contrast to those hierocrats who forgot "not to take a literal form of speech as if it were figurative."[35] To illustrate how the papalist writers wrongly and often maliciously assign figurative meaning to scripture, Dante turns his *disputatio* into a different type of text: the biblical commentary. His commentary, however, also includes instructions for the reader on how to interpret the Bible in line with the tendency to didacticism that is strictly connected to Dante's prophetic vocation.

Dante considers one by one those passages of the Bible that he considers have been "abused" by the hierocrats and offers his own interpretation following, at least as far as he is concerned, Augustinian hermeneutics. Dante's approach to reading the Bible explains why the church felt so threatened by the *Monarchia*. In it, a layman, without formal training in theology, offers a series of literal, non-"allegorized," interpretations of the Bible that in most cases subvert not only the hierocrats' views but also traditional exegesis. Dante practices a literal reading of the sacred text that pays attention to the psychology of its characters and speakers, as well as to the *modus scribendi* of biblical authors. A good example of his procedure, which is both exegetical and polemical, is found in his treatment of one of the most common hierocratic arguments based on the biblical episode concerning the "two swords" in Luke's Gospel (22:35–38).[36] Dante sums up the papalist argument, bolstered by the *Unam sanctam*, Pope Bonifice VIII's bull of 1302 in which, *inter alia*, the poet asserts the pontiff's supreme divinely ordained power, quite neatly:

> Accipiunt etiam illud Luce quod Petrus dixit Cristo, cum ait "Ecce duo gladii hic"; et dicunt, quod per illos duos gladios duo predicta regimina intelliguntur, que quidem Petrus dixit esse ibi ubi erat, hoc est apud se; unde arguunt illa duo regimina secundum auctoritatem apud successorem Petri consistere. (3.9.1)

> [They also take those words spoken by Peter to Christ in Luke, when he says: "Behold, here are two swords"; and they maintain that by those two swords we are to understand the two powers mentioned earlier [temporal and spiritual]; and from this they argue that those two powers as far as their authority is concerned reside with Peter's successor.]

In the hands of the papalists, Luke 22:38 had become a key passage to explain the jurisdictional scope of the church's ministry, as well as a strong biblical argument in defense of the pope's *plenitudo potestatis*. Dante's literal explanation of the episode, instead, makes an interesting logical point: in the Bible, Christ refers to a sword for each apostle, namely, to twelve swords, while Peter's reply refers to two swords: "Ecce gladii duo hic" [Here are two swords]. This prompts Christ's rebuke: "Satis est" [It's enough]. Numerical precision, Dante comments, is not at the center of Jesus's message. Peter has misunderstood him. Peter's reaction, Dante says, was too fast and spontaneous, "festina et inpremeditata" (3.9.9). To reinforce his reading, the poet provides an acute analysis of

Peter's character as an impulsive, superficial, but passionate speaker. The list of episodes he analyzes to support this view is rather lengthy; however, Dante notes: "Iuvat quippe talia de archimandrita nostro in laudem sue puritatis continuasse, in quibus aperte deprehenditur quod, cum de duobus gladiis loquebatur, intentione simplici respondebat ad Cristum" (3.9.17) [It is helpful to have listed these episodes involving our Archimandrite in praise of his ingenuousness, for they show quite clearly that when he spoke of the two swords he was answering Christ with no deeper meaning in mind]. In following this exegetical procedure, Dante wants to show his readers how to interpret the Bible correctly by observing one of Augustine's rules on exegesis, a rule according to which "obscura ex locis apertioribus explicanda" (*De doctrina christiana* 3.26) [obscure passages are to be interpreted by those that are clearer]. This brings the poet-theologian to a daring conclusion: if we need to explain "Peter with Peter," that is to say, if Peter's behavior in Luke 22:38 is explained by Peter's character as it emerges in other sections of the Gospels, the number of the swords he brandishes in Luke 22:38 does not necessarily mean much, because the evangelical text shows how often Peter rambled on and misunderstood the spiritual meaning of Christ's messages.

Incidentally, Dante also highlights the shortcomings of the first pope, a fallible man who misunderstood the words of Christ and was blinded by his zeal, more or less like the current popes who, according to Dante, misinterpret the Bible through an excess of zeal. The point might be interpreted as an oblique commentary on the doctrine of papal infallibility, which, from the eleventh century onward, when it found a strong assertion in propositions 19 and 22 of the *Dictatus papae* (1073–85), had become a focal point in the church's battle for power and authority against the empire. In the early years of the fourteenth century, the debate on papal infallibility had been reignited and challenged from within the church during the conflict between Franciscan factions over the practice of absolute poverty, which the Spirituals saw approved in 1279 in Pope Nicholas III's bull *Exiit qui seminat*, but which the Conventuals and eventually Pope John XXII opposed. It is not difficult to see in Dante's reflections on Peter's passionate personality a commentary on the fallibility of papal interpretation of God's will, and therefore on the possibility, also voiced in *Purgatorio* 20.85–90, of, on the one hand, acknowledging that a pope might err, while, on the other, not denying the full authority of his office.

Universal Monarchy: The Title and Readers of the Treatise

Like the *Comedy*, the *Monarchia* is a hybrid. It is an all-inclusive text that attempts to bring together a variety of hermeneutic approaches to establish what, according to Dante, is the most important truth of all for the achievement of earthly happiness, namely, that the empire founded by Rome is a divinely ordained ontological necessity. In comparison to the wealth of texts concerning politics that emerged in the late thirteenth and early fourteenth centuries, Dante's treatise is very much an *unicum*; and its uniqueness is clearly announced in the title that Dante gave his work. The use of the term *monarchia* in the title is as distinctive as the rest of the text. The term never featured among the standard and repetitive terms, such as *imperium, principatum,* and *regimen*, normally employed by contemporary writers of political treatises.[37] The term *monarchia* had become familiar to Aristotelian scholars who, following the translation of Aristotle's *Nicomachean Ethics* and *Politics*, had started to discuss what makes for good or bad government and what factors are conducive to the preservation of a political constitution. In this context, the term had been used somewhat ambiguously, but, associated with other categories such as *regnum* [kingdom] or *civitas* [city], *monarchia* was generally used to refer to a type of constitution, a collection of fundamental principles that constituted the legal basis of a polity. In the thirteenth century, the word was used by jurists such as Andrea d'Isernia; and it is perhaps because of their influence that the term *monarchia*, once familiar in patristic writings, was used by polemicists engaged in the row between Pope Boniface VIII and Charles the Fair of France regarding their respective power. Interestingly, the term *monarcha* was used by none other than Boniface VIII himself in a letter to Albert I of Germany that he wrote in 1303 to gain his support against Charles IV. In this context, the term *monarchia* was generally deployed as a synonym for the Roman Empire.

This, of course, is the general meaning that Dante attributes to *monarchia* in his treatise: for him the Roman Empire coincides with the "universal monarchy." Nonetheless, his attempts to study the subject from a variety of different angles (philosophy, metaphysics, law, historiography, theology, hermeneutics) clearly shows a desire to demonstrate rigorously why a historical entity, the Roman Empire, is, per se, the best form of political constitution. Yet, for Dante, the monarchy is also a providential and eschatological entity. Thus, as far as he is concerned, the perfect human constitution reflects the will for peace and order decreed by God. The authority of the monarch, as stated by Gratian in his *Decretum*, derives directly from God. It is probably not a coincidence that Dante resorts to the rare concept of *monarchia divina*, namely, God as monarch, to affirm the necessity of the monarchy for the well-being of the world:

> Partes eius bene respondent ad ipsam per unum principium tantum . . . ergo et ipsa ad ipsum universum sive ad eius principem, qui Deus est et monarcha, simpliciter bene respondet per unum principium tantum, scilicet unicum principem. Ex quo sequitur monarchiam necessariam mundo ut bene sit. (1.7.2–3)

> [For its parts are well adapted to it in relation to a single principle . . . and so absolutely speaking it too is well adapted to the universe (or to its ruler, who is God and Monarch) in relation to a single principle, i.e. one ruler. And thus it follows that monarchy is necessary to the well-being of the world.]

Dante thus assigned the terms *monarchia* and *monarcha* to the Roman Empire, to the best constitution and best form of government, to God, and, of course, to the title of his work, thereby closing the circle of divine intervention in history through his own involvement as the prophet-philosopher of God's truth. Yet we would be wrong to think that his political analysis was intended just for those who would be saved on account of their faith and virtue. As Dante surprisingly claims, the *Monarchia* is also meant to educate those who do not share his belief in paradise, namely, pagans:

> Quod si contra veritatem ostensam de inparitate virium instetur, ut assolet, per victoriam David de Golia obtentam instantia refellatur; et si Gentiles aliud peterent, refellant ipsam per victoriam Herculis in Antheum. Stultum enim est valde vires quas Deus confortat, inferiores in pugile suspicari. (2.9.11)

[And if the usual objection should be urged against the truth I have shown (that opponents may be unevenly matched in strength), let the objection be refuted by the victory of David over Goliath; and if the pagans want a different example, let them refute it by the victory of Hercules against Antaeus. For it is very foolish to suppose that strength sustained by God in a champion might be unequal to the task.]

The address to the "gentiles," albeit hypothetical, suggests that Dante wished to address humanity as a whole, including those residing outside the boundaries of Christendom. That he intended for his message to reach everyone, or at least to be valid universally, is supported by the *Monarchia*'s fundamental claim that human beings, whatever their creed, are part of a *humana universitas*. This view is rooted in the philosophical *principium* that Dante establishes in the opening of *Monarchia* I: all humans, even pagans, as *Inferno* 4 makes clear, contribute to the achievement of human earthly perfection that is found in knowledge. The empire is necessary to establish universal peace, which is the prerequisite for bringing to fulfillment the intellectual and moral perfection of the whole of humanity. As Chiesa and Tabarroni note, the emperor is needed not only by Christians but also by everyone, including the "Asyani et Affricani."[38] These populations are juridical subjects even though, as Dante states, they do not accept the authority of the pope:

Quod vero ab aliquo imperatore non receperit, per ea que superius manifesta sunt patet sufficienter. Et quod etiam ab assensu omnium vel prevalentium non habuerit quis dubitat, cum non modo Asyani et Affricani omnes, quinetiam maior pars Europam colentium hoc aborreat? Fastidium etenim est in rebus manifestissimis probationes adducere. (3.14.7)

[But it is clear that if the Church gave itself that power, it did not have it before it gave it; and thus it would have given itself what it did not possess, which is impossible. That it did not receive it from some Emperor is sufficiently clear from what was proved earlier. And who can doubt that it did not receive it from the consent of all men or of the most exceptional among them, given that not only all Asians and

Africans, but also the greater part of those who live in Europe find the idea abhorrent? It is tedious to offer proofs in matters which are self-evident.]

Such universalism, which Dante probably owed to the study of the ancients, as well as to the knowledge disseminated by Italian merchants and missionary friars, is one of the most modern and powerful points of the *Monarchia*'s philosophical and political claims. So far Dante's address to non-Christian readers has gone unnoticed. Yet I consider this to be an important point of entry to understand not only Dante's political thought but also, and more interestingly, the openness of his worldview. Dante is generally defined as the poet of Christendom, writing for Christians. Yet his awareness of the political rights of pagans reveals him to be a universal thinker, a philosopher and not only a believer.

Civic Duties and Peacemaking

As well as contributing to the creation of political science as we know it today, the *Monarchia* created a model of civil engagement that, in the exaltation of the figure of Cicero, finds its pivotal point. The perennial quest for sources, quotations, and influences in the *Monarchia* has too often obscured the importance of the reemergence of the political persona of Cicero in the treatise. As studies on the medieval reception of Cicero have demonstrated, in the early Middle Ages Cicero had been portrayed as a sort of monastic scholar modeled on St. Jerome.[39] Even in the *Moralium dogma philosophorum*, a twelfth-century popular treatise on virtues and vices most probably known to Dante, Cicero is portrayed as a misogynist who advocates the avoidance of active life in favor of meditation and solitude. The study of Aristotle, however, modified the reception and perception of the ancient world and transformed the image of Cicero into that of a moral philosopher. As such he features, for example, in the *Summa theologiae* of Thomas Aquinas. Yet the Roman Cicero as a political and ethical thinker found his real admirers in Italy, where intellectuals were searching for viable and valuable examples of public engagement and proper citizenship to help sustain the existence of the new city-states.[40] Cicero was here understood as a Roman statesman who lived his life to serve the *res publica* and who wrote works whose aim was to create a culture and a practical philosophy for civic living. Although the facts of Cicero's political career remained unknown, his life became a model of the active intellectual worthy of veneration and imitation. Making an important contribution toward this change in the reception of Cicero, Dante's *Monarchia* too celebrates the active life right from its opening lines:

> Longe nanque ab offitio se esse non dubitet qui, publicis documentis imbutus, ad rem publicam aliquid afferre non curat; non enim est lignum, quod secus decursus aquarum fructificat in tempore suo, sed potius perniciosa vorago semper ingurgitans et nunquam ingurgitata refundens. Hec igitur sepe mecum recogitans, ne de infossi talenti culpa quandoque redarguar, publice utilitati non modo turgescere, quinymo fructificare desidero, et intemptatas ab aliis ostendere veritates. (1.1.2–3)

> [For the man who is steeped in the teachings which form our common heritage, yet has no interest in contributing something to the community, is failing in his duty: let him be in no doubt of that; for he is not "a tree planted by the rivers of water, that bringeth forth his fruit in due season," but rather a destructive whirlpool which forever swallows things down and never gives back what it has swallowed. Thinking often about these things, lest some day I be accused of burying my talent, I wish not just to put forth buds but to bear fruit for the benefit of all and to reveal truths that have not been attempted by others.]

Equally, echoes of Cicero's *De officis* reverberate throughout the first and second books. In a way, the humanists' later fascination with the Roman writer took shape in the works of classicizing intellectuals like Dante: his discovery of the classical world testified by the *Comedy* and the *Monarchia* was intimately tied to a strong ethics of participation in the active life. Cicero provided an ideal portrait for anyone who, like Dante, hoped to have an impact on earthly happiness. Yet, as the opening of the *Monarchia* clearly declares, placing his talent and knowledge at the service of the common good was for Dante also an apostolic duty. In his influential *Enarrationes in Psalmos*, Augustine identified the fruit brought about by the tree of life—Christ and/or the Holy Spirit—as the apostles who preach God's word to establish his law.[41] Dante claims for himself a similar apostolic duty, and to do so, as Aquinas's interpretation of Psalm 1 suggests, he expresses his feelings while "lifting his eyes to the entire state of the world and considering how some do well, while others fail. . . . They agree in happiness, which all seek; they differ in the way to happiness, and in the outcome, because some reach it, and others do not."[42]

From his first encounter with Beatrice, his personal bearer of beatitude, in the *Vita nova* (II.5[1.6]) to his discovery of the Aristotelian creed that "la scienza è ultima perfezione della nostra anima, nella quale sta la nostra ultima felicitade" (*Conv.* 1.1.1) [knowledge is the ultimate perfection of our soul, in which resides our ultimate happiness], seeking the way to happiness can perhaps be considered the hallmark of Dante's oeuvre. The *Monarchia* follows in this line of inquiry by developing the *Convivio*'s theory that earthly happiness (and intellectual perfection) can be achieved only if the world is at peace. Again, Dante had long searched for the principle of peace. Having found his personal source of peace in the Christ-like Beatrice,[43] he learned from his involvement in the political affairs of his city the precariousness of personal happiness in unstable political and social conditions often marked by conflict and violence. After seeing his *patria* stained by blood, and experiencing the tragedy of exile, Dante became an advocate for peace. In Florence, he had worked to pacify conflict between opposing factions. After his banishment in 1302, Dante soon rejected the logic of war and vengeance, and, in his *Epistle* 1, written in late winter 1304, he became the mouthpiece of his fellow Florentine exiles in supporting the peacemaking process undertaken by Cardinal Niccolò da Prato, who had been sent by Pope Benedict XI to bring order to Tuscany. In 1306 Dante represented Franceschino Malaspina, Lord of Castiglione del Terziere, in Sarzana, where he concluded a peace with the bishop of Luni. Yet the failure of many local initiatives, coupled to his renewed and broadening access to books, encouraged Dante to expand his political perspectives. Thus, when in 1310 the Emperor Henry VII descended into Italy to restore peace to the peninsula, Dante wrote his *Epistle* 7 to the princes and peoples of Italy inviting them to hail Henry as peacemaker and divine universal ruler.[44] To use Aquinas's words, the poet lifted "his eyes on the entire state of the world" and concluded that there could be no happiness where there was no universal peace. As Dante openly declares, the principle that guides the *Monarchia* is therefore peace taken as the most essential condition for life:[45]

> Unde manifestum est quod pax universalis est optimum eorum que ad nostram beatitudinem ordinantur. Hinc est quod pastoribus de sursum sonuit non divitie, non voluptates, non honores, non longitudo vite, non sanitas, non robur, non pulcritudo, sed pax; inquit enim celestis militia: "Gloria in altissimis Deo, et in terra pax hominibus bone voluntatis." Hinc etiam "Pax vobis" Salus hominum salutabat. . . . Ex hiis ergo que declarata sunt patet per quod melius, ymo per quod optime genus humanum pertingit ad opus proprium. Et per consequens visum est propinquissimum medium per quod itur in illud ad quod, velut in ultimum finem, omnia nostra opera ordinantur, quia est pax universalis, que pro principio rationum subsequentium supponatur. (1.4.2–5)

[Hence it is clear that universal peace is the best of those things which are ordained for our human happiness. That is why the message which rang out from on high to the shepherds was not wealth, nor pleasures, nor honours, not long life, nor health, nor strength, nor beauty, but peace; for the heavenly host said: "Glory to God on high, and on earth peace to men of good will." And that is why the Saviour of men used the greeting "Peace be with you." . . . From the arguments developed so far, it is clear what is the better, indeed the best, way of enabling mankind to engage in the activity proper to humanity; and consequently we see the most direct means of achieving the goal to which all our human actions are directed as to their final end. That means is universal peace, which is to be taken as the first principle for the arguments which follow.]

Dante's appeal was ignored; indeed, it is more correct to say that it remained largely unknown. This was largely due to the *Monarchia*'s very limited circulation, especially after the church condemned it, placing it in the *Index librorum proibitorum* in 1559. In truth, even in the fourteenth century, its circulation and impact remained marginal.[46] Dante's defense of a dying institution like the empire must have seemed at best naive and utopian, at worst conservative and obsolete. Dante's dream of universal peace, knowledge, and happiness continues to haunt those readers who, to this day, remain aware that the poet's "enemies" have never cared for such values.

Notes

1. The most authoritative proposal dates the *Monarchia* to the last years of Dante's life: 1317–18; for recent arguments in support of this dating, see Fenzi, "È la *Monarchia*." This view finds significant support in the reference to the *Paradiso* in *Mon.* 1.12.6: "sicut in Paradiso Comedie iam dixi" [as I have already said in the *Paradiso* of the *Comedy*]. However, it has recently been called into question by Quaglioni, who suggested that the *Monarchia* was probably composed in 1312–13, at the time of Henry VII of Luxembourg's descent into and campaign in Italy, since echoes of the legislation enacted in relation to these events can be found in Dante's text: Quaglioni ed., 843, further arguments at 844–60. Chiesa and Tabarroni, who have also recently edited the *Monarchia*, argue that it was composed in stages over a period of several years from 1312 to 1318: Chiesa and Tabarroni, "Introduzione," lx–lxvi. For the vast bibliography on *Monarchia*, see Chiesa and Tabarroni ed., lxxxvii–cxix.

2. "Est ergo temporalis Monarchia, quam dicunt 'Imperium,' unicus principatus et super omnes in tempore vel in hiis et super hiis que tempore mensurantur" (*Mon.* 1.2.2) [Temporal monarchy, then, which men call "empire," is a single sovereign authority set over all others in time, that is to say over all authorities that operate in those things and over those things which are measured by time].

3. Quaglioni ed., 875.

4. Unless otherwise noted, for translation of passages from the *Monarchia* I am quoting from Dante, *Monarchy*, Shaw ed. and trans.

5. On the originality of this attempt, see Chiesa and Tabarroni ed., 19.

6. The bibliography on the history of the conflict between the Holy Roman emperors and the medieval church is vast: Tierney, *Crisis*, is still a classic study. A recent companion on the medieval papacy provides a good introduction to many aspects of the church's conflict with the empire: Sisson and Larson, *Companion*.

7. The *accessus* is "the custom of medieval commentators on classical authors of prefixing to their works a *schema* generally called an accessus has long been known.... In such a prefatory note they treated of items such as the following: *vita auctoris, titulus operis, intentio scribentis, materia operis, utilitas*, and *cui parti philosophiae supponatur*"; Quain, "Medieval *accessus ad auctores*," 215. Late medieval scholars developed a form of *accessus* based on the four Aristotelian causes that helped to explain a subject: the material, the formal, the efficient, and the final. The formal cause (*causa formalis*) is the form that governs a particular thing or matter, or the genus to which it belongs.

8. The written *quaestio* was built around conflicting statements on a given issue raised by authoritative works, with each claim being illustrated by arguments in favor and against. Statements were supported with *auctoritates*, namely,

quotations from scripture, the fathers, and the philosophers. The *disputatio* or *quaestio disputata* was a classroom debate in which masters and students discussed various interpretations of a theory. For a general overview on these scholastic genres, see Bazán et al, *Questions disputées*.

9. In his *Trattatello*, Boccaccio maintained that Dante had participated in philosophical discussions at the University of Paris: Boccaccio, *Trattatello*, 1st red., Ricci ed., 25–26. It is likely that Dante received only a limited formal education. Anna Pegoretti analyzes Boccaccio's treatment of Dante's Parisian education in Pegoretti, "Curriculum del poeta-teologo."

10. For important observations regarding Dante's scientific method, see Chiesa and Tabarroni, "Introduzione," xxx–xxxiv.

11. See De Rijk, *"Logica modernorum."*

12. See, for example, *Mon.* 2.5.23 and 26; 2.9.11; 3.5.11; 3.7.4 and 8.

13. I quote here Cassell's translation of the *Monarchia*, since, in my view, it provides a more interesting rendition of the verb *phylosophamur* as used here by Dante than Shaw's, who translates the verb as "those things philosophy teaches us."

14. Miethke, "Practical Intentions of Scholasticism."

15. See, for example, Lambertini, "Tra etica e politica."

16. Thomas Aquinas, *Sententia libri metaphysicae* 1.1.1n4.

17. On this point and on the use of the expression in political literature, see Briguglia, *"Inquirere veritatem,"* 3–20. For more information on Bishop Tempier and the 1277 condemnations, see Cachey, chapter 8 of this book, the section "The *Status Quaestionis* on the *Questio.*"

18. Chiesa and Tabarroni, "Introduzione," lxxiv–lxxxiv.

19. See Barański, "Dante and Doctrine."

20. "Volo, inquit, fratres meos discipulos evangelicos esse sicque in notitia veritatis proficere, quod in simplicitatis puritate concrescant, ut simplicitatem columbinam a prudentia serpentina [see Matt. 1:16] non separent, quas Magister eximius ore suo benedicto coniunxit" (Bonaventure, *Legenda* 11.1, Menestò et al. ed.) ["I want my friars," he said, "to be disciples of the gospels and to progress in knowledge of the truth in such a way as to increase in pure simplicity without separating the simplicity of the dove from the wisdom of the serpent which our eminent Teacher joined together in a statement from his own blessed lips"]. The translation is from Bonaventure, *Soul's Journey into God*, trans. Cousins, 281.

21. Boccaccio, *Trattatello*, 1st red., Ricci ed., 195. The translation is from Boccaccio, Bruni, and Villani, *Earliest Lives of Dante*.

22. As Prue Shaw elegantly put it: "Dante now argues not just from principles to conclusions but from events to their meaning" ("Introduction," xviii). Chiesa and Tabarroni ed., 122, note this shift in relation to 2.8.3: "Egli esce qui dal piano della dimostrazione scientifica in senso stretto per passare su quello dell'interpretazione della storia" [He exits from the field of scientific demonstration to that of the interpretation of history].

23. Augustine, *De civitate Dei*, col. 89. Translation from Augustine, *City of God*, trans. Dods.

24. Clark, "Augustine's Virgil."

25. Dante's response to Augustine is similar to that of his contemporary Ptolemy of Lucca, who "was the first, both in the *De regimine* and in another treatise written some twenty years earlier, the *Determinatio compendiosa*, to attack the Augustinian verdict on Roman self-love [and to turn] Augustine's moral on its head. Starting from Augustine's references to Roman heroes, particularly in book 5, chapter 18 of the *City of God*, Ptolemy turned Augustine's moral on its head. He did not attack the great African father directly. Instead he demonstrated an obsequious respect, together with a shameless flair for misquotation" (Davis, "Ptolemy of Lucca," 33).

26. For more information on Dante and Cino, see Tavoni, chapter 6 of this book, the section "The Poets and the Language of *Sì*."

27. Quaglioni's edition and introduction to the *Monarchia* offer the best analysis of Dante's use of and relationship to contemporary legal thought. See also Menzinger, "Dante and the Law."

28. The three most significant treatises by Augustinian friars in defense of the pope's absolute supremacy were Giles of Rome, *De ecclesiastica potestate* (1302), James of Viterbo, *De regimine christiano* (1302), and Augustinus Triumphus, *Summa de potestate ecclesiastica* (completed by 1326). On these works and their ideology, see, for example, Wilks, *Problem of Sovereignty*. See also Barnes, "Historical and Political Writing"; Burns, *Cambridge History*; Kempshall, *Common Good*.

29. I quote here from Cassell's translation.

30. Dante also quotes Augustine's *De quantitate animae* in *Ep.* 13.80, if this is indeed by his hand.

31. Quoted at least twenty-six times, Augustine is the most cited authority after the Bible in Giles of Rome's treatise. As noted by Arquillière, *Agustinismo politico*, 49, Giles quoted Augustine and wrote in an Augustinian "style," but "Es evidente para San Agustín que todo poder procede de Dios así como la mayor dignidad de la Iglesia respecto del poder temporal por tener a su cargo las cosas divinas. Pero esta mayor dignidad de lo espiritual no supone que el poder temporal, cuyo origen divino nadie discute, derive del poder eclesiástico, proceda de la autoridad espiritual" [To Augustine all power derives from God, and the greater dignity of the church, in comparison to temporal power, derives from its dealings with divine matters. But this greater dignity of the church does not imply that temporal power, whose divine origins are never called into doubt, derives from ecclesiastical power and its spiritual authority].

32. Augustine, *De doctrina christiana* 2.9.14. See also *De civitate Dei* 11.3.

33. "Regula in figuratis locutionibus servanda proponitur. Sic eversa tyrannide cupiditatis caritas regnat iustissimis legibus dilectionis Dei propter Deum, sui et proximi propter Deum. Servabitur ergo in locutionibus figuratis regula

huiusmodi, ut tam diu versetur diligenti consideratione quod legitur, donec ad regnum caritatis interpretatio perducatur. Si autem hoc iam proprie sonat, nulla putetur figurata locutio" (*De doctrina christiana* 3.15.23) [The tyranny of lust being thus over-thrown, charity reigns through its supremely just laws of love to God for His own sake, and love to one's self and one's neighbor for God's sake. Accordingly, in regard to figurative expressions, a rule such as the following will be observed, to carefully turn over in our minds and meditate upon what we read till an interpretation be found that tends to establish the reign of love. Now, if when taken literally it at once gives a meaning of this kind, the expression is not to be considered figurative]. Translation from Augustine, *On Christian Doctrine*.

34. The relevance of Augustine's *De doctrina christiana* for Dante's understanding of theology is to be understood in light of the poet's belief that theology itself is to be identified with the study of the Bible and scriptural exegesis. See Barański, "Dante and Doctrine."

35. "Ne propriam quasi figuratam velimus accipere" (*De doctrina christiana* 3.10.14).

36. "Quando misi vos sine sacculo, et pera, et calceamentis, numquid aliquid defuit vobis? At illi dixerunt: Nihil. Dixit ergo eis: Sed nunc qui habet sacculum, tollat; similiter et peram: et qui non habet, vendat tunicam suam et emat gladium. Dico enim vobis, quoniam adhuc hoc quod scriptum est, oportet impleri in me: Et cum iniquis deputatus est. Etenim ea quae sunt de me finem habent." [And he said to them, "When I sent you out with no moneybag or knapsack or sandals, did you lack anything?" They said, "Nothing." He said to them, "But now let the one who has a moneybag take it, and likewise a knapsack. And let the one who has no sword sell his cloak and buy one. For I tell you that this scripture must be fulfilled in me: 'And he was numbered with the transgressors.' For what is written about me has its fulfillment." And they said, "Look, Lord, here are two swords." And he said to them, 'It is enough.'"].

37. Lambertini, "Usi di 'monarchia.'"

38. Chiesa and Tabarroni ed., 222n7.

39. On Cicero in the Middle Ages, see Herren, "Cicero *redivivus apud scurras*," and Ward, "What the Middle Ages Missed." As noted by Briguglia, the appropriation of the political Cicero starts with Brunetto Latini: Briguglia, "'Comun' di Cicerone."

40. Citations from Cicero's *De officis* were used by those, like the judge Albertano da Brescia, who, in his *De amore et dilectione Dei et proximi et aliarum rerum et de forma vite*, written ca. 1238, maintained that dedication to the active life was to be preferred to a contemplative existence. On the role of Cicero in the creation of civic humanism in Italy, see Baron, *In Search* and Garin, *Umanesimo italiano*. For more recent contributions, see Hankins, "'Baron Thesis'" and his edited collection *Renaissance Civic Humanism*.

41. Augustine, *Enarrationes in Psalmos*, col. 67.

42. "Elevantis oculos ad totum statum mundi, et considerantis quomodo quidam proficiunt, quidam deficient. . . . Conveniunt in beatitudine, quam omnes quaerunt; different autem in processu ad beatitudinem, et in eventu huius, quia quidam perveniunt, et quidam non" (Thomas Aquinas, *In psalmos Davidis expositio* 1.1). For the translation, see Thomas Aquinas, *Commentary on the Psalms*.

43. "Io sono a vedere lo principio de la pace" (Vn XXIII.8 [14.8]) [I am contemplating the fountainhead of peace].

44. For further discussion of Epistle 7, see Honess, chapter 4 of this book.

45. A few years later, Marsilius of Padua wrote the *Defensor pacis* (before 1324), a treatise that, like the *Monarchia*, invoked the independence of secular power from religious power as the means to ensure universal peace. On peace in Dante's thought, see Davis, "Remigio de' Girolami", Vasoli, "Pace." See also the essays on peace in Dante collected in Barnes and O'Connell, *War and Peace*.

46. Quaglioni ed., 809–28, offers a good synthesis of the early reception of the *Monarchia*. A detailed analysis of Guido Vernani's *Refutation of the "Monarchia" Composed by Dante* may be found in Cassell, *Monarchia Controversy*. See also Nardi, "Fortuna della *Monarchia*."

CHAPTER 8

Questio de aqua et terra

THEODORE J. CACHEY, JR.

The inner anxiety and the heavy, troubled awkwardness which attend every step of the unself-confident man, the man whose upbringing is inadequate, who does not know what application to make of his inner experience or how to objectify it in etiquette, the tortured and outcast man—it is these qualities which give the poem all its charm, all its drama, and they create its background, its psychological ground.
—Osip Mandelstam, *Conversation about Dante*

The three "other works" Dante wrote during the last fifteen years of his life in exile, years that were primarily dedicated to the composition of the *Commedia*, corresponded each in turn to vital commitments the poet had originally made in connection with the undertaking of the poem. In order to fully appreciate the arc of Dante's life and works, it is therefore important to consider these "other works" in relation to the political, literary-linguistic, and cosmological underpinnings of the poem. In fact, the *Monarchia* provided arguments in support of the poem's political theology, while the *Eclogues* offered a spirited defense of the poet's groundbreaking use of the vernacular language. In the *Questio de aqua et terra* [A question about the water and the land], the poet renewed his long-standing philosophical and poetic engagements with cosmology, a source of inspiration that traced its origins to as far back as the *Vita nova*. Yet, among the three late "other works," our understanding and appreciation of the *Questio* can be said to be still the most subject to further development. In fact, Dante studies have underestimated the importance of the cosmological dimensions of Dante's project when compared to its literary and political aspects. While these are easily translatable and understandable in modern and contemporary critical contexts, Dante's cosmology was based on the Ptolemaic system, which could not be more archaic and remote from us.[1] Certainly, important work on Dante's cosmology has been done, particularly regarding the poem, and especially in relation to the *Paradiso*, as well as to some other of Dante's works, including, for example, the *Rime petrose* and more recently the *Vita nova*.[2] Nevertheless, the *Questio* has remained at the margins, an awkward, even embarrassing "other work" that some Dante scholars might just as easily do without. Indeed, some have recently sought to exclude (yet again) the *Questio* from the canon of Dante's oeuvre.

Questions about whether Dante was the author of the *Questio* go back to the lack of any manuscripts of the treatise from before the *editio princeps*, which appeared in Venice in 1508, edited by the Augustinan friar Giovanni Benedetto Moncetti, a circumstance that led to debates during the nineteenth century about whether Dante wrote the *Questio*.[3] Nonetheless, the attribution of the *Questio* to Dante has been confirmed repeatedly in the history of the modern philological reconstruction of the canon of his works. The controversy peaked between the end of the nineteenth and the beginning of the twentieth century, when the attribution to Dante was confirmed thanks to important studies by Edward Moore, Ernesto Parodi, and Paget Toynbee;[4] and the *Questio*, edited by Ermenegildo Pistelli, entered the Edizione Nazionale of Dante's works directed by Michele Barbi in 1921. Dante's authorship of the work was subsequently cast into doubt by Bruno Nardi in an essay that is still considered fundamental for the understanding of Dante's cultural context if not for whether he wrote the *Questio*.[5] In fact, Francesco Mazzoni persuasively argued for the attribution to Dante against Nardi in his edition and commentary for the Ricciardi edition of Dante's works.[6]

Only recently have doubts about whether Dante wrote the *Questio* again been raised, encouraged by skepticism expressed by Marco Santagata in the edition of Dante's works he directed and in his best-selling life of Dante.[7] These doubts have been raised at the same time that three new editions of the *Questio* have appeared, all of whose editors accept the attribution of the work to Dante.[8] Indeed, it does not appear that anything substantially new has emerged from the recent debate in Italy about the attribution, except for a question that has been raised concerning a possibly anachronistic argument in a single passage.[9] While this question is still under review, it should be said that even if a single anachronistic argument were discovered, it would not be sufficient in and of itself to deny the attribution to Dante. One can, therefore, confidently share the opinion of the editor of the most authoritative recent edition of the work that "according to our current knowledge, the traditional attribution of the *Questio* to Dante Alighieri can be confirmed."[10]

There is little doubt that the lack of a stable interpretive collocation of the *Questio* has contributed to persistent doubts about its attribution. Some readers have found it difficult to accept the work as genuine because of received ideas about what constitutes the fundamental canon of Dante's works that, taken together with certain idioyncracies of the text that we address below, have tended to marginalize the *Questio*. Given this critical situation, if one hopes to achieve an appreciation of the *Questio* and its place in the poet's oeuvre, a good place to begin is by recognizing the continuity of the poet's engagement with cosmology from the beginning of his career. Indeed, the personal and autobiographical dimension of his investment in cosmology spoke to the heart of Dante's identity from the start. His understanding of the nature of the cosmos and his place in it was vital to his assertion of an authoritative status within his culture. His claim to be a divinely predestined poet represented a signature aspect of his authorial identity, which traced its origins back to the sources of Dante's being, that is to say, to his awareness of the providential nature of his existence and of his place in the world. Cosmology was no less central to Dante's project than were his political ideology and his linguistic and rhetorical commitments.

The *Questio* therefore offers an opportunity to reconsider and to reflect upon the poet's investments as a cosmographical authority or "cosmographos" (*Questio*, XIX [53]), as they had developed during the entire course of his poetic career, culminating in the final cantos of the *Paradiso*. More to the point, I want to suggest in this chapter that the *Questio* expresses certain anxieties of the poet about his place in the world, including his cultural authority and that of his poem. These anxieties were driven especially by his exiled status. In fact, the cosmological theme that was initially deployed by the poet as early as the *Vita nova* to address the epiphany of his encounter with Beatrice was subsequently developed under the pressures of exile starting in the late *Rime* and in the *Convivio*.[11] As an antidote to his exiled status, Dante began to develop in the *Convivio* the full-blown cosmological picture of the universe that he would develop further in the *Commedia*. In fact, in Dante's culminating literary response to the experience of exile, he manages poetically to reposition himself, as Curtius brilliantly expressed it, at the intersection of "the astrophysical cosmos of the structure of the world and . . . the metaphysical cosmos of the transcendent."[12] Yet, even as Dante was completing the final cantos of the *Paradiso*, at the point of transition between the end of his residence in Verona and his final move to Ravenna,[13] the apprehensions and anxieties of the exile reappeared symptomatically in the *Questio*, where Dante's bold, not to say overdetermined assertions of authority are shadowed by the author's inner sense of vulnerability.[14] In fact, the uncertainty of the biographers regarding the question of Dante's residence is symptomatic: it suggests an ineffable transition in the Florentine exile's irremediably itinerant existence, and an interpretive key for unlocking the deeper motivations of the work.

Dante's cosmology, no less than the political or linguistic-literary aspects of his poem, came under increasing pressure toward the end of the poet's life, during the time when he was completing the *Paradiso*. He would be called upon in the *Eclogues* to defend his use of the vernacular by an exponent of the emerging humanistic culture that was turning its back on the vernacular as a vehicle for authoritative literary expression;[15] and he had to justify the imperial political theology expressed by the poem in the *Monarchia*, at the same time that that ideology was coming under increasing attack.[16] A no less epochal shift in cosmology was taking place during the same period, involving both the heavens and the earth. I refer to the beginnings of the transition from an Aristotelian place-based cosmos to one that would be characterized by the emergence of early modern space. This shift was foreshadowed in philosophical terms by the bishop of Paris Etienne Tempier's Condemnation of 1277, which implicated, among its 219 prohibited teachings that were under discussion in the Faculty of Arts, important cosmological features of Aristotle's natural philosophy.[17] It was heralded in its terrestrial guise by the birth of the Atlantic age of exploration and discoveries between the end of the thirteenth and the beginning of the fourteenth century, and the revolution in the history of cartography that accompanied it.[18] Dante's awareness of these shifts in the history of space and place would inspire, on the one hand, his magnificent map of the cosmos in *Paradiso* 28.13–42, which has been likened to the "retroverse" or the "3-sphere" conception of the universe of modern-day physics, and, on the other, by his invention of the last voyage and shipwreck of Ulysses in *Inferno* 26, which seems to presage the new Atlantic age of the discoveries and explorations that was just getting underway.[19]

But most importantly, Dante's awareness of contemporary theoretical and cosmo-cartographic shifts in the history of space was focused by the experience of the exile who knew well "sì come sa di sale / lo pane altrui, e come è duro calle lo scendere e 'l salir per l'altrui scale" (*Par.* 17.58–60) [the bitter taste / of others' bread, how salt it is, and know / how hard a path it is for one who goes / descending and ascending others' stairs].[20] It was, in other words, intensified by the movements of the poet from place to place and from court to court, particularly during what proved to be the final transition during the last period of his life and works.[21] Dante felt the pressure of having to defend and consolidate his place in the world in the cosmological domain no less than he did on the linguistic and political fronts as he was finishing the poem, on the eve of his final move from Verona to Ravenna. The vital connection between the theme of cosmology and Dante's personal situation, and in particular his exiled status, can provide a key for appreciating the broader significance of the *Questio*, including the particular vulnerabilities that it expressed. This connection to his personal circumstances ultimately motivated the *Questio*, and it explains the work's awkwardness and its overdetermined aspects. In fact, everything that one really needs to know about Dante's cosmology is contained in the *Commedia*. The *Questio* can seem at one level to be a completely superfluous occasional work, written explicitly to preempt those who, driven by envy, might misrepresent the author's views "ut quereretur utrum aqua in sphere sua, hoc est in sua naturali circunferentia, in aliqua parte esset altior terra que emergit ab aquis, et quam communiter 'quartam habitabilem' appellamus" (*Questio* II [5]) [on the question whether water, in its own sphere, that is in its natural circumference, was in any part higher than the earth which emerges from the waters and which we commonly call the habitable quarter],[22] as he had expressed them orally in his "determination" [determinatio] of the matter held in Verona on January 20, 1320. Why bother? Indeed, the *Questio* appears to add little or nothing to the poet's oeuvre except as a manifestation of the author's edginess and susceptibility. Before addressing the viewpoints of other critics as to what motivated Dante to write the work, the next section will offer a further consideration of Dante's distinctive connection to cosmology and its self-authorizing role along the entire arc of his career.

Dante *Cosmographos*

Already before the exile Dante employed cosmology in his writings as a literary means of contextualizing and interpreting his life within a totalizing vision of the universe. Generally speaking, Dante's approach in his lyric poetry, and, as we have seen, in the *Vita nova*, is distinctive for the way in which it relates cosmological phenomena to autobiographical experience, in particular in relation to the disorienting and sometimes alienating subjective experience of love. Indeed, Claudio Giunta, in his commentary on the *Rime*, has observed that Dante's originality consisted "in the ability that only he has among writers of his time to put into relation . . . cosmology with the most important events of his private life, and to interpret these against the background of that cosmology."[23] This dimension of Dante's intellectual personality underwent an intensification following his exile, as demonstrated by the *Convivio*, which was explicitly undertaken to rehabilitate the author's reputation that had been seriously damaged by his banishment. Dante began to understand cosmology in relation to his existential circumstances in a new way. On the one hand, Dante displays his knowledge of cosmology in the *Convivio* in a relatively external and pedantic manner as a means of establishing his intellectual and cultural authority vis-à-vis his contemporaries, for example, in his accounts of the heavens, the angelic hierarchy, and their relation to the system of the arts and sciences in that work.[24]

More significant for the future direction of Dante's poetic project is the way in which his personal situation as an exile is directly implicated in the cosmological system that he describes in the *Convivio*. In fact, ultimate responsibility for the exile is attributed to the same "dispensator de l'universo" [the Overseer of the universe][25] who providentially inclined

Dante's soul via "universal nature" to the pursuit of knowledge and his own perfection, as stated in the *Convivio*'s first programmatic sentences: "Sì come dice lo Filosofo nel principio della Prima Filosofia, tutti li uomini naturalmente desiderano di sapere. La ragione di che puote essere [ed] è che ciascuna cosa, da providenza di prima natura impinta, è inclinabile alla sua propria perfezione"[26] (*Conv.* 1.1.1) [As the Philosopher states at the beginning of the First Philosophy, all human beings by nature desire to know. The reason for this is that each thing impelled by Nature's providence tends toward its own perfection]. The exiled Dante's personal pursuit of knowledge will subsequently take in the *Commedia* the form of a poetic exploration of the cosmos in the tradition of the twelfth-century Neoplatonic poets of the so-called School of Chartres, Alan of Lille and Bernardus Silvestris. However, the protagonist of the journey through the heavens will no longer be an allegorical figure such as Alan's Fronesis in the *Anticlaudianus* or Bernardus's Natura in *Cosmographia*, but a historical individual, Dante Alighieri, whose poem will serve as the means for overcoming the author's exiled status vis-à-vis both his contemporaries and the Creator.[27] In fact, Dante came to the conclusion that a philosophical approach to knowledge as pursued in the *Convivio* was inadequate to his purpose and that the genre of the cosmological poem represented the opportunity to pursue the truth by means that surpassed those of contemporary philosophers and theologians.[28] Indeed, as the author of a sacred cosmographical poem, "Al qual ha posto mano e cielo e terra" (*Par.* 25.2) [The work so shared by heaven and earth], Dante would make in the poem unprecedented claims for his special access to truth.[29]

The reason why Dante wrote the *Questio* becomes less of a mystery as soon as one begins to reflect on the vital importance of cosmology for the poet and the state of cosmological knowledge during the time that he was writing. Since the time of the *Convivio*, Dante had staked a large part of his reputation on the authority of his cosmological knowledge. In undertaking to write a cosmological poem in the epistemological mode of the twelfth-century Neoplatonic poet-cosmographers, he had significantly raised the stakes and, given the Aristotelian context in which he wrote, in a provocative manner. As mentioned above, cosmological thought at the time was in an unprecedented phase of development and renewal under the stimulus of the works of Aristotle and the commentary tradition associated with those works. Inquiry into the nature of the cosmos was in ferment, characterized by intense debates and controversies, to such an extent that a comprehensive model of the whole might have seemed unattainable; indeed, according to one authoritative historian of science, "No genuine cosmological synthesis was developed during the late Middle Ages."[30]

Yet Dante's *Commedia* stands out in contrast to this evolving cosmographical context. The intellectual debate surrounding cosmological questions had evidently stimulated Dante to pursue through poetry his own higher synthesis of the diverse elements that made up the contemporary cosmological picture.[31] Indeed, starting from the premises of the first sentences of the *Convivio*, to achieve a full understanding of the order of creation was for Dante tantamount to achieving knowledge of the Creator and of himself, including as a creative artist, which meant imitating nature, "che l'arte vostra quella, quanto pote / come 'l maestro fa 'l discente; / sì che vostr'arte a Dio quasi è nepote (*Inf.* 11.105–8) [and when it can, your art would follow nature / just as a pupil imitates his master; / so that your art is almost God's grandchild].[32] In the poem, Dante undertook to present as comprehensive and integrated a vision of the cosmos as was possible, thereby compensating for the lack of such a picture in the doctrinal contributions of the theological and philosophical masters.

At the same time that he was completing the *Paradiso*, which expressed Dante's culminating vision of the universe from the astronomical/astrological and metaphysical perspective of the heavens, the *Questio* offered the opportunity to recapitulate the poet's vision of the sublunary realm of the earth. It was a gesture not unrelated to the retrospective gaze that, from the eighth heaven of the fixed stars and his natal heaven of Gemini, the pilgrim twice casts upon "l'aiuola che ci fa tanto feroci" (*Par.* 22.151 and also *Par.* 27.86) [the little threshing floor that so incites our savagery]. As we will see, the *Questio*, in fact, stands in a complementary relation to the *Paradiso*, containing numerous points of contact, including verbal echoes, with the final cantos of the third canticle. It recapitulates cosmological notions that are vital for the poem and for the *Paradiso* concerning creation, the nature of prime matter, universal nature, and the influence of the heavens on the earth. The poem and the poet's exile were the pretexts for Dante's return to a philosophical and cosmological mode of discourse in the *Questio*, which also explains, as we will see, the awkwardness of this "other work." The poet's attempt to return to the philosophical-cosmological mode of the *Convivio* short-circuits, crossing the wires of a tendentious assertion of authority the poet claimed by virtue of the poem on the one hand, with the expression of continuing anxieties about the exile's social cultural status on the other.

The *Status Quaestionis* on the *Questio*

The awkwardness of the *Questio*, including whether the work's philosophical method and cosmological content are in contradiction with the poem, has represented a significant challenge for Dante scholarship since the third redaction of the commentary on the *Commedia* by Dante's son Pietro (1359–64). Glossing the cosmogonic account of Lucifer's fall given by the poet in *Inferno* 34, Pietro sought defensively to excuse his father's poetic fictions, distinguishing between the scientific treatment of the *Questio* and the mode in which the same matter is treated in the poem "in persona Virgilii transumptive et ficte" [in the mouth of Virgil, in a figural and poetic mode].[33] More recent Dante criticism has since that time made major progress in the editorial reconstruction and critical assessment of the work. Francesco Mazzoni argued convincingly for the attribution of the *Questio* to Dante but considered it to be a scientific palinode with respect to the poem. For Mazzoni, the *Questio* served as a corrective of certain aspects of the poem's account of the creation.[34] According to Giorgio Padoan, on the other hand, the treatise offers simply a scientific perspective on cosmological questions, in contrast to that of the *scriba Dei* of the poem, who wrote instead from the perspective of revealed truth. Far from retracting the bold cosmological discoveries of the poem, Dante sought to bolster the poem's authority by showing that he was perfectly conversant in the principles and methods of natural philosophy. In delineating the boundary between scientific and poetic forms of knowledge, according to Padoan, Dante was careful not to contradict the poem in the *Questio*.[35] For Zygmunt G. Barański, instead, Dante's ostentatious displays of Aristotelian knowledge and method in the treatise are pretexts for the treatise's far-reaching critique of the rationalist position in contemporary epistemological controversies between biblical exegetes and natural philosophers.[36]

My view of the *Questio* as the overdetermined expression of Dante's vulnerabilities about his cultural authority builds upon these critical perspectives but also departs from them. To begin with, Mazzoni's attribution of the work to Dante, taken together with the no less compelling (and more concise) argumentation of Moore, has represented a premise for subsequent critical studies.[37] My reading, in fact, builds on many of the same parallel passages to other works of Dante identified by Moore, in particular the *Convivio*, the *Commedia*, and the *Monarchia*. As we will see, cosmological passages across Dante's oeuvre bear Dante's highly distinctive signature and show a remarkable consistency and coherence. Mazzoni's notion of a palinodic relationship between poem and treatise has, however, proved to be unconvincing in the light of subsequent studies. Indeed, an assessment of recent scholarship reveals that putative points of contrast or contradiction between the *Questio* and the poem, regarding the account of Creation and the fall of the angels in *Paradiso* 29 and the fall of Lucifer in *Inferno* 34, are more apparent than real.[38] Moreover, it is highly unlikely that Dante's purpose in the *Questio* would have been intentionally to undermine the authority of the poem and to deny its truth status. On the contrary, as both Padoan and Barański have emphasized, it is important to note how careful Dante is to avoid areas of potential conflict between the poem and the treatise with regard to the respective purviews of the revealed truth of the poem on the one hand and the philosophical mode of inquiry of the treatise, which is explicitly limited to natural philosophy, on the other.[39] I will return to this point below.

Indeed, Padoan and Barański share the view that the *Questio* is in a complementary relation to the poem. For Barański, however, Padoan failed to recognize a putative *vis polemica* fundamentally informing the treatise. According to Barański, Dante is not respectfully deferring to the authority of the philosophers by adopting their point of view and methodology. Rather, he is setting them up for a devastating critique. The point of the *Questio*, in Barański's view, is to assert the superiority of the epistemological claims and *auctoritas* of the poet and of the poem vis-à-vis the natural philosophers. Barański's characterization of the treatise as a kind of rear-guard action designed polemically to reiterate and reinforce the epistemological claims made in the poem is by far the boldest interpretive intervention on the *Questio* to date. There is, indeed, little doubt that the *Question about the Water and the Land* served as a pretext for addressing preemptively eventual skepticism about the claims of the poem by Dante's contemporary Aristotelian interlocutors. Indeed, as we will see, he reprimands them for their presumption, just as he does the philosophers in the nearly contemporary late cantos of the *Paradiso*.

Yet both Padoan and Barański depended on a perhaps too narrow notion of the critical reception of the *Commedia* that Dante would have been responding to by writing the *Questio*. They anticipate a range of skeptical readers, who would have been diffident toward the poet's claim to be a *scriba Dei* or who might have had the kind of religious reservations that would eventually lead to the Dominicans' condemnation of the *Monarchia*.[40] Instead, the *Questio* responds to the exiled author's more generalized sense of vulnerability in sociopolitical and intellectual terms at the time he wrote it. As we will see in the next section, this authorial susceptibility specific to Dante is quite explicitly revealed by the framing introductory and concluding parts of the text. Moreover, one important and uncontroversial fact worth bearing in mind is that Dante authored the *Questio* before finishing the *Paradiso*. In this respect, the *Questio* is complementary to *Epistola* 13 addressed to Cangrande della Scala, under whose auspices the *Questio* was also composed. In effect, these two occasional "other works" can be seen to frame the anticipated publication of the final canticle. Both works represent pressured attempts by Dante to preempt and to control the contemporary reception of the soon-to-be-completed *Commedia*. Rather than simply a response to critiques of the parts of the poem that were already circulating, the *Questio* expresses Dante's sense of vulnerability at the highly sensitive and pressured time when the *Paradiso* was still to be completed and delivered to the public, on the eve of his decampment from Verona. Indeed, there are reasons to think that Dante may have departed the Ghibelline court of the Scaligeri under some duress.[41] Viewed from this perspective, the *Questio*'s eccentric rhetorical performance would express, not so much a self-possessed polemical response to contemporary skepticism about the poem and its author, as a stressed and preemptive reaction to the exile's vulnerable situation.

The "Truths" of the *Questio*

That the attribution of the *Questio* should have been disputed is remarkable when one considers how many of the text's salient features bear Dante's distinctive signature, starting with the highly individualized, not to say hyperbolic, nature of the text's assertions of authority. In undertaking to definitively resolve the relatively commonplace question of the form and the situation of the water and the land, Dante aims from the outset to put his personal stamp on the debate. The treatment throughout is highly personal, in keeping with an intellectual style that Moore first identified as distinctively Dantean, as demonstrated by numerous parallels with thoughts, forms of expression, and citations found in Dante's acknowledged other works. Dante's assertions of authority, moreover, in both the emphatic introductory and concluding sections and the work's argumentative climax, provide a revealing glimpse, in their overbearing rhetoric, of the anxious situation of the autodidact living in exile who was about to publish a poem that claimed to access truth in a manner that would transcend every other institutional discourse outside scripture. (In fact, Dante was about to present in *Paradiso* 29 his own version of Genesis that would vie with that of the Bible.)[42]

Nonetheless, from an institutional point of view, Dante did not possess the requisite sociopolitical and academic qualifications to intervene in the question of natural philosophy that was at issue in *Questio*. He did not have a formal education or a university degree. As Villani wrote of the poet Dante Alighieri, "This man was a great scholar in almost every branch of learning, although he was a layman [*laico*]," that is to say, according to the *Tesoro della lingua italiana delle origini* (*TLIO*, definition 4.1), "although he was a person of little culture."[43] The pressures surrounding the publication of the great cosmological poem find palpable expression in the tension between those elements of the introduction that express a transcendent sense of the author's authority and those that express an extreme sense of sociocultural vulnerability.

In fact, Dante describes himself at the outset as "inter vere philosophantes minumus" ([1]) [the least of true philosophizers], and the self-characterization represents a defining feature of the work; in fact, it can be said to be completed by his signature in the concluding paragraph of the treatise, where it is pointedly reiterated together with his name: "Determinata est hec phylosophia . . . per me Dantem Alagherium, philosophorum minimum" (XXIV [87]; my emphasis) [This philosophical question was decided . . . by me, Dante Alighieri, least of philosophers].[44] This invocation of the humility topos has occasioned some commentary, and Barański is no doubt correct in his observation that "to simply dismiss the phrase as a modesty topos is to do disservice to a poet who carefully weighed every word he wrote."[45] It is, indeed, a characteristic topic for Dante: for example, the *Convivio* both begins and ends with similar expressions of humility.[46] But the evident contrast between Dante's assertions of authority and his expressions of vulnerable humility invite interpretation. For Moore, it was almost as if Dante "sought to expiate by means of frequent expressions of humility the sin of pride for which he expected to spend extra time in Purgatory."[47] But there is also, I believe, an underlying psychological dimension to this characteristic theme of Dante's in relation to the *Questio* that reflects the awkward situation of an autodidact poet, self-conscious about his limited formal educational training, claiming an *auctoritas* that would exceed that of the philosophical *magistri*. It is not uncommon for highly intelligent people to have a strong sense of their own merit but at the same time to be insecure and as a sort of disclaimer humbly to proclaim their "ignorance." In fact, according to Barański, in light of "his limited formal educational training, it is more than understandable why Dante should have wanted to downplay his 'philosophizing' credentials." But Dante was unmistakeably affirming those credentials at the same time. In characterizing himself as "least among philosophizers [*philosophantes*]" at the beginning of the *Questio*, Dante alludes not so indirectly to his idiosyncratic and vulnerable intellectual and social status as an autodidact. But it is no less significant that by the end of the demonstration he will have self-promoted himself to the professional status of philosopher ("philosophorum," XXIV [87]).[48]

The chancery formula that Dante, "the least among philosophizers," uses to address the public at the start, "Universis et singulis" [To all and each] ([1]), is, indeed, incongruously emphatic and out of place in the context of a treatise ostensibly dedicated to a standard question of natural philosophy, to say nothing of the historical irony that the work remained virtually unknown until it was discovered and published at the beginning of the sixteenth century.[49] It is the same salutation used much more appropriately in the fifth epistle Dante addressed on the occasion of the descent of Emperor Henry VII "Universis et singulis Ytalie Regibus et Senatoribus alme Urbis" [To each and all of the kings of Italy and senators of the holy city]. The form of address, in fact, was typically utilized in "documents that were intended to have universal and patent value, such as decrees, testimonies, rulings or similar documents."[50] Similarly emphatic and, given the context, incongruous is the terminology that the author uses to characterize the exceptionally authoritative nature of his intervention: Dante's use of the verb *placuit* in the phrase "sed placuit de ipsa verum ostendere" (I [3]) [but determined to demonstrate the truth about it], presents his "determinatio" of the question of the position and the form of the water and the earth as no less than a final and unappealable decree. Indeed, the use of *placuit*, as Pastore Stocchi has noted, evokes a classical formula reserved for senatorial decrees that later became characteristic in documents communicating pontifical decisions made during councils and synods, and that were binding pronouncements of correct theological or canonical doctrine.[51]

The compulsive repetition of the word *truth* in various aspects and from various perspectives in the first few lines of the treatise represents a no less striking and characterizing self-authorizing gesture.[52] The author greets those who "shall inspect these letters," [presentes litteras inspecturis], in the name of Christ, who is "the beginning of truth and the light" [in Eo salutem qui est principium veritatis et lumen] ([1]), and informs them that because he had witnessed the question being discussed ineptly at Mantua "following appearance rather than truth," [ad apparentiam magis quam ad veritatem]; and that given that the author had since his youth been nurtured "in the love of truth" [in amore veritatis ex pueritia mea continue sim nutritus] (I [3]); for this reason he decided to undertake to "demonstrate the truth" [placuit de ipsa verum ostendere], for indeed he possessed equally a "love of truth" and a hatred of falsehood [tum veritatis amore, tum etiam odio falsitatis] (I [3]).[53] Accordingly, Dante undertakes the examination of the question at hand, starting with "the principle of the truth to be investigated" [tanquam ad principium investigande veritatis] (II [5]). What Gianfranco Contini, in a magisterial *lectura* on *Paradiso* 28 identified as a "parola fondamentale e rivelatrice" [a fundamental and revelatory word] in that canto,[54] that is, the repetition of the keyword *vero* and its derivatives, emerges here in the nearly contemporary scholastic cosmological treatise on the water and the land as an overdetermined and idiosyncratic verbal tic.[55] The theme of Dante's having been nurtured in the love of truth represents a variant on the opening of the *Convivio* discussed above ("All men naturally desire to know" [*Conv.* 1.1.1]), which also finds a parallel in the first sentence of the *Monarchia*: "Omnium hominum, quod amorem veritatis natura superior impressit" (*Mon.* 1.1.1) [For all men whom the Higher Nature has endowed with a love of truth]. But while in the *Convivio* and in the *Monarchia*, as Pastore Stocchi has noted in his commentary, Dante articulates an "abstract *sententia*," the opening of the *Questio* expresses "the forceful and proud testimony of an unequivocally personal experience."[56]

What is striking about the *Questio*'s deployment of characteristic Dantean themes in the salutation and in its first sentences is both their concentration in the small space of a few lines, their emphatically personal nature, and the fact that the claims that Dante makes at the outset for his authority are out of proportion in the context of a *disputatio* on a cosmological question of natural philosophy. These claims, which evidently derive to a large extent from his personal stake in the cosmological vision of the *Commedia*, come across as hyperbolic and overwrought in the context of the *Questio*. Yet they coincide with other elements present in the same introductory part of the *Questio* that express the author's strong sense of personal vulnerability, starting with his self-identification as Dante Alighieri "de Florentia" [from Florence]. Rather than use the straightforward adjective *florentinus*, Florentine, as in the *salutationes* of Epistles 3 ("To a Pistoian Exile"), 5 ("To the Princes and Peoples of Italy"), 6 ("To the Florentines"), and 7 ("To the Emperor Henry VII"), Dante identifies himself in the *Questio* in a manner similar to the bitter and prideful distancing of the epistle to Cangrande, where he famously describes himself as "florentinus natione non moribus" (*Ep.* XIII [1] and [28]) [Florentine by birth but not by mores].[57] In the *Questio*, according to Padoan, the Florentine exile signals that the city is for him "by now only a place of birth rather than a homeland."[58] Dante seems to underscore his estrangement from his *patria* and the virtually definitive nature of his exile status at this particular crossroads of the journey of his life and works.[59] In light of these signature passages of the *Questio* and the "Letter," Dante's poignant aspiration to return to Florence expressed in the more or less contemporary exordium of *Paradiso* 25.1–9 comes across as resigned, if not sardonic.[60]

We have already noted the close connection between Dante's exile and the theme of cosmology, that is, the way in which, from the time of the *Convivio*, Dante's investigation of the truth with regard to the functioning of the cosmos became inextricably bound up with his experience of exile. In setting aside the *Convivio*, the exiled author undertook the poetic cosmological Bildungsroman of the *Commedia*, a work that was designed to overcome the author's exile by reenvisioning the cosmos and

Dante's place in it, including his own central role in salvation history. Moreover, as we will see, the cosmological substance of the *Questio* reinforces key aspects of Dante's highly personal perspective on and investment in the functioning of the cosmos, particularly as regards the infallibility of the design of universal nature and of the influence of the stars on the sublunary world. In this respect, the *Questio* represents a conceptually redundant (and therefore overdetermined) reiteration of Dante's literary and cosmological solution to the existential challenge of exile that was initially undertaken by the *Convivio* and eventually resolved by the *Commedia*. The awkward redundancy of the *Questio*, however, is symptomatic of the fact that the literary solution of the poem that Dante was still in the process of completing was insufficient to address the continuing sociocultural alienation that the Florentine exile experienced in his everyday life at the end of his time in Verona. Dante's move away from the plurilingual and genre-mixing approach that is otherwise so characteristic of his oeuvre in the relatively formalized *Questio*, a text that largely adheres to generic expectations of the *disputatio ordinaria*, is suggestive of the depth of the crisis he was experiencing.[61]

Thus expressions of vulnerability, such as those regarding Dante's status as an exile and his lack of formal qualifications, contrast with the otherwise transcendent claims that Dante implicitly makes in the introductory and concluding paragraphs. The discrepancy introduces a subtle element of psychological tension into the exordium that emerges explicitly in Dante's preoccupation with his reputation and the integrity of his views, which he describes as vulnerable to the "livor multorum—qui, absentibus viris invidiosis mendatia confingere solent—post tergum bene dicta transmutent" (I [3]) [the spleen of the many who are wont to foist lies, in their absence, upon those they hate, should pervert, behind my back, what I had rightly uttered]. In fact, as we have seen, Dante somewhat incongruously attributes the original motivation for the *Questio* to his fear that "post tergum," behind his back, his views would be misrepresented. The remedy that presented itself to him is that "placuit insuper in hac cedula meis digitis exarata quod determinatum fuit a me relinquere, et formam totius disputationis calamo designare" (I [3]) [it is my further pleasure, in this attestation prepared by my own fingers, to leave a record of my conclusion, and to design with my pen the form of this whole disputation].

These worries about what might be said behind his back recall Dante the exile's lengthy anxiety-ridden explorations of the question of reputation in the *Convivio*; for example, in *Convivio* 1.4–8, where we are told that there are three reasons why someone's presence diminishes the good and the evil that is attributed to that person, whereas in the person's absence both are heightened.[62] Envy is one of these causes, which, while stimulated by one's presence, is at the same time restrained in its operation by the person being there and consequently works more virulently against someone who is absent. Nevertheless, Dante evokes in the *Questio* concerns regarding the integrity of his views and his reputation in a more directly personal way when compared to his general disquisition on the topic of reputation in book 1 of the *Convivio*. His greater sense of vulnerability seems also to be reflected in the emphatic overdetermined "signatory" aspects of the text, including the emphasis on the author's writing of the document in his own hand and even, arguably, the awkwardness of the double computation of the date in the document's last paragraph or colophon: "qui quidem dies fuit septimus a Ianuariis Idibus, et decimus tertius ante Kalendas Februarias" (XXIV [88]) [which day was the seventh from the Ides of January, and the fourteenth before the Kalends of February].[63]

Dante's mention of Mantua at the beginning, "existente me Mantue" (I [2]) [when I was in Mantua], represents an implicit allusion to the author's contingent itinerant status, while his staging the description of the triumphant setting of the *determinatio* in the *sacellum*, the small shrine, of St. Helena's in Verona in the work's conclusion has the effect of turning the *Questio* and the resolution of the philosophical question it treats into a kind of triumphant journey of return to and arrival at the Verona of Cangrande della Scala: "Determinata est hec philosophia dominante invicto domino Cane Grandi de Scala pro Imperio Sacro Sancto Romano . . . in inclyta urbe Verona, in sacello Helene gloriose" (XXIV [87]) [This philosophical question was decided under the lordship of the unconquered Lord Can Grande della Scala, Vicar of the Holy Roman Empire . . . in the illustrious city of Verona in the sanctuary of the glorious Helen]. But the susceptibilities of the exiled author vis-à-vis his contemporaries are evoked even in the triumphant conclusion. In this context, rather than expressing anxieties about those who would misrepresent his ideas and talk behind his back, Dante lashes out at those who did not deign to attend his lecture. In fact, the "determination" was given "coram universo clero Veronensi, preter quosdam qui, nimia caritate ardentes, aliorum rogamina non admittunt, et per humilitatis virtutem, Spiritus Sancti pauperes, ne aliorum excellentiam probare videantur, sermonibus eorum interesse refugiunt" (XXIV [87]) [in the presence of all the clergy of Verona, except certain persons who, burning with excess of charity, will not accept the invitations of others, and who, in the virtue of humility, poor pensioners of the Holy Spirit, lest they should seem to endorse the excellence of others, refuse to be present at their discourses]. Two different kinds of affront to Dante's status and proud sense of his place in the world are therefore highlighted and described in the introduction and in the conclusion of the work: those who would speak behind the poet's back in his absence and those who refused to be present at his discourse, as if to frame the *Questio* and to underscore for us its psychological grounding in the sociocultural and psychological susceptibilities, as Mandelstam put it, of "the unself-confident man."

Autobiographical Cosmology

A reading of the *Questio* through the lens of Dante's difficult existential situation on the eve of his final relocation from Verona to Ravenna and before he had finished the *Paradiso* diverges from the critical perspective of Padoan, who focused on the scholastic procedural aspects of the work, interpreting them primarily in relation to the poet Dante's efforts to demonstrate his credentials to a skeptical scientific community; and from Barański's on the work's polemical *vis* made explicit in the diatribe against those who would presume to seek knowledge that is beyond their capacity to know that emerges at the climax of the treatise. Both these readings tend to overlook the importance of cosmology for Dante as an antidote to the challenges of his existential situation, as well as his personal stake in the cosmological explanations that are central to the treatise. Indeed, the "question about the water and the land" resonated deeply with the spatial quandaries that the exiled Dante faced both theoretically and practically in the struggle to establish and maintain his place in the world. In particular, the final and efficient causes of the emergence of the land that are central to the treatise's argumentative structure reveal

Dante's bedrock faith in "Natura universalis" [universal nature] and in the "dispensator Deus gloriosus" [God, the glorious dispensator] as the forces that, ultimately, not only caused the land to emerge above the waters in the Northern Hemisphere but also elevated the *auctoritas* of the exiled poet, lifting him up to the heavens in the poem.[64]

Certainly Dante, "the least of philosophizers," wanted to demonstrate to his contemporaries that he was a competent scholastic philosopher, and critics have acknowledged and admired his facility in the scholastic idiom that he demonstrates in the syllogistic and formally argumentative sections of the text. After having referenced the discussion in Mantua that was left unresolved (I [2–3]) and having announced his intent to register the "determination" established by him (I [3]), Dante restates the terms of the question, namely, whether water in its own sphere was in any part higher than the land (II [4–5]). He then starts by enumerating, according to the conventions of the *disputatio* "genre," aspects of which he had already theorized and put into practice in the *Convivio*, the objections of those who opposed his point of view, that is, of those who would incorrectly argue in favor of the thesis of the greater elevation of the water with respect to the land (II [6]–VIII. [16]).[65] Moving on to the exposition of his own position, Dante announces the order of the treatment that will follow in five parts):

> In ostendendo sive determinando de situ et forma duorum elementorum, ut superius tangebatur, hic erit ordo: primo, demonstrabitur impossibile aquam in aliqua parte sue circumferentie altiorem esse hac terra emergente, sive detecta. Secundo, demonstrabitur terram hanc emergentem esse ubique altiorem totali superficie maris. Tertio, instabitur contra demonstrata et solvetur instantia. Quarto ostendetur causa finalis et effitiens huius elevationis, sive emergentie, terre. Quinto solvetur ad argumenta superius prenotata. (IX [17])

> [This will be the order. First, the impossibility of the water at any part of its circumference being loftier than this emergent or uncovered land will be demonstrated (chapters X [18]–XIII [29]). Secondly, it will be shown that the emergent land is everywhere loftier than the whole surface of the sea (chapters XIV [30]–[33]). Thirdly, a rejoinder will be urged against the conclusions established, and this

rejoinder will be refuted (XVI [34]–[41]). Fourthly, the final and efficient causes of this elevation or emergence of land will be shown (XVIII [43]–XXIII [78]). Fifthly, the arguments above noted will be answered (XXIII [79]–XXIV [88]).]

Like previous critics, I understand the syllogistic argumentation of the treatise, particularly of the first fourteen chapters, to reflect the layman Dante's desire to affirm his scientific qualifications in front of the contemporary learned community by speaking their language, as it were, just as he had at the beginning of his exile undertaken to rehabilitate his "scientific" reputation in the *Convivio*, albeit by more innovative and plurilingual means. This objective explains, I think, the repeated references to Aristotle; indeed, "Rideret Aristoteles si audiret" (XII [24]) [Aristotle would laugh to hear] the arguments of Dante's opponents in the *Questio*, a signature jibe used also in the *Convivio*.[66] From this perspective, the numerous citations of Aristotle throughout the text are perhaps more a symptom of Dante's insecurities about his professional status than a polemic gesture vis-à-vis the rationalist school that for Barański would be the target of Dante's critique.[67] They also serve to mask Dante's dependence on an array of more or less contemporary authorities on the question from which his own treatment largely derives. By not citing anyone other than Aristotle (and his commentator Avveroes), Dante is careful not to diminish in any way his personal authority.[68]

In the third section, according to Dante's breakdown of the order of the treatise (XVI [34]–XIX [58]), he discusses arguments contrary to those that he has proposed to show that the land is higher than the water and refutes them one by one. As Pastore Stocchi has noted, this section of the *Questio* does not respond to the arguments of Dante's opponents but rather records the phase in scholastic procedure in which "the validity of the conclusions reached [by the author] is tested by making explicit and resolving the internal dialectic of their reasons, as they presented themselves in the labor of the author's own thought."[69] Accordingly, this transitional passage leads to the key argumentative sections of the treatise in which the final and efficient causes of the emergence of the land are revealed, which are first traced to the need for a place in the cosmos that would enable the mixing of the elements, according to the intention of "universal nature":

[44] Propter quod sciendum est quod Natura universalis non frustatur suo fine; unde, licet natura particularis aliquando propter inobedientiam materie ab intento fine frustretur, Natura tamen universalis nullo modo potest a sua intentione deficere, cum Nature universali equaliter actus et potentia rerum—que possunt esse et non esse—subiaceat. [45] Sed intentio Nature universalis est ut omnes forme, que sunt in potentia materie prime, reducantur in actum, et secundum rationem spetiei sint in actu, ut materia prima secundum suam totalitatem, sit sub omni forma materiali, licet secundum partem sit sub omni privatione opposita, preter unam. [46] Nam cum omnes forme que sunt in potentia materie, idealiter sint in actu in Motore celi (ut dicit Comentator in De substantia orbis), si omnes iste forme non essent semper in actu, Motor celi deficeret ab integritate diffusionis sue bonitatis: quod non est dicendum. (XVIII [44]–[46])

[And therefore be it known that universal nature is not baulked of her goal. And so, though particular nature may be baulked of her intended goal by the recalcitrance of matter, yet universal nature can in no sort fail of her intention, since both the actuality and the potentiality of things which may be or not be, are equally subject to universal nature (44). But it is the intention of universal nature that all the forms which are within the potentiality of first matter should be reduced to actuality, and should be actualised in specific fashion, in order that first matter, in its totality, should be submitted to every material form, although in each of its parts it should be submitted to every opposite privation save one (45). For since all forms which are ideally within the potentiality of matter, are actualised in the mover of heaven, as the Commentator says in the *De Substantia Orbis*, if all these forms were not continuously actualised, the mover of heaven would fail of the complete diffusion of his excellence, which may not be uttered (46).]

Pastore Stocchi has drawn attention to Dante's "originality" and the "particular rigor" of his cosmological elucidation here, when compared to the anthropocentric account of Campanus of Novara (one of Dante's important precursors), who attributes the cause of the emergence of the land simply to God's need to create a place for mankind to flourish.[70] However, besides noting Dante's profounder cosmological engagement, which recalls the Aristotelian language and metaphors of his rewriting of the biblical Creation story in *Paradiso* 29, it is important to note Dante's personal investment in the theme of universal nature that "nullo modo potest a sua intentione deficere" [may not be baulked of her intended goal], which is evoked compulsively throughout his oeuvre.[71] One could say that the power of universal nature is the cosmological means upon which the faith of the "happy ending" of the *Commedia* is based, insofar as it represents the mechanism that will lead without fail to the ultimate redemption of the world. Moreover, the cosmological account of the mixing of the elements provides a cosmic analogy or source text for the poetic mixing or plurilingualism of the poem. Dante, the *deus artifex* of the poem, imitates God the Creator in his creation of the world as a place for the aggregation and "reduction to actuality" of all the elements.

As noted above, as far as his explanations of the causes of the emergent land are concerned, Dante states explicitly that he will restrict his research within the limits of natural philosophy: "Propter causam vero effitientem investigandam prenotandum est quod tractatus presens non est extra materiam naturalem, que est hic materia subiecta" (XX [60]) [But for the investigation of the efficient cause we must note in advance that the present treatise does not go beyond the scope of nature].[72] The restriction of the sphere of inquiry to that which is accessible to the scientific inquiry of human reason is noteworthy, since it implies that the question can also be considered "extra materiam naturalem," and we will address in a moment the question of how to interpret Dante's explicit demarcation of this boundary. Meanwhile, the efficient physical cause of the emergence of the land is sought in the influence of the heavens and, by process of elimination, is found to be located in the starry heaven of the eighth sphere. The virtue of the heaven of the fixed stars elevates the land as a magnet attracts iron, as well as by the force of vapors, which, attracted by the stars of that heaven, creates pressure in the internal cavities of the earth:

> et cum ista terra detecta extendatur a linea equinoctiali usque ad lineam quam describit polus zodiaci circa polum mundi, ut superius dictum est, manifestum est quod virtus elevans est illis stellis que sunt in regione celi istis duobus circulis contenta, sive elevet per modum

attractionis—ut magnes attrahit ferrum—sive per modum pulsionis, generando vapors pellentes, ut in particularibus montuositatibus. (XXI [73])

[And since the exposed land stretches from the equinoctial line to the line which the pole of the zodiac describes round the pole of the universe, as was said above, it is manifest that the lifting virtue is in those stars which are in the region of heaven contained between those two circles, whether it elevates it by way of attraction, as the magnet attracts iron, or by way of impulsion, by generating vapours that force it up, as in the case of special mountain ranges. (73)]

What should be emphasized, and what Dante does emphasize in the *Questio*, in a manner that has deep correspondences with the contemporary cosmological vision of *Paradiso*, is, on the one hand, the infallibility and inevitability of God's providential plan as it finds cosmological expression through universal nature, and, on the other, the power of the starry heavens and the constellations to raise up the land and to influence life on earth, just as universal nature and the stars have raised up Dante through the heavens and beyond in the poem. The personal cosmological implications of the providential power of universal nature and the influence of the starry heavens are what drive the *Questio* beneath the treatise's showy display of scholastic Aristotelian competence. It is in these passages that the *Questio* reflects Dante's uniquely personal investment in the cosmological vision of the *Paradiso*. His ascent through the heavens has the same inevitability, the same "exceptional" nature, as the emergence of the land by virtue of universal nature and the eighth heaven.

At this point, Dante answers the question of why the elevation of the land was not circular like the heavens but rather took the form of a half moon: "quod ideo non fuit circularis quaia materia non suffitiebat ad tantam elevationem" (XXI [74]) [because there was not sufficient matter for so great an elevation]. But he declines to explain why the elevation of the land occurred only in the Northern Hemisphere:

[75] Et ad hoc est dicendum, sicut dicit Philosophus in secundo De Celo, cum querit quare celum movetur ab oriente in occidens et non e converso: ibi enim dicit quod consimiles questiones vel a multa stul-

titia vel a multa presumptione procedunt, propterea quod sunt supra intellectum nostrum. [76] Et ideo dicendum ad hanc questionem, quod ille dispensator Deus gloriosus, qui dipensavit de situ polorum, de situ centri mundi, de distantia ultime circumferentie univesri a centro eius, et de aliis consimilibus, hec fecit tamquam melius, sicut et illa. Unde, cum dixit: "Congregentur aque in locum unum, et appareat arida," [Gen. 1:9] simul et virtuatum est celum ad agendum, et terra potentiata ad patiendum. [XXI [75]–[76]])

[To this we must answer according to what the Philosopher says in the Second *De Caelo*, when he asks why the heavens move from east to west, and not the other way. For there he says that such questions arise from great folly or from great presumption, because they transcend our intellect (75). And therefore, we must reply to this question that the great disposer, the glorious God, who made his dispositions concerning the position of the poles, the position of the centre of the universe, the distance of the extreme circumference of the universe from its centre, and other like things, ordained these, even as those, as was best. Wherefore when he said, "Let the waters be gathered together into one place and let the dry land appear," the heaven was at the same time endowed with virtue to act and the earth with potentiality to be acted on. (76)]

At this point, Dante rather abruptly interrupts the continuation of the inquiry with a *reprimendum* directed to those who would seek to know beyond the limits of human reason:

[77] Desinant ergo, desinant homines querere que supra eos sunt, et querant usque quo possunt, ut trahant se ad immortalia et divina pro posse, ac maiora se relinquant! Audiant amicum Iob dicentem: "nunquid vestigia Dei comprehendes, et Omnipotentem usque ad perfectionem reperies?" [Job 11:7]; audiant Psalmistam dicentem: "mirabilis facta est scientia tua ex me: confortata est, et non potero ad eam" [Psalm 138:6]; audiant Ysaiam dicentem: "quam distant celi a terra, tantum distant vie mee a viis vestris" [Isaiah 55:9];—loquebatur equidem in persona Dei ad hominem; audiant vocem Apostoli ad Romanos: "O altitude divitiarum scientie et sapientie Dei, quam

inconprehensibilia iudicia eius et investigabilis vie eius!" [Romans 11:33]; et denique audiant propriam Creatoris vocem dicentis: "quo ego vado, vos non potestis venire."[73] [78] et hec suffitiant ad inquisitionem intente veritatis. (XXII [77]–[78])

[Let men desist therefore, let them desist, from searching out things that are above them, and let them seek up to such point as they may, that they may draw themselves to immortal and divine things to their utmost power and may abandon things too great for them. Let them listen to the friend of Job, when he says: "Wilt thou understand the footprints of God, and search out the Almighty to perfection?" Let them listen to the Psalmist, when he says: "Thy knowledge is wonderful, and has comforted me, and I may not attain to it." Let them listen to Isaiah, when he says: "As far as the heavens are above the earth, so far are my ways above your ways"; for he was speaking in the person of God to man. Let them hearken to the voice of the apostle *Ad Romanos*: "Oh the height of the wealth, of the knowledge, and wisdom of God! how incomprehensible are his judgments and his ways are past finding out." And finally let them hearken to the proper voice of the Creator, when he says: "Whither I go, ye cannot come" (77). And let this suffice for the inquiry into the truth we set before us (78).]

The polemical exhortation marks the work's climax, and the transition to its denouement in the fifth and final part of the treatise, where the five theses of the adversaries evoked in the first section (II [6]–VIII [16]) are rapidly examined and refuted (XIII [79]–[86]), at which point the "determination" is concluded and the author returns to celebrate the authoritative setting and sponsorship of its presentation in the concluding sentences (XXIV [87]–[88]).

Cutting off the inquiry and establishing emphatically the limits of human knowledge at the work's climax are no less expressive of the author's potential vulnerabilities than those found in the introductory and concluding parts of the treatise that we discussed above.[74] Indeed, the key transition from the central cosmological argument of the treatise to its conclusion is characterized by a shifty anxiousness. Dante tendentiously misquotes Aristotle in order to justify his refusal to give a scientific explanation for why the land emerged only in the Northern Hemisphere and thereby manages to avoid other potential objections to his account, including biblical ones.[75] And of course, as many critics have observed, by short-circuiting the investigation precisely when he does, Dante manages to dodge potentially awkward comparisons that would embarrass his interpreters for centuries, beginning with his son Pietro, between the poem's mythical-poetic account of the fall of Satan and the *Questio*'s scientific treatment that "non est extra materiam naturalem."

We can conclude, therefore, that there is little doubt that Dante sought to establish a clear boundary between the investigations of natural philosophy and his own poetic-prophetic *auctoritas* in the poem and that he uses his signature polemical style in marking that boundary in the *Questio*.[76] But what Dante emphasizes in the *Questio* at the same time are the profound correspondences between the cosmological picture of the treatise and the poem that he was in the process of completing, by reinforcing signature aspects of his highly personal investment in the functioning of the cosmos. The highly formalized scholastic treatment of the *Questio* represented a redundant and overdetermined reiteration of Dante's cosmo-poetic response to the existential challenges of exile in the poem. The awkwardness of the work is symptomatic of the continuing sociocultural alienation that the Florentine exile was experiencing during what would prove to be his final transfer from Verona to Ravenna with the *Paradiso* still "in progress." At the heart of the *Questio*, and what constituted Dante's deepest motivation in writing it, was the author's personal stake in the cosmological vision of universal nature and the heaven of the fixed stars elevating the land as part of the providential plan of the "dispensator dell'universo" [the Overseer of the universe], for it was the same "dispensator" that had ordained Dante's exile,[77] and who was ultimately responsible no less inevitably and ineffably for lifting up the poet and guiding his redemptive journey through the heavens of the *Paradiso*, "a l'etterno dal tempo . . . / e di Fiorenza in popol giusto e sano" (*Par.* 31.38–39) [to eternity from time . . . / and to a people just and sane from Florence I came].

NOTES

This chapter is based on the lecture I gave in 2015 as part of the "Dante's Other Works" seminar series held at the University of Notre Dame. It is a thoroughly revised and updated version of Cachey, "Verità." I would like to thank Zyg

Barański, Simon Gilson, Giuseppe Ledda, Paolo Pellegrini, and Chiara Sbordoni for their comments on earlier drafts of this chapter and for their friendship and support.

1. Nevertheless, attempts have been made to establish an analogy or correspondence between Dante's cosmology and the model of the universe of contemporary physics. See Peterson, "Dante and the 3-Sphere"; Osserman, *Poetry of the Universe*; Egginton, "On Dante, Hyperspheres"; Barolini, "Dante and Reality"; and Freccero, *Dante's Cosmos*, who judiciously observes that "the correspondence may be somewhat exaggerated; yet it is undeniable that Dante imagined a finite but boundless cosmos just as cosmologists have ever since Einstein" (7).

2. Cosmology is an anachronistic category when applied to the Middle Ages. Accordingly, the entry in the *Enciclopedia dantesca* (Martinelli, "Cosmologia") consists of just a brief paragragh that cross-references articles by Capasso and Tabarroni, "Astrologia," "Astronomia," and "Cielo," and by Volpini, "Elemento," among others. For the *Paradiso*, see Martinez, "Guinizzellian Protocols," and Mazzotta, "Cosmology and the Kiss"; for the *Rime petrose*, see Durling and Martinez's landmark *Time and the Crystal*; and for the *Vita nova*, see the excellent Chisena, "Astronomia di Dante," as well as, for the *Commedia*, by the same author, "Miti astrali." On Dante and cosmology, see the recent Barsella, "Dante e la *machina mundi*," and Cachey, "Cosmology, Geography, and Cartography." Benchmark studies include Cornish, *Reading Dante's Stars*; Cristaldi, *Verso l'empireo*; Boyde and Russo, *Dante e la scienza*; Ghisalberti, "Cosmologia"; Stabile, "Cosmologia e teologia" and *Dante e la filosofia*; R. Kay, *Dante's Christian Astrology*; Murray, "Purgatory"; and the classic studies of Moore, "Astronomy of Dante" and "Geography of Dante," as well as Boyde, *Dante Phylomythes*.

3. References to the *Questio* that predate the sixteenth-century edition include Pietro Alighieri's in the third redaction of his commentary (*Comentum*; see below), and clear echoes of the treatise in passages of Jacopo Alighieri's *Dottrinale* (4.7–18; 37–42 and 45–54; see *Questio* XVIII [54–55]), as discussed recently by Canonico, "Sulla dimostrazione." Evidence of Jacopo's knowledge of his father's treatise, which is important for the attribution question, was noted at the beginning of the last century (*Quaestio*, Biagi ed., 63–65), but appears since then to have been largely forgotten. For the edition, see Padoan, "Moncetti." Giovanni Benedetto Moncetti da Castiglione Fiorentino, rector of the Augustinian order in Padua and a doctor of theology, discovered the *Questio* and had it printed by Manfredo Bonelli da Monferrato, with a dedicatory letter to Cardinal Ippolito d'Este. For the history of the attribution question, see Rinaldi, "Nota introduttiva," 663–70; and for the editorial history his "Nota al testo," 671–74. For accounts of the *querelle*, see also F. Mazzoni, "'*Questio*,'" and the concise and detailed interventions of Pellegrini, "Riso di Aristotele,' 'Sul testo."

4. Moore, "Genuineness of the *Quaestio*"; Parodi, "'*Quaestio*'"; Toynbee, "Dante and the 'Cursus.'"

5. Nardi, "Caduta di Lucifero."
6. F. Mazzoni, "Punto sulla *Questio*"; and see also Freccero's rebuttal of Nardi, "Satan's Fall."
7. Santagata did not include the *Questio* in the *Opere* of Dante that he directed ("Introduzione," xcix and cxxx n59); see also Santagata's brief treatment of the question in his biography of the poet, *Dante*, 300–301.
8. Pastore Stocchi (2012), Rinaldi (2016), and Caroti (2017).
9. Casadei, "Primi appunti" and "*If* XXXIV e *Pd* XXIX." Fioravanti has drawn attention for a possible anachronism in chapter VIII [16–18] (Roman numerals refer to chapters and arabic numbers refer to periods), which appear to reflect knowledge of a theory of John Buridan (1292–post 1358), for whom the earth had two centers, the *centrum magnitudinis* and the *centrum gravitatis* (Fioravanti, "Alberto di Sassonia," 94–97). But see the responses of Pellegrini, "Sul testo," and Rinaldi, "Note sulla *Questio*," and, most recently, Fioravanti, "Simplicio."
10. For a recapitulation of the history of the question of the attribution, see Rinaldi, "Nota introduttiva," especially 663–70: "Ritengo che, allo stato attuale delle nostre conoscenze la tradizionale atribuzione della *Questio* a Dante Alighieri possa essere confermata" (670).
11. The poet first resorted to cosmology in order to deal with the divinely ordained first encounter with Beatrice at the beginning of his ninth year, fixing his place in the cosmos by framing the encounter in relation to the circulation of the heavens (*Vn* II.1–2 [1.1–2]). For commentary on the cosmological background and the sources of Dante's cosmological knowledge before the exile, see Chisena, "Astronomia." In the *Rime*, the cosmological theme is developed, for example, in the great canzone of exile "Tre donne" [Three women], in which Dante's faith in the justice of his exilic perspective is rooted in the knowledge of the divinely predisposed cosmological cycle of the Nile river. See Martinez, "'Nasce il Nilo,'" 126–31: "The hopes for palingenesis scattered through the 'Tre Donne' rest on the implicit promise of the restorive power suggested by the cycle of the Nile" (131).
12. Curtius, *European Literature*, 366.
13. The biographers of the poet remain uncertain about whether Dante returned to Verona from Ravenna in early 1320 or if the public "determinatio" [determination] of the *Questio* (explicitly dated January 20, 1320 [*Questio*, XXIV [87]), took place in Verona at the end of his residence there, in other words, on the eve of his decampment to Ravenna. According to some recent studies (Santagata, *Dante*, 300–301; Casadei, "Dante tra Verona," 120–22), Dante was already in Ravenna in 1319; according to others, he arrived in Ravenna at the beginning of 1320 (Billanovich, "Tra Dante e Petrarcha," 16–17); Indizio, *Problemi di biografia dantesca*, 108–13; Inglese, *Vita di Dante*, 140–41).
14. I refer here to the author's vulnerability or susceptibility to physical, moral, and cultural harm vis-à-vis contemporary individuals, institutions, and

centers of power. Tylus (*Writing and Vulnerability*, 7–8) notes that minor genres are ideal for investigating authorial vulnerability as a literary cultural category.

15. See Lummus, chapter 9 of this book.

16. Cheneval, "Dante's *Monarchia*," and Coglievina, "Primi momenti della 'fortuna.'" For the *Monarchia*, including the controversies surrounding its dating, see Nasti, chapter 7 of this book.

17. The Condemnation was symptomatic of the tensions between natural philosophy and theology in Dante's time. For some historians of medieval science, Tempier's insistence on God's absolute power led to greater freedom of thought and creativity in the field of cosmological speculation. See Grant, "Condemnation of 1277." Others have challenged this view. See Bianchi, *Vescovo e i filosofi*.

18. On the cosmology of space and place between the medieval and early modern periods, see Casey, *Fate of Place*, especially part two: "From Place to Space," 75–132, Egginton, "On Dante, Hyperspheres," Grant, "Cosmology."

19. The 1291 expedition of two Genoese merchants, Vadino and Ugolino Vivaldi, beyond the Pillars of Hercules was the first known expedition in search of an ocean passage to India. For its possible connections to Dante, see Rogers, "Vivaldi Expedition"; for Dante and cartography of the Due-Trecento, see Cachey, "Cartographic Dante" and "Cosmographic Cartography."

20. Citations from the *Commedia* are from the site of the Società Dantesca Italiana (Petrocchi ed. and Mandelbaum trans., *Divine Comedy*).

21. "The question occurs to me—and quite seriously—how many sandals did Alighieri wear out in the course of his poetic work, wandering about on the goat paths of Italy?" (Mandel'shtam, "Conversation about Dante," 6).

22. Traces of a debate about this question are present in Italy during the Duecento among the intellectuals associated with the court of Frederick II, as witnessed by a chapter of Sydrach, *Libro di Sidrach* (272), titled "Lo re domanda: Quale è più alto la terra o il mare" [The king asks: What is higher the land or the sea]. The question first presented itself when the Aristotelian system of the cosmos and theory of place came into contact with the theological system of the patristic tradition based in the interpretation of the Bible. According to the Aristotelian system, the earth found its place within the surrounding sphere of the water, and that of the water was "contained" in turn by the spheres of air and of fire, "each in its own place" ("ciascuna nel suo luogo proprio" (Nardi, *Caduta di Lucifero*, 244). This vision of the cosmos had to be reconciled with the biblical account of the third day of Creation (Gen. 1:9), which suggested a clear separation of the land and water. Barański ("Segni della creazione," 209 and n18), notes that the question had long been a point of epistemological contention between biblical exegetes and rationalists. Moreover, from the perspective of the Aristotelian system itself, there was a need to account for the anomaly of the emergence of the inhabited land that should have been located beneath the water. All citations are from Rinaldi's edition of the *Questio*; the English trans-

lation used is the one by Wicksteed (occasionally silently modified for greater adherence to the original Latin).

23. Giunta, in his commentary on "Voi ch'intendendo il terzo ciel movete" [Oh you who move the third heaven by intellection] (*Convivio*, Fioravanti ed., 196), notes that, while the idea that the heavens and the angelic hierarchy had an influence on human life was commonplace during the Middle Ages, Dante's originality consisted "nella capacità che lui solo ha, tra gli scrittori del suo tempo, di mettere in rapporto questa cosmologia con gli avvenimenti più significativi della sua vita privata, e di leggere questi sullo sfondo di quella."

24. See especially *Conv.* 2.3.5 and 13–14.

25. "Ahi, piaciuto fosse al dispensatore dell'universo che la cagione della mia scusa mai non fosse stata! ché né altri contra me avria fallato, né io sofferto avria pena ingiustamente, pena, dico, d'essilio e di povertate" (*Conv.* 1.3.3–4) [Oh if only it had been pleasing to the Overseer of the universe that the cause for my self-justification had never been! For others would not have wronged me, nor would I have suffered unjust punishment—the punishment, that is, of exile and poverty]. For the English translation I have used Frisardi.

26. *Convivio*, Fioravanti ed., 95, notes that "La 'prima natura' con la sua 'providenza' è con tutta probabilità da identificare con la 'Natura universale,' che ordina la particolare a sua perfezione" [The "providence" of "prima natura" (first nature) is probably to be identified with "universal nature," which orients the particular to its perfection]. For Dante's concept of universal nature in the *Convivio*, see 1.7.9; 3.4.10; 4.9.2, 26.3; and see below for the role of universal nature in a crucial passage of the *Questio* XVIII [44–49].

27. Ariani, *Lux inaccessibilis*, 40. Ariani is one of the relatively few recent commentators to explore Dante's debts to the poetic and philosophical *auctores* of the so-called School of Chartres. See also Addivinola, "Aspetti della contemplazione"; Prandi, "Ad intuitum" and "Teologia come pittura"; Rossi, "Alain de Lille" and "Tradizione allegorica"; but see also classic studies such as Curtius, "Dante und Alanus"; Dronke, "Boethius, Alanus and Dante"; Wetherbee, *Platonism and Poetry*; and Witke, "River of Light."

28. For a corrective to the received idea of the essentially "philosophical" orientation of the *Convivio*, see Bianchi, chapter 10 of this book (especially the section "*Genus Philosophiae?*"), and Montemaggi, chapter 11 of this book.

29. Cachey, ". . . Alcuna cosa"; and see Hollander, "Al quale ha posto," for a cosmological gloss on *Par.* 25.2, to the effect that "the clay that wrote the *Commedia* has the name of Dante."

30. Grant, "Cosmology," 265.

31. Egginton ("On Dante, Hyperspheres," 213) captures well this context: "Dante wrote the *Divine Comedy* between 1306 and 1321, at a mid-point between the Condemnation and its eventual repeal, a time marked by the tension between Aristotelian hegemony and the prohibition against impinging on the omnipotence of God. It seems logical to imagine that such a time would

offer exciting possibilities to a poet of Dante's age, especially a poet whose immediate task is to write an imaginary journey from the physical to the theological world. In other words, Dante had to make explicit what many thinkers could disregard; he had to build a poetic bridge between worlds that had as yet not been made commensurable."

32. See S. Gilson, "Divine and Natural Artistry."
33. Pietro Alighieri, *Comentum*, 277.
34. See F. Mazzoni, "Introduzione," in particular 717–32.
35. See Padoan, "Introduzione."
36. Barański, "Segni della creazione."
37. See Moore, "Genuineness of the *Quaestio*," 303–74. See also the recent findings of Pellegrini ("Riso di Aristotele," 53–67) that reinforce the conclusions of Moore and Mazzoni as regards the attribution.
38. F. Mazzoni ("'Questio'") found *Inferno* 34 and the cosmology of the *Questio* to contradict one another. Gallarino (*Metafisica e cosmologia*, 54–62 and 131–32) finds reconcilable the account of *Inferno* 34 with the cosmology of the *Questio*. Pasquazi ("Sulla cosmogonia") makes the case against any significant contradiction. Bellomo ("Lucifero," 103) also found the texts compatible but from different perspectives, the poetic and the scientific. But for another point of view, that returns to positions of Nardi, see Casadei, "Primi appunti," and "*If* XXXIV e *Par* XXIX." Regarding putative contradictions between *Inferno* 34 and the *Questio*, see the judicious observations of Rinaldi, "Nota introduttiva," 664–65.
39. See *Questio* XX [60]: "Propter causam vero effitientem investigandam prenotandum est quod tractatus presens non est extra materiam naturalem, que est hic materia subiecta" [But for the investigation of the efficient cause we must note in advance that the present treatise does not go beyond the scope of nature].
40. See also the caveats of Bellomo, "Lucifer," 103.
41. Inglese (*Vita di Dante*, 141) notes that the poltical expediency of Dante's exit from Ghibelline Verona "is indirectly confimed by his involvement—involuntary and in some respects surreal—in the investigation of the witchcraft of the Visconti against Pope John XXII" [L'opportunità, per Dante, di allentare i rapporti con la *Pars Imperii* è indirettamente confermata dalla sua implicazione—del tutto involontaria, e, per certi aspetti surreale—nella vicenda dei sortilegi viscontei contro il papa]. The Milanese cleric Bartolomeo Cagnolato testified at the papal curia in Avignon on September 11, 1320, that Galeazzo Visconti (son of Matteo, the lord of Milan) had summoned Dante to Piacenza in order to commission him to cause by witchcraft the death of the pope. For the episode, see Biscaro, "Dante Alighieri." Billanovich ("Tra Dante e Petrarca," 27–28) believed that the well-known anecdote recounted by Petrarch (Petrarca, *Rerum memorandarum libri* 2.83, Billanovich ed.) describing Dante's "contuber-

nio ingrate" [thankless coexistence] with Cangrande and his courtiers reflected indirectly genuine testimony of the difficult time Dante experienced in Verona.

42. See Boitani, "Poetry and Poetics."

43. "Questi fue grande letterato quasi in ogni scienza, *tutto fosse laico*. . . . Questo Dante per lo suo savere fue alquanto presuntuoso e schifo e isdegnoso e quasi a guisa di filosofo mal grazioso non bene sapea conversare co' laici" (G. Villani, *Nuova cronica* 10.136) [This man was a great scholar in almost every branch of learning, although he was a layman. . . . This Dante was extremely presumptuous, haughty and disdainful due to his knowledge, so that almost like a graceless philosopher he was unable to have conversation with lay (uneducated) persons].

44. Barański ("'With Such Vigilance,'" 62–63) would alter the Wicksteed translation in the first passage cited here, to read "least among those who engage in intellectual activity," in light of the important research of Pegoretti ("Filosofanti"), who has established that *philosophans* could refer to "anyone involved in intellectual activity, and the designation was rarely used to distinguish between different groups of intellectuals or different intellectual traditions." I have here altered the translation to "philosophizers," however, so as not to lose completely the clearly *arriviste* inspiration of Dante's self-definition, as well as the significance of Dante's self-promotion to the secure status of philosopher at the conclusion of the "determination" of the *Questio* (XXIV [87]).

45. Barański, "'With Such Vigilance!,'" 62.

46. *Conv.* 1.1.10: "E io adunque, che non seggio alla beata mensa, ma, fuggito della pastura del vulgo, a' piedi di coloro che seggiono ricolgo di quello che da loro cade" [I therefore, who do not sit at the blessed meal, but, having fled the feeding ground of the common herd, gather at the feet of those who are seated, what falls from them]. Again, at the end of the *Convivio*, the author states that he will follow the example of the humble "good craftsman": "E questo intendo, non come buono fabricatore ma come seguitatore di quello, fare in questa parte" (*Conv.* 4.30.2) [And this is my intention (not as a good craftsman but as one who aspires to be one), in the part now under discussion].

47. Moore, "Genuineness of the *Quaestio*," 328.

48. For Dante's connections to the university faculty of the arts and medicine, in particular in connection with his astronomical and cosmological interests, see Tabarroni, "Ambienti culturali."

49. The observation is made by Pastore Stocchi ed., 28n1.

50. "Documenti che . . . s'intendeva avessero per tutti valore patente e universale di decreto, di attestato, di precetto e simili" (Pastore Stocchi ed., 28n1).

51. Pastore Stocchi ed., 226n3, also notes that in late medieval Latin *placuit* expresses the manifestation of divine will, and in this sense Dante uses it in the poem: "com'altrui piacque" (*Inf.* 26.141 and *Purg.* 1.133).

52. See Barański ("Segni della creazione"), in the section of his chapter titled "La verità della *Questio*," where he emphasizes the epistemological stakes

of the word *verità*. I adopt the plural "le verità" in the title of this section of the chapter to indicate a different critical perspective, focusing less on what the "truth" might mean for Dante than on the subjective psychological resonances of the repetition of the word six times in the space of the first two short paragraphs.

53. The denunciation of those who judge on the basis of appearance, such as those who discussed the question in Mantua "que dilatrata multotiens ad apparentiam magis quam ad veritatem" (I [2]) [many times fiercely debated following appearance rather than truth], is another signature theme of the author of the *Commedia*, which can be illustrated by any number of parallel passages, including Beatrice's nearly contemporary denunciation of the philosophers and theologians of the schools and their speculations about angels in *Paradiso* 29.85–87: "Voi non andate giù per un sentiero / filosofando: tanto vi trasporta / l'amor de l'apparenza e 'l suo pensiero!" [Below, you do not follow one sole path as you philosophize—your love of show and thought of it so carry you astray!]

54. Contini discovered that variations of the "truth" (*vero*) are strategically repeated four times as a leitmotiv, once within each of the four major movements of *Paradiso* 28, the canto in which Dante provides a map of the cosmos and reveals the "true" order of the angelic hierarchy (Contini, "Esempio di poesia dantesca").

55. Luca Azzetta, the recent editor of *Epistola XIII*, has called to my attention a similar insistence on "truth" in the contemporary letter to Cangrande, which was also written under the pressure of the future publication of the still-to-be-completed *Paradiso*: "Et post quam permisit hanc veritatem" (*Ep.* 13.24) [And having established this truth]; translation mine. In his commentary on the letter, Azzetta notes that the first three verses of the *Paradiso*, following the lengthy elucidation of paragraphs 53–56, are presented here without hesitation as "the truth" [hanc veritatem] (389).

56. Pastore Stocchi ed., 226n3: "una sententia astratta diventa ora testimonianza intensa e orgogliosa di una esperienza tutta personale."

57. For the controversies surrounding the attribution of this letter, see Honess, chapter 4 of this book.

58. Padoan ed., *De situ et forma*: "quasi a significare che Firenze gli è ormai solo luogo d'origine più che patria" (2n).

59. Pastore Stocchi ed., 224, highlights the connection between the "de Florentia" of the *Questio* and the "fiera e amara presa di distanza dalla città natia in Ep., XIII 1 e 28" [the proud and bitter distancing from the city of his birth in *Ep.* XIII 1 and 28].

60. *Par* 25.1–9: "Se mai continga che 'l poema sacro / al quale ha posto mano e cielo e terra, / sì che m'ha fatto per molti anni macro, / vinca la crudeltà che fuor mi serra / del bello ovile ov'io dormi' agnello, / nimico ai lupi che li danno guerra; / con altra voce omai, con altro vello / ritornerò poeta, e in sul fonte / del mio battesmo prenderò 'l cappello" [If it should happen . . . If this

sacred poem— / this work so shared by heaven and by earth / that it has made me lean through these long years— / can ever overcome the cruelty / that bars me from the fair fold where I slept, a lamb opposed to wolves that war on it, / by then with other voice, / with other fleece, / I shall return as poet and put on/ at my baptismal font, the laurel crown]. For an overview of the critical disagreement about whether Dante presents himself here as vigorous in his hope for laureation or skeptical about its likelihood, see Hollander's *Paradiso* commentary, 668–69. But for a new perspective of the exordium of *Paradiso* 25, see Lummus, chapter 9 of this book, the section "Dante's Laurel Crown."

61. For discussion of the *disputatio ordinaria* and the distinction between the *disputatio ordinaria* and the *disputatio quodlibetalis*, see Dell'Oso, "How Dante Became Dante," 12–15 and n36. The disputation was often divided into two sessions. In the first, arguments for a given thesis were presented and in a preliminary way, clarified and determined by a student under the supervison of the master. Dante's *Questio* largely corresponds to the expectations for the second session of a disputed question during "which the master himself would make the determination, give his answer and respond to all the opposing arguments" (Sweeney, "Literary Forms," 2.6). For the culture and forms of medieval disputation, see Bazán et al., "Questions disputées"; Glorieux, *Litterature quodlibétique*; Novikoff, *Medieval Culture*; and Schabel, *Theological Quodlibeta*.

62. Moore ("Genuineness of the *Quaestio*," 330–31) had already noted that the theme of envy connected the *Convivio* (1.4) and the *Questio*.

63. See Pastore Stocchi ed., 275, and Rinaldi ed., 751, for numerological explanations of earlier scholars that would account for the redundant manner in which Dante gives the date.

64. The relationship between the *Questio* and the cosmological underpinnings of the poem represents, generally speaking, a still underdeveloped area of research. See for an example of interesting recent developments in this direction: Sarti, "Dante."

65. On *disputatio* in the *Convivio*, see *Conv*. 4.2.15: "Ché prima si ripruova lo falso, e poi si tratta lo vero. . . . Però è da sapere che, tutto che e all'uno e all'altro s'intenda, al trattare lo vero s'intende principalmente; a riprovare lo falso s'intende in tanto in quanto la veritate meglio si fa apparire" [The false is refuted first and then the true is addressed. However, we should keep in mind that although both are intended, the main intention is to attend to the true; attention is given to refuting the false only so that the true may be made more prominent]. For a nuanced account of the *Questio*'s general conformance to the argumentative standards of the academic question or *quaestio*, "come genere letterario, l'espressione, anche se nella fattispecie largamente approssimativa, ci sia consentita per semplicità" [as a literary genre, although in this case the use of the term is fairly approximate for the sake of simplicity], see Pastore Stocchi, "*Quaestio*." For a summary-outline of the treatise, see Rinaldi ed., 688–91.

66. *Conv.* 4.15.6: "Sanza dubio forte riderebbe Aristotile udendo fare spezie due dell'umana generazione" [And without a doubt Aristotle would have a good laugh hearing that the human race has two species].

67. Barański ("Segni della creazione," 206) identifies seventeen citations and allusions to the Philosopher and his works in the *Questio*, noting that in "the apparently rationalist treatise, the name of Aristotle, the supreme authority of the rationalist school, is not correlated as is Dante's to truth" [in questo trattato apparentemente razionalista, il nome di Aristotele, la suprema 'autorità' della scuola razionalista, non è parimenti correlato alla *veritas*].

68. Padoan, "Causa, struttura," 172. F. Mazzoni ed., 709–10, did not discover in the *Questio* any ideas or opinions that do not find correspondence in another earlier or contemporary author, whether regarding the concentricity of the spheres (Giles of Rome and Campanus of Novara), the final cause of the emergence of the lands and the theory of universal nature (Michael Scot, Roger Bacon, Campanus of Novara, Bernard of Trille, Pietro d'Abano, Giles of Rome, Cecco d'Ascoli), or the eighth Heaven of the Fixed Stars as the efficient cause of the emergence of the land (Ristoro d'Arezzo, Pietro d'Abano).

69. Pastore Stocchi, "*Quaestio*," 763: "in cui la validità delle conclusioni raggiunte è saggiata esplicitando e risolvendo le istanze dialettiche interne, quali si sono presentate nel travaglio del pensiero dell'autore stesso."

70. Pastore Stocchi ed., 256n48, calls attention to Dante's personal investement in the theme and speaks of his "profonda originalità nel peculiare rigore dell'esposizione."

71. On the Creation story in the *Paradiso*, see Boitani, "Poetry and Poetics," 125: "It [the *Commedia*] is not simply the journey through the three realms, or Virgil, Beatrice, and the various characters encountered that comprise the *fabulae* and *mythoi*, but also, for us, Dante's system of logic and philosophical lexis, underpinning both the individual passages and the whole structure of the poem." On universal nature, see note 26 above. See also *Conv.* 4.9.2: "Ché se prendere volemo la natura universale di tutto, tanto ha giurisdizione quanto tutto lo mondo, dico lo cielo e la terra, si stende" [For when we consider the jurisdiction of universal nature of all things, we see that it extends throughout creation, by which I mean both heaven and earth]; *Conv.* 3.4.12: "Ancora: è posto fine al nostro ingegno in ciascuna sua operazione, non da noi ma dall'universale natura" [Furthermore, a limit is placed on our ability, in each of its operations not by us but by universal nature]. And compare *Mon.* 1.10.1; 2.3; *Par.* 1.127–29; 8.100–14: "'E non pur le nature provedute / sono in la mente ch'è da sé perfetta, / ma esse insieme con la lor salute / . . . / Vuo' tu che questo ver più ti s'imbianchi?'. / E io: 'Non già; ché impossibil veggio / che la natura, in quel ch'è uopo, stanchi'" ["And in the mind that, in itself, is perfect, / not only are the natures of his creatures / but their well-being provided for; / and thus, whatever his bow shoots must fall / according to a providential end / . . . / Would you have this

truth still more clear to you?"/ I: "No. I see it is impossible for nature to fall short of what is needed"].

72. *Questio* XX [60].

73. Barański, "Segni della creazione," 211, notes that the citation from John's Gospel is the only one of the five biblical references in the passage not to be explicitly associated with a book of the Bible and that it would be best not to associate the "voice of the Creator" with any one of the three possible sources in the passages in John's Gospel [John 7:34; 8:21; 13:33]: "È probabile che le parole di Giovanni abbiano assunto lo *status* di un testo divino semi-indipendente" [It is likely that the words of John had assumed in the Middle Ages the status of a divine statement that was semi-independent].

74. For another reading of this climactic passage in terms of the epistemological debate between biblical exegetes and the "rationalists," see Barański, "Segni della creazione," especially 209–19.

75. Pastore Stocchi ed., 268n75, notes that Aristotle, in the passage cited by Dante (*On the Heavens* 287b, 162–64: "Why does the heaven revolve in one direction rather than the other?"), after having acknowledged that the question might be considered "trivial" or "difficult," concludes nevertheless that "it is better to state what is likely rather than to give up altogether" and goes ahead to offer a hypothesis. According to Pastore Stocchi ed., 269n76, the argument here becomes "sketchy and even evasive." Dante might have found himself in difficulty given the fact that the heavens, according to the account of Genesis, were created on the fourth day while the waters were separated from the land on the third. How could the heavens have caused the emergence of the land above the water?

76. See *Purg.* 3.37–39: "State contenti, umana gente, al quia; / ché, se potuto aveste veder tutto, / mestier non era parturir Maria" [Confine yourselves, o humans, to the *quia*; / had you been able to see all, there would / have been no need for Mary to give birth]. The resonance of the passage from the *Purgatorio* with the one in the *Questio* is highlighted by many modern commentators. But see also *Par.* 19.79–90.

77. See *Conv.* 1.3.3–4, and see note 26 above.

CHAPTER 9

Egloge

DAVID G. LUMMUS

Theocritus syragusanus poeta . . . primus fuit qui greco carmine buccolicum excogitavit stilum. . . . Post hunc latine scripsit Virgilius. . . . Post hunc scripserunt et alii, sed ignobiles, de quibus nil curandum est, excepto inclito preceptore meo Francisco Petrarca.

[The Syracusan poet Theocritus was the first to devise the bucolic style in Greek song. . . . After him Virgil wrote in Latin. . . . After him, other poets wrote, but they are lowly and obscure and we should not concern ourselves with them, except for my famous teacher, Francesco Petrarca.]

—Giovanni Boccaccio to Martino da Signa, 1372–74 (*Epistole* 23.1)

Dante's poetic correspondence with Giovanni del Virgilio, his final two poetic compositions and his only Latin poems, represents one of the most enigmatic moments of Dante's poetic career and one of the most understudied of Dante's works. Already in Boccaccio's brief account of the history of bucolic poetry, Dante's two eclogues are elided, along with other late antique and medieval efforts at reviving the genre.[1] Boccaccio's term *ignobiles*, which here includes Dante, contrasts not with Virgil, however, but with Petrarch. The absent Dante is here the vernacular poet, whose style is lowly and whose fame has not yet brought him to Parnassus. Boccaccio may be indicating with this elision Dante's marked refusal to participate in that Latin Parnassus in the *Egloge*, in which he adeptly defends his vernacular poem and refuses the invitation to write a Latin poem that would win him the laurel crown in Bologna.

Composed between 1320 and 1321, Dante's two eclogues written in response to a metrical letter sent from Bologna by Giovanni del Virgilio to Dante in Ravenna have long been recognized as important for understanding Dante's engagement with municipal concerns at the end of his life and his stance on the *Commedia* at the time of its completion. They can be seen as ad hoc compositions written on the occasion of an unexpected correspondence, but also as a defense of the poetic program of the *Commedia*. They are linked especially with the final cantos of the *Paradiso*, which Dante completed in the same period. These views are not mutually exclusive. Indeed, they both indicate the biographical nature of the poems as a form of self-commentary to which we are accustomed as readers of Dante. Uniquely in Dante's oeuvre, however, the *Egloge* show Dante's direct engagement with a Latin humanistic culture prominent in northern Italy, especially Bologna and Padua. From this biographical perspective, the *Egloge* can be seen as a programmatic manifesto of Dante's poetics instigated by an unexpected provocation. As such, they shed light on Dante's view of himself as a poet and of his aspirations for the *Commedia*.

The *Egloge* as they have been transmitted to us are not a book or a work, although perhaps they could have been, had Dante lived long enough to compose another eight of them.[2] As texts, they are the record of an event that necessarily includes Giovanni del Virgilio's initial metrical letter and eclogue response, forming a total of four compositions, only three of which are eclogues. The text of the *Egloge* is transmitted by eight principal codices from the fourteenth and fifteenth centuries, the oldest of which is Boccaccio's *Zibaldone Laurenziano* (MS BML Pluteo XXIX 8), an autograph notebook of miscellaneous texts. Boccaccio's copy of the four compositions includes glosses by one or more commentators linked with the Emilia-Romagna area in which the exchange took place. The glosses seek to decode the pastoral cypher of names and terms used by Dante and del Virgilio, making possible the identification of historical referents within the text, but leaving unresolved several questions of identification and interpretation.[3]

Recent work on the *Egloge* has sought to root the compositions in the intellectual, political, and urban contexts of Bologna and Ravenna, especially regarding their reception in fourteenth-century Bologna. Three recent critical editions have provided renewed versions and Italian translations of the text and explanatory notes that take advantage of new documentary evidence in explicating some of the more difficult interpretative problems of the poems.[4] Gabriella Albanese and Paolo Pontari have presented convincing evidence, for example, that Giovanni del Virgilio's appointment as a publicly salaried professor of poetry and versification in Bologna was a direct result of his correspondence with Dante, and they have found archival documentation for Dante's circle of friends and admirers in Ravenna.[5] Marco Petoletti's recent work on the *Egloge* has focused instead on the philological questions surrounding the material transmission of the text and on the context of Dante's earliest reception in Ravenna.[6] These studies, together with those of others such as Alberto Casadei, have kept the critical relevance of the *Egloge* firmly linked to Dante's biography, particularly his political concerns, and to the interpretation of the *Commedia*.[7] The *Egloge* still lack a modern scholarly edition accompanied by an English translation.[8] Consequently, perhaps, scholarship on the *Egloge* in the Anglophone world has been more sporadic than that on others of Dante's Latin works, which are more commonly taught and read in English across the university curriculum.[9]

In what follows, I offer a reading of Dante's two eclogues together with Giovanni del Virgilio's metrical letter and eclogue, concluding with a brief reflection on the incipit to *Paradiso* 25.[10] The focus of my reading will be on Dante's masterful manipulation of the pastoral tradition, especially the idyllic landscape, in crafting his response to del Virgilio. Critics have long looked outside of the *Egloge* in order to respond to some of the more enduring questions opened by the correspondence. Why did Dante reject del Virgilio's offer of the laurel crown in Bologna? Did he truly hope to be crowned poet laureate in Florence? Who is the historical referent of Polyphemus? When read on their own terms and not from the perspective of the *Commedia* or from the point of view of Dante's troubled political life, the poems can be seen to have their own internal logic and can provide a useful instrument not only for reconstructing Dante's biography and interpreting passages of the *Commedia* but also for understanding his idea of himself as a poet. To use the words of Jonathan Combs-Schilling, the *Egloge* give readers the opportunity "to peer inside [Dante's] workshop."[11]

The First Exchange

In late 1319 or early 1320, Giovanni del Virgilio wrote to Dante in an effort to bring him to Bologna.[12] One of the most clamorous misjudgments in the history of literature, del Virgilio's Horatian metrical letter opens by attacking Dante's choice to write the *Commedia* in the vernacular: "Tanta quid heu semper iactabis seria vulgo, / et nos pallentes nichil ex te vate legemus?" (*Ecl.* 1.6–7) [Why, alas, do you always throw such serious arguments down to the common folk, and we who are pale from study read nothing from you, a poet?]. The first twenty lines of the poem are a categorical dismissal of Dante's choice to divulge the secrets of heaven and hell to the "gens ydiota" [ignorant people] in the "sermone forensi" (*Ecl.* 1.10; 18) [language of the city square]. Just as Petrarch would write to Boccaccio in *Familiares* 21.15, Dante's poem is criticized for divulging sublime subject matter in a popular style more appropriate to the tavern than to the academy. Del Virgilio's bold attack on Dante's poetics shows a familiarity with (and misunderstanding of) Dante's enterprise in the *Commedia* and an arrogance that he is correct in his assumptions and judgments.

Del Virgilio was a part of the Latinate university culture of the Guelf-dominated municipalities of northern Italy, such as Bologna and Padua, in which a poet like Albertino Mussato was able to achieve a measure of fame and success.[13] On behalf of those who are pale from study, del Virgilio requests of Dante a Latin epic poem that would recount the conflict between Guelfs and Ghibellines following the death of Henry VII. The epic poem he suggests to Dante would start with Henry's death in 1313 during his failed campaign to take Italy, moving on to Ghibelline Uguccione della Faggiola's victory over the Guelf coalition at Montecatini in 1315 and Cangrande della Scala's campaign against Vicenza and Padua in 1317–18, and concluding with King Robert of Naples's naval campaign against the Ghibelline siege of Genoa in 1318–19.[14] While these might be understood as separate topics for a poem, taken together they represent a chronological and geographical progression that could be recounted in epic style, much like Albertino Mussato's *De obsidione Canis Grandis de Verona ante civitatem Paduanam* (1321), though on a larger scale.[15]

Del Virgilio promises Dante fame across the land area of the ancient Roman Empire:

> carmine quo possis Alcide tangere Gades
> et quo te refluus relegens mirabitur Hyster,
> et Pharos et quondam regnum te noscet Helysse.
> Si te fama iuvat, parvo te limite septum
> non contentus eris, nec vulgo iudice tolli.
>   (*Ecl.* 1.30–34)

[With this song you can touch the Pillars of Hercules. For it the Danube will marvel at you and flow backward. The lighthouse of Alexandria and the kingdom that was once Dido's will know of you. If fame delights you, you will not be content to be encircled by a small boundary or to be raised by the judgment of the common people.]

Dante's potential fame is promised by the universality of the Latin language among men of learning, but it is also guaranteed by the importance of the political and militaristic subject of the poem, which would gain him the laurel crown in Bologna. In del Virgilio's eyes, such a recognition by a local community would provide Dante with the opportunity to become a leader to the people ("dux populo") and to help put a stop to their struggles ("tantos hominum compesce labores") (*Ecl.* 1.35–44). Del Virgilio calls on Dante to become a poet of history in a different way than he had been in the *Commedia*. For del Virgilio, the poet's duty was to document and put into historical perspective the immediate struggles of a specific population. This kind of poet needed an urban base of action and a defined public with which to engage, as well as a universal language that could guarantee his poem's impact in the present, its longevity in time, and its general comprehensibility across linguistic boundaries.

Del Virgilio's boldness in his letter to Dante is met by Dante's untimely brilliance and otherworldly certainty.[16] In response to the Bolognese professor's Horatian metrical letter, Dante writes in the form of an eclogue, capitalizing both on the classical genre's lowliness and on its association with natural spaces far from the city. His choice of the eclogue itself is a rebuttal of del Virgilio's proposal, penned in a Horatian voice and evocative of the epic Virgil. With the eclogue, as Zygmunt Barański has noted, Dante boldly aligns himself with the low-style Virgil of the *Bucolica*.[17]

In the poem, Dante represents himself as Tityrus and del Virgilio as Mopsus. As goats pass by, Tityrus sits beneath an oak tree discussing Mopsus with Melibeus, who is understood as representing Florentine notary Dino Perini.[18] Tityrus describes to Melibeus how Mopsus inhabits a kind of magical *locus amoenus*, an idealized place, where he can contemplate men and gods, making music such that wild animals follow him and rivers flow backward. The contrast between the two pastoral landscapes and the attitudes of the two poets is clear from the outset. Dante sits in a simple, humble landscape of shepherds, explaining the classicizing poem of del Virgilio to his unlearned friend, while del Virgilio is represented as a new Orpheus in a highly aestheticized landscape that bends to the poet's will.

Tityrus juxtaposes Mopsus's dedication to the Muses to the pursuits of law students, but his praise quickly drifts into mockery. Tityrus remarks that Mopsus is pale because he spends too much time in the forest and that his bowels are bursting with the milk of the Muses.[19] Dante ironizes the status of del Virgilio by overstating it and highlighting the incommunicability of his style to the uninitiated. Melibeus is nonetheless worried that Tityrus will leave and asks him what he intends to do, since he can imagine that the poet desires to be crowned with laurel. In responding to Melibeus's concern, Tityrus begins by calmly explaining that there is hardly any prestige for poets anymore, but Dante's anger at del Virgilio's earlier attack emerges in his voice: "cum sic dedit indignatio vocem" (*Ecl.* 2.38) [when at that point indignation took over my voice]. This indignation marks the monologue that follows about the potential of receiving the laurel crown in Bologna or Florence:

> Quantos balatus colles et prata sonabunt,
> si viridante coma fidibus peana ciebo!
> Sed timeam saltus et rura ignara deorum.
> Nonne triumphales melius pexare capillos
> et patrio, redeam si quando, abscondere canos
> fronde sub inserta solitum flavescere Sarno?
> (*Ecl.* 2.39–44)

[How many bleats will the hills and fields sound out, if I, with my hair made green, raise a paean with my lyre? But I fear crags and fields that do not know the gods. Would it not be better that I style my triumphal hair and hide it, since it is gray, beneath a woven bough on the shores of my native Arno, I whose hair once shone with youth?]

These lines, together with the opening of *Paradiso* 25, have led generations of readers to believe that Dante entertained the fantasy of returning triumphant to Florence as poet laureate. Tityrus's irony and indignation in the first two lines of the exclamation, however, are continued by his rhetorical question about Florence. What can be said of Bologna's danger for Dante can also be said of Florence, where the threat of violence was justified by the law that governed his exile.

Dante's fear of Bologna makes a certain amount of sense historically. In fact, Boccaccio's glossator explicates the reference to the gods in line 41 politically, noting "imperatorum, quia contraria parti Dantis tunc Bononia erat" (*Glosse* 2.41) [of the emperors, because Bologna was then against the faction of Dante]. Rather too much credit has been given to the glossator's interpretation in this case—probably because it feeds the tendency to read these compositions in a political key. In my view, Dante's fear of Bologna is more general and concerns the status of poetic culture there. The phrase "ignara deorum," which is Virgilian in origin, expresses a general lack of civilization. Virgil uses it in book 8 of the *Aeneid*, when Evander describes the ritual feasting in honor of Hercules as being an empty superstition that does not know the gods ("vana superstitio veterumque ignara deorum," *Aen.* 8.187). With this in mind, it seems that Dante is concerned about the interests of the Bolognese in assigning him the laurel crown, since it may be an empty superstition associated with a profession that seems to have lost all prestige.

When Tityrus poses the rhetorical question about the coronation in Florence, his relationship to the city remains conditional and unreal ("redeam si quando"). He superimposes his past, young self onto his future elderly self. Whereas the question demands a positive response, prefaced as it is by the particle *nonne*, the response reflects an unreality. It would be better, had he not spent the time between his youth and old age in exile. It would be better, if he could turn back time and change the nature of his relationship with Florence. He knows that he cannot go back and that the conditions of his work as a poet include exile for life from the city of his birth.

The eclogue continues with Melibeus reminding Tityrus that he does not have much time left. To this, Tityrus responds that he will only ever accept a laurel crown when he has finished the *Commedia*. Although it is hard to believe that Dante would have imagined returning to Florence under any circumstances, much less as poet laureate, readers have tended to interpret this declaration as a literal expression of Dante's true desires. The historical association of Dante as poet of Florence is so strong that it has obfuscated the irony behind Dante's enthusiasm here.[20] We must not forget that Dante is rebutting a bold-faced insult to his life's work in the *Commedia*. Dante, indeed, asserts himself as poet of Florence—which he figures as the city of his youth, much as he had in the encounter with Cacciaguida in *Paradiso*, and identifies himself entirely as the author of the *Commedia*.

Tityrus invites Mopsus to back off and explains to Melibeus that he does so because of how he insulted the *Commedia*:

> Comica nonne vides ipsum reprehendere verba,
> tum quia femineo resonant ut trita labello,
> tum quia Castalias pudet acceptare sorores?
> (*Ecl.* 2.51–53)

> [Do you not see that he reprehends comic language, both because it sounds worn out on the lips of women and because it shames the Muses to accept it?]

Tityrus then rereads Mopsus's verses to Melibeus, effectively showing him the source of his indignation in the multilayered insults to his poem. Dante rejects del Virgilio's invitation on all accounts. He will not write a Latin poem and he will not accept the laurel crown in Bologna. His fame will be due to the *Commedia*, if to anything at all, and he will be associated with the utopian memory of the Florence of his youth. Dante could not have responded more brilliantly to del Virgilio's pompous invitation. By framing his response as an explanation to a novice in the art of poetry, Dante doubles down on the irony of his enthusiasm and praise throughout. He makes clear that del Virgilio has understood nothing about him as a poet or about his poetic enterprise in the *Commedia*.

Much discussion has been dedicated to the closing lines of this eclogue, in which Tityrus tells Melibeus that he is ready to send Mopsus ten pails of milk from a favorite sheep. The sheep and ten pails have been variously interpreted as Dante's comic Muse and ten cantos of the *Paradiso*, or as Virgil's *Bucolica* and its ten eclogues, or as bucolic poetry in general and ten eclogues composed by Dante.[21]

The Second Exchange

Del Virgilio wastes no time responding to Dante's eclogue with his own. His approach is defensive, as he seems to have realized that he has offended Dante with his invitation. The eclogue opens by establishing the pastoral setting, this time in a verbose description that aims to establish Mopsus as the sole shepherd inhabiting a cave ("nativo . . . antro") in the woodlands on the outskirts of the city (*Ecl.* 3.1–24). Unlike the simple, Virgilian setting of Dante's first eclogue, with two shepherds sitting in the shade of an oak tree, here del Virgilio represents his woodland as a place of abundance and overstimulation. He embraces his pastoral alter ego, Mopsus, whom Tityrus had addressed as a city dweller:

> Si cantat oves et Tityrus hircos
> aut armenta trahit, quianam civile canebas
> urbe sedens carmen? Quando hoc Benacia quondam
> pastorale sonans detrivit fistula labrum,
> audiat in silvis et te cantare bubulcum.
> (*Ecl.* 3.26–30)

[If Tityrus sings of sheep and goats or leads herds, why ever did you sing a civic song sitting in the city? Since the pipes once of Benacus, sounding in the pastoral fashion, wore down his lips, let him hear you too, rustically, sing in the forest.]

The contrast between the city and the simplicity of the pastoral landscape runs across the entire correspondence, with Dante embracing the latter in its difference from the former and del Virgilio seeking to superimpose the former upon the latter. This contrast in setting represents more generally the intellectual and poetic contrast between the two men. The question of the vernacular versus Latin and the question of whether to accept the laurel are mapped onto the landscape of the pastoral.

Del Virgilio's response aims at coaxing Dante to Bologna through flattery. He compares, even equates, Dante and Virgil and offers Bologna as the next best thing to Florence, misunderstanding Dante's indignation as directed solely against that "ingrata urbs" (*Ecl.* 3.38) [ungrateful city]. He communicates to Dante that in Bologna he will be able to pass his time in leisure together with del Virgilio. In a long description of Mopsus's cave, del Virgilio represents a natural world that offers its bounty without labor. He describes it being surrounded by oregano and poppies, wild thyme, garlic, mushrooms, and apples, and inhabited by honey-producing bees (*Ecl.* 3.52–71). Boccaccio's glossator attempted to interpret these items allegorically as representative of different aspects of the Bolognese academy (philosophy, ancient sayings, poetic fables, etc.). Whether or not they are directly allegorical, the overwrought description of intellectual leisure is meant to seduce Dante, who is described as "pulvereus ... in tegmine scabro" (*Ecl.* 3.36) [covered in dust in a coarse mantle].

In this environment, Mopsus promises Tityrus that he will find a following and a school in which to teach:

> Huc ades; huc venient, qui te pervisere gliscent,
> Parrasii iuvensque senes, et carmina leti
> qui nova mirari cupiantque antiqua doceri.
> *Ecl.* 3.67–69)

> [Come here. Here the young and old Parrasians will come, who are burning to see you and who would happily desire to admire your new songs and to be taught the ancient ones.]

There is some disagreement about the reference to ancient and modern songs. Given del Virgilio's disposition toward the vernacular *Commedia*, which he calls *novi canti* in the first line of his metrical letter, it would be reasonable to read the *carmina nova* here as the *Commedia*, or perhaps as both the *Commedia* and the new eclogues. *Antiqua carmina* doubtlessly refers to Latin poetry, although it is unclear whether this is ancient Latin poetry to be taught by Dante or Dante's own Latin poetry.[22] Either way, in the view of someone like del Virgilio, only Latin poetry could be taught, while vernacular poetry could be cause for admiration or wonder.

Assuming that Dante's fear of Bologna is political in nature, del Virgilio tries throughout to evoke a bond of friendship between the two men. Early on, Mopsus expresses his love to Tityrus, using an ancient marriage topos of the elm and the vine:[23]

> nec te crucia, crudelis, et illum,
> cuius amor tantum, tantum complectitur, inquam,
> tam te, blande senex, quanto circumligat ulmum
> proceram vitis per centum vincula nexu.
> (*Ecl.* 3.40–43)

> [and do not cruelly torment yourself or him, whose love embraces you so much, I say, so much, gentle old man, as the vine surrounds the lofty elm with chains tied a hundred times.]

Toward the end, he offers to act as guarantor of the poet's safety in Bologna, calling himself a friend: "Non ipse michi te fidis amanti? / Sunt forsan mea regna tibi despecta?" (*Ecl.* 3.76–77) [Do you not believe me who loves you? Do you perhaps look down upon my kingdoms?]. Pivoting on this presumed friendship in poetry, del Virgilio questions whether Dante's self-claimed fear is only a politically motivated excuse for remaining in Ravenna, where he is paid more lavishly for his services than he could arrange in Bologna. Del Virgilio insinuates that Dante has been bought and paid for by Guido Novello da Polenta (indicated with the pastoral name Iollas):

> Mopse, quid es demens? Quia non permittet Iollas
> comis et urbanus, dum sunt tua rustica dona,
> hisque tabernaculis non est modo tutius antrum,
> quis potius ludat.
> (*Ecl.* 3.80–83)

> [Mopsus, why are you foolish? Because Iollas will not allow it; he is courteous and sophisticated, while your gifts are rustic, and a cave is not now safer than those huts, in which he may sing more opportunely.]

Del Virgilio bypasses Dante's self-defense as a humble, exiled poet who feels nostalgia for the Florence of his youth by insinuating that Dante's dedication to the Muses has been purchased by the wealth of a local lord. He challenges Dante in the name of the Muses and in the name of a friendship in poetry to leave the protection of that lord to become the poet of the city in Bologna, under his personal protection. He concludes by warning that if Dante cannot become that poet, del Virgilio will be forced to reach out instead to his generation's other major poetic voice, Albertino Mussato.[24] In fact, we might think of Mussato as the model of civic poet that del Virgilio would like Dante to become, a poet of history with his feet planted firmly on the ground and embedded within a well-defined urban context. By locating himself within a utopian pastoral landscape, Dante has signaled to del Virgilio his resistance to being defined by any municipality. As Guy Raffa has noted, "Dante shows once and for all the inadequacy of prizes and even public recognition for a project born out of exile and a rich theological imagination."[25]

Written in the summer of his death, Dante's response to del Virgilio—his final work of poetry—takes a bizarre turn. A conversation between Tityrus and Alphesibeus (physician Fiduccio de' Milotti), this poem is recounted in the third person, and its setting is shifted to Sicily.[26] If the models for the correspondence thus far have been Horace and Virgil, here Dante turns to Ovid as his principal example, specifically Ovid's rewriting in *Metamorphoses* 13 of Theocritus's *Idyll* 11 on Polyphemus and Galatea. The opening lines of the poem signal its difference from the first eclogue:

> Velleribus Colchis prepes detectus Eous
> alipedesque alii pulchrum Titana ferebant.
> Orbita, qua primum flecti de culmine cepit,
> currigerium cantum libratim quemque tenebat,
> resque refulgentes, solite superiarier umbris,
> vincebant umbras et fervere rura sinebant.
> Tityrus hec propter confugit et Alphesibeus
> ad silvam pecudumque suique misertus uterque,
> fraxineam silvam, tiliis platanisque frequentem.
> (*Ecl.* 4.1–9)

[Swift Eoos, released from the fleeces of Colchis, and the other wing-footed steeds were bearing the beautiful Titan. The orbit, where it first began to be bent from its summit, held each chariot-bearing wheel in equilibrium, and the things that shine with light, which are usually overcome by the shadows, conquered the shadows and made the fields seethe with heat. On account of this, Tityrus and Alphesibeus fled to the forest, and each felt pity for himself and for his sheep.]

In stark contrast to the simplicity of the first eclogue's setting, these lines situate the typical pastoral moment of retreat from the heat of the sun in cosmological terms, marking the time of day with a reference to myth and astrology.[27] Unlike del Virgilio's Mopsus, who inhabits a cave, Dante's Tityrus is seen out in the open, beneath the stars. We view the pastoral landscape throughout the poem described from this outside perspective, as if the author of the *Commedia* were looking down upon it.[28]

The conversation between Tityrus and Alphesibeus opens with Alphesibeus expressing his surprise that Mopsus enjoys living in the caves of the Cyclopes beneath Aetna (*Ecl.* 4.16–27). He expresses his perplexity by contrasting it with his lack of surprise that living things behave according to their nature, suggesting either that Mopsus lives among the Cyclopes (namely, in Bologna) against his nature as a poet or that he is not a poet. Dante subtly undermines del Virgilio's political allegiance just as del Virgilio has done with Dante in the concluding lines of his eclogue.

The pastoral landscape plays a particularly important role in this eclogue. There is some inconsistency in maintaining the fiction of the pastoral location in Sicily separate from its true geographical references. The caves of the Cyclopes beneath Aetna clearly refer to Bologna, while Dante's Ravenna is indicated by the "roscida rura Pelori" (*Ecl.* 4.46) [dewy fields of Pelorus], or modern-day Punta del Faro near Messina. This identification is all but denied by Tityrus later on in the poem, when he tells Alphesibeus that Mopsus incorrectly thinks that they are in Ravenna—"litora dextra Pado ratus a Rubicone sinistra" (*Ecl.* 4.67) [on the right shore of the Po, to the left of the Rubicon]—while they are really in Sicily. The real-world references emerge once more at verses 84–87, when Alphesibeus expresses to Tityrus his hope that the poet will never accept the laurel along the Reno river, which runs just outside the walls of Bologna. The references to real-world geography confirm the location of Mopsus as del Virgilio in Bologna, whereas they make the presence of Dante as Tityrus in Ravenna ambiguous, asserting that he inhabits instead a nonplace of the pastoral imaginary.

There is no reason to think that this inconsistency is the result of a lack of care on the part of the author or that it was penned by someone other than Dante.[29] Rather, by maintaining the distance between his historical location and that of the imaginary pastoral cypher, Dante reinforces the fact that he is not beholden to his patron in Ravenna, as del Virgilio had insinuated. Dante's main goal in this eclogue, in fact, is to respond to this insinuation and to justify his reluctance to join del Virgilio in Bologna.

As Tityrus and Alphesibeus speak, they are interrupted by the arrival of Melibeus, who brings Mopsus's eclogue in the form of self-playing pipes. Upon hearing the first line of the poem, Alphesibeus expresses his concern that Tityrus will leave for the caves of the Cyclopes, explaining his worries in a mythological code:

> Tibia non sentis quod fit virtute canora
> numninis et similis natis de murmure cannis,
> murmure pandenti turpissima tempora regis
> qui iussu Bromii Pactolida tinxit harenam?
> Quod vocet ad litus Ethneo pumice tectum,
> fortunate senex, falso ne crede favori,
> et Driadum miserere loci pecorumque tuorum.
> Te iuga, te saltus nostri, te flumina flebunt
> absentem et nymphe mecum peiora timentes,
> et cadet invidia quam nunc habet ipse Pachinus.
> Nos quoque pastores te cognovisse pigebit.
> Fortunate senex, fontes et pabula nota
> desertare tuo vivaci nomine nolis.
> *(Egloge* IV.50–62)

[Do you not hear the flute make sounds by virtue of a spirit and similar to the reeds born from the murmur, the murmur that showed the most disgraceful temples of the king, who stained the sands of the Pactolus by order of Bromius? That it calls you to the shore of

Aetna covered in pumice, blessed old man, do not believe the false acclamation, but have compassion for the Draiads of this place and of your sheep. The hills, the crags, the rivers will cry over you if you leave, as will the nymphs with me, fearful of the worst, and the envy that Pachinus now feels will fall upon us. It will also grieve us shepherds to have met you. Blessed old man, do not wish to desert the springs and well-known fields, depriving them of your long-lived name.]

Alphesibeus's exhortation contains two allusions to the myth of Midas. First, the pipes are compared to the reeds that share the news of Midas's donkey ears, which were his punishment for opposing Apollo in his contest against Pan. The allusion to such a punishment by the patron of poetry suggests that poor judgment can result in public shaming. The reference to the Pactolus river alludes to the process by which Midas was able to remove his golden touch, which was the result of greed. Taken together, these allusions may be interpreted as obliquely insinuating that leaving Pelorus for the caves of the Cyclopes would stain the poet's reputation as being motivated by greed. Like Mopsus in del Virgilio's eclogue, Alphesibeus calls on Tityrus's friendship and bond with the landscape itself.

To assuage his fellow shepherd's concern that Tityrus would leave Pelorus out of greed, Tityrus defines his relationship to Mopsus in terms of the love of poetry: "Mopsus amore pari mecum connexus ob illas / que male gliscentem timide fugere Pyreneum" (*Ecl.* 4.65–66) [Mopsus, who is connected with me by an equal love on account of those women who fearfully fled Pyreneus, who burned wrongly for them]. These lines pick back up Mopsus's words in del Virgilio's eclogue about their shared love of poetry. It is peculiar, however, that Dante would choose to reference Pyreneus when speaking of dedication to the Muses. Ovid recounts that Pyreneus trapped the Muses in his house in order to rape them (*Met.* 5.273–93). The juxtaposition of the equitable love between Mopsus and Tityrus and the mad desire of Pyreneus for the Muses opens up an ambiguity about the quality of Mopsus's poetic friendship with Tityrus expressed in del Virgilio's eclogue. This ambiguity echoes, furthermore, the opening discussion about Mopsus's reasons for living among the Cyclopes.

This subtle questioning of del Virgilio's intentions leads into another Ovidian allusion, which has been the source of endless speculation among readers of this exchange. Tityrus explains that he would gladly visit Mopsus if it were not for his fear of Polyphemus:

> Sed quanquam viridi sint postponenda Pelori
> Ethnica saxa solo, Mopsum visurus adirem
> hic grege dimisso, ni te, Polipheme, timerem.
> (*Ecl.* 4.73–75)

[But, although the rocks of Aetna must be placed after the green land of Pelorus, I would leave this flock and go to see Mopsus, if I did not fear you, Polyphemus.]

Following the glossator's note on Tityrus's fear in the first of Dante's eclogues, most commentators link the fear of Polyphemus to Dante's presumed fear of persecution by the Guelfs of Bologna. Although Boccaccio's glossator notes only that Polyphemus was the Cyclops in book 3 of the *Aeneid*, modern commentators have tried to link the Cyclops with different historical figures. The most compelling hypothesis is Fulcieri de' Calboli, who had been recently elected *capitano del popolo* in Bologna and who had been in the city for some months.[30] While it is possible that Fulcieri de' Calboli is the historical referent of Polyphemus, it is not necessarily the case.[31] Dante would have had good reason to fear de' Calboli as a radical Guelf military leader, yet the political situation in Bologna never emerges directly in any of the four poems. Although del Virgilio highlights Dante's political situation in Ravenna, Dante never bows to the petty municipal rivalries that motivate the Bolognese professor. It is only within a critical context that has been shaped by the political concerns of commentators, and their diverse municipal allegiances, that Dante's politics has been represented as central to the exchange.[32] Instead, within the economy of the correspondence, of this eclogue in particular, and of Tityrus's explanation to Alphesibeus specifically, what is at stake and under examination is the nature of Mopsus's relationship with Tityrus. From this perspective, Polyphemus embodies Dante's concerns with del Virgilio *tout court*, as a Bolognese academician and a self-styled cultivator of the Muses, who would instrumentalize Dante as a political poet. In what follows, I would like to suggest that Polyphemus might be more fruitfully considered as an alternative to Mopsus as alter ego for the Bolognese professor. As representative of the effort to bring Dante to Bologna, del Virgilio is the primary cause of Dante's concern and thus the main target of Dante's response.

One of the reasons behind the shift of setting to Sicily was to accommodate and manipulate del Virgilio's description of Mopsus's pastoral location as a cave, which Dante interprets as the "arid rocks of the Cyclopes" at the beginning of his response. As Lino Pertile has noticed, Dante radically transforms del Virgilio's pastoral cave into a place of horror.[33] The invocation of Polyphemus fits into this manipulation of setting. It is also consonant with the worry expressed in the first eclogue about the "fields that do not know the gods," since Cyclopes typically represented the uncouth. Polyphemus, who is described in his role as the pursuer of Galatea, can also be connected with the mention of Pyreneus at the beginning of Tityrus's answer to Alphesibeus. Both are mythological offenders of poetry and potential rapists. Like Pyreneus, who captures the Muses to violate them, Polyphemus pretends to be a pastoral poet in order to coax Galatea away from her lover Acis, whom he eventually assaults. Dante, through Tityrus's fear of Polyphemus, identifies with the vulnerable Galatea. A closer look at the Ovidian source material will show how the mythological episode maps onto Dante's concerns with del Virgilio.

The story of Galatea and Polyphemus is recounted at the end of book 13 of the *Metamorphoses*, with Galatea telling it in the first person to Scylla, who lives in the Straits of Messina near Pelorus. She describes how, in the name of love, Polyphemus transformed himself from someone who hated the gods—"magni cum dis contemptor Olympi" (*Met.* 13.761) [despiser of great Olympus and its gods]—into a seemingly civilized lover, who temporarily changed his appearance and stopped his savage pillaging and killing.[34] The transformation was only brief, since the final expression of his love for Galatea would be the murder of Acis, an episode that Alphesibeus recounts in Dante's second eclogue.[35] In Ovid's tale, Polyphemus is described as a giant parody of the pastoral poet. His staff is a pine tree and his pipe has one hundred reeds. His love song for Galatea invites her to join him in his caves, where the temperature is always perfect and nature bountifully produces apples, grapes, strawberries, cherries, plums, and chestnuts (*Met.* 13.810–30). Polyphemus promises her this bounty, his flock, and more, entreating her: "Iam, Galatea, veni, nec munera despice nostra!" (*Met.* 13.839) ["Now come, Galatea, and don't despise my gifts!"]. His pronouncement of love, however, is followed by his threat to murder his competitor, Acis (*Met.* 13.865–69). When he eventually finds Galatea with Acis, Polyphemus reveals his uncouth self and violently strikes and murders Acis with a piece of the mountainside he had promised to Galatea. Ovid's representation of Polyphemus provides Dante with a model of the false poet, who feigns love only to enact violence.

The applicability of this model to del Virgilio as he is imagined by Dante is striking. It lies unspoken in the lines between Tityrus's mention of the Cyclops's name and Alphesibeus's description of his murderous violence:

"Quis Poliphemon," ait "non horreat" Alphesibeus
"assuetum rictus humano sanguine tingui,
tempore iam ex illo quando Galathea relicti
Acidis heu miseri discerpere viscera vidit?
Vix illa evasit: an vis valuisset amoris,
effera dum rabies tanta perferbuit ira?
Quid, quod Achimenides sociorum cede cruentum
tantum prospiciens, animam vix claudere quivit?"
                                                 (*Ecl.* 4.76–83)

["Who would not shudder at Polyphemus," Alphesibeus said, "who is accustomed to wetting his jaws with human blood, already from that time when Galatea saw him, alas, tear to pieces the bowels of poor Acis, whom she had left behind? She barely escaped herself; or would the power of love have prevailed, while his cruel wrath boiled over with such madness? What to say about the fact that Achaemenides, who only saw him from afar bloody from the slaughter of his companions and was barely able to save his life?"]

We are given no clues about whom or what these names represent, not even by Boccaccio's glossator, who clarifies merely that they are proper names. If we look back at Mopsus's flattering words to Tityrus and compare them to those of Polyphemus to Galatea, with whom Tityrus identifies, a potential correspondence emerges, which indicates that Dante chose to bring up this episode as a way to speak indirectly to del Virgilio about his worries. He wanted to believe del Virgilio, but he was afraid that the professor was more like Polyphemus than Mopsus.

There are several correspondences between Polyphemus's profession of love and Mopsus's approach of Tityrus in del Virgilio's eclogue. Generally, with Polyphemus's love song in mind, we might think more suspiciously about Mopsus's profession of friendship. Furthermore, the list of belongings and the boasting about the abundance of food in his caves finds a parallel in the description of Mopsus's cave. More specifically, Mopsus says that the caves are his dominion ("mea regna") and he asks if Tityrus despises them ("sunt tibi despecta"). This can be compared to Polyphemus's description of his ownership of the natural abundance of his caves and the mountainsides where his sheep dwell—"Sunt mihi, pars montis, vivo pendentia saxo / antra" (*Met.* 13.810) [I have a whole mountainside for my possessions, deep caves in the living rock]—and to his request that Galatea not look down on his gifts ("Nec munera despice nostra," *Met.* 13.839). Dante's use of allusion invites readers to rethink this exaggerated display of overabundance through the filter of Polyphemus's love of Galatea. At one point, Polyphemus tells her that his flock can barely walk because the ewes' udders stretch down to their legs: "praesens potes ipsa videre, / ut vix circumeant distentum cruribus uber" (*Met.* 13. 825–26) [Here you can see for yourself how they can hardly walk for their distended udders]. Mopsus had boasted to Tityrus of his own abundance in similar terms: "Quid tamen interea mugit mea bucula circum? / quadrifluumne gravat coxis umentibus uber?" (*Ecl.* 3.90–91) [But why does my heifer bellow around now? Do her four flowing udders weigh on her wet haunches?]. It is as if Dante's mention of Polyphemus were meant to unveil del Virgilio's source text in the pretend pastoral of the Cyclops. It is also important to note that the invocation of Polyphemus indicates a correspondence between Tityrus and Galatea, who both speak about love to a companion in Pelorus, when their narrative is interrupted by a vocative ("Polypheme") that shifts the discourse to the second person, even if the Cyclops is outside the immediate context of the interlocutors.[36] This correspondence indicates that Dante views his position in this debate as precarious and vulnerable.[37]

Nevertheless, Dante subtly calls into question del Virgilio's overwrought praise and lavish offerings. As a reader of Ovid, del Virgilio would likely have recognized this in the mention of Polyphemus.[38] The invocation of Polyphemus also serves to reiterate Dante's depiction in his first eclogue of Bolognese lands as "fields that do not know the gods." Read together with the invocation of Midas's greed and infamy earlier in the second eclogue, the violence of Polyphemus could correspond to the potential damage to Dante's reputation. Dante may wish to believe that del Virgilio is a Virgilian Mopsus, a friend of the Muses, and not like Pyreneus or Polyphemus, but the eclogue begins with Alphesibeus questioning Mopsus's nature: Why would he live with the Cyclopes? Dante's answer (and challenge) is that del Virgilio may be Polyphemus himself, an uncouth man who pretends to be a poet in order to achieve his desire. Whether or not this is the case, it is clear that Dante's shift of the pastoral setting to Sicily is governed by the Ovidian story of Galatea, which takes on the pastoral genre through parody.[39] With the mention of Polyphemus, Dante is able to deflate the pompous classicism of del Virgilio's eclogue and to maintain his superiority beyond the realms of civic poetry.

In the conclusion he finally responds to del Virgilio's insinuation that he is beholden to his lord in Ravenna, Guido Novello da Polenta. We learn in the final lines of the poem that the conversation has been overheard by Iollas, Guido Novello's pastoral name. The poem concludes:

Callidus interea iuxta latitavit Iollas,
omnia qui didicit, qui retulit omnia nobis:
ille quidem nobis et nos tibi, Mopse, poymus.
(*Ecl.* 4.95–97)

[The astute Iollas meanwhile lay hidden. He heard everything and repeated it all to us. He composed for us and we for you, Mopsus.]

The entire exchange between Tityrus and Alphesibeus has been recorded and told by Iollas. The relationship between Iollas and Tityrus, as Dante and his patron, is one of mutual collaboration that inverts sociopolitical norms. Da Polenta is effectively represented as Dante's scribe. In response to del Virgilio, then, Dante shows himself to be in perfect freedom, with the ruler of the city at his service rather than vice versa. His host remains attentive in the background and takes note; he collaborates but does not intervene. He exists in a Ravenna that is precisely Pelorus, a pastoral environment that never gives way to a civic reality that can control him or his poetry. Here Dante can remain unchained from the duties of the civic poet and fully assume the role of author of the *Commedia*, a work of poetry that belongs to no city and to all.

Dante's Laurel Crown

All evidence suggests that Dante had finished the *Commedia* by the time he wrote this final eclogue. Although the third-person framing mechanism could indicate that Dante did not complete the poem or that the poem was sent to del Virgilio after Dante's death, the framing serves a poetic and narrative purpose, as does the shift of setting from Arcadia to Sicily. The third-person perspective also reasserts Dante's position as author of the *Commedia* and as a *poeta theologus* whose authority originates in heaven, not in any city—not even Florence.

The idea that Dante entertained a fantasy of returning to Florence and, even more, of being crowned poet laureate is founded upon the projection of the opening lines of *Paradiso* 25 onto the specific context of the *Egloge*. As I hope to have shown, the circumstances of the *Egloge* give Dante the opportunity to defend himself as a vernacular poet and as a poet who shuns the municipal concerns associated with the laurel crown. The pastoral is the ideal genre for both purposes: it is the most humble and rustic of the classical genres of poetry. What Dante does not do in the *Egloge* is express any hope of returning to Florence. If we reconsider these lines from *Paradiso* 25 in the light of the *Egloge*, the unreal futurity of his return to Florence emerges:

>   Se mai continga che 'l poema sacro
> al quale ha posto mano e cielo e terra,
> sì che m'ha fatto per molti anni macro,
>   vinca la crudeltà che fuor mi serra
> del bello ovile ov' io dormi' agnello,
> nimico ai lupi che li danno guerra;
>   con altra voce omai, con altro vello

ritornerò poeta, e in sul fonte
del mio battesmo prenderò 'l cappello
   però che ne la fede, che fa conte
l'anime a Dio, quivi intra' io, e poi
Pietro per lei sì mi girò la fronte.
              (*Par.* 25.1–9)

[If it ever happens that the sacred poem, to which both Heaven and earth have set their hand, so that for many years it has made me lean, vanquish the cruelty that locks me out of the lovely sheepfold where I slept as a lamb, an enemy of the wolves that make war on it, with other voice by then, with other fleece I shall return as poet, and at the font of my baptism I shall accept the wreath: for there I entered the faith that makes souls known to God, and later Peter so circled my brow because of it.]⁴⁰

Claire Honess puts it best when she writes of these lines: "It can only be in a metaphorical sense that Dante can receive the poet's *cappello*. . . . It is the poet's wish that his text be read and accepted . . . by its Florentine readers."⁴¹ Dante reiterates the reference to his poem as sacred from *Paradiso* 23, locating it in a place between heaven and earth. Florence oscillates between past and future: it is first the fold where he was a lamb, but it is then transformed into the font where he was baptized. For the poet writing in Ravenna, it does not exist in the present tense. Only in an unrealized future will Dante be able to return as the poet who is as much a part of his poem as God is of creation.

There are also verbal signs that lead us to understand that Dante will return to Florence in the material form of his poem. The "other voice" that he has acquired could be understood as the Dante's poetic voice in the mouth of a reader, while the "other fleece" (as *vello* is translated and interpreted) might be understood as a double entendre, indicating both clothing and the *vellum*, or parchment, through which Dante's voice will be available to future readers.⁴² After all, the subject of the first half of the conditional is the sacred poem itself, and Dante represents himself as a lamb. This kind of transformation into the material form of the book may be connected to the metamorphosis of Marsyas, who is mentioned in *Paradiso* 1 as a figure for the poet, just after a reference to the laurel crown

(*Par.* 1.13–21). Perhaps Dante is hoping there for a poetic inspiration that will figuratively excoriate him, making of his skin the parchment of his book. That is, he is calling on Apollo (God) to help him transform into the poet who will live on in his poem. Although I cannot get into this question in depth here, I would argue that this is the transformation that takes place in the heaven of the fixed stars, in part thanks to the examination on the theological virtues in *Paradiso* 24–26. Thus, if Dante will return triumphantly to Florence, it will be as borne by the poem itself, in which he has already been crowned.[43]

Perhaps Boccaccio was right not to include Dante's *Egloge* in the history of the pastoral he offered to Martino da Signa. Dante's skillful manipulation of the bucolic genre works to differentiate himself from such a Parnassus and to highlight his exceptionality and that of his poem. For modern readers of Dante, whose place in the Parnassus of European literature is undeniable, the value of the *Egloge* lies in their status as the textual documentation of an epochal cultural event. They are important evidence for Dante's early reception and for his late biography. They indicate his concerns and hopes regarding his fame within his own time. Perhaps most importantly, however, the *Egloge* represent from a perspective outside of the *Commedia* Dante's own conception of his great poem and of himself as a poet.

Notes

1. Boccaccio held the *Egloge* in high regard. He noted in his *Trattaello in laude di Dante* that they were "assai belle" (2nd red., 135). In addition to his working copy of the *Egloge* in MS Florence, Biblioteca Medicea Laurenziana–Pluteo XXIX 8 (MS BML Pluteo XXIX 8), the so-called *Zibaldone Laurenziano*, he created an anthology of bucolic poetry that included the pastoral Latin verse of Virgil, Petrarch, himself, Dante and Giovanni del Virgilio (excluding the initial metrical letter), and Checco di Meletto Rossi. MS Florence Biblioteca Medicea Laurenziana–Pluteo XXXIX 26 is a copy of Boccaccio's lost codex produced by the Augustinian friar Iacopo da Volterra.

2. See Petoletti, "Egloge," 159–61, for a succinct discussion of the textual tradition. See also Billanovich, "Giovanni del Virgilio."

3. The full text of these glosses is included as an appendix to Petoletti's edition of the *Egloge*, 632–48. Quotations of the glosses are from this edition and are referenced hereafter as *Glosse*. On Boccaccio's manuscripts of the *Egloge*, see Petoletti, "Boccaccio editore."

4. See Pastore Stocchi ed. (2012), Albanese ed. (2015), and Petoletti ed. (2016). The standard edition for many years was Reggio ed. (1969). I have used Petoletti's edition for quotations throughout. English translations of the *Egloge* are my own.

5. See Albanese and Pontari, "Notariato Bolognese," esp. 86–89, "Il cenacolo ravennate di Dante," and *Ultimo Dante*.

6. See Petoletti, *Dante*. See also the brief overview in Petoletti, "Egloge."

7. See Casadei, "Dante tra Ravenna." Other important and recent work on the *Egloge* in the Italian context includes Allegretti, "Acrostico" and "Dante 'Tityrus annosus'"; Bologna, "Dante e il latte"; Ferrara, "Senso del tempo"; Pertile, "*Egloghe* di Dante"; and Villa, "Problema dello stile umile."

8. See Wicksteed and Gardner's *Dante and Giovanni del Virgilio*. The 1902 edition and translation are outdated and overdue for replacement.

9. See, for example, Annett, "'Veritade ascosa'"; Combs Schilling, "Tityrus in Limbo"; Ferrara, "Ethical Distance"; and Raffa, "Dante's Mocking Pastoral Muse."

10. The reading here provided is a newly reworked and condensed version of my discussion of the *Egloge* in Lummus, *City of Poetry*, 68–98 and 104–9.

11. See Combs-Schilling, "Tityrus in Limbo," 4.

12. The precise dating of the exchange is difficult to establish. It is likely that del Virgilio sent his first missive between the end of 1319 and the beginning of 1320 and that Dante's initial response and del Virgilio's rebuttal were written and sent before the end of 1320. Dante's final response dates to the summer of 1321, just a few months before his death in September. See the synthetic discussion of these issues of dating in Casadei, "Dante tra Ravenna," 122–24.

13. On Mussato and the humanistic culture of northern Italy during this period, see Witt, *In the Footsteps*, 117–73. See also Lummus, *City of Poetry*, 22–62. It is unlikely that Dante and Mussato ever met; on their potential intertextual links, see Lombardo, "Oltre il silenzio" and "Epistola 'dantesca.'" See also Albanese, "*De Gestis Henrici VII Cesaris*" and "'Poeta et historicus.'"

14. These topics are listed in chronological order in veiled pastoral language in del Virgilio's letter. Their meaning was first deciphered by Boccaccio's glossator.

15. On this fascinating Latin poem, see Lummus, *City of Poetry*, 50–60.

16. While Dante is certain of the value of his epic poem, he is also well aware of the vulnerability of his person. See Theodore Cachey's reflections on Dante's vulnerability in the essay on the *Questio* in this book. See also the discussion of Dante's second eclogue below, 317–26.

17. See Barański, "Dante Alighieri," 561–62. For a discussion of the humble style as it is debated in the *Egloghe*, see Villa, "Problema dello stile umile."

18. See Albanese and Pontari, "Cenacolo ravennate," 330–45, for a general discussion of Dante's friends in Ravenna, including Perini.

19. Mopsus is literally described as full up to his throat (i.e., choking) with the milk of the Muses: "vatificis prolutus aquis et lacte canoro / viscera plena ferens et plenus adusque palatum" [filling up his bowels with the milk of song and becoming full up to his throat] (*Egloge* 2.30–32). On the link between the milk imagery in Dante's first eclogue and in *Paradiso* 23, see Pertile, "*Egloghe* di Dante," 153–56.

20. Early commentators, such as Iacopo della Lana and Pietro Alighieri, began the tradition of viewing the incipit to *Paradiso* 25 literally as Dante's desire to return to Florence. See also Boccaccio's ideologically driven description of Dante's desire for the laurel crown in *Trattatello* 1.125–26.

21. Although all answers to this question will never be more than hypotheses (without new and definitive material evidence), see Casadei, *Dante oltre la "Commedia*," 56–60, and Lorenzini, *Corrispondenza bucolica*, 4–7, for a strong case in favor of the latter. For a recent reading that argues plausibly for the former, see Pertile, "*Egloghe* di Dante," 156, where the critic suggests in a close comparative reading between the first eclogue and *Paradiso* XXIII that the milk pails promise the last ten (then yet unwritten) cantos of the *Paradiso*.

22. Other interpretations of these lines see the modern poetry as referring to Dante's eclogues and the ancient poetry as being that of the Roman *auctores*.

23. On the topos of the elm and ivy, see Demetz, "Elm and the Vine."

24. Years later, in 1327, del Virgilio writes to Mussato with an eclogue, shortly before the latter's death, receiving no known reply. See Lorenzini, *Corrispondenza bucolica*, 175–95.

25. Raffa, "Dante's Mocking Pastoral Muse," 273. See also Ferrara, "Ethical Distance," which argues that Dante maintains an ethical distance from earlier political concerns in an effort to explain his refusal of del Virgilio's request to pen a Latin political poem.

26. On Fiduccio de' Milotti, see Albanese and Pontari, "Cenacolo ravennate," 346–75. The awkwardness of Dante's tactics of both relocating the pastoral setting to Sicily and composing it from the perspective of a third person has caused some critics to postulate that he died before completing it or that he did not write it at all. See Pertile, "*Egloghe* di Dante," for a cogent review of the perplexities presented by the poem. See also Allegretti, "Dante 'Tityrus annosus,'" for arguments in favor of the overall coherence between the two eclogues. On the history of challenges to the authenticity of Dante's eclogues, see Petoletti, "Nota introduttiva," 503–4. For a discussion of the question of the authenticity of this eclogue, see Petoletti's note to *Ecl.* 4.70.

27. For a reading of the opening lines as indicating the time of day and not a season, see Casadei, *Dante oltre la "Commedia*," 57.

28. It is likely that Dante completed the *Paradiso* before writing this eclogue. See Casadei, *Dante oltre la "Commedia,"* 196–200. See also Combs-Schilling, "Tityrus in Limbo," 22n19, for a thorough discussion of the question.

29. See Combs-Schilling, "Tityrus in Limbo," 24n32, for a discussion of the question of the shift in setting.

30. For a review of the questions opened by this enigmatic figure, see Petoletti's note to *Ecl.* 4.75. See also the new historical evidence presented in favor of Polyphemus as Calboli in Albanese and Pontari, "Notariato bolognese," esp. 24–37. They note that Calboli was already present in Bologna as *capitano della guerra* in June 1321 before becoming *capitano del popolo* in irregular appointment in July of the same year.

31. Casadei, however, seems to think the question has been resolved in favor of Calboli, as do Albanese and Pontari. See Casadei, "Dante tra Ravenna," 123. See also Ferrara's considerations in "Ethical Distance," 118–21, where the author concludes that "apart from considerations related to danger and personal safety . . . what clearly emerges from his bucolic verses is a fundamentally ethical distance from political involvements" and that "Dante will limit his global ethical and political thought to his all-embracing epic poem" (120–21).

32. The contest over which city should rightly inherit Dante's heritage continues at each anniversary of the poet's birth and death. On the history of the political importance of inheriting Dante's heritage, see Raffa, *Dante's Bones*.

33. See Pertile, "*Egloghe* di Dante," 163.

34. For the text and translation of the *Metamorphoses*, I have used Miller and Goold's Loeb.

35. In his description, Alphesibeus conflates Polyphemus's threats to tear Acis to pieces with his death, which is caused by being crushed by a piece of mountainside launched at him by the Cyclops.

36. Speaking to Scylla and referring to Polyphemus with the third person, Galatea abruptly shifts to addressing him in the second person: "Iamque tibi formae, iamque est tibi cura placendi, / iam rigidos pectis rastris, Polypheme, capillos" (*Met.* 13.864–65) [And now, Polyphemus, you become careful of your appearance, now anxious to please; now with a rake you comb your shaggy locks].

37. In the context of this exchange, Dante's confidence in the value of his vernacular poetry remains unshaken, while the precariousness of his individual being is highlighted.

38. Giovanni del Virgilio himself interpreted Polyphemus in his *Allegorie librorum Ovidii Metamorphoseos* as a figure for corruption, especially moral corruption of the heart. See del Virgilio, *Allegorie* 13.6. See Raffa, "Dante's Mocking Pastoral Muse," 283–84.

39. See also Pertile, "*Egloghe* di Dante," 163, where the critic notes that the *antrum*, or cave, that del Virgilio chooses to describe his pastoral dwelling in his

first eclogue is the determining factor for the choice of Polyphemus, Galatea, and the Sicilian landscape in Dante's response.

40. I have used Durling's translation of the *Paradiso* here.

41. Honess, "Ritornerò poeta . . . ," 102. See also Honess, chapter 4 of this book, where she highlights Dante's own awareness (in *Ep.* 12) that any triumphant return to Florence would be "highly unlikely" (147).

42. For a discussion of the scholarly debate on these lines, see Hollander, "Marsyas as *figura Dantis*." On medieval writers' metapoetic self-consciousness about writing on skin, see S. Kay, *Animal Skins*.

43. Dante's mention of Saint Peter in the last tercet refers to his coronation at the end of *Paradiso* 24.151–53.

CHAPTER 10

Philosophy and the "Other Works"

LUCA BIANCHI

In the preface to the Italian translation of his book *Dante Philomythes and Philosopher*, published in 1984 as *L'uomo e il cosmo*, Patrick Boyde recalls that the original English title aimed at emphasizing that Dante was at one and the same time a poet, a lover of myth, and a philosopher. He further makes clear that his title is inspired by a well-known passage in Aristotle's *Metaphysics* (1.2 982b17–19); and, after explaining the meaning of the word *philomythes*—as he had done in the introduction to the 1981 English edition—he adds: "Il termine filosofo, amante della vera conoscenza, non richiede spiegazioni" [The term *philosopher*, lover of true knowledge, needs no explanation].[1]

This is a good example of an attitude recently criticized by Zygmunt Barański, who has rightly noted that, although the leading Dante scholars "have always been sensitive to the historical and cultural specificities" of his ideas, "they have demonstrated considerably less concern with defining in a philologically refined manner the poet's understanding of the scope and nature of particular broad areas of knowledge, epistemology and intellectual activity, such as 'philosophy,' 'theology,' 'wisdom.'"[2] As a matter of fact, if Boyde was perhaps too optimistic in assuming that today's Italian readers are familiar with the basic dictionary definition of the word *philosopher*, there is no doubt that its meaning in Dante's times was even more controversial. Which kind of intellectuals were qualified as "philosophers" between the end of the thirteenth and the beginning of the fourteenth century? Was Dante deemed a "philosopher"? Did he consider himself to be one? And which (if any) of his works were regarded by himself and by his contemporaries as philosophical works, and ought to be considered as such nowadays?

Answering these questions is much more complex than one might suspect, especially if one bears in mind the peculiar development of scholarship on medieval philosophy. One should never forget that from the end of the nineteenth century onward the history of medieval philosophy grew and acquired the status of an institutionalized discipline on the basis of very strong assumptions concerning what philosophy was during the Middle Ages. Needless to say, medievalists had different opinions on this point, but they all had to face a problem that historians of ancient, modern, and contemporary philosophy could pass over: medievalists felt obliged to argue that philosophy did exist from the sixth to the fourteenth century, although all the major thinkers of this period were *clerici*, often belonging to religious orders, who produced mainly, if not exclusively, works dealing with theology. Thus many medievalists tried to emphasize, first, that philosophy was practiced quite freely and as an autonomous discipline, separate from rational theology; second, that medieval thinkers significantly contributed to the development of philosophical inquiry because, besides discussing the so-called problem of "reason and faith," they worked on the main traditional branches of philosophy. So the first generations of historians of medieval philosophy (from Victor Cousin and Jean-Barthélemy Hauréau to Josef Kleutgen, from Pierre Mandonnet and Martin Grabmann to Maurice De Wulf) tried to show that one can find in the works of medieval thinkers a set of strictly philosophical doctrines, which perfectly conform to the traditional branches of philosophy: logic, epistemology, philosophy of nature, ethics, and metaphysics. Étienne Gilson—who introduced the controversial notion of Christian philosophy—and Fernand Van Steenberghen—who rejected it, distinguishing between philosophy understood in a "broad" sense (a *Weltanschauung*, which in the Middle Ages might be identified with the Christian worldview) and in a "strict" sense (a systematic work of pure reason, separate from theology)—both agreed that one is allowed to "extract" from the writings of great medieval theologians their philosophical theories; and they both agreed that one is therefore allowed to use passages taken from Aquinas's *Summae*, as well as from Scotus's and

Ockam's commentaries on the *Sentences*, to evaluate their contribution to the development of logic, epistemology, ontology, and so on.

There is no need to say that, besides neglecting relevant aspects of the cultural and institutional context in which it was developed, such an approach improperly identified medieval philosophy with a selection of themes discussed in the works of the great thirteenth- and fourteenth-century theologians: previous thinkers were reduced to simple "forerunners"; thirteenth- and fourteenth-century arts masters who taught grammar, logic, and Aristotle's philosophy were seen as minor figures, worthy to be included in the picture only if they were connected with the great theologians; nonscholastic and nonprofessional thinkers (including major figures such as Raymond Lull, Meister Eckhart, and Dante) were often ignored, at times hastily dismissed with vague labels (mystic, polymath, etc.), at times considered as mere "popularizers" of unoriginal views.

Over the last thirty or so years many historians have challenged and deconstructed this approach to medieval philosophy. They have called attention to the fact that the term *philosophia* covered a wide and mutable semantic area during the Middle Ages. They have argued, on the one hand, that the practice of selecting a set of theories contained in theological works and labeling them "philosophy" is totally anachronistic. They have shown, on the other hand, that even thirteenth- and fourteenth-century sophisticated treatments of logical and physical problems had an essential theological background. They have criticized the tendency to superimpose contemporary definitions of philosophy onto those circulating in the Middle Ages and have refuted the idea that scholasticism is the best or even the only expression of it. This new trend (Alain de Libera in the 1990s spoke of "nouveau médiévisme") has allowed historians of the last generations to give due attention to the plurality of conceptions of philosophy that actually existed during the Middle Ages and to enlarge considerably their field of research, challenging hierarchies generally accepted by their predecessors: hierarchies between periods (the myth of the thirteenth century as the golden age of scholasticism, followed by a fourteenth-century "crisis," has been abandoned); hierarchies between disciplines (today nobody identifies the "spirit" of medieval thought with theology or metaphysics); hierarchies between "great" and "minor" authors (for instance, it is now clear to all that the arts master Boethius of Dacia and the theologian Henri of Ghent are both major figures); hierarchies between "original" and "deep" texts, issuing from university teaching and written in Latin, and "popularizing" texts written in the vernacular (one need only think of Nicole Oresme to understand that, in fact, linguistic boundaries did not correspond to intellectual and cultural standards).[3]

So far so good. Medievalists now generally adopt an expanded and inclusive notion of philosophy that, although theoretically rather problematic, is heuristically useful. In this perspective, Ruedi Imbach and his "school" had the great merit of calling attention to the growing interest of laymen in philosophical debates and to the dissemination of the ideal of philosophical life outside university milieus.[4] Yet, when they rightly emphasize that Dante's life and works provide evidence for this major and previously neglected cultural phenomenon, when they make him—together with profoundly different figures such as Francesco Petrarca and Christine de Pizan—a champion of the so-called *philosophie laïque*, they also convey two ideas that, far from being obvious, deserve further investigation: namely that Dante considered himself to be a philosopher and that he regarded several of his works as philosophical texts.[5]

I will discuss these two intertwined issues separately, starting with the first one for a precise reason: departing from Boethius and following the conception of paronymous terms diffused by Latin grammarians, Dante himself maintains in the *Convivio* (3.11.5–6) that it was the concrete term *filosofo* that generated the abstract *filosofia*, which is "lo vocabulo del suo propio atto" [the term for the philosopher's proper activity].[6]

Phylosophie domesticus

It is well known that some of his contemporaries viewed Dante not only as a poet but also as a philosopher and as a theologian. One need only think of Giovanni del Virgilio's epitaph for the *sommo poeta*: "theologus Dantes, nullius dogmatis expers, quod foveat claro philosophia sinu" [Here lies Dante, theologian bereft of no doctrine that Philosophy nurtured at her illustrious breast], or of the gloss to the *Inferno* by Jacopo Alighieri: "illustre filosofo e poeta" [illustrious philosopher and poet], or by Graziolo de' Bambaglioli: "philosophye verum alumpnum et poetam excelsum" [a true pupil of philosophy and a distinguished poet].[7] It is equally well known that one of the most influential sources of this image of Dante is his biography by Giovanni Boccaccio, who writes that during his lifetime "alcuni il chiamarono sempre 'poeta,' altri 'filosofo' e molti 'teologo'" [some always called him "poet," others "philosopher," and many "theologian"]. Boccaccio also adds that Dante was "uomo nel grembo della filosofia nutricato" [a man nourished in the womb of philosophy].[8] It has been pointed out that this presentation depends on what Dante himself wrote in 1315 (*Ep.* 12.3.6), defining himself in his twelfth letter as "phylosophie domestic*us*" [familiar of philosophy].[9] However, it has not been hitherto highlighted, I believe, that, though drawing on this passage, Boccaccio uses a formula that has a clear Boethian flavor, and that Dante did not use in his letter or elsewhere, saying instead in the *Convivio* (1.3.4) that he was "nutrito" [nourished] by Florence.[10] As an attentive reader of the *Consolation of Philosophy*—and a great admirer of Boethius, ready to identify himself with this exiled thinker—Dante was well aware of the deep differences that separated them.[11] Unlike Dante, Boethius was in a position to state that he had been "Eleaticis atque Academicis studiis innutritum" [nourished in the lore of Eleatics and Academics], and "nostro . . . lacte nutritus" [nourished . . . upon the milk] of Lady Philosophy.[12] Dante simply says that he was "phylosophie domestic*us*," an expression that may signify "servant to," or better, "familiar with philosophy."[13] This claim is in fact in keeping with what he had written in a famous autobiographical passage in the *Convivio* (2.12.2–7), namely, that he became fond of the "donna gentile" [gracious lady]—the allegorical figure of philosophy—after the death of his first love, Beatrice, in 1290, and that this second love, to which he came rather late by medieval standards, was not filial (like Boethius's love) but passionate and violent. Consequently, Dante describes it by merging the sapiential language of the Solomonic books of the Old Testament, the erotic metaphors of the *Song of Songs*, and the sexual allusions of courtly literature.[14]

In the *Questio de aqua et terra*—provided it is by his own hand—Dante addresses his ideal audience as formed by men "in phylosophia nutriti" [nourished by philosophy] but speaks of himself as "inter vere philosophantes minimus" (21.71; and see 1.2). Is this "a formula whose adjectival modesty masks its substantive hubris," as Albert Ascoli claims? Or should we take it more seriously, as Barański suggests?[15] The sincerity of such a topos (undoubtedly reminiscent of St Paul's self-description as "minimus apostolorum" [the least of the apostles] in 1 Cor. 15:9) is difficult to evaluate, but what interests me here is less the alternative between arrogance and humility than the precise rendering of the phrase, which, in my opinion, does not mean "the least among the philosophers" (as in the variant reading that we find at the end of the *Questio*, "philosophorum minimum" [24.86]), but "the least among those who truly do philosophy."[16]

This is a subtle yet significant distinction, in the light of two elements. First, thanks to Anna Pegoretti we know that the Latin expression *philosophantes*—as well as the Italian *filosofanti* used by Dante in an autobiographical passage of the *Convivio* (2.12.7)—was sometimes used as a synonym of *philosophi*, was sometimes applied to theologians in a pejorative sense, but often designated in general all those who studied and practiced philosophy broadly understood as the highest form of knowledge, including therefore theologians and other intellectuals of various kinds.[17] Second, throughout the long Middle Ages, not only did a multiplicity of conceptions of philosophy exist and cohabit—as I have already noted—but also different paradigms of the philosopher were available.

As far as *philosophia* was taken in its generic sense of love for wisdom and for the most perfect way of life, it could be identified with true knowledge and virtue, and therefore with Christian beliefs and practices: in this perspective, which develops the patristic view of philosophy as *imitatio Christi*, one might call "philosophers" all Christians and in particular eremites and monks. During the twelfth century, the influence of Latin authors such as Seneca, Cicero, Macrobius, and Boethius grew considerably, and several ancient philosophers were regarded by Peter Abelard and John of Salisbury as endowed with a special revelation that allowed them to grasp key doctrines of the Christian faith. Yet Abelard was convinced that this revelation was grounded in natural reason and was the result of a process of personal purification. Consequently, he felt free to argue that ancient philosophers established a model of moral perfection that was still effective for Christians.[18] Moreover laymen, often working in the princely courts, started producing texts on natural, moral, and political philosophy.[19]

When translations from Greek and Arabic made accessible not only a large corpus of previously unknown philosophical works but also a variety of tracts on hermeticism, alchemy, natural magic, and physiognomy, other paradigms of the philosopher came to the fore, including that of the ḥakīm, a wise man who, in the Islamic world, was engaged in secular learning and served a ruler as an adviser on medical, astrological, and ethical matters. This explains why translators of medical and philosophical texts from Arabic (such as Stephen of Pisa, Gerard of Cremona, and Philip of Tripoli) were referred to as "philosophers": Theodore of Antioch—a Jacobite Syrian Orthodox Christian educated in Mosul and Baghdad, who served the Emperor Fredrick II as diplomat, translator, astrologer, and physician—was generally presented as "the emperor's philosopher."[20]

Nonetheless the major change occurred precisely in the period of Dante's youth, when the institutionalization of the teaching of philosophy in university arts faculties and the adoption as "textbooks" of newly available Aristotelian treatises on natural philosophy, metaphysics, and ethics caused a realignment of the notion of philosophy, now conceived as a specific form of knowledge that used only rational principles and methods to address a precise set of problems and was based on a well-identified corpus of *auctoritates*—mainly, though not exclusively, the works authored by, or ascribed to, the Stagirite. In this context, most thirteenth-century theologians carefully distinguished between the *sancti*, namely, the fathers and other authoritative Christian thinkers, and the *philosophi*, namely, ancient pagan and contemporary non-Christian thinkers. Indeed, they regarded philosophy as a form of worldly wisdom that expressed what the human mind might reach by its own means, and therefore had its raison d'être, but only before Christianity or outside Christendom—mainly in the Muslim world. Undoubtedly, these theologians were convinced that philosophy (and notably the Neoplatonized versions of Aristotle's thought that circulated in that period) still had a deep meaning for Christian culture, because they maintained that many of its conclusions represented what was rationally true. At the same time, they believed that these conclusions ought to be integrated into a higher form of wisdom, developed from new premises grounded on religious revelation. Therefore, although all great thirteenth-century theologians obviously did philosophy, they (Thomas Aquinas included) did not label themselves "philosophers."[21]

In their fight to introduce a new conception of philosophy as an autonomous discipline, independent of revelation, which ought to be appreciated and practiced in itself and not simply as a component of the theological enterprise, arts masters, such as Siger of Brabant, Boethius of Dacia, and their Parisian colleagues, tried to distinguish themselves from masters of theology, who not only formed a well-identified and self-conscious group but also enjoyed a higher social and cultural status. Precisely for this reason, these arts masters proudly presented themselves as the descendants of the ancient philosophers and started calling themselves *philosophi, viri philosophici, homines philosophici,* or even, in Italy, *layci et saeculares philosophi*.[22] Neglected for a long time by medievalists—who, as I noted earlier, paradoxically wrote histories of philosophy in which little or no place was given to the only group of thinkers who, during the thirteenth and fourteenth centuries, considered themselves to be "philosophers"—the emergence of this new class of professional philosophers, who dared to apply to themselves the term *philosophi*, while giving it a very specific sense, was not unknown to Dante.[23] Even if one admits that the *Questio* is authentic and that, in a single passage, Dante claimed to be the least not only among the *philosophantes*, but also among the *philosophi*, the fact remains that his self-portrait was that of a *litteratus* who, among other things, did philosophy in a general sense of the word, but in a manner very different from that of contemporary professional philosophers. A layman, an amateur essentially, since he was self-taught, who started studying philosophy at the age at which most arts masters had already completed their mandatory period of regency, Dante did not deem himself inferior to them—as witnessed for instance in his tendency to impart pedantic lessons of logic.[24] At the same time, he was and always felt himself to be an outsider,[25] who loved philosophy with the passion and freshness of the neophyte, yet always bent it to his ethical, political, and, in particular, literary purposes.

It is now generally accepted that, especially in the *Convivio* and in the *Monarchia*, Dante heavily depends on late thirteenth-century professional thinkers who taught the arts, theology, and law. I will consider this point in due course, but I would like to stress here that, although these thinkers were among his favorite sources, they were also one of the main targets of his criticisms.[26] Convinced that the growth of the universities had produced a commodification of knowledge, in the *Convivio* Dante harshly rebuked specialists of various disciplines, theologians included, for seeking wisdom "in quanto per quella guadagnano denari o dignitate" and "per acquistare moneta o dignitate" (1.9.3; 3.11.10) [for the sake of gaining money or position; to gain money or prestige]. He acutely detected the fundamental tension between the model of philosophy as a perfect way of life and its professionalization in the arts faculties, and, taking very seriously Aristotle's claim that philosophy aims at satisfying the desire for knowledge shared by all human beings, he refused the elitism of professional philosophers. Dante thus carefully distinguished "quelli pochi che seggiono a quella mensa dove lo pane delli angeli si manuca" [those few who sit at the meal where the bread of angels is eaten] from "quelli che colle pecore hanno comune cibo" (*Conv.* 1.1.7) [those whose food is shared with sheep]; and claiming that he had the opportunity to take his place "a' piedi di coloro che seggiono" [at the feet of those who are seated] and to gather "di quello che da loro cade" (*Conv.* 1.1.10) [what falls from them], he envisaged a project of popularization of philosophy (whatever this notion might mean in the *Convivio*).[27] Left unfinished, this project marked a turning point in Dante's formation as a thinker, so that several themes sketched out in the vernacular *Convivio* were developed in Latin treatises such as the *De vulgari eloquentia* and the *Monarchia*. But what are the outputs of this great intellectual enterprise?

Genus Philosophiae?

This leads us to the second problem that I mentioned: the extent to which Dante considered his texts to be philosophical. Ruedi Imbach, whose essays on Dante's thought mark a major step in recent scholarship, stated a few years ago that Dante's "overtly philosophical oeuvre" consists of five texts: the *Convivio*, the *De vulgari eloquentia*, the *Monarchia*, the *Questio de aqua et terra*, and *Epistle* 13 to Cangrande della Scala.[28] I have neither the space nor the competence to discuss, in general terms, what philosophical texts may be, if and how we should accord them a special status, and why they might differ from other texts (poetry, fiction, history, etc.). Nevertheless, I noted that one of the most important outcomes of the *nouveau médiévisme* was to encourage historians to recognize that it is anachronistic to superimpose today's definitions of philosophy onto medieval thinkers, who used the term to refer to a large and variable set of intellectual experiences, doctrines, and productions. Consequently, this would imply that the distinction between philosophical and nonphilosophical works is historically determined and depends on changeable and changing notions of philosophy adopted in different periods and contexts. Therefore, can we be sure that texts that we now find significant in our reconstruction of the development of past philosophical thought were conceived as obviously philosophical by their authors and their intended audiences?

Let me therefore make a few comments on Imbach's list, starting with the two writings whose authenticity is still controversial. The *Questio de aqua et terra* is clearly presented as a philosophical text: the author refers to it as "hec philosophia" (24.87), a phrase that should likely be amended to "hec questio" [this question] and, if not, can mean nothing more than "this philosophical question."[29] The author declares that his purpose is to resolve a problem of Aristotelian cosmology without going "extra materiam naturalem" (20.60) [beyond the boundaries of natural matter]. Yet the *Questio* is also presented as the written version of a dispute, originally arisen in Mantua and resolved not only on a separate occasion (as generally happened) but also in another place, namely, the little church of Sant'Elena in Verona. This in itself is rather extraordinary. However, if one accepts Dante's authorship, other elements are even more puzzling. A disputation implies the presence of disputants, normally advanced students who provide *pro* and *contra* arguments. Thus the question arises: Who played this role, supposedly in Mantua, introducing the arguments, five of which were actually taken into account in Verona (2.6)? Although we are aware of the existence in the latter city of a community of masters and students, we are simply told that the audience was constituted by "universo clero veronensi" (24.87) [the entire Veronese clergy]; and yet the exact meaning of this formula is far from clear. Moreover, a question, either ordinary or quodlibetal, could be "determined" (1.3) only by a master, namely, a *magister*, and, given that Dante did not have this degree, we are obliged to make a few challenging assumptions. First, that in order to consolidate his intellectual reputation, his intent was to act as if he were a master in a city through which he happened to be passing: an important Ghibelline city that did not house a *studium generale* but had a body of masters teaching different disciplines.[30] Second, that he was invited (or at least allowed) by local authorities to perform this role, or, more precisely, given the nature of the problem examined, the role of an arts master. Third, that explaining why land emerges from water in the Northern Hemisphere, he not only emphasized that God's providential design cannot be completely understood by limited human forms of knowing but also quoted extensively from the Bible, something that arts masters rarely did in their disputations, during which, as we will see, they were careful to speak "philosophically" or "naturally."

The letter to Cangrande belongs instead to a completely different literary genre. Here the author dedicates the *Paradiso* to the Lord of Verona, offers an introduction to the *Commedia* as a whole, and expounds the first canto of the *Paradiso*. Therefore the *Epistle* constitutes—if it is entirely authentic, as Luca Azzetta has convincingly argued—the last of Dante's self-commentaries and can hardly be regarded in itself as a philosophical contribution for the simple reason that it offers a "philosophical reading" of another text.[31]

But what about the other works included in the so-called *opere minori*, notably the *Convivio*, the *De vulgari eloquentia*, and the *Monarchia*, the three interrelated writings that sometimes find a place, however limited, in our histories of medieval philosophy? There is no doubt that they all contain a substantial amount of philosophical material and provide evidence of Dante's deep, though not always firsthand, knowledge of thinkers such as Aristotle, Avicenna, Averroes, Albert the Great, and Thomas Aquinas. Moreover, it has recently been suggested that these three works follow a common "vena razionalista" [rationalistic vein] and that the *Convivio* and the *Monarchia* should be read against the background of the philosophical tradition developed by late thirteenth-century arts masters.[32] Dante did indeed borrow—to a different extent and for different purposes—principles, ideas, and quotations from these thinkers. He also adopted some of their values and ideals; he imitated their methods, their argumentative procedures, their jargon; he displayed the same logical and hermeneutical skills that were proper to university-trained scholars.[33] Yet the status that Dante assigned to these three masterpieces remains controversial, and their affinity to late thirteenth- and early fourteenth-century philosophical literature is far from evident. Consequently, in the fourteenth century as well as now, one might well resist the temptation of placing them on the same bookshelf as works of "medieval philosophy."

Indeed, it can be argued that it is misleading to label the *Convivio* a "philosophical treatise,"[34] and Barański has recently done so by highlighting primarily its exceptional formal aspects that bear little relationship to those of a philosophical tractate: its textual hybridity (the combined use of commentary, compilation, and question), its digressive character, its use of metaphor, and its recourse to the *stylus satiricus*.[35] One might add that its doctrinal content too is anything but that commonly found in standard philosophical texts of the late Middle Ages. It is true that in their commentaries Francis Cheneval, Thomas Ricklin, and Gianfranco Fioravanti have convincingly shown that in books 1–3 Dante heavily depends on the literary genre of introductions to philosophy widespread in the arts faculties from the 1250s and that, following this model, he offers a definition of philosophy, a celebration of philosophy, an analysis of the "impediments" [impedimenta] to philosophical life, and a division of philosophy. But does this mean that the *Convivio* as a whole was conceived as a work of philosophy? I would not venture to claim as much, and for at least four reasons.

First, even though Dante was clearly interested in showing that the canzoni that he had written during the 1290s convey a deep philosophical message, the general aim and structure of the *Convivio* remain an enigma. We know that the subject matter of all the poems that Dante intended to comment upon was love and virtue (*Conv.* 1.1.14) and that some of the unwritten books would probably have dealt with virtues such as justice, temperance, liberality, and humility. At the same time, we do not know whether Dante envisioned tackling only moral topics or whether he had more ambitious and wide-ranging encyclopedic projects. Second, however important and however philosophical it might be, the prose of the *Convivio* is explicitly subordinated to the previously written canzoni because its declared task (see 1.5–6) is to reveal their hidden meaning.[36] Third, the main purpose of the first three books is to offer the "food" of knowledge to men and women without university training and to make them eager to sample the pleasures of the philosophical life. In doing so, Dante vernacularizes materials largely employed by Parisian and Italian arts masters in their opening lectures on the Aristotelian corpus, but this does not mean that he simply repeats accepted views: his language, his syncretistic approach, his emphasis on the limits of human knowledge, and, above all, his complex, not to say ambiguous, notions of "philosophy" and "wisdom" are extremely original. The fact remains, however, that the *Convivio*, for more than half of its parts in prose, is less a piece *of* philosophy than a piece *about* philosophy (or about what today might be called "metaphilosophy"). Finally, only in book 4 does Dante eventually start doing philosophy in a more concrete way, addressing a specific question—the nature of true nobility and its connection to virtue—which undoubtedly had a great ethical and political significance and involved relevant problems of metaphysics and natural philosophy. Yet Dante focuses on this issue precisely because it was relatively little scrutinized by professional thinkers, either philosophers or theologians.[37] And if Dante discusses it by reproducing the scholastic technique of the disputed question, he also goes beyond late medieval philosophical inquiry in at least three ways. First, he makes extensive use of the Latin poets (most notably Virgil).[38] Second, he declares that, besides solving the problem of nobility according to natural philosophy ("per modo naturale"; 4.21.1), he is willing to treat it theologically ("per modo teologico" or "per via teologica"; 4.21.1 and 11). Third, he insists on the practical consequences of an incorrect conception of nobility and reacts against error on this issue in violent terms: "Rispondere si vorrebbe non colle parole ma col coltello a tanta bestialitade" (4.14.11) [The answer to such subhuman stupidity would have to be not with words but with a sword]—an assertion that has often been glossed, but without highlighting a significant point. Dante here not only departs from the impersonal style of scholastic method but also adopts the language used by theologians and censors against errors in matters of faith, thereby, giving a religious coloring to his *quaestio de nobilitate*.[39]

If one may convincingly maintain that the *Convivio* is much more than a "philosophical treatise," the case of the *De vulgari eloquentia* is no less problematic. At the opening of the text (1.1.1–2), Dante stresses the novelty of his work, announces that it will offer a "de vulgaris eloquentie doctrina" [theory of eloquence in the vernacular], and carefully defines its "subject." It has been argued that, in so doing, "he portrays himself as the bold founder of a new branch of knowledge."[40] But where might this be placed in the system of arts and disciplines? Despite his penchant for the divisions of philosophy—one has only to think of chapters 13 and 14 of the second book of the *Convivio*—nowhere does Dante clearly resolve this question; and this seems to me a telling silence. However this may be, in the first part of his treatise, Dante provides a universal history and theory of language; in the second, unfinished part, he outlines an art of poetry, examining different styles and forms used by vernacular writers. The effort of giving philosophical foundation to the notion of the "illustrious vernacular" [volgare illustre] is evident. However, it is also evident that the *De vulgari eloquentia* has not only a philosophical but also a historical, exegetical, political, and literary dimension and that the problem of nobility is no less important here than in the *Convivio*.⁴¹ The greatest impulse to read the *De vulgari eloquentia* as mainly concerned with the philosophy of language was given by Maria Corti's influential book *Dante a un nuovo crocevia*, published in 1981, where Dante's conception of language was presented as a development of that elaborated by late thirteenth-century modistic grammarians, most notably Boethius of Dacia. This interpretation, however, is no longer tenable. Immediately criticized by authoritative historians of medieval grammar and logic, it has been conclusively refuted by Costantino Marmo, who has shown, first, that the relationship between Dante and Parisian *modistae*, through the alleged intermediation of Gentile of Cingoli, is highly speculative; second, that Corti gave a totally distorted view of the modistic project of investigation, because, following Geoffrey L. Bursill-Hall, she read it in terms of Noam Chomsky's model of deep structure; and third, that Corti seriously misunderstood the *De vulgari eloquentia*, ascribing to Dante an idea that he never held, namely that God did not give human beings a specific language "but rather a universal generative (deep) structure that Adam was going to use in making up his language and naming things."⁴²

Ruedi Imbach and Irène Rosier-Catach have elegantly highlighted that, in the *De vulgari eloquentia*, the existence of the "illustrious vernacular" is demonstrated by using the *reductio ad unum* principle, taken from Aristotle's *Metaphysics*, which Dante also exploits, in a political sense, in the *Convivio* (4.4.5–6) and more extensively in the *Monarchia*—a masterpiece that one cannot qualify as a "minor work" without some embarrassment.⁴³ Along with the use of a rather technical Latin, of a more impersonal style, of well-formed syllogisms, and of other logical tools, the systematic recourse to general principles that lay the foundation for further discussion demonstrates Dante's intention to approach scientifically the much-debated and politically pressing problem of the relationship between church and empire. But does "scientifically" mean "philosophically"?

At a first glance, one might give a positive answer, especially because the need for a universal monarchy is demonstrated by assuming, without qualms, the fundamental premise that the goal and the highest happiness of human beings consist in the complete actualization of their intellectual potentialities. Dante then argues that this requires the efforts of a "multitudo" (1.3.8) [multitude] of individuals who can "liberrime atque facillime" [most freely and readily] attend to their "fere divinum" [almost divine] intellectual activity "in quiete sive tranquillitate pacis" (1.4.2) [in the calm or tranquility of peace] under the guidance of a supreme emperor. The Aristotelian inspiration of the premise is evident. According to some scholars, Dante gave a particular reading of Aristotle's doctrine of intellectual happiness, advancing a sort of "political Averroism," or at least giving a social and political version of the ideal of philosophical life disseminated by the so-called radical Aristotelians.[44] Other scholars maintain instead that there are no traces of "Averroism" in the *Monarchia* and that Dante's political thought, more generally, has nothing "unorthodox" about it.[45] It goes without saying that I am unable to take a stance here on such complex problems, whose full examination would require an attentive reading of two controversial passages: one from the first book, where, arguing that the pursuit of knowledge is a collective task, Dante hints at Averroes's doctrine of the unity of the potential intellect; and the other from the third book, where he maintains that the empire and the church are mutually independent because divine providence has given humanity two ends (temporal and spiritual), which must be reached by two different means (the teachings of philosophy and spiritual teachings). My only, trifling remark is that, however interpreted, philosophical theories on the (earthly and heavenly) ends of human life represent at the same time the starting point and the point of arrival of the long journey Dante made in order to answer the three main questions that he raises in the *Monarchia* and that, during this journey, rich philosophical matter, taken mainly from the Aristotelian tradition, interacts fruitfully with other materials drawn from a vast array of theological, exegetical, political, and juridical texts, from pagan and Christian literature, and from historiography. The two most recent annotated editions and translations of the treatise provide overwhelming evidence of this. While Diego Quaglioni has the great merit of revealing the hitherto underrated presence and importance of the *Digest* in the treatise, Paolo Chiesa and Andrea Tabarroni elegantly argue that, although in the prologue to the first book, by tacitly comparing himself to great "scientists" of the past, Dante claims for himself the role of founder of a new political science, in the second and the third books he progressively presents himself as a prophet, destined not only to disclose "veritates occultas" (1.1.5) [hidden truths] but to fight for truths that make men free.[46] However one evaluates the controversial image of Dante as a prophet, Chiesa and Tabarroni demonstrate that, for the poet, a rational inquiry into the origin, nature, and scope of the universal monarchy cannot be carried out using exclusively philosophical principles and logical methods: it also entails the interpretation of biblical passages; the discussion of theological, ecclesiological, and political doctrines; and the analysis of the events of the past within a providential conception of history.[47]

"Dephilosophizing" Dante's "Other Works"?

To avoid misunderstandings, I hasten to make clear that my goal is neither to launch abstract discussions about the "degree of philosophicity" of Dante's *opere minori* nor to suggest that they ought to be "dephilosophized." It is evident that a wide range of philosophical interests and concerns plays an essential role in all these works. Nonetheless, since these interests and concerns were neither the only nor, in most cases, the principal ones, it seems to me that, when one reads these works as a historian of philosophy, one should emphasize not only their philosophical dimension but also the risk of neglecting or underrating other relevant aspects. Thus one should draw attention to what Dante borrows from philosophical sources but also underscore how he rethinks and reshapes them from a perspective that is always his own, precisely because it is not exclusively, not uniquely philosophical.[48]

From this point of view, it might be instructive—I am not aware that this has so far been done—to examine the presence of the word *philosophy* and related terms in Dante's "other works." In the Latin works, including all the *Epistles* and the *Questio de aqua et terra*, one can find forty-five occurrences of *phylosophus*, eight of *phylosophia*, four of the verb *phylosophor*, three of the adjective *phylosophicus*, and two of *philosophantes*. In the Italian works, one can find ninety-one occurrences of the noun *filosofo* (in more than half the cases used to refer to the Stagirite), fifty-six occurrences of the noun *filosofia*, six of the adjective *filosofica* (always in the feminine gender), three of the verb *filosofare*, two of the adverb *filosoficamente*, one of *filosofante* (adjective), and one of *filosofanti* (noun). This means that the terms related to the notion of philosophy have sixty-two occurrences in the Latin works and 160 occurrences in the "minor" Italian works, for a total of 222 occurrences.[49] To make a comparison—an extremely rough one because of the different size of their respective works—the two major theologians of the second half of the thirteenth century, who rightly have a major place in our histories of philosophy but, as I pointed out earlier, never described themselves as philosophers, employ these terms much more frequently: Bonaventure around 1,000 times and Thomas Aquinas more than 7,000 times. We are therefore obliged to recognize that, compared to other intellectuals of his age, Dante has recourse to the notion of "philosophy" in a significant but rather limited way, and this is even more striking if one considers four facts. First, around one-third of the occurrences of the Latin terms dealing with this concept are in works (six in the epistle to Cangrande and fourteen in the *Questio de aqua et terra*) whose authenticity, however plausible it might be, is still controversial. Second, more than a half of these occurrences (thirty-eight out of sixty-two) are in the *Monarchia*. Third, in this as in the other Latin works, in most cases they simply are references to "the Philosopher" par excellence, namely Aristotle, and introduce quotations and sayings extracted from his works.[50] Fourth, more than two-thirds (158 out of 222) of all references to *philosophy* and related terms in both the Latin and Italian works are in the *Convivio*, namely, the work where, as we have seen, rather than doing philosophy Dante declares his love for this form of knowledge, invites others to practice it, explains its origin, its nature, and its limits, and extensively quotes "the Philosopher."

It is equally useful to call attention to another point. Dantists agree that the "other works" are extremely original, complex, and idiosyncratic for several reasons, first of all, their literary forms and genres, the variety of their styles and registers, the energy and the creativity of their language, and the richness of their sources. It is instead often overlooked that, however philosophical they might be or appear to us to be, these works have two features that make them profoundly different from any other text written in Dante's times, either by professional philosophers (arts masters such as Boethius of Dacia and Siger of Brabant) or by the *theologi philosophantes* (notably Albert the Great and Thomas Aquinas).

Dante's "other works" contain several elements that had little place in contemporary philosophical literature broadly understood. Late medieval philosophical texts—and even most theological works, with the significant exception of some quodlibetal questions and sermons—generally discussed highly theoretical topics and aimed at presenting universally valid truths, which were supposed to transcend spatial and temporal contingencies. Unsurprisingly, they hardly ever presented geographical or historical evidence to support these truths: only in encyclopedias and in a few treatises, such as Albert the Great's *De natura locorum* and Roger Bacon's *Opus Maius*, can one find important, though often speculative remarks concerning geography, geopolitics, and world history. Because of their subject matter, the impact of geography and history in Dante's "other works" is instead substantial: the linguistic geography of Europe and Italy in the *De vulgari eloquentia* (I.8 and 10. 4–7);[51] the geography of climate and of religions in the *Monarchia* (1.14.6; 3.14.7); the history of language in the *De vulgari eloquentia* (I.4–9); the history of philosophy in the *Convivio* (3.11.3–5; 4.6.9–16);[52] and the history of ancient Rome and of the church in the *Convivio* (4.5.6–20) and in the *Monarchia* (1.16.1–4; 2.4.7–10; 3.10–11).

Moreover, Dante's "other works" also contain materials that could not have any sort of place in the writings of professional philosophers. Between the mid-thirteenth century and the first decades of the fourteenth century, at least three elements characterized a properly philosophical approach, differentiating it from other forms of intellectual inquiry. First, there was the Aristotelian idea that metaphors are not suitable to scientific discourse, that the "infimus modus persuadendi" [the worst way of arguing]—as Siger of Brabant put it—is that which proceeds "per metaphoras et fabulas" [through metaphors and fables] and that therefore a "fable"—as Dante himself claims in *Convivio* 4.14.15—cannot be taken into account when "filosoficamente disputando" [disputing philosophically].[53] Second, there was a need to maintain a clear distinction between the point of view of the philosopher and that of the Christian believer, between rationally demonstrated truths and the truths of faith. Third, one finds the practice of "speaking naturally," excluding supernatural phenomena and causes that are beyond the powers of human intellection.[54] As a consequence, in this period, philosophical literature strictly understood (the works that issued from the arts faculties, but also the Aristotelian commentaries and the treatises on noetics and ontology authored by theologians such as Albert the Great, Thomas Aquinas, and Giles of Rome) dismissed metaphorical language, made little use of religious *auctoritates*, carefully avoided disputing purely theological questions, and in particular did not take into account miracles and other events freely and directly produced by God. Now, there is no need to recall that, in Dante's "other works," metaphors are everywhere; biblical quotations—often interpreted in original ways—abound and interact with profane sources;[55] religious *exempla* are employed together with anecdotes and fantastic tales; and theological issues emerge frequently, even in the *De vulgari eloquentia*, where two paragraphs (1.2.2–3 and 3.1) are devoted to the question of the language of angels.[56]

No less pervasive are references to miracles and God's interventions in nature and in human history. If miracles are simply evoked in the *De vulgari eloquentia* (1.4.6), they are notoriously at the heart of the second book of the *Monarchia*. Here, reorganizing, developing, and qualifying what he had written in the fourth book of the *Convivio* (4.5.17–20), Dante tries to demonstrate that the Roman Empire's claim for absolute authority over the world is legitimate because it reflects the divine will. God's will—Dante argues—may be known through various "signs," and specifically through the numerous miracles performed to establish power of the Romans and the judgment implicitly formulated by God when granting them victory in "duels" with their enemies. Albert Ascoli noted that this "mode of argument itself tends to vitiate Dante's claim to have proceeded on rational grounds."[57] One may add that pages of this kind, which the Dominican theologian Guido Vernani would find ridiculous and unworthy of refutation, have no parallel in any philosophical text redacted in the first decades of the fourteenth century, and this is not by chance.[58] As a matter of fact, no professional philosopher ventured to examine what depends exclusively on God's inscrutable will; and no professional philosopher would have ever presented himself, as Dante clearly does, as an authorized interpreter of his will, capable of detecting in the events of Roman history the traces of God's "braccia" [arms], "mani" [hands] (*Conv.* 4.5.17–20), and "digitus" [finger] (*Mon.* 2.4.2), that is, of the preternatural interventions God performed in order to realize a providential design that must be revealed to mankind.[59]

If Dante's fascination with speculations on divine plans and interventions neatly distinguishes his approach from that of the arts masters who professionally taught philosophy, his use of the notion of the miracle in the *Convivio* distances him from contemporary theologians too. It is well known that in *Convivio* 3.7.15–17 Dante argues as follows: Christian faith is founded on the miracles performed by Jesus and his saints, but many people are doubtful about them and "non possano credere miracolo alcuno sanza visibilmente avere di ciò esperienza" (16) [cannot believe anything miraculous without having experience of it visibly]; philosophy, allegorically represented by the *donna gentile*, is "una cosa visibilmente miraculosa, della quale li occhi delli uomini cotidianamente possono esperienza avere, [e]d a noi faccia possibili li altri" (16) [a visibly miraculous thing, which the eyes of human beings can have daily experience of, making other miracles possible for us].[60] Later, in the fourteenth chapter (3.14.14), Dante repeats that faith "ha sua origine" [has its origin] from Lady Philosophy, because through her humans rationally explain "molto . . . che sanza lei pare maraviglia" [much . . . of what without her seems marvelous] and are thus induced to understand that "ogni miracolo" [every miracle] can exist because it has its cause in a "più alto intelletto" [higher intellect].[61]

These passages are puzzling and have been a matter for debate among scholars. As ever, Giovanni Busnelli and Giuseppe Vandelli tried to read them in accordance with Thomas Aquinas's thought, spurring the reaction of Étienne Gilson, who convincingly argued that by the time he wrote the *Convivio* Dante promoted the independence of philosophy and maintained that it is useful to faith in itself, and not because it is the handmaid of a scientific theology such as that envisaged by Thomas Aquinas.[62] Going further, Gianfranco Fioravanti has recently pointed out the similarities between Dante's position and that of the "radical" Aristotelian Boethius of Dacia, who insisted that, far from contradicting the Christian religion, philosophy paves the way for it because, while considering "solum . . . virtutes causarum naturalium" [only . . . the powers of natural causes], it also stimulates thought about what is possible according to "causam superiorem quam sit natura" [a cause that is higher than nature].[63] Though ingenious, Fioravanti's suggestion, I believe, leaves unanswered one problem. Dante only hints at the potential utility for the Christian faith of the distinction between natural and supernatural causes and, far from developing an epistemological reflection, insists that theological virtues, first of all faith, have their "origin" in philosophy; and he qualifies philosophy in itself as "a visibly miraculous being," whose simple and testable existence enables reluctant believers to admit that miracles that are no longer visible and are known only thanks to the testimony of scripture are actually possible. This is, as far as I know, a unique and amazing way of understanding the function of philosophy: Aquinas never imagined anything of the kind, as opportunely recalled by Gilson;[64] nor, I would add, did Boethius of Dacia. Indeed, the Danish arts master precisely used miracles as a criterion for distinguishing philosophy, conceived as a form of knowledge based exclusively on rational arguments, from faith, whose truths are proved by God's supernatural interventions. In his treatise *On the Eternity of the World* he claimed that philosophy "nec innititur . . . revelationibus et miraculis" [does not rest on revelations and miracles], while faith "in multis innititur miraculis et non rationibus" [in many instances rests on miracles and not on rational arguments].[65]

Furthermore, the idea of philosophy at work in the *Convivio* is neither that of Boethius of Dacia nor, again, that of Thomas Aquinas. Much has been written on this idea by scholars, and for this reason I have not so far commented on this controversial topic. From Bruno Nardi onward, the religious character of Dante's second love has been emphasized.[66] I do not intend to challenge this widely accepted view, but I will argue that greater importance should be given to two elements. First, when in the third book of the *Convivio* Dante explains the meaning of *philosopher* and *philosophy*, he offers a purely etymological definition of these terms, which lacks the religious flavor of the most diffused definitions that even Parisian arts masters always repeated to their students,[67] but depends on the definitions provided by the two—lay!—thinkers who marked his intellectual formation. Thus, when he writes that the "nome di 'filosofo' . . . tanto vale quanto 'amatore di sapienza'" (3.11.5) [term *philosopher* . . . is equivalent to "a lover of wisdom"], he is quoting almost verbatim Brunetto Latini's *Rettorica*;[68] and when a few lines later (3.11.6) he adds that "filosofia non è altro che amistanza a sapienza" [philosophy is nothing other than friendship to wisdom], Dante is rewriting a passage from Boethius.[69] Second, and more important, in the following two chapters, besides introducing the oft-repeated definition of philosophy as "amoroso uso di sapienza" [a loving exercise of wisdom], Dante explains that philosophy pertains differently to God and to the "altre intelligenze" [other intelligences];[70] he distinguishes "la divina filosofia" (3.12.12–13) [divine philosophy] from "la filosofia humana" (3.13.3) [human philosophy];[71] and although he does not examine in depth the meaning of this uncommon and unstudied distinction, he openly declares that the philosophy praised in his treatise is precisely "human philosophy."[72]

We are now in a position to better appreciate Dante's enigmatic presentation of philosophy as "una cosa visibilemente miraculosa, della quale li occhi delli uomini cotidianamente possono esperienza avere" [a visibly miraculous thing, which the eyes of human beings can have daily experience of]. Starting from the assumption that miracles provide "principalissimo fondamento" [the main foundation] of Christian faith, Dante recognizes that those performed in the past cannot be seen but only believed, and thus he feels that the skepticism of those who "non possano credere miracolo alcuno sanza visibilemente avere di ciò esperienza" [are unable to believe any miracle unless they have visible evidence of it] can be bypassed only by showing them a miracle that is perceived "cotidianamente," namely, daily (3.7.16). Too little attention has been paid to this key term. We know that, following the methodological imperative formulated by the Dominican theologian Albert the Great, arts masters often declared, with undisguised pride, that they did philosophy without caring about miracles.[73] Professional theologians instead devoted long questions to miracles, distinguishing those that are above (*supra*), beside (*praeter*), and against (*contra*) nature, and presenting the sacrament of the Eucharist as the best instance of the constant manifestation of God's power: a *cotidianum miraculum*, a daily miracle.[74] Only someone who was neither a professional philosopher nor a professional theologian could dare to present philosophy as a miracle that occurs and can be seen daily like the Eucharist but that, unlike the Eucharist, does not presuppose faith and instead generates it.[75] Also for this reason philosophy is, as Dante wrote at the beginning of the *Convivio* (1.1.7 and 1.10), the "bread of angels" that should be given to a large audience, including those who do not have the chance to sit at the "beata mensa" [blessed table] of the wise. Indeed, all (or better almost all[76]) ought to know, to commend, and to love "human philosophy," the earthly personification of a "divine philosophy" that coincides with the Word of God, Christ, physically present in the consecrated bread offered each day at the altar.[77]

Notes

1. Boyde, *Uomo nel cosmo*, 18; the translation is my own. I am grateful to Anna Pegoretti for helpful comments on earlier drafts of this chapter.
2. The few exceptions to the rule come, significantly, from a Dante

scholar who was above all a historian of philosophy; see Maierù, "Sull'epistemologia di Dante" and "Dante di fronte alla *Fisica*." The quotation is from Barański, "Dante and Doctrine," 12n6.

3. The scholarship on these matters is immense: see at least Imbach and Maierù, *Studi di filosofia medievale*; de Libera, *Penser au Moyen Âge*, 68–75, and "Retour de la philosophie médiévale?"; Imbach, *Dante*, 1–3; Bianchi, "Testi e contesti"; König-Pralong, "Histoire." Useful information on the different uses of *philosophia* and related terms during the Middle Ages may be found in Portalupi, "*Philosophia* e lemmi affini."

4. See Imbach, *Dante*, 129–48; Imbach, "*Translatio philosophiae*"; Cheneval, "Einleitung," xxxviii–li. On the so-called *déprofessionalisation* of the ideal of philosophical life and its dissemination outside the universities (with references to Dante and Eckhart), see de Libera, *Penser au Moyen Âge*, 23–24, 334–35.

5. See Imbach, "*Translatio philosophiae*," in particular 152–53. Significantly enough, Imbach ends this essay, devoted to Dante's conception of philosophy, by quoting (166) a passage of the *Critique of Pure Reason* ("Method of Transcendentalism," chap. 3, "The Architectonic of Pure Reason") where Kant distinguishes the "scholastic" and the "cosmic concept" of philosophy and concludes: "In that sense it would be very boastful to call oneself a philosopher." In *Dante*, Imbach pointed out the poet's original contribution to philosophy (see in particular 134–41, 173), and, in his concluding remarks (249; translation is my own), he already hinted at a parallel between Dante and Kant, emphasizing their common stance regarding the "primacy of practical reason."

6. On this passage and its sources, see Migliorini Fissi, "Onde *filos* e *sofia* . . ." (on grammarians as a source for Dante on this point, see in particular 211–13); Bartuschat, "'Filosofia' di Brunetto Latini." English translations from the *Convivio* are from Frisardi unless otherwise stated.

7. The epitaph by Giovanni del Virgilio is quoted in Boccaccio, *Trattatello*, Fiorilla ed., 1st red., 91; 2nd red., 65; the translation is from Bollettino. Jacopo Alighieri, *Chiose all' "Inferno," Proemio*, 1.5, Bellomo ed.; Bambaglioli, *Commento. Proemio*, 1, Rossi ed. (the translations from these texts are my own).

8. Boccaccio, *Trattatello*, Fiorilla ed., 1st red., 26 and 164.

9. The translation is taken from Dante, *Dantis Alagherii Epistolae*, ed. Toynbee.

10. Frisardi has "bread," but "nourished" is closer to the original. In the *Questio de aqua et terra* 1.3 (my emphasis), the author says: "cum *in amore veritatis* a pueritia mea continue sim *nutritus*" [since I have been nourished from my childhood in the love of truth]; the translation is my own. Reference to "childhood" makes it clear that here "love of truth" cannot simply be identified with philosophy, as is often assumed.

11. On Dante's readiness to identify himself with Boethius, see Bianchi,

"'Heterodox' in Paradise?," 96–97. The most recent comprehensive study on Boethius in Dante is Lombardo, *Boezio in Dante*.

12. Boethius, *De consolatione philosophiae* 1. pr. 1.10; 1. pr. 2.2, and *Consolation of Philosophy*, Cooper trans.

13. The formula is uncommon. I have found it only in the *Chronicle of the Czechs*, redacted by Cosmas of Prague at the beginning of the twelfth century: see Cosmas of Prague, *Cosmae pragensis Cronica Boemorum* 2.28, Breholz ed.

14. See Dronke, *Dante's Second Love*, in particular 26–30, where differences between Boethius's personified Philosophy and Dante's *donna gentile* are examined (without noticing that Boethius's emphasis on the fact that he was nourished by Lady Philosophy is not present in Dante). On the sexual connotations, see Dronke, *Dante's Second Love*, 38; Nasti, "'Vocabuli d'autori,'" 136–53; Dante, *Convivio*, Fioravanti ed., 477–79, 493–94.

15. See Ascoli, *Dante*, 233n10; Barański, "'With Such Vigilance,'" 62, and "Sulla formazione intellettuale," 36. It is worth noting that a similar topos was even used by Thomas Aquinas at the end of one of his most polemical treatises, the *De unitate intellectus*, well known in Italian milieus frequented by Dante. Here Thomas defined himself as "minimus" [the least] among men "veritatis zelatores" [zealous for truth].

16. See Cachey, "Verità," 154–55. Cachey acutely emphasizes the sense of anxiety and vulnerability of the author (see also 143, 149, 157).

17. See Pegoretti, "Filosofanti."

18. On the "disappearance" of the philosophers at the beginning of the Christian era, see Fioravanti, "Da Agostino" and "Morte e rinascita," 11–13. On Abelard's conception of philosophy, see at least Valente, "Philosophers and Other Kinds." Evidence of the rich plurality of meanings of *philosophy* and related terms during the Middle Ages is provided by Portalupi, "*Philosophia* e lemmi affini," and Pegoretti, "Filosofanti."

19. See Caiazzo, "*Rex illitteratus*." William of Conches complains, however, that in his times "vix invenitur philosophus" [a philosopher is hardly found]; the translation is my own. See *Dragmaticon philosophiae* 6.1.5, Ronca ed.

20. On the *ḥakīm* as a model for Latin culture, see Burnett, *Arabic into Latin*, IV, 1–78; IX, 225–85.

21. The scholarship on the institutionalization of the teaching of philosophy in thirteenth-century universities is too extensive to be listed here. However, as far as Paris is concerned, see at least Bianchi, *Censure et liberté intellectuelle*, 89–127. On Italian arts masters' self-description as "philosophers," see Fioravanti, "Filosofi e gli altri," 91–105. As regards Thomas Aquinas, see Porro, *Tommaso d'Aquino*, 13–15, 68–69. Ironically enough, professional philosophers did consider Aquinas as a philosopher: see, for instance, Siger of Brabant, *De anima intellectiva* 3 (Bazán ed.), who calls Albert the Great and Thomas Aquinas "praecipui viri in philosophia" [leading men in philosophy]; the translation

is my own.

22. See at least Bianchi, "*Viri philosophici*," 275–79, and Bianchi, "Johannes de Malignes," 304–7; Fioravanti, "Morte e rinascita," 13–15, and "Filosofi e gli altri," 104.

23. On how medievalists' histories of philosophy ignored the new class of professional philosophers, see Bianchi, "Aristotelismi della scolastica," 20–22.

24. According to the statute of 1215 (*Chartularium Universitatis Parisiensis*, Denifle and Chatelain ed., 1:78), Parisian arts masters could not start teaching before they were twenty-one years old. One of the oaths imposed on incepting masters was that they would teach for at least two years, but in the fourteenth century the average length of regency was about five years; see Courtenay, *Teaching Careers*, 15 and 21. For Dante's logic lessons, see, for example, *Mon.* 1.11.8, 14.1–3; 2.5.22 and 24, 10.9–10; 3.4.4–5. It is remarkable that, according to Chiesa and Tabarroni, "Introduzione," xxv, cxxviii–cxxxv, Dante may have added some of these passages in a later redaction of the text.

25. See Robiglio, "Philosophy and Theology," 142–43. Chiesa and Tabarroni, "Introduzione," xxv, affirm instead that when he wrote the *Monarchia* Dante considered himself to be a philosopher: "Egli sembra . . . ritenere tale qualifica [i.e., "la qualifica di *philosophus*"] ormai pacificamente accolta e consolidata, al punto da spingersi ad accomunarsi ai sapienti in un plurale collettivo ('ut ex his patet que de caelo phylosophamur,' II 2 3)" [He seems . . . to consider this title as by now peacefully accepted and consolidated, to the point that he goes so far as to associate himself with the wise, speaking in a collective plural ("ut ex his patet que de caelo phylosophamur" [as is clear from those things that we philosophize about the heavens], II 2 3)]. One might argue, however, that this sentence hardly provides evidence for general claims about Dante's self-consciousness, and Chiesa and Tabarroni's own translation of *Mon.* 2.2.3— "come *si studia* in filosofia nel *De caelo*" (81) seems at odds with their interpretation. One might further note that Prue Shaw and Diego Quaglioni go perhaps too far when they transform the verb *philosophamur* into a noun that has the status of the subject of the sentence: "as it is clear from those things *philosophy teaches* us about the heavens" (*Monarchy*, Shaw ed. and trans., 32); "come è evidente da quel che del cielo *ci insegna la filosofia*" (Quaglioni ed., 1065) [as it is clear from what philosophy teaches us about the heavens]. Nonetheless, the use of the first person in the plural of the verb *philosophari* (very infrequent; see Portalupi, "*Philosophia* e lemmi affini," 289) does not necessarily mean that Dante included himself among the philosophers: it might simply hint at his sense of belonging to a learned community. On his knowledge of Aristotle's *De caelo*, see Fioravanti, "'Come dice il filosofo,'" 42–43, 49–50.

26. This point is opportunely underscored by Fioravanti, "Prima trattazione 'sottile,'" 100–103.

27. See Imbach, *Dante*, 129–48, and "*Translatio philosophiae*"; Gentili,

Uomo aristotelico, 127–65.

28. Imbach, "*Translatio philosophiae*," 152–53.

29. See Stefano Caroti's remarks in his edition of the *Questio*, xxxvii n153.

30. Evidence of a tradition of teaching the liberal arts in Verona is provided by the statutes of the city, as is opportunely mentioned by Piron in his review of Rinaldi's edition of the *Questio*, 149.

31. Imbach, "*Translatio philosophiae*," 152; the translation is my own.

32. Tavoni, *Qualche idea su Dante*, 30–34 (quotation on 31), 52.

33. See Cheneval, "Einleitung," lxxxiii–cv; Fioravanti, "Introduzione," 30–36, 63–65, and "Prima trattazione 'sottile,'" 98–100; Chiesa and Tabarroni, "Introduzione," xxxii–xxxiii, lxxiv–lxxviii. Dante's use of scholastic methods and jargon had already been pointed out by Segre, *Lingua, stile e società*, 227–70.

34. See Barański, "'Oh come è grande,'" 9, and "Sulla formazione intellettuale," 35. The idea that the *Convivio* is a "philosophical treatise" is still widely diffused. In fact, the designation repeatedly appears even in one of the finest articles on the *Convivio*: see Leo, "Unfinished *Convivio*," 74, 92; at 82, 90, and 99 the *Convivio* is presented as an ethical treatise.

35. Camozzi Pistoja, "Quarto trattato del *Convivio*," has emphasized the satirical dimension of the fourth book of the *Convivio*. On the "hybridity" of the *Convivio*, see Barański, "'Oh come è grande,'" 11, 14–15.

36. On this point, see Ascoli, *Dante*, 132, 210–15 (and n66).

37. See Fioravanti, "Introduzione," 66–79, and "Prima trattazione 'sottile,'" 100–101. This is not to say, however, that the problem had not been examined from a philosophical perspective; see at least Delle Donne, "Disputa sulla nobiltà," and Guillelmus de Aragonia, *De nobilitate animi*.

38. See Leo, "Unfinished *Convivio*," 94–100.

39. I have slightly modified Frisardi's translation because Robiglio, "Nobiltà di spada," 203–4, appositely argues that, in Dante's time the term *coltello* refers not to a knife but to a short sword. Robiglio, however, suggests a different interpretation of the passage, since he assumes that Dante here is hinting at dueling. Examples of the language of theologians denouncing errors in matters of faith are provided by William of Auvergne's *De universo*, 693bB, 785bB, 802aE: "Ut circa illud *non ratione* disceptandum sit, *sed magis igne, et gladio persequendum*" [One should not rationally debate about it but rather persecute it by fire and sword]; "Contra errorem igitur istum *non est tam ratione disceptandum, quam igne, et gladio pugnandum*" [One should rather fight by fire and sword against this error than debate rationally]; "In destructione autem hujus erroris *non rationibus, aut probationibus* utendum est, *sed igne, et gladio*, omnique poenali genere exterminii" [In order to destroy this error one should not use arguments or proofs, but the fire and the sword, and any kind of correctional extermination]. Translations are my own.

40. Barański, "Dante and Doctrine," 54. In his commentary on *De vulgari*

eloquentia 1.1, Enrico Fenzi provides a different interpretation of the term *doctrina* and insists on the "approccio eminentemente storico-descrittivo di Dante" [Dante's eminently historical and descriptive approach].

41. On this point, see Rosier-Catach, "Uomo nobile," 170–74, and "Du vulgaire illustre."

42. Marmo, "Had the Modistae Any Influence," 13. On the controversial thesis of the influence of the *modistae* in the *De vulgari eloquentia*, see also Maierù, "Dante al crocevia?," 740–47; Lo Piparo, "Dante linguista anti-modista."

43. Imbach and Rosier-Catach, "De l'un au multiple." See also, among others, Imbach, "Appunti," 47–48; Tavoni, *Qualche idea su Dante*, 61–62. Attention to this point, however, had already been drawn by Stabile in an article first published in 1997 and now included in *Dante e la filosofia*, 261, 266–67.

44. A recent assessment of Dante's "Averroism" may be found in Marenbon, "Dante's Averroism"; for my critique of his claims, see Bianchi, "Averroismo di Dante," 80–84.

45. On the *Monarchia*, among recent works, see Stocchi Perucchio, "Limits of Heterodoxy." For a general discussion about Dante's "orthodoxy," see Barański, "Temptations" and "(Un)orthodox Dante"; Bianchi, "Dante eterodosso?"; Falzone, "Eresia ed eterodossia."

46. Quaglioni, "Introduzione," 870–75; Chiesa and Tabarroni, "Introduzione," xxiii–xxxiv, lxxiv–lxxxiv.

47. According to Boccaccio, *Trattatello* 16.195, Fiorilla ed., 1st red., Dante demonstrates in the first book the need for the empire "by disputing logically," namely, "loicalmente"; in the second the providential role of Rome "per argomenti istoriografi" [by means of historical arguments]; in the third the independence of the empire from the church "per argomenti teologi" [by means of theological arguments]. Things are, of course, much more complicated; see also the next subsection.

48. The approach that I advocate, however, is well represented in recent Dante studies: one need only think of Fioravanti's excellent and well-balanced commentary to the *Convivio*, or of the intelligent introduction by Chiesa and Tabarroni to their richly annotated edition and translation of the *Monarchia*. See also Imbach, "Appunti," 44, who explores the "philosophical dimension" of the *De vulgari eloquentia* by examining (i) which philosophical principles are used; (ii) how they are used; and (iii) how Dante modifies them. On Dante's original reworking of materials borrowed from a plurality of sources, see S. Gilson, "Sincretismo e scolastica."

49. It is worth noting that the Italian terminology is richer than the Latin one. The *Commedia*, however, features only one occurrence of the noun *filosofia*, two of the adjective *filosofico*, and one of the verb *filosofare*. It goes without saying that in the Italian works philosophy is often personified.

50. For a systematic analysis of all explicit references to Aristotle's works,

see Fioravanti, "'Come dice il filosofo,'" who provides evidence of Dante's wide and often firsthand knowledge of them.

51. See Stabile, *Dante e la filosofia*, 229–30, 253–70; F. Bruni, "Geografia di Dante," 243–53.

52. I am aware that speaking of the "history of philosophy" is totally anachronistic. As a matter of fact, in these and in other passages, Dante intermingles doxographical materials with general remarks on the development of philosophy in ancient times; see Fioravanti, "Dossografie filosofiche."

53. See Aristotle, *Topics* 6.2 139b18–140a1; as for Siger, see *Quaestiones in Metaphysicam* 3.q.17, rep. Cambridge, Maurer ed., 117; rep. Munich, Dunphy ed., 138; translations are my own.

54. See Bianchi, "Loquens ut naturalis," with further bibliography.

55. See Chiesa and Tabarroni, "Introduzione," lxix–lxx; Cremascoli, "Bibbia nella *Monarchia*"; Nasti, "'Vocabuli d'autori,'" 160–62.

56. See Rosier-Catach, "Solo all'uomo," 441–53; Fenzi, "Introduzione," xlix–l.

57. Ascoli, *Dante*, 255.

58. Vernani, *De reprobatione Monarchie* 2.3, Chiesa and Tabarroni ed., 344: "Sed quod Deus voluerit quod Romani regnarent voluntate beneplaciti, probat per miracula. Que probatio est potius deridenda quam dissolvenda" [But that God willed the Romans to rule by the "will of His good pleasure" our writer tries to prove by miracles—a proof that is more to be mocked than refuted; *Refutation of the "Monarchia,"* Cassell trans.].

59. On Dante's prophetism in the *Monarchia*, see Chiesa and Tabarroni, "Introduzione," lxxv, lxxxiv–lxxxv; on Dante's conception of miracles, Steinberg, "Dante's Constitutional Miracles," is fundamental. Steinberg acutely examines (see in particular 436–40) how, in the *Monarchia*'s section on miracles, Dante reworks material from the *Convivio*.

60. See also *Conv.* 3.8.20: "E questo conferma quello che detto è di sopra nell'altro capitolo, quando dico ch'ella è aiutatrice della fede nostra" [And this confirms what was said in the previous chapter, where I state that she is an aid to our faith].

61. I follow here Ryan's translation (Dante, *Banquet*).

62. E. Gilson, *Dante et la philosophie*, 113, 116–22. See also Dronke, *Dante's Second Love*, 34, who writes that in *Convivio* 3.7.15–18 Dante "now claims for the Donna Gentile precisely the status of incarnate divine miracle, blessed in her effects, which he had claimed for Beatrice in the *Vita Nuova*." What then follows, in my opinion, is less convincing.

63. See *Convivio*, Fioravanti ed., 494–95.

64. E. Gilson, *Dante et la philosophie*, 120–22.

65. Boethius of Dacia, *De aeternitate mundi*, Green-Pedersen ed., 336, 364; English translation by Wippel, *On the Eternity*.

66. See at least Nardi, *Dante*, 163–64, and *Nel mondo di Dante*, 216–17;

Corti, *Felicità mentale*, 83–85; Nasti, *Favole d'amore*, 93–110; Barański, "Dante and Doctrine," 38–45, and "'Oh come è grande,'" 24; Moevs, *Metaphysics of Dante's Comedy*, 82–88.

67. I refer, for instance, to the following definitions, disseminated in the Middle Ages by Isidore of Seville, Hugh of Saint Victor, al-Farabi, Gundissalinus, and Ysaac: "Philosophia est divinarum humanarumque rerum cognitio" [Philosophy is the knowledge of divine and human things]; "Philosophia est assimilatio operibus Creatoris per virtutem humanam" [Philosophy is an assimilation to the works of the Creator through human virtue]; "Philosophia est cura, studium et sollecitudo mortis" [Philosophy is the care, zeal, and solicitude for death]. They are quoted in all the introductions to philosophy edited by Lafleur, *Quatre introductions*, 181, 258–59, 308–10 (the first one is also in those edited by Imbach, "Einfürungen in die Philosophie," 487–88). See also John of Dacia, *Divisio scientiae* 5–7, Otto ed., who first defines philosophy as "amor sapientiae," then adds several more religiously oriented definitions, including Alcuin's definition of philosophy as "inquisitio naturarum humanarum deique apprehensio" [the search of human natures and apprehension of God]. Translations are my own.

68. Migliorini Fissi, "Onde *filos* e *sofia* . . . ," 204–5. On the relationship—and the differences—between Brunetto's and Dante's conception of philosophy, see Bartuschat, "'Filosofia' di Brunetto Latini."

69. Boethius, *In Isagogen Porphyrii*, Brandt ed., 7: "Est enim philosophia amor et studium *et amicitia quodammodo* sapientiae" [Philosophy is indeed the love, the pursuit, and in a certain sense the friendship of wisdom]; the translation is my own. Often neglected, this source was pointed out in *Convivio*, Vasoli ed., 421n6.

70. I follow here Ryan's translation (*Banquet*), which seems to me better than Frisardi's: "a loving use of wisdom."

71. "È adunque la divina filosofia della divina essenza, però che in esso non può essere cosa alla sua essenzia aggiunta; ed è nobilissima, però che nobilissima è la essenzia divina; ed è in lui per modo perfetto e vero, quasi per etterno matrimonio" (*Conv*. 3.12.13) [Divine philosophy, therefore, is of the divine essence, for no thing can be added in him to his essence; and she is most noble, because the divine essence is most noble; and she is in him perfectly and truly, as if through eternal marriage].

72. "De la quale Filosofia umana seguito poi per lo trattato, essa commendando" (*Conv*. 3.13.3) [And I go on to discuss human philosophy throughout the treatise, praising it]. The distinction between human and divine philosophy recalls but does not coincide with the standard distinction between *scientia divina* and *scientia humana*. Writing a half century after Dante, Conrad of Megenberg declares that the theologian is a philosopher as far as he practices "divine philosophy" (*Yconomica* 3.1.4: "Theologus philosophus est a philosophia divina"); and in his commentary on the 1277 prohibited articles he establishes

what is "impossible according to human philosophy [*philosophie humane*]" against what is "possibile according to divine philosophy [*philosophie divine*]" (*Yconomica* 3.1.13) (Krüger ed., *Ökonomik*, vol. 3). The distinction between human and divine philosophy, however, is anything but common, and as far as I know, the only antecedent to Dante can be found in the vernacular commentary on Boethius's *Consolation of Philosophy* (II, t. 87) authored by Notker of St. Gallen: "Philosophia téilet síh in diuina et humana" (the passage is quoted and translated into Italian in Sturlese, *Storia della filosofia tedesca*, 39–40).

73. Albert the Great's expression "Nihil ad me de Dei miraculis, cum ego de naturalibus disseram" [When I am discussing natural things, God's miracles are nothing to me; the translation is my own] is to be found in his paraphrase of the *De generatione et corruptione* 1.22. It was so well received that it was included in the *Auctoritates Aristotelis*; see Bianchi, "Loquens ut naturalis," 47–48, with references to arts masters, from Siger of Brabant to John of Jandun.

74. The main works on the medieval conception of miracles are mentioned in Bianchi, "*Cotidiana miracula.*"

75. Note that in *Conv.* 3.7.16, Dante insists on the adverb *visibilmente*, used twice in two lines, and on the possibility of experiencing philosophy with one's own "eyes." Strangely, Leo, "Unfinished *Convivio*," does not take into account this decisive passage in his analysis of vision in Dante's works. My reading, however, may confirm his thesis (79) that "in the *Convivio* Dante presents himself within the limits of the Christian faith as a normal *viator.*"

76. On Dante's qualifications regarding the audience of the *Convivio*, see Bianchi, "Noli comedere"; Pegoretti, "'*Da questa nobilissima perfezione*.'"

77. The Eucharistic value of the metaphor of the "bread of angels" is underscored by Fioravanti, "Pane degli angeli," 198–200. See also Barański, "'Oh come è grande,'" 21–25. Camozzi Pistoja, "Testo come eucarestia," likely goes too far when he argues that the *Convivio* as a whole has a strong "Eucharistic characterization."

CHAPTER 11

Theology and the "Other Works"

VITTORIO MONTEMAGGI

The theological dimensions of Dante's works have been the subject of increasing scholarly attention in recent decades.[1] Significant possibilities were opened up for this in the twentieth century by scholars such as Erich Auerbach, Kenelm Foster, Étienne Gilson, Bruno Nardi, and Charles Singleton, who, in their different ways and working within different academic contexts and traditions, explored the rich and complex relationship between the literary and the theological in Dante.[2] The work of scholars such as Zygmunt Barański, Piero Boitani, Steven Botterill, Anna Maria Chiavacci Leonardi, John Freccero, Peter Hawkins, Robert Hollander, Robin Kirkpatrick, Giuseppe Mazzotta, and Lino Pertile further opened up a wide range of conceptual and methodological possibilities for broader and deeper study of this fundamental aspect of Dante's writing.[3] Building on all this, since the turn of the century, scholarly attention has turned to Dante's theology in even more deliberate, systematic, and methodologically wide-ranging fashion, including interdisciplinary work across the disciplines of Dante studies and theology.[4]

For the purposes of the present essay, a key work to highlight in the latter respect is Christian Moevs's *The Metaphysics of Dante's "Comedy."* Moevs's book proposes a radical reorientation of scholarly attention to how Dante speaks about God and about the relationship between reality and God. According to Moevs, in order to engage fully with Dante's work, we need to be open, even in a scholarly context, to carrying out interpretation in recognition of central aspects of the understanding of reality that Dante shared with the theologians of his age and with the theological traditions he is drawing on. In particular, Moevs emphasizes the importance, in our interpretations of Dante, of taking seriously Dante's idea of the utter and radical dependence of all that is on God.

Moevs's aim is to show how all of reality, for Dante, is ultimately nothing other than an expression of divine being, truth, and love. It follows that the relationship between a human being and God is ultimately not a relationship between two beings: the relationship between creature and Creator is that between a manifestation of being and the truth and love in which being originates, has its ground, and is nourished. If accepted, such a view of Dante's work has extremely significant interpretive implications, both conceptual and methodological. In particular, it requires acknowledgment that certain conventional assumptions concerning academic work might need in some way to be modified, at least to the extent that as scholars we might wish to engage with Dante's thought according to epistemological parameters closer to Dante's own. As Moevs puts it, for Dante, "God, as the ultimate subject of all experience, cannot be an object of experience: to know God is to know oneself as God, or (if the expression seems troubling) as one 'with' God or 'in' God."[5] This challenges us to consider the possibility that in studying Dante's theology we might need in some way to transcend our sense of epistemological duality between ourselves as subjects and the object of our study.

The latter challenge can be approached in a number of ways. One of these is to explore the difference that can be made to the study of Dante's theology by seeing it primarily as a living expression of Dante's own spiritual exploration of divinity; that is, of the truth or love in (and as) which all has its being. As I have argued elsewhere, this also calls for openness to interpreting Dante's work as the expression of his wish to engage through it with us as readers on our own spiritual journeys. In this sense, to study Dante's theology will coincide to some extent with accepting Dante's invitation to his readers to realize that the meaningfulness of his theology ultimately resides in readers' own living engagement with Dante's work.[6]

Another way of approaching the challenge outlined above is to focus, less on "theology" understood as lived encounter with Dante's text as spiritual journeying, than on the various ways "theology" might be understood relative to the medieval religious contexts in which Dante developed his work as part of his exploration of divinity. Indeed, recent scholarship has been showing just how rich Dante's engagement was with the religious culture of his day in its intellectual, artistic, and liturgical dimensions.[7]

In relation to all of the above, another extremely important point of reference is recent work by Barański, who argues that it would be historically and philologically inaccurate to think that Dante might have viewed himself as a "theologian" or his work as "theology."[8] We thus need to exercise interpretive caution in referring to Dante's "theology." Indeed, reflection on the topic of the present essay ought to proceed with at least three important considerations in mind as to what thinking about "theology and the 'other works'" might mean: (1) to reflect on our topic is to reflect on the relationship between Dante's works and the various dimensions of the religious culture of his day; (2) to reflect on our topic is to reflect on the theological significance of Dante's works for us today; and (3) to reflect on our topic is to reflect on what possible points of connection might be between (1) and (2).

The present chapter is written primarily from the perspective of point (3) above. My aim is to suggest a reading of the relationship between theology and the "other works" that might offer a broad perspective that can fruitfully inform further, more detailed and wide-ranging work. Indeed, while there has been much interest in the theological dimensions of Dante's works in recent times, such interest has for the most part focused in one way or another on the *Commedia*, either in itself or as a lens through which to engage with Dante's works as a whole. Much remains to be done on the relationship between theology and the "other works" in their own right. As this volume shows, however, the work that has been done on the "other works" to date and that this volume builds on and takes forward provides important interpretive foundations. Having had the privilege of attending the lecture series in which this volume originates, in this essay I attempt to reflect on the "other works" primarily in the light of the fresh insights that those lectures opened up and that the present volume confirms and expands.[9]

At the same time, it is important to acknowledge one very significant way in which existing scholarship has already begun to shift our perception of the relationship between theology and the "other works." Through an enriched sense of Dante's engagement with his religious contexts, scholars have concretely begun to show that we ought to pay closer attention to how Dante's writing in the "other works" might be read as his original reworking of forms of theology not usually taken into consideration by scholars. Key examples here are the readings of the *Convivio* offered by Barański and Paola Nasti that show that the *Convivio*, long considered a "philosophical" rather than a "theological" text, can in fact be read as the result of Dante's conscious reworking of forms of theological writing such as the *comentum*, the *compilatio*, and the *quodlibet*.[10] As suggested by these examples, there is certainly more to the relationship between theology and the "other works" than has so far met the scholarly eye. The aim of this essay is to contribute to these trends by suggesting an overarching perspective from which Dante's authorship of the "other works" might be considered of theological significance, both for us today and in relation to the theology of his day.

Overall, the reflections offered in this essay are meant to issue in questions: open-ended invitations to consider the theological dimensions of Dante's writing. I hope that this way of proceeding can, precisely in its interrogative open-endedness, fruitfully contribute to our ongoing engagement with Dante's works. In this spirit—and not that of presuming to offer some kind of "master narrative"—I suggest a unifying thread that might, while respecting the differences between the "other works," help us consider their theological significance, both individually and as a whole. The primary idea I would like to propose in this essay—my unifying thread—is that if we wish to explore the relationship between theology and the "other works," then we need to ask: What is the existential and spiritual relationship that Dante envisages between himself and his readers? To ask of each text what kind of a text it is reveals to us something of the nature of what we are reading. To ask of each text what kind of relationship it wishes to establish between Dante and ourselves is more richly to reveal something of the truth in which, according to Dante, all texts and all persons are grounded. The latter perspective, I suggest, takes us more fully into the realm of the theological.

This suggestion is offered, specifically, in connection with a general consideration made by Barański in a discussion on Dante and theology during the lecture series on which the present volume is based: for Dante, to refer to "theology" would ultimately be to refer to the interpretation of scripture. This is indeed an accurate definition of Dante's understanding of theology. But it is important to reflect on what we might mean by it, so as to engage more fully with its implications.[11] In line with medieval interpretation of scripture more generally, to say that for Dante theology ultimately coincides with the interpretation of scripture is emphatically *not* to refer to an easily definable—or containable—phenomenon. It is certainly not as simple as saying that there is a text or set of texts—scripture—and that the aim of theology is to offer an interpretation of it, in the sense of "interpretation" that we generally employ in the academy today, based on a dualism between the subject doing the interpretation and his or her object of study. Dante did think that many theologians failed at their job and interpreted scripture in unhelpfully dualistic ways.[12] He also felt, however, that even in the hands of a layman like himself scripture ought to be engaged with, not simply as a text to be objectively interpreted, but as a text the interpretation of which can coincide with the very origin of our being, and of reality as a whole. Dante would not have considered himself a theologian in the technical sense. But he certainly practiced the activity at the heart of theology: that is, he engaged with scripture as a source of life, for himself and for his readers. Whatever else we might say about Dante's engagement with scripture, and of its presence in his "other works," we can helpfully think of the latter as a crucial dimension of Dante's engagement with Revelation; that is, with the self-manifestation in creation of divinity, of the Word of God, the supreme written embodiment of which, for Dante and for medieval theologians more generally, is scripture. In this sense, it is impossible to mark a clear-cut separation between those aspects of Dante's works that explicitly engage with scripture and all those other dimensions of his works that, broadly speaking, have to do with Dante's conception of his relationship to truth itself—in the light of which he produces works he believes can have a transformative and salvific effect on those who engage with them.

In other words, to think of the relationship between theology and Dante's "other works" is to think of the ways in which Dante writes as informed by a sense of truth speaking in him to us. It would of course be impossible to offer a single interpretive key that can explain how this works in each of the "other works" or to describe all the different authorial strategies Dante employs in his writings to engage with and communicate truth to his readers. This is in significant measure because Dante's own understanding of himself and his writing changes throughout his life. In this regard, the contributions to the present volume by Theodore Cachey,

David Lummus, and Christopher Kleinhenz offer illuminating perspectives on our present topic, particularly in connection with the various literary mechanisms by which Dante constructs his authorial self in his works, and the interpretive dynamics by which we might read or recognize this self. What seems to remain more or less constant throughout Dante's oeuvre, however, is Dante's sense of the real difference that his voice can make in the world, as something in and through which truth might be seen more clearly.[13] In this sense, Dante's engagement with scripture—his practicing the activity at the heart of theology—is one of the defining characteristics of the "other works," one of the primary reasons that accounts for their boldness and originality as texts and the rich, complex, and surprising ways in which they escape easy categorization.

As phrased above, with an emphasis on "truth" instead of "God" alongside "scripture," the language of this essay may seem to have moved closer to philosophical rather than theological rhetoric. Indeed, in some of the "other works," especially the *Convivio*, Dante himself can be seen to be moving in that direction. As Luca Bianchi's contribution to the present volume shows, however, philosophy and theology in the "other works" are closely intertwined. Even when Dante seems to adopt philosophical rhetoric or methodology at the expense of theological ones, as he clearly seems to do in the *Convivio*, he does so in ways that seem designed to invite reflections on the nature of philosophy itself that might highlight its theological goals and underpinnings.

More specifically, it is important to note that Dante's engagement with scripture throughout the "other works," understood along the terms outlined so far, is such as to warrant an overall understanding of Dante's engagement with "truth" as distinctly theological in one primary, crucial sense. Engagement with truth, for Dante, is an embodied, incarnated phenomenon, inextricable from an understanding of how the whole human person—body and soul—participates in truth. This incarnational sense of engagement with truth can ultimately be tied to Dante's understanding of the Incarnation as the core of Revelation and of a conception of existence as grounded in divinity and directed back toward it, through divinity's own presence in creation. At different junctures of his life, Dante might be seen to engage in different ways with this inherently theological understanding of existence, as defined by the Incarnation of the Word. It is plausible to suggest, however, that the boldness and energy with which

Dante speaks to his readers in at least a significant portion or aspect of each of the "other works" derive from a sense that the human person can embody in his or her experience the divine truth in which Dante believes the cosmos has its beginning and end.

It is of course in the *Commedia* that Dante most explicitly and extensively gives expression to the understanding of the relationship between humanity and divinity outlined above. In the poem, we find a conscious presentation of the journey of deification as inseparable from a living, incarnated participation in such a journey on the part of both author and reader. This does not happen so explicitly or extensively in the "other works." However, in the light of what has been said above, and of the work presented in this volume as a whole, I believe it is a perspective from which it can be fruitful to explore Dante's writing as a whole. Our guide question in what follows, therefore, will be: *To what extent and in what ways can the "other works" be seen as manifestations of Dante's (changing) understanding of human personhood—and therefore also human authorship—as having an essentially, and irreducibly, divine dimension?*

In approaching this question, it is important, methodologically, to include ourselves as readers in an understanding of the significance of the relationship between theology and Dante's "other works." To emphasize again a point already outlined above, to study the relationship between theology and the "other works" is not only to study how theology, as some kind of identifiable entity, might be present *in* the "other works." It is, perhaps more importantly, to study how Dante might have understood the practices of writing and of reading themselves as coinciding with the same truth revealed in scripture and in Christ, and therefore as potentially salvific, both for him and for his readers.

Despite some prominent recent trends in Dante scholarship wishing to emphasize a more or less radical departure on Dante's part from the theological at particular junctures in his career, it does seem more sensible to suppose that, throughout his life, Dante maintained, overall, a broadly orthodox, if radically innovative, relationship with Christian belief and practice. This aspect of Dante's existence did indeed manifest itself, textually, in some profoundly interesting ways. This is true, in one way or other, of each of the "other works." In what follows, I wish to highlight some of the most significant examples of this, relative to our guiding question stated above.

One such example is offered by the *Monarchia*. The text is generally regarded as significant theologically in relation to questions regarding ecclesiastical authority and its relationship to political authority. This is certainly the case. In the *Monarchia*, Dante offers a substantial intervention to contemporary debates concerning the relationship between church and empire, in a series of arguments that draw on a number of sources, including scripture. In her contribution to this volume, however, Nasti presents an important set of considerations for interpreting the work anew, especially with regard to Dante's approach to argument and to engagement with his sources. She shows, in particular, how at different points in the text Dante might be seen consciously to present us with argumentative strategies relatable, in specific technical terms, to different kinds of intellectual disciplines: philosophy, civil law, history, and—ultimately and most significantly—biblical exegesis. Nasti further argues that, uniting all of these different strands of Dante's thought, and therefore giving coherence to the text as a whole, is Dante's foregrounding of interpretive practices that we might define as literary. For instance, Dante privileges literary *auctoritates* over historical and political ones; and he gives great importance in his arguments to detailed and psychologically nuanced interpretations of human character and action.

From the latter perspective, the way Dante frames the text from its inception is especially significant:

> Omnium hominum quos ad amorem veritatis natura superior impressit hoc maxime interesse videtur: ut, quemadmodum de labore antiquorum ditati sunt, ita et ipsi posteris prolaborent, quatenus ab eis posteritas habeat quo ditetur. Longe nanque ab offitio se esse non dubitet qui, publicis documentis imbutus, ad rem publicam aliquid afferre non curat; non enim est lignum, quod secus decursus aquarum fructificat in tempore suo, sed potius perniciosa vorago semper ingurgitans et nunquam ingurgitata refundens. Hec igitur sepe mecum recogitans, ne de infossi talenti culpa quandoque redarguar, publice utilitati non modo turgescere, quinymo fructificare desidero, et intemptatas ab aliis ostendere veritates.[14] (*Mon.* 1.1.1–3)

> [For all men whom the Higher Nature has endowed with a love of truth, this above all seems to be a matter of concern, that just as they

have been enriched by the efforts of their forebears, so they too may work for future generations, in order that posterity may be enriched by their efforts. For the man who is steeped in the teachings which form our common heritage, yet has no interest in contributing something to the community, is failing in his duty: let him be in no doubt of that; for he is not "a tree planted by the rivers of water, that bringeth forth his fruit in due season" [Psalms 1:3], but rather a destructive whirlpool which forever swallows things down and never gives back what it has swallowed. Thinking often about these things, lest some day I be accused of burying my talent [see Matt. 25:14–30], I wish not just to put forth buds but to bear fruit for the benefit of all, and to reveal truths that have not been attempted by others.][15]

Dante frames his text, from the outset, with a clear sense of his perceived responsibility not simply to speak what he believes to be true but to do so nourishingly, as an expression of his own healthy spiritual development, just as a tree might produce fruit that in turn provides the seed out of which other trees might grow. In this sense, Dante's emphasis on the importance of his work can be seen not simply as a statement of his perceived superiority but as an invitation for us to consider what fruit might be derived from Dante's text, in the light of recognition of the specific characteristics of Dante's voice. Dante's is clearly a confident voice; a voice confident of its particular intellectual and interpretive talent, which it wishes to offer for the benefit of others, and of society as a whole. In this sense, Nasti argues, Dante can be seen to present himself—as literary author—as being in a privileged position to address the questions the text is going to raise: to interpret, that is, nothing other than the way in which society ought to be ordered so as to respect the order willed by God for the cosmos.

With regard to Dante's idea of how society should be ordered, the most famous statement of the *Monarchia* is to be found in its last chapter. Here we find Dante's statement of a double end for human existence: an earthly one, to be pursued through philosophical virtue under the guidance of the emperor and political authorities; and a heavenly one, to be pursued through theological virtue under the guidance of the pope and ecclesiastical authorities.[16] In the light of the reading proposed by Nasti, the most significant aspect of the conclusion to the *Monarchia* is not the particular political theory it presents but the theological dynamics of the authority that Dante ascribes to himself so as to confidently present such a theory. The literary intellectual here presents himself as the spokesperson of divinity, the faithful interpreter of the divine will for the unfolding of creation. Thus our reading of the text is envisaged by Dante not as a detached or dualistic affair but as sharing in the divine responsibility of allowing creation to unfold the way it was created to be. Readers are called to respond to Dante's text by ordering their lives in keeping with the correct exercise of philosophical and theological virtue, which on Dante's terms would in itself be tantamount to the incarnated expression of truth.

In short, the theology of the *Monarchia* is not to be found simply in how Dante engages with scripture during the course of his argument but, even more significantly, in how he presents himself as spokesperson for the divine will that scripture itself incarnates; and, crucially, in our openness to transform our lives, individually and communally, in response to such a voice. We can thus follow up our guiding question with another open-ended interrogative, specifically related to the *Monarchia*: *To what extent is it important to see the theology of the "Monarchia" as residing not simply in what Dante presents to his readers in the text but also in the transformative impact he envisions his text can have in the world, in and through the relationship established between his readers and his truth-bearing authorial voice?*

In the *Epistles* too, Dante strongly presents his voice as truth-bearing. This is especially so in his letters addressing political and ecclesiastical concerns, which can be connected in one way or another to the question of the relationship between church and empire addressed by Dante at a more general level in the *Monarchia*. In her chapter in this volume, Claire Honess draws particular attention to Dante's conscious use of scriptural rhetoric in these letters. In this we see, once again, strong evidence of Dante's engagement with scripture, an engagement that cannot be dismissed simply as a rhetorical exercise but that ought to be taken as a living sign of Dante's confidence in the ability of his voice to embody truth. Even more energetically than in the *Monarchia*, we see in Dante's so-called political letters something that transcends political theory. The interest of these texts lies, not simply in the particular political vision they present, but in the fact that Dante—lay, literary intellectual—presents himself, through engagement with scripture, as spokesperson for divinity and faithful interpreter of God's will for creation.

The letter to the Italian cardinals is particularly striking in this respect. Written in mid-1314 and addressed to the Italian cardinals involved in the papal election following the death of Clement V, it voices Dante's anger at the corruption of ecclesiastical institutions, which have become legalistic machines instead of living and faithful interpreters of theological tradition, as embodied especially in the writings of the fathers. Dante thus consciously presents himself as a layman who, even if a lowly sheep in the ecclesial flock, is able to interpret correctly what the divine will is for the church. And in doing so he once again puts his subtle literary skills in service of his engagement with scripture. In a striking passage, for instance, he considers the claim some might make that he is overstepping his mark because he is reaching out to touch divine things without authority, like Uzzah, who was punished for touching the ark.[17] Dante responds that, in fact, he is merely trying to correct the path of the oxen pulling the cart on which the ark travels. With both wit and profundity, Dante thus displays his ability to interpret image and metaphor, while at the same time proposing a theologically sophisticated understanding of the relationship between ecclesiastical institutions and divinity itself:

> Forsitan "et quis iste, qui Oze repentinum supplicium non formidans, ad arcam, quamvis labantem, se erigit?" indignanter obiurgabitis. Quippe de ovibus pascue Iesu Christi minima una sum; quippe nulla pastorali auctoritate abutens, quoniam divitie mecum non sunt. Non ergo divitiarum, sed gratia Dei sum id quod sum, et "zelus domus eius comedit me." Nam etiam "in ore lactentium et infantium" sonuit iam Deo placita veritas, et cecus natus veritatem confessus est, quam Pharisei non modo tacebant, sed et maligne reflectere conabantur. Hiis habeo persuasum quod audeo. Habeo preter hec preceptorem Phylosophum qui, cuncta moralia dogmatizans, amicis omnibus veritatem docuit preferendam. Nec Oze presumptio quam obiectandam quis crederet, quasi temere prorumpentem me inficit sui tabe reatus; quia ille ad arcam, ego ad boves calcitrantes et per abvia distrahentes attendo. Ille ad arcam proficiat qui salutiferos oculos ad naviculam fluctuantem aperuit.[18] (*Ep.* 11.5)

> [Will you, perhaps, reproach me indignantly, "Who is this who does not fear the sudden punishment of Uzzah, but sets himself up as the protector of the Ark, no matter how unsteady it may be?" [see

2 Sam. 6:6–7]. I am, without doubt, the least of the sheep in the pasture of Jesus Christ, and certainly I am not taking advantage of my pastoral authority since I possess no wealth. It is, therefore, not by riches but by the grace of God that I am what I am [see 1 Cor. 15:9–10], and "zeal for his house devours me" [Psalms 68:10 (69:9)]. For that truth which is pleasing to God proceeds even from the mouths of babes and sucklings [Psalms 8:3 (8:2)], and a man born blind has proclaimed the truth that the Pharisees not only do not acknowledge, but rather maliciously contradict [see John 9]. These things give me the courage of my convictions. Besides, I also have the authority of Aristotle, who, in setting out the principles of ethics, taught that truth is more important than friendship. Nor am I sullied by the stain of the sin of Uzzah, although some have thought to accuse me of similar presumption, as though I had spoken out rashly; for, whereas Uzzah reached out his hand to the Ark itself, I reach out to the recalcitrant oxen who are pulling it off course. I pray that God, who turned the salvific power of his gaze onto the little boat tossed by the waves [Matt. 8:23–27, Mark 4:35–40, Luke 8:22–25], will also come to the aid of the Ark.]¹⁹

In the *Epistles* too, then, Dante's work clearly displays a theological dimension. And, as with the *Monarchia*, we see this as lying primarily in Dante's understanding of the role his writing can play in the world in and through its transformative impact on its readers. We can, here too, follow up our guide question with other open-ended interrogatives specifically related to the *Epistles*: *What does Dante's engagement with scripture as presented in the "Epistles" tell us about his understanding of his voice as truth-bearing? What can we learn from the "Epistles" about Dante's understanding of himself as a person who can speak truthfully not just about but for divinity? And what, in turn, does this tell us of his understanding of how his texts might have acted as moments of transformative human encounter, as words that might aid his readers in their journey toward salvation?*

The *De vulgari eloquentia*, too, clearly has a confident theological character, especially in the way that, in the first eight chapters of the work, Dante sets up his discussion of Italian vernacular poetry. In these chapters, Dante's engagement with scripture is indeed a very prominent aspect of the text, especially in Dante's extended meditation on the vernacular itself, based on a highly creative reading of Genesis. Dante, who is writing in Latin, offers an impassioned defense of the greater value with respect to Latin of the vernacular, on the grounds that the vernacular is the language that we all learn from childhood, in intimate embodied fashion, from those closest to us. He also offers a detailed account of the beginnings of the vernacular itself in the Earthly Paradise, in the language first spoken by Adam, as expression of his intimate relationship with God. Having done so, Dante then addresses in *De vulgari eloquentia* 1.6 the question of which particular language it was that Adam spoke. He concludes that it must have been Hebrew: this was the language spoken by Christ, and it would be unreasonable to suppose that Christ spoke any language other than that with which humanity was first created.

In his lecture on the *De vulgari eloquentia*, the late Steven Botterill emphasized the importance of the chapter in which Dante reflects on the relationship between the language spoken by Adam and that spoken by Christ.[20] He drew particular attention to the fact that the heart of the chapter is in fact neither about Adam nor about Christ, but about Dante. Here Dante criticizes the short-sighted view of many who confuse their own vernacular with the vernacular spoken by Adam, thinking their own vernacular to be the highest possible form of language. He then presents himself as someone who is intimately tied to his particular birthplace and its vernacular but who is also acutely conscious that this cannot be considered the best language in the world:

> Nam quicunque tam obscene rationis est ut locum sue nationis delitiosissimum credat esse sub sole, hic etiam pre cunctis proprium vulgare licetur, idest maternam locutionem, et per consequens credit ipsum fuisse illud quod fuit Ade. Non autem, cui mundus est patria velut piscibus equor, quanquam Sarnum biberimus ante dentes et Florentiam adeo diligamus ut, quia dileximus, exilium patiamur iniuste, rationi magis quam sensui spatulas nostri iudicii podiamus. Et quamvis ad voluptatem nostrum sive nostre sensualitatis quietem in terries amenior locus quam Flornetia non existat, revolventes et poetarum et aliorum scriptorum volumina, quibus mundus universaliter et membratim describitur, ratiocinantesque in nobis situationes varias mundi locorum et eorum habitudinem ad utrunque polum et circulum equatorem, multas esse prependimus firmiterque censemus

et magis nobiles et magis delitiosas et regiones et urbes quam Tusciam et Florentiam, unde sumus oriundus et civis, et plearasque nationes et gentes delectabiliori atque utiliori sermone uti quam Latinos.[21] (*Dve* 1.6.2–3)

[For whoever is so misguided as to think that the place of his birth is the most delightful spot under the sun may also believe that his own language—his mother tongue, that is—is pre-eminent among all others; and, as a result, he may believe that his language was also Adam's. To me, however, the whole world is a homeland, like the sea to fish—though I drank from the Arno before cutting my teeth, and love Florence so much that, because I loved her, I suffer exile unjustly—and I will weigh the balance of my judgement more with reason than with sentiment. And although for my own enjoyment (or rather for the satisfaction of my own desire), there is no more agreeable place on earth than Florence, yet when I turn the pages of the volumes of poets and other writers, by whom the world is described as a whole and in its constituent parts, and when I reflect inwardly on the various locations of places in the world, and their relations to the two poles and the circle at the equator, I am convinced, and firmly maintain, that there are many regions and cities more noble and more delightful than Tuscany and Florence, where I was born and of which I am a citizen, and many nations and peoples who speak a more elegant and practical language than do the Italians.][22]

In commenting on this passage, Botterill drew particular attention to its autobiographical significance, in terms of what it tells us about the spirit with which Dante approached the composition of the work. The way in which Dante refers to Florence, to his exile, and to his studies allows us to perceive in Dante an author consciously trying to foreground the particularity of his personal experience as the source of his particular authority with respect to the questions he is addressing. Even in the *De vulgari eloquentia*, then, Dante seems, not to be speaking to us in merely theoretical terms, but to be grounding those in a keen sense of the particular value of his particular voice. And, even here, this presentation of particularity resonates with strong theological overtones. While Dante clearly says that he cannot consider his vernacular as on a par with that spoken by Adam and Christ, he does nonetheless prominently invite us to reflect on his particularity as part of an argumentative trajectory that links the two. He might speak a different vernacular from Adam and Christ, but his particular experience grants him the authority to be one who can correctly interpret how to understand the relationship between the language spoken by the first human being and that spoken by the Redeemer of humanity (*Dve* 1.6.5–6). And, once again, the argumentative strategies Dante pursues are strongly literary in character, especially insofar as in the opening chapters of *De vulgari eloquentia* Dante uses his literary skills to offer a new exegesis of Genesis. Akin to what we saw in the *Monarchia* and the *Epistles*, in the *De vulgari eloquentia* too Dante uses his literary skills to engage with scripture in novel ways. He presents himself as offering to his fellow human beings something of theological value that only he—given his particular intellectual abilities—is able to offer. As Dante puts it at the very beginning of the work, given that no one else has been able to do it, he will aim to speak of the eloquence "necessary" to all men, women, and children, and to do so as inspired by the "Verbo aspirante de celis" (*Dve* 1.1.1) [Word that comes from above]. Inspired by the Word, the literary author aims to enlighten all human beings as to how to use words.

For the purposes of the present chapter, it is indeed extremely significant to note that Dante's treatise on poetry should open with a confident presentation on Dante's part of himself as a faithful interpreter of scripture, especially in relation to the question of the language spoken by Adam and Christ. Dante appears to want to tell his readers that his understanding of poetry in the Italian vernacular is based on a truthful understanding of language itself as enshrined in scripture. He thereby presents himself as both poet and theorist of poetry, carrying out an essential theological function: that of revealing to his readers how, in the very way we speak, to be true to the way we were created to speak, and that of thereby helping to heal the communal fractures that follow from an incorrect understanding and use of vernacular language. These are the same kind of fractures that have led to Dante's exile and that, as Dante argues in *De vulgari eloquentia* 1.7–8, originate in the presumption of Babel. By theorizing about the Italian vernacular, one could say, Dante imagines himself able to heal the communal fractures existing in the Italian peninsula by bringing all speakers of the Italian vernacular together under his scripturally sanctioned conception of it.

Dante might speak a different language from that of Adam and Christ, but his text is presented as able to have a salvific effect. In claiming to be able to discern correctly what scripture teaches us about language, Dante seems to be presenting himself as having a salvific, Christic function: that of speaking, and allowing others to speak, in ways that can in some measure redeem the kind of fractures effected by Babel, especially insofar as these manifest themselves in linguistic disunity and the kind of imperfect communities this generates. Once again, then, Dante can be seen not only as engaging with scripture *in* his text but as speaking with a confident energy deriving from his perception that his voice is itself consonant with the truth embodied in scripture and incarnate in Christ. This allows us to raise, even in connection to the *De vulgari eloquentia*, an open-ended interrogative following our guide question stated above: *To what extent does the theological significance of the "De vulgari eloquentia" reside as much in what Dante says in the text as in the way in which he envisions the transformative impact of his voice on his readers, through his scripturally informed presentation of language itself?*

The latter question is especially significant if asked in conjunction with reflection on the *Convivio*. While Dante in the *Convivio* formally states that Latin is superior to the vernacular, it is in the vernacular that the text is written; and, in book 1.1, Dante presents his use of the vernacular in imagery that is strongly Eucharistic. By writing in the vernacular, Dante tells us, he wishes to provide vital intellectual and spiritual nourishment to those who normally do not have access to the kind of material the *Convivio* presents.[23] In this, Dante's use of the vernacular in the *Convivio* is consistent with what is suggested above about the *De vulgari eloquentia*: Dante writes with a keen sense of the salvific power of his vernacular voice and authorial personhood, power that is akin to that of the divine Word itself.

However, in other respects the case for a theological significance for the *Convivio* would not appear to be as straightforward to make as with the *De vulgari eloquentia*. Indeed, the *Convivio* is explicitly written as a celebration of philosophy and is a text in which Dante's interest and focus seem more explicitly to be philosophical rather than theological. A number of readers have in fact seen in this text Dante's attempt to depart from a Christian theological vision in favor of more radical and unorthodox philosophical frameworks available in his time. True, Dante's direct engagement with scripture does not seem as marked in this text as in others. Yet, as Bianchi and Simon Gilson in their different ways point out in their contributions to the present volume, a close reading of the text reveals that little in Dante's celebration of philosophy in the *Convivio* is actually unorthodox from a Christian theological point of view. This, coupled with the bold and broad engagement with different branches of knowledge that Gilson shows Dante to be performing in the *Convivio*, leads us to suggest that even the *Convivio* can have rich theological significance.

The suggestion is all but explicitly confirmed at the end of book 3. The final chapter of book 3 focuses directly on wisdom, the love of which the *Convivio* as a whole is intended to celebrate. In the first part of the chapter, the way Dante refers to wisdom suggests he is indeed here speaking of philosophy as an intellectual discipline in itself, somehow detached from living engagement with Christian Revelation. Yet gradually, as the chapter progresses, scripture becomes increasingly prominent through extended reference to the book of Wisdom and the book of Proverbs, thought by Dante to have been authored by Solomon. Here Dante refers specifically to Wisdom as at one with God and as the origin and end of creation. Following this we get another, stronger and even more striking reference to Revelation. Dante once again refers to the pivotal moment of salvation history: the Incarnation of divinity itself in human form:

> O peggio che morti che l'amistà di costei fuggite, aprite li occhi vostri e mirate: ché, innanzi che voi foste, ella fu amatrice di voi, aconciando e ordinando lo vostro processo; e poi che fatti foste, per voi dirizzare in vostra similitudine venne a voi. E se tutti al suo conspetto venire non potete, onorate lei ne' suoi amici e seguite li comandamenti loro, sì come [quelli] che nunziano la volontà di questa etternale imperadrice; non chiudete li orecchi a Salomone che ciò vi dice, dicendo che "la via de' giusti è quasi luce splendiente, che procede e cresce infino al die de la beatitudine": andando loro dietro, mirando le loro operazioni, che essere debbono a voi luce nel cammino di questa brevissima vita. (*Conv.* 3.15.17–18)

> [O worse than dead, you who shun her friendship, open your eyes and observe: for before you came to be she was your lover, preparing and planning the form of your life; and after you were created, to

direct you aright, she came to you as one like yourselves. And if you cannot all attain to the sight of her, honour her in her friends and follow their commands, as those who proclaim to you the will of this eternal empress—do not be deaf to Solomon's words when he speaks in this vein, declaring that "the way of the just is like a resplendent light, which spreads and grows brighter until the daytime of happiness" [Proverbs 4:18]—pursue them and observe their actions, which should be a light for you on the journey through this fleeting life.][24]

On the evidence of this passage, it would seem that even in the *Convivio* Dante's understanding of his intellectual enterprise is inseparable from his understanding of how it might fit within salvation history, both in terms of the relationship between his subject matter and the Incarnation and in terms of his understanding of how his work might contribute to the process of salvation itself by inviting others, through his work, to a closer relationship with truth. If we connect this to the Eucharistic imagery with which Dante presents his enterprise to readers in book 1, we clearly seem to have in the *Convivio* another confidently powerful statement on Dante's part of his perception of the theological value of his authorial voice. In writing the *Convivio* Dante is doing nothing other than attempting to offer us vital intellectual and spiritual nourishment in recognition of the fact that the wisdom underlying and reflected in the cosmos offered itself to us for our salvation in human form. This allows us to pose for the *Convivio*, too, open-ended interrogatives that follow from our overarching guide question: *To what extent is the celebration of wisdom offered in the "Convivio" ultimately and consciously rooted in Dante's living engagement with Christian Revelation? And, to what extent might the theological significance of the text once again be seen to lie not just in what the text says but in the way Dante addresses his readers as an author who believes his voice can contribute to their salvation?*

Unlike the *Convivio*, the *Vita nova* has long been recognized by commentators as theological and as the work with the closest affinity to the theological dimensions of the *Commedia*, especially in connection with the presentation of Beatrice as a heavenly figure. Yet even the *Vita nova* is not generally recognized as theological in itself, as a whole. Barański's contribution to the present volume, however, invites us to reconsider this question. Barański argues that the *Vita nova* ought to be read as consciously composed by Dante with scripture and scriptural interpretation as primary points of reference. According to Barański, this text, which is ostensibly about Dante's earthly love for Beatrice and which is only in part explicitly engaging with scripture, was in fact written by its author as a text that can embody within itself the authority of the biblical model. Barański proposes that in its form as self-commentary the *Vita nova* is explicitly written as a new kind of literature, one that not only serves to document a spiritual regeneration in its author through his love for Beatrice but also aims to have a spiritually regenerative effect for readers in opening up for them the possibility for a renewed perception, understanding, and engagement with the experience of love. Moreover, all of this is done not only through recourse to scriptural reference but also through use of scripture as the primary model.

In light of the above, the key narrative and poetic turn in the text to a poetics of praise, in and around "Donne ch'avete intelletto d'amore" [Ladies who have understanding of love], reveals on a metaliterary level Dante's conception of himself as an author whose poetry seeks to have on readers the same regenerative effect that Beatrice has on him, which, as suggested by the canzone, is in itself comparable to the salvific effect of Christ. The *Vita nova* can thus as a whole be seen as Dante's attempt to partake, as love poet, in the salvific work of scripture. In yet another way, we see the lay, literary intellectual engaging with scripture so as to fashion his voice as truth-bearing—or as love-bearing, we might more accurately say in the case of the *Vita nova*.

In turn, this suggests a richer reading than usually proposed of how the *libello* stands in relation to Dante's works as a whole relative to theology. The *Vita nova* ought to be regarded as theologically significant not simply insofar as, unlike any of the other "other works," it contains elements (especially the presentation of Beatrice) that seem clearly to look toward and prepare for the more explicitly theological enterprise of the *Commedia*. The *Vita nova* ought to be considered theological, more generally and significantly, insofar as it shows how Dante, already in the earlier phases of his literary career, consciously conceives of himself as an author whose voice can fruitfully partake in divinity and in the salvific work of the Word of God. In this, the *Vita nova* seems not so much to stand out from the other "other works" as to suggest further interpretive interrogatives: *To what extent can the "Vita nova" too, like the other texts we have considered, be seen as an expression of Dante's engagement with scripture as the primary point of reference for fashioning his authorial voice? What do we learn from the "Vita nova" about Dante's perception of his voice as salvific for his readers?*

The significance of these questions, as of all of the questions raised so far, is enhanced if we turn to the *Rime* and, in particular, to one crucial, general feature of the *Rime* and of our interpretation of them that Manuele Gragnolati brings to light in his contribution to the present volume. Gragnolati highlights the process of self-construction that is evident both in Dante's own relationship to his *Rime* and in any editorial attempt to order them in coherent fashion. This idea is crucial for our engagement with the question of the relationship between theology and the "other works" for two interconnected reasons.

First, there is what the idea tells us about Dante's self-understanding as literary author. As Gragnolati shows, from as early as the time of the composition of the *Vita nova* Dante is relating to his already existing *rime* through a conscious refashioning of their meaning so as to fit the overall narrative and conceptual trajectory of the work. If we pair this with the reading of the *Vita nova* suggested above, we are presented with the image of an author who perceives in his early lyrical output intellectual, ethical, existential, and spiritual possibilities to be fruitfully discovered (or elaborated afresh!), even after the poems' initial composition, in engagement with scripture. The early *rime* might or might not have been composed as the expression of theological activity, but their insertion in the *Vita nova* signals to us that at least some of them became an integral part of Dante's gradual understanding of himself as a literary author in whom divinity—or love—speaks. By extension, in the light of the reading of the "other works" presented above, the same might be said of what we learn about Dante's relationship with his lyric poetry from its insertion in the *Convivio* and the *De vulgari eloquentia*.

The second reason for which Gragnolati's perspective on the *Rime* is crucial for reflecting on the relationship between theology and the "other works" has to do with our own engagement with Dante's writing. As Gragnolati shows, the long, complex, and multifaceted editorial history of the *Rime* tells us that confrontation with the question of the ordering of Dante's lyric poetry necessarily generates in scholarly interpreters responses that have to do with not only technical philological and literary questions but also ideological and existential assumptions concerning what literature is, and what its value is, for the interpreter and the interpreter's culture. Often these assumptions are subconscious and/or unspoken. In any case, however, to fashion an ordering of the *Rime* is not just thereby to comment on the texts themselves; it is also to fashion for ourselves an author: a conception of who Dante is and what some of the deeper motivations might be for him to write the way he does. As Gragnolati shows, the *Rime* taken on their own ultimately resist any kind of systematic fashioning in this way. This ought to be acknowledged and respected, and this caution against systematic fashioning ought by extension to be applied critically even to the overall reading of the "other works" proposed here. But there is in Gragnolati's reading of the editorial history of the *Rime* an important lesson that I believe has significant value for our present task of reflecting on the relationship between theology and the "other works." Gragnolati's insights remind us that *any* interpretive encounter with Dante's work is also an encounter with Dante himself—an encounter, however, whereby Dante's character is determined in significant measure by our own spoken or unspoken assumptions concerning personhood and authorship.

There is great responsibility in this encounter, from a theological point of view too. In interpreting Dante's work, we are also interpreting Dante himself: we are fashioning for ourselves, and for anyone engaging with our work, an image of a person; we impose on a fellow human being an identity that might or might not correspond to their actual person, but through which, in any case, their person lives on. We all have our different idea as to who Dante is or might have been. Yet we would not be engaging with his work if we did not somehow share the belief that his work is in some sense significant for us today. We might or might not agree with Dante's idea of truth. Yet we would not be engaging with his work academically if we did not believe that there is some kind of truth or meaningfulness that transcends our individual selves and that allows us to engage in intellectual debate, moving toward an ever-richer comprehension of our literary and intellectual heritage and its ongoing significance. We might or might not consider the theological as such to be important. Yet we would not be reflecting on the relationship between theology and the "other works" if we did not believe that there is something significant to learn from the theological dimensions of Dante's writing.

What I would like to propose, in conclusion, is that, to give ourselves the richest opportunity for reflecting on the relationship between theology and the "other works," it is important that we consciously interpret these as moments of human encounter between ourselves and Dante. We might like the Dante we encounter or not. We might agree with his claims to be speaking for divinity or not. But unless we are open to encountering Dante as a fellow human being offering us his voice on a common journey toward an ever-richer understanding of ourselves and the world we are part of, we close ourselves off from the theological heart—and art—of Dante's writing.

One of the most important currents in Dante scholarship at the moment is the study of what is referred to as Dante's intellectual formation. I would like to suggest that in order for us to engage with the theological significance of Dante's work, study of Dante's intellectual formation ought to be characterized in part by study of Dante's conscious perception of himself as an author through whom truth speaks, and of the ways in which this perception is consciously presented in Dante's engagement with scripture and with Revelation more broadly. In their different ways, the "other works" offer us a remarkable record of a human being attempting to live out—in as truthful a manner as he is capable of—his responsibility to aid other human beings on their journey. As proud or as humble as we might think Dante to be in thinking of himself in this way, our engagement with his work along these lines can be a fruitful experience. At the very least it will allow us to explore, consciously, critically, communally, our own understanding of our relationship with truth. We might or might not think of this explicitly as a theological, spiritual, or salvific activity. But, on the interpretive terms I have tried to outline above, I believe Dante might suggest to us that, in any case, this is in essence an activity that brings us closer to nothing other than truth itself. Be that as it may, reflecting on the relationship between theology and the "other works" is significant both for what it can tell us about Dante and for what it can allow us to discover about ourselves.

Our overarching guide question was: *To what extent and in what ways can the "other works" be seen as manifestations of Dante's (changing) understanding of human personhood—and therefore also human authorship—as having an essentially, and irreducibly, divine dimension?* In the light of the various ways in which this question was addressed above, the open-ended interrogative I would like to end with is: *What is at stake for us, as scholars and more generally, in responding to the various ways in which Dante's "other works" invite us to recognize an irreducibly divine dimension in Dante's voice, and therefore also in our own?* It is in this kind of question, I believe, that the significance of reflection on "theology and the 'other works'" ultimately lies.

Notes

1. It would be impossible to offer a comprehensive bibliography on Dante and theology, which is vast and dates back to the earliest commentaries to Dante's work. The references given here are meant to be indicative of main strands of recent work. Where possible, reference is made to works available in English. (Because of the Covid-19 pandemic in 2020, when completing the chapter I did not have access to all of the works referred to, or to all of the editions and translations of Dante's works I would normally have used.)

2. See, for example, Auerbach, "'Figura'" and "St Francis"; Foster, "Teologia" and *Two Dantes*; E. Gilson, *Dante et Béatrice* and *Dante and Philosophy*; Nardi, *Dante* and *Nel mondo di Dante*; Singleton, *Dante's "Commedia"* and *Journey to Beatrice*. See also Curtius, "Poetry and Theology"; Lansing, *Dante and Theology*.

3. See, for example, Barański, *Dante e i segni*; Boitani, *Tragic and the Sublime*; Botterill, *Dante and the Mystical Tradition*; Chiavacci Leonardi, commentary to her edition of the *Commedia*; Freccero, *Poetics of Conversion*; Hawkins, *Dante's Testaments*; Hollander, *Allegory in Dante's "Commedia"*; Kirkpatrick, *Dante's "Paradiso"*; Mazzotta, *Dante's Vision*; Pertile, *Puttana e il gigante*. See also Kleinhenz, "Dante and the Bible"; Hawkins, "Dante and the Bible"; Ryan, "Theology of Dante."

4. See, for example, DeLorenzo and Montemaggi, *Dante, Mercy, Beauty*; Honess and Treherne, *Reviewing Dante's Theology*; Ledda, *Bibbia di Dante*, *Dante poeta cristiano*, *Preghiera e liturgia* and *Teologie di Dante*; Lombardo, Parisi, and Pegoretti, *Theologus Dantes*; Montemaggi and Treherne, *Dante's "Commedia."* See also Franke, *Revelation of the Imagination*; Montemaggi, *Reading Dante's "Commedia"*; Nasti, *Favole d'amore*; Took, *Conversations with Kenelm*; Webb, *Dante's Persons*. Increasing interest in theological reflection on Dante's work is further seen, for instance, in the theological contributions to Corbett and Webb, *Vertical Readings*, and in the theological inflection of Kirkpatrick's commentary in *Divine Comedy*, Kirkpatrick ed. and trans. See also Iannucci, "Theology"; Williams, "Theology of the *Comedy*." Some of the most important current manifestations of interest in the study of the theological dimensions of

Dante's work are ongoing collaborative projects addressing the question of the origins and contexts of Dante's theological imagination. These include the AHRC-funded project "Dante and Late Medieval Florence: Theology in Poetry, Practice and Society," run by the University of Leeds and the University of Warwick, and the conferences and seminars around the question of Dante's intellectual formation organized by the Devers Program in Dante Studies and the Center for Italian Studies at the University of Notre Dame. I am greatly indebted to participation in these initiatives.

5. Moevs, *Metaphysics of Dante's "Comedy,"* 5.
6. Montemaggi, *Reading Dante's "Commedia,"* 31–88.
7. See especially the works referred to in note 4 above.
8. Barański, "Dante and Doctrine" and "(Un)orthodox Dante."
9. The "other works" in this chapter are treated roughly in inverse chronological order to emphasize continuity between them, while also not wishing to suggest that it might be possible or desirable to offer a single "master narrative" for interpreting Dante's development as an author. Space does not allow for reference to all of the "other works." The present chapter focuses more closely on *Monarchia*, *Epistles*, *De vulgari eloquentia*, *Convivio*, *Vita nova*, and *Rime*. I hope this can nonetheless provide perspectives that might, even if more indirectly, fruitfully be brought to bear on the interpretation also of Dante's *Questio de aqua et terra* and *Eclogues*, and perhaps also on the *Fiore* and the question of its attribution.
10. Barański, "'Oh come è grande'"; Nasti, "'Vocabuli d'autori.'"
11. For broader reflection on Dante's work relative to medieval definitions of theology, see Robiglio, "Philosophy and Theology."
12. This can be seen, for instance, in passages of the *Commedia* in which Dante points to the failure of exegetes who are motivated by individualistic and materialistic interests (e.g., *Par.* 9.133–38 and 29.85–145). It is also evident in Dante's engagement with scripture in the "other works" explored in this chapter.
13. I am especially grateful to Theodore Cachey for his advice on this question. See also Montemaggi, *Reading Dante's "Commedia,"* 246–47.
14. Text from Dante, *Monarchia*, Shaw ed. and trans.
15. Translation from Dante, *Monarchia*, Shaw ed. and trans.
16. For some of the metaphysical and theological implications of this, see Moevs, *Metaphysics of Dante's "Comedy,"* 77, 156–57.
17. For broader reflection on how Dante's treatment of this passage of scripture might be connected to medieval debates concerning the relation between the political and the theological, see Menziger, "Law."
18. Text from Dante, *Epistole*, ed. Pistelli.
19. Translation from Dante, *Four Political Letters*, trans. Honess.
20. As noted in the preface, Steven Botterill, to whose memory this book is dedicated, gave a lecture on the *De vulgari eloquentia* in the original series of

lectures. Mirko Tavoni generously agreed to contribute the chapter on the *De vulgari eloquentia* to the present volume.
21. Text from Dante, *De vulgari eloquentia*, ed and trans. Botterill.
22. Translation from Dante, *De vulgari eloquentia*, ed and trans. Botterill.
23. See also Barański, "'Oh come è grande,'" 20–26.
24. Translation from Dante, *Banquet*, Ryan trans.

BIBLIOGRAPHY

Primary Works

Alanus ab Insulis. *Literary Works*. Edited and translated by Winthrop Wetherbee. Cambridge, MA: Harvard University Press, 2013.
Alighieri, Dante. *The Banquet*. Translated by Christopher Ryan. Saratoga, FL: ANMA Libri, 1989.
———. *La canzone montanina*. Edited by Paola Allegretti. Verbania: Tararà, 2001.
———. *Commedia*. Edited by Anna Maria Chiavacci Leonardi. 3 vols. Milan: Mondadori, 1991–97.
———. *La Commedia secondo l'antica vulgata*. Edited by Giorgio Petrocchi. 2nd ed. 4 vols. Florence: Le Lettere, 1994.
———. *Convivio*. Edited by Franca Brambilla Ageno. 3 vols. Florence: Le Lettere, 1995.
———. *Il Convivio*. Edited by Giovanni Busnelli and Giuseppe Vandelli with an introduction by Michele Barbi. 2 vols. Florence: Le Monnier, 1934.
———. *Convivio*. Edited by Gianfranco Fioravanti. Canzoni edited by Claudio Giunta. In Dante Alighieri, *Opere*, 2:3–805. Milan: Mondadori, 2011–14.
———. *Convivio*. Edited by Cesare Vasoli. Canzoni edited by Domenico De Robertis. Milan: Ricciardi, 1988.
———. *Convivio: A Dual-Language Critical Edition*. Edited and translated by Andrew Frisardi. Cambridge: Cambridge University Press, 2018.
———. *Dante's Lyric Poetry*. Edited by Kenelm Foster and Patrick Boyde. 2 vols. Oxford: Oxford University Press, 1967.
———. *Dante's Lyric Poetry: Poems of Youth and of the "Vita Nuova."* Edited by Teodolinda Barolini. Translated by Richard Lansing. Toronto: Toronto University Press, 2014.
———. *Dantis Alagherii Epistolae: The Letters of Dante*. 2nd ed. Edited by Paget Toynbee. Oxford: Clarendon Press, 1966.
———. *De l'éloquence en vulgaire*. Edited by Irène Rosier-Catach. Paris: Fayard, 2011.

———. *De situ et forma acque et terre*. Edited by Giorgio Padoan. Florence: Le Monnier, 1968.

———. *Detto d'Amore*. In Dante Alighieri, *Il "Fiore" e il "Detto d'Amore" attribuibili a Dante Alighieri*, edited by Gianfranco Contini, 483–512. Edizione Nazionale a cura della Società Dantesca Italiana, vol. 1. Milan: Mondadori, 1984.

———. *Detto d'Amore*. In Dante Alighieri, *Il "Fiore" e il "Detto d'Amore" attribuibili a Dante Alighieri*, edited by Gianfranco Contini, vol. 1, pt. 2 of *Opere minori*, 553–798. Milan: Ricciardi, 1984.

———. *The Detto d'Amore*. In Dante Alighieri, *The Fiore and the Detto d'Amore: A Late 13th-Century Italian Translation of the Roman de la Rose, Attributable to Dante Alighieri*. Translated by Christopher Kleinhenz and Santa Casciani. Notre Dame, IN: University of Notre Dame Press, 2000. [For *Detto* editions that do not attribute the work to Dante, see below, listings under the title *Detto d'Amore* rather than under an author.]

———. *De vulgari eloquentia*. Edited and translated by Steven Botterill. Cambridge: Cambridge University Press, 1996.

———. *De vulgari eloquentia*. Edited by Enrico Fenzi. Rome: Salerno, 2012.

———. *De vulgari eloquentia*. Edited by Aristide Marigo. Florence: Le Monnier, 1938.

———. *De vulgari eloquentia*. Edited by Pier Vincenzo Mengaldo. Critical ed. Padua: Antenore, 1968.

———. *De vulgari eloquentia*. Edited and translated with commentary by Pier Vincenzo Mengaldo. In Dante Alighieri, *Opere minori*, 2:1–237. Milan: Ricciardi, 1979–88.

———. *De vulgari eloquentia*. Edited by Mirko Tavoni. In Dante Alighieri, *Opere*, 1:1065–547. Milan: Mondadori, 2011.

———. *De vulgari eloquentia: Sobre la elocuencia en lengua vulgar*. Edited by Raffaele Pinto. Madrid: Cátedra, 2018.

———. *The Divine Comedy*. Edited and translated by Robin Kirkpatrick. 3 vols. London: Penguin, 2006–7.

———. *The Divine Comedy*. Translated by Allen Mandelbaum. Berkeley: University of California Press, 1980–82.

———. *Egloge*. Edited by Gabriella Albanese. In Dante Alighieri, *Opere*, 2:1593–783. Milan: Mondadori, 2011–14.

———. *Egloge*. In Dante Alighieri, *Epistole, Ecloge, Quaestio de aqua et terra*, edited by Manlio Pastore Stocchi. Rome: Antenore, 2012.

———. *Egloge*. Edited by Marco Petoletti. In Dante Alighieri, *Epistole. Egloge. Questio de aqua et terra*, edited by Marco Baglio, Luca Azzetta, Marco Petoletti, and Michele Rinaldi, 489–650. Rome: Salerno, 2016.

———. *Le Egloghe di Dante*. Edited by Giovanni Reggio. Florence: Olschki, 1969.

———. *Epistola XIII*. Edited by Luca Azzetta. In Dante Alighieri, *Epistole. Egloge. Questio de aqua et terra*, edited by Marco Baglio, Luca Azzetta, Marco Petoletti, and Michele Rinaldi, 271–487. Rome: Salerno, 2016.

———. *Epistolae: The Letters of Dante*. Edited and translated by Paget Toynbee. 2nd ed. Oxford: Clarendon Press, 1966.

———. *Epistole*. Edited by Marco Baglio. In Dante Alighieri, *Epistole. Egloge. Questio de aqua et terra*, edited by Marco Baglio, Luca Azzetta, Marco Petoletti, and Michele Rinaldi, 1–227. Rome: Salerno, 2016.

———. *Epistole*. Edited by Ermenegildo Pistelli. Florence: Società Dantesca Italiana, 1960. www.danteonline.it.

———. *Epistole*. Edited by Claudia Villa. In Dante Alighieri, *Opere*, 2:1417–592. Milan: Mondadori, 2011–14.

———. *Il Fiore*. In Dante Alighieri, *Fiore. Detto d'Amore*, edited by Paola Allegretti. Florence: Le Lettere, 2011.

———. *Il Fiore*. In Dante Alighieri, *Tutte le opere*, edited by Luigi Blasucci, 735–75. Florence: Sansoni, 1965.

———. *Il Fiore*. In Dante Alighieri, *Il "Fiore" e il "Detto d'Amore" attribuibili a Dante Alighieri*, edited by Gianfranco Contini, 1–467. Edizione Nazionale a cura della Società Dantesca Italiana, vol. 1. Milan: Mondadori, 1984.

———. *Il Fiore*. In Dante Alighieri, *Il "Fiore" e il "Detto d'Amore" attribuibili a Dante*, edited by Gianfranco Contini, vol. 1, pt. 2 of *Opere minori*, 799–827. Milan: Ricciardi, 1984.

———. *The Fiore*. In Dante Alighieri, *The Fiore and the Detto d'Amore: A Late 13th-Century Italian Translation of the Roman de la Rose, Attributable to Dante Alighieri*. Translated by Christopher Kleinhenz and Santa Casciani. Notre Dame, IN: University of Notre Dame Press, 2000.

———. *Il Fiore*. In Dante Alighieri, *Il Fiore; Detto d'Amore*. Edited by Luca Carlo Rossi. Milan: Mondadori, 1996.

———. *Il Fiore (The Flower)*. Edited by John Took. Lewiston, NY: Edwin Mellen Press, 2004. [For *Il Fiore* editions that do not attribute the work to Dante, see below, listings under the title *Il Fiore* rather than under an author.]

———. *Four Political Letters*. Translated by Claire Honess: London: MHRA, 2007.

———. *Das Gastmahl IV*. Edited and commented by Ruedi Imbach and translated by Thomas Ricklin, with Roland Béhar. Hamburg: Meiner, 2004.

———. *The Inferno; Purgatorio; Paradiso*. Edited by Robert Hollander. 3 vols. New York: Anchor Books, 2000–2007.

———. *Libro de las canciones y otro poemas*. Edited by Juan Varela-Portas de Orduña (coord.), Rossend Arqués Corominas, Raffaele Pinto, Rosario Scrimieri Martín, Eduard Vilella Morató, and Anna Zembrino. Madrid: Akal, 2014.

———. *Monarchia*. Edited by Paolo Chiesa and Andrea Tabarroni, with Diego Ellero. Rome: Salerno, 2013.
———. *Monarchia*. Edited by Diego Quaglioni. In Dante Alighieri, *Opere*, 2:807–1415. Milan: Mondadori, 2011–14.
———. *Monarchy*. Edited and translated by Prue Shaw. Cambridge: Cambridge University Press, 1996.
———. *Paradiso*. Vol. 3 of *The Divine Comedy of Dante Alighieri*. Edited and translated by Robert M. Durling. Annotated by Ronald L. Martinez and Robert M. Durling. Oxford: Oxford University Press, 2011.
———. *La quaestio de aqua et terra di Dante Alighieri*. Edited by Vincenzo Biagi. Modena: G. T. Vincenzi e nipoti, 1907.
———. *Quaestio de aqua et terra*. In Dante Alighieri, *Epistole, Ecloge, Quaestio de aqua et terra*, edited by Manlio Pastore Stocchi. Rome: Antenore, 2012.
———. *Quaestio de aqua et terra*. Translated by Philip H. Wicksteed. In *The Latin Works of Dante*, 387–426. New York: Greenwood Press, 1969.
———. *Questio de aqua et terra*. Venice: Manfredo de Monteferrato, 1508.
———. *Questio de aqua et terra*. Edited by Stefano Caroti. doi: 10.14640/QuadernidiNoctua4.
———. *Questio de aqua et terra*. Edited by Francesco Mazzoni. In Dante Alighieri, *Opere minori*, 2:693–880. Milan: Ricciardi, 1979–88.
———. *Questio de aqua et terra*. Edited by Ermenegildo Pistelli. In *Le opere di Dante*, edited by Michele Barbi, 465–80. Florence: R. Bemporad e Figlio Editori, 1921.
———. *Questio de aqua et terra*. Edited by Michele Rinaldi. In Dante Alighieri, *Epistole. Egloge. Questio de aqua et terra*, edited by Marco Baglio, Luca Azzetta, Marco Petoletti, and Michele Rinaldi, 651–751. Rome: Salerno, 2016.
———. *Rime*. Edited by Michele Barbi. Florence: Bemporad, 1921.
———. *Rime*. Edited by Gianfranco Contini. Turin: Einaudi, 1995.
———. *Rime*. Edited by Domenico De Robertis. 5 vols. Florence: Le Lettere, 2002.
———. *Rime*. Edited and commented by Domenico De Robertis. Florence: SISMEL and Edizioni del Galluzzo, 2005.
———. *Rime della maturità e dell'esilio*. Edited by Michele Barbi and Vincenzo Pernicone. Florence: Le Monnier, 1969.
———. *Le rime della maturità e dell'esilio*. Edited by Marco Grimaldi. Rome: Salerno, 2019.
———. *Rime della "Vita nuova" e della giovinezza*. Edited by Michele Barbi and Francesco Maggini. Florence: Le Monnier, 1956.
———. *Rime giovanili e della Vita nuova*. Edited by Teodolinda Barolini. With notes by Manuele Gragnolati. Milan: BUR Rizzoli, 2009.
———. *A Translation of the Latin Works of Dante Alighieri*. Translated by A. G. F. Howell and Philip H. Wicksteed. New York: Greenwood Press, 1969.

———. *Tutte le opere*. Edited by Alessandro Della Torre. Florence: Barbèra, 1919.

———. *Vita nova*. Edited by Guglielmo Gorni. Turin: Einaudi, 1996.

———. *La vita nuova*. Rev. ed. Edited by Michele Barbi. Florence: Bemporad, 1932.

———. *Vita nuova*. Edited by Domenico De Robertis. Milan: Ricciardi, 1980.

———. *Vita nuova*. Edited by Donato Pirovano. In *Vita nuova; Rime*, edited by Donato Pirovano and Marco Grimaldi. Rome: Salerno, 2015.

———. *Vita nuova: Italian Text with Facing English Translation*. Edited by Dino S. Cervigni and Edward Vasta. Notre Dame, IN: University of Notre Dame Press, 1995.

Alighieri, Jacopo. *Chiose all'"Inferno."* Edited by Saverio Bellomo. Padua: Antenore, 1990.

———. *Il Dottrinale*. Edited by Giovanni Crocioni. S. Lapi: Città di Castello, 1895.

Alighieri, Pietro. *Comentum super poema "Comedie" Dantis: A Critical Edition of the Third and Final Draft of Pietro Alighieri's Commentary on Dante's "The Divine Comedy."* Edited by Massimiliano Chiamenti. Tempe: Arizona Center for Medieval and Renaissance Studies, 2002.

Angiolieri, Cecco. *Il Fiore: Nuove congetture testuali e interpretazioni*. Edited by Menotti Stanghellini. Monteriggioni: Ind. Grafiche Pistolesi Editrice, 2009.

Aristotle. *On the Heavens*. Translated by W. K. C. Guthrie. Cambridge, MA: Harvard University Press, 1939.

Augustine. *The City of God*. Translated by Marcus Dods. In *From Nicene and Post-Nicene Fathers*, edited by Philip Schaff, vol. 2. Buffalo, NY: Christian Literature Publishing, 1887. www.newadvent.org/fathers/1201.htm.

———. *De civitate Dei*. In PL 41, cols. 13–804.

———. *De doctrina christiana libri quator*. In PL 34, cols. 15–122.

———. *Enarrationes in Psalmos*. In PL 36, cols. 67–1027.

———. *On Christian Doctrine*. In *From Nicene and Post-Nicene Fathers*. https://faculty.georgetown.edu/jod/augustine/ddc3.html.

Bambaglioli, Graziolo de'. *Commento all'"Inferno" di Dante*. Edited by Luca Carlo Rossi. Pisa: Scuola Normale Superiore, 1998.

Bene Florentinus. *Candelabrum*. Edited by Gian Carlo Alessio. Padua: Antenore, 1983.

Biscioni, Antonio Maria. *Prose di Dante Alighieri e di Messer Gio. Boccaccio*. Florence: Gaetano Tartini and Santi Franchi, 1723.

Boccaccio, Giovanni. *Epistole*. Edited by Ginetta Auzzas. In *Tutte le opere di Giovanni Boccaccio*, edited by Vittore Branca, vol. 5, pt. 1. Milan: Mondadori, 1992.

———. *The Life of Dante (Trattatello in laude di Dante)*. Translated by Vincenzo Zin Bollettino. New York: Garland, 1990.

———. *Trattatello in laude di Dante*. Edited by Maurizio Fiorilla. In *Le Vite di Dante dal XIV al XVI secolo: Iconografia dantesca*. Edited by Monica Berté, Maurizio Fiorilla, Sonia Chiodo, and Isabella Valente, 11–154. Rome: Salerno, 2017.

———. *Trattatello in laude di Dante*. Edited by Bruno Maier. Milan: Rizzoli, 1965.

———. *Trattatello in laude di Dante*. Edited by Pier Giorgi Ricci. In *Tutte le opere di Giovanni Boccaccio*, edited by Vittore Branca, vol. 3. Milan: Mondadori, 1974.

Boccaccio, Giovanni, Leonardo Bruni, and Filippo Villani. *The Earliest Lives of Dante*. Translated by James Robinson Smith. New York: Henry Holt, 1901.

Boethius. *The Consolation of Philosophy*. Translated by W. V. Cooper. London: Dent, 1902.

———. *De consolatione philosophiae. Opuscula theologica*. Edited by Claudio Moreschini. Munich: Teubner, 2005.

———. *In Isagogen Porphirii commenta*. Edited by Samuel Brandt. Vienna: Tempsky, 1906.

Boethius of Dacia. *De aeternitate mundi*. Edited by Nicolaus G. Green-Pedersen. In *Boethii Daci opera*, 6.2:335–66. Copenhagen: G. E. C. Gad, 1976.

———. *On the Eternity of the World*. In *On the Supreme Good, On the Eternity of the World, On Dreams*, translated by John F. Wippel. Toronto: Pontifical Institute of Mediaeval Studies, 1987.

Bonaventure of Bagnoregio. *Legenda maior sancti Francisci*. In *Fontes franciscani*. Edited by Enrico Menestò, Stefano Brufani, Giuseppe Cremascoli, Emore Paoli, Luigi Pellegrini, and Stanislao da Campagnola, 777–961. Assisi: Edizioni Porziuncola, 1995.

———. *The Soul's Journey into God; The Tree of Life; The Life of St. Francis*. Translated and introduced by Ewert H. Cousins, 178–328. New York: Paulist Press, 1978.

Bruni, Leonardo. *Le vite di Dante e del Petrarca*. Edited by Antonio Lanza. Rome: Archivio Guido Izzi, 1987.

Campano da Novara. *Campanus of Novara and Medieval Planetary Theory: "Theorica planetarum."* Edited and translated by Francis S. Benjamin Jr. and G. J. Toomer. Madison: University of Wisconsin Press, 1971.

Castelvetro, Lodovico. "Spositione a XXIX canti dell'Inferno di Lodovico Castelvetro. Introduzione, edizione critica e commento. Appendice: le postille all'incunabolo Alpha K.1.13." Edited by Vera Rebaudo. PhD diss., University of Ca' Foscari, 2015.

Chartularium Universitatis Parisiensis. Edited by Heinrich Denifle and Émile Chatelain. 4 vols. Paris: Delalain, 1889–97.

Cicerone. *Pro Ligario, Pro Marcello, Pro rege Deiotaro (orazioni cesariane) volgarizzamento di Brunetto Latini*. Edited by Cristiano Lorenzi. Pisa: Edizioni della Normale, 2018.

Conrad of Megenberg. *Ökonomik*. Edited by Sabine Krüger. Vols. 1–3 of *Die Werke des Konrad von Megenberg*. Monumenta Germaniae Historica: Staatsschriften des späteren Mittelalters. Stuttgart: Hiersemann, 1984.

Cosmas of Prague. *Cosmae pragensis Cronica Boemorum*. Edited by Berthold Breholz. Monumenta Germaniae Historica: Scriptores rerum germanicarum, n.s., 2. Berlin: Weidmann, 1923.

Dante da Maiano. *Rime*. Edited by Rosanna Bettarini. Florence: Le Monnier, 1969.

del Virgilio, Giovanni. *Allegorie librorum Ovidii Metamorphoseos*. In Fausto Ghisalberti, "Giovanni del Virgilio espositore delle *Metamorfosi*," 43–107. *Il giornale dantesco* 34, n.s., 4 (1933): 1–110.

Detto d'Amore. In *Poemetti allegorico-didattici del secolo XIII*. Edited by Luigi Di Benedetto, 349–64. Bari: Laterza, 1941.

Detto d'Amore. Edited by Luciano Formisano. In *Il Fiore e il Detto d'Amore*, vol. 1 of *Opere di dubbia attribuzione e altri documenti danteschi*. Rome: Salerno, 2012.

Detto d'Amore. In *Il "Fiore" e il "Detto d'Amore*," edited by Ernesto Giacomo Parodi, appendix to *Le opere di Dante*. Florence: Bemporad, 1922. Reprinted in "Opere di Dante," *Enciclopedia dantesca*, 2nd ed., 6: 999–1002. Rome: Istituto della Enciclopedia Italiana, 1984.

Detto d'Amore. Edited by Luigi Vanossi. In *La teologia poetica*, 111–22.

"*Detto d'Amore*: Antiche rime imitate dal 'Roman de la Rose.'" Edited by Salomone Morpurgo. *Il propugnatore*, n.s., 1 (1888): 18–61.

Il Fiore. In *Poemetti allegorico-didattici del secolo XIII*, edited by Luigi Di Benedetto, 229–347. Bari: Laterza, 1941.

Il Fiore. In *Il Fiore e il Detto d'Amore*, edited by Luciano Formisano, vol. 1 of *Opere di dubbia attribuzione e altri documenti danteschi*. Rome: Salerno, 2012.

Il Fiore. In *"Il Fiore" e "Il Detto d'Amore*," edited by Claudio Marchiori. Genoa: Tilgher, 1983.

Il Fiore. Edited by Giuseppe Mazzatinti. In Mazzatinti, *Inventario dei manoscritti italiani delle biblioteche di Francia*, 3:611–730. Rome: Presso i Principali Librai, 1888.

Il Fiore. In *Il "Fiore" e il "Detto d'Amore" attribuiti a Dante Alighieri: Testo del XIII secolo*, edited by Guido Mazzoni. Florence: Alinari, 1923.

Il Fiore. In *Il "Fiore" e il "Detto d'Amore*," edited by Ernesto Giacomo Parodi, appendix to *Le opere di Dante*. Florence: Bemporad, 1922. Reprinted in "Opere di Dante," *Enciclopedia dantesca*, 2nd ed., 6: 967–96. Rome: Istituto della Enciclopedia Italiana, 1984.

Il Fiore. In *Poemetti del Duecento*, edited by Giuseppe Petronio, 175–375. Turin: UTET, 1951.

Il Fiore, poème italien du XIIIe siècle, en CCXXXII sonnets, imité du Roman de la Rose par Durante. Edited by Ferdinand Castets. Paris: Maisonneuve, 1881.
Foscolo, Ugo. *La Commedia di Dante Alighieri.* Vol. 1, *Discorso sul testo e su le opinioni diverse prevalenti intorno alla storia e alla emendazione critica della Commedia di Dante.* London: William Pickering, 1825.
Giamboni, Bono. *Delle storie contra i Pagani di Paolo Orosio libri VII.* Edited by Francesco Tassi. Florence: Baracchi, 1849.
———. *"Il libro de' vizî e delle virtudi" e "Il trattato di virtù e di vizî."* Edited by Cesare Segre. Turin: Einaudi, 1968.
Gregory the Great. *Moralia in Iob.* Edited by Paolo Siniscalco. 3 vols. Rome: Città Nuova Editrice, 1992–97.
Guillaume de Lorris and Jean de Meun. *The Romance of the Rose.* Translated by Charles Dahlberg. Princeton, NJ: Princeton University Press, 1995.
———. *Le Roman de la Rose.* Edited by Félix Lecoy. 3 vols. Paris: Champion, 1965–70.
Guittone d'Arezzo. *Lettere.* Edited by Claude Margueron. Bologna: Commissione per i testi di lingua, 1990.
Jerusalem Bible. London: Darton, Longman and Todd, 1974.
John of Dacia. *Divisio scientiae.* In *Johannis Daci Opera,* edited by Alfred Otto, 1:1–42. Copenhagen: G. E. C. Gad, 1955.
Lancia, Andrea. *Chiose alla "Commedia."* Edited by Luca Azzetta. 2 vols. Rome: Salerno, 2012.
Latini, Brunetto. *La rettorica.* Edited by Francesco Maggini. Florence: Galletti e Cocci, 1915.
———. *Tesoretto.* In Brunetto Latini, *Poesie,* edited by Stefano Carrai, 3–155. Turin: Einaudi, 2016.
L'Ottimo commento della "Divina Commedia": Testo inedito d'un contemporaneo di Dante citato dagli Accademici della Crusca. Edited by Arnaldo Torri. 3 vols. Pisa: Capurro, 1827–29.
Monti, Vincenzo, ed. *Convito de Dante Alighieri ridotto a lezione migliore.* Padua: Tipografia della Minerva, 1827.
Il Novellino. Edited by Alberto Conte. Rome: Salerno, 2001.
Ovid. *Metamorphoses.* Translated by Frank Justus Miller. Revised by G. P. Goold. 2 vols. Cambridge, MA: Harvard University Press, 1926.
Petrarca, Francesco. *Rerum memorandarum libri.* Edited by Giuseppe Billanovich. Florence: Sansoni, 1943.
Pietro di Dante. *Il "Commentarium" di Pietro Alighieri nelle redazioni ashburnhamiana e ottoboniana.* Edited by Roberto Della Vedova and Maria Teresa Silvotti. Florence: Olschki, 1978.
Prosper Aquitanus. *Liber epigrammatum.* Edited by Albertus G. A. Horsting. Berlin: De Gruyter, 2016.

Siger of Brabant. *De anima intellectiva.* In Sigier de Brabant, *Questiones in tertium de anima; De anima intellectiva; De aeternitate mundi,* edited by Bernardo Bazán, 70–112. Louvain: Publications Universitaires and Béatrice-Nauwelaerts, 1972.

———. *Quaestiones in Metaphysicam: Édition revue de la reportation de Munich: Texte inédit de la reportation de Vienne.* Edited by William Dunphy. Louvain-la-Neuve: Éditions de l'Institut Supérieur de Philosophie, 1981.

———. *Quaestiones in Metaphysicam: Texte inédit de la reportation de Cambridge: Édition revue de la reportation de Paris.* Edited by Armand Maurer. Louvain-la-Neuve: Éditions de l'Institut Supérieur de Philosophie, 1983.

Silvestris, Bernard. *The Cosmographia of Bernardus Silvestris.* Edited and translated by Winthrop Wetherbee. New York: Columbia University Press, 1990.

Sydrach. *Il libro di Sidrach: Testo inedito del secolo XIV.* Edited by Adolfo Bartoli. Bologna: G. Romagnoli, 1868.

Testi fiorentini del Dugento e dei primi del Trecento. Edited by Alfredo Schiaffini. Florence: Sansoni, 1926.

Thomas Aquinas, Saint. *Commentary on the Psalms.* http://hosted.desales.edu /w4/philtheo/loughlin/ATP/Psalm_1.html.

———. *Sententia libri metaphysicae.* Edited by Roberto Busa and Enrique Alarcón. Turin: Marietti, 1950.

Vernani, Guido. *De reprobatione "Monarchie" composite a Dante.* In Dante Alighieri, *Monarchia,* edited by Paolo Chiesa and Andrea Tabarroni with Diego Ellero, 327–66. Rome: Salerno, 2013.

———. *Refutation of the "Monarchia" Composed by Dante.* In Anthony K. Cassell, *The "Monarchia" Controversy,* 174–97. Washington, DC: Catholic University of America Press, 2004.

Villani, Filippo. *De origine civitatis Florentie et de eiusdem famosis civibus.* Edited by Giuliano Tanturli. Padua: Antenore, 1997.

———. *Expositio seu comentum super Comedia Dantis Allegherii.* Edited by Saverio Bellomo. Florence: Le Lettere, 1989.

Villani, Giovanni. *Nuova cronica.* Edited by Giuseppe Porta. 3 vols. Parma: Fondazione P. Bembo and Guanda, 1990–91.

Virgil. *Eclogues. Georgics. Aeneid. Appendix Vergiliana.* Translated by H. Rushton Fairclough. Revised by G. P. Goold. 2 vols. Cambridge, MA: Harvard University Press, 1916–18.

William of Aragon. *De nobilitate animi.* Edited by William D. Paden and Mario Trovato. Cambridge, MA: Harvard University Press, 2012.

William of Auvergne. *De universo.* In *Guilielmi Alverni [. . .] opera omnia,* 593–1074. Facsimile reproduction of the 1674 Paris edition. Frankfurt: Minerva, 1963.

William of Conches. *Dragmaticon philosophiae.* Edited by Italo Ronca. Turnhout: Brepols, 1997.

Secondary Sources

Abrame-Battesti, Isabelle. "La trivialisation du *Roman de la Rose* dans le *Fiore*." In "Du 'Roman de la Rose' au 'Fiore' attribué à Dante," edited by Claude Perrus, special issue, *Arzanà* 1 (1992): 43–69.

Addivinola, Gabriella. "Aspetti della contemplazione nel Paradiso: Alcune osservazioni sul sincretismo dantesco." In *Mystique, histoire et littérature: Itinéraires de recherche (XIIIe–XXe siècles, domaine franco-italien)*, edited by Massimo Lucarelli and Elisabetta Lurgo, 27–55. Alessandria: Edizioni dell'Orso, 2019.

Ahern, John. "*Epistles*." In *The Dante Encyclopedia*, edited by Richard Lansing, 352–55. New York: Garland, 2000.

Albanese, Gabriella. "*De Gestis Henrici VII Cesaris*: Mussato, Dante e il mito dell'incoronazione poetica." In *Enrico VII, Dante e Pisa a 700 anni dalla morte dell'imperatore e dalla "Monarchia" (1313–2013)*, edited by Giuseppe Petralia and Marco Santagata, 161–202. Ravenna: Longo, 2016.

———. "'Poeta et historicus': La laurea di Mussato e Dante." In *"Moribus antiquis sibi me fecere poetam": Albertino Mussato nel VII centenario dell'incoronazione poetica (Padova 1315–2015)*, edited by Rino Modonutti and Enrico Zucchi, 3–45. Florence: SISMEL and Edizioni del Galluzzo, 2017.

Albanese, Gabriella, and Paolo Pontari. "Il cenacolo ravennate di Dante e le *Egloge*: Fiduccio de' Milotti, Dino Perini, Guido Vacchetta, Pietro Giardini, Menghino Mezzani." *Studi danteschi* 82 (2017): 311–427.

———. "Il notariato bolognese, le *Egloge* e il Polifemo dantesco: Nuove testimonianze manoscritte e una nuova lettura dell'ultima egloga." *Studi danteschi* 81 (2016): 13–93.

———, eds. *L'ultimo Dante e il cenacolo ravennate: Catalogo della Mostra (Ravenna, Biblioteca Classense, 9 settembre–28 ottobre 2018)*. Ravenna: Longo, 2018.

Alexander, David. "Dante and the Form of the Land." *Annals of the Association of American Geographers* 76, no. 1 (1986): 38–49.

Alfie, Fabian. *Dante's "Tenzone" with Forese Donati: The Reprehension of Vice*. Toronto: University of Toronto Press, 2011.

———. "Durante's *Ars amandi*: A Structural Reading of the *Fiore*." *Forum Italicum* 36 (2002): 5–24.

———. "Wolves in Sheep's Clothing: Jean de Meun, Durante and Bindo Bonichi." *Rivista di studi italiani* 18 (2000): 34–59.

Allegretti, Paola. "Un acrostico per Giovanni del Virgilio." *Studi danteschi* 69 (2004): 289–94.

———. "Dante 'Tityrus annosus' (*Egloghe*, IV.12)." In *Dante the Lyric and Ethical Poet / Dante lirico e etico*, edited by Zygmunt G. Barański and Martin McLaughlin, 168–208. London: Legenda, 2010.

---. "La *Decretale* dello scandalo (*Fiore*, sonetti 37 e 219)." *Studi danteschi* 74 (2009): 275–97.

---. "È il *Fiore* adespoto? La questione della tradizione indiretta." *Studi danteschi* 81 (2016): 247–71.

---. "Il rapporto tra il *Roman de la Rose* e il *Fiore*: I modelli del volgarizzamento, alcune particolarità della *dispositio*." *Studi danteschi* 73 (2008): 251–305.

Alvino, Giuseppe. "Ancora sulla serie *Roman de la Rose–Fiore–Commedia*: Alcune verifiche sui riscontri inediti." In *Sulle tracce del Dante minore*, edited by Thomas Persico and Riccardo Viel, 141–54. Bergamo: Società Dante Alighieri, Comitato di Bergamo, Sestante Edizioni, 2017.

---. "La memoria del *Fiore* in Dante: Alcuni inediti riscontri." *Rivista di studi danteschi* 15 (2015): 259–84.

Annett, Scott. "'Una veritade ascosa sotto bella menzogna': Dante's *Eclogues* and the World beyond the Text." *Italian Studies* 68 (2013): 36–56.

Ardizzone, Maria Luisa, ed. *Dante and Heterodoxy: The Temptations of 13th Century Radical Thought*. Newcastle: Cambridge Scholars, 2014.

---. *Reading as Angels Read: Speculation and Politics in Dante's Banquet*. Toronto: University of Toronto Press, 2016.

Arduini, Beatrice. "Un episodio della tradizione quattrocentesca del *Convivio*: Il codice Riccardiano 1044." In *Per Franco Brioschi: Saggi di lingua e letteratura italiana*, edited by Silvia Morgana and Claudio Milanini, 69–80. Milan: Cisalpino, 2007.

---. "Il ruolo di Boccaccio e di Marsilio Ficino nella tradizione del *Convivio* di Dante." In *Boccaccio in America: 2010 International Boccaccio Conference, American Boccaccio Association, University of Massachusetts Amherst, April 30–May 1*, edited by Elsa Filosa and Michael Papio, 95–103. Ravenna: Longo, 2012.

Ariani, Marco. *Lux inaccessibilis: Metafore e teologia della luce nel "Paradiso" di Dante*. Rome: Aracne, 2010.

Armour, Peter. "Lettura dei sonetti LXI–XC." In *Lettura del "Fiore"* [= *Letture classensi* 22], edited by Zygmunt G. Barański, Patrick Boyde, and Lino Pertile, 53–74. Ravenna: Longo, 1993.

---. "The *Roman de la Rose* and the *Fiore*: Aspects of a Literary Transplantation." *Journal of the Institute of Romance Studies* 2 (1993): 63–81.

Arquillière, Henri-Xavier. *El agustinismo político*. Granada: Editorial Universidad de Granada, 2005.

Ascoli, Albert R. *Dante and the Making of a Modern Author*. Cambridge: Cambridge University Press, 2008.

---. "*Epistle to Cangrande*." In *The Dante Encyclopedia*, edited by Richard Lansing, 348–52. New York: Garland, 2000.

———. "Palinode and History in the Oeuvre of Dante." In *Dante Now: Current Trends in Dante Studies*, edited by Theodore J. Cachey Jr., 155–86. Notre Dame, IN: University of Notre Dame Press, 1995.

———. "'Ponete mente almeno come io son bella': Prose and Poetry, *Pane* and *Vivanda*, Goodness and Beauty, in *Convivio* I." In *Dante's "Convivio" or How to Restart a Career in Exile*, edited by Franziska Meier, 115–43. Bern: Lang, 2018.

———. "Tradurre l'allegoria: *Convivio* II, i." *Critica del testo* 14, no. 1 (2011): 153–76.

Auerbach, Erich. *Dante: Poet of the Secular World*. Chicago: University of Chicago Press, 1961.

———. "'Figura.'" In *Scenes from the Drama of European Literature*, translated by Ralph Manheim, 11–78. Minneapolis: University of Minnesota Press, 1984.

———. *The Literary Language and Its Public in Late Latin Antiquity and in the Middle Ages*. Princeton, NJ: Princeton University Press, 1993.

———. "St. Francis." In *Scenes from the Drama of European Literature*, translated by Ralph Manheim, 79–100. Manchester: Manchester University Press, 1984.

Austin, John L. *How to Do Things with Words: The William James Lectures Delivered at Harvard University in 1955*, edited by J. O. Urmson. Oxford: Oxford University Press, 1962.

Azzetta, Luca. "Le chiose alla *Commedia* di Andrea Lancia, l'*Epistola a Cangrande*, e altre questioni dantesche." *L'Alighieri* 21 (2003): 5–76.

———. "'Di questo parla l'autore in una chiosa d'una sua canzone': The *Convivio* through the Eyes of Its First Readers." In *Dante's "Convivio" or How to Restart a Career in Exile*, edited by Franziska Meier, 247–81. Bern: Lang, 2018.

———. "Nota sulla tradizione del *Convivio* nella Firenze di Coluccio Salutati." *Italia medioevale e umanistica* 58 (2017): 293–303.

———. "La tradizione del *Convivio* negli antichi commenti alla *Commedia*: Andrea Lancia, l'*Ottimo Commento* e Pietro Alighieri." *Rivista di studi danteschi* 5, no. 1 (2005): 3–34.

Baldelli, Ignazio. "Lingua e stile delle opere in volgare di Dante." In *Enciclopedia dantesca*, Appendice, 55–112. Rome: Istituto della Enciclopedia Italiana, 1970–78.

———. "La prosa del *Convivio*." In *Enciclopedia dantesca*, Appendice, 88–93. Rome: Istituto della Enciclopedia Italiana, 1970–78.

Banella, Laura. *La "Vita nuova" del Boccaccio: Fortuna e tradizione*. Rome: Antenore, 2017.

Barański, Zygmunt G. "*Comedìa*: Notes on Dante, the Epistle to Cangrande and Medieval Comedy." *Lectura Dantis* 8 (1991): 26–55.

———. "Il *Convivio* e la poesia: Problemi di definizione." In *Contesti della "Commedia": Lectura Dantis Fridericiana*, edited by Francesco Tateo and Daniele Maria Pegorari, 9–64. Bari: Palomar, 2004.

———. "Dante Alighieri: Experimentation and (Self-)Exegesis." In *The Cambridge History of Literary Criticism*, vol. 2, *The Middle Ages*, edited by Alastair J. Minnis and Ian Johnson, 561–82. Cambridge: Cambridge University Press, 2005.

———. "Dante and Doctrine (and Theology)." In *Reviewing Dante's Theology*, edited by Claire E. Honess and Matthew Treherne, 1:9–63. Bern: Lang, 2013. Also in *Dante, Petrarch, Boccaccio: Literature, Doctrine, Reality*, 45–81. Cambridge: Legenda, 2020.

———. *Dante e i segni: Saggi per una storia intellettuale di Dante Alighieri*. Naples: Liguori, 2000.

———. *Dante, Petrarch, Boccaccio: Literature, Doctrine, Reality*. Cambridge: Legenda, 2020.

———. "Dante 'poeta' e 'lector': 'Poesia' e 'riflessione tecnica' (con divagazioni sulla *Vita nova*)." *Critica del testo* 14, no. 1 (2011): 81–110.

———. "Dante's Biblical Linguistics." *Lectura Dantis* 5 (1989): 105–43.

———. "The Ethics of Literature: The *Fiore* and Medieval Traditions of Rewriting." In *The "Fiore" in Context: Dante, France, Tuscany*, edited by Zygmunt G. Barański and Patrick Boyde, 207–32. Notre Dame, IN: University of Notre Dame Press, 1997.

———. "Il *Fiore* e la tradizione delle *translationes*." *Rassegna europea di letteratura italiana* 5–6 (1995): 31–41.

———. "Genesis, Dating, and Dante's 'Other Works.'" In *The Cambridge Companion to Dante's "Commedia,"* edited by Zygmunt G. Barański and Simon Gilson, 208–28. Cambridge: Cambridge University Press, 2019.

———. "*Inferno* I." In *Lectura Dantis Bononiensis*, edited by Emilio Pasquini and Carlo Galli, 11–40. Bologna: Bononia University Press, 2011.

———. "'Lascio cotale trattato ad altro chiosatore': Form, Literature, and Exegesis in Dante's *Vita nova*." In *Dantean Dialogues: Engaging with the Legacy of Amilcare Iannucci*, edited by Maggie Kilgour and Elena Lombardi, 1–40. Toronto: University of Toronto Press, 2013.

———. "Lettura dei sonetti I–XXX." In *Lettura del "Fiore"* [= *Letture classensi* 22], edited by Zygmunt G. Barański, Patrick Boyde, and Lino Pertile, 13–35. Ravenna: Longo, 1993.

———. "*Magister satiricus*: Preliminary Notes on Dante, Horace and the Middle Ages." In *Language and Style in Dante*, edited by John C. Barnes and Michelangelo Zaccarello, 13–61. Dublin: Four Courts Press, 2013.

———. "The 'New Life' of 'Comedy': The *Commedia* and the *Vita Nuova*." *Dante Studies* 113 (1995): 1–29.

———. "'Oh come è grande la mia impresa' (*Conv.* IV. vii. 4): Notes towards Defining the *Convivio*." In *Dante's "Convivio" or How to Restart a Career in Exile*, edited by Franziska Meier, 9–26. Bern: Lang, 2018.

———. "On Dante's Trail." *Italian Studies* 72 (2017): 1–15.

———. "The Roots of Dante's Plurilingualism: 'Hybridity' and Language in the *Vita nova*." In *Dante's Plurilingualism: Authority, Knowledge, Subjectivity*, edited by Sara Fortuna, Manuele Gragnolati, and Jürgen Trabant, 98–121. Oxford: Legenda, 2010.

———. "I segni della creazione: Il mistero della *Questio de aqua et terra*." In *Dante e i segni: Saggi per una storia intellettuale di Dante Alighieri*, 199–215. Naples: Liguori, 2000.

———. "Sulla formazione intellettuale di Dante: Alcuni problemi di definizione." *Studi e problemi di critica testuale* 90 (2015): 31–54.

———. "The Temptations of a Heterodox Dante." In *Dante and Heterodoxy*, edited by Maria Luisa Ardizzone, 164–96. Newcastle: Cambridge Scholars, 2014.

———. "'Tres enim sunt manerie dicendi . . .': Some Observations on Medieval Literature, 'Genre,' and Dante." In *Dante, Petrarch, Boccaccio: Literature, Doctrine, Reality*, 209–56. Cambridge: Legenda, 2021.

———. "(Un)orthodox Dante." In *Reviewing Dante's Theology*, edited by Claire Honess and Matthew Treherne, 2:253–330. Bern: Lang, 2013.

———. "'Valentissimo poeta e correggitore de' poeti': A First Note on Horace and the *Vita nova*." In *Letteratura e filologia fra Svizzera e Italia: Studi in onore di Guglielmo Gorni*, edited by Maria Antonietta Terzoli, Alberto Asor Rosa, Giorgio Inglese, and Paola Allegretti, 1:3–17. Rome: Edizioni di Storia e Letteratura, 2010.

———. "'With Such Vigilance, with Such Effort!' Studying Dante 'Subjectively.'" *Italian Culture* 33 (2015): 55–69.

Barański, Zygmunt G., and Patrick Boyde, eds. *The "Fiore" in Context: Dante, France, Tuscany*. Notre Dame, IN: University of Notre Dame Press, 1997.

Barański, Zygmunt G., Patrick Boyde, and Lino Pertile, eds. *Lettura del "Fiore"* [= *Letture classensi* 22]. Ravenna: Longo, 1993.

Barber, Joseph A. "Prospettive per un'analisi statistica del *Fiore*." *Revue des études italiennes* 31 (1985): 5–24.

———. "A Statistical Analysis of the *Fiore*." *Lectura Dantis* 6 (1990): 100–22.

Barbi, Michele. "Introduzione." In Dante Alighieri, *La vita nuova*, xiii–cccix. Edited by Michele Barbi. Florence: Bemporad, 1932.

———. "Razionalismo e misticismo in Dante" [1933]. In *Problemi di critica dantesca. Seconda serie (1920–1937)*, 2–86. Florence: Sansoni, 1964.

Barnes, John C. "Historical and Political Writing." In *Dante in Context*, edited by Zygmunt G. Barański and Lino Pertile, 354–70. Cambridge: Cambridge University Press, 2015.

———. "Lettura dei sonetti CXXI–CL." In *Lettura del "Fiore"* [= *Letture classensi* 22], edited by Zygmunt G. Barański, Patrick Boyde, and Lino Pertile, 91–108. Ravenna: Longo, 1993.

———. "Uno, nessuno e tanti: Il *Fiore* attribuibile a chi?" In *The "Fiore" in Context: Dante, France, Tuscany*, edited by Zygmunt G. Barański and Patrick Boyde, 331–62. Notre Dame, IN: University of Notre Dame Press, 1997.

Barnes, John C., and Daragh O'Connell, eds. *War and Peace in Dante: Essays Literary, Historical and Theological*. Dublin: Four Courts Press, 2015.

Barolini, Teodolinda. "Aristotle's *Mezzo*, Courtly *Misura*, and Dante's Canzone *Le dolci rime*: Humanism, Ethics, and Social Anxiety." In *Dante and the Greeks*, edited by Jan Ziolkowski, 163–79. Washington, DC: Dumbarton Oaks, 2014.

———. "'Cominciandomi dal principio infino a la fine' (V.N., XXIII, 15): Forging Anti-narrative in the *Vita Nuova*." In *"La gloriosa donna de la mente": A Commentary on the "Vita Nuova,"* edited by Vincent Moleta, 119–40. Florence: Olschki; Perth: University of Western Australia, 1994.

———. "Critical Philology and Dante's *Rime*," *Philology* 1 (2015): 91–114.

———. "Dante and Reality/Dante and Realism (*Paradiso*)." *Spazio filosofico* 8 (2013): 199–208.

———. "Dante and the Lyric Past." In *Dante and the Origins of Italian Literary Culture*, 23–45. New York: Fordham University Press, 2006.

———. *Dante and the Origins of Italian Literary Culture*. New York: Fordham University Press, 2006.

———. "Dante's Lyric Poetry: From Editorial History to Hermeneutic Future." In *Dante's Lyric Poetry: Poems of Youth and the Vita Nuova (1283–1292)*, edited by Teodolinda Barolini, 13–28. Toronto: University of Toronto Press, 2014.

———. *Dante's Poets: Textuality and Truth in the "Comedy."* Princeton, NJ: Princeton University Press, 1984.

———. "Difference as Punishment or Difference as Pleasure: From the Tower of Babel in *De vulgari eloquentia* to the Death of Babel in *Paradiso* 26." *Textual Cultures* 12, no. 1 (2019): 137–54.

———. "Editing Dante's *Rime* and Italian Cultural History: Dante, Boccaccio, Petrarca . . . Barbi, Contini, Foster-Boyde, De Robertis." In *Dante and the Origins of Italian Literary Culture*, 245–78 and 433–41nn. New York: Fordham University Press, 2006.

———. "For the Record: The Epistle to Cangrande and Various 'American Dantisti.'" *Lectura Dantis* 6 (1990): 140–43.

———. "Guittone's *Ora parrà*, Dante's *Doglia mi reca*, and the *Commedia*'s Anatomy of Desire." In *Dante and the Origins of Italian Literary Culture*, 47–69. New York: Fordham University Press, 2006.

———. *The Undivine Comedy: Detheologizing Dante*. Princeton, NJ: Princeton University Press, 1992.

Baron, Hans. *In Search of Florentine Civic Humanism*. Vol. 1, *Essays on the Transition from Medieval to Modern Thought*. Princeton, NJ: Princeton University Press, 1988.

Barsella, Susanna. "Dante e la *machina mundi*: Modelli cosmologici e l'Epistola XIII." *Studi danteschi* 84 (2019): 205–68.

Bartoli Langeli, Attilio. "Scrivere all'imperatrice." In *Le lettere di Dante: Ambienti culturali, contesti storici e circolazione dei saperi*, edited by Antonio Montefusco and Giuliano Milani: 429–54. Berlin: De Gruyter, 2020.

Bartuschat, Johannes. "La 'filosofia' di Brunetto Latini e il *Convivio*." In *Il Convivio di Dante*, edited by Johannes Bartuschat and Andrea A. Robiglio, 33–51. Ravenna: Longo, 2015.

Bartuschat, Johannes, and Andrea A. Robiglio, eds. *Il Convivio di Dante*. Ravenna: Longo, 2015.

Bausi, Francesco. "Doglia mi reca ne lo core ardire." In Dante Alighieri, *Le quindici canzoni lette da diversi*, 2:197–253. Lecce: Pensa Multimedia, 2012.

Bazán, Bernardo, John Wippel, Gérard Fransen, and Danielle Jacquart, eds. *Les questions disputées et les questions quodlibétiques dans les facultés de théologie, de droit et de médecine*. Turnhout: Brepols, 1985.

Beggiato, Fabrizio. "Cielo." In *Enciclopedia dantesca*, 5:564–68. Rome: Istituto della Enciclopedia Italiana, 1970–78.

Bellomo, Saverio. "L'Epistola a Cangrande, dantesca per intero: 'A rischio di procurarci un dispiacere.'" *L'Alighieri* 45 (2015): 5–19.

———. "Fiore" and "Detto d'Amore." In *Filologia e critica dantesca*, 2nd ed., 199–205, 207–11. Brescia: Editrice La Scuola, 2012.

———. "Lucifero e la cosmogonia poetica di Dante: Lettura di *Inferno* XXXIV." *L'Alighieri* 43 (2014): 91–106.

Beltrami, Pietro G. *La metrica italiana*. 5th ed. Bologna: il Mulino, 2011.

Benedetto, Luigi Foscolo. "Di alcuni rapporti tra il *Detto d'Amore* ed il *Fiore*." *Giornale storico della letteratura italiana* 81 (1923): 76–92.

———. *Il "Roman de la Rose" e la letteratura italiana*. Halle: Niemeyer, 1910.

Benucci, Alessandro. "De la tour de Babel à l'*ydioma tripharium*: La carte linguistique de l'Europe romane selon le *De vulgari eloquentia* de Dante." In *Romania: Réalité(s) et concepts*, edited by Anne-Marie Chabrolle-Cerretini, 41–65. Limoges: Editions Lambert-Lucas, 2013.

Berisso, Marco. "Cosa chiedere al *Fiore*." In *Per Enrico Fenzi: Saggi di allievi e amici per i suoi ottant'anni*, edited by Paolo Borsa, Paolo Falzone, Luca Fiorentini, Sonia Gentili, Luca Marcozzi, Sabrina Stroppa, and Natascia Tonelli, 241–59. Florence: Le Lettere, 2020.

———. "Il Dante di De Robertis e il *Libro delle canzoni*." In *Dante a Verona 2015–2021*, edited by Edoardo Ferrarini, Paolo Pellegrini, and Simone Pregnolato, 247–66. Ravenna: Longo, 2018.

Bernardi, Marco. *Orazio: Tradizione e fortuna in area trobadorica.* Rome: Viella, 2018.
Bernardo, Aldo S. "Sex and Salvation in the Middle Ages: From the *Romance of the Rose* to the *Divine Comedy.*" *Italica* 67 (1990): 305–18.
Bertoni, Giulio. "La prosa della *Vita Nuova* di Dante." In *Lingua e cultura (Studi linguistici)*, 167–222. Florence: Olschki, 1939.
Bianchi, Luca. "Gli aristotelismi della scolastica." In *Le verità dissonanti: Aristotele alla fine del medioevo*, edited by Luca Bianchi and Eugenio Randi, 3–30. Rome: Laterza, 1990.
———. "L'averroismo di Dante: Qualche osservazione critica." *Le tre corone* 2 (2015): 71–109.
———. *Censure et liberté intellectuelle à l'Université de Paris (XIIIe–XIVe siècles).* Paris: Les Belles Lettres, 1999.
———. "*Cotidiana miracula*, comune corso della natura e dispense al diritto matrimoniale: Il miracolo fra Agostino e Tommaso d'Aquino." *Quaderni storici* 44 (2009): 313–28.
———. "Dante eterodosso? Vecchie polemiche e nuove prospettive di ricerca." In *Theologus Dantes: Tematiche teologiche nelle opere e nei primi commenti*, edited by Luca Lombardo, Diego Parisi, and Anna Pegoretti, 19–36. Venice: Edizioni Ca' Foscari, 2018.
———. "A 'Heterodox' in Paradise? Notes on the Relationship between Dante and Siger of Brabant." In *Dante and Heterodoxy*, edited by Maria Luisa Ardizzone, 78–105. Newcastle: Cambridge Scholars, 2014.
———. "Johannes de Malignes." In *Portraits de maîtres offerts à Olga Weijers*, edited by Claire Angotti, Monica Brinzei, and Mariken Teeuwen, 297–307. Porto: Fédération Internationale des Instituts d'Études Médiévales, 2012.
———. "Loquens ut naturalis." In *Le verità dissonanti: Aristotele alla fine del medioevo*, edited by Luca Bianchi and Eugenio Randi, 33–56. Rome: Laterza, 1990.
———. "'Noli comedere panem philosophorum inutiliter': Dante Alighieri and John of Jandun on Philosophical Bread." *Tijdschrift voor filosofie* 75 (2013): 335–55.
———. "Testi e contesti nel 'nuovo medievismo' italiano." In *Cinquant'anni di storiografia filosofica in Italia: Omaggio a Carlo Augusto Viano*, edited by Enrico Donaggio and Enrico Pasini, 109–22. Bologna: il Mulino, 2000.
———. "'Ultima perfezione' e 'ultima felicitate.'" In *Edizioni, traduzioni e tradizioni filosofiche (secoli XII–XVI): Studi per Pietro B. Rossi*, edited by Luca Bianchi, Onorato Grassi, and Cecilia Panti, 315–28. Rome: Aracne, 2018.
———. *Il vescovo e i filosofi: La condanna parigina del 1277 e l'evoluzione dell'aristotelismo scolastico.* Bergamo: Lubrina, 1990.
———. "*Viri philosophici*: Nota sui prologhi dei commenti all'*Etica* e ai *Meteorologica* erroneamente attribuiti a Giacomo di Douai (ms. Paris, BnF, lat.

14698)." In *Scientia, Fides, Theologia: Studi di filosofia medievale in onore di Gianfranco Fioravanti*, edited by Stefano Perfetti, 253–87. Pisa: Edizioni ETS, 2011.

Biasin, Michael. "Indagine su Dante e il mondo confraternale: Le laude e la eulogia di san Domenico." *Le tre corone* 7 (2020): 25–62.

Billanovich, Giuseppe. "Giovanni del Virgilio, Pietro da Moglio, Francesco da Fiano." *Italia medioevale e umanistica* 6 (1963): 203–34.

———. "Tra Dante e Petrarca." *Italia medioevale e umanistica* 8 (1965): 1–44.

Biscaro, Girolamo. "Dante Alighieri e i sortilegi di Matteo e Galeazzo Visconti contro papa Giovanni XII." *Archivio storico lombardo* 47 (1920): 446–81.

Black, Robert. *Humanism and Education in Medieval and Renaissance Italy*. Cambridge: Cambridge University Press, 2001.

Boitani, Piero. "The Poetry and Poetics of the Creation." In *Dante's "Commedia": Theology as Poetry*, edited by Vittorio Montemaggi and Matthew Treherne, 95–130. Notre Dame, IN: University of Notre Dame Press, 2010.

———. *The Tragic and the Sublime in Medieval Literature*. Cambridge: Cambridge University Press, 1989.

Bologna, Corrado. "Dante e il latte delle Muse." In *Atlante della letteratura italiana*, vol. 1, *Dalle origini al Rinascimento*, edited by Sergio Luzzatto and Gabriele Pedullà, 145–55. Turin: Einaudi, 2010.

Borgognoni, Adolfo. "Il *Fiore*." *La rassegna settimanale di politica, scienza, lettere ed arti*, no. 198 (October 16, 1881): 247–49.

Borsa, Paolo. "Identità sociale e generi letterari: Nascita e morte del sodalizio stilnovista." *Reti medievali rivista* 18, no. 1 (2017): 271–303.

Botterill, Steven. *Dante and the Mystical Tradition: Bernard of Clairvaux in the "Commedia"*. Cambridge: Cambridge University Press, 1994.

———. "*Dante Studies* and the Study of Dante." *Annali d'italianistica* 8 (1990): 88–102.

Bowsky, William M. *Henry VII in Italy: The Conflict of Empire and City-State, 1310–1313*. Lincoln: University of Nebraska Press, 1960.

Boyde, Patrick. *Dante Phylomythes and Philosopher: Man in the Cosmos*. Cambridge: Cambridge University Press, 1981.

———. *Dante's Style in His Lyric Poetry*. Cambridge: Cambridge University Press, 1971.

———. "Lettura dei sonetti CCXI–CCXXXII." In *Lettura del "Fiore"* [= *Letture classensi* 22], edited by Zygmunt G. Barański, Patrick Boyde, and Lino Pertile, 155–78. Ravenna: Longo, 1993.

———. "The Results of the Poll: Presentation and Analysis." In *The "Fiore" in Context: Dante, France, Tuscany*, edited by Zygmunt G. Barański and Patrick Boyde, 363–78. Notre Dame, IN: University of Notre Dame Press, 1997.

———. "*Summus minimusve poeta?* Arguments for and against Attributing the *Fiore* to Dante." In *The "Fiore" in Context: Dante, France, Tuscany*, edited by Zygmunt G. Barański and Patrick Boyde, 13–45. Notre Dame, IN: University of Notre Dame Press, 1997.

———. *L'uomo nel cosmo: Filosofia della natura e poesia in Dante*. Translated by Elisabetta Graziosi. Bologna: il Mulino, 1984. Originally published as *Dante Philomythes and Philosopher: Man in the Cosmos* (Cambridge: Cambridge University Press, 1981).

Boyde, Patrick, and Vittorio Russo, eds. *Dante e la scienza*. Ravenna: Longo, 1995.

Branca, Vittore. "Poetica del rinnovamento e tradizione agiografica nella *Vita Nuova*." In *Studi in onore di Italo Siciliano*, 1:123–48. Florence: Olschki, 1966.

———. "Tradizione francescana del linguaggio agiografico della *Vita Nuova*." In *Letteratura italiana e ispirazione cristiana*, edited by Carlo Ballerini, 17–43. Bologna: Patron, 1980.

Breschi, Giancarlo. "Ancora su *Fiore* CCXI 13." In *Sotto il segno di Dante: Scritti in onore di Francesco Mazzoni*, edited by Leonella Coglievina and Domenico De Robertis, 65–74. Florence: Le Lettere, 1998.

Briguglia, Gianluca. "Lo comun' di Cicerone e la 'gentilezza' di Egidio Romano: Alcune considerazioni su pensiero politico e lingue volgari nel tardo medioevo." *Rivista di storia delle idee politiche e sociali* 44, no. 3 (2011): 397–411.

———. *"Inquirere veritatem": Osservazioni sui prologhi dei trattati politici di Giovanni di Parigi, Egidio Romano, Giacomo da Viterbo (1301–1303)*. Florence: Olschki, 2008.

Brilli, Elisa. "Enrico VII, Dante e gli 'universaliter omnes Tusci qui pacem desiderant.'" In *Le lettere di Dante: Ambienti culturali, contesti storici e circolazione dei saperi*, edited by Antonio Montefusco and Giuliano Milani: 395–428. Berlin: De Gruyter, 2020.

———, ed. "Forum Dante and Biography." *Dante Studies* 136 (2018): 133–231.

Brownlee, Kevin. "The Conflicted Genealogy of Cultural Authority: Italian Responses to French Cultural Dominance in *Il Tesoretto*, *Il Fiore*, and *La Commedia*." In *Generation and Degeneration: Tropes of Reproduction in Literature and History from Antiquity through Early Modern Europe*, edited by Valeria Finucci and Kevin Brownlee, 262–86. Durham, NC: Duke University Press, 2001.

———. "Jason's Voyage and the Poetics of Rewriting: The *Fiore* and the *Roman de la Rose*." In *The "Fiore" in Context: Dante, France, Tuscany*, edited by Zygmunt G. Barański and Patrick Boyde, 167–84. Notre Dame, IN: University of Notre Dame Press, 1997.

———. "The Practice of Cultural Authority: Italian Responses to French Cultural Dominance in *Il Tesoretto*, *Il Fiore*, and the *Commedia*." *Forum for Modern Language Studies* 33 (1997): 258–69.

Brownlee, Kevin, and Sylvia Huot, eds. *Rethinking the "Romance of the Rose": Text, Image, Reception*. Philadelphia: University of Pennsylvania Press, 1992.

Brugnoli, Giorgio. "Introduzione." In Dante Alighieri, *Epistole*, edited by Arsenio Frugoni and Giorgio Brugnoli, vol. 2 of *Opere minori*, 512–21. Milan: Ricciardi, 1979–88.

Brugnolo, Furio. "Conservare per trasformare: Il *transfer* lirico in Dante (*Vita Nuova* e dintorni)." In *Vita nova. Fiore. Epistola XIII*, edited by Manuele Gragnolati, Luca Carlo Rossi, Paola Allegretti, Natascia Tonelli, and Alberto Casadei, 25–65. Florence: SISMEL and Edizioni del Galluzzo, 2018.

Bruni, Francesco. "La geografia di Dante nel *De vulgari eloquentia*: Mappe e carte geografiche." In Dante Alighieri, *De vulgari eloquentia*, edited by Enrico Fenzi, 241–61. Rome: Salerno, 2012.

Burnett, Charles. *Arabic into Latin in the Middle Ages: The Translators and Their Intellectual and Social Context*. Farnham: Ashgate, 2009.

Burns, James H., ed. *The Cambridge History of Medieval Political Thought, c.350–c.1450*. Cambridge: Cambridge University Press, 1988.

Buzzetti Gallarati, Silvia. "La memoria di Rustico nel *Fiore*." In *Studi di filologia medievale offerti a D'Arco Silvio Avalle*, 65–98. Milan: Ricciardi, 1996.

———. "Postilla oitanica al *Fiore*." *Critica del testo* 15 (2012): 325–61.

Bynum, Caroline Walker. "Did the Twelfth Century Discover the Individual?" In *Jesus as Mother: Studies in the Spirituality of the High Middle Ages*, 82–109. Berkeley: University of California Press, 1982.

Cabaillot, Claire. "Un exemple de 'naturalisation': Le *Fiore*." In "Du 'Roman de la Rose' au 'Fiore' attribué à Dante," edited by Claude Perrus, special issue, *Arzanà* 1 (1992): 15–42.

Cachey, Theodore J., Jr. "'. . . Alcuna cosa di tanto nodo disnodare' (*Convivio*, III, viii, 3): Cosmological Questions between the *Convivio* and the *Commedia*. In *Dante's "Convivio" or How to Restart a Career in Exile*, edited by Franziska Meier, 55–76. Oxford: Peter Lang, 2019.

———. "Cartographic Dante." *Italica* 86, no. 3 (2010): 325–54.

———. "Cartographic Dante: A Note on Dante and the Greek Mediterranean." In *Dante and the Greeks*, edited by Jan M. Ziolkowski, 197–226. Washington, DC: Dumbarton Oaks Research Library and Collections, 2014.

———. "Cosmographic Cartography of the Perfect 28s." In *Vertical Readings in Dante's "Commedia*," edited by George Corbett and Heather Webb, 3:111–38. Cambridge: Open Book, 2015–17.

———. "Cosmology, Geography, and Cartography." In *Dante in Context*, edited by Zygmunt G. Barański and Lino Pertile, 221–40. Cambridge: Cambridge University Press, 2015.

———. "*Questio*." In *Dante*, edited by Roberto Rea and Justin Steinberg, 163–78. Rome: Carocci, 2020.

———. "Le verità (e l'imbarazzo) della *Questio* di Dante." In *Dante poeta cristiano e la cultura religiosa medievale: In ricordo di Anna Maria Chiavacci*

Leonardi, edited by Giuseppe Ledda, 137–65. Ravenna: Centro dantesco dei Frati Minori Conventuali, 2018.

Caiazzo, Irene. "*Rex illitteratus est quasi asinus coronatus*: I laici e la filosofia nel secolo XII." *Freiburger Zeitschrift für Philosophie und Theologie* 63 (2016): 347–80.

Callegari, Danielle. "Dante's Nutritional Vernacular: Food, Hunger, and Consumption from *Convivio* to *Commedia*." PhD diss., New York University, 2014.

Camargo, Martin. *Ars dictaminis, ars dictandi*. Turnhout: Brepols, 1991.

Camboni, Maria Clotilde. *Fine musica: Percezione e concezione delle forme della poesia dai Siciliani a Petrarca*. Florence: SISMEL, 2017.

———. "Philologie et langue dans le *Rime* de Dante." *Chroniques italiennes web* 15, no. 1 (2009): 1–12.

Camozzi Pistoja, Ambrogio. "Il quarto trattato del *Convivio*: O della satira." *Le tre corone* 1 (2014): 27–53.

———. "Testo come eucarestia: Linguaggio parabolico nel *Convivio* di Dante." *Studi danteschi* 84 (2020): 57–99.

Candido, Igor. "Per una rilettura della *Vita Nova*: La prima *visio in somniis*." *Lettere italiane* 71 (2019): 21–50.

Canettieri, Paolo. "Il *Fiore* e il *Detto d'Amore*." *Critica del testo* 14, no. 1 (2011): 519–30.

Canonico, Camilla. "Sulla dimostrazione della sferica forma della terra e dell'aqua: Jacopo Alighieri e la *Questio de aqua et terra*." Paper presented at AlmaDante, International Dante Conference, University of Bologna, June 24, 2020.

Capasso, Ideale, and Giorgio Tabarroni. "Astrologia." In *Enciclopedia dantesca*, 1:427–30. Rome: Istituto della Enciclopedia Italiana, 1970–78.

———. "Astronomia." In *Enciclopedia dantesca*, 1:431–35. Rome: Istituto della Enciclopedia Italiana, 1970–78.

———. "Cielo." In *Enciclopedia dantesca*, 1: 998–1005. Rome: Istituto della Enciclopedia Italiana, 1970–78.

Cappello, Giovanni. "La *Vita Nuova* tra Guinizzelli e Cavalcanti." *Versants* 13 (1988): 47–66.

Carrai, Stefano. *Dante elegiaco: Una chiave di lettura per la "Vita nova."* Florence: Olschki, 2006.

———. "Il doppio congedo di *Tre donne intorno al cor mi son venute*." In *Le rime di Dante*, edited by Claudia Berra and Paolo Borsa, 197–212. Milan: Cisalpino, 2010.

Casadei, Alberto. *Dante: Altri accertamenti e punti critici*. Milan: Franco Angeli, 2019.

———. *Dante oltre la "Commedia."* Bologna: il Mulino, 2013.

———. "Dante tra Ravenna e Verona: Dati storici e questioni di poetica." In *Dante: Altri accertamenti e punti critici*, 120–32. Milan: Franco Angeli, 2019.

———. "*If* XXXIV e *Pd* XXIX in relazione alla *Questio de aqua et terra*." In *Dante: Altri accertamenti e punti critici*, 189–211. Milan: Franco Angeli, 2019.

———. "Una nuova epistola di Dante? Alcuni dubbi preliminari." In *Dante: Altri accertamenti e punti critici*, 278–86. Milan: Franco Angeli, 2019.

———. "Primi appunti su *Inf.* XXXIV in relazione alla *Questio de aqua et terra*." In *Lecturae Dantis: Dante oggi e letture dell'"Inferno*,*"* edited by Sergio Cristaldi [= *Le forme e la storia* 9 (2016): 299–315].

———. "Sull'autenticità dell'*Epistola a Cangrande*." In *Ortodossia ed eterodossia in Dante*, edited by Carlota Cattermole, Celia de Aldama, and Chiara Giordano, 803–30. Madrid: La Discreta, 2014.

Casapullo, Rosa. *Storia della lingua italiana: Il Medioevo*. Bologna: il Mulino, 1999.

Casciani, Santa. "'Consider the Rose, Where It Grows': Jean de Meun and Dante." In *Italiana 8: Pluralism and Critical Practice: Essays in Honor of Albert N. Mancini*, edited by Paolo A. Giordano and Anthony Julian Tamburri, 1–13. Lafayette, IN: Bordighera, 1999.

Casey, Edward S. *The Fate of Place: A Philosophical History*. Berkeley: University of California Press, 1998.

Cassata, Letterio. "Sul testo del *Fiore*." *Studi danteschi* 58 (1986): 187–237.

Cassell, Anthony K. *The Monarchia Controversy: An Historical Study with Accompanying Translations of Dante Alighieri's "Monarchia," Guido Vernani's "Refutation of the Monarchia Composed by Dante" and Pope John XXII's Bull, "Si Fratrum.*" Washington, DC: Catholic University of America Press, 2004.

Castellani, Arrigo. "Le *cruces* del *Fiore*." *Studi linguistici italiani* 15, n.s., 8 (1989): 100–105.

Castets, Ferdinand. "Introduction." In *Il fiore, poème italien du XIIIe siècle*, edited by Ferdinand Castets, ix–xxiv. Paris: Maisonneuve, 1881.

Cattermole, Carlota, Celia de Aldama, and Chiara Giordano, eds. *Ortodossia ed eterodossia in Dante Alighieri*. Madrid: Ediciones de La Discreta, 2014.

Ceccherini, Irene. "Il *Convivio*." In *Dante: Fra il settecentocinquantenario della nascita (2015) e il settecentenario della morte (2021)*, edited by Enrico Malato and Andrea Mazzucchi, 2:383–400. Rome: Salerno, 2016.

Cervigni, Dino S., and Edward Vasta. "Introduction." In *Vita Nuova: Italian Text with Facing English Translation*, edited by Dino S. Cervigni and Edward Vasta, 1–44. Notre Dame, IN: University of Notre Dame Press, 1995.

Cheneval, Francis. "Dante's *Monarchia*: Aspects of Its History of Reception in the 14th Century." In *Moral and Political Philosophies in the Middle Ages: Proceedings of the Ninth International Congress of Medieval Philosophy, Ottawa, 17–22 August 1992*, edited by B. Carlos Bazán et al., 1474–85. New York: Legas, 1995.

———. "Einleitung zu den Bücheren I–IV." In Dante Alighieri, *Das Gastmahl: Erstes Buch. Italienisch-Deutsch*, edited and commented by Francis Cheneval and translated by Thomas Ricklin, xi–cv. Hamburg: Meiner, 1996.

Chiamenti, Massimiliano. "*Aï faus ris*: L'unicità, ossia *the otherness* di una poesia di Dante." *L'Alighieri* 33 (2009): 9–22.

———. "Il modulo della negazione: Sul filo di *Bibbia—Fiore—Commedia*." In *La Scrittura infinita: Bibbia e poesia in età medievale e umanistica*, edited by Francesco Stella, 187–92. Florence: SISMEL and Edizioni del Galluzzo, 2001.

Chiesa, Paolo, and Andrea Tabarroni. "Introduzione." In Dante Alighieri, *Monarchia*, edited by Paolo Chiesa and Andrea Tabarroni with Diego Ellero, xix–lxxxvi. Rome: Salerno, 2013.

Chisena, Anna G. "L'astronomia di Dante prima dell'esilio: Gli anni della *Vita nova* (con un'appendice sul *Convivio*)." *L'Alighieri* 53 (2019): 25–52.

———. "Miti astrali e catasterismi nel cielo dantesco: Le Orse, Boote e la Corona di Arianna." *L'Alighieri* 50 (2017): 57–78.

Clark, Gillian. "Augustine's Virgil." In *The Cambridge Companion to Virgil*, edited by Charles Martindale and Fiachra Mac Góráin, 77–87. Cambridge: Cambridge University Press, 2019.

Coglievina, Leonella. "L'attribuzione del *Fiore* a Dante: Un problema risolto." In *Dante Alighieri 1985: In memoriam Hermann Gmelin*, edited by Richard Baum and Willi Hirdt, 229–42. Tübingen: Stauffenburg, 1985.

———. "Un frammento estravagante: *Fiore* XCVII 1–4." *Studi danteschi* 56 (1984): 213–16.

———. "Primi momenti della 'fortuna' della *Monarchia* di Dante." In *Dante: Letture critiche e filologiche*, edited by Rudy Abardo, 141–56. Rome: Edizioni di Storia e Letteratura, 2014.

Colombo, Angelo. "Karl Witte e Vincenzo Monti postillatori del *Convivio*: Un esercizio di filologia dantesca nella Milano del primo Ottocento." In *Vie Lombarde e Venete: Circolazione e trasformazione dei saperi letterari nel Sette-Ottocento fra l'Italia settentrionale e l'Europa transalpine*, edited by Helmut Meter, Furio Brugnolo, and Angela Fabris, 219–31. Berlin: De Gruyter, 2011.

Combs-Schilling, Jonathan. "Tityrus in Limbo: Figures of the Author in Dante's *Eclogues*." *Dante Studies* 133 (2015): 1–26.

Contini, Gianfranco. "Un esempio di poesia dantesca (Il canto XXVIII del *Paradiso*)." In *Un'idea di Dante*, 191–213. Turin: Einaudi, 1976.

———. "Fiore, Il." In *Enciclopedia dantesca*, 2:895–901. Rome: Istituto della Enciclopedia Italiana, 1970–78.

———. *Un'idea di Dante*. Turin: Einaudi, 1976.

———. "Introduzione." In Dante Alighieri, *Il "Fiore" e il "Detto d'Amore," attribuibili a Dante Alighieri*, edited by Gianfranco Contini, vol. 1, pt. 2 of *Opere minori*. Milan: Ricciardi, 1984.

———. "Introduzione." In Dante Alighieri, *Rime*, edited by Gianfranco Contini, with an essay by Maurizio Perugi, liii–lxx. Turin: Einaudi, 1995.

———. "Un nodo della cultura medievale: La serie *Roman de la Rose—Fiore—Divina Commedia*." *Lettere italiane* 25 (1973): 162–89. Reprinted in Contini, *Un'idea di Dante*, 245–83. Turin: Einaudi, 1976.

———. "Nota al testo." In Dante Alighieri, *Rime*, edited by Gianfranco Contini, with an essay by Maurizio Perugi, 283–304. Turin: Einaudi, 1995.

———. "Preliminari sulla lingua del Petrarca." In *Varianti e altra linguistica*, 169–92. Turin: Einaudi, 1970.

———. "Santorre Debenedetti, il *Fiore* e il *Detto d'Amore*." In *Frammenti di filologia romanza: Scritti ecdotici e linguistica (1932–1989)*, edited by Giancarlo Breschi, 1:449–57. Florence: Edizioni del Galluzzo, 2007.

———. "Sul testo del *Fiore*." In *Frammenti di filologia romanza: Scritti ecdotici e linguistica (1932–1989)*, edited by Giancarlo Breschi, 1:431–48. Florence: Edizioni del Galluzzo, 2007.

Corbett, George, and Heather Webb, eds. *Vertical Readings in Dante's "Comedy."* 3 vols. Cambridge: Open Book, 2015–17.

Cornish, Alison. *Reading Dante's Stars*. New Haven, CT: Yale University Press, 2000.

———. *Vernacular Translation in Dante's Italy: Illiterate Literature*. Cambridge: Cambridge University Press, 2011.

Corrado, Massimiliano. *Dante e la questione della lingua di Adamo ("De vulgari eloquentia," I 4–7; "Paradiso," XXVI 124–38)*. Rome: Salerno, 2010.

Corti, Maria. *Dante a un nuovo crocevia*. Florence: Libreria commissionaria Sansoni, 1981.

———. *La felicità mentale: Nuove prospettive per Cavalcanti e Dante*. Turin: Einaudi, 1983.

———. *Percorsi dell'invenzione: Il linguaggio poetico e Dante*. Turin: Einaudi, 1993.

Courtenay, William J. *Teaching Careers at the University of Paris in the Thirteenth and Fourteenth Centuries*. Notre Dame, IN: University of Notre Dame Press, 1988.

Cremascoli, Giuseppe. "La Bibbia nella *Monarchia* di Dante." In *La Bibbia di Dante: Esperienza mistica, profezia e teologia biblica in Dante*, edited by Giuseppe Ledda, 31–47. Ravenna: Centro dantesco dei Frati Minori Conventuali, 2011.

Cristaldi, Sergio. "Empireo e cosmo nel *Convivio*." In *Non di tesori eredità: Studi di letteratura italiana offerti ad Alberto Granese*, edited by Rosa Giulio, 39–80. Naples: Guida, 2015.

———. *Verso l'empireo: Stazioni lungo la verticale dantesca*. Acireale: Bonanno, 2013.

———. *La "Vita Nuova" e la restituzione del narrare*. Soveria Mannelli: Rubbettino, 1994.
Croce, Benedetto. *La poesia di Dante*. 2nd rev. ed. Bari: Laterza, 1921.
Culler, Jonathan. "Philosophy and Literature: The Fortunes of the Performative." *Poetics Today* 21 (2000): 503–19.
Cursietti, Marco. "Ancora per il *Fiore*: Indizi cavalcantiani." *La parola del testo* 1 (1997): 197–218.
Curti, Elisa. "Bembo lettore di Dante e Boccaccio." In *Tra due secoli: Per il tirocinio letterario di Pietro Bembo*, 222–27, 241–61. Bologna: Gedit Edizioni, 2006.
Curtius, Ernst Robert. "Dante und Alanus ab Insulis." *Romanische Forschungen* 62 (1950): 28–31.
———. *European Literature and the Latin Middle Ages*. Translated by William R. Trask. Princeton, NJ: Princeton University Press, 1953.
———. "Poetry and Theology." In *European Literature and the Latin Middle Ages*, translated by William R. Trask, 214–27. Princeton, NJ: Princeton University Press, 1953.
D'Agostino, Alfonso. "Itinerari e forme della prosa." In *Storia della letteratura italiana*, vol. 1, *Dalle origini a Dante*, edited by Enrico Malato, 527–630. Rome: Salerno, 1995.
D'Ancona, Alessandro. "Il *Romanzo della Rosa* in italiano." In *Varietà storiche e letterarie*, serie 2, 1–31. Milan: Treves, 1885.
Davie, Mark. "The *Fiore* Revisited in the *Inferno*." In *The "Fiore" in Context: Dante, France, Tuscany*, edited by Zygmunt G. Barański and Patrick Boyde, 315–27. Notre Dame, IN: University of Notre Dame Press, 1997.
———. "Lettura dei sonetti CLI–CLXXX." In *Lettura del "Fiore"* [= *Letture classensi* 22], edited by Zygmunt G. Barański, Patrick Boyde, and Lino Pertile, 109–30. Ravenna: Longo, 1993.
Davis, Charles T. "Education in Dante's Florence." *Speculum* 40 (1965): 415–35.
———. "Ptolemy of Lucca and the Roman Republic." *Proceedings of the American Philosophical Society* 118, no. 1 (1974): 30–50.
———. "Remigio de' Girolami and Dante: A Comparison of Their Conceptions of Peace." *Studi danteschi* 36 (1959): 105–36.
De Bonfils Templer, Margherita. "Il dantesco amoroso uso di Sapienza: Sue radici platoniche." *Stanford Italian Review* 7 (1987): 5–27.
———. "La *donna gentile* del *Convivio* e il boeziano mito d'Orfeo." *Dante Studies* 101 (1983): 123–44.
———. "Le due *ineffabilitadi* del *Convivio*." *Dante Studies* 108 (1990): 67–78.
———. "'La prima materia degli elementi.'" *Studi danteschi* 58 (1986): 275–91.
de Libera, Alain. *Penser au Moyen Âge*. Paris: Seuil, 1991.
———. "Retour de la philosophie médiévale?" *Le débat* 72 (1992): 155–69.

Delle Donne, Fulvio. "Una disputa sulla nobiltà alla corte di Federico II di Svevia." *Medioevo romanzo* 23 (1999): 3–20.

———. "Tra retorica e poetica: Una lettera amatoria in prosa e versi attribuita a Pier della Vigna." In *Itinerari del testo per Stefano Pittaluga*, edited by Cristina Cocco et al., 1:369–81. Cagliari: Dipartimento di Antichità, Filosofia e Storia, 2018.

Dell'Oso, Lorenzo. "How Dante Became Dante: His Intellectual Formation in Florence between *Laici* and *Clerici* (1294–1296)." PhD diss., University of Notre Dame, 2020.

———. "Per la formazione intellettuale di Dante: I cataloghi librari, le tracce testuali, il *Trattatello* di Boccaccio." *Le tre corone* 4 (2017): 129–61.

———. "Tra Bibbia e 'letteratura di costumanza': Un ipotesi su 'Ecce Deus fortior me' (*Vita nova*, II 4)." In *Dante e la cultura fiorentina*, edited by Zygmunt G. Barański, Theodore J. Cachey Jr., and Luca Lombardo, 221–40. Rome: Salerno, 2019.

DeLorenzo, Leonard J., and Vittorio Montemaggi, eds. *Dante, Mercy, and the Beauty of the Human Person*. Eugene, OR: Cascade, 2017.

Demetz, Peter. "The Elm and the Vine: Notes toward the History of a Marriage Topos." *PMLA* 73, no. 5.1 (1958): 521–32.

De Rijk, Lambertus M. *"Logica modernorum": A Contribution to the History of Early Terminist Logic*. Assen: Van Gorcum, 1962.

De Robertis, Domenico. "Un *Convivio* copiato dal Manetti." In *Editi e rari: Studi sulla tradizione letteraria tra Tre e Cinquecento*, 216–20. Milan: Feltrinelli, 1978.

———. *Il libro della "Vita Nuova."* 2nd ed. Florence: Sansoni, 1970.

———. "Sulla tradizione estravagante delle rime della *Vita Nuova*." *Studi danteschi* 44 (1976): 5–84.

———. "La traccia del *Fiore*." In *The "Fiore" in Context: Dante, France, Tuscany*, edited by Zygmunt G. Barański and Patrick Boyde, 187–205. Notre Dame, IN: University of Notre Dame Press, 1997.

De Robertis, Teresa, and Giuliano Milani. "Il contesto fiorentino." In *Intorno a Dante*, edited by Luca Azzetta and Andrea Mazzuchi, 67–89. Rome: Salerno, 2018.

De Robertis Boniforti, Teresa. "Nota sul codice e la sua scrittura." In *The "Fiore" in Context: Dante, France, Tuscany*, edited by Zygmunt G. Barański and Patrick Boyde, 49–81. Notre Dame, IN: University of Notre Dame Press, 1997.

De Sanctis, Francesco. *Storia della letteratura italiana*. 2 vols. Naples: Morano, 1870–71.

Diacciati, Silvia. "Dante: Relazioni sociali e vita pubblica." *Reti medievali rivista* 15, no. 2 (2014): 243–70.

Diacciati, Silvia, and Enrico Faini. "Ricerche sulla formazione dei laici a Firenze nel tardo Duecento." *Archivio storico italiano* 175 (2017): 205–37.

Di Fonzo, Claudia. "Dal *Convivio* alla *Monarchia* per il tramite del *De officiis* di Cicerone: L'imprescindibile paradigma ciceroniano." *Tenzone* 14 (2013): 71–122.

Dionisotti, Carlo. *Geografia e storia della letteratura italiana.* Turin: Einaudi, 1967.

Dragonetti, Roger. "Specchi d'amore: il *Romanzo della Rosa* e il *Fiore*." *Paragone* 374 (1981): 3–22.

Dronke, Peter. "Boethius, Alanus and Dante." *Romanische Forschungen* 78 (1966): 119–25. Reprinted in *The Medieval Poet and His World*, 431–38. Rome: Edizioni di Storia e Letteratura, 1984.

———. *Dante's Second Love: The Originality and the Contexts of "Convivio."* Leeds: Society for Italian Studies, 1997.

Duhem, Pierre. *Medieval Cosmology: Theories of Infinity, Place, Time, Void, and the Plurality of Worlds.* Translated by Roger Ariew. Chicago: University of Chicago Press, 1985.

———. *Le système du monde.* 10 vols. Paris: Librairie Scientifique A. Hermann et Fils, 1913–59.

Durling, Robert, and Ronald Martinez. *Time and the Crystal: Studies in Dante's Rime Petrose.* Berkeley: University of California Press, 1990.

Dusio, Cristina. "Un nuovo manoscritto del *Convivio* (Roma, Bibl. Dell'Accad. dei Lincei e Corsiniana, 44 B 5)." *Rivista di studi danteschi* 16, no. 1 (2016): 116–33.

Egginton, William. "On Dante, Hyperspheres, and the Curvature of the Medieval Cosmos." *Journal of the History of Ideas* 60, no. 2 (1999): 195–216.

Eisner, Martin. *Boccaccio and the Invention of Italian Literature: Dante, Petrarch, Cavalcanti, and the Authority of the Vernacular.* Cambridge: Cambridge University Press, 2013.

Eliot, Thomas Stearns. *Dante.* 1929. Reprint, London: Faber and Faber, 1965.

Faini, Enrico. "Prima di Brunetto: Sulla formazione intellettuale dei laici a Firenze ai primi del Duecento." *Reti medievali rivista* 18, no. 1 (2017): 189–218.

Falzone, Paolo. "Il *Convivio* di Dante." In *La filosofia in Italia al tempo di Dante*, edited by Carla Casagrande and Gianfranco Fioravanti, 225–64. Bologna: il Mulino, 2016.

———. "Il *Convivio* di Dante secondo Maria Corti: Appunti e considerazioni." *Il giornale di filosofia: Filosofia italiana*, 2007. www.giornaledifilosofia.net/public/filosofiaitaliana/scheda_fi.php?id=35.

———. *Desiderio della scienza e desiderio di Dio nel "Convivio" di Dante.* Naples: Società Editrice il Mulino, 2010.

———. "Eresia ed eterodossia nella *Commedia*: Equivoci, punti fermi, zone d'ombra." In *Per il testo e la chiosa del poema dantesco* [= *Letture classensi* 47], edited by Giorgio Inglese, 43–72. Ravenna: Longo, 2018.

———. "'Sì come dice Alberto in quello libro che fa dello intelletto': La citazione del *De intellectu et intelligibili* di Alberto Magno in *Convivio* III, VII, 3–4." In *Letteratura e filologia tra Svizzera e Italia: Studi in onore di Guglielmo Gorni*, edited by Maria Antonietta Terzoli, Alberto Asor Rosa, Giorgio Inglese, and Paola Allegretti, 1:37–56. Rome: Edizioni di Storia e Letteratura, 2010.

Fasani, Remo. "Ancora per l'attribuzione del *Fiore* al Pucci." *Studi e problemi di critica testuale* 6 (1973): 22–66.

———. "L'attribuzione del *Fiore*." *Studi e problemi di critica testuale* 39 (1989): 5–40.

———. "Il *Fiore* e Brunetto Latini." *Studi e problemi di critica testuale* 57 (1998): 305–31.

———. *Il "Fiore" e il "Detto d'Amore" attribuiti a Immanuel Romano*. Ravenna: Longo, 2008.

———. "Il *Fiore* e la poesia del Pucci." *Deutsches Dante-Jahrbuch* 49–50 (1974–75): 82–141.

———. *La lezione del "Fiore."* Milan: All'Insegna del Pesce d'Oro, 1967.

———. *Metrica, lingua e stile del "Fiore."* Florence: Cesati, 2004.

———. *Il poeta del "Fiore."* Milan: All'Insegna del Pesce d'Oro, 1971.

Fenzi, Enrico. "Ancora sulla *Epistola* a Moroello e sulla 'montanina' di Dante (*Rime*, 15)." *Tenzone* 4 (2003): 43–84.

———. "Dal *Convivio* al *De vulgari eloquentia*: Appunti di lettura." In *Il Convivio di Dante*, edited by Johannes Bartuschat and Andrea A. Robiglio, 83–104. Ravenna: Longo, 2015.

———. "È la *Monarchia* l'ultima opera di Dante? (a proposito di una recente edizione)." *Studi danteschi* 72 (2007): 215–38.

———. "Introduzione." In Dante Alighieri, *De vulgari eloquentia*, edited by Enrico Fenzi, xix–cxxv. Rome: Salerno, 2012.

———. "*Sollazzo* e *leggiadria*: Un'interpretazione della canzone dantesca *Poscia ch'amor*." *Studi danteschi* 63 (1991): 191–280.

Ferrante, Joan. *The Political Vision of the "Divine Comedy."* Princeton, NJ: Princeton University Press, 1984.

Ferrara, Sabrina. "Ethical Distance and Political Resonance in the *Eclogues* of Dante." In *Ethics, Politics and Justice in Dante*, edited by Giulia Gaimari and Catherine Keen, 111–26. London: UCL Press, 2019.

———. "'Io mi credea del tutto esser partito': Il distacco di Dante da Cino." In *Cino da Pistoia nella storia della poesia italiana*, edited by Rossend Arqués Corominas and Silvia Tranfaglia, 99–111. Florence: Cesati, 2016.

———. "Il senso del tempo nelle *Egloghe* di Dante, uomo e poeta." *Italianistica* 44, no. 2 (2015): 199–208.

Filippini, Francesco. "Dante degli Abati probabile autore del *Fiore*." *Giornale dantesco* 26 (1923): 35–43.

———. "Un possibile autore del *Fiore*." *Studi danteschi* 4 (1921): 109–19.

Fioravanti, Gianfranco. "Alberto di Sassonia, Biagio Pelacani e la *Questio de aqua et terra*." *Studi danteschi* 82 (2017): 81–97.

———. "'Come dice il filosofo': Dante e la *littera* di Aristotele." *Italianistica* 48 (2019): 11–50.

———. "Il *Convivio* e il suo pubblico." *Le forme e la storia*, n.s., 7, no. 2 (2014): 13–21.

———. "Da Agostino a Sidonio Apollinare: Come scomparvero i filosofi in Occidente." In *La filosofia medievale tra antichità ed età moderna: Saggi in memoria di Francesco Del Punta (1941–2013)*, edited by Amos Bertolacci, Agostino Paravicini Bagliani, and Mario Bertagna, 73–100. Florence: Edizioni del Galluzzo, 2017.

———. "Dossografie filosofiche nel *Convivio* di Dante." In *L'antichità classica nel pensiero medievale*, edited by Alessandro Palazzo, 267–77. Porto: Fédération Internationale des Instituts d'Études Médiévales—Faculdade de Letras de Universidade do Porto, 2011.

———. "I filosofi e gli altri." In *La filosofia in Italia al tempo di Dante*, edited by Carla Casagrande and Gianfranco Fioravanti, 91–122. Bologna: il Mulino, 2016.

———. "Introduzione." In Dante Alighieri, *Convivio*, edited by Gianfranco Fioravanti, canzoni edited by Claudio Giunta. In Dante Alighieri, *Opere*, 2:5–79. Milan: Mondadori, 2011–14.

———. "Morte e rinascita della filosofia: Da Parigi a Bologna." In *La filosofia in Italia al tempo di Dante*, edited by Carla Casagrande and Gianfranco Fioravanti, 11–24. Bologna: il Mulino, 2016.

———. "La nobiltà spiegata ai nobili: Una nuova funzione della filosofia." In *Il "Convivio" di Dante*, edited by Johannes Bartuschat and Andrea A. Robiglio, 157–63. Ravenna: Longo, 2015.

———. "Il pane degli angeli nel *Convivio* di Dante." In *Nutrire il corpo, nutrire l'anima nel Medioevo*, edited by Chiara Crisciani and Onorato Grassi, 191–200. Pisa: ETS, 2017.

———. "Presenze bibliche nel *Convivio* di Dante." In *La Bibbia nella letteratura italiana*, vol. 5, *Dal Medioevo al Rinascimento*, edited by Grazia Melli, Marialuigia Sipione, and Pietro Gibellini, 249–57. Brescia: Morcelliana, 2013.

———. "La prima trattazione 'sottile' della nobiltà: *Convivio*, Trattato Quarto." *Rivista di filosofia neo-scolastica* 1 (2013): 97–104.

———. "Simplicio: Chi era costui?" *Studi danteschi* 86 (2019): 189–96.

Fischer-Lichte, Erika. *Ästhetik des Performativen*. Frankfurt: Suhrkamp, 2004.
Fleming, John V. "Jean de Meun and the Ancient Poets." In *Rethinking the "Romance of the Rose*," 81–100. Philadelphia: University of Pennsylvania Press, 1992.
Formisano, Luciano. "Commentare il *Fiore*." In *Leggere Dante oggi: I testi, l'esegesi: Atti del Convegno-seminario di Roma 25–27 ottobre 2010*, edited by Enrico Malato and Andrea Mazzucchi, 163–79. Rome: Salerno, 2012.
———. "Le postille di Ernesto Giacomo Parodi al *Fiore* e al *Detto d'Amore*." *Studi e problemi di critica testuale* 90 (2015): 439–59.
———. "Qualche riflessione sul *Fiore*." *Critica del testo* 19, no. 1 (2016): 191–204.
———. "Le rime del *De vulgari eloquentia*. 1. Le rime provenzali e francesi." In Dante Alighieri, *De vulgari eloquentia*, edited by Enrico Fenzi, 267–338. Rome: Salerno, 2012.
Foster, Kenelm. "Introduction." In *Dante's Lyric Poetry*, edited by Kenelm Foster and Patrick Boyde, 2 vols., 1:ix–xliii. Oxford: Clarendon Press, 1967.
———. "Teologia." In *Enciclopedia dantesca*, 5:564–68. Rome: Istituto della Enciclopedia Italiana, 1970–78.
———. *The Two Dantes and Other Studies*. Berkeley: University of California Press, 1977.
Foster, Kenelm, and Patrick Boyde, eds. *Dante's Lyric Poetry*. Vol. 2, *Commentary*. Oxford: Clarendon Press, 1967.
Franke, William. *The Revelation of the Imagination: From Homer and the Bible through Virgil and Augustine to Dante*. Evanston, IL: Northwestern University Press, 2015.
Fratta, Aniello. "La lingua del *Fiore* (e del *Detto d'Amore*) e le opere di Francesco da Barberino." *Misure critiche* 14 (1984): 45–62.
Freccero, John. *Dante: The Poetics of Conversion*, edited by Rachel Jacoff. Cambridge, MA: Harvard University Press, 1986.
———. *Dante's Cosmos*. Binghamton, NY: Center for Medieval and Renaissance Studies, State University of New York at Binghamton, 1998.
———. "Satan's Fall and the *Quaestio de Aqua et Terra*." *Italica* 38, no. 2 (1961): 99–115.
Friis-Jensen, Karsten. *The Medieval Horace*, edited by Karin M. Fredborg et al. Rome: Edizioni Quasar, 2015.
Frosini, Giovanna. "Volgarizzamenti." In *Storia dell'italiano scritto*, vol. 2, *Prosa letteraria*, edited by Giuseppe Antonelli, Matteo Motolese, and Lorenzo Tomasin, 17–72. Rome: Carocci, 2014.
Gagliardi, Antonio. *La tragedia intellettuale di Dante: Il "Convivio."* Catanzaro: Pullano, 1994.
Gallarino, Marco. *Metafisica e cosmologia in Dante: Il tema della rovina angelica*. Bologna: il Mulino, 2013.

Gallo, Ernest. "Matthew of Vendôme: Introductory Treatise on the Art of Poetry." *American Philosophical Society Proceedings* 118 (1974): 51–92.

Gambale, Giacomo. *La lingua di fuoco: Dante e la filosofia del linguaggio.* Rome: Città Nuova, 2012.

Garin, Eugenio. *L'umanesimo italiano.* Bari: Laterza, 1952.

Gaunt, Simon. "Discourse Desired: Desire, Subjectivity and *Mouvance* in *Can vei la lauzeta mover*." In *Desiring Discourse: The Literature of Love, Ovid through Chaucer*, edited by James Paxson and Cynthia Gravlee, 89–110. Selinsgrove, PA: Susquehanna University Press, 1998.

Gentili, Sonia. *L'uomo aristotelico: Alle origini della letteratura italiana.* Rome: Carocci, 2005.

Ghisalberti, Alessandro. "La cosmologia nel Duecento e Dante." *Letture classensi* 13 (1984): 33–48.

Gianferrari, Filippo. "Dante and Thirteenth-Century Latin Education: Reading the *Auctores Minores*." PhD diss., University of Notre Dame, 2017.

———. "*Pro Patria Mori*: From the *Disticha Catonis* to Dante's Cato." *Dante Studies* 135 (2017): 1–30.

Gillespie, Vincent. "The Study of Classical Authors from the Twelfth Century to c. 1450." In *The Cambridge History of Literary Criticism*, vol. 2, *The Middle Ages*, edited by Alastair Minnis and Ian Johnson, 145–235. Cambridge: Cambridge University Press, 2005.

Gilson, Étienne. *Dante and Philosophy.* Translated by David Moore. New York: Harper and Row, 1963.

———. *Dante et Béatrice: Études dantesques.* Paris: Vrin, 1974.

———. *Dante et la philosophie.* 3rd ed. Paris: Vrin, 1972.

Gilson, Simon A. "Divine and Natural Artistry in Dante's *Commedia*." In *Art and Nature in Dante*, edited by John C. Barnes, 153–86. Dublin: Four Courts Press, 2014.

———. "Qualche considerazione su Dante, l'enciclopedismo medievale e Servasanto da Faenza." In *Dante e l'enciclopedismo*, edited by Giuseppe Ledda. Ravenna: Longo, forthcoming.

———. "Reading the *Convivio* from Trecento Florence to Dante's Cinquecento Commentators." *Italian Studies* 54, no. 2 (2009): 266–95.

———. "Sincretismo e scolastica in Dante." In *Studi e problemi di critica testuale* 90 (2015): 317–39.

Ginzburg, Carlo. "Dante's *Epistle to Cangrande* and Its Two Authors." *Proceedings of the British Academy* 139 (2006): 195–216.

Giunta, Claudio. "L'amore come destino." In *Dante the Lyric and Ethical Poet / Dante lirico e etico*, edited by Zygmunt G. Barański and Martin McLaughlin, 119–36. Oxford: Legenda, 2010.

———. "Che differenza c'è tra commentare la poesia moderna e commentare la poesia medievale (con esempi dalle rime di Dante)." *Chroniques italiennes web* 13, no. 1 (2008): 1–42.

———. "Nota al testo." In Dante Alighieri, *Rime*, edited by Claudio Giunta. In Dante Alighieri, *Opere*, 2 vols., 1:59–74. Milan: Mondadori, 2011–14.

———. "Un nuovo commento alle *Rime* di Dante." *Paragone letteratura* 81–83 (2009): 3–26.

———. *Versi a un destinatario: Saggio sulla poesia italiana del Medioevo*. Bologna: il Mulino, 2002.

Glorieux, Palemon. *La littérature quodlibétique de 1260 à 1320*. 2 vols. Le Saulchoir, Kain (Belgium): Revue des sciences philosophiques et théologiques, 1925–35.

Gorni, Guglielmo. "Appunti sulla tradizione del *Convivio*." *Studi di filologia italiana* 55 (1997): 5–22.

———. "Dante, Durante e Dante Allegri." In *Dante prima della "Commedia,"* 253–63. Fiesole: Cadmo, 2001.

———. *Dante prima della "Commedia."* Fiesole: Cadmo, 2001.

———. "Il gemello del *Fiore*, ossia *Il Detto d'Amore*." In *Storia di un visionario*, 69–74. Bari: Laterza, 2008.

———. *Lettera nome numero: L'ordine delle cose in Dante*. Bologna: il Mulino, 1990.

———. "Una *pulzelletta* per messer Brunetto." In *Il nodo della lingua e il verbo d'amore: Studi su Dante e altri duecentisti*, 49–69. Florence: Olschki, 1981.

———. "Ser Durante, chi era costui?" In *Dante: Storia di un visionario*, 41–68. Bari: Laterza, 2008.

———. "Sul *Fiore*: Punti critici sul testo." In *The "Fiore" in Context: Dante, France, Tuscany*, edited by Zygmunt G. Barański and Patrick Boyde, 87–108. Notre Dame, IN: University of Notre Dame Press, 1997.

Gorra, Egidio. "Il codice H 438 della Biblioteca della Facoltà di Medicina di Montpellier (già Bouhier E, 59)." In Giuseppe Mazzatinti, *Inventario dei manoscritti italiani delle biblioteche di Francia*, 3:419–610. Rome: Presso i Principali Librai, 1888.

Gragnolati, Manuele. *Amor che move: Linguaggio del corpo e forma del desiderio in Dante, Pasolini e Morante*. Milan: il Saggiatore, 2013.

———. "Authorship and Performance in Dante's *Vita nova*." In *Aspects of the Performative in Medieval Culture*, edited by Manuele Gragnolati and Almut Suerbaum, 123–40. Berlin: De Gruyter, 2010.

———. "Una performance senza gerarchia: La riscrittura bi-stabile della *Vita nova*." In *Vita nova. Fiore. Epistola XIII*, edited by Manuele Gragnolati, Luca Carlo Rossi, Paola Allegretti, Natascia Tonelli, and Alberto Casadei, 67–85. Florence: SISMEL and Edizioni del Galluzzo, 2018.

———. "Trasformazioni e assenze: La *performance* della *Vita nova* e le figure di Dante e Cavalcanti." *L'Alighieri* 35 (2010): 5–23.

———. "Without Hierarchy: Diffraction, Performance, and Re-writing as *Kippbild* in Dante's *Vita nova*." In *Renaissance Rewritings*, edited by Irene

Fantappiè, Helmut Pfeiffer, and Tobias Roth, 9–24. Berlin: De Gruyter, 2017.

Gragnolati, Manuele, Luca Carlo Rossi, Paola Allegretti, Natascia Tonelli, and Alberto Casadei, eds. *Atti degli incontri sulle Opere di Dante*. Vol. 1. *Vita Nova. Fiore. Epistola XIII*. Florence: SISMEL and Edizioni del Galluzzo, 2018.

Grant, Edward. "The Condemnation of 1277, God's Absolute Power, and Physical Thought in the Late Middle Ages." *Viator* 10 (1979): 211–44.

———. "Cosmology." In *Science in the Middle Ages*, edited by David C. Lindberg, 265–302. Chicago: University of Chicago Press, 1978.

Grayson, Cecil. "Dante and the *Roman de la Rose*." In *Patterns in Dante: Nine Literary Essays*, edited by Cormac Ò Cuilleanáin and Jennifer Petrie, 189–203. Dublin: Four Courts Press, 2005.

———. "*Nobilior est vulgaris*: Latin and Vernacular in Dante's Thought." In *Centenary Essays on Dante*, 54–76. Oxford: Oxford University Press, 1965.

Grimaldi, Marco. "Boccaccio editore delle canzoni di Dante." In *Boccaccio editore e interprete di Dante*, edited by Luca Azzetta and Andrea Mazzucchi, 137–57. Rome: Salerno, 2014.

———. "Nota ai testi." In Dante Alighieri, *Vita Nuova; Rime*, edited by Donato Pirovano and Marco Grimaldi, 313–23. Rome: Salerno, 2015.

Guenée, Bernard. "Lo storico e la compilazione." In *Aspetti della letteratura latina nel secolo XIII*, edited by Claudio Leonardi and Giovanni Orlandi, 57–76. Florence: La Nuova Italia, 1986.

Guglielminetti, Marziano. *Memoria e scrittura: L'autobiografia da Dante a Cellini*. Turin: Einaudi, 1977.

Hainsworth, Peter. "Lettura dei sonetti XCI–CXX." In *Lettura del "Fiore"* [= *Letture classensi* 22], edited by Zygmunt G. Barański, Patrick Boyde, and Lino Pertile, 75–89. Ravenna: Longo, 1993.

Hall, Ralph G., and Madison U. Sowell. "*Cursus* in the Can Grande Epistle: A Forger Shows His Hand." *Lectura Dantis* 5 (1989): 89–104.

Hankins, James. "The 'Baron Thesis' after Forty Years and Some Recent Studies of Leonardo Bruni." *Journal of the History of Ideas* 56, no. 2 (1995): 309–38.

———, ed. *Renaissance Civic Humanism: Reappraisals and Reflections*. Cambridge: Cambridge University Press, 2000.

Harrison, Robert Pogue. "The Bare Essential: The Landscape of *Il Fiore*." In *Rethinking the "Romance of the Rose": Text, Image, Reception*, edited by Kevin Brownlee and Sylvia Huot, 289–303. Philadelphia: University of Pennsylvania Press, 1992.

———. *The Body of Beatrice*. Baltimore: Johns Hopkins University Press, 1988.

Hawkins, Peter S. "Dante and the Bible." In *The Cambridge Companion to Dante*, edited by Rachel Jacoff, 120–35. Cambridge: Cambridge University Press, 1993.

———. *Dante's Testaments: Essays in Scriptural Imagination*. Stanford, CA: Stanford University Press, 1999.

———. "Religious Culture." In *Dante in Context*, edited by Zygmunt G. Barański and Lino Pertile, 319–40. Cambridge: Cambridge University Press, 2015.

Herren, Michael W. "Cicero *redivivus apud scurras*: Some Early Medieval Treatments of the Great Orator." In *Cicero Refused to Die: Ciceronian Influence through the Centuries*, edited by Nancy Deusen, 39–45. Leiden: Brill, 2013.

Hirsh, John C. "The Prose Structure of the *Vita Nuova*." *Neophilologus* 64 (1980): 402–4.

Hollander, Robert. *Allegory in Dante's "Commedia."* Princeton, NJ: Princeton University Press, 1969.

———. "'Al quale ha posto mano e cielo e terra': *Paradiso* (25.2)." *Electronic Bulletin of the Dante Society of America*, January 1997. www.princeton.edu/~dante/ebdsa/rh97.html (accessed 30 June 2020).

———. *Dante: A Life in Works*. New Haven, CT: Yale University Press, 2001.

———. "Dante's Deployment of the *Convivio* in the *Comedy*." *Electronic Bulletin of the Dante Society of America*, October 7, 1996. www.princeton.edu/~dante/ebdsa/html.

———. *Dante's Epistle to Cangrande*. Ann Arbor: University of Michigan Press, 1993.

———. "Marsyas as *Figura Dantis*: *Paradiso* 1.20." *Electronic Bulletin of the Dante Society of America*, April 27, 2010. www.princeton.edu/~dante/ebdsa/hollander042710.html.

———. "Response to Henry Ansgar Kelly." *Lectura Dantis* 14–15 (1994): 96–110.

Honess, Claire E. "'Ecce nunc tempus acceptabile': Henry VII and Dante's Ideal of Peace." *The Italianist* 33 (2013): 484–504.

———. *From Florence to the Heavenly City: The Poetry of Citizenship in Dante*. Oxford: Legenda, 2006.

———. "'Ritornerò poeta . . .': Florence, Exile, and Hope." In *"Se mai continga . . .": Exile, Politics and Theology in Dante*, edited by Claire E. Honess and Matthew Treherne, 85–103. Ravenna: Longo, 2013.

Honess, Claire, and Matthew Treherne, eds. *Reviewing Dante's Theology*. 2 vols. Oxford: Lang, 2013.

Hooper, Laurence E. "Dante's *Convivio*, Book 1: Metaphor, Exile, *Epoché*." Supplement, *Modern Language Notes* 127, no. 1 (2012): S86–S104.

———. "Exile and Rhetorical Order in the *Vita nova*." *L'Alighieri* 52 (2011): 5–27.

Hult, David F. *Self-Fulfilling Prophecies: Readership and Authority in the First "Roman de la Rose."* Cambridge: Cambridge University Press, 1986.

Hunt, Richard William. "The Introductions to the *Artes* in the Twelfth Century." In *Studia medievalia in honorem R. M. Martin*, 85–112. Bruges: "de Tempel," 1948.

Huot, Sylvia. "Authors, Scribes, *Remanieurs*: A Note on the Textual History of the *Romance of the Rose*." In *Rethinking the "Romance of the Rose": Text, Image, Receptien*, edited by Kevin Brownlee and Sylvia Huot, 203–33. Philadelphia: University of Pennsylvania Press, 1992.

———. "The *Fiore* and the Early Reception of the *Roman de la Rose*." In *The "Fiore" in Context: Dante, France, Tuscany*, edited by Zygmunt G. Barański and Patrick Boyde, 153–66. Notre Dame, IN: University of Notre Dame Press, 1997.

———. *The Romance of the Rose and Its Medieval Readers: Interpretation, Reception, Manuscript Transmission*. Cambridge: Cambridge University Press, 1993.

Iannucci, Amilcare A. "Theology." In *The Dante Encyclopedia*, edited by Richard Lansing, 811–15. New York: Garland, 2000.

Imbach, Ruedi. "Appunti di uno storico della filosofia sul *De vulgari eloquentia*." In *Le opere minori di Dante nella prospettiva della Commedia* [= *Letture classensi* 38], edited by Johannes Bartuschat, 41–62. Ravenna: Longo 2009.

———. *Dante, la philosophie et les laïcs: Initiations à la philosophie médiévale*. Vol. 1. Fribourg: Éditions Universitaires; Paris: Éditions du Cerf, 1996.

———. "Einfürungen in die Philosophie aus dem XIII. Jahrhundert." *Freiburger Zeitschrift für Philosophie und Theologie* 38 (1991): 471–93.

———. "*Translatio philosophiae*: Dante et la transformation du discours scolastique." In *Le défi laïque: Existe-t-il une philosophie de laïcs au Moyen Âge?*, edited by Ruedi Imbach and Catherine König-Pralong, 147–66. Paris: Vrin, 2013.

Imbach, Ruedi, and Alfonso Maierù, eds. *Gli studi di filosofia medievale fra Otto e Novecento: Contributo a un bilancio storiografico*. Rome: Edizioni di Storia e Letteratura, 1991.

Imbach, Ruedi, and Irène Rosier-Catach. "De l'un au multiple, du multiple à l'un: Une clef d'interprétation pour le *De vulgari eloquentia*." *Mélanges de l'École française de Rome. Moyen Âge* 117 (2005): 509–29.

Indizio, Giuseppe. *Problemi di biografia dantesca*. Longo: Ravenna, 2014.

———. "Supplemento a *Fiore*, CXXIV e CXXVI: L'Inquisizione tra fede e azione politica." *Rivista di studi danteschi* 9, no. 1 (2009): 99–113.

Inglese, Giorgio. "*Fiore* XLIX 3: 'Al buono amico, che non fu di Puglia.'" *Giornale storico della letteratura italiana* 193, no. 642 (2016): 280–82.

———. *Vita di Dante: Una biografia possibile*. Rome: Carocci, 2015.

Irvine, Martin. *The Making of Textual Culture: "Grammatica" and Literary Theory, 350–1100*. Cambridge: Cambridge University Press, 1994.

Italia, Sebastiano. "L'empireo, la Prima Mente e il Protonoè nel *Convivio*." *Le forme e la storia*, n.s., 7, no. 2 (2015): 55–66.

Iwakura, Tomotada. *Il pensiero linguistico di Dante Alighieri*. Rome: Aracne, 2011.

Jacoff, Rachel. "The Post-palinodic Simile in *Paradiso* VIII and IX." *Dante Studies* 98 (1980): 111–22.

Jennaro-MacLennan, Luis. *The Trecento Commentaries on the "Divina Commedia" and the "Epistle to Cangrande."* Oxford: Clarendon Press, 1974.

Kay, Richard. *Dante's Christian Astrology*. Philadelphia: University of Pennsylvania Press, 1994.

Kay, Sarah. *Animal Skins and the Reading Self in Medieval Latin and French Bestiaries*. Chicago: University of Chicago Press, 2017.

———. *Subjectivity in Troubadour Poetry*. Cambridge: Cambridge University Press, 1990.

Keen, Catherine. *Dante and the City*. Stroud: Tempus, 2003.

———. "Florence and Faction in Dante's Lyric Poetry: Framing the Experience of Exile." In *"Se mai contigna...": Exile, Politics, and Theology in Dante*, edited by Claire E. Honess and Matthew Treherne: 63–83. Ravenna: Longo, 2013.

———. "A Florentine *Tullio*: Dual Authorship and the Politics of Translation in Brunetto Latini's *Rettorica*." In *The Afterlife of Cicero*, edited by Gesine Manuwald, 1–16. London: Institute of Classical Studies and University of London, 2016.

Kelly, F. Douglas. *Internal Difference and Meanings in the "Roman de la Rose."* Madison: University of Wisconsin Press, 1995.

Kelly, Henry Ansgar. "*Cangrande* and the Ortho-Dantists." *Lectura Dantis* 14–15 (1994): 61–95.

———. "Reply to Robert Hollander." *Lectura Dantis* 14–15 (1994): 111–15.

———. *Tragedy and Comedy from Dante to Pseudo-Dante*. Berkeley: University of California Press, 1989.

Kempshall, Matthew S. *The Common Good in Late Medieval Political Thought*. Oxford: Clarendon Press, 1999.

Kirkpatrick, Robin. *Dante's "Paradiso" and the Limitations of Modern Criticism*. Cambridge: Cambridge University Press, 1978.

Kleinhenz, Christopher. "Dante and the Bible: Biblical Citation in the *Divine Comedy*." In *Dante: Contemporary Perspectives*, edited by Amilcare A. Iannucci, 74–93. Toronto: University of Toronto Press, 1997.

Kleinhenz, Christopher, and Santa Casciani. "Introduction to the *Detto d'Amore*." In Dante Alighieri, *The Fiore and the Detto d'Amore: A Late 13th-Century Italian Translation of the Roman de la Rose, Attributable to Dante Alighieri*, edited and translated by Christopher Kleinhenz and Santa Casciani, 503–7. Notre Dame, IN: University of Notre Dame Press, 2000.

Kleinhenz, Christopher, and Santa Casciani. "Introduction to the *Fiore*." In Dante Alighieri, *The Fiore and the Detto d'Amore: A Late 13th-Century Italian Translation of the Roman de la Rose, Attributable to Dante Alighieri*, edited and translated by Christopher Kleinhenz and Santa Casciani, 3–34. Notre Dame, IN: University of Notre Dame Press, 2000.

König-Pralong, Catherine. "L'histoire de la philosophie médiévale depuis 1950: Méthodes, textes, débats." *Annales. Histoire, sciences sociales* 64 (2009): 143–69.

Lafleur, Claude. *Quatre introductions à la philosophie au XIIIe siècle*. Montreal: Institut d'Études médiévales; Paris: Vrin, 1988.

Lambertini, Roberto. "Tra etica e politica: La *prudentia* del principe nel *De regimine* di Egidio Romano." *Documenti e studi sulla tradizione filosofica medievale* 3, no. 1 (1992): 77–144.

———. "Usi di 'monarchia' prima di Dante: Alcune osservazioni." In *Autorità e consenso: Regnum e monarchia nell'Europa medievale*, edited by Maria Pia Alberzoni and Roberto Lambertini, 361–74. Milan: Vita e Pensiero, 2017.

Langheinrich, Bernhard. "Sprachliche Untersuchung zur Frage der Verfassenschaft Dates am *Fiore*." *Deutsches Dante-Jahrbuch* 19 (1937): 97–196.

Lansing, Richard, ed. *Dante and Theology: The Biblical Tradition and Christian Allegory*. Vol. 4 of *Dante: The Critical Complex*. New York: Routledge, 2003.

———. "Dante's Intended Audience in the *Convivio*." *Dante Studies* 110 (1992): 17–24.

Lannutti, Maria Sofia. "'Ars' e 'scientia,' 'actio' e 'passio': Per l'interpretazione di alcuni passi del *De vulgari eloquentia*." *Studi medievali* 41, no. 1 (2000): 1–38.

Lannutti, Maria Sofia, and Massimiliano Locanto, eds. *Tracce di una tradizione sommersa: I primi testi lirici italiani tra poesia e musica*. Florence: SISMEL, 2005.

Lanza, Antonio. "Il *Fiore* e il *Detto d'Amore*: Ser Durante, non Dante Alighieri: Storia di un miraggio." In *Primi secoli: Saggi di letteratura italiana antica*, 69–80. Rome: Archivio Guido Izzi, 1991.

Lausberg, Heinrich. *Handbuch der literarischen Rhetorik*. 2 vols. Munich: Max Hueber, 1960.

Lazzerini, Lucia. "Il *Fiore*, il *Roman de la Rose* e i precursori d'*oc* e d'*oïl*." In *The "Fiore" in Context: Dante, France, Tuscany*, edited by Zygmunt G. Barański and Patrick Boyde, 137–51. Notre Dame, IN: University of Notre Dame Press, 1997.

———. Review of *Il "Fiore" e il "Detto d'Amore,"* edited by Gianfranco Contini (1984). *Medioevo romanzo* 11 (1986): 133–43.

Ledda, Giuseppe, ed. *La Bibbia di Dante: Esperienza mistica, profezia e teologia biblica in Dante*. Ravenna: Centro dantesco dei Frati Minori Conventuali, 2011.

———, ed. *Dante poeta cristiano e la cultura religiosa medievale in ricordo di Anna Maria Chiavacci Leonardi*. Ravenna: Centro dantesco dei Frati Minori Conventuali, 2019.

———, ed. *Preghiera e liturgia nella Commedia*. Ravenna: Centro dantesco dei Frati Minori Conventuali, 2013.

———, ed. *Le teologie di Dante*. Ravenna: Centro dantesco dei Frati Minori Conventuali, 2015.

Lee, Alexander. *Humanism and Empire: The Imperial Ideal in Fourteenth-Century Italy*. Oxford: Oxford University Press, 2018.
Lee, Charmaine. *La soggettività nel Medioevo*. Manziana (Rome): Vecchiarelli, 1996.
Leo, Ulrich. "The Unfinished *Convivio* and Dante's Rereading of the *Aeneid*." In *Sehen und Wirklicheit bei Dante*, 71–104. Frankfurt: Klostermann, 1957.
Leonardi, Lino. "Attualità di Contini filologo." In *Gianfranco Contini, 1912–2012: Attualità di un protagonista del Novecento*, edited by Lino Leonardi, 65–80. Florence: Edizioni del Galluzzo, 2014.
———. "Il *Fiore*, il *Roman de la Rose* e la tradizione lirica italiana prima di Dante." In *The "Fiore" in Context: Dante, France, Tuscany*, edited by Zygmunt G. Barański and Patrick Boyde, 233–69. Notre Dame, IN: University of Notre Dame Press, 1997.
———. "'Langue' poetica e stile dantesco nel *Fiore*: Per una verifica degli 'argomenti interni.'" In *Studi di filologia medievale offerti a D'Arco Silvio Avalle*, 237–91. Milan: Ricciardi, 1996.
———. "Nota sull'edizione critica delle *Rime* di Dante a cura di Domenico De Robertis." *Medioevo romanzo* 28 (2004): 63–113.
———. Review of *Fiore. Detto d'Amore*, edited by Paola Allegretti, and *Il Fiore e il Detto d'Amore*, edited by Luciano Formisano. *Medioevo romanzo* 37 (2013): 219–25.
Librandi, Rita. "Ristoro, Brunetto, Bencivenni e la *Metaura*: Intrecci di glosse e rinvii tra opere di uno scaffale scientifico." In *Lo scaffale della biblioteca scientifica in volgare*, edited by Rita Librandi and Rosa Piro, 101–22. Florence: SISMEL and Edizioni del Galluzzo, 2006.
Lokaj, Rodney. "Le fonti biblico-patristiche quali vettori tematici nella lettera XI ai Cardinali." In *Le lettere di Dante: Ambienti culturali, contesti storici e circolazione dei saperi*, edited by Antonio Montefusco and Giuliano Milani: 509–30. Berlin: De Gruyter, 2020.
Lombardi, Elena. "Il pensiero linguistico nella *Vita Nova*." In *Vita nova. Fiore. Epistola XIII*, edited by Manuele Gragnolati, Luca Carlo Rossi, Paola Allegretti, Natascia Tonelli, and Alberto Casadei, 115–34. Florence: SISMEL and Edizioni del Galluzzo, 2018.
Lombardo, Luca. "'Alcibiades quedam meretrix': Dante lettore di Boezio e i commenti alla *Consolatio philosophiae*." *L'Alighieri* 52 (2018): 5–36.
———. *Boezio in Dante: La "Consolatio philosophiae" nello scrittoio del poeta*. Venice: Edizioni Ca' Foscari, 2013.
———. "Un'epistola 'dantesca' di Albertino Mussato." *L'Alighieri* 51 (2018): 37–62.
———. "Oltre il silenzio di Dante: Giovanni del Virgilio, le epistole metriche di Mussato e i commentatori danteschi antichi." *Acta historiae* 22, no. 1 (2014): 17–40.

———. "Primi appunti sulla *Vita nova* nel contesto della prosa del Duecento." *L'Alighieri* 60 (2019): 21–41.

———. "*Quasi come sognando*: Dante e la presunta rarità del *libro di Boezio* (*Convivio* II xii 2–7)." *Mediaeval Sophia: Studi e ricerche sui saperi medievali* 12 (2012): 141–52. www.mediaevalsophia.net/12-luglio-dicembre-2012.

———. "'Talento m'è preso di ricontare l'insegnamento dei phylosophi': Osservazioni sulla prosa dottrinale a Firenze nell'età di Dante." In *Dante e la cultura fiorentina*, edited by Zygmunt G. Barański, Theodore J. Cachey Jr., and Luca Lombardo, 33–58. Rome: Salerno, 2019.

Lombardo, Luca, Diego Parisi, and Anna Pegoretti, eds. *Theologus Dantes: Tematiche teologiche nelle opere e nei primi commenti*. Venice: Edizioni Ca' Foscari, 2018.

López Cortezo, Carlos. "La presencia de *Il Fiore* en la *Vita Nuova* (Caps. V y VI)." *Tenzone* 1 (2000): 27–49.

Lo Piparo, Franco. "Dante linguista anti-modista." In *Italia linguistica: Idee, storia, strutture*, edited by Federico Leoni, Daniele Gambarara, Franco Lo Piparo, and Raffaele Simone, 9–30. Bologna: il Mulino, 1983.

Lorenzini, Simona. *La corrispondenza bucolica tra Giovanni Boccaccio e Checco di Meletto Rossi: L'egloga di Giovanni del Virgilio ad Albertino Mussato*. Florence: Olschki, 2011.

Lummus, David G. *The City of Poetry: Imagining the Civic Role of the Poet in Fourteenth-Century Italy*. Cambridge: Cambridge University Press, 2020.

Maffia Scariati, Irene. "*Fiore Inferno in fieri*: Schede di letture in parallelo." In *The "Fiore" in Context: Dante, France, Tuscany*, edited by Zygmunt G. Barański and Patrick Boyde, 273–313. Notre Dame, IN: University of Notre Dame Press, 1997.

———. "Spigolature sulle *Letture classensi* del *Fiore*: Il 'Salvaggio loco' e il nome di Durante." *Rassegna europea di letteratura italiana* 4 (1994): 35–52.

Maierù, Alfonso. "Dante al crocevia?" *Studi medievali* 24 (1983): 735–48.

———. "Dante di fronte alla *Fisica* e alla *Metafisica*." In *Le culture di Dante: Studi in onore di Robert Hollander*, edited by Michelangelo Picone, Theodore J. Cachey Jr., and Margherita Mesirca, 127–49. Florence: Cesati, 2004.

———. "Sull'epistemologia di Dante." In *Dante e la scienza*, edited by Patrick Boyde and Vittorio Russo, 157–72. Ravenna: Longo, 1995.

Malato, Enrico. "Amor cortese e amor cristiano da Andrea Cappellano a Dante." In *Lo fedele consiglio de la ragione: Studi e ricerche di letteratura italiana*, 126–227. Rome: Salerno, 1989.

Maldina, Nicolò. "Raccogliendo briciole: Una metafora della formazione dantesca tra *Convivio* e *Commedia*." *Studi danteschi* 81 (2016): 131–64.

Mandel'shtam, Osip. "Conversation about Dante." In *Selected Essays*, translated by Sidney Monas, 3–44. Austin: University of Texas Press, 1977.

Manzi, Andrea. "Dante e le fonti manoscritte della lirica delle Origini: Ricognizioni bibliografiche e bilanci." *Critica letteraria* 41, no. 1 (2013): 4–29.
Marchesi, Simone. "La rilettura del *De officiis* e i due tempi della composizione del *Convivio*." *Giornale storico della letteratura italiana* 178 (2001): 84–107.
Marcozzi, Luca. "L'epistola di Dante ai fiorentini: Memoria scritturale, profetismo e tracce umanistiche dell'invettiva dantesca." In *Le lettere di Dante: Ambienti culturali, contesti storici e circolazione dei saperi*, edited by Antonio Montefusco and Giuliano Milani: 329–52. Berlin: De Gruyter, 2020.
———. "Stilnovisti ed elegia latina." In *La poesia in Italia prima di Dante*, edited by Franco Suitner, 187–202. Ravenna: Longo, 2017.
Marenbon, John. "Dante's Averroism." In *Poetry and Philosophy in the Middle Ages: A Festschrift for Peter Dronke*, edited by John Marenbon, 349–74. Leiden: Brill, 2001.
Marigo, Aristide. *Mistica e scienza nella "Vita Nuova" di Dante: Le unità di pensiero e le fonti mistiche, filosofiche e bibliche*. Padua: Drucker, 1914.
Marmo, Costantino. "Had the *Modistae* Any Influence on Dante? Thirty Years after Maria Corti's Proposal." In *Dante and Heterodoxy*, edited by Maria Luisa Ardizzone, 1–17. Newcastle: Cambridge Scholars, 2014.
Martinelli, Luciana. "Cosmologia." In *Enciclopedia dantesca*, 2:235. Rome: Istituto della Enciclopedia Italiana, 1970–78.
Martinez, Ronald L. "Guinizellian Protocols: Angelic Hierarchies, Human Government, and Poetic Form in Dante." *Dante Studies* 134 (2016): 48–111.
———. "Mourning Beatrice: The Rhetoric of Threnody in the *Vita nuova*." *MLN* 113 (1998): 1–29.
———. "'Nasce il Nilo': Justice, Wisdom and Dante's Canzone 'Tre donne intorno al cor mi son venute.'" In *Dante Now: Current Trends in Dante Studies*, edited by Theodore J. Cachey Jr., 115–53. Notre Dame: University of Notre Dame Press, 1995.
———. "The Poetics of Advent Liturgies: *Vita Nuova* and *Purgatorio*." In *Le culture di Dante: Studi in onore di Robert Hollander*, edited by Michelangelo Picone, Theodore J. Cachey Jr., and Margherita Mesirca, 271–304. Florence: Cesati, 2004.
Mazzoni, Francesco. "Introduzione." In Dante Alighieri, *Questio de aqua et terra*, edited by Francesco Mazzoni, vol. 2 of *Opere minori*, 693–737. Milan: Ricciardi, 1979–88.
———. "Il punto sulla *Questio de aqua et terra*." *Studi danteschi* 39 (1962): 39–84.
———. "La *Questio de aqua et terra*." *Studi danteschi* 34 (1957): 163–204.
Mazzoni, Guido. "Se possa *Il Fiore* essere di Dante Alighieri." In *Raccolta di studii critici dedicata ad Alessandro D'Ancona festeggiandosi il XL anniversario del suo insegnamento*, 657–92. Florence: G. Barbèra, 1901.
Mazzotta, Giuseppe. "Cosmology and the Kiss of Creation (*Paradiso* 27–29)." *Dante Studies* 123 (2005): 1–21.

———. *Dante, Poet of the Desert: History and Allegory in the "Divine Comedy."* Princeton, NJ: Princeton University Press, 1979.

———. *Dante's Vision and the Circle of Knowledge.* Princeton, NJ: Princeton University Press, 1993.

Mazzucchi, Andrea. "A proposito della *consecuzione R[ose]—F[iore]—Angiolieri*: Un supplemento d'indagine sulla *danteità* del *Fiore*." *Studi danteschi* 63 (1991): 313–34.

———. "Proposte per una nuova edizione commentata del *Convivio*." In *Leggere Dante oggi: I testi, l'esegesi*, edited by Enrico Malato and Andrea Mazzucchi, 81–107. Rome: Salerno, 2012.

———. *Tra "Convivio" e "Commedia": Sondaggi di filologia e critica dantesca.* Rome: Salerno, 2004.

McKenzie, Kenneth. "The Symmetrical Structure of the *Vita Nuova*." *PMLA* 18 (1905): 341–55.

Meier, Franziska, ed. *Dante's "Convivio" or How to Restart a Career in Exile.* Bern: Lang, 2018.

Mengaldo, Pier Vincenzo. "Introduzione." In Dante Alighieri, *De vulgari eloquentia*, edited by Pier Vincenzo Mengaldo, vii–cxxv. Padua: Antenore, 1968.

———. *Linguistica e retorica di Dante.* Pisa: Nistri Lischi, 1978.

Menzinger, Sara. "Dante and the Law: The Influence of Legal Categories on Fourteenth Century Political Thought." *Roma Tre Law Review* 1 (2019): 74–90.

———. "Law." In *Dante in Context*, edited by Zygmunt G. Barański and Lino Pertile, 47–58. Cambridge: Cambridge University Press, 2015.

Miethke, Jürgen. "Practical Intentions of Scholasticism: The Example of Political Theory." In *Universities and Schooling in Medieval Society*, edited by William Courtenay and Jürgen Miethke, 211–28. Leiden: Brill, 2000.

Migliorini Fissi, Rosetta. "'Onde *filos* e *sofia* . . .' (*Conv.* III xi 5 e *Rett.* 17, 6)." *Studi danteschi* 55 (1978): 179–214.

Milani, Alessio. "Il *Fiore*: Aspetto metrico del testimone e regolarizzazione nell'edizione Contini." *Per leggere* 12 (2007): 97–120.

Minnis, Alastair. *"Magister amoris": The "Roman de la Rose" and Vernacular Hermeneutics.* Oxford: Oxford University Press, 2001.

———. *Medieval Theory of Authorship.* 2nd ed. Aldershot: Scolar Press, 1988.

———. "'Nolens auctor sed compilari reputari': The Late Medieval Discourse of Compilation." In *La méthode critique au moyen âge*, edited by Mireille Chazan and Gilbert Dahan, 47–63. Turnhout: Brepols, 2006.

Minnis, Alastair J., and Alexander Brian Scott, eds. *Medieval Literary Theory and Criticism c.1100–c.1375.* Oxford: Clarendon Press, 1988.

Moevs, Christian. *The Metaphysics of Dante's "Comedy."* Oxford: Oxford University Press, 2005.

Moleta, Vincent. "The *Vita Nuova* as a Lyric Narrative." *Forum Italicum* 12 (1978): 369–90.
Monaci, Ernesto. *Crestomazia italiana dei primi secoli*. Second fascicule. Città di Castello: Lapi, 1889.
———. "Una redazione italiana inedita del *Roman de la Rose*." *Giornale di filologia romanza* 1 (1878): 238–43.
Montefusco, Antonio. "Competenze, prassi e legittimità profetica del Dante *dictator illustris*: Elementi di un'interpretazione sociologico-retorica delle epistole." In *Le lettere di Dante: Ambienti culturali, contesti storici e circolazione dei saperi*, edited by Antonio Montefusco and Giuliano Milani: 105–30. Berlin: De Gruyter, 2020.
———. "Contini e il 'nodo': L'avventura del *Fiore* (tra *Roman de la Rose* e *Commedia*)." *Ermeneutica letteraria* 10 (2013): 55–65.
———. "Le lettere di Dante: Circuiti comunicativi, prospettive editoriali, problemi storici." In *Le lettere di Dante: Ambienti culturali, contesti storici e circolazione dei saperi*, edited by Antonio Montefusco and Giuliano Milani: 1–39. Berlin: De Gruyter, 2020.
———. "*Mostrando allor se·ttu·ssé forte e duro* [LX.3]: Amicizia, precettistica erotica e cultura podestarile-consiliare nel *Fiore*." *Arzanà* 13 (2010): 137–70.
———. "Novità per il *Fiore*? Prime osservazioni a partire da due edizioni recenti." *Rivista di studi danteschi* 13 (2013): 397–421.
———. Review of *Fiore. Detto d'Amore*, edited by Paola Allegretti, and *Il Fiore e il Detto d'Amore*, edited by Luciano Formisano. *L'Alighieri* 44 (2014): 157–63.
Montemaggi, Vittorio. *Reading Dante's "Commedia" as Theology: Divinity Realized in the Human Encounter*. New York: Oxford University Press, 2016.
Montemaggi, Vittorio, and Matthew Treherne, eds. *Dante's "Commedia": Theology as Poetry*. Notre Dame, IN: University of Notre Dame Press, 2010.
Montuori, Francesco. "Le rime del *De vulgari eloquentia*. 2. Le rime italiane." In Dante Alighieri, *De vulgari eloquentia*, edited by Enrico Fenzi, 339–439. Rome: Salerno, 2012.
Moore, Edward. "The Astronomy of Dante." In *Studies in Dante: Third Series*, 1–108. Oxford: Clarendon Press, 1903.
———. "The 'Battifolle' Letters Sometimes Attributed to Dante." *Modern Language Review* 9, no. 2 (1914): 173–89.
———. "The Genuineness of the *Quaestio de aqua et terra*." In *Studies in Dante: Second Series*, 303–74. Oxford: Clarendon Press, 1899.
———. "The Geography of Dante." In *Studies in Dante: Third Series*, 109–43. Oxford: Clarendon Press, 1903.
Moroldo, Arnaldo. "Emprunts et réseaux lexicaux dans le *Fiore*." *Revue des langues romanes* 92 (1988): 127–51.

Morpurgo, Salomone. "*Detto d'Amore*, antiche rime imitate dal *Roman de la Rose*." *Il propugnatore*, n.s., 1 (1888): 16–61.

Mostra di manoscritti, documenti e edizioni (VI centenario della morte di G. Boccaccio). 2 vols. Certaldo: A cura del Comitato promotore, 1975.

Muner, Mario. "La paternità brunettiana del *Fiore* e del *Detto d'Amore*." *Motivi per la difesa della cultura* 9 (1971): 274–320.

———. "Perché il *Fiore* non può essere di Dante (e a chi invece potrebbe attribuirsi)." *Motivi per la difesa della cultura* 7 (1968–69): 88–105.

Murray, Alexander. "Purgatory and the Spatial Imagination." In *Dante and the Church: Literary and Historical Essays*, edited by Paolo Acquaviva and Jennifer Petrie, 61–92. Dublin: Four Courts, 2007.

Nardi, Bruno. *La caduta di Lucifero e l'autenticità della "Quaestio de aqua et terra."* Turin: SEI, 1959.

———. *Dal "Convivio" alla "Commedia" (sei saggi danteschi)*. Edited by Ovidio Capitani. Rev. ed. Rome: Istituto Italiano per il Medio Evo, 1992.

———. *Dante e la cultura medievale*, edited by Paolo Mazzantini. 2nd ed. Rome: Laterza, 1983. First published 1942 by Edizioni di Storia e Letteratura (Rome).

———. "Fortuna della *Monarchia* nei secoli XIV e XV." In *Nel mondo di Dante*, 163–205. Rome: Edizioni di Storia e Letteratura, 1944.

———. *Nel mondo di Dante*. Rome: Edizioni di Storia e Letteratura, 1944.

Nasti, Paola. *Favole d'amore e "saver profondo": La tradizione salomonica in Dante*. Ravenna: Longo, 2007.

———. "Religious Culture." In *The Cambridge Companion to Dante's "Commedia,"* edited by Zygmunt G. Barański and Simon Gilson, 158–72. Cambridge: Cambridge University Press, 2019.

———. "Storia materiale di un classico dantesco: La *Consolatio Philosophiae* fra XII e XIV secolo: Tradizione manoscritta e rielaborazioni esegetiche." *Dante Studies* 134 (2016): 142–68.

———. "'Vocabuli d'autori e di scienze e di libri' (*Conv*. II xii 5): Percorsi sapienzali di Dante." In *La Bibbia di Dante: Esperienza mistica, profezia e teologia biblica in Dante*, edited by Giuseppe Ledda, 121–78. Ravenna: Centro dantesco dei Frati Minori Conventuali, 2011.

Nieddu, Laura. "Processo all'immagine di un *Fiore* forense." *Forum Italicum* 53 (2019): 281–95.

Novati, Francesco. *Attraverso il Medio Evo: Studi e ricerche*. Bari: Laterza, 1905.

Novikoff, Alex J. *The Medieval Culture of Disputation: Pedagogy, Practice, and Performance*. Philadelphia: University of Pennsylvania Press, 2013.

Orelli, Giorgio. "Un sonetto del *Fiore*." *Paragone* 296 (1974): 37–52.

Osserman, Robert. *The Poetry of the Universe*. New York: Anchor Books, 1995.

Pacioni, Marco. "L'*auctoritas* poetica e il personaggio Cavalcanti nella *Vita Nova*." In *Auctor/Actor: Lo scrittore personaggio nella letteratura italiana*, edited by Gilda Corabi and Barbara Gizzi, 41–61. Rome: Bulzoni, 2006.

Padoan, Giorgio. "Cause, struttura e significato del *De situ et figura aque et terre*." In *Il lungo cammino del poema sacro: Studi danteschi*, 163–80. Florence: Olschki, 1993.

———. "Introduzione." In *De situ et forma acque et terre*, edited by Giorgio Padoan, vii–xxxi. Florence: Le Monnier, 1968.

———. "Moncetti." *Enciclopedia dantesca*, 3:1004–5. Rome: Istituto della Enciclopedia Italiana, 1970–78.

———. "La *Quaestio de aqua et terra*." *Cultura e scuola* 14 (1965): 758–67.

Palma di Cesnola, Maurizio. "La battaglia del *Fiore*: Omaggio a Remo Fasani." *Studi e problemi di critica testuale* 59 (1999): 5–42.

———. "Un Durante francese? Proposta per il *Fiore*." In *"Per correr miglior acque . . .": Bilanci e prospettive degli studi danteschi alle soglie del nuovo millennio*, 2:1007–23. Rome: Salerno, 2001.

———. "*Fiore*: La battaglia attributiva." In *Questioni dantesche: Fiore, Monarchia, Commedia*, 13–42. Ravenna: Longo, 2003.

Paolazzi, Carlo. "Il 'comico' tra *Donna pietosa* e i canti proemiali dell'*Inferno*: Scheda per l'attribuzione del *Fiore* a Dante." *Lettere italiane* 28 (1976): 137–59.

———. *La "Vita Nuova": Legenda sacra e historia poetica*. Milan: Vita e pensiero, 1994.

Papi, Fiammetta. "Aristotle's Emotions in Giles of Rome's *De regimine principum* and in its Vernacular Translations (with a Note on Dante's *Convivio* III, 8, 10)." *Annali della Scuola Normale Superiore di Pisa*, 5th ser., 8, no. 1 (2016): 73–104.

Parkes, Malcolm B. "The Influence of the Concepts of *Ordinatio* and *Compilatio* on the Development of the Book." In *Scribes, Scripts and Readers: Studies in the Communication, Presentation and Dissemination of Medieval Texts*, 35–70. London: Hambledon, 1991.

Parodi, Ernesto Giacomo. "Prefazione." In *Il Fiore e il Detto d'Amore*, edited by Ernesto Giacomo Parodi, v–xx. Appendix to *Le opere di Dante*. Florence: Bemporad, 1922.

———. "La *Quaestio de aqua et terra* e il cursus." *Bollettino della Società Dantesca Italiana* 24 (1917): 168–69.

Pasquazi, Silvio. "Sulla cosmogonia di Dante (*Inferno* XXXIV e *Questio de aqua et terra*)." In *D'Egitto in Ierusalemme*, 121–56. Rome: Bulzoni, 1985.

Pastore Stocchi, Manlio. "Epistole." In *Enciclopedia dantesca*, 2:703–10. Rome: Istituto della Enciclopedia Italiana, 1970–78.

———. "*Quaestio de aqua et terra*." In *Enciclopedia dantesca*, 4:761–65. Rome: Istituto della Enciclopedia Italiana, 1970–78.

Pegoretti, Anna. "*Civitas diaboli*: Forme e figure della religiosità laica nella Firenze di Dante." In *Dante poeta cristiano e la cultura religiosa medievale: In ricordo di Anna Maria Chiavacci Leonardi*, edited by Giuseppe Ledda, 65–116. Ravenna: Centro dantesco dei Frati Minori Conventuali, 2018.

———. "Il *curriculum* del poeta-teologo: Boccaccio e il viaggio di Dante a Parigi." *Studi sul Boccaccio* 47 (2019): 129–58.

———. "'*Da questa nobilissima perfezione molti sono privati*': Impediments to Knowledge and the Tradition of Commentaries on Boethius' *Consolatio Philosophiae*." In *Dante's "Convivio," or How to Restart a Career in Exile*, edited by Franziska Meier, 77–97. Oxford: Peter Lang, 2018.

———. "L'empireo in Dante e la 'divina scienza' del *Convivio*." In *Theologus Dante: Tematiche teologiche nelle opere e nei primi commenti*, edited by Luca Lombardo, Diego Parisi, and Anna Pegoretti, 166–88. Venice: Edizioni Ca' Foscari, 2018.

———. "Filosofanti." *Le tre corone* 2 (2015): 11–70.

———. "On Grammar and Justice: Notes on *Convivio*, II.xii. 1–7." In *Ethics, Politics and Justice in Dante*, edited by Giulia Gaimari and Catherine Keen, 14–29. London: UCL Press, 2019.

Peirone, Luigi. *"Il Detto d'Amore" tra "Il Fiore" e Dante*. Genoa: Tilgher, 1983.

———. *Tra Dante e "Il Fiore": Lingua e parola*. Genoa: Tilgher, 1982.

Pellegrini, Paolo. "La quattordicesima epistola di Dante Alighieri: Primi appunti per una attribuzione." *Studi di erudizione e di filolgia italiana* 7 (2018): 5–20.

———. "Il riso di Aristotele e l'autenticità della *Questio de aqua et terra* di Dante." *L'Alighieri* 49 (2017): 53–68.

———. "Sul testo della *Questio de Aqua et Terra* di Dante (o del dialogo tra filologia e filosofia)." *L'Alighieri* 52 (2018): 117–35.

Pèrcopo, Erasmo. "Il *Fiore* è di Rustico di Filippo?" *Rassegna critica della letteratura italiana* 12 (1907): 49–59.

Perrus, Claude. "Avant-propos." In "Du 'Roman de la Rose' au 'Fiore' attribué à Dante," edited by Claude Perrus, special issue, *Arzanà* 1 (1992): 7–14.

———, ed. "Du 'Roman de la Rose' au 'Fiore' attribué à Dante." Special issue, *Arzanà* 1 (1992).

Persico, Thomas. *Le parole e la musica: Poesia ed esecuzione dalla "Vita nuova" alla "Divina Commedia."* Rome: Aracne, 2019.

Pertile, Lino. "*Cantica* nella tradizione medievale e in Dante." *Rivista di storia e letteratura religiosa* 27 (1992): 389–412.

———. *Canto-cantica-Comedìa* e l'Epistola a Cangrande." *Lectura Dantis* 9 (1991): 105–23.

———. "Dante Looks Forward and Back: Political Allegory in the Epistles." *Dante Studies* 115 (1997): 1–17.

———. "Le *Egloghe* di Dante e l'antro di Polifemo." In *Dante the Lyric and Ethical Poet / Dante lirico e etico*, edited by Zygmunt G. Barański and Martin McLaughlin, 153–67. London: Legenda, 2010.

———. "Lettera aperta a Robert Hollander sui rapporti tra *Commedia* e *Convivio*." *Electronic Bulletin of the Dante Society of America*, October 8, 1996. www.princeton.edu/~dante/ebdsa/html.

———. "Lettura dei sonetti CLXXXI–CCX." In *Lettura del "Fiore"* [= *Letture classensi* 22], edited by Zygmunt G. Barański, Patrick Boyde, and Lino Pertile, 131–53. Ravenna: Longo, 1993.
———. *La puttana e il gigante: Dal Cantico dei cantici al Paradiso Terrestre di Dante*. Ravenna: Longo, 1998.
———. "Sulla cronologia e il pubblico del *Convivio*." *Le tre corone* 7 (2020): 11–24.
Peterson, Mark A. "Dante and the 3-Sphere." *American Journal of Physics* 47, no. 12 (1979): 1031–35.
Petoletti, Marco. "Boccaccio editore delle egloghe e delle epistole di Dante." In *Boccaccio editore e interprete di Dante*, edited by Luca Azzetta and Andrea Mazzucchi, 159–83. Rome: Salerno, 2014.
———, ed. *Dante e la sua eredità a Ravenna nel Trecento*. Ravenna: Longo, 2015.
———. "Egloge." In *Dante*, edited by Roberto Rea and Justin Steinberg, 149–62. Rome: Carocci, 2020.
———. "Nota introduttiva." In Dante Alighieri, *Egloge*, edited by Marco Petoletti, 491–504. Rome: Salerno, 2016.
Petrocchi, Giorgio. "Biografia." In *Enciclopedia dantesca*, Appendice, 1–53. Rome: Istituto della Enciclopedia Italiana, 1970–78.
Picchio Simonelli, Maria. "Pubblico e società nel *Convivio*." *Yearbook of Italian Studies* 4 (1980): 41–58.
Picone, Michelangelo. "Dante rimatore." *Letture classensi* 24 (1995): 171–87.
———. "Il *Fiore*: Struttura profonda e problemi attributivi." *Vox romanica* 33 (1974): 145–56.
———. "Glosse al *Detto d'Amore*." *Medioevo romanzo* 3 (1976): 394–409.
———. "Osservazioni sul testo del *Detto d'Amore*." *Studi e problemi di critica testuale* 13 (1976): 5–18.
———. *Percorsi della lirica duecentesca*. Fiesole: Cadmo, 2003.
———. *Scritti danteschi*. Edited by Antonio Lanza. Ravenna: Longo, 2017.
———. "*Vita Nuova*." In *The Dante Encyclopedia*, edited by Richard Lansing, 874–78. New York: Garland, 2000.
———. "*Vita Nuova" e tradizione romanza*. Padua: Liviana, 1979.
———. "La *Vita Nuova* fra autobiografia e tipologia." In *Dante e le forme dell'allegoresi*, edited by Michelangelo Picone, 59–69. Ravenna: Longo, 1987.
Pietrobono, Luigi, ed. *Il poema sacro: Saggio d'una interpretazione generale della "Divina Commedia."* 2 vols. Bologna: Zanichelli, 1915.
Pinto, Raffaele. *Dante e le origini della cultura letteraria moderna*. Paris: Champion, 1994.
———. "La grammatica in Dante." *Quaderns d'Italià* 18 (2013): 15–44.
———. "Introducción." In *De vulgari eloquentia: Sobre la elocuencia en lengua vulgar*, edited by Raffaele Pinto, 7–138. Madrid: Cátedra, 2018.
———. *Le "Rime" di Dante: Libro di canzoni o rime sparse?* London: RECEPTIO Academic Press, 2020.

Piron, Sylvain. Review of Dante Alighieri, *Questio de aqua et terra*, edited by Michele Rinaldi. *L'Alighieri* 50 (2017): 146–51.

Pirovano, Donato. *Il dolce stil novo*. Rome: Salerno, 2014.

———. "Nota introduttiva." In Dante Alighieri, *Vita Nuova; Rime*, edited by Donato Pirovano and Marco Grimaldi, 3–35. Rome: Salerno, 2015.

Porcelli, Bruno. "La nominazione dei protagonisti nel *Fiore*, nella *Vita nuova*, nella *Commedia*." *Italianistica* 27 (1998): 221–31.

Porro, Pasquale. *Tommaso d'Aquino: Un profilo storico-filosofico*. Florence: Carocci, 2012.

Portalupi, Enzo. "*Philosophia* e lemmi affini nel *Thesaurus formarum*." In *"In principio erat verbum": Mélanges offerts en hommage à P. Tombeur*, edited by Benoît and Michel Tock, 253–300. Turnhout: Brepols, 2005.

Prandi, Stefano. "'Ad intuitum supercelestium formarum': Alain de Lille e la *Commedia*." In *Dante poeta cristiano e la cultura religiosa medievale: In ricordo di Anna Maria Chiavacci Leonardi*, edited by Giuseppe Ledda, 117–35. Ravenna: Centro dantesco dei Frati Minori Conventuali, 2018.

———. "Teologia come pittura: Alain de Lille e Dante (*Purg*. XI, 82–84)." In *La parola e l'immagine: Studi in onore di Gianni Venturi*, edited by Marco Ariani, Arnaldo Bruni, Anna Dolfi, and Andrea Gareffi, 99–116. Florence: Olschki, 2010.

Quadlbauer, Franz. *Die antike Theorie der "Genera dicendi" im lateinischen Mittelalter*. Vienna: Hermann Böhlaus, 1962.

Quaglio, Enzo. "Per l'antica fortuna del *Fiore*." *Rivista di studi danteschi* 1 (2001): 120–27.

Quaglioni, Diego. "Introduzione." In Dante Alighieri, *Monarchia*, edited by Diego Quaglioni, vol. 2 of Dante Alighieri, *Opere*, 809–83. Milan: Mondadori, 2014.

Quain, Edwin A. "The Medieval *Accessus ad Auctores*." *Traditio* 3 (1945): 215–64.

Raffa, Guy. *Dante's Bones: How a Poet Invented Italy*. Cambridge, MA: Harvard University Press, 2020.

———. "Dante's Mocking Pastoral Muse." *Dante Studies* 114 (1996): 271–91.

Rajna, Pio. "La questione del *Fiore*." *Il marzocco* 26, no. 3 (January 16, 1921): 1. Reprinted in *Scritti di filologia e linguistica italiana e romanza*, edited by Guido Lucchini, 765–71. Rome: Salerno, 1998.

Ramacciotti, Sister Mary Dominic. *The Syntax of "Il Fiore" and of Dante's "Inferno" as Evidence in the Question of the Authorship of "Il Fiore."* Washington, DC: Catholic University of America, 1936.

Rea, Roberto. "Amore e ragione nella *Vita Nuova*." *Studi romanzi*, n.s., 14 (2018): 165–95.

———. "La *Vita Nuova* e le *Rime*: *Unus philosophus alter poeta*: Un'ipotesi per Cavalcanti e Dante." In *Dante fra il settecentocinquantenario della nascita*

(2015) e il settecentenario della morte (2021): Atti delle Celebrazioni, del Forum e del Convegno internazionale di Roma: maggio-settembre 2015, edited by Enrico Malato and Andrea Mazzucchi, 331–60. Rome: Salerno, 2016.

Reggio, Giovanni. "Niccolò da Prato." In *Enciclopedia dantesca*, 4:46–47. Rome: Istituto della Enciclopedia Italiana, 1970–78.

Renier, Rodolfo. "Di una imitazione italiana del *Roman de la Rose*." *Preludio* 5 (1881): 242–46.

Reynolds, Barbara. "Introduction." In Dante, *Vita Nuova*, rev. ed., translated by Barbara Reynolds, xiii–xxix. London: Penguin Books, 2004.

Reynolds, Suzanne. *Medieval Reading: Grammar, Rhetoric and the Classical Text*. Cambridge: Cambridge University Press, 1996.

Richards, Earl Jeffrey. *Dante and the "Roman de la Rose": An Investigation into the Vernacular Narrative Context of the "Commedia."* Tübingen: Niemeyer, 1981.

———. "The *Fiore* and the *Roman de la Rose*." In *Medieval Translators and Their Craft*, edited by Jeanette Beer, 265–83. Kalamazoo, MI: Medieval Institute Publications, 1989.

Rinaldi, Michele. "Nota al testo." In *Questio de aqua et terra*, edited by Michele Rinaldi, 671–87. In Dante Alighieri, *Epistole. Egloge. Questio de aqua et terra*, edited by Marco Baglio, Luca Azzetta, Marco Petoletti, and Michele Rinaldi, 651–751. Rome: Salerno, 2016.

———. "Nota introduttiva." In *Questio de aqua et terra*, edited by Michele Rinaldi, 651–70. In Dante Alighieri, *Epistole. Egloge. Questio de aqua et terra*, edited by Marco Baglio, Luca Azzetta, Marco Petoletti, and Michele Rinaldi, 651–751. Rome: Salerno, 2016.

———. "Note sulla *Questio de aqua et terra* a partire da una recente edizione (e con un contributo iconografico)." *Rivista di studi danteschi* 17 (2017): 111–33.

Rinoldi, Paolo. "In margine ad una recente edizione del *Fiore*." *Lettere italiane* 66 (2014): 393–44.

Robey, David. "The *Fiore* and the *Comedy*: Some Computerized Comparisons." In *The "Fiore" in Context: Dante, France, Tuscany*, edited by Zygmunt G. Barański and Patrick Boyde, 109–34. Notre Dame, IN: University of Notre Dame Press, 1997.

Robiglio, Andrea A. "La nobiltà di spada in Dante: Un appunto su *Convivio* IV xiv 11." In *Il Convivio di Dante*, edited by Johannes Bartuschat and Andrea A. Robiglio, 191–204. Ravenna: Longo, 2015.

———. "Philosophy and Theology." In *Dante in Context*, edited by Zygmunt G. Barański and Lino Pertile, 137–58. Cambridge: Cambridge University Press, 2015.

Rogers, Francis M. "The Vivaldi Expedition." *Annual Report of the Dante Society, with Accompanying Papers* 73 (1955): 31–45.

Roman de la Rose Digital Library. http://romandelarose.org/.

Roncaglia, Aurelio. "Sul 'divorzio' tra musica e poesia nel Duecento italiano." In *L'Ars nova italiana del Trecento. 4. Atti del 3º Congresso internazionale, sul tema La musica al tempo di Boccaccio e i suoi rapporti con la letteratura*, edited by Agostino Ziino, 365–97. Certaldo: Centro di studi sull'Ars nova italiana del Trecento, 1978.

Rosenstein, Roy. "Mouvance." In *Handbook of Medieval Studies: Terms, Methods, Trends*, edited by Albrecht Classen, 2:1538–547. Berlin: De Gruyter, 2010.

Rosier-Catach, Irène. "Dante et le langage: Ni modiste ni cabbaliste." In *Dante et l'Averroïsme*, edited by Alain de Libera et al., 79–115. Paris: Collège de France and Les Belles Lettres, 2019.

———. "Du vulgaire illustre, le 'plus noble de tous,' à la noblesse du *Convivio*." In *Il "Convivio" di Dante*, edited by Johannes Bartuschat and Andrea A. Robiglio, 105–34. Ravenna: Longo, 2015.

———. "Man as a Speaking and Political Animal: A Political Reading of Dante's *De vulgari eloquentia*." In *Dante's Plurilingualism: Authority, Knowledge, Subjectivity*, edited by Sara Fortuna, Manuele Gragnolati, and Jürgen Trabant, 34–51. Oxford: Legenda, 2010.

———. "Présentation." In Dante Alighieri, *De l'éloquence en vulgaire*, edited by Irène Rosier-Catach, 9–64. Paris: Fayard, 2011.

———. "'Solo all'uomo fu dato di parlare': Dante, gli angeli, gli animali." *Rivista di filosofia neo-scolastica* 98 (2006): 435–65.

———. "L'uomo nobile e il volgare illustre." In *Ortodossia ed eterodossia in Dante Alighieri*, edited by Carlota Cattermole, Celia de Aldama, and Chiara Giordano, 165–89. Madrid: Ediciones de La Discreta, 2014.

Rossi, Luciano. "Alain de Lille, Jean de Meun, Dante: 'Nodi' poetici e d'esegesi." *Critica del testo* 7, no. 2 (2004): 851–75.

———. "Dante, la *Rose* e il *Fiore*." In *Studi sul canone letterario del Trecento: Per Michelangelo Picone*, edited by Johannes Bartuschat and Luciano Rossi, 9–32. Ravenna: Longo, 2003.

———. "De Jean Chopinel à Durante: La série *Roman de la Rose—Fiore*." In *De la Rose: Texte, image, fortune*, edited by Catherine Bel and Herman Braet, 273–98. Louvain: Peeters, 2006.

———. "Du nouveau sur Jean de Meun." *Romania* 121, nos. 483–84 (2003): 430–60.

———. Review of *The "Fiore" in Context: Dante, France, Tuscany*, edited by Zygmunt G. Barański and Patrick Boyde. *Aevum* 72, no. 2 (1998): 598–603.

———. "Jean de Meun e Guido Guinizelli a Bologna." In *Bologna nel Medioevo: Atti del Convegno, Bologna, 28–29 ottobre 2002, con altri contributi di filologia romanza*, 87–108. Bologna: Pàtron, 2004.

———. "La tradizione allegorica: Da Alain de Lille al *Tesoretto*, al *Roman de la Rose*." In *Le tre corone: Modelli e antimodelli della "Commedia,"* edited by Michelangelo Picone, 143–79. Ravenna: Longo, 2008.

Ryan, Christopher. "The Theology of Dante." In *The Cambridge Companion to Dante*, edited by Rachel Jacoff, 136–52. Cambridge: Cambridge University Press, 1993.

Santagata, Marco. *Dante: Il romanzo della sua vita*. Milan: Mondadori, 2012.

———. "La donna del miracolo." In *Amate e amanti: Figure della lirica amorosa fra Dante e Petrarca*, 13–61. Bologna: il Mulino, 1999.

———. "Introduzione." In Dante Alighieri, *Le opere*, edited by Marco Santagata, Claudio Giunta, Guglielmo Gorni, and Mirko Tavoni, 1:viii–cxxxii. Milan: Mondadori, 2011.

Sarolli, Gian Roberto. "Il numero nelle opere di Dante." In *Enciclopedia dantesca*, 4:88–96. Rome: Istituto della Enciclopedia Italiana, 1970–78.

Sarteschi, Selene. "Dalla *Rettorica* di Brunetto Latini alla *Vita Nova*." In *Il percorso del poeta cristiano: Riflessioni su Dante*, 33–51. Ravenna: Longo, 2006.

Sarti, Luna. "Dante and the Water Cycle in the *Commedia*: God, Physics, and Flowing Waters." *Dante Studies* 137 (2019): 1–22.

Sasso, Gennaro. *La lingua, la Bibbia, la storia: Su "De vulgari eloquentia" I*. Rome: Viella, 2015.

Sbacchi, Diego. "L'andamento ternario della *Vita Nuova*." *Rivista di letteratura italiana* 35 (2017): 9–22.

———. "Due luoghi della *Vita Nuova*: La camera e il fiume." *Lettere italiane* 65 (2013): 15–28.

———. "Le indicazioni orarie nella *Vita Nuova*." *Lettere italiane* 67 (2015): 127–39.

Scafi, Alessandro. *Mapping Paradise: A History of Heaven on Earth*. London: British Library, 2006.

Scartazzini, Giovanni Andrea, ed. *La "Divina Commedia," riveduta nel testo e commentata da G. A. Scartazzini*. 3 vols. Leipzig: Brokhaus, 1874–82.

Schabel, Christopher, ed. *Theological Quodlibeta in the Middle Ages*. 2 vols. Leiden: Brill, 2006–7.

Scott, John A. *Perché Dante?* 2nd rev. ed. Rome: Aracne, 2019.

———. *Understanding Dante*. Notre Dame, IN: University of Notre Dame Press, 2004.

———. "The Unfinished *Convivio* as the Pathway to the *Comedy*." *Dante Studies* 113 (1995): 31–56.

Sebastio, Leonardo. "'Ragion la Bella' nel *Fiore*: Preistoria o genesi dell'idea di cultura in Dante." In *Dante: Summa Medievalis: Proceedings of the Symposium of the Center for Italian Studies, SUNY Stony Brook*, edited by Charles Franco and Leslie Morgan, 52–86. Forum Italicum Supplement: Filibrary 9. Stony Brook, NY: Forum Italicum, 1995.

———. *Strutture narrative e dinamiche culturali in Dante e nel "Fiore."* Florence: Olschki, 1990.

———. "Tra *Roman de la Rose* e *Il Fiore*." *L'Alighieri* 29 (1988): 18–36.

Segre, Cesare. "Introduzione." In *La prosa del Duecento*, edited by Cesare Segre and Mario Marti, vii–xliii. Milan: Ricciardi, 1959.

———. *Lingua, stile e società: Studi sulla storia della prosa italiana*. Milan: Feltrinelli, 1976.

Senior, Diane. "The Authority and Autonomy of the *Fiore*." *Forum Italicum* 32 (1998): 305–31.

———. "Love, Sex, and Gender in Durante's *Fiore*." *The Italianist* 17 (1997): 29–43.

Shaw, Prue. "Introduction." In Dante, *Monarchy*, edited by Prue Shaw, ix–xxxiv. Cambridge: Cambridge University Press, 1996.

Singleton, Charles S. *Dante's "Commedia": Elements of Structure*. Baltimore: Johns Hopkins University Press, 1977.

———. *An Essay on the "Vita Nuova."* 1949. Reprint, Baltimore: Johns Hopkins University Press, 1977.

———. *Journey to Beatrice*. Baltimore: Johns Hopkins University Press, 1958.

Sisson, Keith, and Atria A. Larson, eds. *A Companion to the Medieval Papacy: Growth of an Ideology and Institution*. Leiden: Brill, 2016.

Somaini, Francesco. "L'epistola V e l'ipotesi di un dossier dantesco per Enrico VII." In *Le lettere di Dante: Ambienti culturali, contesti storici e circolazione dei saperi*, edited by Antonio Montefusco and Giuliano Milani: 287–328. Berlin: De Gruyter, 2020.

Sparrow, Katie. "Dante's Self-Characterization in the *Vita nova*: *Auctoritas* through Love and Writing." MA thesis, University of Notre Dame, 2018.

Spitzer, Leo. "Osservazioni sulla *Vita Nuova* di Dante." In *Studi italiani*, 95–146. Milan: Vita e Pensiero, 1976.

Stabile, Giorgio. "Cosmologia e teologia nella *Commedia*: La caduta di Lucifero e il rovesciamento del mondo." *Letture classensi* 12 (1983): 139–73.

———. *Dante e la filosofia della natura: Percezioni, linguaggi, cosmologie*. Florence: SISMEL and Edizioni del Galluzzo, 2007.

———. "Dante oggi: Il *Convivio* tra poesia e ragione." *Critica del testo* 14, no. 1 (2011): 345–99.

Steinberg, Justin. *Accounting for Dante: Urban Readers and Writers in Late Medieval Italy*. Notre Dame, IN: University of Notre Dame Press, 2007.

———. "Author." In *The Oxford Handbook of Dante*, edited by Manuele Gragnolati, Francesca Southerden, and Elena Lombardi, 3–16. Oxford: Oxford University Press, 2021.

———. *Dante and the Limits of the Law*. Chicago: University of Chicago Press, 2013.

———. "Dante's Constitutional Miracles (*Monarchia* 2.4 and *Inferno* 8–9)." *Lettere italiane* 68 (2016): 431–44.

———. "Messianic and Legal Time in Dante's Political Epistles." In *Le lettere di Dante: Ambienti culturali, contesti storici e circolazione dei saperi*, edited by

Antonio Montefusco and Giuliano Milani, 371–94. Berlin: De Gruyter, 2020.

Stillinger, Thomas C. *The Song of Troilus: Lyric Authority in the Medieval Book.* Philadelphia: University of Pennsylvania Press, 1992.

Stocchi Perucchio, Donatella. "The Limits of Orthodoxy in Dante's *Monarchia*." In *Dante and Heterodoxy*, edited by Maria Luisa Ardizzone, 197–224. Newcastle: Cambridge Scholars, 2014.

Stoppelli, Pasquale. *Dante e la paternità del "Fiore."* Rome: Salerno Editrice, 2011.

Storey, H. Wayne. "Following Instructions: Remaking Dante's *Vita Nova* in the Fourteenth Century." In *Medieval Constructions in Gender and Identity: Essays in Honor of Joan M. Ferrante*, edited by Teodolinda Barolini, 117–32. Tempe, AZ: MRTS, 2005.

Sturlese, Loris. *Storia della filosofia tedesca nel medioevo: Dagli inizi alla fine del XII secolo.* Florence: Olschki, 1990.

Sweeney, Eileen. "Literary Forms of Medieval Philosophy." In *The Stanford Encyclopedia of Philosophy*, edited by Edward N. Zalta. https://plato.stanford.edu/archives/sum2019/entries/medieval-literary/.

Tabarroni, Andrea. "Ambienti culturali prossimi a Dante nell'esilio: Lo studio bolognese di arti e medicina." In *Dante: Fra il settecentocinquantenario della nascita (2015) e il settecentenario della morte (2021): Atti delle Celebrazioni in Senato, del Forum e del Consiglio internazionale di Roma: maggio-ottobre 2015*, edited by Enrico Malato and Andrea Mazzucchi, 1:327–48. Rome: Salerno, 2016.

Tanturli, Giuliano. "Come si forma il libro delle canzoni?" In *Le rime di Dante*, edited by Claudia Berra and Paolo Borsa, 117–34. Milan: Cisalpino, 2010.

———. "L'edizione critica delle *Rime* e il libro delle canzoni di Dante." *Studi danteschi* 68 (2003): 250–66.

Tartaro, Achille. "La prosa narrativa antica." In *Letteratura italiana*, vol. 3, *Le forme del testo*, pt. 2, *La prosa*, edited by Alberto Asor Rosa, 623–714. Turin: Einaudi, 1984.

Tavoni, Mirko. "Che cosa è la poesia? Chi è poeta?" In *Qualche idea su Dante*, 295–334. Bologna: il Mulino, 2015.

———. "Che cosa erano il volgare e il latino per Dante." In *Dante e la lingua italiana*, edited by Mirko Tavoni, 9–27. Ravenna: Longo, 2013.

———. "*Convivio* e *De vulgari eloquentia*: Dante esule, filosofo laico e teorico del volgare." *Nuova rivista di letteratura italiana* 17, no. 1 (2014): 11–54.

———. "Dante e il 'paradigma critico della contingenza.'" *Dante Studies* 136 (2018): 201–12.

———. "Dante e la scoperta del Paradiso terrestre in mezzo all'Oceano." *Studi danteschi* 84 (2019): 1–14.

———. "*De vulgari eloquentia*." In *Dante*, edited by Roberto Rea and Justin Steinberg, 79–94. Rome: Carocci, 2020.

———. "Le *Epistole* I e II nella vita di Dante (fatti, personaggi, date, testualità, ideologia)." In *Le lettere di Dante: Ambienti culturali, contesti storici e circolazione dei saperi*, edited by Antonio Montefusco and Giuliano Milani: 201–32. Berlin: De Gruyter, 2020.

———. "L'esilio dantesco fra testi e documenti (sul *De vulgari eloquentia*, Bologna e il 'paradigma critico della contingenza')." *Medioevo letterario d'Italia* 14 (2017): 23–33.

———. "L'idea imperiale nel *De vulgari eloquentia*." In *Enrico VII, Dante e Pisa: A 700 anni dalla morte dell'Imperatore e dalla "Monarchia" (1313–2013)*, edited by Giuseppe Petralia and Marco Santagata, 215–33. Ravenna: Longo, 2016.

———. "Introduzione." In Dante Alighieri, *De vulgari eloquentia*, edited by Mirko Tavoni, vol. 1 of Dante Alighieri, *Opere*, v–xcviii. Milan: Mondadori, 2011–14.

———. "Lingua parlata e lingua scritta in Dante: Appunti metalinguistici e linguistici." In *L'antinomia scritto/parlato*, edited by Franca Orletti and Federico Albano Leoni, 89–115. Città di Castello: I libri di Emil, 2020.

———. "Il pane degli angeli (*Convivio* I i 7–*Paradiso* II 10–15)." In *Esercizi di lettura per Marco Santagata*, edited by Annalisa Andreoni, Claudio Giunta, and Mirko Tavoni, 51–62. Bologna: il Mulino, 2017.

———. "Perché i volgari italiani sono quattordici (*De vulgari eloquentia* I x 7)?." In *"Una brigata di voci": Studi offerti a Ivano Paccagnella per i suoi sessantacinque anni*, edited by Chiara Schiavon and Andrea Cecchinato, 133–47. Padua: CLEUP, 2012.

———. *Qualche idea su Dante*. Bologna: il Mulino, 2015.

———. "Volgare e latino nella storia di Dante." In *Dante's Plurilingualism: Authority, Knowledge, Subjectivity*, edited by Sara Fortuna, Manuele Gragnolati, and Jürgen Trabant, 52–68. Oxford: Legenda, 2010.

———. "*Ydioma Tripharium* (Dante, *De vulgari eloquentia*, I 8–9)." In *History and Historiography of Linguistics*, edited by Hans-Josef Niederehe and Konrad Koerner, 233–47. Amsterdam: J. Benjamins, 1990.

Tavoni, Mirko, and Emmanuele Chersoni. "Ipotesi d'interpretazione della 'suprema constructio' (*De vulgari eloquentia* II vi)." *Studi di grammatica italiana* 31 (2012): 131–58.

Teeuwen, Mariken. *The Vocabulary of Intellectual Life in the Middle Ages*. Turnhout: Brepols, 2003.

Terracini, Benvenuto. "La prosa poetica della *Vita Nuova*." In *Analisi stilistica: Teoria, storia, problemi*, 207–49. Milan: Feltrinelli, 1966.

Tesi, Riccardo. *La lingua della grazia: Indagini sul "De vulgari eloquentia."* Padua: Esedra, 2016.

———. *Storia dell'italiano: La formazione della lingua comune dalle fasi iniziali al Rinascimento*. Milan: Zanichelli, 2007.

Tierney, Brian. *The Crisis of Church and State, 1050–1300*. Englewood Cliffs, NJ: Prentice Hall, 1964.
Todorović, Jelena. *Dante and the Dynamics of Textual Exchange: Authorship, Manuscript Culture, and the Making of the "Vita Nova."* New York: Fordham University Press, 2016.
Tomazzoli, Gaia. "Funzioni delle metafore nelle epistole arrighiane." In *Le lettere di Dante: Ambienti culturali, contesti storici e circolazione dei saperi*, edited by Antonio Montefusco and Giuliano Milani: 147–64. Berlin: De Gruyter, 2020.
Tonelli, Natascia. *Fisiologia della passione: Poesia d'amore e medicina da Cavalcanti a Boccaccio*. Florence: Edizioni del Galluzzo, 2015.
———. "Ragione e i suoi consigli nei sonetti del Fiore." *Tenzone* 6 (2005): 231–47.
———. "Rileggendo le *Rime* di Dante secondo l'edizione e il commento di Domenico De Robertis: Il libro delle canzoni." *Studi e problemi di critica testuale* 73 (2006): 9–59.
———. "Le rime." *Critica del testo* 14, no. 1 (2011): 207–32.
———, ed. *Sulle tracce del "Fiore."* Florence: Le Lettere, 2016.
———. "I tempi della poesia, il tempo della prosa: A proposito di alcune visioni della *Vita Nuova*." In *Atti degli incontri sulle Opere di Dante*, vol. 1, *"Vita Nova." "Fiore." "Epistola XIII,"* edited by Manuele Gragnolati, Luca Carlo Rossi, Paola Allegretti, Natascia Tonelli, and Alberto Casadei, 173–94. Florence: SISMEL and Edizioni del Galluzzo, 2018.
Took, John. *Conversations with Kenelm: Essays on the Theology of the "Commedia."* London: Ubiquity Press, 2013.
———. *Dante*. Princeton, NJ: Princeton University Press, 2020.
———. *Dante: Lyric Poet and Philosopher: An Introduction to the Minor Works*. Oxford: Clarendon Press, 1990.
———. "Dante and the *Roman de la Rose*." *Italian Studies* 37 (1982): 1–25.
———. "Dante and the *Rose*: The *Fiore* and the *Detto d'amore*." In *Dante*, 133–59. Princeton, NJ: Princeton University Press, 2020.
———. "The *Detto d'amore* and the *Fiore*." In *Dante, Lyric Poet and Philosopher: An Introduction to the Minor Works*, 29–43. Oxford: Clarendon Press, 1990.
———. "Introduction." In *Il Fiore (The Flower)*, edited by John Took, xiii–lxix. Lewiston, NY: Edwin Mellen Press, 2004.
———. "Lettura dei sonetti XXXI–LX." In *Lettura del "Fiore"* [= *Letture classensi* 22], edited by Zygmunt G. Barański, Patrick Boyde, and Lino Pertile, 37–51. Ravenna: Longo, 1993.
———. "Towards an Interpretation of the *Fiore*." *Speculum* 54 (1979): 500–27.
Torraca, Francesco. "Il *Fiore*." In *Studi di storia letteraria*, 242–71. Florence: Sansoni, 1923.

Toynbee, Paget. "Dante and the 'Cursus': A New Argument in Favour of the Authenticity of the *Quaestio de aqua et terra*." *Modern Language Review* 13 (1918): 420–30.

———. "Introduction." In *Dantis Alagherii Epistolae: The Letters of Dante*, 2nd ed., edited by Paget Toynbee, xiii–liv. Oxford: Clarendon Press, 1966.

Trovato, Mario. "Against Aristotle: Cosmological Vision in Dante's *Convivio*." *Essays in Medieval Studies* 20 (2003): 31–46.

———. "Il primo trattato del *Convivio* visto alla luce dell'*accessus ad auctores*." *Misure critiche* 6 (1976): 5–14.

Trovato, Paolo. *Il testo della "Vita Nuova" e altra filologia dantesca*. Rome: Salerno, 2000.

Turco, Jeffrey. "Restaging Sin in Medieval Florence: Augustine, Brunetto Latini, and the Streetscape of Dante's *Vita nuova*." *Italian Studies* 73 (2018): 15–21.

Tylus, Jane. *Writing and Vulnerability in the Late Renaissance*. Stanford, CA: Stanford University Press, 1993.

Valente, Luisa. "Philosophers and Other Kinds of Human Beings according to Peter Abelard and John of Salisbury." In *Logic and Language in the Middle Ages: A Volume in Honour of Sten Ebbesen*, edited by Jakob L. Fink, Heine Hansen, and Ana María Mora-Márquez, 105–23. Leiden: Brill, 2013.

Vallone, Aldo. "Il *Fiore* come opera di Dante." *Studi danteschi* 56 (1984): 141–67.

Vanossi, Luigi. *Dante e il "Roman de la Rose": Saggio sul "Fiore."* Florence: Olschki, 1979.

———. "*Detto d'Amore*." In *Enciclopedia dantesca*, 2:393–95. Rome: Istituto della Enciclopedia Italiana, 1970–78.

———. Review of Gianfranco Contini's two 1984 editions of *Il "Fiore" e il "Detto d'Amore" attribuibili a Dante Alighieri*, Mondadori (Edizione Nazionale) and Ricciardi. *Giornale storico della letteratura italiana* 162 (1985): 453–58.

———. *La teologia poetica del "Detto d'Amore" dantesco*. Florence: Olschki, 1974.

Van Peteghem, Julie. "The Vernacular Roots of Dante's Reading of Ovid in the *Commedia*." *Italian Studies* 73 (2018): 223–39.

Varela-Portas de Orduña, Juan. "El *Libro de las canciones*, ¿una nueva obra de Dante?" In Dante Alighieri, *Libro de las canciones y otro poemas*, edited by Juan Varela-Portas de Orduña (coord.), Rossend Arqués Corominas, Raffaele Pinto, Rosario Scrimieri Martín, Eduard Vilella Morató, and Anna Zembrino, 5–107. Madrid: Akal, 2014.

Vasoli, Cesare. "La Bibbia nel *Convivio* e nella *Monarchia*." In *Dante e la Bibbia*, edited by Giovanni Barblan, 19–39. Florence: Olschki, 1988.

———. "*Convivio* di Dante e l'enciclopedismo medievale." In *L'enciclopedismo medievale*, edited by Michelangelo Picone, 363–81. Ravenna: Longo, 1994.

———. "Fonti albertiane nel *Convivio* di Dante." In *Albertus Magnus und der Albertismus: Deutsche philosophische kultur des Mittelalters*, edited by J. F. M. Maarten Hoenene and Alain De Libera, 33–49. Leiden: Brill, 1995.

———. "La pace nel pensiero di Dante, di Marsilio da Padova e di Guglielmo d'Ockham." In *Otto saggi per Dante*, 41–64. Florence: Le Lettere, 1995.

Vecce, Carlo. "'Ella era uno nove, cioè uno miracolo' (*Vn* XXIX. 3): Il numero di Beatrice." In *"La gloriosa donna de la mente": A Commentary on the "Vita Nuova,"* edited by Vincent Moleta, 161–79. Florence: Olschki; Perth: University of Western Australia, 1994.

Vela, Claudio. "Per la misura del *Detto d'Amore*." *Antico/Moderno* 4 (1999): 91–103.

Viel, Riccardo. "L'impronta del *Roman de la Rose*: I gallicismi del *Fiore* e del *Detto d'Amore*." *Studi danteschi* 71 (2006): 129–90.

Villa, Claudia. "Per una tipologia del commento mediolatino: *L'Ars Poetica* di Orazio." In *Il commento ai testi*, edited by Ottavio Besomi and Carlo Caruso, 19–46. Basel: Birkhäuser, 1992.

———. "Il problema dello stile umile (e il riso di Dante)." In *Dante the Lyric and Ethical Poet / Dante lirico e etico*, edited by Zygmunt G. Barański and Martin McLaughlin, 138–52. London: Legenda, 2010.

———. "Tempi dell'epistolario dantesco: L'epistola al Malaspina." In *Le lettere di Dante: Ambienti culturali, contesti storici e circolazione dei saperi*, edited by Antonio Montefusco and Giuliano Milani: 233–42. Berlin: De Gruyter, 2020.

Vinay, Gustavo. "Ricerche sul *De vulgari eloquentia*. 1. Lingua artificiale, naturale e letteraria." *Giornale storico della letteratura italiana* 136 (1959): 236–74 and 367–88.

Viscardi, Antonio. "La favella di Cacciaguida e la nozione dantesca del latino." *Cultura neolatina* 2 (1942): 311–14.

Vitale, Vincenzo. "Pagan Gods as Figures of Speech: Dante's Use of Servius in the *Vita Nova*." *Italian Studies* 76, no. 3 (2021): 219–29.

Volpini, Enzo, "Elemento." *Enciclopedia dantesca*, 2:648–51. Rome: Istituto della Enciclopedia Italiana, 1970–78.

Ward, John O. "What the Middle Ages Missed of Cicero, and Why." In *Brill's Companion to the Reception of Cicero*, edited by William H. F. Altman, 307–26. Leiden: Brill, 2015.

Webb, Heather. *Dante's Persons: An Ethics of the Transhuman*. Oxford: Oxford University Press, 2016.

Weijers, Olga. *Dictionnaires et répertoires au Moyen Âge: Une étude du vocabulaire*. Turnhout: Brepols, 1991.

Wetherbee, Wintrop. *Platonism and Poetry in the Twelfth Century: The Literary Influence of the School of Chartres*. Princeton, NJ: Princeton University Press, 1972.

Wicksteed, Philip H., and Edmund Gardner. *Dante and Giovanni del Virgilio, Including a Critical Edition of the Text of Dante's "Ecloghae Latinae" and of the Poetic Remains of Giovanni del Virgilio*. Westminster: Constable, 1902.

Wieruszowski, Hélène. "An Early Anticipation of Dante's 'cieli e scienze.'" *Modern Language Notes* 61, no. 4 (1946): 217–28.

Wilks, Michael. *The Problem of Sovereignty in the Later Middle Ages: The Papal Monarchy with Augustinus Triumphus and the Publicists*. Cambridge: Cambridge University Press, 1963.

Williams, Anna N. "The Theology of the *Comedy*." In *The Cambridge Companion to Dante*, 2nd ed., edited by Rachel Jacoff, 201–17. Cambridge: Cambridge University Press, 2007.

Wirth, Uwe. "Der Performazbegriff im Spannungsfeld von Illokution, Iteration und Indexikalität." In *Performanz: Von Sprachphilosophie zu den Kulturwissenschaften*, edited by Uwe Wirth, 9–53. Frankfurt: Suhrkamp, 2002.

Witke, Edward Charles. "The River of Light in the *Anticlaudianus* and the *Divina Commedia*." *Comparative Literature* 11 (1959): 144–56.

Witt, Ronald G. "The Arts of Letter-Writing." In *The Cambridge History of Literary Criticism*, vol. 2, *The Middle Ages*, edited by Alastair Minnis and Ian Johnson, 68–83. Cambridge: Cambridge University Press, 2005.

———. *In the Footsteps of the Ancients: The Origins of Humanism from Lovato to Bruni*. Leiden: Brill, 2000.

Wunderli, Peter. "*Mortuus redivivus*: Die Fiore-Frage." *Deutsches Dante-Jahrbuch* 61 (1986): 35–50.

Zaccagnini, Guido. *La vita dei maestri e degli scolari nello Studio di Bologna nei secoli XII e XIV*. Geneva: Olschki, 1926.

Zanni, Raffaella. "Il *De vulgari eloquentia* fra linguistica, filosofia e politica." *Critica del testo* 14, no. 1 (2011): 279–343.

———. "Tra *curialitas* e *cortesia* nel pensiero dantesco: Una ricognizione e una proposta per *De vulgari eloquentia* I, xviii, 4–5." In *Ortodossia ed eterodossia in Dante Alighieri*, edied by Carlota Cattermole, Celia de Aldama, and Chiara Giordano, 233–49. Madrid: Ediciones de La Discreta, 2014.

Zinelli, Fabio. "Dante TQ." *L'indice dei libri del mese*, January 2012, 27.

Zingarelli, Nicola. "La falsa attribuzione del *Fiore* a Dante Alighieri." *Rassegna critica della letteratura italiana* 27 (1922): 236–54.

Zink, Michel. *La subjectivité littéraire autour du siècle de saint Louis*. Paris: PUF, 1985.

Zumthor, Paul. *Essai de poétique médiévale*. Paris: Seuil, 1972.

CONTRIBUTORS

Zygmunt G. Barański is Serena Professor of Italian Emeritus at the University of Cambridge and R. L. Canala Professor of Romance Languages and Literatures Emeritus at the University of Notre Dame. He has published extensively on Dante, on medieval Italian literature, on Dante's fourteenth- and twentieth-century reception, and on twentieth-century Italian literature, film, and culture. His most recent book is *Dante, Petrarch, Boccaccio: Literature, Doctrine, Reality* (2020). For many years he was senior editor of *The Italianist*, and until 2021 he held the same position with *Le tre corone*.

Luca Bianchi is professor of history of medieval philosophy and currently serves as head of the Department of Philosophy at the State University of Milan. He has published extensively on medieval, Renaissance, and early modern thought. His books include *Il vescovo e i filosofi: La condanna parigina del 1277 e l'evoluzione dell'aristotelismo scolastico* (1990); *Censure et liberté intellectuelle à l'Université de Paris* (1999); *Studi sull'aristotelismo del Rinascimento* (2003); and *Pour une histoire de la "double vérité"* (2008).

Theodore J. Cachey, Jr., is professor of Italian at the University of Notre Dame. He has published on Dante, Petrarch, and Boccaccio, as well as on the history of the Italian language, on Italian travel literature, and on the relationship between cartography and literature. He directs the Devers Family Program in Dante Studies at Notre Dame and is director of the Center for Italian Studies there. He is the founder and coeditor, with Zygmunt G. Barański and Christian Moevs, of the Devers Series in Dante and Medieval Italian Literature published by the University of Notre Dame Press.

SIMON GILSON is Agnelli-Serena Professor of Italian at the University of Oxford and fellow of Magdalen College. He is the author of *Dante and Renaissance Florence* (2005) and *Reading Dante in Renaissance Italy: Florence, Venice and the "Divine Poet"* (2018).

MANUELE GRAGNOLATI is professor of Italian literature at Sorbonne Université, associate director of the ICI Berlin Institute for Cultural Inquiry, and senior research fellow at Somerville College, Oxford. He is the author of the monographs *Experiencing the Afterlife: Soul and Body in Dante and Medieval Culture* (2005) and *Amor che move: Linguaggio del corpo e forma del desiderio in Dante, Pasolini e Morante* (2013). He has collaborated with Teodolinda Barolini on the edition of Dante's *Rime giovanili e della "Vita Nuova"* (2009) and has coauthored, with Francesca Southerden, *Possibilities of Lyric: Reading Petrarch in Dialogue* (2020). He is the coeditor of several volumes on Dante and the Middle Ages, including *Aspects of the Performative in Medieval Culture* (2010); *Dante's Plurilingualism* (2010); *Metamorphosing Dante* (2011); *Desire in Dante and the Middle Ages* (2012); *Vita nova. Fiore. Epistola XIII* (2018); *Dante's Modernity* (2020); and the *Oxford Handbook of Dante* (2021).

CLAIRE E. HONESS was professor of Italian studies at the University of Leeds, UK, where she worked from 2003 until 2021. She served as head of Italian, as head of the School of Languages, Cultures and Societies, and, most recently, as dean of the Leeds Doctoral College. She was chair of the Society for Italian Studies in the UK and Ireland from 2015 to 2018. Her research interests focus on the way in which Dante uses political images and ideas in his writing. Her book *From Florence to the Heavenly City: The Poetry of Citizenship in Dante* was published in 2006, and she has also translated four of the poet's letters on political themes.

CHRISTOPHER KLEINHENZ is the Carol Mason Kirk Professor of Italian Emeritus at the University of Wisconsin-Madison, where he has taught courses in medieval Italian literature, particularly Dante, Petrarch, Boccaccio, and the early lyric tradition. In addition to over one hundred articles, he has published more than fifteen books and essay collections, including *Dante intertestuale e interdisciplinare: Saggi sulla "Commedia"*

(2015) and *Approaches to Teaching Dante's "Divine Comedy"* (2020). For fifteen years he was the editor of *Dante Studies* and currently serves as coeditor of the *Rivista internazionale di ricerche dantesche* and *Letteratura cavalleresca italiana*. He received the *Fiorino d'oro* from the Società Dantesca Italiana in 2008 and was named a Fellow of the Medieval Academy of America in 2009.

DAVID G. LUMMUS is an assistant professor of Italian at the University of Notre Dame. He is the author of *The City of Poetry: Imagining the Civic Role of the Poet in Fourteenth-Century Italy* (2020). He has coedited (with Martin Eisner) *A Boccaccian Renaissance: Essays on the Early Modern Impact of Giovanni Boccaccio and His Works* (2019) and has edited *The Decameron Sixth Day in Perspective* (2021).

VITTORIO MONTEMAGGI is senior lecturer in religion and the arts in the Department of Theology and Religious Studies at King's College London, where he also contributes to the work of the Centre for the Arts and the Sacred at King's. His work focuses primarily on the writings of Dante Alighieri and of Primo Levi and also explores authors as different as Gregory the Great, Catherine of Siena, Shakespeare, and Roberto Benigni. He is the author of *Reading Dante's "Commedia" as Theology: Divinity Realized in Human Encounter* (2016) and coeditor of *Dante's "Commedia": Theology as Poetry* (2010) and *Dante, Mercy, and the Beauty of the Human Person* (2017).

PAOLA NASTI is associate professor of Italian at Northwestern University. Her research focuses on medieval Italian literature and religious culture, as well as its textual and intellectual history. Her first book, *Favole d'amore e "saver profondo": La tradizione salomonica in Dante* (2007), explored how the medieval Bible provided Dante with narrative, intellectual, and rhetorical models. The study of scriptural intertextuality in Dante's works continues to be her primary scholarly interest, and in a number of long articles she has investigated Dante's theology of the church, his representation of holiness, and his treatment of Passion narratives. She coedited the first volume on the Dante commentaries in the Anglophone world, *Interpreting Dante: Essays on the Traditions of Dante Commentary* (2013).

MIRKO TAVONI, formerly professor of Italian linguistics and Dante studies at the University of Pisa, has published a number of studies on Dante, including a translation of and commentary on the *De vulgari eloquentia* (2011) and the volume *Qualche idea su Dante* (2015). He is the editor of *Dante e la lingua italiana* (2013) and, with Bernhard Huss, *Dante e la dimensione visionaria fra medioevo e prima età moderna* (2019). He is a member of the Scientific Board of the Vocabolario Dantesco, a project developed by the Accademia della Crusca, and of the Vocabolario Dantesco Latino. He is one of the editors of the *Nuova rivista di letteratura italiana* and is preparing a collection of essays in Renaissance linguistics.

INDEX OF NAMES

Abelard, Peter, 338, 356n18
Abrame-Battesti, Isabelle, 68n126
Adam, 190, 193–94, 197, 375–78
Aeneas, 249–50
Ahern, John,148n15
Alain de Libera, 335
Alan of Lille, 97, 175, 276
Albanese, Gabriella, 308, 331n30
Albertano da Brescia, 268n40
Albert the Great, 161, 164–65, 168, 174, 177, 343, 349, 350, 354, 356n21, 362n73
Albumasar, 163, 175
Alessandro d'Ancona, 49
al-Farabi, Abu Nasr, 361n67
Alfie, Fabian, 38, 65n87
Alfraganus, 175
Alighieri, Jacopo, 51, 296n3, 336
Alighieri, Pietro, 128, 170, 278, 295, 296n3, 330n20
Allegranza, Pietro, 2
Allegretti, Paola, 49, 50, 55, 60n32, 70n135
Amico di Dante. *See* Lippo Pasci dei Bardi
Andrea d'Isernia, 258
Andreoli, Raffaello, 173
Anonimo Fiorentino, 171
Apuleius, 248
Aquinas, Thomas (saint), 161, 164, 168, 177, 182n11, 189, 207, 242, 243, 261, 263, 269n42, 334–35, 343, 349, 350, 352, 353, 356n15, 356n21
Ariani, Marco, 299n27
Aristotle, 7, 100, 110, 123n118, 156, 161, 162, 164, 166–67, 176, 177, 189, 201, 204, 206, 207, 223, 224–25, 227, 240–42, 243, 244, 258, 261, 263, 265n7, 273, 276, 289, 292–93, 298n22, 304n66, 305n75, 333, 335, 339, 341, 343, 346, 347, 348, 349, 374
Armour, Peter, 38, 58n18
Arnault Daniel, 9–10, 207, 208, 209, 210, 213
Arquillière, Henri-Xavier, 267n31
Ascoli, Albert, 19, 180, 337, 351
Auerbach, Erich, 13, 363
Augustine (saint), 75, 84, 97, 158, 177, 190, 248–49, 250, 252, 253–54, 257, 262–63, 267n25, 267n31, 267n33
Augustinus Triumphus, 253, 267n28
Augustus (emperor), 228, 233–34
Austin, John, 14, 32n32
Averroes, 343, 347
Avicenna, 165, 343
Azzetta, Luca, 302n55, 343
Azzo VIII of Este (marquis), 210

Bacon, Roger, 304n68, 350
Baldelli, Ignazio, 168

Barański, Zygmunt, 30n2, 38–39, 40, 55, 58n19, 58n23, 61n43, 69n127, 278, 279–80, 281–82, 287, 289, 298n22, 301n44, 301n52, 304n67, 305n73, 311, 333, 337, 343–44, 363, 365, 366, 380–81
Barbi, Michele, 2, 5, 8, 20–22, 23, 26, 27, 28, 32n34, 80, 91, 117n33, 178, 271
Barolini, Teodolinda, 1, 2, 12, 14, 15, 18, 24, 25, 26, 28, 33n45, 127, 180, 218n10
Battifolle (countess), 127, 130–32, 134, 148n10, 149n30
Beatrice, 6, 7, 8, 12, 17, 18, 19, 71–72, 73, 77–78, 79, 81, 82, 83, 84, 85, 87, 89, 91, 93, 94–95, 108, 114n3, 160, 162, 263, 273, 297n11, 302n53, 337, 380, 381
Bellomo, Saverio, 300n38
Bembo, Pietro, 172
Benedict XI (pope), 132, 263
Benivieni, Girolamo, 171
Bennasutti, Luigi, 173
Benvenuto da Imola, 128, 171
Bernard of Trille, 304n68
Bernardus Silvestris, 276
Bernart de Ventadorn, 13, 30
Bertran de Born, 179, 207, 208–9
Bianchi, Luca, 184n37, 368, 379
Billanovich, Giuseppe, 300n41
Biscioni, Antonio Maria, 173, 182n16
Boccaccio, Giovanni, 2, 23, 24, 27–28, 29, 104, 125, 126, 127, 128, 146, 149n21, 170, 172, 240, 246–47, 248, 306–7, 309, 312, 315, 323, 328, 328n1, 330n20, 337, 359n47
Boethius, 75, 97, 106, 120n68, 158, 162, 167, 174, 175, 177, 335, 336, 337, 338, 339–40, 346, 349, 352, 353, 356n14, 361n69
Boitani, Piero, 304n71, 363

Bonaventure, Saint, 244–45, 266n20, 349
Boncompagno da Signa, 175
Boniface VIII (pope), 202, 235, 256, 258
Bono Giamboni, 91, 123n118
Botterill, Steven, xiii, xv, 363, 375–76
Boyde, Patrick, 2, 7, 8, 11, 17, 22, 25, 26, 58n23, 333
Brambilla Ageno, Franca, 170
Branca, Vittore, 74
Brilli, Elisa, 150n43
Brownlee, Kevin, 55
Brunetto Latini, 44, 53, 54, 65n87, 67n102, 67nn105–6, 75, 90–91, 97, 109, 110–13, 123n118, 159, 177, 252, 353
Bruni, Leonardo, 125, 126
Buridan, John, 297n9
Bursill-Hall, Geoffrey L., 346
Busnelli, Giovanni, 178, 352

Cacciaguida, 133, 135, 141, 145, 146, 313
Cachey, Theodore J., Jr., 329n16, 356n16, 367–68
Caesar, Julius, 238, 245
Cagnolato, Bartolomeo, 300n41
Camozzi Pistoja, Ambrogio, 358n35, 362n77
Canettieri, Paolo, 67n105
Cangrande della Scala, 126, 127–28, 129, 280, 286, 309, 343
Capella, Martianus, 97
Capellanus, Andreas, 37
Campanus of Novara, 290, 304n68
Casadei, Alberto, 300n38, 308, 331n31
Casamassima, Emanuele, 57n2
Casciani, Santa, 49, 66n88
Casella, 179, 211
Cassata, Letterio, 63n64
Cassell, Anthony, 266n13
Castelvetro, Lodovico, 172

Index of Names

Castets, Ferdinand, 38, 49, 64n69
Cavalcanti, Guido, 3, 4–5, 8, 9, 11, 12, 17, 19, 31n9, 33n40, 54, 55, 81, 84, 100, 108, 109, 172, 199, 204, 212–13
Cecco Angiolieri, 9, 34n50, 49, 54, 68n118
Cecco d'Ascoli, 304n68
Cervigni, Dino S., 116n32
Charles Martel, 227
Charles of Valois, 210
Charles the Fair, 258
Checco di Meletto Rossi, 328n1
Cheneval, Francis, 344
Chiamenti Massimiliano, 5
Chiaro Davanzati, 108
Chiavacci Leonardi, Anna Maria, 363
Chiesa, Paolo, 246, 260, 265n1, 347–48, 357n25, 359n48
Chomsky, Noam, 346
Christ, 19, 136, 137, 138, 139, 147, 166, 228–29, 233–34, 237–38, 245, 256, 257, 262–63, 283, 351, 373–74, 375–78, 381
Christine de Pizan, 336
Cicero, 89, 90, 97, 110, 111, 162, 167, 174, 177, 232–33, 251–52, 261–62, 338
Cino da Pistoia, 10–11, 12, 16, 21, 199, 204, 205–6, 207, 215, 216, 219n20, 251
Clement V (pope), 142, 235, 373
Combs-Schilling, Jonathan, 309
Conrad of Megenberg, 361n72
Constantin (emperor), 236–37
Contini, Gianfranco, 1–2, 12–13, 15, 21–22, 26, 27, 30n2, 32n25, 49, 50, 52, 53, 58n16, 62n59, 63n64, 66n90, 214, 283, 302n54
Corti, Maria, 178, 346
Curtius, Ernst Robert, 273

Daniel (prophet), 244, 245
Dante da Maiano, 3, 16, 54
Dante degli Abati, 54
David (king), 222, 234, 245, 259–60
Dell'Oso, Lorenzo, 123n118, 303n61
De Robertis, Domenico, 3, 5, 22–25, 27, 28, 55, 72, 122n95
De Robertis Boniforti, Teresa, 57n2, 100
De Sanctis, Francesco, 31n7
Dronke, Peter, 356n14, 360n62
Durante di Giovanni, 38, 50, 54, 69n127

Egginton, William, 299n31
Enrichetto delle Querce, 2

Fabbruzzo dei Lambertazzi, 201, 204
Falzone, Paolo, 178, 180
Fasani, Remo, 67n102, 68n126
Fenzi, Enrico, 359n40
Ferrara, Sabrina, 331n31
Ficino, Marsilio, 171
Fioravanti, Gianfranco, 174, 178, 297n9, 299n26, 344, 352, 359n48
Folgore da San Gimignano, 4, 54, 67n102
Folquet de Marseille, 209, 210
Forese Donati, 8–9, 12, 31n15
Formisano, Luciano, 49, 50, 56, 67n98, 67n116, 68n126, 70n136
Foscolo, Ugo, 173
Foster, Kenelm, 2, 7, 8, 11, 17, 22, 25, 26, 363
Francesco da Barberino, 54
Francesco da Buti, 128, 171
Francis of Assisi (saint), 244–45
Freccero, John, 296n1, 363
Frederick I, 235
Frederick II, 166, 199, 203, 204, 206, 235, 298n22, 339
Fulcieri de' Calboli, 321, 331nn30–31

Galatea, 322–25, 331n36
Galen, 222,
Gaunt, Simon, 13, 30
Gentile of Cingoli, 346
Gerardo da Borgo San Donnino, 59n30
Gerard of Cremona, 339
Ghislieri, Guido 201, 204
Giacomo da Lentini, 215
Giles of Rome, 177, 202, 252–53, 267n28, 267n31, 304n68, 350
Gilson, Étienne, 334, 352, 353, 363
Gilson, Simon, 379
Giovanni del Virgilio, 306, 307, 308, 309, 310–11, 311, 313–22, 323–26, 328n1, 329n12, 330n24, 331nn38–39, 336
Giuliani, Giambattista, 173
Giunta, Claudio, 10, 26–27, 33n45, 274, 299n23
Godfrey of Fontaines, 243
Gorni, Guglielmo, 32n33, 51, 80, 91, 97, 117n33, 170
Gorra, Egidio, 49
Gragnolati, Manuele, 33n40, 181n2, 382–83
Gratian, 259
Grayson, Cecil, 67n99
Graziolo de' Bambaglioli, 336
Gregory the Great (pope), 121n83
Grimaldi, Marco, 27
Guido da Montefeltro, 179
Guido da Pisa, 128, 149n21
Guido delle Colonne, 199, 215
Guido Novello da Polenta, 316, 325
Guillaume de Lorris, 36–37, 38, 41, 42–43, 44, 51, 59n24
Guillaume Durand, 54
Guinizelli, Guido, 5, 9, 12, 44, 53, 81, 84, 200–201, 204, 205, 209
Guiraut de Bornelh, 207, 208, 209

Guittone d'Arezzo, 3, 4, 43, 44, 53, 54, 55, 62n52, 84, 108, 122n98, 210
Gundissalinus, Dominicus, 361n67

Harrison, Robert Pogue, 59n24, 62n50
Hawkins, Peter, 363
Henri of Ghent, 335
Henry VII (emperor), 126, 127, 134, 135, 136–39, 140–41, 142, 143, 144, 145, 147, 235, 263, 265n1, 282, 309
Hollander, Robert, 97, 179, 180, 302n60, 363
Homer, 91, 99, 100
Honess, Claire, 327, 372
Horace, 99, 167, 317
Hugh of St. Victor, 177, 361n67
Huot, Sylvia, 37, 38, 55, 58n21

Iacopo della lana, 330n20
Imbach, Ruedi, 160, 174, 176, 336, 341, 342, 346, 355n5, 359n48
Inglese, Giorgio, 147n5, 300n41
Innocent III (pope), 253
Irnerius of Bologna, 252
Isaiah (prophet), 136, 139, 245, 293–94
Isidore of Seville, 361n67

Jacopo della Lana, 128
James of Viterbo, 243, 253, 267n28
Jean de Meun, 36–37, 38, 42, 43, 51, 53, 58n12, 65n87
Jeremiah (prophet), 94, 97, 100, 139, 140, 143
Jerome (saint), 261
Jezabel, 82
Job, 293–94
Johannes de Sacrobosco, 175
John XXII (pope), 257
John of Dacia, 361n67
John of Paris, 243

Index of Names   453

John of Salisbury, 252, 338
John the Baptist (saint), 19, 138, 139
John the Evangelist (saint), 238, 305n73
Justinian (emperor), 251
Juvenal, 167

Kant, Immanuel, 355n5
Keen, Catherine, 145
Kirkpatrick, Robin, 363
Kleinhenz, Christopher, 49, 368

Lancia, Andrea, 170
Lang, Abby, 57n3
Lapo Gianni, 199, 204
Lazzerini, Lucia, 55
Leo, Ulrich, 362n75
Leonardi, Lino, 28, 53, 55
Leonardo da Vinci, 171
Levi, 236
Libri, Guglielmo, 36
Lippo Pasci dei Bardi, 43, 54, 67n102
Livy, 174, 232, 248
Lorenzo de' Medici, 171
Lucan, 99, 140, 151n63, 168, 177, 232, 248
Luke the Evangelist (saint), 233–34, 256–57
Lull, Raymond, 335
Lummus, David, 302n60, 368

Macrobius, 338
Maggini, Francesco, 20–21
Magi, the, 236
Malaspina, Franceschino, 263
Malaspina, Moroello, 11, 145
Malato, Enrico, 27
Mandelstam, Osip, 287
Manfred, 199, 204
Margaret of Brabant, 127, 130–32, 134, 149n30
Marigo, Aristide, 74, 218n11

Marmo, Costantino, 346
Marsilius of Padua, 269n45
Mary, Blessed Virgin, 82, 89, 305n76
Mazzatinti, Giuseppe, 49, 63n62, 64n69
Mazzoni, Francesco, 271, 278, 279, 300n38, 304n68
Mazzoni, Guido, 49, 62n59
Mazzotta, Giuseppe, 363
Mazzucchi, Andrea, 168
Meister Eckhart, 335
Mengaldo, Pier Vincenzo, 214
Midas, 320
Milani, Giuliano, 63n64, 122n95
Milton, Thomas, 172
Moevs, Christian, 363–64
Monaci, Ernesto, 49, 63n60, 63n65
Moncetti, Giovanni Benedetto, 271, 296n3
Monte Andrea, 53, 108
Montefusco, Antonio, 56, 62n59, 69n132
Monti, Vincenzo, 173
Moore, Edward, 173, 271, 279, 281, 282, 303n62
Morpurgo, Salomone, 49
Mussato, Albertino, 309, 310, 317, 329n13, 330n24

Nardi, Bruno, 178, 184n43, 271, 353, 363
Nasti, Paola, 175, 366, 370–71
Neckham, Alexander, 175
Niccolò da Prato, 132, 133–34, 263
Nicholas III (pope), 257
Noah, 195
Notker of St. Gallen, 361n72
Novati, Francesco, 64n72
Novellino, 91, 122n98

Onesto da Bologna, 201, 204
Orelli, Giorgio, 66n88

Oresme, Nicole, 336
Orosius, 91, 248
Ottimo Commento, 170
Ovid, 97, 99, 116, 160, 168, 177, 248, 317, 320, 322–23, 325

Padoan, Giorgio, 278, 279–80, 284, 287
Paolazzi, Carlo, 66n88
Parodi, Ernesto Giacomo, 49, 50, 53, 58n16, 64n71, 68n126, 271
Pasquazi, Silvio, 300n38
Pastore Stocchi, Manlio, 283, 284, 289, 290, 301n51, 302n59, 303n63, 303n65, 304nn69–70, 305n75
Paul (saint), 136, 137, 238, 244, 245, 293–94, 337–38
Pegoretti, Anna, 301n44, 338
Pellegrini, Paolo, 126
Pèrcopo, Erasmo, 67n106
Perini, Dino, 311
Pernicone, Vincenzo, 8, 20–21
Perrus, Claude, 69n127
Pertile, Lino, 58n23, 65n84, 179, 322, 331n39, 363
Peter (saint), 256–57
Peter of Auvergne, 242
Petoletti, Marco, 308
Petrarch, Francis, 2, 10, 30n2, 81, 128, 172, 307, 309, 328n1, 336
Petrocchi, Giorgio, 62n59
Philip of Tripoli, 339
Picone, Michelangelo, 14–15, 32n34, 53, 66n93
Piendibeni, Francesco, 127
Pietrobono, Luigi, 178
Pietro d'Abano, 304n68
Pirovano, Donato, 27
Pistelli, Ermenegildo, 271
Plato, 162, 164, 175
Poliziano, Angelo, 2, 171

Polyphemus, 321–25, 331n36
Pontari, Paolo, 308, 331n30
Porcelli, Bruno, 59n26
Proba, Faltonia Betitia, 248
Pseudo-Dionysius, 164
Ptolemy, 161
Ptolemy of Lucca, 252, 267n25
Pucci, Antonio, 54, 67n102, 68n126
Pythagoras, 164

Quaglioni, Diego, 221, 347, 357n25

Raffa, Guy, 317
Rea, Roberto, 33n40
Remigio de' Girolami, 252
Ricklin, Thomas, 344
Rinaldi, Michele, 297n10, 300n38, 303n63, 303n65
Ristoro d'Arezzo, 304n68
Robert (king), 309
Robiglio, Andrea A., 358n39
Romano, Immanuel, 54, 67n102
Rosier-Catach, Irène, 346
Rossi, Luca Carlo, 49, 50
Rossi, Luciano, 53, 59n30
Rustico Filippi, 9, 54, 67n106

Salutati, Coluccio, 171
Santagata, Marco, 271
Sarti, Luna, 303n64
Saul (king), 137, 236
Scartazzini, Giovanni, 173, 183n25
Scot, Michael, 175, 304n68
Scott, John, 179, 180
Scotus, Duns, 334–35
Sebastio, Leonardo, 56
Segre, Cesare, 168
Seneca, 110, 163, 167, 338
Shaw, Prue, 266n13, 266n22, 357n25
Siger of Brabant, 48, 52, 339–40, 349, 350, 356n21
Singleton, Charles S., xiii, 74, 363

Solomon (king), 167, 244, 245, 379–80
Somaini, Francesco, 151n56
Sordello, 198
Stanghellini, Menotti, 49
Statius, 166, 168, 177
Steinberg, Justin, 77, 360n59
Stephen of Pisa, 339
Stoppelli, Pasquale, 53, 63n66, 69n129
Storey, Wayne, 105
Sydrach, 298n22
Sylvester (pope), 236

Tabarroni, Andrea, 246, 260, 265n1, 301n48, 347–48, 357n25, 359n48
Tanturli, Giuliano, 28
Tasso, Torquato, 172
Tempier, Etienne (bishop), 243, 273, 298n17
Terino da Castelfiorentino, 16–17
Theocritus, 317
Theodore of Antioch, 339
Tomazzoli, Gaia, 152n65
Tommaseo, Niccolò, 173
Tommaso da Faenza, 204
Tonelli, Natascia, 28, 31n9
Took, John, 50, 56, 182n10
Torraca, Francesco, 68n119, 173
Toynbee, Paget, 136, 271
Trovato, Mario, 180
Tuccio Manetti, Antonio, 171

Ugolino Buzzola Manfredi, 204
Uguccione della Faggiola, 309
Ulysses, 273
Uzzah, 373–74

Valla, Lorenzo, 236
Vandelli, Giuseppe, 352
Vanossi, Luigi, 48, 53, 55, 56, 64n75, 65n84, 67n98, 68n121
Van Steenbergen, Fernand, 334
Varela-Portas de Orduña, Juan, 28
Vasoli, Cesare, 174
Vasta, Edward, 116n32
Vernani, Guido, 351
Viel, Riccardo, 53
Villa, Claudio, 146
Villani, Filippo, 52, 126, 128
Villani, Giovanni, 170, 171, 182n19, 281, 301n43
Virgil, 99, 109, 132–33, 165–66, 168, 177, 188, 197–98, 222, 231, 248, 249–50, 278, 306, 311, 312, 315, 317, 328n1, 345
Visconti, Galeazzo, 300n41
Vitale, Vincenzo, 122n98
Vivaldi, Ugolino, 298n19
Vivaldi, Vadino, 298n19

William of Auvergne, 358n39
William of Conches, 175, 177
William of Ockham, 334–34
Witt, Ronald, G., 130
Witte, Karl, 173
Wittgenstein, Ludwig, 20

Ysaac, 361n67

Zumthor, Paul, 32n28

www.ingramcontent.com/pod-product-compliance
Lightning Source LLC
Chambersburg PA
CBHW071354300426
44114CB00016B/2063